Vol. 23 No. 1
February 1981

JOURNAL OF INTERAMERICAN STUDIES

and WORLD AFFAIRS

A Publication of the Center for Advanced International Studies,
The University of Miami

SAGE PUBLICATIONS

Journal of INTERAMERICAN STUDIES
and WORLD AFFAIRS

The editors and publisher wish to acknowledge with gratitude the assistance and encouragement of the Center for Advanced International Studies, University of Miami, in providing ancillary services and support for this journal.

Journal of
INTERAMERICAN
STUDIES
and WORLD AFFAIRS

Vol. 23
No. 1
February
1981

CONTENTS

The Peruvian External Debt: Problem and Prospect
PEDRO-PABLO KUCZYNSKI 3

Antarctica, Latin America, and the International System in the 1980s: Toward a New Antarctic Order?
CARLOS J. MONETA
Translated by MARJORY MATTINGLY URQUIDI 29

The Associated States and Independence
GEORGE C. ABBOTT 69

Britain and Chile, 1851-1886: Anatomy of a Relationship
JOHN MAYO 95

SAGE PUBLICATIONS / *Beverly Hills* *London*

Policy: The **JOURNAL OF INTERAMERICAN STUDIES AND WORLD AFFAIRS** reflects the interests of the scholarly community and interested public concerned with the social, economic, political, and cultural aspects of life in Latin America (including the Caribbean), particularly in those instances where the subject is of concern to more than one of the traditional disciplines. As these concerns change, so will the content of the journal.

Articles which have special relevance for interrelationships between American nations and of those nations with the rest of the world will be given special consideration. An effort will be made to include occasional articles that state an unusual or even discordant position on a subject of broad interest to be supplemented by critical comments of authorities representing differing positions on the topic. The editors continue to welcome articles by scholars from all parts of the world.

Manuscripts should be submitted in duplicate to: Editor, **JOURNAL OF INTERAMERICAN STUDIES AND WORLD AFFAIRS**, Box 24-8134, University of Miami, Coral Gables, Florida 33124. Manuscripts should be typewritten, double-spaced, with footnotes, references, tables, and charts on separate pages, and should follow the current journal style. A brief biographical paragraph describing each author's current affiliation, research interests, and recent publications should accompany the manuscript.

Correspondence regarding book reviews should be sent directly to: Book Review Editor, **JOURNAL OF INTERAMERICAN STUDIES AND WORLD AFFAIRS**, Box 24-8134, University of Miami, Coral Gables, Florida 33124.

JOURNAL OF INTERAMERICAN STUDIES AND WORLD AFFAIRS is published four times annually—in February, May, August, and November.

Subscriptions: Regular institutional rate $36.00 per year. Individuals may subscribe at a one-year rate of $18.00. Add $2.00 for subscriptions outside the United States. Orders from the U.K., Europe, the Middle East, and Africa should be sent to the London office (address below). Noninstitutional orders **must** be paid by personal check.

Second class postage paid at Beverly Hills, California. ISSN 0022-1937

This journal is abstracted or indexed in **Historical Abstracts, Human Resources Abstracts, Sage Urban Studies Abstracts, International Political Science Abstracts, Public Affairs Information Service, Current Contents, Social Sciences Citation Index, Social Sciences Index, ABC POL SCI,** and **United States Political Science Documents.**

Back Issues: Information about availability and prices of back issues may be obtained from the publisher's order department (address below). Write to London office for sterling prices.

Inquiries: Address all correspondence and permissions requests to SAGE PUBLICATIONS, Inc., 275 South Beverly Drive, Beverly Hills, California 90212. Inquiries and subscriptions from the U.K., Europe, the Middle East, and Africa should be sent to SAGE PUBLICATIONS Ltd, 28 Banner Street, London EC1Y 8QE, England. Other orders should be sent to the Beverly Hills office.

Advertising: Current rates and specifications may be obtained by writing to the Advertising Manager at the Beverly Hills office (address above).

Claims: Claims for undelivered copies must be made no later than three months following month of publication. The publisher will supply missing copies when losses have been sustained in transit and when the reserve stock will permit.

Change of Address: Six weeks' advance notice must be given when notifying of change of address. Please send old address label along with the new address to insure proper identification. Please specify name of journal. POSTMASTER: Send change of address to: Journal name, c/o 275 South Beverly Drive, Beverly Hills, CA 90212.

PEDRO-PABLO KUCZYNSKI
Halco (Mining) Co.
Pittsburgh, PA 15212

THE PERUVIAN EXTERNAL DEBT
Problem and Prospect

Peru, in the period 1976-1979, along with half a dozen or so other countries occupied the center stage in the discussion of developing countries, which fact serious difficulties in meeting their external debt service and which face equally if not more serious problems of internal adjustment—especially little if any economic growth—as they try to raise themselves out of their financial crises. The countries which might be on such a problem list[1] each have their own specific problems. All of them, in one way or another, have had a major fiscal problem which has absorbed the bulk of domestic credit into the public sector and created strong pressures to borrow abroad. Of course, the individual causes of the public sector problem vary. In several countries, especially those which export copper, adverse export prices since 1974 have contributed significantly to development problems. The "list" of countries will no doubt change and quite probably expand in the next year or two, especially if there is an almost inevitable recession in the United States.

Unlike some of these other countries, in 1979 Peru staged a dramatic recovery in its external and internal finances. The form and speed of the financial recovery suggests something about the origins of the crisis which began in 1974-1975. On one hand, recovery was clearly helped by a sharp rise in commodity export

---

AUTHOR'S NOTE: This study was written at the end of 1978 for a seminar organized by the Council on Foreign Relations and therefore concentrates on events up to that point, with a review of the main changes up to February 1980.

Journal of Interamerican Studies and World Affairs, Vol. 23 No. 1, February 1981 3-27

TABLE 1
Commitments of Publicized Euro-Currency Syndicated Loans to Non-OPEC Developing Countries
(in millions of current U.S. dollars)

	1970	1971	1972	1973	1974	1975	1976	1977	1978	1979
BRAZIL	87	257	579	740	1,672	2,152	3,323	2,814	5,634	6,278
MEXICO	56	295	196	1,588	948	2,311	1,993	2,727	7,250	8,243
PERU	-	-	134	434	442	334	395	189		596
OTHER NON-OPEC LDCs	157	384	572	1,775	3,190	3,402	5,399	7,764	14,018	20,294
TOTAL	300	936	1,481	4,537	6,252	8,199	11,019	13,494	26,903	35,411

SOURCE: Morgan Guaranty Trust Co. (1970-1979).

prices and its coincidence with the friction of long-planned investments in petroleum development. On the other hand, the size and speed of the financial improvement of 1979 would not have been possible without the tough fiscal and monetary measures which were taken by the new civilian economic team brought in by the military authorities in mid-1978.

The history of the Peruvian financial crisis in the late 1970s, the subject of this essay, is perhaps instructive because it helps clarify some of the questions in the present debate on the external debt of some developing countries. To what extent is the problem one of domestic development policies, controllable internally, or one that arises from externally induced problems—such as oil import costs and inflation in basic industrial imports as well? Is this external-internal dichotomy a false one, and is the basic problem simply a reflection of inadequate domestic savings, a key feature of underdevelopment? Given an approach to these questions, is the answer more debt—through recycling, special international facilities, and so on—more aid, or will the problem simply fade away? The case of Peru does not necessarily provide answers to these questions, but an historical account of what happened in Peru may shed light on them.

The sections that follow will examine the circumstances peculiar to Peru which contributed to its debt problem and analyze how the debt expanded in the 1970s. I will then look into the future, trying to highlight the elements which in my view are likely to determine whether Peru can emerge from its present development predicament and whether, given the prospects, Peru will for many years have the doubtful privilege of making frequent pilgrimages to that so far rather exclusive gathering spot, the "Club of Paris."[2] Finally, more general conclusions will be drawn on the possible relevance of the Peruvian experience to other developing countries and to the future attitudes of lenders and policy makers in capital-exporting countries.

I

Peru has had serious economic problems for the last four or five years. Economic growth has virtually stopped and real per capita income fell about 10% in the period 1975-1978. According to official statistics, domestic inflation had accelerated to about 75% in 1978 and about 65% in 1979. The balance of payments showed sharp deficits up to 1978, and international payments were more or less maintained through a patchwork of measures, including large-scale short-term borrowing, forced credits for imports (a form of delayed payments), partial refinancing of external debt and, of course, through a major contraction of economic growth and hence a slowdown in imports. Without the partial debt refinancing which Peru obtained in 1976 and again, but on a much larger scale, in 1978, it undoubtedly would have been forced to suspend service on the external debt. The external debt problem of Peru, which has been but one manifestation of its overall development problem, was one of the most serious among those faced by a number of developing countries and thus attracted considerable attention in the debate on whether major international banks, specifically U.S. banks, have overexposed themselves in credits to some of these countries.

There is no single economic cause of the debt problem of Peru. In a narrow sense, Peru obviously overborrowed, and it did so at terms which were too onerous in relation to realistic possibilities of obtaining new loans to pay off old maturities and for purposes (basically large-scale financing of the budget deficit) which were unproductive. On the other side of the coin, the fact should not be forgotten that over the last fifteen or twenty years, Peru has received relatively little development aid from Washington, including the World Bank, in large part because of the dispute with the U.S. government from 1963 to 1974 on the question of the International Petroleum Company, an Exxon subsidiary (Kuczynski, 1977: ch. 5). As a result, the external debt has for many years suffered from an overly short maturity profile.

In a more fundamental sense, however, substantial government spending (basically for government subsidies to the urban sector and for military outlays) together with an overextension of government activity combined to create a very large public sector deficit, which was the root cause of the financial problem. No one can deny that Peru had bad luck in the 1970s in the sense that an oil boom which had, perhaps optimistically, been hoped for did not materialize; that fishmeal production for export virtually disappeared; and that copper prices collapsed after the dizzy heights of the international commodity boom which ended in 1974. On the other hand, even with these problems, a debt and international payments crisis would quite probably have been avoided had it not been for the magnitude of the fiscal deficit. Furthermore, the lack of public information and debate allowed the problem to fester unseen until it finally exploded in 1976. Thus, if causes of the problem had to be ranked, I would put at the head of the list two very different but interrelated phenomena, namely the unusually large deterioration of public finances and the absence—due to the policy of the military government—of internal criticism and information.

Outside observers are bound to ask how a military government, which seemed to project an image of order and unity together with social reform—an unusual combination among the Latin American military—got itself into the predicament of recent years. The major change carried out by the regime, the land reform begun in 1969, had little impact on the immediate financial situation. The problems were elsewhere. Institutionally, the three military services were not always united nor were the various leaders of the army itself. Serious differences and rivalries, both personal and ideological, thus existed among the members of the cabinet. This led to a lack of coordination in economic policy, a tendency perhaps made more acute by the first head of the junta, General Juan Velasco Alvarado, during the 1968-1975 period. Critical advice was frowned upon, and the limited number of civilians knowledgeable in economic matters were not encouraged to give advice; moreover, they were reluctant to do so after the experiences of the management of the Central Reserve Bank, who fled the country when they were arrested on trumped-up charges in April 1969. Another consideration was that in the feverish and excited atmosphere of the first years of the regime, objections were almost automatically viewed as counterrevolutionary. Moreover, the outside press, international agencies and outside observers in general—both academic and in business—seemed to support the objectives of the new government, which thus felt itself vindicated internationally.

II

The overexpansion of the public sector without a concomitant increase in its revenues was the root problem in Peru's economy in the 1970s. To be sure, this has not been the only economic problem which Peru has faced—exceptionally low sugar and copper prices in the period 1975-1978 were another problem—but it has by itself made the difference between what would have been a problem and what has become a crisis. If internal criticism had been allowed to flourish and if proper public statistics had been available, the magnitude of the problem would have become known by 1972-1973, just as major external borrowing was beginning to take place to bridge the gap. The figures in Table 2 are clear enough. The trouble is that they were not available except to a handful of government officials and, in partial form, to the two international organizations—the I.M.F. and the World Bank—which generally have access to this kind of statistics. Major international money center banks probably also knew

TABLE 2

Peru: Public Sector Deficit as a Percentage of GDP

TOTAL PUBLIC SECTOR	1971	1972	1973	1974	1975	1976	1977	Est[1] 1978	Proj[1] 1979
Current Revenue	23.0	24.0	23.3	31.0	32.7	32.7	32.1	32.5	33.0
Current Expenditure	20.1	21.2	22.4	28.7	34.0	33.2	35.7	34.0	30.5
Capital Outlays Net of Capital Revenue	5.3	5.7	6.3	8.5	9.2	8.7	6.2	5.0	4.7
TOTAL DEFICIT	-2.4	-3.0	-5.4	-6.2	-10.5	-9.1	-9.8	-6.5	-2.2
of which Central Govt.	-3.1	-3.7	-4.0	-3.1	- 5.6	-6.4	-7.5	-4.5	-0.5
State Enterprises[2]	0.3	0.1	-2.1	-4.3	- 4.9	-2.7	-2.3	-2.0	-2.7
Other Public Sector[3]	0.4	0.6	0.8	1.2					

NOTES:

1. Author's estimate and projection.
2. Excludes state banks.
3. Principally nonenterprise agencies, Social Security, local governments; excludes state banks.

about the data. However, even to this day, these figures, rearranged from the 1977 and 1978 reports of one of the international financial agencies, are not generally available to the public.

Both in the case of the central government and of the state enterprise, expenditures rose faster than revenues, even though the latter also increased rapidly. By 1973, the signs of a deteriorating fiscal position were becoming evident, although the lack of accurate and public data concealed the problem from view until well into 1974. By then the public sector deficit was running at a rate of 6% of GNP. By 1975, the deficit was above 10% of GNP, a level unsustainable without extraordinarily large external capital inflows. Until 1977, despite an attempt to reverse the trend in 1976, the deficit continued at about the same unusually high level.

Two main reasons, plus a number of subsidiary ones, lie behind the much faster rate of growth of expenditures than of current revenues. First, the role of the public sector after 1971 became rapidly overextended in relation to its managerial abilities, especially in a growing list of state-controlled enterprises such as those involving fisheries, sugar, import trade, distribution of foodstuffs, distribution of raw materials, plus—later on—electricity distribution, chemicals, cement, and newspapers. Government employment assumed a large role: by 1977, it provided about 500,000 jobs, not counting the armed forces—about

85,000—and state enterprises—about 140,000—or double the level of 1970-1971. The total labor force in 1977 was about 5.5 million, of which probably about 40% were less than fully employed. Second, the expansion of the public sector was combined with an intensification of the long-standing policy in Peru, as in many other developing economies, of subsidizing city dwellers at the expense of the countryside and the farm. This objective was attained through a fixed and gradually increasingly overvalued exchange rate which encouraged imports, especially of food, and the direct subsidization of imported food and gasoline, both of which are predominately consumed by urban masses. The state marketing agency kept food prices low in local currency despite the rapid increase in world grain prices in 1972-1973; the same happened with petroleum prices from 1974 onward, resulting in growing budgetary deficits for both agencies. Not only were imports directly encouraged by their relatively low prices, but as inflation accelerated with expanded central bank credit—either directly or through its equivalent, the release of commercial bank reserve requirements for lending to the public sector—the vicious circle of growing imports and increasing subsidies intensified. Migration to the city accelerated and the pressures for employment in the public sector increased, creating a relatively small but, in relative terms, privileged social group. It would be quite wrong to infer that this cycle has been unique to Peru. Egypt, for example, has gone through similar problems in the last twenty years, and many other developing countries for years have had policies that tend to subsidize the city at the expense of the countryside.

In Peru, the speed of the change was combined with patterns of spending which made the fiscal problem more accurate. Military expenditures expanded rapidly. Purchases of defense equipment from abroad were substantial at the beginning of the 1970s and again in 1977, although no exact dollar amount can be put on these purchases. Data on current military expenditures show a rapid and fairly continuous rise in real terms, accounting for 40% of central government current outlays in 1977 compared to 23% in 1971, and this as a proportion of a rising real volume of government expenditure. The other important tendency was that of public sector investment, which was deliberately expanded in the mid-1970s, partly in order to offset the lack of activity of the private sector. While private construction continued at a fast pace until 1975, most of the rest of private investment was held back—partly as a result of the Industrial Community Law of 1970, under which a profit-sharing plan was designed to gradually give labor up to 50% of the voting stock in large industrial enterprises. Another factor was the state takeover of basic industries and activities, particularly the marketing of exports and imports.

The problem of public investment in directly productive activities was that much of it was uneconomic. Although the cause in general can be described as poor planning, in several cases initial doubts about certain major projects were set aside and large commitments for external borrowing and domestic expenditures were made on the basis of incomplete evidence. Since the government discouraged press criticism and little information was publicly available, there could not be much discussion of these decisions. Examples of major projects of certain value were the fishing complex at Paita, a fishing port on the North Coast (lack of fish and distance from the major domestic market); a new Bagasse newsprint plant; and the Majes irrigation project (excessively high capital cost and poor soils); a number of poorly planned petrochemical ventures undertaken by PetroPeru; and the setting up of a new airline. In addition, the terms of the financing of the Trans Andean oil pipeline were burdensome. Half a dozen or so major public investment projects of this type represent about U.S. $1.5 billion of external debt contracted between 1971 and 1976, largely through supplier credits and commercial bank loans.[3]

The tendency toward internal and external disequilibrium was accentuated by a number of other developments in the balance of payments, some the result of deliberate policy and others externally induced. For a variety of reasons, the major mining investments envisaged in the late 1960s did not materialize in the 1970s, with the important exception of the Cuajone copper mine. The expropriations of foreign-controlled mining companies—Cerro and Marcona in particular—which were carried out as the world commodity price boom of the early 1970s was beginning to peter out, together with labor unrest in the mines, led to the stagnation of mining production up to 1976. Cotton production also fell by the mid-1970s as coastal agriculture shifted to food crops, and fishmeal production fell drastically after overfishing and a change in ecology in the early 1970s. All in all, the volume of Peru's exportable production was less in the mid-1970s than it had been 12 or 13 years earlier.[4]

The growth in export earnings which took place up to 1974 was thus exclusively the result of favorable export prices—a repetition of the phenomenon which had occurred in the mid-1960s—and turned downward as these prices began to level off. In the meantime, import prices continued upward, albeit at a slower pace than in the early 1970s. Moreover, the reliance of the domestic economy upon imports increased as the sixth exchange rate became increasingly overvalued. At the fixed exchange rate maintained until September 1975, the price of imports in Soles became increasingly attractive as domestic inflation accelerated. Imports rose as a percentage of GDP from 11% in 1972 to 18% in 1975. Given the high rates of effective protection against imports of final consumer products, enterprises were indirectly encouraged to import them in "intermediate" form (an "essential" import, according to import control authorities) so that total imports of consumer and intermediate goods as a percentage of total national consumption rose from 7% in 1972 to 11% in 1975. The higher cost of oil imports accounted for only one-quarter of that increase. The rest was the unintended result of an economic policy which encouraged consumption and imports—primarily benefitting the urban population—and tended to discourage saving and production for export.

III

The medium and long-term external debt of the public sector or guaranteed by it increased six times in nominal terms from the end of 1968 to 1977, not counting short-term debt. Peru is, of course, not the only country that has had a rapid increase in its external debt. For all non-OPEC developing countries during the same period, the increase was about four times. Yet the case of Peru stands out. First of all, the present debt is high by most conventionally accepted standards, such as in relation to exports, to GDP, or to per capita income. Second, the growth of external debt to such levels took place under a government which had as one of its major political aims the reduction of dependence on the outside world.[5] Paradoxically, as was noted above, the reliance upon imports and external financing in general increased substantially during the 1970s, despite a complex mechanism of controls intended to achieve the opposite result. Third, as a result of the limited access of Peru to long-term loans from international agencies, the proportion of official long-term loans from such agencies in the external public debt of Peru has for many years been low: In 1977, it was only 7%. The average maturity of the medium- and long-term external public debt in that year was about 4 years, an unusually short period for most developing countries.

There is no uniform way in which to measure external debt and its impact. The World Bank, which is the most comprehensive and consistent source of information on the external debt of developing countries, publishes data on the external debt of the public sector or guaranteed by the latter. The information includes both outstanding, or disbursed and due debt and undisbursed, or available debt, both of them relevant measures, depending on the purpose of the measurement. Because of the need to make the statistics reliable and comparable among countries, the data are published after a considerable delay, a factor of some consequence at a time of rapidly growing debt. The data do not in general include the external unguaranteed debt of the private sector, an omission which is minor in the case of most countries. Brazil, which has a relatively large private sector debt, publishes comprehensive data on it. Nor do the data include short-term debt. Under normal circumstances, such debt is said to be "self-liquidating," because much of it is for export or import financing over short periods. However, in an economy facing external payment problems, an increase in the short-term debt is often the sign—if published information exists—that something may be amiss. The Central Bank is likely in such circumstances to draw down short-term credit lines from abroad. Also, minimum terms may be prescribed for import payments so that in effect foreign suppliers are forced to extend credit or else not sell.

In fact, beginning approximately in 1975 this is what happened in Peru. At the end of 1978, the international reserves of the Peruvian banking system were negative by U.S. $1.2 billion, which means that Peru owed about U.S. $1.6 billion in outstanding short-term lines, after about U.S. $400 million held abroad by the Central Bank in working balances. While the lending banks are for the time being "rolling over" or renewing these lines, the interest is nevertheless an important part of debt service. At present euro and U.S. domestic rates, the interest bill on the negative reserves was on the order of U.S. $200 million in 1978. There was also an obligation, probably substantially smaller, for deferred current import payments, either in the form of actual interest on letters of credit or on arrears, or through higher prices for the merchandise charged by the exporter in order to offset the credit costs.

In addition to these conceptual problems, the measurement of the Peruvian debt was made difficult by possible omissions and inconsistencies in the data supplied to foreign creditors. The record of Peru's external public and guaranteed medium- and long-term debt as of mid-December 1978, such as original maturities over one year, is shown in Table 3. In addition, a very rough estimate of short-term debt has been made.

The government in mid-1978 declared that the outstanding external debt totalled U.S. $8.3 billion,[6] but this number may be on the high side because it appears to include unguaranteed private sector debt, in particular for the Cuajone copper mine. On the other hand, it is not clear to what extent the government data or the ones above include all defense purchases, so that there is a possibility of the outstanding debt being marginally higher. If undisbursed debt is included, on the grounds that funds available will no doubt be drawn down and will therefore affect future debt service, the totals shown in Table 3 rise by about

TABLE 3
External Public and Guaranteed Debt Outstanding, 1969-1978
(U.S. $ million, current prices)

END OF PERIOD	1969	1972	1973	1974	1975	1976	1977	EST. JUNE 1978
A. TOTAL Medium & Long-Term Outstanding	853	1,240	1,583	2,297	3,179	3,851	4,684	5,100
International Agencies	140	265	275	282	296	317	406	480
Governments & Suppliers[1]	475	619	693	928	1,121	1,289	1.452	1,570
Private Banks)		330	560	948	1,344	1,683	1,878	1,850
Other, including other) known defense[2])	238	26	55	139	418	562	948	1,200
B. TOTAL Short-Term Debt	-	-	37	480	545	1,367	1,607	1,766
Net Reserve Liabilities[3]	-	-	-	-	-	752	1,100	1.211
Trade Credit[4]	-	-	37	480	545	615	507	555
C. TOTAL Known Outstanding Obligations (A + B)	854	1,240	1,620	2,777	3,724	5,218	6.291	6,866

SOURCE: International Monetary Fund (1969-1978) and author's estimates.

NOTES:

1. Classified together, since in practice the bulk of supplier credits is insured by the government of the exporter; includes only a small amount of concessional aid.
2. U.S. medium-term Commodity Credit Corp. credits for food grains; petroleum imports credits from Ecuador and Venezuela; known defense equipment not included above.
3. Reserve assets less reserve liabilities.
4. Import registrations, for which import payment authorized, less actual payments; in practice, roughly equivalent to delayed–i.e., above 90 days–payments for which longer-term arrangements do not exist. Although not legally guaranteed by the state, the payments in local currency have been collected, so that the official banking system is in practice liable for the payment of these arrears to outside creditors.

U.S. $1.5 billion, so that the total external obligations of the public sector, both long-term and short-term—net of assets held abroad by the banking system—were probably in the range of $8 to $8.5 billion at the end of 1978.

The rapid growth of Peru's external debt began in 1973. From then on, foreign commercial banks accounted for about half of all new commitments until 1976. We shall turn later to the question of why the banks lent. By early 1976, because of the increasingly evident balance of payments problem, the banks essentially withdrew from making significant new medium- and long-term commitments. However, their exposure continued to increase rapidly in 1976 and 1977 as the central bank and other state banks drew down available short-term lines in order to maintain the flow of payments. By the end of 1976—when the doors of the banks closed as the stabilization program begun in that year failed to take hold—borrowing at relatively short terms increased for essential supplies, primarily grains from the United States financed at medium-term by the Commodity Credit Corporation and petroleum from Ecuador and Venezuela. These items, together with defense purchases in 1977, account for the ballooning of "other" debt in 1977-1978. In addition, early in 1978 the authorities obtained short-term loans from Mexico, Venezuela, Spain, and other countries as well as a $25 million deposit from Occidental Petroleum. On top of this general purpose financing, in the 1970s Peru made relatively heavy use of supplier credits for machinery and defense equipment imports. The growth of the external debt was therefore not simply the result of lending by commercial banks.

The rapid deterioration in the balance of payments in 1975 coincided with the worsening of the public sector deficit to 10% of GNP in that year. Both the fiscal and balance of payments problems were exacerbated by the sharp decline of copper prices, which affected both export earnings and tax revenue from the major mining companies. At first the commercial banks reacted slowly to the adverse turn of events—a major syndicated loan for the oil pipeline was put together in the third quarter of the year—but by early 1976 they had withdrawn from making new medium-term commitments as they began to doubt the ability of the government to implement an effective stabilization program, despite the strenuous efforts of the civilian finance minister of the day. In May 1977, one of Peru's leading businessmen was brought in as minister, but he was unsuccessful in his attempt over the next few weeks to obtain cohesive support within the government for the difficult measures needed. The biggest obstacle was the lack of cohesion among various blocs in the predominantly military cabinet. The financial and economic deterioration accelerated until the most recent attempt, begun in mid-1978 by a new economic team to work out a stabilization program.

The major domestic element of the new program has been a large-scale adjustment in the price system, including interest rates, the exchange rate—which has been depreciated more or less in line with domestic inflation—and the prices charged by

TABLE 4
Estimated Debt Service on Existing Medium- and Long-Term External Public Debt as of December 1977[1]
(in millions of U.S. dollars)

	ACTUAL 1977	EST. 1978	1979	1980	PROJECTED 1981	1982	1983
1. ORIGINALLY SCHEDULED	642	798	1,504	1,106	983	714	600
Amortization	396	706	947	862	750	535	450
Interest	246	342	401	292	226	172	150
2. AFTER REFINANCING	642	548	695	652	1,126	1,127	1,000
Amortization	396	506	515	362	750	835	750
Interest	246	292	180	290	376	292	250
3. SERVICE ON NEW DEBT[2]	-	-	80	100	140	210	280
4. TOTAL SERVICE [2,3]	642	548	775	752	1,266	1,337	1,280
5. EXPORT EARINGS[3] NEEDED TO KEEP DEBT SERVICE RATIO AT 35%	1,830	1,550	2,215	2,150	3,620	3,820	2,860
6. POSSIBLE EXPORT[3] EARNINGS	1,726	1,800	2,100	3,600	?	?	?

SOURCE: International Monetary Fund (1969-1978), line 1, plus author's estimates, lines 2-6. Information as of mid-1979.

NOTES:
1. Excludes interest on short-term debt, which adds about $200 million annually in 1978 and 1979.
2. Assumes net capital inflows, excluding direct investment, of $400 million annually in 1979-1983, a rather low figure in relation to export and GNP growth targets.
3. Merchandise exports, f.o.b.

state enterprises, particularly petrol and rice. The program, which represents a major reversal of previous financial policies, has provided the basis for a standby credit agreement with the International Monetary Fund, under which Peru will progressively be allowed to draw up to SDR 184 million—about U.S. $243 million at 1980 exchange rates over a two-year period, subject to quarterly targets on public finances, domestic credit expansion, and international reserves, as well as limits on external borrowing. The program agreed with the IMF has in turn made possible a partial refinancing of the external debt service due in 1979 and 1980. The implementation of the financial recovery program since it was put into effect in mid-1978 has been remarkably successful: The backlog of import payment arrears has been sharply reduced, international reserves have recovered sharply—partly because of an improvement in copper export prices—and the public sector deficit has been cut back to a manageable size. On the other hand, the government has yet to work out an effective development program, and the social impact of high unemployment and continued inflation could become devastating.

IV

The brief and perhaps somewhat classical interpretation given above of the recent economic difficulties of Peru and the accompanying external debt problems is bound to raise many questions, both about the future outlook and about whether something can be learned from the past. The first and most obvious question is whether Peru will in the future be able to overcome its most recent economic problems. To a considerable extent, of course, the economic outcome will depend on political variables. A Constituent Assembly was elected in mid-1978 and is at work on a new constitution which would permit, sometime in 1980, the first presidential and parliamentary elections since 1963. The elections to the Assembly, in which the Acción Popular party of ex-President Fernando Belaúnde refused to participate, showed a polarization of the electorate between the radical left, splintered but vocal and carrying one-third of the votes, and the center and right, ranging from the dominant APRA party to the largely Lima-based Social Christian party—in reality the followers of a leading politician of the previous regime. APRA (Alianza Popular Revolucionari Americana), formerly a revolutionary and still a very well-organized party, was highly dependent on its aged leader, Víctor Raúl Haya de la Torre, who died in 1979. The party has undoubtedly drifted rightward over the years. So far APRA has not shown its hand in the ongoing economic debate in Peru, and it probably does not have a comprehensive economic recovery program. Add to this a very young electorate, most of whom have never voted, and there are obvious elements of instability in a future civilian regime, which would be one of Peru's all too infrequent experiments with elected government.

The emerging class of young economic technocrats, which is larger than might be expected, has so far not been attracted to the major parties it perceives as either too ideological or excessively dependent on personalities. Many of these "técnicos" have been peripherally involved with the military government without actively participating in it. Such a group, well-trained but relatively inexperienced, will hold the key to the implementation of an economic program and to the accompanying and much-needed reform of the cumbersome administration apparatus. How they can be brought into the administration should be a major priority for a new government.

In the meantime, however, the recent debt refinancing obtained by Peru as a result of the measures worked out in mid-1978 with the International Monetary Fund gives Peru only a limited time to work out and start a development program that will reverse long-standing economic biases. The bulge of debt service has been pushed back from 1979-1980 to 1981-1983. Debt service obligations will continue at extremely high levels and will probably be unsustainable without major capital inflows, a windfall gain on commodity export prices, or unusually successful measures to reverse the stagnation in the volume of exportable production which has been a feature of the last fifteen years, or a combination of all three.

It is fairly clear that whatever economic program is worked out by a new administration, following the difficult but necessary financial measures already launched by the present civilian economic team will not only have to undo some of the measures of the last ten years but also tackle the longer-term problems of Peruvian development. Among them are the lack of incentives for agricultural and mining development—the two pillars of future economic growth—as well as the need to reorient the manufacturing sector away from an excessive reliance on protection from imports and towards a greater ability to compete and to put its considerable excess capacity to use by exploiting export opportunities. A promising start has been made on the latter point with the Expert Promotion Decree-Law of November 1978. To the extent that Peru is successful in launching and carrying out an economic recovery and development program, the debt problem will recede in importance as Peru tackles its basic development issues.

In November 1978, the major lenders to Peru—with the normal exception of the international financial agencies—agreed in principle on a large-scale refinancing of about $1.5 billion in interest and principal repayments due in 1979 and 1980. About $700 million of this is due to commercial banks, $600 million to European, North American, and Japanese suppliers and governments, and the remainder to lenders from centrally planned economies plus Latin American central banks. There is no doubt that the general agreement, even though it was subject to negotiations with each individual lender—by and large now complete—represents a major achievement. Nevertheless, the agreement still leaves open the question of whether Peru can effectively resume its economic growth with its perspective debt burden. Substantial debt servicing capacity is going to be taken up during the period 1982-1985/1986 with servicing old debt—namely the $1.5 billion of refinancing plus other past debt—so that little will be left to service new debt needed for new investment. That is, unless a major international commodity price boom gets underway again (an unpredictable event) and unless a new administration can quickly get productive investment moving again.

It has been argued by some observers of the external debt of developing countries that the maturity structure of external debt is not a key variable, as long as new capital inflows keep coming. In the case of countries emerging from a major financial and economic crisis, however, the maturity structure has to be a major factor in the recovery, since otherwise not enough time is provided for new investment to generate output and income. In the case of Peru, therefore, unless the new borrowing can be obtained at long term, future governments are likely to become fairly frequent candidates for refinancing, with all the problems of stop-and-go growth and development which this process entails. The IMF, in an annex to the last background report of its staff to the Executive Board, says almost as much:

> Given that no major expansion in export volume is expected after 1978, and that, even under the most conservative assumptions, some newly contracted debt will have to be repaid during this period, it is unlikely that the ratio of service payments to merchan-

> dise exports will actually fall below 40% during these five years unless there is a marked improvement in world prices for Peru's exports. If, for example, new debt contracted from 1978 through 1981 were to follow the pattern of 1974-1977, total debt service payments in 1982 would be U.S. $1.4 billion, rather than the U.S. $700 million currently scheduled [Latin America Economic Report, 1978].

These numbers go up after the refinancing, which was not included in the quoted text.

The rough projections of debt service below, based on the limited information publicly available (with the bulk of the refinancing repayable in 1982-1986), show that a significant rise in export prices—of the size which occurred in 1979—would be needed on top of a healthy increase in export volume to sustain such a service with ease. Military government spokesmen have stated that the new arrangements will enable Peru to keep the ratio of the service on medium- and long-term external debt to merchandise exports at or below 35%. There is, of course, nothing sacrosanct about such a ratio, since it is the overall health of the balance of payments which matters. But even taking such a figure at face value, the simple estimation in the table below shows that Peru will need a very high level of exports in 1981-1982 to even come close to such a proportion. Put in plain language, short of unusually favorable commodity export prices, Peru might well face a continuing balance of payments problem for several years to come, which would put a serious constraint upon development prospects.

In fact, in 1979 the combination of a successful financial recovery program and unexpectedly buoyant exports—due to the recovery of copper prices, the boom in silver, and the coming into full force of oil exports in a seller's market—enabled the authorities to undo part of the refinancing arrangements for 1979-1980 and revert partially to the original debt service schedules. Merchandise exports in 1979 boomed to U.S. $3.5 billion, of which $700 million were due to petroleum. The partial reversal of the refinancing will lighten the debt burden of future years, although it will continue to be heavy. The health of the balance of payments will continue to be precarious: The unusually favorable export conditions of 1979 could evaporate in the wake of a world recession, and imports, which have reflected the depressed domestic economy in Peru, are bound to expand once economic growth resumes. Equally important is the fiscal constraint imposed by the high debt service. In short, Peru must overcome its internal servicing problem, presently in the public sector, and increase its export volume if the high level of debt service is not to place the Peruvian economy excessively at the mercy of the vagaries of export prices.

V

Beyond the first issue—how Peru will manage in the future—the second issue raised by the Peruvian external debt problem is the role of foreign lenders. Were they overeager? Did they show due diligence in making their credit analyses? What should their relationship be to the International Monetary Fund? As said earlier, foreign commercial banks were only one of several categories of lenders to Peru; supplier credits are not far behind in importance in the structure of the Peruvian external debt. On the other hand, questions about the attitude and role of foreign lenders in Peru and in other countries with debt problems have tended to focus on commercial banks, for several reasons. First, banks have provided the major new element of international lending in the 1970s, thus sharply changing the balance between official and private lending to the richer and larger developing countries. Second, banks have become for such countries the main source of freely disposable foreign capital: Their loans are not tied to specific imports or projects and are thus available for general purpose or deficit financing. Third, bank loans have naturally tended to have shorter maturities than loans from official or semiofficial sources, such as supplier credits, so that they loom large in immediate debt service. The shorter maturities by themselves do not necessarily imply a larger net foreign exchange requirement each year to service debt, as long as lending banks are willing and in a position to provide new loans to replace the old ones.

In Peru, foreign banks are the largest single creditor: As of mid-1978, they held about one-third of the medium- and long-term debt outstanding and the bulk of the short-term debt, so that altogether they were owed about 45% of the external obligations of the public sector.

There is little doubt that the lead banks—the majority of them U.S. money-center banks—which organized loan syndicates to Peru in the early and mid 'seventies thought that they had a credit-worthy customer. An apparently stable military government but with a reformist drive, a relatively solid fiscal position, due in part to the fact that the new government had kept the tax measures padded by the Belaúnde administration in mid-1968, and especially the prospect of major new foreign exchange earnings in copper and oil—all seemed highly positive factors. Some of these prospects were, of course, only hopes, and financial and fiscal information was inadequate and delayed. Even so, the few analyses publicly available from international agencies—an economic report on Peru having been published by the World Bank in December 1973 (IBRD, 1973), based on a visit eleven months earlier, and the Bank having convened a "consultative group" of official and private lenders in 1972 and again in 1975—seemed to suggest that, despite some problems, the basic variables of the economy were in good order. With this kind of evidence, the banks, which were attracted by the profitability and relative safety of loans to sovereign governments of developing countries, were naturally eager to consider such lending.

Without falling into the trap of writing history backwards, I believe that there were enough signs from 1971-1975 that should have moderated the enthusiasm of some banks toward Peru. For one thing, the loans to Peru, at least among major U.S. banks, tended to be concentrated in relatively few banks while others consistently refused to participate, thus giving at least a prima facie indication that they were not satisfied with the creditworthiness of the borrower. Moreover, there were certainly signs during that period which cast doubt on the ability of the government to manage the rapidly expanding public sector. The nationalization and/or expropriations of basic industries, major mining enterprises, foreign trade, and so on, were accompanied by widespread labor unrest and discussions and divisions within the government itself which certainly suggested that all was not well. The major banks did undertake their own economic analyses, but these suffered from the inadequacy of the data and their generally narrow focus. A glance at the offering memoranda—equivalent to a prospectus for a loan—for loans to Peru in the period 1972-1974 shows for most of them a level of analysis in which can be described as cursory. The same comment can be made about the prospectuses for loans to other countries. Little is said about such important variables as price and exchange policies or the admittedly hard-to-judge area of the quality of economic management. Most of these documents provided only a partial view for the smaller banks seeking information, while already well-informed larger banks would presumably not need to read them.

The question of the quality of credit analysis and information brings in the role of the International Monetary Fund in the solution of problems such as those which Peru faced. The Fund is the major source of current financial information on developing economies. For perfectly understandable reasons, the Fund does not normally make the confidential information which it obtains from governments available to commercial institutions, specifically the banks which today hold such a large part of the debt of most of the largest developing countries. Yet, the International Monetary Fund in the 1970s has played an increasingly important role in working out programs to help overcome the external payments problems of developing countries in financial trouble, for which service on bank debts is a major part of the external payments burden.

In the early 1970s, it looked as if the Fund would have a limited role because its resources had grown more slowly than international trade and lending and therefore were falling short of the size of potential problems. But recent increases in quotas and the growing number of countries in financial distress in the wake of the 1974-1975 recession have given the Fund renewed vigor. The Fund should probably take the opportunity of its expanded role to think through whether there are significant improvements possible in the way it is helping developing countries put together their stabilization programs. The Fund has now been in that business for more than 25 years, and the basic analytic tools have remained the same. More than before, the judgments of the Fund have a wide impact that goes well beyond the amount of balance-of-payments credits which it is willing to contribute itself.

In the case of Peru, the program agreed to with the Fund in mid-1978 is doubtedly well conceived in the sense that the fiscal, exchange rate, price, and monetary measures were and are absolutely essential. The IMF has not "bailed out" the banks, since it insisted that the refinancing be part of the financial package. On the other hand, the fact that the banks insisted in Peru, as in other cases, that there be an agreement with the Fund before they would consider a refinancing gives the Fund tremendous leverage. (In 1976, the U.S. banks had tried to help organize and monitor by themselves the short-lived stabilization program of that year, but the effort failed, partly because of the domestic difficulties of financial stabilization.) In the old days, the King of Spain used to send his "visitadores" or inspectors to see if the colonies were behaving; the visitadores of today are upright, well-trained economists who work in a professional international organization where the plaintiff has a vote and a seat on the board. But the word of these inspectors can still be of overwhelming importance. In the case of Peru as in other countries, the program worked out by the government and supported by the Fund focuses largely on short-term financial questions, an emphasis that is needed but may turn out to have been excessive. It says little about how the patient is going to be encouraged to invest and produce after the initial recovery period.

VI

I have emphasized the availability of economic information as a crucial element. That may be a truism, but in Peru the internal lack of information and criticism was no doubt a major element in allowing the fiscal and financial situation to deteriorate as far as it did. Internationally, the case of Peru points up the existence of gaps in the assessment of credit risks. The issue is not that of "controlling" the euro-currency loan market, where most of the growth of international credit in the 1970s has been funded—by definition the euro market is uncontrolled and effective controls would simply displace it to a further and uncontrolled market—but whether the existing mechanisms of international credit information are adequate. The United States monetary authorities have in the last couple of years begun to take an interest in the question and now publish country exposure data for U.S. banks every six months. The Federal Reserve and the other bank supervisory authorities are now pooling their economic assessments on developing countries for the purpose of supervising the international portfolios of U.S. banks and their foreign branches and subsidiaries. But the lending institutions still do not get the information and, except for the largest ones, are not sufficiently equipped to obtain it and analyze it. The international financial institutions are not in a comfortable position to provide their confidential credit assessments, since their access to data would be restricted if they passed them on to the public; moreover, since the country being analyzed is itself a member of the evaluating institution, the final document may not give the full opinion of the staff doing the analysis. With about $100 billion of bank credits to developing countries, $60 billion of them from U.S. banks, there may be a need for an independent source of information and analysis, perhaps a kind of international Standard and Poor's of Moody's. Both borrowing governments and major lenders would be less than enthusiastic about such a venture; on the other hand, the large number of smaller lenders might well be interested in such an idea and make its operation a requirement for their continued participation in international credits to a number of countries. The large sums at stake certainly justify some cooperative effort in order to forestall the volatility of debt-connected crises which could endanger the stability of international capital flows.

CONCLUSION

The new civilian government of Fernando Belaúnde Terry was inaugurated July 28, 1980. The presidential and parliamentary elections earlier in the year were the first since 1963, an interval which reflects the sporadic and relatively infrequent experimentation of Peru with constitutional rule. The civilian government inherits an economy very different from that which it left in 1968. It is true to say that there have been major institutional changes in the sense that the state has—largely unsuccessfully—taken over large areas of the economy, from foreign trade and marketing to sugar mills, several basic industries, and even newspapers. There was, of course, the major redistribution of land ownership begun in 1969. At the same time, the employment problem has become much more acute; agriculture has remained virtually stagnant and, overhanging these problems, the external debt is ten times larger and several times more burdensome in relative terms than it was twelve years ago. The debt question, as I have tried to show in this article, is a reflection of Peru's own development problem, including its ability to manage its financial affairs. On the other hand, the debt question could substantially limit the room for maneuver of the new administration. This means that the Peruvian economy continues to be heavily dependent on the vagaries of commodity export prices. In order to begin changing this pattern, among many other requirements will be not only a tremendous effort on the part of the incoming administration, but also a large and active contribution by outside official lenders, who have so far played only a small role in the economic fortunes of Peru.

NOTES

1. The following might be mentioned, with the latest estimate of their outstanding external public debt at the end of 1978: Turkey, $12 billion; Peru, $8 billion; Zaire, $2+ billion; North Korea, about $2 billion; Zambia, $1+ billion; Jamaica, $1+ billion and Gabon, $1 billion. This total, about $25 billion, represented 10% to 12% of the external public debt of non-OPEC developing countries at the time. In rough numbers, about $10 billion or $11 billion of the $25 billion was owed to commercial banks.

2. When the Belaúnde government, through Finance Minister Manuel Ulloa, requested a partial refinancing of the Peruvian external debt in June 1968, I had the unfortunate task of calling for a meeting of the "Club," but it refused to meet. I therefore chaired my own meeting in London.

3. The largest commitment by far is the pipeline at a total cost of about U.S. $800 million, of which $330 million is a Japanese supplier credit apparently denominated in

Yen, even though the oil exports to Japan which support the debt service on the loan are, naturally enough, priced in U.S. dollars.

4. Using data from International Financial Statistics (1979), with 1975 = 100, the average export volume in 1974-1976 was 101 compared to 118 in 1961-1963, while export prices were respectively 116 and 21 in the two periods.

5. See, for example, Peru (1971: ch. 1), which states the following among the three major goals of development policy: "C. Strengthening national sovereignity, which will entail a drastic reduction of the present dependency and vulnerability of the economy by guaranteeing national control of domestic resources, by changing the traditional pattern of international economic relations."

6. The actual dollar amount is larger because the World Bank and the Interamerican Development Bank account for their loans at the original exchange rates. Since the loans are to a large degree repayable in currencies which have appreciated in relation to the dollar, the actual amount outstanding in U.S. dollars is larger than accounted.

REFERENCES

IBRD [International Bank for Reconstruction and Development] (1973) Current Economic Position and Prospects of Peru. December. Washington, DC: Author.

International Financial Statistics (1979-) Yearbook. Washington, DC: International Monetary Fund. (Monthly publication)

International Monetary Fund (1969-1978) Annual consultation reports. (unpublished)

KUCZYNSKI, P. P. (1977) Peruvian Democracy under Economic Stress: An Account of the Belaunde Adminstration. Princeton, NJ: Princeton Univ. Press.

Latin America Economic Report [London] (1978) "Peru's debt rescheduling only staves off problems." November 24: 2.

Morgan Guaranty Trust (1970-1979) World Financial Markets. New York: Author.

Peru (1971) Plan Nacional de Desarrollo, 1971-1975, Section 2, May. Supreme Decree 015-71-PM. Lima.

Pedro-Pablo Kuczynski was appointed Minister of Energy and Mines in the present Peruvian government of Fernando Belaúnde after this article was written; he was the economic adviser and manager of the Central Reserve Bank of Peru during the previous Belaúnde administration. Kuczynski has been active in international financial and industrial organizations, taught economics at the University of Pittsburgh, and is the author of Peruvian Democracy under Economic Stress: An Account of the Belaúnde Administration, 1963-1968 (Princeton, 1977) *and numerous articles.*

Publisher's Note: The following information is printed in accordance with U.S. postal regulations: Statement of Ownership, Management and Circulation (required by 39 U.S.C. 3685). 1. Title of Publication: JOURNAL OF INTERAMERICAN STUDIES AND WORLD AFFAIRS. 1A. Publication No.: 0022-1937. 2. Date of Filing: October 1, 1980. 3. Frequency of Issue: Quarterly. 3A. No. of Issues Published Annually: 4. 3B. Annual Subscription Price: institutions, $36.00; individuals, $18.00. 4. Location of Known Office of Publication: 275 South Beverly Drive, Beverly Hills (Los Angeles), California 90212. 5. Location of the Headquarters or General Business Offices of the Publishers: 275 South Beverly Drive, Beverly Hills (Los Angeles), California 90212. 6. Names and Complete Addresses of Publisher, Editor, and Managing Editor: Publisher: Sara Miller McCune, 1102 South Oakhurst Drive, Los Angeles, California 90035; Editor: John P. Harrison, University of Miami, Box 24-8134, Coral Gables, FL 33124; Managing Editor: None. 7. Owner (If owned by a corporation, its name and address must be stated and also immediately thereunder the names and addresses of stockholders owning or holding 1% or more of total amount of stock. If not owned by a corporation, the names and addresses of the individual owners must be given. If owned by a partnership or other unincorporated firm, its name and address, as well as that of each individual must be given.): Sage Publications, Inc., 275 South Beverly Drive, Beverly Hills, California 90212; Sara Miller McCune, 1102 South Oakhurst Drive, Los Angeles, California 90035; George D. McCune, 1102 South Oakhurst Drive, Los Angeles, California 90035; Marvin Sirot, Mohawk Lane, Greenwich, Connecticut 06830; Gustave Sirot, Wingate Road, Guilford, Connecticut 06340; John B. Hurford, 220 East 63rd Street, New York, New York 10021; Albert L. Zesiger, 1125 Fifth Avenue, New York, New York 10028; Judith C. Zesiger, 1125 Fifth Avenue, New York, New York 10028; Morris Janowitz, 1357 E. 55th Place, Chicago, Illinois 60637. 8. Known Bondholders, Mortgagees, and Other Security Holders Owning or Holding 1% or More of Total Amount of Bonds, Mortgages or Other Securities: None. 9. For Completion by Nonprofit Organizations Authorized to Mail at Special Rates (Section 132.122, PSM): Not Applicable.

10. Extent and Nature of Circulation	Av. No. Copies Each Issue During Preceding 12 Months	Actual No. of Copies of Single Issue Published Nearest to Filing Date
A. Total no. copies printed (net press run)	1766	1859
B. Paid circulation:		
1. Sales through dealers and carriers, street vendors and counter sales	162	148
2. Mail subscriptions	1196	1221
C. Total paid circulation (sum of 10B1 and 10B2)	1358	1369
D. Free distribution by mail, carrier or other means: samples, complimentary, and other free copies	46	50
E. Total distribution (sum of C & D)	1404	1419
F. Copies not distributed:		
1. Office use, left-over, unaccounted, spoiled after printing	362	440
2. Returns from news agents	0	0
G. Total (sum of E, F1 and 2—should equal net press run shown in A)	1766	1859

11. I certify that the statements made by me above are correct and complete. (Signed) Gary Polinsky, General Manager. 12. 39 U.S.C. 3626 provides in pertinent part: "No person who would have been entitled to mail matter under former section 4359 of this title shall mail such matter at the rates provided under this subsection unless he files annually with the Postal Service a written request for permission to mail matter at such rates." In accordance with the provisions of this statute, I hereby request permission to mail the publication named in item 1 at the reduced postage rates presently authorized by 39 U.S.C. 3626. (Signed) Gary Polinsky, General Manager.

CARLOS J. MONETA
United Nations Institute for Training & Research (UNITAR)
New York

ANTARCTICA, LATIN AMERICA, AND THE INTERNATIONAL SYSTEM IN THE 1980s

Toward a New Antarctic Order?

The Antarctic Treaty was signed by twelve countries in 1959.[1] This group, together with those countries having territorial claims prior to signing the treaty—Argentina, Australia, Chile, France, New Zealand, Norway, and the United Kingdom—would try with great difficulty to reconcile the opposing interests of (1) countries that for decades had been actively defending their claims of sovereignty over sectors of Antarctica; (2) superpowers that, while not asserting any claims of their own—although certainly reserving the right to do so in the future—did not accept those of other countries; and (3) a number of countries that had been invited to participate in the treaty because they had been active in Antarctica during the International Geophysical Year.

In 1979, the Tenth Meeting of the Antarctic Treaty Consultative Parties was held in Washington. In the intervening twenty years, several countries had agreed to the treaty and one country, Poland, had changed its status to consultative party. The primary political objectives of the United States and other great powers that led to the signing of the treaty were to prevent the continent from being drawn into the Cold War between the Soviet Union and the United States, to work for a limited internationalization of the continent, and to reach a compromise solution among the

---

EDITOR'S NOTE: The translation of this article is by Marjory Mattingly Urquidi.

Journal of Interamerican Studies and World Affairs, Vol. 23 No. 1, February 1981 29-68

countries with and without claims so that issues of sovereignty would be temporarily "frozen" and treaty members would have access to all of Antarctica. These are still the objectives, but their realization is threatened by major changes occurring in the world system. In addition to the entry of new members, the group of countries that originally drafted the Antarctic Treaty must face a broad range of problems, many of which are not adequately provided for in the treaty. These include an escalation in the conflicts linked to territorial claims and to East-West strategic rivalry; the discovery of important natural resources; and the appearance on the scene of such extraneous actors as transnational corporations, international agencies, and developing countries with increasing and diverging interests in the continent and its adjacent areas.[2] Some examples follow.

In 1975, Senator Pell recommended to the U.S. Senate Subcommittee on the Ocean and Environment that private industry—especially the sector concerned with heavy mineral and oil—should be part of the official U.S. delegation to the Meetings of the Antarctic Treaty Consultative Parties. Meanwhile, the Head of the U.S. Department of Energy Resources of the Office of Geological Research stated that the recoverable oil resources in the Antarctic had been estimated at about 15 billion barrels (Washington Post, 1975).

Efforts of the United Nations agencies to participate in some of the activities considered in the treaty—for example, environmental protection and exploitation of the living resources of the Antarctic Ocean—have not been encouraged by the treaty members, which so far have managed to prevent any outside intervention (Sollie, 1979: 205).[3]

Treaty members have adopted the same attitude regarding any action linking the Antarctic question, directly or indirectly, to UNCLOS (United Nations Conference on the Law of the Sea). Several attempts have been made by some of the developing countries—for example, the Arab countries in 1976 and Brazil in 1979—to include the "Antarctic question" in the agenda of the UNCLOS conference, arguing that the regime of the "Common Heritage of Mankind" should be applied to Antarctica.[4]

In an appraisal of the strategic interests of the Soviet Union vis-à-vis the restrictions imposed by UNCLOS on the military use of oceans, a U.S. expert on maritime policy and strategy (Mangone, 1978: 69) stated that "no law-of-the-sea treaty in the long run will be able to deny to the United States or the Soviet Union the utilization of the oceans for their vital security needs. . . . For the United States, in particular, sea control to support its allies and to protect international trade, including crucial petroleum supplies, would not be abandoned for legal articles only approved by the developing nations of Asia, Africa and Latin America."

In turn, the leading Soviet authority on naval strategy, Admiral Gorshkov, Commander-in-Chief of the Fleet, described the function of that branch of the armed forces in his country's global competition with the United States.[5] He stressed that the navy is used as a foreign policy instrument designed to demonstrate that the United States no longer dominates the seas, adding that the Soviet Union is increasingly concerned with maintaining its presence in all the oceans where it has strategic interests (Moneta, 1974).[6]

The foregoing present only some of the conflictive aspects of the growing importance of Antarctica in several spheres: (a) the global international system; (b) the regional Latin American subsystem; and (c) the strictly Antarctic subsystem. In the context of security and strategy—the exploration of Antarctica, the exploitation and conservation of its marine and continental resources, and the claims of sovereignty over vast portions of its territory—are matters that increasingly attract the attention of the national, international, and transnational actors. As Antarctica becomes a definite part of the complex of major problems confronting these actors, it also becomes a new and active subsystem of the international system.

Bearing this in mind, this article will present some thoughts on the problems related to the emergence and characteristics of the "New Antarctic Order" that in future years will result from the interaction of political, strategic, economic, scientific, and technological factors that are already operating within and outside the framework of the Antarctic Treaty.

THE "TRANSITION" STATE OF THE INTERNATIONAL REGIME: ANTARCTICA VIS-A-VIS UNCLOS

Although it is still premature to predict the final outcome of the next sessions of the United Nations Conference on the Law of the Sea (UNCLOS), it is possible to identify some of the basic issues. Most center around disagreements concerning boundaries, uses, and jurisdiction by the various categories of actors: the developing and industrialized countries; countries with and without a coastline; the traditionally great maritime powers; and the medium-size and small countries with coastal navies.

These problems arise from a fundamental change in the concept of the use of ocean space promoted by the developing countries in their attempt to achieve a worldwide redistribution of resources and power.

Indeed, the traditional attitude, based on use—for example, fishery and transport (with its corresponding military implications)—is being replaced by a political vision incorporating new concepts of territorial space. The ocean without frontiers is being transformed into a sea with Exclusive Economic Zones (EEZ) where uses expanded, including new activities.

The growing authority of the state on the ocean is clearly seen in a national sense in the significant expansion of space that, under different regimes, can be controlled and exploited by the Nation-State. These changes, led by the developing countries, include a new and vast Exclusive Economic Zone (EEZ); special rights for countries in disadvantageous geographical locations, archipelagos, and landlocked countries, and legal regime of the continental shelf and the possibilities offered by shared utilization of the seabed and deep ocean floor situated outside national jurisdictions under the regime of the "Common Heritage of Mankind."[7]

These basic changes in political-economic objectives (the idea of appropriation), together with the new and more-intensive use of ocean resources made possible by technology, constitute the area in which there will be conflicts of jurisdiction and sovereignty between UNCLOS and the regime of the Antarctic Treaty.

Current issues refer chiefly to the legal status of Antarctica and the utilization of its resources in the continental shelf and surrounding waters.

Clearly, present concern with the future of Antarctica is inextricably bound up with the latter's petroleum and gas potential and its already proven wealth of krill and other species. The different legal positions should be viewed politically since they largely express rationalizations—proposed in order to establish rules of distribution and the use of privileged values—of the political, economic, and strategic interests that are involved.

Although there will be no attempt to discuss the different interpretations,[8] what should be pointed out is that the subsoil of the legal flora is made up of a layer of *realpolitik*. Countries with territorial claims argue convincingly that their acquisitions are well grounded and not to be denied on the basis of a law that does not take circumstances into account and that the time has come to adapt the law to major advances in all spheres—Informal Composite Negotiating Text (ICNT) a precise example of this. Furthermore, several of these territorial acquisitions show signs of permanent occupation.[9]

By refusing to recognize such claims, the United States and the Soviet Union are placed in an excellent relative position.[10] Principles such as free access to the development of natural resources and the establishment of nonpreferential and uniform rules making the resources of all Antarctica available to treaty members form part of official U.S. policy (U.S. Congress [Senate], 1975b: 5) and they also suit the Soviets. Consequently, whereas the possibilities of resource exploration and exploitation are theoretically equal, in practice they turn out to be totally asymmetrical[11] because of the huge differences in the financial, scientific, and technological capabilities of the advanced members of the treaty as compared with the developing countries.

The latter, with the exception of those who are consultative members of the Antarctic Treaty, find it expedient to adopt the position of *Res Communis,* since it maximizes the possibility of their participating in the benefits derived from the exploitation of resources that otherwise would be beyond their grasp because of the technological and economic inadequacies making them ineligible to accede to the treaty.

This reference to political realities suggests that the evolution of international law and its legitimacy are not just the result of a consensual acceptance of privileged values but that they are also the expression of relations of power and of radically different social, political, and economic functions that are going through dynamic transformations.

The values and interests of the international community should therefore be reconciled—insofar as possible—with those of the member countries of the treaty. Specific problems arise at different levels: (a) the extent to which the international community will accept the Antarctic Treaty; and (b) the treaty's own lack of precise definitions regarding resource exploration and exploitation, as well as the geographical limits that may be applied to this international agreement.

It may be considered that the actions and declarations to date of the actors in the international system imply acceptance of the treaty by the totality of the Nation-States. Nonetheless, there have already been signs of opposition, one of which is found in the evolution of the United Nations Conference on the Law of the Sea (UNCLOS). Statements made in this forum—such as those of the conference chairman and of other delegates[12]—indicate the Third World's growing interest in having principles and mechanisms of international cooperation adopted that would enable it to share in Antarctic resources.

Actually, what is at issue is not the treaty itself but how it may be used by a few countries to legitimize their monopoly of its benefits. Insofar as the treaty members are willing to look for a formula that will substantially take care of the economic interests of the developing countries, the doors are clearly open for negotiation.

The Antarctic Treaty members are keenly aware of the new situation and seem prepared to try to meet the needs of all parties. At the end of the Tenth Meeting of Consultative Parties, they issued a press communique reaffirming their rights and at the same time accepting their responsibilities to find ways within the treaty framework not only to solve their internal problems but also to balance effective treatment of these resource issues against the need to protect the interests of all mankind in the Antarctic (U.S. Department of State, 1979b). Overall, this document, together with the statements of the various delegations (e.g., U.S. Department of State, 1979a) is a reaffirmation of the provisions of the treaty and of the determination of the parties to maintain the system when new issues related to Antarctic resources come to the forefront (U.S. Department of State, 1979a, 1979b).

It is evident that the treaty, which has been in force for twenty years and which has achieved many of its objectives, is now recognized internationally as a "special case" by a law that is evolving and not subject to the strict criteria of traditional international law (Guyer, 1977: 153-154). It is not only logical but simple justice to acknowledge that treaty members (Van Essen, 1975-1976: 95-96), as well as the rest of the world community, have rights. In its new stage, the treaty should be developed as an instrument capable of resolving the problems of the ownership, control, administration, and regulation of natural resources among its own members and between these and the international community.

CONFLICTS LINKED TO RESOURCE EXPLOITATION

Although their size and commercial value are still a matter of discussion, deposits of copper, manganese, uranium, coal, platinum, chrome, beryl, cobalt, nickel, titanium, gold, and silver exist in Antarctica. Almost all are found in the Antarctic Peninsula, with extensive fields of iron and coal concentrated in the Prince Charles Mountains and the Trans-Antarctica mountain range, respectively (Wright and Williams, 1975; FNF, 1973).

There are mineral nodules on the deep ocean floor, but their mining is not expected to be economically feasible for some time to come, and meanwhile there are other, more accessible areas in the world offering greater potential. The situation in the seas around Antarctica, however, is different; the continental shelf seems to have deposits of petroleum and gas in amounts that vary according to the sources and experts consulted (Wright and Williams, 1975: 53-55; FNF, 1973; Tinker and Holdgate, 1979; Tinker, 1979), but that are between 15 billion and well over 50 billion barrels of oil. Again, the waters surrounding the Antarctic Peninsula, which are claimed variously by Argentina, Chile, and Great Britain (i.e., the Weddell Sea), are the richest. The shelves of the Weddell and Bellingshausen Seas (Argentina, Chile, and Great Britain), together with the Ross Sea (New Zealand) and the Amundsen Sea (unclaimed) are considered the most promising areas (Wright and Williams, 1975; FNF, 1973).

The Southern Ocean also contains renewable resources, especially the small crustacean krill which is high in protein value. Krill exploitation is still in the experimental stage; its catch very limited—less than 200,000 tons per year mainly by the Soviet Union, Japan, and Poland[13]—and its biological cycle not fully understood. There is also a possibility that the krill could not be directly used for human consumption, since it is now used only for feeding animals. It is estimated that approximately 100 million tons of krill could be harvested annually, compared with the present worldwide total marine catch of 70 million tons (Kimball, 1980).

The largest concentrations of krill are found chiefly within the 200-mile limit off the coasts of the Antarctic Peninsula and in the waters of the Weddell Sea around the Orcadas (Orkney), Georgias (King George), and Sandwich Islands—that is, the Antarctic sectors disputed by Argentina and Great Britain.

What regime will govern all this wealth? The articles of the Antarctic Treaty do not refer specifically to resource exploration and exploitation (FNF, 1973: L-1) but only to the preservation and conservation of living resources (art. IX, par. 1f). Nevertheless, the treaty contains other provisions (FNF, 1973: L-1, L-2) that furnish a legal framework for the member states to act in this matter. Thus, a convention, not yet approved [Editor's note: Although the convention had not been approved at the time this article was written, it has since been approved] was drafted for the conservation of renewable marine resources, and it also extends treaty jurisdiction to the "Antarctic convergence." The principles and text of a future convention on mineral resources and hydrocarbons have been under study since the start of this decade.[14]

In the case of marine resources, which are receiving immediate attention, the issue of sovereignty seems to be linked to the regime that will be agreed on. By applying its provisions to the area south of 60° South Latitude, the treaty establishes that nothing in it "shall prejudice or in any affect the rights, or the exercise of the rights, of any State under international law with regard to the high seas within that area" (art. VI). Given the advances of UNCLOS on the continental shelf and the Exclusive Economic Zone (EEZ) regimes,[15] it may be asked what area will be considered high seas, since there are member countries with territorial claims associated with the right to EEZ (FNF, 1973) and other members that do not recognize it.[16] Will countries outside the treaty accept a jurisdiction extending to 60° South Latitude? As far as the Antarctic convergence? Or, as many experts have proposed,[17] will a kind of Exclusive Economic Zone be recognized that surrounds the entire Antarctic continent and the islands included within the 60° South Latitude?

As regards living resources, the agreement uses a legal device—the results of which cannot be predicted—to try to reconcile the new requirements related to the EEZ of UNCLOS with the positions of states that do not recognize claims and wish to be guaranteed free access to the 200 miles of Antarctic coastline. It is therefore at least doubtful that the same mechanism can be successfully applied to the exploitation of oil and gas in the continental shelf.

Still to be considered are resources that will be exploited in the future such as icebergs—Antarctica encompasses 90% of the world supply of fresh water—which some of the Arab states have already shown interest in exploiting.[18]

These new regimes may be the source of any number of possible jurisdictional disputes: the binding character of the regimes on third states; the coordination of activities and the demarcation of areas of jurisdiction as between nations; the jurisdiction of the Antarctic Treaty and of UNCLOS, with a typical case being the future relations of treaty members with the Authority created by

UNCLOS in the administration of resources located outside national jurisdictions.

A simple enumeration of some of the most likely points of cooperation or conflict—several of which are already a fact—among the different actors gives an idea of the magnitude of the problems that will have to be faced.

WITHIN THE FRAMEWORK OF THE ANTARCTIC TREATY

—states with claims vs. states without claims
—as between states with claims; e.g., Argentina, Chile, and Great Britain
—as between states without claims; e.g., USA and USSR
—states with fisheries vs. states without fisheries
—conservationist states, which do not yet want to undertake exploitation at least of some of the resources vs. states such as the United States and the Soviet Union, which advocate immediate exploitation
—states with significant scientific-technological and financial resources vs. states lacking in such resources; i.e., developed countries vs. developing countries
—states with status of consultative party vs. signatory states; e.g., Argentina and/or Chile vs. Brazil

WITHIN THE CONTEXT OF THE "GLOBAL SYSTEM-ANTARCTIC SUBSYSTEM"

—member states of the Antarctic Treaty vs. nonmember states, which in turn can be divided into states with consultative status vs. nonmember states, signatory states vs. nonmember states, and so on
—member states vs. transnational entities such as transnational corporations and nongovernmental associations
—member states vs. international agencies such as Food and Agriculture Organization and the United Nations Environment Program
—member states vs. subnational entities such as ecological groups

In practice, this simple presentation can be extended to a variety of combinations, such as member states without resources and nonmember states with resources vs. member states with resources. Furthermore, this list should include polarizations arising from security factors. The most probable result will be a subsystem of growing complexity that will develop functional-sectoral links of a cooperative-conflictive nature among the different actors of the global system at the subnational, national, and transnational levels. The polarizations and alliances emerging from the conventional North-South and East-West coordinates will be appreciably modified in the light of these new factors.

One of the essential elements for effectively improving the negotiating position of the developing countries, whether or not they are members of the Antarctic Treaty, will be the ability to clearly perceive the structural changes, the impact of new political and economic forces, the contradictions generated, and the consequent opportunities to resolve such contradictions by formulating more unorthodox strategies.

THE ANTARCTIC SUBSYSTEM VIS-A-VIS PROBLEMS OF STRATEGIC SECURITY: UNCLOS AND ASPECTS OF STRATEGIC SECURITY

In recent decades there have been important changes in the strategic perceptions and capabilities of the actors with maritime interests. The traditional powers have experienced increasing uncertainty over signs of their loss of naval supremacy, given the appearance of the Soviet Union as a new sea power with global possibilities, as well as the emergence of several Third World countries having regional potential.[19]

These new events have affected their ability to control ocean activities in peacetime—that is, in this period of local conflicts limited in scope. Nonetheless, thanks to their financial resources and technological advances, they have maintained some predominance in the military area and in the field of economic activities, where they act in conjunction with the transnationals.

The ideology rationalizing naval supremacy—freedom of the seas—had to give way to the revindication ideologies of the territorialization and internationalization of ocean space. Although the status quo was broken, the military objectives of maintaining strategic naval control and of using marine resources remain, even if they must be adapted to the new conditions. Consequently, naval strategy and diplomacy are going to be affected by economic, political, and technological changes (Booth, 1979: 329-330).

UNCLOS has been perceived by United States and British specialists (Osgood, 1974; Booth, 1979; Mangone, 1978; Hollick, 1974; Morris, 1976; Knight, 1974; Buzan, 1976; Hill, 1976) since it entails restrictions on the use of the four dimensions of ocean space—seabed, subsoil, surface, and air space—necessary to satisfy security objectives. The latter are to maintain: (a) strategic nuclear capability vis-à-vis the Soviet Union through the possibility of overflights by military planes and the unannounced passage of submerged nuclear submarines through straits and zones beyond the twelve-mile limit; (b) the ability to hold maneuvers and to send U.S. naval forces to remote areas; (c) military intelligence operations—e.g., through devices placed to detect underwater activities in the continental shelf; and (d) protection of population, commercial interests, and access to critical resources (Osgood, 1974: 78-79; Knight, 1974: 22-24; U.S. Congress [Senate], 1977).

The USSR and the U.S. navies coincide in their mission of strategic nuclear deterrent, as well as in their conduct of military intelligence operations and naval maneuvers. There is no doubt that the Soviet Union is actively preparing itself so that, in case of conflicts in areas distant from its territory, its forces can be rapidly deployed to such areas.[20] At the present stage, however, it places primary importance on developing its ability to "show the flag" in remote Third World theaters, thereby acting as a deterrent, and to "deny access" to western lines of communication (Morris, 1976: 66-67; Mangone, 1978: 72; Gorshkov, 1974).

Since the Soviet navy continues to globalize its strategy, it can be expected to increase its presence in the Indian Ocean and the South Atlantic, where its interests are beginning to go beyond the merely subregional.

These security interests meant that the great powers directed their policy in UNCLOS toward ensuring (a) their access to distant bodies of water through the right of free passage; (b) limitations on the extent to which the EEZ would enhance the already existing power of control and jurisdiction exercised by coastal states; (c) the right of military planes to fly over international waters; (d) freedom of scientific research; and (e) the possibility of installing detection equipment in the continental shelf.

In strategic terms, the basic scenario consists in maintaining global competition with the Soviet Union for an indefinite period "in which moderated great-power competition will be punctuated by continual disturbances on the peripheries of the developed world" (Osgood, 1974: 114)—that is, the tensions and conflicts in the developing regions are expected to increase.

For regional or subregional naval powers, UNCLOS is not an obstacle but rather a legal umbrella under which it can improve its negotiating position vis-à-vis the great powers. The new oceanic territories entail greater vigilance and therefore larger and more modern naval forces. Technological innovation, by introducing into naval warfare missiles that can be mounted on intermediate and small vessels, offers some deterrent potential to the fleets of medium-size countries if conflicts with the great powers develop in the course of local operations.

It is possible to observe a mutual influence—unfortunately, asymmetrical—between security factors and the new oceanic regime. Even if strategic operations can be affected by UNCLOS they generally retain their predominance. In this connection, it should be pointed out that the text under negotiation in UNCLOS accepts, by omission, certain privileges for military interests (Booth, 1979: 341). Thus, navies can conduct military exercises in the EEZ of other states, construct platforms for military use and for mounting nonnuclear weapons and can avoid submitting disputes related to military activities to the mechanisms provided by the negotiating text for solving conflicts, thereby appreciably conditioning the effectiveness of UNCLOS in preserving oceans for pacific uses.

Since the medium-size and smaller powers are not immediately affected by the nuclear deterrent strategy—unless, of course, it breaks down—they are relatively more likely to be involved in direct and localized confrontations with actors at their level.

There are therefore various considerations that bear on the security aspects of the Antarctic subsystem and its zones of influence.

—UNCLOS and strategic security factors affect each other, but the latter predominate in case of conflict. In "peacetime" the states, especially the traditional naval powers, are able to maintain an active naval presence in the desired theater of operations.
—The new legal regime and technological advances nonetheless offer greater opportunities for independent action by developing countries in defense of their interests.
—The problems still not solved by UNCLOS, together with the numerous points of friction that will appear if the UNCLOS negotiating text is finally approved and applied, offer a broad field of action for the exercise of naval diplomacy based on military power.
—The South Atlantic and its zone of influence—Antarctic Peninsula, Queen Maud Land, Bellingshausen and Weddell Seas—are gradually becoming more valuable from a security standpoint because of the shifting of the lines of strategic East-West confrontation in Africa south of the Sahara; the presence of the naval forces of both superpowers in the Indian Ocean; the importance of sea lanes connecting the Pacific and Atlantic Oceans (Antarctica-Latin America) and the Atlantic and Indian Oceans (Antarctica-Africa); and the bilateral or subregional conflicts of varying consequence that erupt in the Latin American Southern Cone, South Africa, and the African Horn.

THE CHANGING EMPHASIS IN THE STRATEGIC CONCEPT OF ANTARCTICA: THE PREEMINENCE OF ECONOMIC INTERESTS

During the Second World War, Antarctica acquired some military significance because of the English observatories installed there that provided valuable meteorological information. Furthermore, German submarines prowling the waters north of the Antarctic Peninsula harassed ships transporting food to Europe from the Atlantic coast of Latin America.

Because of Antarctica's marginal geographical location and its lack of population and known resources, the continent and its surrounding waters were of little strategic importance for a number of years, facilitating the nonmilitarization agreement.

Nevertheless, Antarctica, or at least part of its territory, could not be dismissed altogether since it represented a potential base for missile attack against the southern countries of Latin America and Africa, as well as New Zealand and Australia. Moreover, the Antarctic Peninsula facilitates any attempt at control of the Pacific-Atlantic-Indian Ocean sea lanes by actors having the necessary military, technological, and logistic resources.

As has been pointed out earlier, the signing of the Antarctic Treaty achieved one of its objectives, which was to remove Antarctica from the cold war scheme by prohibiting its militarization (art. 1, par. 1). This made it possible to prevent the introduction of nuclear and even conventional forces, even though the latter regularly operated as suppliers of logistic services and in pursuit of scientific activities (art. 1, par. 2). Nevertheless, the danger of isolated acts of hostility or of a future militarization, whether partial or temporary, is not to be discarded in the light of a series of possibilities.

—return to cold war politics, due to the evolution of the USA-USSR strategic equilibrium at a global, sectoral, or regional level; e.g., Persian Gulf, Indian Ocean, Africa
—formal or de facto breakdown of the Antarctic Treaty, due to the impossibility of reaching an agreement among its members for the exploration and exploitation of natural resources or in the face of pressure by other factors of the international system
—use of military force by countries to settle the conflict of totally or partially overlapping territorial claims
—penetration of the Antactic continent or ocean space by third parties that are not members of the treaty and that do not accept treaty regulations

Some of these possibilities should be commented on, however briefly. To date, the "neutralization" of the continent and its jurisdictional waters has satisfied the security requirements of the United States and the Soviet Union, but the strategic equilibrium may be altered in a way that would induce the superpowers to run the risk of changing the rules of the game. There is a broad range of potential geopolitical-strategic disequilibria in Soviet-North

American relations that would have serious repercussions on the treaty—for example, the "loss" of South Africa or of control of the Indian Ocean by the United States.

On the other hand, even today there are factors that may be speculated about. What if nuclear submarines of either or both superpowers make trips to waters covered by the treaty to obtain scientific-military information? Might they not already have potential support points on the coasts of the continent? For this purpose, the inspection operations carried out by treaty members may be adequate to identify installations or special equipment, but they would not detect activities such as the first mentioned.

The remaining scenarios selected are focused on conflicts of sovereignty and resource distribution. In the case of the great powers, strategic concerns are shifted to the exploitation of marine resources (U.S. Congress [House], 1978: 78-90). Thus, for example, Ann Hollick (1974: 1-2) states that "in 1973 and 1974 the warfare between global strategic and coastal economic interests was subtly transformed into a conflict between political strategy and resource-oriented economic perspectives . . . political compromises have evolved steadily away from positions favoring military-strategic interests to positions more congenial to coastal and economic interests."

These changes in the positions adopted by the great western powers and, in particular, by the United States and the Soviet Union[21] in the UNCLOS discussions are paralleled in the Antarctic Treaty negotiations.[22] The most important difference resides in the Soviet Union's opposition to the commercial exploration and exploitation of nonrenewable resources,[23] which seems to respond to economic and political-strategic concerns rather than to the reasons formally cited. The latter are related to protection of the environment, the lack of urgency to undertake exploitation given the existence of reserves in other, more accessible, parts of the world, and the need to maintain a legacy of natural resources for coming generations.[24]

To determine with any precision the probability of a given scenario of conflict, as well as the numerous viable combinations of cooperative or adversary relationships among the various actors, is beyond the scope of this article. Nevertheless, mention can be made of the general objectives pursued by the different actors that will influence the evolution of the process.

STRATEGIC-ECONOMIC OBJECTIVES OF THE UNITED STATES

A 1970 White House memorandum contained the guidelines laid down by President Nixon for U.S. policy in Antarctica. This document reiterated the desire of the United States that (1) the Antarctic Treaty should remain in force; (2) the continent should continue to be used for pacific purposes; and (3) scientific research should be promoted, with emphasis on "the prediction and assessment of resources" (U.S. White House, 1975: 30).

These objectives were confirmed and even expanded in the reports submitted to the Senate in 1975 by the assistant secretary of state, also head of the Antarctic Policy Group.[25] The reports reaffirmed the need to protect U.S. rights and interests, to guarantee freedom of exploration and scientific research, to ensure free access to the development (understood as "use") of natural resources, to establish nonpreferential rules for activities to be carried out for this purpose, and to have an orderly administrative system for the area (U.S. White House, 1975: 5). Its basic principles were again corroborated in 1979 by the statements of the U.S. delegate to the Tenth Meeting of the Consultative Parties (U.S. Department of State, 1979a).

The major objectives thus set forth propose freedom of movement throughout the treaty area to continue scientific exploration, now oriented toward future commercial exploitation. This freedom of movement is to be based on principles that ensure equal opportunity for all and that lay the groundwork for a common administrative mechanism to regulate activities.

A regime of mineral exploitation is sought under the treaty or through other agreements linked to it. But what would happen if, because of the opposition of the Soviet Union, countries with claims or other similar factors, this were not possible? If we turn to the most recent antecedent—conflict over the regime of exploitation of ocean space beyond national jurisdictions—we find that (a) the United States seriously considered the alternative (and even discussed it with various countries) of a "mini-treaty" between the industrialized countries and some of the emerging powers—e.g., Brazil—to exploit resources outside the scope of the United Nations negotiations (Morris, 1979: 171); and (b) it was believed possible that measures of opposition might include "resorts to low-level violence" (U.S. Congress [House], 1978: 102). It was therefore decided that if it became necessary to defend commercial exploitation of mineral resources in the seabed, "linking the mining operation to the military deterrence continuum by suitable official statements and military demonstrations might be effective against single-nation threats" (U.S. Congress [House], 1978: 103). A Third World common front could be better confronted "by negotiating an offsetting defense agreement among the industrialized countries similar to the fishing protection agreements in the North Sea" (U.S. Congress [House], 1978: 103). Furthermore, "in addition to the military responses enumerated above, political and economic measures, both negative and positive, could be taken to strengthen deterrence" (U.S. Congress [House], 1978: 103).

Experts and government delegates who have attended the consultative meetings are fully aware that a mini-treaty might be concluded between the United States and other industrialized powers outside the scope of the Antarctic Treaty for the exploitation of Antarctic minerals—especially the continental shelf oil—inasmuch as it has been suggested on various occasions in informal conversations. Although this possibility has undoubtedly exerted pressure in the negotiations and has had an effect on the decisions of the developing member countries, there is still another element involved. The political and even economic cost of a mini-treaty—assuming that the Soviet Union would remain passive, which cannot be safely taken for granted—would be excessive for another of the actors on the world scene: the transnational corporations.

OBJECTIVES OF THE TRANSNATIONAL CORPORATIONS

It may be asked what the most suitable scenarios are for the transnational corporations (TNCs). Since their objective is to obtain maximum returns, they require various conditions such as a climate of legal and political stability guaranteeing the security of their investments.

Obviously, the ideal situation is presented in the model implicit in the principles set forth in the U.S. position during the negotiations conducted in the meetings of the treaty consultative parties and, with some variations, in the position of European countries like England. It was earlier expressed in the model advanced in UNCLOS by the heavy-mineral exterprises:[26] the concession of exclusive licenses, backed by the authorizing country; a minimal payment for exploitation rights; and the greatest possible freedom to control all the stages of the production and marketing processes. If "uniform legal-political rules of the game" have to be drawn up, they will be accepted insofar as these requirements are met.

What would happen if the regime that the Antarctic Treaty members seek to apply is considered too unfavorable by the TNCs? Given the subsystem's potential for internal instability (e.g., the active opposition of some members), and for generalized external pressures (e.g., a common front by the developing countries against an exclusionary regime of resource-exploitation in Antarctica), the TNCs will be obliged to assess carefully the costs and benefits of an agreement between a few selected countries as compared with a more orderly and stable, albeit less attractive, regime.

In UNCLOS, the initial TNC position—which was to request the U.S. government to negotiate rights of tenure (U.S. Congress [House], 1977: 66-67)—gradually shifted to a reluctant acceptance of the proposed regime of an International Sea-Bed Authority (United Nations, 1979); that is, an accomodation seems to have been reached between the developed and developing countries and the TNCs. This mini-max exercise suggests that it is preferable to obtain relatively fewer advantages in exchange for the security of stable conditions. As the director of the Department of Marine Resources of Kennecott Copper Corporation said, "The worse thing that could happen to us would be to have the treaty put us out of business" (U.S. Congress [House], 1977: 67).

Therefore, although from a military standpoint it is natural to talk about the defense of commercial operations—and for some enterprises, to request it—the TNCs have apparently lost much of their confidence that the governments of industrial powers will be able to perform these functions efficiently, as in the past (U.S. Congress [House], 1977: 67). The new strategies by which the TNCs adapt to fluid international conditions might very well serve to recommend an agreement that would satisfy at least minimally the countries with claims—especially the developing countries—and that would also provide for some distribution of benefits to the Third World, as against an exclusive mini-club of industrialized countries exposed to great pressures and the possible use of violence. In any case, differences of opinion have begun to appear in the TNC sector.[27]

OBJECTIVES OF THE SOVIET UNION

Unless the Soviet Union remains at least passive, no regime designed to restrict the mining of mineral resources to the industrialized countries can be successfully implemented. Although no attempt will be made to predict that country's behavior, some idea of the course it will take can be gathered from observation of the positions it has adopted at consultative meetings and the activities it has undertaken in Antarctica.

Notwithstanding its expressed support of a moratorium on commercial exploration and exploitation, the Soviet Union has, in practice, demonstrated its interest in stepping up its exploration for minerals and hydrocarbons. Its scientists and technicians are working in the Ross Sea and the Antarctic Peninsula areas, both potentially rich in minerals and hydrocarbons (Slevich, 1977: 148-149) where they have installed several scientific stations.[28] The Soviet Union is also interested in the Weddell Sea, south of the Antarctic Peninsula, which appears to contain valuable deposits of petroleum and gas. Furthermore, Soviet and U.S. geologists consider that the Dufek Zone of the Pensacola mountains has an abundance of minerals (Wright and Williams, 1975; Slevich, 1977: 149).

Throughout the 1970s, new USSR bases were established encircling the Antarctic continent (Auburn, 1977: 149). This combined an economic criterion in terms of resource exploration, the geopolitical objective being to have bases located in most of the claimed Antarctic territories while constructing additional ones in the unclaimed sector that had previously been almost exclusively the domain of the United States.

By these activities the Soviet Union ensures (1) that it will exercise an implicit but effective veto over any attempt by a country to make good its territorial claims, or that it will at least be in a position to negotiate terms with that country; (2) that it will have selective access and future participation in all the Antarctic areas; and (3) that through the bases it has established in the zones already occupied by the other superpower, it will come into "strategic contact" of a deterrent nature with the United States.

The ocean "areas of influence" of Antarctica in the South Atlantic and the zone of the Pacific-Atlantic and Atlantic-Indian Ocean accesses, including the latter's western flank, are becoming steadily more important to the United States and the Soviet Union and of course to the maritime countries of Latin America's Southern Cone.[29] In the economic sphere, the Soviet Union fishes intensively along the African coast and is preparing to accelerate its exploitation of krill in the subantarctic waters where the United States has less interest in this resource and consequently has still not developed the technology to exploit it.

Taking into account the situation of the subregion and the capabilities of both naval powers, as well as their commitments to client states in other areas of the world where an arms equilibrium must be maintained in local waters, it seems unlikely that there will be a significant increase of force in this region—unless there are radical changes in the strategic balance such as those already mentioned. It is to the advantage of both the United States and the Soviet Union to keep Antarctica nonmilitarized, thereby preserving that aspect of detente.

The industrialized European countries adhering to the Antarctic Treaty have neither the interest nor the capability to participate in the strategic game of maritime security in this region. Exceptions might be in certain areas of influence as would be the case of the United Kingdom in the African Horn and the Latin American Southern Cone or the serious threat that would be presented by an attack on, for example, the Malvinas (Falkland) Islands or South Africa. European efforts are centered on the exploration of natural resources, as seen in the preparation of an Antarctic expedition that will be shared by ten countries of that continent (de Gerlache de Gomery, 1973). Since 1979 British geologists have been studying the prospects of mineral deposits along an extensive belt of the Antarctic coast (New Scientist, 1979).

THE INTERESTS OF THE LATIN AMERICAN MEMBER COUNTRIES OF THE ANTARCTIC TREATY AND THEIR PARTICIPATION IN THE INTERNATIONAL SYSTEM

Given the characteristics of the political and economic models prevailing in Argentina, Chile, and Brazil—and in Uruguay, as a possible candidate to accede to the treaty[30]—which the groups in power consider to be in defense of the "national interest" and which interact with neoliberal economic policies,[31] the participation of these countries in the world economy is based on a mixture of elements of laissez faire, an attempt to be fully integrated into the western capitalist system, and the reformist model of the New International Economic Order (NIEO); for example, proposals of the Charter of Rights and Duties of States. None of these Latin American countries supports the third choice, which would be to sever their connections with the world system. (Cox, 1979; Moneta, 1978).[32]

It should be stressed that many of the underlying principles of the reformist proposal made by the developing countries seeking a NIEO—the transfer and generation of technology, sovereignty over natural resources, restrictions on transnational corporations—will play an important role in intensifying or moderating conflicts in the context of the future Antarctic agreement on the exploitation of living and mineral resources.

What will the effect of participation be in the world system on the basic behavior of countries involved in Antarctica?

Because of the neoliberal characteristics of their models and their limited financial, scientific, and technological resources, Argentina and Chile would, in principle, accept agreements with other states and with the TNCs permitting them to maintain the forms of legal sovereignty and yielding them some economic benefits. Nevertheless, the geopolitical constants of such nationalist values as the commitment to defend what is considered to be national territory, which have continued even under governments of divergent political cast, introduce a reformist component into their strategy. They can therefore undertake implicit or explicit agreements with actors of differing ideologies to support them in the negotiations of the consultative parties and to enhance their individual ability to explore and exploit resources.

Thus, Argentina and Chile have taken advantage of the Soviet Union's proposal of a moratorium on the exploitation of mineral resources to try to delay the discussion and adoption of decisions on this question (Moneta, 1974-1975a; FNF, 1973). With some exceptions both countries have sought and obtained the support of the Third World for the position they maintain in the Antarctic Treaty as countries with claims. As a member of several groups of developing countries, Argentina in particular, succeeded in having the English occupation of the Malvinas (Falkland) Islands condemned.[33]

In 1978 Chile initiated conversations with the Republic of China to develop joint scientific research projects in Antarctica including natural resources (La Prensa, 1978).

These ideologically heterodox arrangements still have no appropriate equivalent when it is a matter of designing cooperative exploration and exploitation policies of this magnitude for countries of similar rank but with conflicting interests in other areas—as in the case of Argentina and Chile—or for countries within or outside the region that do not belong to the Treaty.[34] It should be pointed out, however, that Chile and Argentina have continued their collaboration, albeit very weakened, vis-à-vis external actors even during the worst moments of the Beagle conflict.

These countries have still not begun to profit from the vast possibilities open to them if they should decide to cooperate within the framework of the Antarctic sector. Taken together and added to their favorable geographical location, their financial, scientific, and technological resources would give them much more leverage as regards the other actors and would enable them to develop more autonomous and effective policies in the mining of hydrocarbons and the exploitation of krill. Nevertheless, to date both states have, in an individual and competitive way, turned to the TNCs and the industrialized countries. Thus, for example, Chile is developing an active fishery program to study the utilization and marketing of krill and other species on the basis of joint ventures established with South Korea, Spain, Taiwan, West Germany, France, and the Republic of China. Argentina, which is behind in this respect since it had not previously paid much attention to fishery in the Southern Ocean, is carrying out a program through agreements with Japan, South Korea, West Germany, and Spain (Kimball, 1980). If the Beagle dispute could be settled, this situation might change in the future since there is some awareness in both countries of the political and economic costs of maintaining such geopolitical conflicts that are largely holdovers from the last century and that in scale and perspective are not in accord with the challenges both will face in the decades ahead.

The case of Brazil is qualitatively different. It only recently became interested in Antarctica[35] thanks to the new strategic dimension of its status as an emerging power and in the hope of being able to share in exploitation of the natural resources, especially hydrocarbons, since it imports 80% of its oil. Its leaders are therefore more flexible as to objectives and policies.

Brazil, which acceded to the Antarctic Treaty in 1976 (Greño Velasco, 1976) and is at present constrained by treaty provisions (art. IV; par. 2) from making official territorial claims, is conscious of the weight of the forces that de facto orient the Antarctic process toward a collective ownership among a limited number of members. Given its excellent economic links with the industrialized countries and its advanced industrial and technological development making it one of the first noncentral countries potentially capable of mining the ocean (Morris, 1979), Brazil has much to gain and nothing to lose by its association with the treaty and with any subsequent agreements originating in the latter.

Furthermore, Brazil is not limited to relying on its own efforts; like any of the other members, it can serve as a vehicle for outside transnational or national actors that want indirect access to the Antarctic continent. The first informal meeting of experts, held in Norway in 1973 to analyze the problems relative to the exploration and future exploitation of mineral resources in Antarctica (FNF, 1973: L-3, L-11, L-13; Moneta, 1974-1975a: 25-26), discussed the possibility that transnationals might try to conduct their operations through nations where they have their head offices or through branch offices located in other nation-states participating in the treaty. The same recourse might be employed by a national or supranational actor outside the Antarctic Treaty through agreements with a member state. According to a recent press release, still unconfirmed, the European Economic Community and Brazil are studying the possibility that the former provide the technological and financial assistance needed by Brazil to explore Antarctic resources.[36]

Uruguay has shown interest in taking part in the scientific activities in Antarctica, even though it has still not made any territorial claims or asked to sign the treaty.[37] Since it is a relatively less-developed country, its most practical strategy would appear to be an agreement with Argentina and Brazil, or with one of them, enabling it to carry out some scientific activity and later to be associated with these countries in the exploitation stage. A second alternative, but without much chance of success, would be to try to become the host country for a transnational corporation.

From a security standpoint, Argentina and Chile naturally differ in their objectives regarding the superpowers and the other actors that do not recognize their territorial claims. Their principal aim is to continue to exercise their sovereignty through diplomatic and scientific-technical activities and through their actual presence in these sectors.

If a minimally satisfactory agreement is concluded among the Antarctic Treaty members, Argentina and Chile would attempt to obtain the best possible conditions for ensuring their effective participation in the collective decisions, obtaining maximum economic benefits, and safeguarding their sovereignty in some form. Vis-à-vis outside actors, they would be likely to join the other members in a common policy to maintain an exclusive regime in Antarctica.

If, however, no understanding is reached, Argentina and Chile may be tempted to employ nonpacific means to preserve at least part of their rights. Although this would undoubtedly be a last resort, "military diplomacy" is not to be discounted since they used it against each other in the 1940-1950 period when they occupied and held military exercises on the Antarctic Islands; and Argentina used it against Great Britain in 1943, 1952, and 1953. The most recent incident of this kind was in 1976, when an Argentine destroyer opened fire on an English ship conducting geological studies to investigate the existence of hydrocarbons in the continental shelf surrounding the Malvinas (Falkland) Islands over which Argentina claims sovereignty.

In a broader context, the incidents precipitating the use of a "naval presence" after the Second World War show that medium-size and even small countries—Iceland with Great Britain, Ecuador and Perú with the United States, Argentina with Poland and the Soviet Union—have on numerous occasions used their limited naval forces in defense of their territories and natural resources. These cases also demonstrate that great powers are rather reluctant to respond in the same way because of the inherent political costs. In general, their response has been to utilize the broad range of economic measures at their disposal such as restrictions on financial assistance and trade.

LATIN AMERICA AND THE ANTARCTIC SUBSYSTEM

The changes that have occurred in the international system in the seventies, together with indigenous national and regional factors, have substantially modified the possibilities and requirements of Latin American nations. These states that are individually endowed with potential viability—Mexico, Argentina, Brazil, and Venezuela—have begun to go beyond the borders of Latin America to penetrate other regions and sectors of international activity at the ideological, political, eonomic, and cultural levels.

Thus, for example, Mexico extends its political-ideological influence internationally, especially in the developing world through the Charter of Rights and Duties of States. Its area of economic influence reaches to the Caribbean and, at a sectoral level, according to the oil policy it adopts.

In the same way, Cuba and Brazil have penetrated Africa through different political-economic projects, and Brazil currently plans to participate in Antarctica where until now only Chile and Argentina have been active. Furthermore, in light of the "defrontcão" legal argument based on the Theory of Sectors which justifies an eventual territorial claim, Brazil has deliberately opened the way to claims by such other South American states as Uruguay, Perú, and Ecuador.[38]

In brief, we are facing a very dynamic situation characterized by the breakdown of the regional limits to the action of some Latin American states and a growing sectoral and functional interdependence due to the changes in the world system and in areas that are altogether new for some of these states.

In this context, what will the interactions of the Antarctic system be with the Latin American subsystem and the world system that can affect the interests of the leading and some of the secondary actors in the Latin American subsystem? It is possible to indicate a number of the areas and issues that in principle will hold varying degrees of interest for the latter.

EVOLUTION OF THE NEW INTERNATIONAL ORDER (NIO)

As already stated, settlement of the Antarctic problem will be a test case of how the new international regime will evolve. In the eighties, Antarctica will be an example of the course to be taken by the conflicts between developed and developing countries and of possible solutions for resource exploration and exploitation now the subject of legal debate. Having initiated the NIO, Latin America will follow with interest the ways in which it will be applied in Antarctica.

UNITED NATIONS CONFERENCE ON THE LAW OF THE SEA (UNCLOS)

The potential conflicts between the International Authority that will administer marine resources located beyond national jurisdictions—assuming approval of the results of the United Nations Conference on the Law of the Sea—and the Antarctic Treaty members, stem from Latin America's interest in the vast ocean space endowed with a wealth of renewable and nonrenewable resources lying relatively close to part of its coastline. What is and what is not agreed to will determine how the benefits derived from marine resource exploitation will be distributed. It will also condition the implementation of the UNCLOS principles and regulations to which Latin America has made a positive contribution.

THE INTERNATIONAL AND REGIONAL ENERGY SITUATION

Once the offshore deposits of petroleum and gas in Antarctica are confirmed and gradually brought into production—both prospects well within the technological capabilities of the eighties and nineties—there will be an appreciable change in the political and economic situation of the oil-exporting countries and of those external states and entities like the transnationals, whether or not they are members of the Antarctic Treaty, that share in their exploitation.

Thus, the industrialized powers—in particular the United States—will have direct or indirect access to new sources of energy over which they will have more and better control. The oil-exporting countries should keep this in mind, since their negotiating position regarding the industrialized oil-importing countries may be adversely affected.

In the regional context, Argentina and Chile and possibly Brazil will obtain new sources of energy production, a situation that will substantially modify their economic situation and the policies they will adopt at the international and regional levels. Argentina might become an exporter—it is already on the verge of becoming one even without these resources—and Chile, which still has to import almost 50% of its oil, will be able to meet domestic demand. Furthermore, Brazil's critical energy shortage would be significantly eased. It can safely be predicted that when these new economic resources become available, there will be an increase in the economic growth rate and the regional political activities of these countries.

Consequently, on the regional energy scene Mexico and Venezuela might be joined by two or perhaps three important new actors and, in the case of Argentina and Brazil, by countries with a relatively advanced nuclear technology. Therefore, there will be a change in the distribution of power, considered in terms of the ownership of critical resources and of the capability to exert economic influence in Latin America.

LATIN AMERICA AND THE COUNTRIES OF THE REGION THAT ARE MEMBERS OF THE ANTARCTIC TREATY

The foregoing discussion indicates that some Latin American countries will be extremely interested in how the Antarctic subsystem conflicts may be resolved or heightened. It should not be forgotten that the Latin American member countries of the Antarctic Treaty seek political support to strengthen their positions against regional competitors or against external actors that are treaty members; on the other hand, if the cooperative concept is reaffirmed, they will seek economic support to participate technically and financially in the exploration and exploitation of the energy resources.

THE CONDITIONING FACTORS OF COOPERATION AND CONFLICT IN THE ANTARCTIC TREATY: TECHNOLOGICAL VIABILITY

The considerations presented so far have depended basically on the technological variable. The technology assumptions of this article, until now implicit, rest on the possibility of advances in the systems and means of offshore oil drilling, commercial exploitation, production, storage, transportation, and pollution control that will make exploitation feasible in ten to twenty years.

Opinions in this field vary widely. According to the report of a group of experts on mineral exploration and exploitation convoked by the Antarctic Treaty members (SCAR, 1977; King, 1979: 57-58), technology already existed in 1977 for perforation from mobile structures to depths of more than 1,000 meters in areas free of large icebergs, conditions rarely found in Antarctica. Although present technology does not seem to hold the promise of revolutionary advances in surface units (King, 1979: 18), it is making rapid progress in the design of underwater units, which would eliminate the problems caused by icebergs. It is to be hoped that this technology will be perfected in five or ten years (King, 1979: 5).

In production, the greatest strides are expected in the underwater sector (Offshore, 1979: 163, 168; New York Times, 1980: C-3). In transportation, the Arctic oil industry has led the way with pipelines and other innovations, such as highly maneuverable and resistant tankers accompanied by icebreakers, that can easily be transferred to Antarctica (Offshore, 1979). Furthermore, there have been basic qualitative changes in overland transportation using new vehicles that travel on an air cushion (Offshore, 1979: 162-164), and an effort is being made to coordinate an air-bus system to cross Antarctica (Smith and Dana, 1973). Finally, the new models of submerged storage tanks that are already in use in the Middle East need only minor modifications to be adapted to the harsh Antarctic climate.

To summarize, technological difficulties can be overcome in the near future, perhaps in ten years, if the necessary resources are made available for research. Marketing of petroleum depends largely on world prices and exploitation costs, which will certainly be higher in Antarctica than in more accessible and hospitable regions; but one of the determinants of cost is technology, which has been making remarkable progress. Oil price rises have outstripped all calculations made by experts and if the international situation continues to generate conflictive factors, particularly around the Persian Gulf, petroleum may be assigned a "political" price by the United States and other industrialized countries; that is, there would be a political determination to invest in areas that are more "secure" from a geopolitical standpoint. Such areas will certainly include Antarctica, but not as a first priority.

Assuming that such a political determination exists and that a basic decision is made by the leading transnational corporations to invest in research and development—as is already indicated by the numerous applications for commercial hydrocarbon exploration submitted by private companies in several industrialized countries[39]—it is just a question of time until the financial-technological obstacles are overcome. The favorable attitude of the TNCs is partly because access to Antarctica is, from a technological standpoint, the logical continuation of their work in difficult terrains requiring the new technology initiated in the North Sea exploitation. Current exploration and exploitation in the Arctic region furthers this process, which would culminate in Antarctica. It is, after all, basically a matter of transferring what has been learned and applied in the Arctic and other areas to a new region for which part of the necessary technology already exists or is about to be developed.

An examination of those having the technological innovations that are essential to effective commercial exploration and exploitation of hydrocarbons reveals that a relatively small group of TNCs, including Exxon and Shell, together with a few research centers in the developed countries, are in control of such knowledge. Therefore, the developing member countries of the

Antarctic Treaty—and countries that might be incorporated into future treaty conventions on exploitation—will depend to a large extent on those corporations to carry out their own exploitation. As is well known, past relations of this type have given rise to situations that do not exactly represent an encouraging precedent. There will be a tendency to repeat positions equivalent to those taken in UNCLOS on deep ocean mining—for example, disputes between developed and deloping countries over the model, functions, and faculties of the authority vis-à-vis the transnational corporations.

Nevertheless, the experience gained by the developing countries in their negotiations with the TNCs will improve their chances of autonomous viability provided they can increase their leverage through effective cooperation in the political, economic, and technological spheres. This implies, however, a political determination, even if it is on a sectoral and functional level; an accurate assessment of limits and opportunities; and great flexibility and pragmatism. In light of existing conflicts, these characteristics will not be easily attained; but the way lies open. As an example, Latin American multinational corporations for the exploration and exploitation of hydrocarbons might be organized around an Argentine-Chile axis, with Brazil as an eventual participant, for activities in Antarctica. Granted that they will undoubtedly require technological assistance and external financing, the basic conditions will have changed significantly. Similarly, selective undertakings shared with other countries—which might include Antarctic Treaty members like Norway and some OPEC and Third World nations that, although "medium-size," nevertheless can contribute technological expertise—could be an effective means of preventing such useless competition as new territorial claims by Latin American countries; they would, instead, muster the political support of the Latin American community and, eventually, of other countries of the developing world.

Whether the Latin American members of the treaty reach an agreement or whether they find it impossible to reconcile their opposing interests, this support will be necessary. None of the models so far proposed and very informally discussed as possible solutions—for example, international agreements with United Nations participation; recognition of territorial claims; joint sovereignty (Spitzenbergen Model)—will relieve Argentina and Chile of their fundamental inadequacies when an attempt is actually made to undertake resource exploitation, nor will it eliminate the need to create a favorable political-economic climate. The above strategy, recommended by the new shape of the regional subsystem and of the world system, is for the good of both nations, Latin America, and the developing countries as a whole.

NOTES

1. Consultative members signing the Antarctic Treaty in 1959 were Argentina, Australia, Belgium, Chile, France, Japan, New Zealand, Norway, South Africa, USSR, United Kingdom, and the United States. Signatory members and their years of signing were Brazil, 1976; Czechoslovakia, 1962; Denmark, 1965; Federal Republic of Germany, 1978; German Democratic Republic, 1974; Netherlands, 1967; and Romania, 1971.

2. Antarctic Treaty countries that have unofficially expressed interest in presenting territorial claims: Belgium, Brazil, Colombia, Peru, and Uruguay.

3. Sollie believes, however, that this negative attitude is exaggerated. For the U.S. position, see U.S. Congress [Senate] (1975a).

4. Confidential conversations held with members of national delegations who took part in the meetings of the Conference on the Law of the Sea.

5. See sources such as Gorshkov (1974), whose collection of articles was published in English by the U.S. Naval Academy.

6. Course on International Politics, 1963-1969, and paper on the same topic presented at the First National Congress on Geopolitics, Universidad Nacional de Mendoza in August 1974.

7. In its Resolution 2749, XXV, the UN General Assembly declared in December 1979 that the deep sea floor and its subsoil were beyond the limits of national jurisdiction and also that the resources of the zone are the common heritage of mankind. The same text is contained in ICNT [Informal Composite Negotiating Treaty].

8. Different opinions on this issues are expressed by specialists such as Guyer (1977: 157-164), Auburn (1977: 155-156), U.S. Congress [Senate] (1975a: 18-20), FNF (1973), Wilson (1978), Bernhardt (1974-1975), and Hannessian (1965).

9. The underlying principles of the positions adopted by Latin American countries with consultative status (Argentina and Chile) and signatory members (Brazil) are discussed in detail by Pinochet de la Barra (1976), Puig (1960), and de Castro (1976). To date, Brazil has not asserted any official claim to Antarctic territory.

The territorial occupation and exercise of sovereignty most in line with traditional international law regarding activities and time span are in the sectors included in the disputed claims of Argentina, Chile, and Great Britain. Argentina, in particular, has established a civilian population and schools and has registered births of children of Argentine citizens in the sector over which it claims sovereignty.

10. Mutually recognized territorial claims in Antarctica: Argentina and Chile (reciprocal); and Australia, France, New Zealand, Norway, and the United Kingdom (mutual).

11. Countries with head offices of transnational and national corporations conducting research on mineral nodules are Belgium, Federal Republic of Germany, France, Japan, United Kingdom, USSR, and the United States (United Nations, 1971; UNCTAD, 1974; Moneta, 1979). Countries with research and development capability in offshore hydrocarbons in Antarctic conditions (state, private, or transnational corporations headquartered in that country) are Belgium, Federal Republic of Germany, Japan, Norway, USSR, United Kingdom, and the United States (Offshore, 1979a, 1978). Countries with the financial capability to carry out exploration and exploitation in Antarctica independently are the Federal Republic of Germany, German Democratic Republic (probable), Japan, United Kingdom, USSR, and the United States. To determine financial capability, account was taken of general financial and economic indicators and of investments made previously in ocean exploration and exploitation of hydrocarbons in terms of estimated costs of exploration and exploitation in Antarctica. Member countries of the Antarctic Treaty—or countries expected to join in the near future—requiring financial and/or technological assistance to carry out exploration and exploitation of hydrocarbons and minerals in Antarctica are Argentina, Australia, Belgium, Brazil, Chile, Czechoslovakia, Denmark, German Democratic Republic, New Zealand, Romania, South Africa, and Uruguay.

12. For example, various statements to this effect by Ambassador Amerasinghe (Sri Lanka), chairman of the conference.

13. Some data on catch levels of krill by Antarctic Treaty members (in metric tons) are: USSR, 1977—105, 049; Poland, 1976—21, and 1977—6,966; Japan, 1976—2,226 and 1977—10,517. See Kimball (1980).

14. This topic was first given careful consideration at an unofficial meeting of experts held in Norway in 1973—their conclusions contained in FNF (1973). At the Ninth Meeting of Treaty Consultative Parties held in London in 1977, consideration was given to the organization of a regulated system for resource exploration and exploitation that would not affect the environment.

15. Antarctic Treaty countries with territorial claims prior to signing the treaty: Argentina, Australia, Chile, France, New Zealand, Norway, and the United Kingdom

16. Today this is a universally accepted principle.

17. See, among others, Van Essen (1975-1976: 95-96), Sollie (1979: 207). For a different appraisal of these possibilities, see Wilson (1978).

18. In the bibliography on this subject, see Hannessian (1974), Ludwigson (1978: 29-33), Newsweek (1977), and Wall Street Journal (1977: 1).

19. Although specialists do not agree on which countries should be in this category, Brazil, Chile, Argentina, India, Spain, and Japan are usually included. See Wemyss (1974: 26), Hayes (1980), Morris (1977), Moneta (1980).

20. See figures on construction and type of Soviet units in Jane's Fighting Ships [London] and New York Times (1979).

21. For the Soviet Union, see Hollick (1974), Yakolev (1978: 34), and Yarolavtsev (1975).

22. The following is the tentative assessment of the position of the Antarctic Treaty members regarding commercial exploration and exploitation of offshore minerals and hydrocarbons:

Country	*Position*
Soviet Union	Opposed to exploration (explor.) and exploitation (exploit.); requests moratorium
Argentina	Same
Chile	Same
Poland	Same
France	Position not clear; tends to favor explor. and exploit.
Japan	Opposed to explor. and exploit. on ecological grounds; position changed in recent years–now favors commercial criterion
United Kingdom	Favors explor. and exploit. of resources
Belgium	Position not clear
Brazil	Not part of Consultative Committee; known to favor explor. and exploit. of resources
Fed. Republic of Germany	Not part of Consultative Committee; believed to favor explor. and exploit. of resources
German Dem. Rep.	Not part of Consultative Committee; position still not known
U.S.A.	Favors explor. and exploit. of resources

Position of Antarctic Treaty members regarding Antarctic fishery (statistical data do not include krill):

Country	*Position*
Soviet Union	In favor (catch, 1977: 257,829 tons)
German Dem. Rep.	In favor (catch, 1977-1978: 10,305 tons)
Poland	In favor (catch, 1977-1978: 63,523 tons)
United States	Opposed; favors restricted fishery on ecological grounds
France	In favor
Australia	In favor; preparations underway to participate
Argentina	In favor, with certain restrictions; preparations underway to participate
Chile	In favor; preparations underway to participate
Japan	In favor

SOURCE: Statistical data from Food and Agriculture Organization and Kimball (1980).

23. The Soviet position was made clear at the meeting of experts held in Norway (FNF, 1973), and it has continued basically unchanged to date.

24. Arguments put forth by the Soviet experts at the informal meeting of experts held in Norway (FNF, 1973).

25. The Antarctic Policy Group (APG) is responsible for the coordination and direction of all policies developed by the various U.S. agencies participating in Antarctic activities. See U.S. Executive Office of the President (1971).

26. See U.S. Congress [House] (1976), in particular the parts referring to Deep Sea Ventures, Inc.

27. For an analysis of the evolution of the attitude of the oil corporations on this matter, see the journals *Offshore, Ocean Industry*, and *Ocean World* for 1978-1979.

28. The most important of these is "Druzhnaya" (77° 34' South; 40° 13' West), on the Filchner Barrier. It was constructed in 1976 near the former Argentine base "General Belgrano."

29. See the Argentine journals *Estrategia* [Buenos Aires], especially 43-44, 1977, and *Geopolítica* [Buenos Aires]; Millia (1979), Moneta (1980); also, the Uruguayan journal *Geopolítica* [Montevideo] and *Geosur* (1979, published by the South American Association of Geopolitical and International Studies).

30. See footnote 2.

31. The positions adopted by the governments of the Antarctic Treaty member states regarding programs of resource exploration and exploitation are the results of conflictive or competitive interactions among the political, economic, scientific-technological, and security concerns of the internal ruling groups and their transnational links.

32. In the context of the different proposals for the NIEO, two models of dissociation are presented: (1) that the S-S (South-South) supported by part of the Third World countries, which believe that only a collective effort—based on mutual, horizontal support—can increase their possibilities for a more autonomous development; and (2) the N-N (North-North) supported by the most conservative of the developed countries, which would like to see greater cooperation among the industrialized nations so that, through their scientific-technological advances, they could become more independent of the Third World countries in energy and raw materials.

33. Although the Malvinas (Falkland) Islands are not located within the Antarctic Treaty limits, the political aspects of a solution to this problem indirectly affect the outcome of the conflicting claims by Argentina and England to overlapping Antarctic sectors. Argentina has succeeded in having the issue of these islands included in the U.N. General Assembly resolutions in several declarations by nonaligned countries as well as in other economic and political Third World forums.

34. There are, however, unorthodox proposals that depart from traditional attitudes and study new alternatives in this sphere. See, for example, Palermo (1979) and Moneta (1975-1975b).

35. For the circumstances of Brazil's accession to the Antarctic Treaty, see Greño Velasco (1976).

36. Radio newscast in Mexico City on December 4, 1979.

37. This country (Uruguay) has an Antarctic-Institute-accorded official status in 1975 and a Commission on Antarctic Studies, organized in 1970 under the auspices of the Foreign Office, to advise the government on Antarctic activities. Furthermore, there have been several announcements of the intention of sending a scientific expedition.

38. Geopolitical experts in Peru and Ecuador have already made public statements on the need to assert the rights of those countries.

39. Countries that have received applications for licenses to explore and exploit hydrocarbons commercially in Antarctica are Australia, Japan, New Zealand, the United Kingdom, and the United States. This list is simply indicative and is based on numerous published sources. It is therefore possible that other countries have received applications of this kind.

REFERENCES

AUBURN, F. (1977) "Offshore oil and gas in Antarctica." German Yearbook of Int. Law 20.

BERNHARDT, J. (1974-1975) "Sovereignty in Antarctica." California Western Int. Law J. 5: 85-112.

BOOTH, K. (1979) "The military implications of the changing law of the sea," pp. 328-362 in J. K. Gamble (ed.) Law of the Sea: Neglected Issues, Proceedings Law of the Sea Institute, Twelfth Annual Conference, October 1978. The Hague, Netherlands: University of Utrecht.

BUZAN, B. (1976) Seabed Politics. New York: Praeger.

COX, R. (1979) "Ideologies and the new international economic order." Int. Organization 2: 257-300.

DE CASTRO, T. (1976) Rumo a Antártida. Rio de Janeiro: Freitas Bastos.

DE GERLACHE DE GOMERY, G. (1973) "A proposed Antarctic European expedition." Antarctic J. 8 (January-February): 15.

FNF [Fridtjof Nansen Foundation] (1973) "Antarctic resources." Report from meeting of experts at the FNF meeting on mineral exploration at Polhogda, Norway, May 30-June 10.

GORSHKOV, S. G. (1974) Red Star Rising at Sea. Annapolis, MD: Naval Academy.

GREÑO VELASCO, J. E. (1976) "La adhesión de Brasil al tratado Antártico." Revista de Política International 146 [Madrid]: 71-89.

GUYER, R. (1977) "The Antarctic system," pp. 153-225 in Collected Courses of the Hague Academy of International Law. Leyden: Sijthoff.

HANNESSIAN, J. (1974) "Overview: some international legal considerations," pp. 57-72 in G. S. Schatz (ed.) Science, Technology and Sovereignty in the Polar Regions. Lexington, MA: D.C. Heath.

——— (1965) "National interests in Antarctica." New Zealand Antarctic Society.

HAYES, D. (1980) "Brasil y el Atlántico Sur: cambio de perspectiva sobre un tema importante" in C. Moneta (ed.) Geopolítica y Política de Poder en el Atlántico Sur. Buenos Aires: Editorial Pleamar.

HILL, C. A. (1976) "U.S. law of the sea position and its effects on the operating navy: a naval officer's view." Ocean Development and Int. Law 3: 341-359.

HOLLICK, A. (1974) "Bureaucrats at sea," pp. 1-73 in A. Hollick and R. Osgood, New Era of Ocean Politics. Baltimore: Johns Hopkins Press.

KIMBALL, L. (1980) "Exploración y explotación del krill: el presente y las perspectivas futuras," in C. Moneta (ed.) Geopolítica y Política de Poder en el Atlántico Sur. Buenos Aires: Editorial Pleamar.

KING, R. E. (1979) "Offshore '79: drilling is increasing in deep water and arctic areas." World Oil 189, 1.

KNIGHT, G. (1974) "Special domestic interests and United States policy," pp. 10-43 in R. Yirsing (ed.) International Relations and the Future of the Ocean Space. Columbia: Univ. of South Carolina Press.

LUDWIGSON, J. (1978) "Bringing home the iceberg." Ocean World (January): 29-33.

MANGONE, G. (1978) Marine Policy for America: The United States at Sea. Lexington, MA: D. C. Heath.

MICHALET, C. (1976) Le Capitalisme Mondial. Paris: Presse Universitaire de France.

MILLIA, F. [ed.] (1979) La Antártida: Un Espacio Geopolítico. Buenos Aires: Editorial Pleamar.

MONETA, C. (1980) "Aspectos conflictivos de las relaciones afro-latinoamericanas: las vinculaciones políticas, económicas y militares de Sudafrica con los paises del Atlántico sudamericano," in C. Moneta, Geopolítica y Política de Poder en el Atlántico Sur. Buenos Aires: Editorial Pleamar.

——— (1979) "Intereses Argentinos en el Atlántico sur: el caso de las riquezas mineras en alta mar," pp. 119-129 in F. Millia (ed.) La Antártida: Un Espacio Geopolítico. Buenos Aires: Editorial Pleamar.

——— (1978) "El uso de los modelos de simulación global como instrumento político en el sistema mundial." Estudios del Tercer Mundo 1, 4: 71-121.

——— (1974-1975a) "Antártida Argentina: los problemas de 1975-1990." Estrategia [Buenos Aires] (November-December 1974; January-February 1975): 31-32; 5-33.

——— (1974-1975b) "Los problemas antárticos en la década del 80." Ciclo de conferencias, CEINAR (Centro de Estudios Internacionales Argentinos), Buenos Aires.

——— (1974) La Estrategia Naval Soviética en el Indoco y Atlántico Sur: Algunas Consideraciones. Buenos Aires: Universidad del Salvador, Facultad de Ciencias Políticas y Sociales.

MORRIS, E. (1979) "Brazil at the Third United Nations Conference on the Law of the Sea." Ocean Development and Int. Law: J. of Marine Affairs 7: 1; 2: 131-177.

——— (1977) "Have U.S. security interests really been sacrificed? A reply to Admiral Hill." Ocean Development and Int. Law 4: 381-397.

——— (1976) The Russian Navy: Myth and Reality. Briarcliff Manor, NY: Stein & Day.

La Nación [Buenos Aires] June 10.

New Scientist [London] (1979) "Cold fronts ahead for Antarctic research." October 25.

Newsweek (1977) July 4: 72.

New York Times (1980) January 15: C-3.

——— (1979) "Russian navy: a new interest in the third world." December 10.

O'CONNOR, J. (1973) The Fiscal Crisis of the State. New York: St. Martin's Press.

Offshore (1979a) June 20.

——— (1979b) "Industry 'crushes' frozen obstacles." February.

——— (1978) June 20.

OSGOOD, R. (1974) "U.S. security interest in ocean law," pp. 75-90 in A. Hollick and R. Osgood, New Era of Ocean Politics. Baltimore: Johns Hopkins Press.

PALERMO, A. (1979) "China, Chile y algunas otras cuestiones Antárcticas." Geopolítica: 13-14.

PINOCHET DE LA BARRA, O. (1976) La Antártida Chilena. Santiago: Andrés Bello.
La Prensa [Buenos Aires] (1978) November 13.
PUIG, G. (1960) La Antártida Argentina ante el derecho internacional. Buenos Aires: De Palma.
SCAR [Scientific Committee on Scientific Research] (1977) Report of group of specialists on the environmental impact assessment of mineral exploration and exploitation in Antarctica. An international council with a mobile headquarters.
SLEVICH, L. (1977) [1973 original ed., Leningrad: Russian Soviet Federated Socialist Republic] Basic Problems of Antarctic Exploration, cited in F. Auburn, German Yearbook of Int. Law 20.
SMITH, P. M. and J. B. DANA (1973) "Airbus: an international air transportation system for Antarctica." Antarctic J. 8, 1: 16-19.
SOLLIE, F. (1979) "Trends and prospects for regimes for living and mineral resources in the Antarctic," in J. K. Gamble (ed.) Law of the Sea: Neglected Issues. Proceedings Law of the Sea, Twelfth Annual Conference, October 23-26, 1978. The Hague, Netherlands: University of Utrecht.
TINKER, J. (1979) "Antarctic: towards a new internationalism." New Scientist [London] (September 13): 799-801.
——— and M. HOLDGATE (1979) Oil and Minerals in the Antarctic. The Bellagio Report. United Kingdom: Scott Polar Research Institute.
TransCanada Pipelines (1972) "Polar gas pipeline." November.
UNCTAD [U.N. Conference on Trade and Development] (1974) TD/B484-3.
United Nations (1979) Documento ONU A/Conf. 62/Wp.10/Rev. 1, 28 April.
——— (1971) Documento ONU A/AC 138/36, May.
U.S. Congress [House] (1978) "Deep seabed minerals: resources, diplomacy, and strategic interest," pp. 78-90 in Subcommittee on International Organizations of the Committee on International Relations. Washington, DC: Government Printing Office.
——— (1977) Hearings Before the Subcommittee on International Organizations of the Committee on International Relations, Ninety-fifth Congress, First Session.
——— (1976) "Mineral resources of the deep seabed." Hearings May 18, 20, and 24 Before the Subcommittee on Mines and Mining of the Committee on Interior and Insular Affairs, Ninety-fourth Congress, Second Session.
U.S. Congress [Senate] (1977) "Congress and the oceans: marine affairs in the 94th congress." Committee on Commerce, Science, and Transportation. Washington, DC: Government Printing Office.
——— (1975a) "Legal status of areas south of 60° S latitude." Hearings Before the Subcommittee on Oceans and International Environment of the Committee on Foreign Relations, U.S. Senate, Ninety-fourth Congress, First Session: 18-20.
——— (1975b) Statement of Assistant Secretary of State Dixy Lee Ray on U.S. Antarctic Policy to Subcommittee on Oceans and International Environment, May 15.
U.S. Department of State (1979a) "Antarctica: 10th meeting of treaty consultative parties." Department of State Bulletin 79, No. 2032, (November).
——— (1979b) October 10 press communique. U.S. Department of State Bulletin 79, No. 2032 (November): 23.
U.S. Executive Office of the President (1971) Circular N.A.-51, revised. August 4. Washington, DC: Executive Office of the President.
U.S. White House (1975) Office of the White House Press Secretariat. October 13.
VAN ESSEN, A. (1975-1976) "L'Antartique et la droit de la mer." Revue Iranienne des Relations Internationales [University de Teheran] 5-6 (hiver).

Wall Street Journal (1977) October 5: 1.

Washington Post (1975) "Estimating the Antarctic oil resources." March 12.

WEMYSS, A.F.C. (1974) "The part played by naval forces in the international scene." South African Institute of Int. Affairs [Johannesburg] 5, 4: 26.

WILSON, G. (1978) "Antarctica, the southern ocean, and the law of the sea." JAG J. [Judge Advocate General, U.S. Air Force Bulletin] 30 (summer): 47-85.

WRIGHT, N. A. and P. L. WILLIAMS (1975) "Mineral resources of Antarctica." U.S. Geological Survey Circular 705: 35-67. Washington, DC: Government Printing Office.

YAKOLEV, I. (1978) "The world ocean and international cooperation." Int. Affairs [Moscow] 6 (June): 31.

YAROLAVTSEV, V. (1975) "The world ocean and international law." Int. Affairs [Moscow] 2 (February): 61-71.

Carlos J. Moneta, Special Fellow with the United Nations Institute for Training and Research (UNITAR), has been Professor of International Politics at the Universities of El Salvador and Mar del Plata in Argentina and Visiting Professor at the University of California—Los Angeles and National University of Mexico (UNAM). In 1962 he was head of the Orcadas scientific base in the Argentine Antarctic and represented Argentina in 1973 at the Conference of Antarctic Experts in Oslo, Norway, on the exploration and exploitation of mineral resources in the Antarctic. He has published books and numerous articles on international politics. His Geopolítica y Política de Poder en el Atlántico Sur *is forthcoming.*

GEORGE C. ABBOTT
International Economic Studies
University of Glasgow, Scotland

THE ASSOCIATED STATES AND INDEPENDENCE

The British experience with federations is not a happy one. Attempts to combine its smaller and poorer colonies into some form of larger political and economic union as part of its decolonization process are generally reckoned to have failed. Almost without exception, the individual colonies decided to go it alone, to seek independence on their own, that is.

The former West Indian colonies are a case in point. Notwithstanding several attempts to bring them closer together, they have shown a remarkable tenacity to retain their individual existence and identity. The 1958 Federation, the most ambitious attempt to weld them into a nation, ended in failure after only three years and much internal wrangling. The larger islands of Jamaica and Trinidad and Tobago went on to become independent on their own. A further attempt to amalgamate the remaining units, the so-called "Little Eight" into a Federation of the Eastern Caribbean also failed, after which Barbados sought independence on its own. This left the Windward Islands (Dominica, Grenada, St. Lucia and St. Vincent) and the Leeward Islands (Antigua, Montserrat, and St. Kitts-Nevis and Anguilla) facing a most uncertain political and constitutional future.

The response of the British government to this peculiar situation was to offer them Associated Statehood, a sort of three-quarter house to independence. This was clearly intended to be a holding operation until a more permanent form of government could be worked out, including independence which the islands

Journal of Interamerican Studies and World Affairs, Vol. 23 No. 1, February 1981 69-94

were free to take simply by giving six months notice and satisfying certain constitutional requirements.

Considering the pace at which political and constitutional developments had moved since the end of World War II, most observers expected these islands to proceed forthwith to independence, since there was now nothing to stop them from becoming independent separately. But after five years, only Grenada had taken the plunge, admittedly under the most unusual, some would say unconstitutional, circumstances. The others showed no great enthusiasm for moving on to independence. Nevertheless, after what would seem an inordinately long time in political and constitutional limbo, they have finally decided to take independence. Within the year they should all be free, independent and self-governing nations.

While this prospect may bring relief in some quarters, it gives rise to grave misgivings in others. The question of their viability, or their lack of it, is still a major cause for concern internationally. How will they manage? Will their economies be able to support the cost of independence and meet their urgent economic and social dependent needs at the same time? Was the federal idea really misconceived and inappropriate in their case? These questions are as pertinent now as when the issue of independence and the form it should take was first raised.

THE FEDERAL IDEA

The most obvious characteristic of these islands is their size. They are very small island economies separated from each other by stretches of water which, though less than a hundred miles in most instances, have served to enhance their separate and individual identities. To smallness and separateness must be added limited natural resources. They rely heavily on export agriculture, since they have no mineral wealth to speak of and limited scope for industrialization.

As export-oriented economies, they are extremely susceptible to the vagaries of world trade in primary products as well as adverse developments in the international economy generally, while domestically, rising populations are a potential source of social and political tension and unrest, given the islands' limited resources and severe unemployment problem. Being small they also suffer from limited domestic markets and the diseconomies of scale in production. In effect, they are small, high-cost producers with a limited range of possibilities internally as well as internationally. Their basic economic and social characteristics are given in Table 1.

It is not necessary to elaborate on the data in this table; the picture is obvious. The islands suffer from a number of disadvantages which derives basically from their size, which was, in fact, the very problem federation was intended to accommodate. As small, discrete economies of marginal significance internationally, they were clearly not in a position to meet the cost of independence with all the paraphernalia and requirements of a modern state and at the same time carry through their ambitious plans for accelerated economic and social development from their own resources, the underlying presumption and requirement on which the granting of independence and self-government rested. As a former colonial secretary bluntly put it:

> If self-government is to be successful and enduring, it must rest upon firm economic and social infra-structure. It is possible to win easy applause by the spectacular grant of self-government before these foundations are laid; but that could only lead to the failure of self-government. . . . I want to see the Colonies with an adequate and sound economic basis which will meet the needs of Government and people, and provide a reasonable standard of life. Unless we can do that, talk about self-government is really humbug. Political responsibility goes ill with financial dependence [Daily Gleaner, 1943].

Individual colonies were therefore required to show that they were capable of maintaining their political and financial independence, standing on their own as it were, before independence and self-government could be granted. Those that could not were advised to federate in order to improve the prospects of their political and economic viability.

TABLE 1
Basic Economic and Social Characteristics:
Leeward and Winward Islands

		LEEWARDS			WINDWARDS			
	UNIT	ANT.	MRAT	S.K.-N.A.	DCA	GDA	ST.L.	ST.V.
Area	Km^2	442	98	357	751	344	616	388
Population (1976)	'000	71	13	66	76	96	110	100
Rate of Growth (1970-1976)	%p.a.	1.4	1.4	0.5	1.1	0.4	1.2	1.2
Density (1976)	per Km^2	161	133	185	101	279	179	258
Urban Population (1975)	%	33.8	11.1	34.1	-	-	-	-
National Income (1976)	$USm:	37	13	41	34	59	65	37
Per Capita Income (1976)	$US	509	1036	587	420	614	598	339
Life Expectancy	Years	62	52	60	58	63	57	59
Piped Water per Dwelling House	%	21.0	29.2	9.8	-	-	11.7	25.0
Illiteracy Rate	%	11.3	19.5	11.8	40.6	23.6	48.3	23.8
Enrollment Ratio (1) (1975)		114	-	95	74	99	63	79
Expenditure on Education as % of Total Public Expenditure (1975)	%	14.5	-	10.8	-	20.5	16.8	-
Pop.: Per Hospital Bed (1975)		154	116	182	234	144	202	170
Pop.: Per Physician (1975)		-	1667	5833	5385	4000	4231	3500
Expenditure in Public Health as % of Total Public Expenditure (1975)	%	14.8	9.5	12.6	8.5	-	8.8	12.2

SOURCE: United Nations (1979: Tables 6.1A, p. 474, and 6.10, pp. 582-583, as amended).

NOTES:
1. The number of pupils enrolled at the first and secondary level (including pupils of all possible ages) as a percentage of the estimated school-age population for those levels–i.e., generally the population aged 5-19).
2. A dash (–) denotes data not available or not reported separately.

The West Indian colonies fell into the second category. Individually, they were too small to make it on their own. The cost would be too high. A federation would considerably improve their chances. It would expedite the process of political development within the region. It would remove existing inequalities and standardize the rate of political and constitutional advance of its members. Each unit would enter as an equal member and become independent within the federation. It would facilitate the transfer of power to local hands, and it would satisfy the growing demand for independence and self-determination. The pooling of resources would also induce a degree of financial and economic stability compatible with political independence.

In terms of economic advantages, a federation would spread the cost of establishing and maintaining a modern state among the different units. It would avoid duplication of effort and the establishment of administrative, diplomatic, and other services for each unit. It would be responsible for the region's economic and social development. It would rationalize industrial development and plan and promote the expansion of trade within the region as well as internationally. Finally, it would be able to speak for the region as a whole in matters of international importance.

The case for a federation also rested on the good work which had already been done—and was being done—by a growing number of regional organizations set up for the purpose of fostering regional cooperation and development. The Development and Welfare Organization, for example, was charged with the specific functions of promoting the economic development of the region and of supplying the skilled, technical, and administrative personnel to carry out these functions. It built roads, bridges, schools, hospitals, clinics, and health centers. It undertook major projects of irrigation and afforestation. It provided the technical expertise for agricultural extension services and similar basic facilities. In short, it set about building the social and economic infrastucture on which independence and self-government was to be based.

Other regional organizations played an equally significant role in helping to bring the islands together and to encourage them to think and act as a unit. However, once federation become a reality, the old feeling of insularity and parochialism resurfaced and put the weak federal structure under immense strain. The whole thing finally collapsed when Jamaica, the largest unit, withdrew from the federation.

It is not necessary to go into the reasons why federation collapsed. This is already adequately covered in the literature (Archibald, 1962; Bobb, 1966; Lowenthal, 1961; Mordecai, 1968; Springer, 1962). However, two points in particular are worth mentioning in the present context. First, the question of finance played a major role in determining the structure, the way it functioned, and finally, the collapse of the federation itself. Second, the relative ease with which Jamaica and Trinidad and Tobago moved on to independence seemed to belie the claim that the islands were too small and too poor to become independent on their own.

Together these two factors, perhaps more than anything else, set the operational constraints for subsequent federal discussions. They featured prominently in discussions on the proposed Federation of the Eastern Caribbean. Although the islands had agreed to establish this federation, and had done a considerable amount of detalied negotiations on its structure and format, when they saw the Report of the Fiscal Commissioner (HMSO, 1963) setting out the financial implications and requirements of federation, some of them immediately began to express grave misgivings about the exercise. Antigua decided the cost was too high. It would require, among other things, the continuation of grant-aid status, something which the island had decided to rid itself of by 1963. It also objected to the proposal that the federal government should control import duties and post office revenues, on the grounds that on a per capita basis it would have to bear a proportionately higher share of the cost of federation than any of the other units.

Barbados also expressed grave doubts about the financing of the new federation: it feared that it would have to bear the cost of carrying the other islands. In particular, it found the idea of federating with a group of grant-aid colonies financially unattractive as well as a potential liability to its own political and constitutional development. It was by no means certain, for example, that the new federation would be fully independent from the start. In addition, many people were disillusioned at the slow progress of the federal talks and the intense internal bickering of the other governments. These considerations were sufficient to cause the Barbados government to reappraise its own political and constitutional future. In 1965 it issued a White Paper which, while not ruling out the possibility of further federal talks, committed Barbados to seeking independence on its own (Barbados Government, 1965a, 1965b). It was no doubt considerably encouraged in this decision by the ease with which both Jamaica and Trinidad and Tobago appeared to be coping with independence on their own.

ASSOCIATED STATEHOOD

Once Antigua and Barbados withdrew from further discussions, the proposed Eastern Caribbean Federation folded up. The British government seems to have accepted the failure of these talks as a clear indication that the islands wished to proceed to independence as separate units, and accordingly took steps to accommodate them. It proposed a new form of association called Associated Statehood to replace the existing colonial relationship. Under the terms of this new relationship, each colony was to be granted full control of its internal affairs—including the right to amend its constitution and the power to end association with Britain and declare itself independent. In the meantime, Britain accepted full responsibility for their external affairs and defense.

The new constitutional proposals[1] were widely discussed throughout the islands, where they received a fair measure of support. Following a series of conferences in London, the necessary legislation was incorporated and enacted in the West Indies Act of 1967. Statehood was set for various dates during that year for each of the islands. Then things suddenly started going wrong. There was a constitutional crisis in St. Kitts-Nevis and Anguilla which ended with Anguilla seceding unilaterally from the state. In St. Vincent, the deep and irreconcilable differences between the government and opposition parties delayed the granting of statehood by almost two years. Even when it was finally taken, the personal differences of leading politicians continued to plague the island's political and constitutional development.

Developments in the other islands were no less chaotic. Instead of preparing themselves for the business of independence and trying to put their economies in order, local politicians set about each other. Personal differences were blown out of proportion and tended to divide rather than unite the state. There also developed the peculiar syndrome of the party in power claiming to be in favor of independence but really being reluctant to take the plunge, while the opposition parties took the line either that the state was not ready for independence and/or could not make it on its own, or that the present leaders were incompetent and could not be trusted to lead the country to independence. In a curious way, therefore, both parties ended up on the same side of the fence.

Developments took a more bizarre turn in Grenada. Having won a convincing victory over the opposition, Gairy decided that this gave him a mandate to proceed to independence. He therefore dispensed with the constitutional requirement of a referendum and asked the British government to terminate association. The opposition parties argued that his actions were unconstitutional, but to no avail. Deep feelings of resentment were aroused among the electorate, who feared that he would become a dictator once the restraining influence of the British government was withdrawn. Their fears were further compounded when a campaign attracting over 19,000 signatures, 46% of the electorate, was ignored.

Notwithstanding widespread opposition, Gairy pushed on with his plans for independence. The run-up period was marked by intense political, social, and industrial unrest. There were riots and shootings. Shops and premises were looted and burned, and leaders of the opposition were beaten up and imprisoned. By the time the island became independent, the opposition had either been silenced or driven underground. The economic and commercial life of the island ground to a halt. Relations between Gairy and the opposition did not improve with independence. In fact, his actions became more outrageous and idiosyncratic. He was eventually ousted in a bloodless coup in March 1979 by Maurice Bishop, the leader of the New Jewel Movement, and his ministers imprisoned. Gairy himself was out of the island at the time.

Developments in Grenada are not, however, sufficient by themselves to explain why the other islands remained for so long as Associated States. Statehood was, after all, intended to be a stop-gap arrangement and could have been ended any time they chose. As it turned out, the process has taken almost 15 years to complete. There are several other reasons why they were reluctant to take the plunge. First, they had gotten themselves into an awful dilemma. On the one hand, they had refused independence within a federal framework, and on the other, when independence was offered to them separately, they were equally reluctant to accept it. What is more, they had no alternative proposals to offer. In effect, what they appeared to be saying was, we want independence, but not as a group and not as individual units, and we have no suggestions. The responsibility for resolving the impasse was thus handed back to Britain.

However, there was no way in which the problem could be resolved within the existing terms of reference. Having accepted the view that federation was both ill conceived and unworkable, the British government had no alternative but to try to sell independence on its own to each unit. It is difficult, though, to see just how they could have succeeded, given that one of the reasons federation was rejected was precisely because it was being imposed from outside, i.e., being advocated by the British government. For their part, the states lacked the political will and necessary internal cohesion to move to independence on their own. Faced with this situation, the status quo seemed the least embarrassing alternative all round.

Second, and in a more positive vein, the Associated States were in fact on to a good thing. Statehood allowed them to enjoy the best of all possible worlds. Politically, they enjoyed full internal self-government. This meant that they could run their own affairs as they chose. They could decide their own level of administrative services, the number of ministries, elected representatives, the nature and form of local government, levels of public expenditure, and so on. As the figures in Table 2 show, they quickly acquired a massive political superstructure and a sprawling bureaucracy.

In 1973, the Windward and Leeward Islands had a total of 47 ministries for their combined population of 476,000. These carried a total establishment of 16,046 persons at a cost of EC$55.4 million, or 42% of their combined estimated public expenditure. By comparison, Barbados—their nearest neighbor and erstwhile partner in the aborted Eastern Caribbean Federation—had 12 ministries, almost quarter the number for a population of 236,000 (i.e., half the same population).

The cost of supporting this top-heavy political and administrative structure was largely borne by the British government. During the first five years of statehood, their overall budgetary deficit

TABLE 2
Leewards and Windwards Establishments and Emoluments

ISLANDS	ESTIMATED POPULATION 1970 CENSUS	NUMBER OF MINISTRIES	SIZE OF ESTABLISH-MENTS	TOTAL EMOLUMENTS % m R.V.	EMOLUMENTS AS % OF TOTAL ESTIMATED EXPENDITURE
Grenada	94,000	8	3,067	10.8	53.0
St. Vincent	87,000	7	3,073	9.3	53.8
St. Lucia	101,000	6	2,875	9.1	41.9
Dominica	71,000	6	2,065	8.4	51.7
Antigua	65,000	8	2,442	8.9	25.3
St. Kitts	46,000	7	1,921	6.5	39.3
Montserrat	12,000	5	603	2.4	45.9
TOTAL	476,000	47	16,046	55.4	42.0
Barbados	236,000	12	9,660	54.7	39.0

SOURCE: Technical Committee (1975, 43: Table 1).

rose from EC$5.3 million to EC$12.5 million. Over the corresponding period U.K. budgetary aid declined from EC$7.5 million to EC$4.6 million, mainly because of the government's decision to shift the emphasis of its aid program from budgetary to capital aid. The latter rose from EC$8 million to EC$31 million. While it appeared, therefore, that the islands were reducing their dependence on Britain for budgetary aid, what they were in fact doing was simply switching various items of public expenditure to their capital budgets, which were mainly financed by C D and W capital aid funds.

But this only partially solved the problem. The real difficulty lay in finding the funds to pay salaries and to maintain basic economic and social services. On average, administration and social services absorbed about 75% of total government expenditure. The position in 1975 was put in the following terms:

> There have been press reports of difficulties being experienced by certain Governments in meeting monthly salary obligations; and at least one Government in the Region has cited requests which it has received for providing budgetary assistance to some countries. Moreover, it is possible that the situation will get worse in 1975 if there is any basis for the unconfirmed report that the overall deficit of the seven islands could increase by anything between EC$6 million and EC$10 million [ISER, 1975: 15].

Third, Associated Statehood relieved them of the cost and responsibility of providing for their own defense and external affairs. They were thus free to utilize their resources to develop their economies. Unfortunately, many of them concentrated on politically motivated projects and other forms of expenditure aimed at securing their own position internally. Expenditure on police and internal security, for example, shot up overnight, adding to the already overburdened cost of administration.

Finally, as states in association with Britain—i.e., not yet fully independent—they had a claim on British aid and technical assistance. The British government for its part not only recognized this claim, but set up a Development Division in Barbados in order to strengthen and promote their development and to facilitate the transfer to full independence. Like its predecessor, the Development and Welfare Organization, this division has performed a very useful role in laying the economic and social infrastructure for independence. However, its very success may in fact have resulted in delaying independence, since once the islands became independent they would lose their moral claim on and direct access to British aid. This is not to say that British aid would automatically dry up, but rather that independence would end their special relationship with Britain. Therefore, the longer it was delayed, the better from their point of view. In brief, there was no real financial or economic incentive for them to take independence.

ONWARD TO INDEPENDENCE

Associated Statehood was clearly an embarrassment to Britain. Instead of being a temporary staging post, it turned into a constitutional nightmare. To begin with, Britain was responsible for the states' defense and security, but powerless to enforce authority; required to safeguard their territorial integrity against external aggression, but unable to intervene in internal political disputes and antistate activities, a distinction which in the context of these states was largely artificial; and expected to provide the

TABLE 3
Average Annual Growth Rate of Per Capita Income in Real Terms for the Windward and Leeward Islands: 1970-1977

ISLANDS	%
LEEWARDS	
Antigua	-3.7
St. Kitts-Nevis	1.6
WINDWARDS	
Dominica	-4.1
Grenada	-3.2
St. Lucia	0.7
St. Vincent	-2.2

SOURCE: World Bank (1979)

finance for their development, but not have any say in determining how, where, when, and why the funds were spent.

As if that were not enough, Britain was often the subject of much unwarranted criticism by the UN Committee on Colonialism for delaying independence, when in fact, the problem was how to get them to take it.

Now that they have been coaxed, cajoled, perhaps even pushed into independence, it is worthwhile looking at some of the problems they face. Taking first their growth rates, although there have been some isolated patches of prosperity, the islands as a group have not experienced any growth in real output for a long time. Table 3 shows their average annual rate of growth of per capita incomes in real terms for each of the Windward and Leeward Islands for the period 1970 to 1977.

Although these estimates are tentative, they paint a very depressing picture. Only St. Kitts-Nevis (1.6% per annum) and St. Lucia (0.7% per annum) registered any growth in real per capita incomes during the period under review. The other islands recorded substantial and frightening falls of real per capita incomes. In Dominica the figure averaged –4.1% per annum, and in Antigua and Grenada it reached –3.7% per annum and –3.2% per annum, respectively. In other words, not only are these islands not growing, they are having to dissave at an alarming rate in order to maintain existing standards of living.

The islands themselves have undergone a certain amount of structural change within the limits of their size and resource base. During the early sixties, for example, agriculture accounted for about 36% of their combined GDP. By the seventies it had dropped to 25%. Most recent estimates put it at 23%. Part of the fall was due to adverse conditions in world export markets for their cash crops. Bananas did well during the sixties only to fall off badly later. During this time export agriculture in the Leeward Islands virtually collapsed, the most obvious example being the sugar industry in Antigua, which ceased operations. In addition, domestic agriculture throughout the region remained stagnant for a long time.

The change has also been due to the islands' efforts to diversify production and to expand into mining and manufacturing. In 1965, mining and other forms of industrial activities accounted for about 3% of total GDP. By 1972 it had risen to 5%. It is currently estimated at 6%. Several manufacturing projects have already been completed, such as footwear, garments, and assembly of television sets, and others are in various stages of completion—a flour mill, glass fibre factory and petroleum refinery. These will undoubtedly help to strengthen their economies and increase exports. It will be a very long time, though, before this sector expands beyond its present marginal role.

Table 4 gives estimates of their combined GDP at current factor cost for 1972 to 1977. Their reliance on agriculture is amply demonstrated. As the figures slow, this is still the most important sector. In common with other primary producers, the Associated States benefited from buoyant export prices between 1974 and 1976. However in terms of volume, exports actually fell. Within this sector bananas continue to do well though it has recently experienced a number of setbacks, including adverse weather conditions, rising cost of fertilizers and other inputs, and labor shortages.

After agriculture, distribution made the largest contribution to GDP, reflecting the extent to which these islands have been converted to service economies. While this has undoubtedly

TABLE 4
Gross Domestic Product at Current Factor Cost for the Windward and Leeward Islands: 1972-1977

						($EC million)
SECTORS	1972[1]	1973[1]	1974[1]	1975[2]	1976[2]	1977[2]
Export Agriculture	25.8	29.2	43.0			
Other Agriculture				93.4	117.9	115.3
Livestock & Fishing	25.5[3]	27.9[3]				
Mining & Manufacturing	15.4	16.3	17.1	-	-	-
Construction	40.9	40.6	43.8	-	-	-
Distribution	60.6	63.0	75.9	88.6	90.0	109.0
Government[5]	54.9	62.7	72.8	80.4	93.0	101.0
Others	83.1	91.6	140.3[4]	-	-	-
Hotels	(20.2)	(19.8)	-	-	-	-
TOTAL	306.2	331.3	392.9	422.8	497.4	536.7

SOURCE: Aggregated and compiled on the basis of data supplied CEPAL and published in CEPAL/CARIB (1978, 14: Table 1).

NOTES:
1. Provisional estimates.
2. Government estimates.
3. Include Antigua's export agriculture.
4. GDP for other Agriculture, Livestock, and Fishing are included in "Other."
5. Include Public Utilities.
– Not available.

helped to sustain their sagging economies, it is potentially a source of instability and overdependence on external factors. Tourism, for example, has picked up quite considerably in Antigua and Dominica, but as the experience of Grenada shows, this industry is extremely susceptible to internal political instability.

In current values, the contribution of the government sector virtually doubled between 1972 and 1977. Percentagewise, however, its contribution hardly changed. It averaged about 18% throughout. This makes the public sector one of the principal agents of employment and economic change. However, its overwhelming emphasis on basic infrastructure and social services means that there are not enough revenue-earning projects to sustain current levels of public spending. In 1977 total government recurrent expenditure exceeded revenue by some EC$22 million. Any attempt to expand present levels of government expenditure will undoubtedly aggravate the deficit.

This is really the crux of the problem. Government expenditures have consistently outstripped revenue collections. In 1973 the former totalled EC$117 million as against EC$95 million for

TABLE 5
Aggregated Government Revenue and Expenditure of the Windward and Leeward Islands: 1975-1977

YEAR	RECURRENT REVENUE	GOVERNMENT EXPENDITURE TOTAL	RECURRENT	CAPITAL
1975	131	175	137	38
1976	148	229	165	64
1977	165	281	187	95

SOURCE: Compiled from data presented in the Statistical Annex (CEPAL/CARIB, 1978a).

the latter. Over the next two years the deficit dropped to EC$6 million, due mainly to improved revenue collection, higher export and import duties, and consumption taxes. The position between 1975 and 1977 is shown in Table 5.

Within the space of two years, government revenues rose by EC$34 million, a very respectable performance all around. There were also some notable shifts in the pattern of contribution. Income tax, for example, rose from 21% of total revenue in 1974 to 26% in 1977, while import duties fell from 24% to 19% over the same period. However, these changes were not sufficient to offset the requirements of recurrent expenditure, which rose by a clear EC$50 million. Faced with such heavy and persistent deficits on current account, these islands are quite unable to finance their own development and have to rely on external finance to meet the cost of their capital requirements. Between 1975 and 1977 the cost of their capital budget rose from $38 million to EC$94 million, an increase of $56 million in two years. Most of this had to come from external sources in the form of concessional aid flows, since the islands have no international reserves to speak of, and their low credit rating does not allow them to borrow on commercial terms.

Notwithstanding the substantial increase in local revenues, the islands are in a very tight spot financially. They cannot balance their budgets, and their development plans are almost wholly dependent on external resources. So far they have been very fortunate. Since 1974 there has been a massive increase in the net

TABLE 6
Net Total Financial Flows Received by the Windward and Leeward Islands: 1973-1977

ISLANDS	1973	1974	1975	1976	1977
LEEWARDS					
Antigua	0	3.0	2.6	3.4	5.5
Montserrat	0	2.7	4.5	3.4	3.1
St. Kitts-Nevis, Anguilla	0	3.6	3.3	3.7	3.4
WINDWARDS					
Dominica	0.6	4.0	8.0	5.9	6.2
Grenada	0.1	1.9	3.2	2.7	3.2
St. Lucia	0.9	7.8	10.5	8.8	6.6
St. Vincent	0.3	3.8	6.1	4.4	4.0
TOTAL	1.9	26.8	38.2	32.3	32.0

SOURCE: United Nations (1979: 396-397).
NOTE: Amounts less than US $1 million are recorded as "0."

total financial flows which they receive. As the figures in Table 6 show, up to 1973, these amounted to less than $2 million.[2] In 1974 they jumped to U.S.$26.8 million, reached a maximum of U.S.$38.2 million in 1975, and then fell back to $32 million in 1977.

There are three points worth making about the figures in this table. First, the vast majority of these funds are concessional in character, with ODA funds (i.e., funds given specifically for developmental purposes) being the principal subgroup. In most instances they run as high as 90% of total net flows. Second, most of the funds are bilateral, with Britain being the main contributor for obvious reasons. Several of the islands believe that once they become independent this pattern will change dramatically. Independence will widen their options and they will be able to play the aid donor's market, so to speak. This was certainly one of Gairy's main reasons for rushing into independence, but as the post-independence experience of Grenada has shown, there is unlikely to be any great rush of donors willing to take up where Britain has left off. Grenada in fact received less than the other islands between 1973 and 1977.

TABLE 7
Value of Exports and Imports and the Trade Balance for the Windward and Leeward Islands: 1972-1978

YEAR	EXPORTS f.o.b.	IMPORTS c.i.f.	TRADE BALANCE CURRENT VALUE	% OF IMPORTS
1972	49	160	-111	-69.4
1973	68	164	- 96	-58.5
1974	82	207	-125	-60.4
1975	90	223	-133	-59.6
1976	99	235	-136	-57.9
1977	111	274	-163	-59.5
1978	152	296	-144	-48.6

SOURCE: Compiled from data presented in United Nations (1979: 4-5, 14-15, 44).

Third, the islands attract very little investment capital. Non-concessional flows, both public and private, total less than $1 million in most years. Dominica and St. Lucia are the notable exceptions. In the case of the former island, they reached $1.3 million in 1976 and 1977. The figures for St. Lucia were $1.4 million and $2.4 million, respectively. These islands are clearly heading for trouble. Net total financial flows for Dominica doubled between 1974 and 1975. They then fell from a maximum of $8 million in 1975 to $6.2 million in 1977, the equivalent of about 85% of the country's total recurrent revenue for that year. Net total flows for St. Lucia amounted to $34.7 million over the four years 1974 through 1977, the highest total for the islands.

This steadily worsening financial situation must be set alongside the performance of the islands' export sectors. Comprehensive data on their balance of payments are not available. The data in the following table must therefore be interpreted with caution since they tell only part of the story. Nevertheless, they are sufficiently clear to enable a broad analysis to be made. In straightforward value terms, both exports and imports have moved steadily upward. Between 1972 and 1978, the former increased by over U.S.$100 million, from $49 million in 1972 to $152 million in 1978, and the latter rose from $160 million to $296 million.

Although it is only a rough indication of imbalance in the overall balance of payments, the trade balance has continued to widen ominously. In 1972 it stood at –$111 million. It fell to –$96 million the following year, but since then has risen to –$144 million. In 1977 it reached a maximum of –$163 million. The possibility of reducing the gap is limited by (1) their overdependence on a few primary commodities for their export earnings, and (2) the diversified and essential nature of imports—e.g., petroleum and petroleum products, machinery, manufactured goods, and other capital goods for development. In 1976 the ratio of imports to GDP averaged 82%. By 1977 the average proportion had risen to 92%. Exports, on the other hand, averaged 34% of aggregate GDP in 1976 and 1977.

In brief, therefore, the Associated States face very serious economic and financial problems. Their budgetary deficits have risen sharply in recent years. The cost of independence will undoubtedly increase these deficits and force them to rely, to an even greater extent, on external resources to bridge the gap. However, their ability to raise funds externally is severely constrained by their lack of reserves and low credit rating. The situation with their balance of payments is just as bad. Export earnings are unlikely to increase sufficiently to pay for their imports or to support a modest increase in living standards. Imports, on the other hand, will continue to surge upward as the cost of development and independence rises. As the situation deteriorates, they will need substantial injections of additional long-term concessional funds to prevent their economies from collapsing. The question then is, who will take on the job of subsidising them indefinitely, and how can this be squared with independence?

FRAGMENTATION OR INTEGRATION?

It is on the political front, however, that the new states will face the sternest test to their independence. The collapse of the 1958 Federation set off a train of events which is still working its way through the region. By opting out of a federation which was specially fashioned to accommodate them, both Jamaica and

Trinidad and Tobago opened the way for fragmentation to be accepted as an alternative strategy of political development. Until then, the cohesion and political unity of the region was regarded as the sine qua non of independence and the lifeblood of the new nation.

It was precisely for this reason that the British government refused to entertain a request from Nevis to be separated from St. Kitts in 1959. The federal government, to which the request was also referred, took the view that separation would establish a dangerous precedent, as it would encourage similar secessionist movements to emerge and flourish and would compromise the constitutional integrity and authority of the new nation. Within the space of two years, the very members who were most vehemently opposed to separation had themselves opted out of the federation, making fragmentation a fact of life.

Having accepted the principle of individual independence in the case of Jamaica and Trinidad and Tobago, the British government had no alternative but to extend it to the other members. Any island which did not want to be integrated with the others could opt out of further federal discussions, and several of them did just that. Grenada opted out of the federal discussions for the "Little Eight" and decided to seek unitary association with Trinidad and Tobago. The latter threw out the proposal, and Grenada was back on its own. Having withdrawn from further federal discussions, Antigua and Barbados were also on their own. In fact, they were all on their own. The forces of fragmentation had once more triumphed over integration.

Fragmentation however, confronted them with the problem of deciding their own future. Barbados chose independence, while Montserrat decided to revert to its former status as a Crown colony, the opposite end of the political and constitutional spectrum, so to speak. The others could not make up their minds whether to go forward or backward. When they finally decided to move forward, they ran into all sorts of trouble. Anguilla refused to remain with St. Kitts and made a unilateral declaration of independence, starting the process of fragmentation all over again. This time though, there was one important new development. Unlike the previous process when the larger units broke away from the smaller ones, it was now the smallest member of the union which had decided to go it alone. In other words, the principle was reversible.[3]

The British government does not appear to have contemplated this possibility. It was simply assumed that islands like Anguilla, Nevis, Barbuda, Bequia, and other Grenadines, which politically, administratively, and in all other respects were an integral part of a larger colonial entity, would wish to remain together. The possibility of further fragmentation within the region was thus, if not ignored, assumed to be so impractical and unrealistic as not to warrant discussion. Consequently, when Anguilla broke away from St. Kitts, the British government was caught between two fundamental and irreconcilable constitutional principles. On the one hand, it was required to uphold the constitutional authority and territorial integrity of the State; on the other, it had to respect the right of the people of Anguilla to determine their own future. To satisfy the first would have meant abrogating its responsibility in respect of the second, and vice versa.

It eventually settled for the second alternative, and Anguilla became a ward of the British government in 1969. It has been administered directly ever since. In 1976 it was given its own ministerial system. It has also received a considerable amount of British aid for roads, schools, water, electricity, and improvements to other economic and social infrastructure. In 1978 it had a total budgetary expenditure of £900,000, of which £220,000, almost 25%, was budgetary support from the British government. In terms of total per capita aid, it currently receives about £130 per annum, making it one of the largest per capita recipients of British aid. Anguilla appears, thus, to have done very well out of the crisis. It enjoys a higher standard of living than would have been possible with St. Kitts, and it has a substantial amount of control over its own affairs.

Unfortunately, Anguilla and the problems it represents have turned out to be a major headache for the British government. By allowing it to break away from St. Kitts and later underwriting its development, the British government offered dependence on British aid as an effective alternative to integration. Incidentally, it employed precisely the same strategy when it allowed Montserrat to revert to being a colony. As the figures in Table 1 indicate, Montserrat has done very well out of this arrangement—much better, in fact, than would have been possible under integration with any of the other islands. Its basic social and economic characteristics compare favorably with the other Windward and Leeward Islands. From being the poorest of the lot, it has moved to the top in terms of per capita income. In 1976 it had a per capita income of U.S.$1036, almost twice that of the other islands. It has its own ministerial system and receives budgetary aid to the tune of £180,000 per annum, approximately 10% of its total budgetary expenditure. In 1978 the total per capita aid was £60.

In both cases fragmentation paid off. There is, in fact, no real incentive for them either to become independent or to be integrated with any of the other units. However, as long as they remain outside the mainstream of developments in the other islands, they are a potential source of political instability within the region. Secessionist elements in Nevis, Barbuda, and elsewhere draw comfort and encouragement from the way in which Anguilla benefited from fragmentation. It is probably only a matter of time before they, too, throw caution and the constitution to the wind, and break away.

Britain is thus faced with a dual problem. First, it has to get the reluctant starters back on course and progressively reduce their dependence on British aid, so that they will accept the economic necessity to move closer to their former partners and eventually be reintegrated with them. Second, it must discourage further attempts at fragmentation. So far it has managed to do this successfully. It has taken a firm line with places like Nevis and Barbuda. The possibility of other Anguillas before independence may therefore be discounted. Its actions are, however, regarded in some quarters as simply keeping the lid on things while hurrying the islands on to independence. Once this is achieved, separatist movements will again emerge in full force to threaten the peace and stability of the new states. In other words, the process of fragmentation is not yet over, and Britain's efforts to contain it will eventually prove counterproductive.

This may well be so. Judged by the experience of those that have already become independent, the region seems to have entered a new and disturbing era of political instability. The coup in Grenada, a novel experience for this part of the world, showed that opposition parties are no longer prepared to respect the constitution and that the democratic process has broken down. Any group which is strong or determined enough can seize power. Revolution has, in fact, finally come to the area, and the way is now open for coups and countercoups.

Dominica experienced a serious political crisis closely resembling that which occurred in Grenada immediately after independence. St. Vincent also had to contend with an attempt by disaffected elements to seize power in the Grenadines less than six months after becoming independent. Other crises will doubtless follow. Although these troubles may manifest themselves in different forms, they are symptomatic of the same basic problem—namely, the inability of each unit to provide the necessary political stability to make a success of independence on its own. None of them has the resources to resist, suppress, or otherwise contain a major uprising or civil disorder for any length of time. These were precisely the type of political problems which federation would have enabled them to overcome. Ironically, therefore, the very islands which turned their backs on integration now find themselves in need of the protection, stability and additional economic and financial resources which a federation provides for small units. In other words, the need for integration is greater now than at any time in the history of these islands.

This brings one to the obvious question: Was federation really ill conceived and inappropriate for these islands? Notwithstanding all that has been written about the collapse of the 1958 Federation, doubts still remain as to whether it was given a fair chance. Its trial period was set for five years. It lasted less than three years. When this is put alongside all the other difficulties which it encountered in its brief and uneventful life, one is entitled to question the bona fides of West Indian leaders. Did they really want it to succeed?

This is not the place to undertake a full-scale analysis of what went wrong, but the almost indecent haste with which the whole exercise was wound up suggests that perhaps they wanted it to fail. Why did the other islands leave it all to Jamaica to decide the fate of the federation? Why did they not take steps to ensure that the decision went in favor of staying in, if that was what they wanted? Why did the British government also do nothing to influence the outcome of the referendum? It could, for example, have called for a referendum in the other islands, or made counter proposals before the event. It simply sat back and waited. It seems either to have misread the situation completely, or, like the constituent members, it too lacked the political will to make federation work. Neither of which is, of course, the same as saying that federation, or some form of amalgamation, is misconceived and inappropriate for these islands.

The Windward and Leeward Islands did, in fact, have separate federal governments before the 1958 Federation was established. The latter, for example, was established in 1871 between Antigua, St. Kitts-Nevis and Anguilla, Montserrat, and the British Virgin Islands. Its headquarters were located in Antigua and, on balance, it functioned reasonably well. It was wound up in 1956 to enable the units to enter the new federation as individual members. The federal idea was thus not an entirely new experience for the region. More to the point, why should these earlier exercises have worked while the latter failed so abysmally?

Until these questions are answered definitively, the case for integration remains. Indeed, it has been urged on these islands repeatedly and, in any number of ways, as their best chance of survival. International organizations and major aid-giving agencies, for example, are not geared for dealing with small individual units. They prefer to operate through regional organizations. It spreads their administrative costs, saves time and effort, and makes life a lot easier for them. Canada and the United States presently channel most of their aid through the Caribbean Development Bank. They are unlikely to open additional channels to accommodate individual islands. Further, given their growing dependence on aid for budgetary and developmental purposes, it is to their advantage to amalgamate and centralize specific services as a cost-reducing exercise and to strengthen their case for additional assistance. In any event, donors are likely to insist on these measures as part of any aid deal. It is therefore a case of doing voluntarily now what may have to be done involuntarily at a later stage.

Various reports have also pointed to the imbalance between the political and administrative structure, on one hand, and the poor economic performance and limited range of possibilities on the other. Their recommendations have invariably come down on the side of integration as the best means of reducing the disparity of improving the overall prospects of independence. One report for example, recommended:

> The Leeward and Windward Islands should proceed to independence and enter into a scheme of constitutional association for the purpose of functioning as a single entity in their relations with other states and with international bodies.[4]

Integration is thus very much a live issue. It is being actively canvassed inside as well as outside the region. Several regional organizations are also doing much good work in laying the foundations for regional integration and economic cooperation. Of these, the most ambitious is the Caribbean Regional Integration Movement (CARICOM) which, despite the balance-of-payments difficulties of individual members, has managed to expand the volume of intraregional trade as well as open up new markets overseas. Excluding trade within the Eastern Caribbean Common Market, CARICOM's intraregional trade as a proportion of its total exports increased from 4.7% in 1960 to 8.3% in 1976. In addition, the community has been taking on more of the cost of financing its collective deficits, with the richer members providing balance-of-payments support and special funds for the poorer members.

The Caribbean Development Bank (CDB) is another regional institution which is helping to integrate the islands. It functions as a bank as well as one of the region's principal development agencies. Between 1970 and 1977, it approved loans totalling over $140 million, of which just over $49 million, or 35.2% went to the more developed countries (MDCs), and $91 million, or 64.8% went to the less developed (LDCs). In addition, loans from its "soft funds" ran to over $85 million. The vast majority of these funds, 93%, went to the LDCs. There has, therefore, been an overwhelming concentration of activities in the poorer members which, in terms of contribution, pay less than 2% of the bank's resources.

In summary, the islands have a long history of cooperation in the field of financial and economic matters. Politically, however, they have shown a predisposition for individual action. This is due as much to their geography and history as to their desire to be a part of the postwar process of decolonization. In common with other colonies, they wanted to achieve independence as separate units as a symbol of their individual struggle and national identity. The strength of these forces was sufficient to fragment the region. The collapse of the 1958 Federation was a traumatic experience from which they have not yet fully recovered. However, the growing number of regional organizations and common services are acting as a synthesizing force, and it may not be long before the islands come to accept their common identity and mutuality of interests, the basis of any integration process.

NOTES

1. See HMSO (1965). Montserrat was excluded from these proposals as the British government intended to discuss the constitutional future of that island with its leaders at a later stage.
2. As the data are recorded in millions of U.S. dollars, amounts less than this basic unit show up as "0." It is possible, therefore, that they significantly underestimate the amount of aid they actually received in that year.
3. For a fuller discussion of this point, see Abbott (1971).
4. A summary of the report's proposals appeared in the ISER Report (1975).

REFERENCES

ABBOTT, G. C. (1971) "Political disintegration: the lessons of Anguilla." Government and Opposition. 6 (winter): 58-74.

ARCHIBALD, C. (1962) "The failure of the West Indies federation." World Today [London] 18 (June): 233-242.

Barbados Government (1965a) Constitutional Proposals for Barbados. Bridgetown, Barbados: Government Printing Office.

——— (1965b) The Federal Negotiations, 1962-1965. Bridgetown, Barbados: Government Printing Office.

BOBB, L. E. (1966) "The federal principle in the British West Indies: an appraisal of its use." Social and Econ. Studies 15 (September): 239-265.

Daily Gleaner (1943) Jamaica, October 10.

Her Majesty's Stationary Office [HMSO] (1963) Fiscal Proposals for an Eastern Caribbean Federation. London: Author.

ISER [Institute of Social and Economic Research] (1975) "The political economy of independence for the Leeward and Windward Islands. Report of a technical committee established by the governments of St. Vincent, St. Lucia, and St. Kitts-Nevis, and Anguilla, March 8. (mimeo)

LOWENTHAL, D. [ed.] (1961) The West Indies Federation. London: Oxford Univ. Press.

MORDECAI, J. (1968) The West Indies: The Federal Negotiations. London: Allen & Unwin.

SPRINGER, H. W. (1962) "Reflections on the failure of the first West Indian federation." Occasional Paper in International Affairs 4. Center for International Affairs, Harvard, July.

United Nations [UNCTAD] (1979) Handbook of International Trade and Development Statistics. New York: Author.

World Bank (1979) World Bank Atlas: Population, Per Capita Product and Growth Rates, 1979. Washington, DC: Author.

George C. Abbott is Senior Lecturer in the Department of International Economic Studies, University of Glasgow, Scotland. He holds degrees from London and Yale and has written widely on the problems of the ministates, the West Indies in particular. His research interests include the debt problem, on which he has recently written a book entitled International Indebtedness and the Developing Countries.

JOHN MAYO
Department of History
University of the West Indies
Cave Hill Campus, Barbados, W.I.

BRITAIN AND CHILE, 1851-1886
Anatomy of a Relationship

Introduction

In 1880, the famous Chilean politician and historian, Benjamin Vicuña Mackenna, wrote:

> There does not exist in the whole globe a country whose prosperity or adversity has a more direct influence as regards Chile than that which affects the welfare of the vast empire of Great Britain, the modern Rome [Chilean Times, 1880].

Five years later, a disgusted U.S. citizen visiting Valparaíso, the republic's principal port, exclaimed "this city is nothing more than an English colony" (Curtis, 1888: 455). The Yankee exaggerated, the Chilean did not; both were noting the phenomenon that existed elsewhere on the globe, a nation whose political independence and absence of constitutional ties with Britain could not disguise its economic dependence upon her. Historians have termed this situation "informal empire" and ascribed its creation to the "imperialism of free trade" (Gallagher and Robinson, 1953: 1-15).[1] Today, nobody disputes the reality of such relationships, but there is considerable controversy over how they were created and their effects on participants. "The basic fact is that British industrialization caused an ever-extending and intensifying development of overseas regions" (Gallagher and Robinson, 1953: 5). Some deny that what took

Journal of Interamerican Studies and World Affairs, Vol. 23 No. 1, February 1981 95-120

place was, in fact "development," claiming instead that the process was one of "under-development" and the inevitable result of the capitalist system in operation (Frank, 1971), but such disagreements only emphasize that the trading ties between the metropolis, Britain, and her economic periphery—countries such as Uruguay, Argentina, Chile, or even Japan—were extremely close. Taking two very dissimilar examples, Britain never supplied less than 43% of Japan's imports in the years between 1873 and 1883 and occupied a still more dominant position in Chile's trade, in 1870 buying 60% of the republic's exports and supplying 45% of its imports; ten years later the respective figures were nearly 78%, and again 45% (Fox, 1969: 369; Mamalakis, 1976: 32).[2] In Uruguay and Argentina, too, Britain possessed great influence, based on her economic strength (Winn, 1975, 1976; Ferns, 1960).

The common denominator of these relationships was Britain's economic predominance: as the first of the industrial nations, she could supply the finished goods undeveloped countries wanted, as well as provide a market for their produce. British ships carried the trade which was often organized and financed by British merchants. In short, Britain could offer a more complete range of goods, services, and capital more cheaply and more efficiently than her competitors, and at the same time buy at least some of the produce of her trading partners. In these circumstances, the expansion of British trade was inevitable. In examining the effects of this process in Chile, it is hoped that some progress will be made in explaining the creation of "dependency" and the reality of "informal empire," in which the republic's status might be described as that of an "informal dominion." This term takes account of the fact that the republic's political independence as a sovereign nation was always fully accepted by Britain, despite the strong economic links between the two countries. In this sense, Chile's position more exactly paralleled those of the self-governing colonies in Australasia, Canada, and South Africa, rather than the Pacific Islands, or Persian Gulf states, where British residents tendered "advice" which became policy.

The Role of the British Government

The British government played a negligible role in the establishment of British interests in Chile. During most of the nineteenth century, the government acted to protect British subjects and trade only when and where it considered they were discriminated against or suffering personal injustice; such interventions usually ended as soon as the local authorities removed the immediate causes of grievance.[3] Even in such cases, British commercial demands were limited to "a fair field and no favour." Once these conditions existed, the British government took no active steps to support the commercial operations that were the foundation of the "informal empire" (Platt, 1973, 1968a, 1968b, 1968c). It did not need to: its laissez-faire policies in trade, including the export of capital, were all the encouragement British entrepreneurs needed. In any event, Chile presented no cause for intervention on any grounds. The republic's government treated all foreigners equally and fairly. When Consul General Thomson did take up a fancied case of grievance in 1863, he found himself deserted by the British community when he attempted to secure compensation for an injured merchant, while his successor managed to save face only when he took up the cudgels for a ship's captain in 1874. Consequently, governmental relations were largely confined to the banalities of diplomatic intercourse, and Santiago was not a popular posting for aspiring young diplomats; Harold Rumbold, the first Briton to hold ministerial rank at Santiago and perhaps the ablest British diplomat to serve there, applied almost continuously for relief throughout his term (Rumbold Private Letters, 1873, 1874, 1875).

This is not to say that Britain's diplomats ignored their country's commercial interests. In 1853 the British chargé protested against an export duty which supposedly discriminated in favor of the French and took the opportunity to stress the advantages of free trade on the Chileans (P.R.O. 1853). As Chile did not adopt free trade for another decade, Britain's influence was scarcely overweening. Another example of British intervention in Chilean policy-making occurred in the early 1860s when the Foreign Office, at the request of the Pacific Steam Navigation Company (P.S.N.C.) instructed the chargé at Santiago to use his "best efforts" "to secure to British trade the right of coasting trade with Chilean ports" (P.R.O., 1861b, 1861c). This was a controversial step, as it had long been Chile's policy to preserve the coastal trade for native vessels. Whether the British intervention had any influence is debatable. When the chargé approached President Pérez, the president explained that Chileans wished to keep the trade for themselves, though he himself favoured opening it, but that the P.S.N.C. in any case benefited as the coasting trade was then "pro tempore" open to all foreign steamers (P.R.O., 1861a). In 1864 the new customs ordinance opened the trade definitively (Brazil and River Plate Mail, 1865). This act has been vigorously condemned by modern Chilean historians (e.g. Encina, 1949, XIV: 644). On the surface, this appears to be one issue in which British pressure may have influenced Chilean policy. The historian of Chile's merchant marine believes this to be the case, though he admits there is no evidence (Véliz, 1961: 138). When the measure, so beneficial to British shipping, was passed, the British chargé, William Taylour Thomson, claimed no credit, a natural step, had he been able to do so. And if there is no evidence of continuing British pressure, there is ample proof of Chile's move towards free trade and laissez-faire policies by the 1860s; the 1864 customs ordinance was its culmination (Will, 1964; Sater, 1976: 313-315). On balance, then, it seems that British desires duplicated Chilean plans, not that they induced them.

This incident was exceptional. Over the whole thirty-five years here considered, the evidence is compelling that the British government was content to limit its support of British subjects and their interests to the traditional fields of securing equality of treatment with other foreigners and safety of persons and property, always subject to limitations imposed by precedent and international law, which were objectives that Chile's domestic order, stability, and government policy in any case secured. Nor is there evidence that Britons in Chile wanted more: although several merchants became members of Parliament on their return from Chile, and H. H. Gibbs, head of Antony Gibbs & Sons, was on the board of the Bank of England for many years, these positions appear to have had no commercial significance in Chile. Relations between the Britons in Chile and their government at home simply were not a factor in the former's success or in the formation of policy by the latter. Neither needed the other, and Chile was too unimportant commercially and strategically—as well as too well run—to arouse either imperial ambitions or sufficient exasperation in the British government to persuade it to interfere in the republic.[4] If passivity be a policy, it was the one the London authorities followed, by default if nothing else.

Chilean Background

In these circumstances of governmental indifference, then, the builders of "informal empires" must be found elsewhere. In the case of Chile and Britain, the builders were the Britons who went to Chile, where they sold foreign goods and services on the local market and organized the return trade that paid form them. The destruction of the Spanish empire gave them their opportunity, while the cause of their success was the technological disequilibrium between advanced Britain and undeveloped Latin America, leading to increased production in the former and increased demand in the latter. The men who took advantage of this situation and organized the trade were, in Latin America, often expatriate merchants. Their attitudes and actions and the reception they received in a particular country determined the nature and extent of their own nation's influence in that country. Examination of the case of Chile demonstrates that the Anglo-Chilean connection was the result of the collaboration of British merchants and Chilean capitalists, based on Chile's capacity to export raw materials. The determinants of the relationship were Chilean ability and willingness or need to absorb British goods and services.

Though economic success could increase both the capacity and desire to trade, government's role in nineteenth-century Chile was limited. Stability, a friendly welcome to foreigners, along with a relatively efficient and honest bureaucracy and spending on such projects as railways created a congenial climate for expansion, but growth and change depended largely on collaboration between the foreigner and local commercial interests. If the latter wished to expand, they could produce more, and so finance it. If they were interested in change, they could buy the necessary instruments and technology with the proceeds of increased production. The Britons and other foreigners were, in the last analysis, dependent on local interest and desire for their goods and services; their authority derived from their ability to satisfy this demand, and it was in their interest to suggest and support the conditions creating it. Consequently, their position grew stronger with their success in convincing the Chileans of their need for the proffered services and goods, but at the same time it became potentially weaker, for two reasons. The British faced growing competition not only from other foreigners but theoretically from Chileans as well, if the government introduced protection or Chilean capitalists invested their capital in industry.

In the second half of the nineteenth century Chilean competition did not materialize and the British were able to hold off foreign challenges with relative ease. This happy result for the British merchants was certainly the outcome of their own labors rather than government action, but it also demonstrated their acceptance by Chile. They remained the agents of British commercial expansion in Chile, but were innovative only to the extent acceptable to Chileans. If Chile did become a dependency of Britain, it was still the republic that called the tune—and it was one to which the Britons in Chile were happy to dance.

The trade figures for Chile between 1850 and 1890 demonstrate the effectiveness of the "imperialism of free trade" (see Table 1). Britain took an increasing share of Chile's exports in both real and relative terms—from just over 30% in 1850 to nearly 70% in 1890—and invariably provided over a third of Chile's imports.

Chile's exports comprised raw materials and agricultural products, almost exclusively copper, nitrates, and wheat, with copper the most important up to the time of the War of the Pacific

TABLE 1
Britain's Share of Chile's Imports and Exports

YEAR	1850 %	1860 %	1870 %	1880 %	1890 %
Exports	32.0	75.3	60.4	77.7	67.1
Imports	34.6	33.5	45.1	45.3	43.3

NOTE: Based on Mamalakis (1976: 32).

from 1879-1883, when nitrates superseded it. Textiles were the largest single item in Chile's imports from Britain: nearly three-eighths in 1858, nearly one-half in 1866, and one-third in 1880 (P.P., 1862, 57: 313, 315, 319; 1867-1868, 70: 987-988, 990; Estadística Comercial, 1881, 26: 200). Other items included coal (used to refine both copper and nitrate), hardware, rails and engines for the new railways, agricultural machinery, and mining equipment.

Chile was one of the most stable Latin American countries as the 1850s began, and during this decade the government implemented policies designed to bring some of the most obviously useful instruments of modern society to the republic. Public expenditure reflected rather than caused the republic's prosperity, revenue being heavily dependent on duties raised on exports, but while private enterprise remained the motor of the economy, government spending could both encourage change and provide opportunities for businessmen. The administration, therefore, supported railway construction, the introduction of the telegraph, uniform postal rates, and other improvements to communications (Encina, 1949, 13: 419, 424, 429, 460; Edwards, 1932: 232, 364, 365). Also during the 1850s, foreigners and Chileans founded the Banco de Valparaíso in 1855, which was the first legally authorized joint-stock bank to survive in Chile, and the legislature passed the 1860 banking law that regulated, rather lightly, the industry during the years here considered (Encina, 1949, 13: 547, 549). In the 1860s the government moved as far towards free trade as it was to do during the century. Government policies, then, were such as would encourage foreign trade and attract foreign traders. The British led the field.

They first came during the wars for independence. In the decade of 1808-1818, the first in which the ports were open to ships of all nations, none of the forty most important merchants in Chile was British, but in the next decade, fifteen were (Rector, 1976: 250-253). The men who established and maintained Britain's dominant position in Chile's economy were largely to continue in this occupation. However, the first generation of Britons in Chile were immigrants, not transients, and they became the progenitors of the Chilean families whose names became famous in the republic later in the century—Edwards, Ross, Blest, McIver, for example—not of a continuing Anglo-Chilean connection. Their children took the nationality of the land of their birth and often of their mothers and usually an occupation very different from the mercantile pursuits of their fathers. So the sons of Joshua Waddington (1792-1876), who had arrived in 1817 and married a Chilean, entered politics (one was a Minister of Finance under Montt), became land owners, invested in the new railways and banks, but avoided the commission trade in which their father remained active until his retirement.

In their concentration on the professions, politics, investments, or the land, these British-named Chileans merely reflected the strength of the values of the society in which they lived. Chile's hierarchical society accepted middle-class pursuits such as trade more as stepping stones to higher status than as lifetime occupations, which meant successful Chileans left them when possible. Equally, however, Chileans needed such services, so their society, top and bottom, welcomed the foreigners providing them.

This deliberate abstention from the import-export trade, not just by the sons of successful British immigrants but also by the families of successful Chilean merchants, left the field open to foreigners, particularly Britons, who established a continuing grip on the business through the mechanism of the self-perpetuating partnerships of merchants, the commission houses. Some arrived on the scene very early and outlasted the individual merchants of the independence era. Antony Gibbs & Sons had a house in Chile in the 1820s—and does now; Duncan Fox & Sons founded in the 1840s, and Balfour Williamson & Co., founded in 1851, are also still in operation. By the 1850s such houses had outlived the pioneers, and in the decades to come they were to dominate the import-export trade. Their activities were major determinants both of the role of the British community in Chile and of the effects on Chile's developement that membership of Britain's "informal empire" had—and perhaps still have.

The British Community

Trade and related activities brought the British. Both the kind of jobs they did and where they chose to live reflected this. There were never many of them; between 1854 and 1885 the British population in Chile grew from 1,934 to just over 5,000. Table 2 shows the importance of Valparaíso, Chile's principal port, where well over a quarter of the Britons in Chile lived. Few Britons were to be found outside Valparaíso or the export provinces of Atacama, Coquimbo, Concepción, and after their conquest from Bolivia and Peru, Antofagasta and Tarapacá.

Throughout this period the British were the most skilled national group in the country. In 1880, Vicuña MacKenna noted that 3261, or 76.4% of the 4267 Britons—including naturalized Britons—had skilled trades or professions (Chilean Times, 1880) in 1875. Census employment statistics show that in 1865, 67.9% of the 2147 employed Britons were merchants, carpenters, miners, sailors, engineers, artisans, or smelters, and 74.4% of the 4112 British workers were employed in those same categories in 1885 (Censo, 1866: 376, 378; Censo, 1889, 1890, 2: 14). In 1865, the census counted Britons in 54 trades or professions; in 1875, in 69; and in 1885, in 64. Other than merchants, Britons in Chile worked in one of two broad fields: as skilled artisans in the country's mines and nascent industries or for the new public utilities; or as providers of services or entertainment, often for fellow members

TABLE 2
Britons in Chile: Principal Locations

Year	Total British Population	Valparaiso %	Export Provinces %	Santiago %	Other %
1854	1,934	36.7	50.9	6.7	5.7
1865	3,092	39.0	47.5	6.2	7.3
1875	4,109	43.8	37.2	9.3	9.7
1885	5,184	29.5	54.5	4.5	4.5

NOTE: Calculated from Censo (1858, 1866, 1876, 1889-1890). Percentages are taken to the first decimal place. The new nitrate provinces included for the first time in 1885 contained 23.4% of the total.

of the British community but not exclusively so. Such were the clergymen and teachers, the doctors, the gardeners, the artists, and the barbers. Britons were principally to be found employed in trade and in the modernizing sectors of the economy: mining, financial services, and what industry there was. They lived where these activities took place—the major port and the mining centers in the north. In central Chile, where most Chileans lived, few Britons were to be found, with the major exception of Valparaíso; the small communities at Santiago and Concepción were dwarfed by those in Atacama and Coquimbo provinces and later by those in the nitrate provinces. The Britons in the nitrate provinces account for the whole of the increase in British numbers between 1875 and 1885; indeed, there was a small decline elsewhere.

The very small number of Britons in Santiago, the capital, is noteworthy (see Table 2). None of the major British houses maintained a partner there in this period, relying instead on a Chilean lawyer or an English agent, such as the ubiquitous Charles Swinburne, to handle matters for them. Politics did not loom large in commerce, although the British did have contacts with the Chilean political class, often the same people in whose wheat and ores they dealt; these relations were therefore closer than their partners in Britain had with government there, though this seems to have had no direct political or economic consequences. Generally, Britons were well satisfied with conditons in Chile—and said so.

In 1876, their own newspaper observed "it is scarcely possible to speak of Chile and of the Chilean character otherwise than in terms of warmest commendation for the present, and of hopefulness for the future"(Chilean Times, 1876). British diplomats agreed, if less enthusiastically. As Rumbold (memo, 1883) sardonically observed:

> The New world, which it was Mr. Cannings's boast to have called into being to redress the balance of the old, has been a thoroughly disappointing creation with the exception, I think, of Chile. In that country alone . . . are to be found traditions of statesmanship and good administration.

And despite occasional tension, both the Chilean commercial community and the government seemed happy to have the Britons—and other foreigners. When President Montt opened the Bolsa Comercial (a gathering place for businessmen, forerunner of a stock exchange) at Valparaíso in 1858, he specifically celebrated the role of foreigners —and of his own government— in his address to the assembled merchants (El Mercurio, 1858b).[5]

In this favorable climate, the British could operate in any part of the economy they chose. They concentrated on the import-export and modern sectors of the economy (often but not always the same). It is convenient now to consider their contributions in particular industries before returning to the central role of the commission house.

New Business Opportunities

In 1854 Congress passed a law governing limited liability companies, which opened the way for joint-stock banks. The first of these was the Banco de Valparaíso, established in 1855; British influence is clearly demonstrated by the membership of the directorate between 1855 and 1894, when the bank merged with others to form the Banco de Chile. Of the 57 men who served on its Valparaíso board, 28 had British names, and 3 of its 6 presidents were Britons: James C. Hayne of William Gibbs & Co.; Bartholomew Browne of Huth, Gruning & Co.; and H. H. Hammond of Graham, Rowe & Co. (Banco de Chile, 1944: 18). In 1863, 4 of the 7 directors were partners in British houses (El Mercurio, 1863a). Although British stock-ownership was considerable, amounting to some 300 of the first emission of 1400 shares (N.V. 1855b), by itself it did not justify the prominent positions assumed by Britons in management. The reason lies elsewhere and appears to be a simple one.

Britons knew how to run banks. Before the successful launching of the Banco de Valparaíso, credit was available from a number of sources: the privately wealthy, the private banks associated with mining families such as the Ossas and Edwards, or the import-export houses, foreign and national. Only the British had real experience with large-scale banking operations over a long time, and given their good relations with wealthy Chileans, their advancement was natural. Certainly, the bank—and subsequent ones—was run according to British practice: the provision of working capital, rather than financing fixed capital (Habakkuk, 1962: 174). As Williamson of Williamson, Balfour—which was a shareholder in the younger Banco Nacional de Chile—put it: "Let people with means seek to develop the resources of the country themselves and not cumber you [the Banco Nacional] with working their spare capital" (Balfour, Williamson Papers, 1877).

An example shows what this meant in practice. In 1875 the Banco de Valparaíso turned down a request from the Compañia de salitres y ferrocarril de Antofagasta to open a current account of 520,000 pesos to continue construction of a railway (Actas, 1875a), despite the backing of the company by William Gibbs & Co. and Agustín Edwards, respectively the most important British house in Chile and the most successful Chilean capitalist of the era (Bermudez, 1963: ch. 4). Instead, it put its money into a loan of 350,000 pesos to the Santiago municipality at 10% a year, ½% commission six-monthly, amortization of at least 25,000 pesos each six months, as well as acting as the city's bankers during the five years of the loan (Actas, 1875b).

Such practices made for safety, but gave the banks a limited role. Apparently both Britons and Chileans were satisfied. No British bank succeeded in establishing itself in the country until the advent of Colonel North and the nitrate era; meanwhile, the Chileans went on hiring Britons to fill executive positions.

The same pattern appears in the establishment of a domestic insurance industry. The British supported the first Chilean insurance company, founded in the 1850s, and in 1858, four of its nine directors were Britons (Valparaíso Mercantile Reporter, 1852; El Mercurio, 1858a). In 1859, 16 of the 35 underwriters of Lloyds de Valparaíso were also British, mostly partners in commission houses (Duncan, Fox Papers, 1859). Here, however, the British did not leave the field to the locals, the commission houses themselves entering the business through agencies from companies at home (Platt, 1977: 54; Hunt, 1951, 1: 78). They soon made their mark. In 1864, 5 British companies bore £ 35,200 of the insured loss in a fire estimated to have cost £ 70-80,000, while three Chilean firms paid £ 9,000 (Brazil and River Plate Mail, 1864). Such losses did not deter them, and they remained important in the industry after the period here considered.

Britons were equally active in transport, directly or indirectly. They participated in the construction and running of all the railroads, helped finance some, and acquired shares in others. A British loan of seven million pesos in 1857 enabled the government to continue the Santiago-Valparaíso railway after private interests failed to raise the necessary capital. Individual Britons helped build it and then run it (Gay, 1972, 2: 351; Chilean Times, 1886). They also participated in the privately financed mining lines in the north, such as the Copiapó-Caldera line, the Coquimbo line, and Carrizal and Cerro Blanco railway (Gay, 1869: 2; Balfour, Williamson Papers, 1884: 2, 3; El Mercurio and Chilean Times, 1876-1886). These acquired stock exchange quotation in England, and after 1875 the majority of the shareholders in the Copiapó and Coquimbo lines lived in Britain—an indication of their profitability and of the need of Chileans to sell during the depression of the late 1870s.

Chilean shipping policies also favored foreigners, the British in particular. Whether this was the result of British pressure has been discussed. It is sufficient to note that Britons in Chile, as well as British shipowners, profited from chartering and insuring ships, as well as repairing them, while Chileans benefited from efficient transport of their bulky goods. This was a form of dependence, but given the general lack of Chilean interest in investing in shipping, it was unavoidable.

Agriculture was perhaps the only important area of the Chilean economy Britons ignored and for good reason. Unlike North America, Chile had little unowned land, and this was on the borders of, or in, Indian territory, and required laborious clearing. Though haciendas in the central valley changed hands, few Britons, and they settlers, competed with the constant Chilean demand. As transients, they had no ambition for the status land-ownership conferred, and as businessmen they understood the disinclination of Chilean landowners to invest in their estates (Bauer, 1975: 69-70). Instead, they supplied modern equipment, when asked, and processed and dealt in agricultural produce.

Industry in this era was largely of the artisan type, based on skills rather than capital, and was devoted principally to processing or repairing. However, the War of the Pacific gave it a considerable boost (Kirsch, 1977: 5-6); Britons were in the forefront of this development. An authority on industrialization in Chile notes that they "regarded their business more as integral parts of the Chilean domestic economy than as segments of a foreign one" (Pfeiffer, 1952: 139), and certainly far more of them than of the commission merchants remained in Chile. Among the principal Chilean foundries were Henderson, Finch y Cia., Balfour, Lyon y Cia., Brower & Hardie, and Lever, Murphy y Cia., whose names denote their origins. Still, these firms commanded far less capital than the commission houses,[6] clearly an indication of the relative failure of such enterprises to attract the interest of capitalists, despite the membership of their proprietors in the British community.

Commission Houses

The commission houses were, without exception, limited-term partnerships of merchants. The more important had houses in both Britain and Chile, often having slightly different names, indicating both their separate legal existences and sometimes different partners. So Antony Gibbs & Sons of London was William Gibbs & Co. in Valparaíso, and the house itself acted as shareholder in the Chilean firm for the London partners, while the partners in Chile participated as individuals. Though the partnerships were limited in term, usually three or five years, they could be and usually were renewed almost automatically, so that the short lives of the houses were a theoretical rather than a practical factor in conducting business.

But if the fixed term could largely be ignored in practice, the houses and their partners did operate under real constraints, formal or informal. Articles of partnership required the partners to devote all their time to the house (hence the popularity of Lloyds de Valparaíso as a painless and profitable means of working partners' surplus funds), some prohibited speculation, others laid down what companies the partners could or could not invest in and one even prohibited its partners from marrying Chilean ladies, in case it compromised the firm's English nationality (Huth Papers, 1862; Balfour, Williamson Papers, 1851). The limited period of partnership was also a constraining factor because houses had to remain sufficiently liquid to pay off retiring or deceased partners, but more important than any of these were capital resources.

The basis of the commission business was capital. They had to give purchasers of their goods credit, and for longer periods than in Britain (Duncan, Fox Papers, 1857). In the same way, suppliers required advances to cover their expenses until their goods were sold. It was a profitable business, as the merchants charged between 8% and 12% a year for their money, as well as charging commission—usually totalling between 5% and 7%—on sales, insurance and freight (e.g., N.V., 1856). It was also a safe one, if the advances were conservative, as they were covered by the goods advanced on, whether copper, silver, wheat, or flour. The principal danger merchants feared was the possibility of being trapped into an *habilitación* (financing) agreement.

Chilean mining law required that mines be worked at a certain level, otherwise the mine could be claimed by anyone. Consequently, the temptation was to continue advancing funds to miners to protect advances already made, in effect accepting an open-ended commitment to find money in the hope of future profits. Such was an habilitación. In bad times, or with low-grade ores, or bad management, this could involve crippling expense; between 1859 and 1872, Robert Walker saw a debt of 100,000 pesos grow to 660,000 (N.V., 1872). Even if such an arrangement were ultimately profitable, it locked up funds, which was anathema to the commission houses. Gibbs (Papers, 1859) spoke for all when reminding their Valparaíso partners that funds should be "actively employed in shipments from one side or the other, and not upon dead work."

For although the houses had considerable capital by Chilean standards, it was not great in an absolute sense, and their prospects of acquiring more were limited by their own decision to remain partnerships. Consequently, such firms' resources were limited to the partners' fortunes and creditworthiness, plus what cash deposits their good name brought in from cautious investors, with Gibbs borrowing at 6% and lending at 12% (Gibbs Papers, 1858a) and amounts raised from selling bills on their British correspondents. The result was that a well-run house was always fully stretched, whatever its resources. Gibbs employed some 3.25 million pesos on the west coast in each of the years from 1853-1857, earning about 10% on this sum (Gibbs Papers, 1858b). In 1858 their London house sold £ 889,000, or about 4,845,000 pesos, on their own or their constituents' behalf. Some William Gibbs & Co. bought outright on the coast, for cash. The rest was "influenced" to Antony Gibbs, i.e., to be sold on commission; to procure this business, the house had to make cash advances (Gibbs Papers, 1859). Clearly the Chile firm made thorough use of its capital, but there was little room for error.

This essentially middleman role was the essence of British activity and influence in Chile. Gibbs continued as it had begun, despite owning nitrate and copper mines: during the decade 1871-1880, the Valparaíso house never influenced less than 4 million pesos per annum to their London friends, and in six of those years it was more than 7 million (Gibbs Papers, 1886). Other firms followed in the same path. Balfour Williamson began in 1851 with £ 15,000 of borrowed capital and traded up to a value of £ 751,270 in 1884 (Balfour Williamson Papers, 1851, 1884). What competition there was came from other foreigners, not Chileans. In 1858-1859, 91 of the 113 import-export houses in the country were foreign (Memoria de Hacienda, 1860), and although this proportion changed as more Chileans entered the business, the British maintained their predominance and their position as the most influential foreigners in the Chilean economy as measured by their share of trade, the position of Britons in Chilean enterprises, and, particularly after the War of the Pacific and the acquisition of the nitrate provinces, in investment. What results had this on Chile?

British Merchants and Chilean Attitudes

It is particularly important that the principal British participants, in terms of capital and skills, in the "ever-extending and intensifying development" of Chile in the second half of the nineteenth century, were merchants. They used money and marketing skills and contacts, not manufacturing or mining or farming, to make money. While individual Britons did well in mining and the country's young industries, either they became Chilean or, like the merchants, returned home with their fortunes. Either way, they made little lasting impact on the country, and the fundamentally mercantile outlook of the British in Chile remained unchanged even after Britons invested in nitrate (much of which in any case came from company floatations in London, not from the resident British community): nitrate stocks appeared to represent—and in most years did represent—a very sound, easily realizable asset, and consequently a suitable means of working spare funds.

Commerce was a conservative occupation. The merchants were only incidentally innovators in Chilean society. Having no share in the production of the articles they sold, their instinct was to drop unprofitable lines, not to seek solutions to manufacturing problems that might cause losses—unless forced to do so. This happened when they had to protect an investment, usually in mining, and helps to explain both their horror of habilitaciónes and their cautious investments—which were rarely large. They preferred to use their money in their own businesses, putting spare funds, when available, into institutions whose management they could influence, whose returns seemed assured, and out of which they could quickly get. They therefore supported banks, insurance companies, established railways, and utility companies in some towns. Outside of the commission business they knew, they shunned risk.

Such an attitude essentially limited the role of Britons, important though it was in the modernization of Chile, to participating in and organizing the import-export trade efficiently and providing skills needed in the modern sectors of the economy. And, crucially, there was little demand for more. To understand why, something must be said of Chilean society.

In this era, there was no shortage of Chileans with money to invest. Profitable trade in agriculture and mining products created, maintained, or increased many great fortunes, so that before the War of the Pacific the bulk of the republic's productive resources in mines and land remained in Chilean hands. In 1882, *El Mercurio* listed 59 private fortunes of a million or more pesos, totalling $178,500,000, and this without any significant contribution from nitrate, in which the Chilean stake had largely disappeared before 1879 (El Mercurio 1882; O'Brien, 1976: 89). Chileans also controlled most of the joint-stock companies, whatever the foreign role in working them. However, this meant no differing entrepreneurial values among the men who controlled the various sectors of the economy: all were members or wished to be members of the elite landowning class that dominated the country. The members of this group showed great flexibility in admitting the newly rich and impregnating them with their own values, which basically meant a continuation of the social status quo, for they had an essentially static view of society.

The workings of government demonstrated this. Whatever its virtues, such an honesty, efficiency, and the successful maintenance of the rule of law and tranquility in the country at large, it remained a government of the elite, for the elite, and by the elite. Its policies reflected this. For example, with loans raised and responsibility expended on the railways, the country benefited. However, the principal direct beneficiaries were the landed class, whose social and economic mobility was immediately increased. In general, they supported modernization of sectors of the country's economy, investing largely but selectively to bring this about so that they and the republic might benefit from international trade. They had no desire for change as such, however, particularly in the hierarchical society they dominated. And so change came slowly, particularly in the countryside, where the mass of Chilians lived. Although the nitrate provinces and the modernizing urban sector, particularly Santiago and Valparaíso, gradually produced a working class that provided the impetus for radical politics, this movement was only embryonic before 1886 and found little echo in the rural areas. Indeed, nitrate wealth and elite determination together underpinned the Parliamentary Republic, despite increasing strains caused by exclusion from politics of precisely those elements of the population created by the economic advances of the nineteenth century. What change there was, was in degree, not in kind.

This meant that Chile in 1886 remained as dependent on foreign markets for her mining produce as in 1851—although she now consumed much of her agricultural production. The production by Brower & Hardie of ten cars for the Valparaíso Tramway Co in 1885 (Chilean Times, 1885) indicated the beginning of some manufacturing capacity, but essentially the country remained as dependent on foreign sources for manufactured goods as thirty years before and hence on exports to pay for them. The British obviously helped create this situation, and their role has been the subject of considerable examination by Chilean historians.

One, Hernán Ramírez Necochea (1960: 95), regards British participation in Chile's economy before 1879 as motivated by the desire to make the republic into a producer of raw materials and consumer of manufactured goods through free trade and other measures. After that year he believes an alliance of merchant-banker capitalism, feudalism, and foreign—mainly British—mining capitalism worked to perpetuate this position, to the distress, even destruction, of industry not associated with these sectors (1956: 58-59).

Claudio Véliz (1963) takes a similar stance, ascribing the continuation of free trade to the influence of a united front of mining and agricultural exporters and the great importing firms of Valparaíso. Another scholar writes that "the merchant community [Chilean and foreign] controlled the import-export economy and was not interested in the creation of an industrial capacity that would challenge their primary source of wealth," and so they refused "to participate in the development of local industry by withholding the necessary capital" (Pregger Román, 1975: 210-211).

Some general points may be made. First, some secondary industry did develop during this period, particularly during and after the War of the Pacific, but even before this the foundries of Valparaíso were able to repair and maintain, if not construct, the machinery used in the mines and mills of the export industries (El Mercurio, 1863b). Second, the government was no enemy of protection, and acted increasingly, if piecemeal, to aid infant industries (Sater, 1976). It seems, then, that both government policy and actual experience undermine the contention that there was a formal or informal alliance of interests, with or without British participation, dedicated to the preservation of free trade and an export-based economy. And yet the British did contribute greatly, both positively and negatively, to the direction Chile's economy took. Their commitment to the country was essentially limited, especially in terms of capital and time. The form of business organization they chose kept down the absolute amounts of money they employed, while their ultimate intention to retire to England, which many, including the most successful, did, precluded long-term investment of the funds they had. Only commitment of their skills was unqualified, and the sectors in which they worked were the most modern in the country. Operating in collaboration with the local elite, their joint success was so great as to render unnecessary the exercise of new initiatives by the latter. But if the British were not themselves innovators, the surviving records indicate both that they did nothing to hinder those who were, and also that there were few of these indeed—in any event mostly associated with the British.

What the British did, then, was to link Chile firmly with the world economy, in which the republic earned great sums, and to assist in the modernization of sectors of the economy. Beyond this, their role was passive—in itself a contribution to Chile's skewed development, but not the only cause. Other reasons must be sought.

The success of the ruling elite in keeping the lion's share of the profits was one. The mass market in Chile was too small to support competitive large-scale industry throughout this period. The agrarian workforce remained poor, and the demand from the slowly increasing numbers of industrial and mining workers remained too small to stimulate investment.

Nor did the investing habits of the elite help. In 1873, Rumbold noted the distribution of some 158.5 million pesos invested in Chilean industry by Chileans: about 125 million was in mining and banking; 33.5 million in railways, steam navigation, insurance, and other companies; while only one industrial undertaking, a paper factory, with a capital of 130,000 pesos appeared, which seemed to confirm what the minister identified as "as the national preference for those modes of acquiring wealth which involve the least possible labour" (P.R.O., 1873). More charitably, they can be used to demonstrate an understandable desire on the part of investors to stick to things they knew (mining), or in which they could gain expert asistance (banking, insurance, railways), and a tendency to use their money where they could watch it. Any underdeveloped country can utilize only that portion of modern technology and technique of which it is informed; and the nature of the Chilean elite and of their closest foreign collaborators, the Britons *in Chile*, was quite simply not innovative in these areas. Further, the British themselves were quite as unwilling as the Chileans to risk their money outside the areas they knew, and their example might well have influenced their hosts.

This highly selective and, in some ways, cautious business climate made it easy for the Britons to defend their position. Even as Britain's industrial strength faced fiercer competition from Europe and the United States, the other pillars of Britain's power—finance, trade, and shipping—held firm. These had always been an essential prop of the British community, and together with their position in the Chilean economy—itself a great assistance in persuading people to buy British—and their new and uncharacteristic nitrate investment, ensured Britain's continued predominance.

Chile was, then, clearly a dependency of the British economy. This position brought both gains and losses. Profitable participation in the world market, modernization of sectors of the economy, and the introduction of new technology all pointed towards progress in nineteenth-century eyes. Against those could be set the noninnovative character of the British presence and, possibly, the unsuitability of some British principles and business practices accepted by the Chileans. For example, free trade, which in Chile was in any case only relative because of the revenue-raising duties always imposed, may have prevented the republic from industrializing behind protective barriers. It is significant, however, that the country did develop industries such as foodstuffs and metal repairing that benefited from the protection given by distance, which may have been the most effective possible. The experience of the Australian colony of Victoria indicates the powerful protective effect of distance, even in an avowedly protectionist environment (Serle, 1971: 5-6, 76-77). Again, the refusal of British-influenced banks to finance fixed capital and of Britons to invest in industry doubtless affected particular enterprises and influenced Chilean investors. However, it must be remembered that there was no shortage of Chilean capital during much of this period, and, a slightly different point, that the British refusal to invest in industry may have been the most rational economic decision for foreigner and native alike. For dependency was not the product of the economic decisions of a powerful British mercantile presence with the Royal Navy in the background to preserve Chile in her primary producing role. The evidence, indeed, suggests strongly that the economic activities of Briton and Chilean alike made eminent commercial sense in the context of the times.

Rather, dependency resulted from a number of factors, of which the attitudes of the Britons within Chile and the pervading power and attendant pressures of the British economy were only a part. Another factor was Chile's traditional social structure, which condemned the bulk of the population to a near-subsistence existence and so perpetuated a tiny domestic market. That the elite was content with this situation was fundamental in its perpetuation, as also was the fact that the economic needs of this class were satisfactorily met by the import-export sector. The result was development, but hardly progress.

Conclusion

Chile, then was clearly part of Britain's "informal empire," an "informal dominion" whose political and social independence was greatly influenced by economic dependence upon the United Kingdom. Influenced, but not controlled, by the administrators of this "empire" were merchants, not politicians, whose masters were the Chilean and British economies, not electorates. Chile became an "informal dominion" through the working of economic processes and without ever being subjected to the formal British imperial process. Consequently, the modernizing effects of the British presence had little immediate effect upon the host society. Indeed, the increased wealth and power that Chile's landowning ruling elite gained through their collaboration with, and use of, the Britons in their midst, together with the windfall of nitrate, allowed the perpetuation of nineteenth-century political patterns well into the twentieth century.

NOTES

1. C.R. Fay (1934) appears to have coined the term "informal empire."
2. Britain's share of Japanese exports ranged from 9.28% to 27.41% in the same period (Fox, 1969: 369).
3. The most important cases occurred in Asia. See Fairbank (1969) and Fox (1969).
4. This mutual lack of interest is clearly demonstrated in the P.R.O.F.O. 16 series for government, and in the Gibbs, Balfour, Williamson, and the Duncan, Fox Papers for the commercial. However, J. L. Rector (1976) demonstrates the application of naval pressure in favor of British merchants. Perhaps the answer lies in the interpretation given to his orders by the naval commander involved.
5. Its five-member directorate consisted of two Britons, a North American, a Frenchman, and a Chilean named Smith.
6. In 1853, when Gibbs had 3.25 million pesos capital, Henderson, Finch y Cia. had a capital of 90,000 pesos (NV, 1855b).

REFERENCES

Actas [Actas del consejo jeneral de administración] (1875a) Banco de Valparaíso, oficina de Santiago. Sesión 12, March 22.

——— (1875b) Manuscrito, Banco de Chile. Sesión 11, March 11.

Balfour, Williamson Papers (1884) "S. Williamson to A. Balfour, October 22." Williamson Letterbooks IV. University College Library, London.
——— (1877) "S. Williamson to C. McCulloch, January 31." Williamson Letterbooks 4. University College Library, London.
——— (1851) Articles of Partnership. January 11. University College Library, London.
Banco de Chile (1944) Reseña Histórica, 1894-1944. Santiago: Author.
BAUER, A. (1975) Chilean Rural Society from the Spanish Conquest to 1930. Cambridge, England: Cambridge Univ. Press.
BERMUDEZ, O. (1963) Historia del salitre desde sus origines hasta la guerra del Pacífico. Santiago: Ediciones de la Universidad de Chile.
Brazil and River Plate Mail [London] (1865) January 7.
——— (1864) April 22.
Censo (1889-1890) Sesto censo jeneral de la república de Chile 1885. Valparaíso: Imprenta de La Patria.
——— (1876) Quinto censo jeneral de la población de Chile 1875. Valparaíso: Emprenta del Mercurio.
——— (1866) Censo jeneral de la república de Chile 1865. Santiago: Imprenta Nacional.
——— (1858) Censo jeneral de la república de Chile 1854. Santiago: Imprenta del Ferrocarril.
Chilean Times [Valparaíso] (1886) September 11, March 20, March 26.
——— (1885) May 16.
——— (1880) May 15.
——— (1876) July 1.
CURTIS, W. E. (1888) The Capitals of Spanish America. New York: Harper & Row.
Duncan, Fox Papers (1859) "Lloyds de Valparaíso Policy, August 1." Duncan Fox y Cia., Santiago.
——— (1857) "J. P. Lynill to S. Myer, Valparaíso, July 15." Old Letters, 1854-1859. Duncan Fox y Cia., Santiago.
EDWARDS, A. (1932) El gobierno de don Manuel Montt, 1851-1861. Santiago: Editorial Nascimento.
ENCINA, F. A. (1940-1952) Historia de Chile desde la prehistoria hasta 1891. Santiago: Editorial Nascimento.
Estadística Comercial [de la república de Chile] (1881) Valparaiso: Universo de G. Helfmann.
FAIRBANK, J. K. (1969) Trade and Diplomacy on the China Coast. Stanford, CA: Stanford Univ. Press.
FAY, C. R. (1934) Imperial Economy and its Place in the Formation of Economic Doctrine, 1600-1932. Oxford: Oxford Univ. Press.
FERNS, H. S. (1960) Britain and Argentina in the Nineteenth Century. Oxford: Oxford Univ. Press.
FOX, G. (1969) Britain and Japan, 1858-1883. Oxford: Oxford Univ. Press.
FRANK, A. G. (1971) Capitalism and Underdevelopment in Latin America. London: Penguin.
GALLAGHER, J. and R. ROBINSON (1953) "The imperialism of free trade." Economic History Rev. 6, 1: 1-15.
GAY, C. (1862, 1869) História física y política de Chile. Agricultura. Santiago, Chile: ICIRA [Instituto de Capitación e Investigación en Reforma Agraria]. (original edition Paris, facsimile reprint 1972).
Gibbs Papers (1972) "Value of shipments, 1868-1886; December 31." Gibbs Ms 11033A/4. Guildhall Library, London.

——— (1859) "A. Gibbs & Sons to W. Gibbs & Co., April 8." Gibbs Ms 11471/1. Guildhall Library, London.

——— (1858a) "A. Gibbs & Sons to W. Gibbs & Co., December 15." Gibbs Ms. 11471/1. Guildhall Library, London.

——— (1858b) "A. Gibbs & Sons to W. Gibbs & Co. August 24." Gibbs Ms. 11471/1. Guildhall Library, London.

HABAKKUK, H. J. (1962) American and British Technology in the Nineteenth Century: The Search for Labour-Saving Inventions. Cambridge, England: Cambridge Univ. Press.

HUNT, W. (1961, 1951) Heirs of Great Adventure. London: n.p.

Huth Papers (1848-1865) Guildhall Library, London.

KIRSCH, H. W. (1977) Industrial Development in a Traditional Society. The Conflict of Entrepreneurship and Modernization in Chile. Gainesville: Univ. of Florida.

MAMALAKIS, M. J. (1976) The Growth and Structure of the Chilean Economy. New Haven, CT: Yale.

Memoria de Hacienda (1860) Santiago: Imprenta Nacional.

El Mercurio [Valparaíso] (1882) April 24.

——— (1863a) February 6.

———(1863b) January 26.

——— (1858a) March 13.

——— (1858b) March 6.

N.V. [Notarial de Valparaíso] (1872) "Agreement between R. Walker and A. Edwards, April 10." Archivo nacional de Chile, Santiago.

——— (1856)"Agreement between Myers, Bland & Co. and Ramon Lecaros, December 15." Archivo nacional de Chile, Santiago.

——— (1855a)" Registration of statutes, November 28." Archivo nacional de Chile, Santiago.

——— (1855b) "Registration of Henderson, Finch y Cia., January 31." Archivo nacional de Chile, Santiago.

O'BRIEN, T. F. (1976) "British investors and the decline of the Chilean nitrate entrepreneurs." Ph.D. dissertation, University of Connecticut.

P.P. [Parliamentary Papers] (1867-1868) Great Britain.

——— (1862) Great Britain.

PFEIFFER, J. B. (1952) "Notes on the heavy equipment industry in Chile, 1800-1910." Hispanic Amer. Historical Rev. 32 (February): 139-161.

PLATT, D.C.M. [ed.] (1977) Business Imperialism. Oxford: Oxford Univ. Press.

——— (1973) "Further objections to an 'imperialism of free trade.'" Economic History Rev. 26 (February): 77-91.

——— (1968a) Finance, Trade and Politics in British Foreign Policy, 1815-1914. Oxford: Oxford Univ. Press.

——— (1968b) "The imperialism of free trade—some reservations." Economic History Rev. (August): 296-306.

——— (1968c) "Economic factors in British policy during the 'new Imperialism.'" Past and Present 39 (April): 120-138.

PREGGER ROMAN, C. G. (1975) "Dependent development in nineteenth century Chile." Ph.D. dissertation, Rutgers University.

P.R.O. [Public Record Office] (1873) "H. Rumbold to Earl Granville, September 16." F.O. 16/177. London Foreign Office Records, Santiago, Chile.

——— (1861a) "W. T. Thomson to Earl Russell, Santiago, November 2. " F.O. 16/117. London Foreign Office Records, Santiago, Chile.

——— (1861b) "Foreign Office to W. T. Thomson, June 29." F.O. 16/117. London Foreign Office Records, Santiago, Chile.

——— (1861c) "Pacific Steam Navigation Co. to Foreign Office, June 8." F.O. 16/119. London Foreign Office Records, Santiago, Chile.

——— (1853) "E.A.J. Harris to Foreign Office; November 6, September 23, May 22." F.O. 16/83. London Foreign Office Records, Santiago, Chile.

RAMIREZ NECOCHEA, H. (1960) Historia del imperialismo en Chile. Santiago: Empresa Editorial Austral.

——— (1956) Historia del movimiento obrero. Santiago: Talleres Gráficos Lautaro.

RECTOR, J. L. (1976) "Merchants, trade and commercial policy in Chile, 1810-1840." Ph.D. dissertation, Indiana University.

Rumbold Private Letters (1873, 1874, 1875) In possession of Sir Anthony Rumbold, Dorset, England.

Rumbold Memo (1883) May 11.

SATER, W. (1976) "Economic nationalism and tax reform in late nineteenth century Chile." Americas 33, 2: 311-335.

SERLE, G. (1971) The Rush to be Rich: A History of the Colony of Victoria, 1883-1889. Melbourne: Univ. of Melbourne.

Valparaíso Mercantile Reporter (1852) July 15.

VELIZ, C. (1963) "La mesa de tres patas." Desarrollo Económico 3 (April-September): 231-247.

——— (1961) Historia de la marina mercante de Chile. Santiago: Ediciones de la Universidad de Chile.

WILL, R. M. (1964) "The introduction of classical economics into Chile." Hispanic Amer. Historical Rev. 54 (February): 1-21.

WINN, P. (1976) "British informal empire in Uruguay in the nineteenth century." Past and Present 73 (November): 100-126.

——— (1975) El imperio informal británico en el Uruguay en el siglo XIX. Montevideo: Ediciones de la Banda Oriental.

John Mayo, Lecturer in history at the Cave Hill campus of the University of the West Indies-Barbados, received his Ph.D. from Oxford University on the role of the British in 19th century Chile. He has taught at the Universities of Papua, New Guinea, and Hawaii, where he developed his interest in Britain's commercial penetration of the west coast of Latin America and the Pacific generally.

Vol. 23 No. 2
May 1981

JOURNAL OF INTERAMERICAN STUDIES

and WORLD AFFAIRS

A Publication of the Center for Advanced International Studies,

The University of Miami

SAGE PUBLICATIONS

Journal of INTERAMERICAN STUDIES and WORLD AFFAIRS

The editors and publisher wish to acknowledge with gratitude the assistance and encouragement of the Center for Advanced International Studies, University of Miami, in providing ancillary services and support for this journal.

Journal of
INTERAMERICAN
STUDIES
and WORLD AFFAIRS

Vol. 23
No. 2
May
1981

CONTENTS

Civil-Military Relations in Colombia: A Societal Explanation
J. MARK RUHL 123

The Andean Pact and the Amazon Treaty: Reflections of Changing Latin American Relations
ELIZABETH G. FERRIS 147

Human Rights Policy: Basic Human Needs and Economic Implications for LDCs
FRANCISCO E. THOUMI 177

REVIEW ESSAYS

Portraits of Venezuela
DANIEL H. LEVINE 203

Education, Ethnicity, and Humanism: Recent Trends in Mexican Intellectual History
HENRY C. SCHMIDT 225

BOOKS RECEIVED 233

SAGE PUBLICATIONS / *Beverly Hills* *London*

Policy: The **JOURNAL OF INTERAMERICAN STUDIES AND WORLD AFFAIRS** reflects the interests of the scholarly community and interested public concerned with the social, economic, political, and cultural aspects of life in Latin America (including the Caribbean), particularly in those instances where the subject is of concern to more than one of the traditional disciplines. As these concerns change, so will the content of the journal.

Articles which have special relevance for interrelationships between American nations and of those nations with the rest of the world will be given special consideration. An effort will be made to include occasional articles that state an unusual or even discordant position on a subject of broad interest to be supplemented by critical comments of authorities representing differing positions on the topic. The editors continue to welcome articles by scholars from all parts of the world.

Manuscripts should be submitted in duplicate to: Editor, **JOURNAL OF INTERAMERICAN STUDIES AND WORLD AFFAIRS,** Box 24-8134, University of Miami, Coral Gables, Florida 33124. Manuscripts should be typewritten, double-spaced, with footnotes, references, tables, and charts on separate pages, and should follow the current journal style. A brief biographical paragraph describing each author's current affiliation, research interests, and recent publications should accompany the manuscript.

Correspondence regarding book reviews should be sent directly to: Book Review Editor, **JOURNAL OF INTERAMERICAN STUDIES AND WORLD AFFAIRS,** Box 24-8134, University of Miami, Coral Gables, Florida 33124.

JOURNAL OF INTERAMERICAN STUDIES AND WORLD AFFAIRS is published four times annually—in February, May, August, and November.

Subscriptions: Regular institutional rate $36.00 per year. Individuals may subscribe at a one-year rate of $18.00. Add $2.00 for subscriptions outside the United States. Orders from the U.K., Europe, the Middle East, and Africa should be sent to the London office (address below). Noninstitutional orders **must** be paid by personal check.

Second class postage paid at Beverly Hills, California. ISSN 0022-1937

This journal is abstracted or indexed in **Historical Abstracts, Human Resources Abstracts, Sage Urban Studies Abstracts, International Political Science Abstracts, Public Affairs Information Service, Current Contents, Social Sciences Citation Index, Social Sciences Index, ABC POL SCI,** and **United States Political Science Documents.**

Back Issues: Information about availability and prices of back issues may be obtained from the publisher's order department (address below). Write to London office for sterling prices.

Inquiries: Address all correspondence and permissions requests to SAGE PUBLICATIONS, Inc., 275 South Beverly Drive, Beverly Hills, California 90212. Inquiries and subscriptions from the U.K., Europe, the Middle East, and Africa should be sent to SAGE PUBLICATIONS Ltd, 28 Banner Street, London EC1Y 8QE, England. Other orders should be sent to the Beverly Hills office.

Advertising: Current rates and specifications may be obtained by writing to the Advertising Manager at the Beverly Hills office (address above).

Claims: Claims for undelivered copies must be made no later than three months following month of publication. The publisher will supply missing copies when losses have been sustained in transit and when the reserve stock will permit.

Change of Address: Six weeks' advance notice must be given when notifying of change of address. Please send old address label along with the new address to insure proper identification. Please specify name of journal. POSTMASTER: Send change of address to: Journal name, c/o 275 South Beverly Drive, Beverly Hills, CA 90212.

J. MARK RUHL
Department of Political Science
Dickinson College
Carlisle, Pennsylvania

CIVIL-MILITARY RELATIONS IN COLOMBIA
A Societal Explanation

In spite of the reestablishment of civilian democracy in Ecuador and Peru, military government continues to be the norm in Latin America. In recent years, many scholars have examined the rise of military regimes in the region in order to gain a better understanding of the dynamics of civil-military relations. Few analysts, however, have studied civil-military relations in the handful of nations where civilian government has persisted. The purpose of this analysis is, therefore, to contribute to a broader understanding of Latin American military behavior by attempting to explain the Colombian armed forces' atypical obedience to civilian authority.

Conceptual Framework

Students of Latin American politics draw upon a number of general theorists in order to account for the high incidence of

AUTHOR'S NOTE: I would like to thank three anonymous referees as well as Shirley Hall, Robert Nilsson, Gene Rosi, Fred Woerner, Harry Dull, Ron McDonald, and Penny Homolash for their comments on an earlier draft of this article. The support of the Dickinson College Research and Development Fund is also acknowledged with appreciation.

Journal of Interamerican Studies and World Affairs, Vol. 23 No. 2, May 1981 123-146

military government in the region. The most commonly used theoretical framework is provided by Huntington (1968), whose theory of political decay figures prominently in the works of such scholars as Stepan (1971, 1973) and O'Donnell (1973, 1976). Huntington (1968: 194) argues:

> the most important causes of military intervention in politics are not military but political and reflect not the social and organizational characteristics of the military establishment but the political and institutional structure of the society.

Specifically, Huntington suggests that as a nation becomes more highly socially mobilized, for example, more literate and more urban, societal demands for greater material well-being and social equality will increase significantly. Under these circumstances, political order becomes much more difficult to maintain. Indeed, unless these new societal demands are satisfied or civilian political institutions become strong enough to manage them, a condition of political decay indicated by political violence, failing civilian regimes, and military intervention will result. Huntington refers to such societies as "praetorian" since, although all social forces become politicized and compete with one another directly in the absence of adequate institutional buffers, the armed forces usually dominate because of their superior coercive capabilities.

Many analysts assert, therefore, that military government is common in contemporary Latin America because most of the countries in the region have become praetorian societies. Latin American social mobilization levels have risen markedly in recent decades, while efforts to broaden the distribution of economic benefits or to construct strong civilian political institutions generally have been unsuccessful. Consequently, most Latin American nations are characterized by political decay and civilian governmental collapse. O'Donnell (1976: 203), for example, argues that Argentina's high level of social mobilization, coupled with economic stagnation and civilian political failure, created a situation of mass praetorianism in which military intervention became a frequent occurrence. Stepan's (1971) classic study of

Brazilian civil-military relations also links military intervention to the praetorian condition. With ample reference to Huntington, Stepan carefully documents a praetorian pattern of rising social mobilization, a stalled economy, and weak political institutions that precipitated the 1964 military coup. Many other scholars also draw upon Huntington's theory and the praetorian concept. McDonald (1975), for example, uses the model to explain the Uruguayan military's takeover of government power during the early 1970s.

In short, military intervention will be most probable under praetorian conditions in which civilian political institutions become overburdened because of the pressures of socioeconomic change.[1] Thus, in order to understand why civilian government has persisted in Colombia, it is necessary to analyze Colombian society to evaluate the degree to which conditions deviate from the praetorian pattern. Therefore, the following analysis examines the nature of social and economic change in Colombia and the character of Colombian civilian political institution before directly discussing the activities of Colombia's armed forces.

Social and Economic Change in Colombia

A number of scholars (Campos and McCamant, 1972; Leal Buitrago, 1973) have designated Colombia as a modern society ripe for every manner of major political disorder—from military coup to social revolution. Indeed, many commonly used quantitative measures indicate that Colombia has begun to approach a potentially dangerous level of social mobilization; three-quarters of the adult population are literate, and over two-thirds of the nation live in cities (Wiarda and Kline, 1979: 5). Such statistics as these, coupled with other data documenting the expansion of mass communication and transportation networks, are used to show the erosion of the traditional passive peasant society and the rise of the more aware and potentially demanding population that Huntington has linked to political instability.

A number of qualifying observations need be introduced to modify this misleading perspective. Compared to the rest of Latin America, Colombia's rate of social mobilization has been especially rapid, particularly with respect to urbanization. In 1951, only 39% of the population lived in cities; therefore, a great number of urban dwellers in contemporary Colombia must still be first generation migrants (Schoultz, 1972). Empirical research by Mangin (1967), Peattie (1972), and others has shown that new migrants are less frustrated and demanding than the general urban population; studies of Bogotá's slum barrios by Van Es and Flinn (1973) confirm these findings for Colombia's largest city. The new migrant may feel that he has improved his status and opportunities simply by entering the more sophisticated, hopeful, urban environment where his access to public services is much improved. The former peasant also tends to retain his traditional rural social deference and is uninterested in joining active political groups.

Furthermore, recent research by Cornelius (1974) and Handelman (1975) demonstrates that most members of the second and later generations of the urban poor may remain politically passive as long as they lack regular industrial employment and as long as antisystem political movements seem too weak to pose a serious threat to the existing government. As members of the urban marginal class sporadically employed in the unstable service sector, i.e., domestic servants and street vendors, such individuals are forced to devote most of their energies to daily survival.

For these reasons, it appears that Colombia's social mobilization level, as indicated by the high percentage of the population living in urban areas, has been consistently inflated by the unusually high number of new migrants and the marginally employed that it encompasses. Many of the children of the 1950-1980 migrants have not yet come of political age. That factor, coupled with the lack of urban industrial employment in Colombia, due in part to its capital-intensive industrial sector, has further inhibited the politicization of second generation urban dwellers.

By modernizing later than many Latin American industrial sectors, Colombian industry has been able to make use of the most technologically sophisticated modes of production which require far fewer workers. In this urban environment of chronic unemployment, labor unions tend to be relatively small and cooptable. Thus, although Colombia's urban population is large and outbreaks of urban violence do occur, the nation's urban centers do not pose the mobilized threat to the system that is represented by the older and better organized urban concentrations of Argentina, Chile or Uruguay.

Rural Colombia also has not become as socially mobilized as its rising literacy level and declining isolation might imply. The "demobilizing" effect of *La Violencia*, 1946-1957, may be the most important factor contributing to the surprisingly low level of rural demands. Fals Borda (1965) and others claim that this brutal experience of interparty conflict, which cost over 200,000 lives, accelerated the breakdown of traditional rural society. Although Colombian peasants may no longer be as firmly controlled by traditional authority structures, they are still not ready for political action because of their fears of further violence. Instead, Dix (1967: 382) notes that studies of refugees from La Violencia revealed a widespread condition of confusion and valuelessness. Thus, this unique historical experience seems to keep rural Colombia a less politically active area than one might expect, given the impact of socially mobilizing forces.

In short, this analysis suggests that Colombia's actual level of social mobilization is substantially lower than that indicated by standard quantitative measures given (1) the high percentage of urban dwellers who are either new migrants and/or economically marginal, and (2) the traumatic rural experience of La Violencia. Consequently, although Colombia is much more socially mobilized than it was thirty years ago, societal demands are apparently lower and more manageable than many scholars have suggested.

Pressures on the civilian elite have been increasing, however, because the Colombian economy with a GDP of $1,100 per capita (Colombia Today, 1980: 6) has not yet been able to satisfy very many of the mass expectations that modernization has generated; Colombia suffers from the common structural problems that plague most Latin American economies. For instance, although domestic industry has expanded in recent years, Colombia is still dependent on its agricultural sector and particularly on the success of its coffee exports; coffee has traditionally provided at least 70% of total export earnings. This dependency level was reduced to about 50% during the 1973-1975 period through export diversification, but the performance of the Colombian economy still remains precariously bound to fluctuating world coffee demand.

The 1975-1977 boom in world coffee prices obviously benefited Colombia, despite the difficult inflationary side-effects it caused; however, this windfall began to erode in 1978 as world production returned to more normal levels. Coffee sales are especially important to the performance of the Colombian economy and a price fall, therefore, is more serious because much of the rest of the agricultural sector is inefficient and unproductive. For example, the domestic agricultural sector still cannot fulfill Colombia's basic food requirements.

The industrial sector also confronts fundamental problems. Colombia has industrialized to its present modest level with 19.2% of the GNP in manufacturing, largely by manufacturing consumer goods that previously were imported (Wiarda and Kline, 1979: 5). However, with fewer imported consumer goods remaining to be substituted, or 9% of 1979 imports, Colombia now is attempting the extremely costly and much more difficult step of developing intermediate and capital goods industries (Colombia Today, 1980: 6). In order to gradually expand industry in this fashion, Colombia must acquire considerable export earnings as well as substantial foreign investment. Domestic private sources of investment never have been sufficient while public investment has been hindered by the government's traditionally weak revenue foundation; taxes are still too closely related to export success. Thus, when coffee and other export earnings fall and foreign investment becomes scarce, Colombian industry stagnates.

Depending on coffee exports and characterized by inefficient agriculture and semideveloped industry, the growth of the Colombian economy has been inconsistent and marked by double-digit inflation. In the 1970s, GDP growth rates were more promising than usual, averaging about 6% per year due to strong legitimate and clandestine (drug-related) export earnings and improved government planning.

Nevertheless, the benefits of this economic expansion have not been shared equally. Distribution of income, like distribution of land in Colombia, is highly inequitable. The top 20% of the population earns more than 60% of total income, while under 5% of land holdings encompass over 65% of arable land (Urrutia and Berry, 1975). The majority of Colombians, including those who have been socially mobilized, remain underemployed, desperately poor, and undernourished—whether they live in the cities or in the countryside. In fact, mass economic benefits are so minimal that Colombia's adjusted moderate level of social mobilization might have caused praetorian conditions had it not been for the nation's strong civilian political institutions.

Colombian Political Institutions

The key to Colombia's stable civil-military relations lies in the present effectiveness and legitimacy of traditional political party leadership. The multiclass Liberal and Conservative parties still dominate Colombian political life, although the fierce interparty rivalry that characterized Colombia's nineteenth-century history and later led to La Violencia no longer exists. Frightened by the potential for class violence that La Violencia suggested, and having experienced a brief and unpleasant period of military dictatorship under populist General Gustavo Rojas Pinilla from 1953 to 1957, the nation's social elite decided to bury past partisan differences (Wilde, 1978). Under the National Front agreement, the two parties agreed to divide legislative and bureaucratic positions equally and to alternate the presidency every four years from 1958 to 1974. This form of coalition government proved to be a highly successful means of elite compromise.

The National Front governments gradually increased the elite's ability to manage economic development and institute modest social reforms. The Colombian bureaucracy was enlarged and professionalized, particularly through the development of new decentralized agencies (Bailey, 1977). The greatest increase in governmental action took place after the 1966 election of Liberal President Carlos Lleras Restrepo, who greatly improved the government's financial base. Lleras also was responsible for stimulating Colombian nontraditional exports by adopting a more flexible exchange rate and by dismantling protective trade barriers that had become counterproductive (Berry et al., 1980: 301-304). Other National Front regimes were not as successful in their efforts to direct Colombia's difficult economy, but the era as a whole showed a marked improvement in governmental performance. Some moderate social reforms, such as increased educational expenditures and a small agrarian reform, also were implemented.

The first two post-National Front governments, that of Liberal Alfonso López Michelsen (1974-1978) and that of his successor, Julio César Turbay Ayala (1978-1982), have continued to govern in this tradition of pragmatic reform and careful economic management. For example, when faced with the rising inflation rate of 30% and a large budget deficit upon taking office, López instituted a harsh economic austerity policy. His stabilization program entailed wage restrictions, fiscal controls, and reduced governmental subsidies, which resulted initially in unemployment, falling industrial activity, and considerable popular opposition. In fact, the additional inflationary stress caused by the coffee bonanza forced López to maintain these unpopular policies throughout his entire term, and the violent general strike of September 1977 suggested some of the unrest these conservative policies generated. Nevertheless, by 1978, the positive longer-term effects of López's austerity program were evident to most observers as the Turbay government inherited a falling inflation rate, steady economic growth, and a very favorable foreign reserve position. Careful economic policies have been continued under Turbay; however, declining coffee prices and a rising trade deficit have contributed to both a new wave of inflation, which was 29% in 1979, and a slower pace of GDP growth, 5% in 1979 (Latin American Weekly Report, 1980e). Large increases in minimum wage rates and an ambitious, publicly financed national development plan have not been sufficient to defuse labor unrest which has remained high since Turbay assumed office.

Although López chose a distinctly nonpopulist response to Colombia's economic problems, he pursued a variety of more broadly poplular reform measures as well. His tax reform increased governmental revenues by drawing more heavily on the wealthier classes; he also expanded educational opportunities in Colombia at the expense of the private schools. Moreover, López maintained a rather nationalistic foreign policy by recognizing Cuba, supporting Panama on the canal issue, and forcing previously foreign-owned banks to become 51% Colombian-owned. Turbay's opposition to Nicaragua's Somoza before the dictator's downfall in 1979 can be viewed as part of the same pattern although the Turbay government subsequently has not been as pro-Sandinista as some of its Andean Pact partners. Relations with Cuba also cooled in 1980. López and Turbay have traveled this cautious path between conservative economic policy and more moderate social and foreign policies with the support of much of the Conservative party. The traditional parties have continued the principle of minority cabinet and administrative participation.

Despite the fact that some of the civilian political elite's policies have been unpopular, especially during periods of economic stress, mass support for the traditional parties has persisted. In the pre-National Front years, the two traditional patron-client parties could take widespread mass support for granted because of the tradition of hereditary party identification, but the elite's popular base did seem in doubt during the latter part of the National Front. In fact, former General Gustavo Rojas organized the populist *Alianza Nacional Popular* (ANAPO) to oppose the National Front and, in April 1970, this lower-class-based group captured almost 36% of the congressional vote and nearly elected its leader to the presidency.

Nevertheless, this apparent threat to the traditional parties dissipated between 1970 and 1974 when normal Liberal-Conservative electoral competition was restored. ANAPO could no longer run candidates under the Liberal and Conservative labels to which Colombians historically have been attached. Thus, in 1974, after adopting a more leftist political platform, the ANAPO presidential candidate, María Eugenia Rojas, the daughter of the general, managed to win only about 10% of the presidential vote and finished a distant third to Liberal Alfonso López Michelsen who won 56% and Conservative Alvaro Gómez Hurtado, 32%. Four years later in the 1978 election, the traditional parties' share of the total vote actually increased to 96% as Turbay won a narrow victory over Conservative Belisario Betancur. Neither ANAPO nor the small, factionalized Marxist opposition generated more than token support although a high abstention rate of 59% indicated some erosion of traditional party loyalties (Ruhl, 1978).

In short, Colombian civilian political institutions have been sufficiently strong and legitimate to maintain political order and to avoid the praetorian syndrome that Huntington and other theorists have linked to military intervention. In the future, Colombia's rising social mobilization and structural economic deficiencies may lead to the unstable politics that characterize much of Latin America, but currently there is neither a sense of national economic crisis nor of political collapse that would encourage the armed forces to become an alternative government.

Colombian Military Tradition

This article has offered a societal explanation for the maintenance of civilian government in Colombia. Although other scholars (Maingot, 1970) have emphasized the influence of Colombia's military tradition of nonintervention, this analysis, in congruence with Huntington's theory, considers the social, economic, and political variables discussed above to be far more important in explaining current civil-military relations. Nevertheless, Colombia's civil-military tradition probably does play a positive, if marginal, role in current military behavior and should be discussed briefly.[2]

Although the Colombian armed forces' obedience to civilian rule is rare in contemporary Latin America, such a relationship is not irregular from the perspective of Colombia's own history; civilian control of the military has been the norm since the early years of independence. During the independence struggle, Colombia's creole aristocracy found Bolívar's racially mixed army distasteful but necessary. However, after hostilities ceased, the civilian elite quickly moved to reduce the military's size and influence.Thus, despite the fact that Colombia experienced innumerable violent civil wars during the nineteenth century, the tiny national army with its few poorly trained officers recruited from marginal classes, played no appreciable role in these Liberal-Conservative conflicts.

When partisan hostility subsided at the beginning of the twentieth century, a professional military finally was created in Colombia with Chilean assistance. Nevertheless, during the untroubled period of partisan compromise which lasted until the 1930s, the civilian elite still had no reason to be apprehensive that the nation's small but growing armed forces might interfere in politics. The 6,000-man Colombian army remained one of Latin America's smallest and least respected military institutions. In the 1930s, however, the elite compromise began to fracture as Liberals attempted to upset the Conservative hegemony and inaugurate an era of political reform. Ultimately, this renewed political conflict resulted in the total political breakdown of La Violencia in the late 1940s. As civil violence between the traditional parties increased, the Colombian military gained influence and finally took control of the government when reactionary Conservative dictator Laureano Gómez alienated both Liberals and moderate Conservatives. Indeed, the bloodless 1953 coup by armed forces chief General Gustavo Rojas Pinilla had broad public support.

Colombia's only military government, from 1953 to 1957, began successfully. An amnesty program reduced rural violence and high coffee prices permitted the Rojas government to cultivate mass support through social welfare activities. Nonetheless, Rojas' attempts to build a personal political base independent of the traditional parties angered civilian politicians and military officers alike. Moreover, in 1956, after coffee revenues began to fall, Rojas could no longer maintain his government's extravagant spending on either social or military projects. After attempting to interfere in the legal electoral process in 1957, Rojas was deposed by a junta of brother officers, who returned power to the now reconciled traditional parties.

Thus, in addition to the factors discussed earlier, Colombia's long civil-military tradition perhaps also encourages the contemporary armed forces to refrain from intervention in civilian politics. In the last century, only one military government has held power and its record was not an impressive one. Given the current competence of civilian leadership, especially when compared with the obvious inadequacies of the 1953-1957 military regime, it is not difficult to understand why the Colombian military has remained in the barracks.

The Role of the Colombian Military

What are the functions of a civilian-controlled military in Latin America? When civil-military tensions have emerged, how have they been managed in Colombia? In order to answer these questions, the following analysis describes the Colombian military's role and its relationship to civilian leadership during the 1958-1980 period.

NATIONAL FRONT (1958-1974)

The armed forces' principal function under the National Front was that of controlling rural violence. Some armed groups of the La Violencia epoch had never disbanded and had turned to banditry. In addition, other small guerrilla units had developed Marxist orientations and had established "independent republics" in inaccessible regions. As the military moved to eradicate these problems, the institution increased in size and became more professionalized. The key figure responsible for these institutional changes within the armed forces was General Alberto Ruiz Novoa, who served as Minister of War between 1962 and 1965.

Most Colombian politicians supported professionalization and expansion measures because a strong armed forces were needed to combat disorder. Between 1961 and 1965, the armed forces grew from under 23,000 to over 37,000 men. Military expenditures rose from about 17% to over 20% of the governmental budget (Steinberg, 1960-1965; Villegas, 1972: 187-189).[3] The larger more professional military effectively brought the rural disorder under control by means of a U.S.-inspired counter-guerrilla strategy, which combined armed repression with civic action.

The military's successful counterinsurgency program stood in sharp contrast to the civilian government's economic and social difficulties in the early National Front years. In addition, General Ruiz began publicly to criticize the civilian political elite for its inability to deal with the underlying problems of economic underdevelopment and social inequality, which he felt made guerrilla movements possible. Given the military's recent successes, the reformist general also insisted that the armed forces should have a much larger role in the nation's development process. Disturbed by Ruiz's controversial statements, President Guillermo León Valencia forced the general's resignation in early 1965. Neither Ruiz nor any units under his command offered resistance.

During the later years of the National Front, the civilian political elite greatly improved its ability to manage the economy and the compromise program of moderate social reform as discussed earlier. Civil-military frictions decreased and the armed forces were permitted to expand to 64,000 men to meet the new Marxist guerrilla threats represented by the *Ejército de Liberación Nacional* (ELN) and the *Fuerzas Armadas Revolucionarias Colombianas* (FARC).[4] The student-led ELN was Castroite in orientation and usually conducted operations in rural Santander, Antioquia, and Bolívar. The less homogeneous FARC, on the other hand, although supported by the regular Communist party, was composed of less ideologically sophisticated guerrilla groups surviving from the La Violencia era. Operating primarily in Tolima and south-central Colombia, the FARC was estimated to be the larger of the two small groups.

The armed forces relied on armed repression to deal with these new guerrillas, and by the end of the National Front period, the army had reduced the guerrillas' ability to carry out major operations against the government. Actually, neither the ELN nor the FARC ever posed a serious danger to the National Front's survival because of the guerrillas' inability to generate popular support in rural Colombia. Indeed, the only serious threat to the traditional elite was ANAPO and, when the 1970 election results were disputed, the armed forces further demonstrated its loyalty by suppressing ANAPO rioters and by holding candidate Rojas under house arrest.

LOPEZ ADMINISTRATION (1974-1978)

Between 1975 and 1978, the Colombian guerrillas staged a resurgence which forced the army to increase counterinsurgency actions. The ELN executed several kidnappings of prominent people and ambushed many army patrols. The group was especially active in remote southern Bolívar where it occasionally overran small villages. However, the military actually was more persistently involved with the FARC which was active in many more areas, i.e., Antioquia, Tolima, Magdalena, Boyacá, Caquetá, and Meta. The two guerrilla organizations might have become even more of a problem for the government, but they were unable to unite in support of a single political program. A third guerrilla organization, the *Ejército Popular de Liberación* (EPL), which surfaced after 1974, also was unable to cooperate with either of the two more important movements because of its allegedly Maoist orientations. In 1975, the army eliminated the EPL's founder, Pedro León Arboleda, after which this group was less active.

In addition, public order was upset during the López Michelsen Administration by workers' striking violently against the government's strict austerity program and by students' demonstrating in labor's support. The armed forces were employed by the government to repress both types of disruption. Although the military's most important role has been to maintain public order, the regular armed forces also were used by the government in a variety of other ways. For example, the military continued to undertake colonization and civil defense projects begun during the National Front period and acted to control drug, emerald, and coffee smuggling.

The Colombian military served the López Michelsen government well. Moreover, the pattern of secure civilian control over the armed forces persisted. The only significant civil-military incident which occurred during the 1974-1978 period was the dismissal of highly respected army commander General Alvaro Valencia Tovar in June 1975. Valencia Tovar was asked to resign because he had clashed publicly with his superior, Defense Minister General Varón Valencia, over the alleged insubordination of two officers who had been too vocal in their criticism of the defense minister over a question of assignments. Some sources suggest that this confrontation was essentially accidental and that López simply chose to end the conflict by ousting the junior of the two generals (Visión, 1975). Other sources, however, maintain that events were purposely designed to result in Valencia Tovar's dismissal. It had been implied that López may have become uncertain about the willingness of Valencia Tovar, who had a reputation as one of the few reformist officers in the army, to use the force necessary to suppress violent worker and student opposition generated by the economic austerity measures (See Latin America Political Report, 1975).[5] Regardless, clearly no attempt at improper military pressure on civilian authorities was involved in this incident.

Finally, it should be noted that the traditionally low prestige of the Colombian military further declined during the López administration because of repeated charges of corruption among high ranking officers. A number of major figures were accused of accepting bribes from foreign arms suppliers and other sources.

In addition, the army's reputation was damaged further during the López period by the spectacular trial of the alleged ELN assassins of Inspector General, General Ramón Rincón Quiñones, in which the defense claimed that superior officers had ordered the general killed in order to halt his investigation of corruption in the military. In an *El Tiempo* editorial, now retired General Valencia Tovar lamented the fact that corruption had brought the armed forces' image to a new low (El Tiempo, 1976).

TURBAY ADMINISTRATION (1978-1980)

Guerrilla activity has increased further in the first two years of President Julio César Turbay's administration. The ELN and EPL have been less active than in past years but the FARC has expanded its operations considerably. For example, in a typical week in mid-1979, the FARC was reported to have assaulted villages in Cauca and ambushed troops in Caldas while a military court in Medellín was finding 59 persons guilty of belonging to a FARC urban network (Latin America Political Report, 1979). Indeed, in February 1980, a FARC communiqué claimed that the movement now had 11 geurrilla "fronts" (Latin America Weekly Report, 1980d).

The most spectacular guerrilla operations of the Turbay era, however, have been carried out by the *Movimiento de Abril 19* (M-19), a relatively new guerrilla group which claims to have originated in the radical wing of ANAPO in response to the "stolen" election of April 19, 1970, in which ANAPO's candidate, General Rojas, allegedly was deprived of victory. The movement first gained national attention in 1974 by stealing the sword of Simón Bolívar from a museum, but, between 1974 and 1978, M-19 engaged in few significant guerrilla activities. In 1979 and 1980, however, M-19 vastly increased its role in Colombian politics by staging numerous sensational terrorist operations. M-19 shocked the nation in early 1979 by raiding Bogotá's principal military arsenal and escaping with thousands of weapons. In February 1980, the group gained worldwide media attention with its capture of U.S. Ambassador Diego Asencio and other diplomatic hostages by means of an armed assault on a reception at the Dominican embassy.

In response to the rising level of guerrilla activity, the Colombian army enlarged its counterinsurgency campaign during the Turbay administration.[6] Armed with a new, tougher security statute which suspends some civil rights of those arrested as "subversives" and raises penalties for political crimes, the military relentlessly has pursued suspected members of M-19 and other guerrilla organizations. Search-and-destroy sweeps by Colombian army brigades have kept the FARC on the run in rural Colombia and urban military units have detained literally thousands of suspected guerrillas.

To date, the Colombian armed forces generally have been successful in meeting the new guerrilla threat. For example, within a few weeks of M-19's arsenal assault, most of the stolen arms had been recovered and many of the guerrillas involved were placed in custody. In fact, the imprisonment of so many M-19 members by the military probably instigated the dramatic seizure of the Dominican embassy. In return for the diplomatic hostages, M-19 initially demanded the release of over 300 prisoners.

The establishment press praised the soldiers for their swift and effective action against these dangerous guerrilla elements. Nevertheless, the military's heavy-handed use of the new security legislation also resulted in the indiscriminate detention of many prominent leftist journalists, artists, and scholars, such as sociologist Orlando Fals Borda and 75-year-old poet Luís Vidales, whose connection to M-19 or other such groups was considered dubious. In addition, many prisoners accused military units of using torture during interrogation. These claims stimulated the Colombian left, Amnesty International, and a number of prominent Liberal and Conservative politicians to level severe criticism at President Turbay and his defense minister, General Luís Carlos Camacho Leyva, for their abuse of human rights. Although the government officially denied most allegations of prisoner abuse, there is little doubt that the army has been guilty of both arbitrary arrest and systematic torture.

In light of these harsh methods and of the increasing visibility of the armed forces in this context of growing turmoil, a number of commentators have argued that the military has been using this new situation to gain control of Colombian politics at the expense of traditional civilian authorities. The inauguration of the new security statute in 1978 caused Echeverry (1978) and other Colombian scholars to warn against the militarization of Colombian politics. Later, amidst the growing army-guerrilla confrontation of 1979, Warren Hoge (1979) summarized the feelings of a number of analysts when he reported that

> some critics are warning that the nation is following the same path as Uruguay, once Latin America's model social democracy, where the military capitalized on an antiterrorist campaign to co-opt a civilian president and eventually assume control.

Is the Colombian military gradually wresting power from civilian leadership? Is civilian democracy soon to be replaced by military dictatorship? As has been often the case in the past, press comment concerning military control over Colombian civilian decision-making has been based on speculation rather than on genuine evidence. No public disputes over policy between President Turbay and General Camacho Leyva have surfaced, hence journalists have based most of their claims on rumors of behind-the-scenes power struggles. Unfortunately, much of this type of information is contradictory. For example, the leftist British newsletter, *Latin America Weekly Report*, asserted one week that the Colombian military opposed President Turbay's amnesty plan for ending the guerrilla problem and that the president and the armed forces' high command "are continuing the subterranean struggle over control of policy towards the armed opposition" (Latin America Weekly Report, 1980c). Without explaining the discrepancy, a few weeks later, the same journal claimed that the government's amnesty program was "masterminded by the hard-line minister of defense General Luís Carlos Camacho Leyva" (Latin America Weekly Report, 1980f).

If one examines the reports of growing military influence in Colombia, one finds that these judgements largely have come from (1) foreign newspapers and periodicals such as *Le Monde* or the *New York Times*, whose reporters have little more than a superficial knowledge of Colombian politics; and (2) leftist and particularly Marxist foreign and domestic sources, which have a vested interest in discrediting the Colombian civilian government. Before traditional assessments of Colombian civil-military relations are discarded, more credible evidence from more objective and knowledgeable sources must become available. While it is true that General Camacho Leyva meets almost daily with President Turbay and apparently has become a trusted adviser, there simply is no genuine evidence that he also has become a military overlord. In fact, a more plausible view is that the unpopular general, who has been discredited by his brother Alfonso's alleged link to the international narcotics trade, is being used to draw criticism away from the civilian authorities.

Colombia is not immune to military intervention. However, for the armed forces to intervene, the praetorian conditions discussed earlier in this article must materialize. In spite of the gross exaggeration of recent reports, no political collapse on the Uruguayan model is imminent. The Colombian economy was not performing particularly well in 1980, but current difficulties simply are not comparable to the decades of economic stagnation that preceded the end of democracy in Uruguay. The Colombian political elite is gradually losing public support because of the failure to institute promised reforms, the suspected links of some of its members to the drug trade, and the weakening of traditional party loyalties. Nonetheless, the Liberal and Conservative elites still retain considerable legitimacy and no recent left alternative has shown signs of successfully attracting substantial mass support.

Finally, although obviously troubling, the recent urban guerrilla problem simply is not serious enough to initiate a pattern of gradual military takeover. M-19 has generated minimal popular support and has not posed the type of continuing embarrassment to civilian political elites that the Tupamaros represented

represented in Uruguay. Significantly, the M-19 seizure of the Dominican embassy failed to accomplish its objectives. When the siege ended in April 1980, the guerrillas secured safe conducts to Cuba for themselves but failed to win freedom for any political prisoners. Indeed, the Turbay government gained considerable prestige by regaining the diplomatic hostages without major concessions or bloodshed.

Conclusions and the Future

Although military government is the norm in Latin America, Colombia continues to maintain a tradition of civilian control over the armed forces. This article has related the Colombian case to Huntington's theory in order to explain the Colombian military's deviance. Essentially, the Colombian military remains obedient to civilian authority because the civilian political elite continues to demonstrate its unity, its governmental capabilities, and its substantial popular support. The praetorian atmosphere of political decay and of civilian institutional collapse that Huntington and others have associated with modernization pressures in most Latin American nations is not present in Colombia, despite social mobilization pressures and serious obstacles to economic growth and distribution. Civilian failures have not proved serious enough or long enough in duration to encourage the more professionalized Colombian armed forces of today to reject its traditional role, much less to contemplate a "bureaucratic-authoritarian" regime on the Brazilian or Argentine pattern discussed by O'Donnel (1973, 1976).

Nevertheless, Colombia's calm civil-military relations are not certain to continue. Indeed, many factors suggest that the civilian political elite will be tested severely in the next decade. Social mobilization is increasing, literacy is rising, and peasants continue to migrate to Colombia's urban centers at alarming rates.

Time also may erode some of the factors discussed earlier that have rendered societal demands manageable until now.

Memories of La Violencia, for example, one day must begin to fade. In addition, the children of earlier urban migrants will come of age in the cities and may be more subject to political organization than were their peasant parents.

In short, the potential for greatly increased demands for redistribution clearly exists. The Colombian economy, on the other hand, indicates no such potential for growth and expansion. Export dependency, low agricultural productivity, and a semideveloped industrial sector indicate a precarious economic future. It is possible that careful governmental management and favorable export prices will result in better economic performance than expected; although this may be the case, rising social mobilization and poor income distribution patterns suggest that the imbalance between societal demands and their fulfillment will increase nonetheless. Thus, although Huntington's theoretical framework explains Colombia's stable civil-military relations today, it also predicts serious stresses for the future.

As Colombia approaches the higher modernization levels achieved by Argentina, Chile, and Uruguay, the civilian political elite may find orthodox economic policies more difficult to impose on the populace. Party identification ties also may begin to weaken decidedly. Indeed, the high 1978 absention rate suggests that the erosion of traditional partisan loyalties is accelerating. In such a context, Colombian presidents may find it necessary to confront the impossible choices that many other Latin American civilian leaders have faced already.

Some future Colombian leaders will choose economic austerity and accept higher levels of civil violence and opposition while others may turn to inflationary populism. If the civilian elite can maintain competency and legitimacy in the troubled times ahead, the traditional pattern of Colombian civil-military relations will continue. The Colombian army will remain like the Mexican military—a major support of the civilian elite. However, if Colombia lapses into the praetorian condition, military intervention will become a distinct possibility. An Uruguayan pattern of economic deterioration and rising urban guerrilla violence obviously would undermine traditional civil-military relations in Colombia; however, to write the obituary for Colombian democracy now on the basis of the relatively minor difficulties that have occurred to date would be premature. The remarkably adaptable and resilient Colombian civilian elite should not be underestimated.

Colombian civil-military relations currently are atypical of Latin America. Although military governments rule most countries in the region, Colombia remains one of the very few nations in which civilian rule persists. Nevertheless, as modernization progresses and the Colombian civilian elite faces increasing socioeconomic pressures, the durability of the traditional civil-military relationship described here will become much less certain. My own expectation is that civilian control of the Colombian military will continue, at least throughout the next decade, despite regular journalistic and academic predictions of growing military power and impending coups. However, the Chilean and Uruguayan experiences make one hesitate to speculate beyond the short run, because both cases cogently demonstrate how quickly traditional military roles can change in contemporary Latin America.

NOTES

1. See Ruhl (1980a) for a fuller discussion of the literature on military intervention in Latin America.

2. For a more detailed examination of Colombian military history, see Maingot (1970), Maullin (1973), Studer (1975), and Ruhl (1980a).

3. The figures cited in Maullin (1973: 83) are somewhat different. Official Colombian military expenditure statistics vary from one source to another and are not considered highly reliable.

4. The only other civil-military conflict in the period took place in February 1969, when President Carlos Lleras Restrepo removed army chief General Pinzón Caicedo because of an article the general wrote in a military journal criticizing civilian interference with the armed forces' budget.

5. The conservative political attitudes of the Colombian officer corps are documented in Ruhl (1980a). A good example of current military thinking is Landazábal Reyes (1975).

6. At present, the Colombian military has 65,800 men under arms, but military spending represents only about 1% of GNP. Moreover, per capita expenditures on the Colombian armed forces are low in comparison with other Latin American nations; for

example, Colombia spends $8 per capita, while Argentina spends $105 per capita (Latin America Weekly Report, 1980a).

REFERENCES

BAILEY, J. J. (1977) "Pluralist and corporatist dimensions of interest representation in Colombia," pp. 259-302 in J. M. Malloy (ed.) Authoritarianism and Corporatism in Latin America. Pittsburgh, PA: Univ. of Pittsburgh Press.

BERRY, R. A., R. G. HELLMAN, and M. SOLAUN (1980) Politics of Compromise: Coalition Government in Colombia. New Brunswick, NJ: Transaction.

CAMPOS, J. T. and J. F. McCAMANT (1972) Cleavage Shift in Colombia: Analysis of the 1970 Elections. Sage Comparative Politics Series 3. Beverly Hills: Sage.

Colombia Today (1980) Vol. 15, No. 3. New York: Colombia Information Service.

CORNELIUS, W. A. (1974) "Urbanization and political demand making: political participation among the urban poor in Latin American cities." Amer. Pol. Science Rev. 68 (September): 1125-1146.

DIX, R. H. (1967) Colombia: The Political Dimensions of Change. New Haven, CT: Yale Univ. Press.

ECHEVERRY, A. (1978) El poder y los militares: un análisis de los ejercitos del continente y Colombia. Bogotá: Editorial Suramerica.

FALS BORDA, O. (1965) "Violence and the breakup of tradition in Colombia," pp. 188-205 in C. Veliz (ed.) Obstacles to Change in Latin America. London: Oxford Univ. Press.

HANDELMAN, H. (1975) "The political mobilization of urban squatter settlements: Santiago's experience and its implications for urban research." Latin American Research Rev. 10 (Summer): 35-72.

HOGE, W. (1979) New York Times (November 14).

HUNTINGTON, S. P. (1968) Political Order in Changing Societies. New Haven, CT: Yale Univ. Press.

LANDAZABAL REYES, F. (1975) Factores de violencia. Bogotá: Tercer Mundo.

Latin American Political Report (1979) February 22.

——— (1975) June 13.

Latin America Weekly Report (1980a) September 19.

——— (1980b) August 8.

——— (1980c) June 27.

——— (1980d) February 22.

——— (1980e) January 11.

LEAL BUITRAGO, F. (1973) Análisis historico del desarrollo politico nacional, 1930-1970. Bogotá: Tercer Mundo.

MAINGOT, A. P. (1970) "Colombia," pp. 127-195 in L. N. McAlister (ed.) The Military in Latin American Socio-Political Evolution: Four Case Studies. Washington, DC: American Institute for Research.

MANGIN, W. (1967) "Latin American squatter settlements: a problem and a solution." Latin American Research Rev. 2 (Summer): 65-98.

MAULLIN, R. (1973) Soldiers, Guerrillas and Politics in Colombia. Lexington, MA: D. C. Heath.

McDONALD, R. H. (1975) "The rise of military politics in Uruguay." Inter-American Economic Affairs 28 (Spring): 25-43.

O'DONNEL, G. A. (1976) "Modernization and military coups: theory, comparisons and the Argentine case," pp. 197-243 in A. Lowenthal (ed.) Armies and Politics in Latin America. New York: Holmes & Meier.

——— (1973) Modernization and Bureaucratic-Authoritarianism: Studies in South American Politics. Berkeley, CA: Univ. of California Press.

PEATTIE, L. R. (1972) The View from the Barrio. Ann Arbor, MI: Univ. of Michigan Press.

RUHL, J. M. (1980) Colombia: Armed Forces and Society. Latin American Monograph Series 1. Syracuse: NY: Syracuse University.

——— (1978) "Party system in crisis?: an analysis of Colombia's 1978 elections." Inter-American Economic Affairs 32 (Winter): 26-45.

SCHOULTZ, L. (1972) "Urbanization and changing voting patterns: Colombia, 1946-1970." Pol. Science Q. 87 (March): 22-45.

STEINBERG, S. H. [ed.] (1960-1965) Statesman's Yearbook. Vol. 31, 97-102. New York: St. Martin's Press.

STEPAN, A. C. (1973) "The new professionalism of internal warfare and military role expansion," pp. 47-65 in A. C. Stepan (ed.) Authoritarian Brazil: Origins, Policies and Future. New Haven, CT: Yale Univ. Press.

——— (1971) The Military in Politics: Changing Patterns in Brazil. Princeton, NJ: Princeton Univ. Press.

STUDER, R. W. (1975) "The Colombian army: political aspects of its role," Ph.D. dissertation, University of Southern California.

URRUTIA, M. and A. BERRY (1975) La distribución del ingreso en Colombia. Medellín: Editorial Lealón.

VAN ES, J. C. and W. L. FLINN (1973) "A note on determinants of satisfaction among urban migrants in Bogotá, Colombia." Inter-American Economic Affairs 27 (Autumn): 15-28.

VILLEGAS, J. (1972-1973) "Presupuestos nacionales de ingreso y gustos, 1871-1970." DANE Boletín Mensual Estadistica (Bogotá) 22, 257-258 (December-Janaury): 171-194.

Visión (1975) June 15 (Mexico City).

WIARDA, H. J. and H. F. KLINE (1979) Latin American Politics and Development. Boston, MA: Houghton-Mifflin.

WILDE, A. W. (1978) "Conversations among gentlemen: oligarchical democracy in Colombia," in pp. 28-81 in J. J. Linz and A. Stepan (eds.) The Breakdown of Democratic Regimes: Latin America. Baltimore, MD: Johns Hopkins Univ. Press.

J. Mark Ruhl is Assistant Professor of Political Science and Director of the Latin American Studies Program at Dickinson College in Carlisle, Pennsylvania. His recent articles include those in Albert Berry et al. Politics of Compromise: Coalition Government in Colombia *(New Brunswick: Transaction Books, 1980) and various journals.*

ELIZABETH G. FERRIS
Miami University
Oxford, Ohio

THE ANDEAN PACT AND THE AMAZON TREATY
Reflections of Changing Latin American Relations

The pattern of Latin American regional cooperation has changed greatly during the past five years. New organizations, such as SELA (Latin American Economic System) and OLADE (Latin American Energy Organization), have been formed, while other groups, such as CACM (Central American Common Market), have become moribund. These changes in regional organizations are primarily the result of changes occurring in the developmental orientations and governmental capabilities of the member governments. In this study, two quite different organizations, the Andean Pact and the Amazon Pact, are examined to shed light on the dynamics of contemporary Latin American international relations and to explore new theoretical approaches in the study of regional cooperation schemes.

In 1968, the Andean Pact was formed by five Spanish American nations in an effort to accelerate the economic development of their members and also to counter growing Brazilian power in Latin America. The five original member nations of the Andean

AUTHOR'S NOTE: Research support from the Faculty Research Committee of Miami University is gratefully acknowledged. Useful comments and suggestions were offered by Jennie K. Lincoln and referees of this journal.

Journal of Interamerican Studies and World Affairs, Vol. 23 No. 2, May 1981 147-175

Pact—Bolivia, Chile, Colombia, Ecuador, and Peru—felt that their progress in integration would be much greater in a group that excluded Brazil and Argentina. Although the Andean Pact was designed to further the cause of Latin American integration generally, it was also the product of dissatisfaction with the distribution of benefits within LAFTA (Latin American Free Trade Association). Nine years after the Pact's formation, following sporadic progress in the group and Chile's withdrawal, Brazil called for the formation of an Amazon Pact which would include the five current Andean Pact members. Initial opposition to the Brazilian-proposed organization came from Venezuelan President Carlo Andrés Pérez, who argued that the new Amazon organization might weaken the Andean Pact. By the summer of 1978, the Venezuelan objections had been overcome, and the Treaty of Amazon was signed by representatives of Bolivia, Colombia, Educador, Peru, and Venezuela (the current Andean Pact members), as well as Brazil, Suriname, and Guyana. The Brazilian initiative signals a change in direction of Brazil's foreign policy; Brazil's traditional position of remaining aloof from Latin American organizations and attempts to form common stands has shifted significantly. The Andean countries' response to the Brazilian initiative also represents a shift in their relations with Brazil and a shift in their view of the integration process. Furthermore, in recent years the direction of the Andean Pact has shifted away from economic programs designed to accelerate national economic development and has turned toward increased institutionalization of collective processes and of coordination of foreign policy positions toward the rest of the world.

The emergence of the Amazon Pact and the changing orientation of the Andean Pact can best be understood by examining the foreign policies of the member governments. These two organizations, so different in orientation and scope, represent the two main thrusts in contemporary Latin American foreign policies: on the one hand, pragmatic issue-centered cooperation and, on the other, increasing "collectivization" of foreign policy. Both of these trends are, in turn, the product of the diminished national capabilities of the members.

Brazil, in a significant departure from its traditional foreign policy stance, has sought international cooperation in developing the Amazon in part because of diminished national capabilities in other areas and in part because of a changing conception of development. The Andean Pact as an organization is shifting away from specific economic developmental strategies toward foreign policy coordination for precisely the same reasons: Its members are seeking a type of development different from that sought by the founding members—at the same time that their capabilities for pursuing the initial objectives of integration have diminished.

An analysis of these two groups provides some understanding of the changes in Latin American international politics as well as enables us to develop new theoretical tools for understanding these changes. The Amazon and Andean Pacts were selected for comparison because they represent South American subregional efforts to deal with common economic problems at two very different points in time. The international environment and national conceptions of development changed greatly between 1969 and 1978 and these changes are reflected in the different mechanisms and goals created by the two organizations.

Traditionally, Latin American cooperative efforts were analyzed through the use of integration theory with the level of analysis clearly focused on the group.[1] However, integration theories—despite their theoretical richness—never quite fit the Latin American case. As many scholars have pointed out, integration theory seemed unable to deal with change or with the often paramount role of external actors.[2] Furthermore, integration theorists' basic assumption of progressively increasing cooperation between member nations limited its applicability in the case of Latin American integration efforts. In the past several years, however, integration theory seems to have been at least partially revitalized as scholars have sought to link the concepts of integration, development, and dependency to increase integration theories' relevance to Latin America. Lynn Mytelka (1979), for example, argues that for countries of lesser development to be successful in their integration efforts, they must include strategies to reduce their dependence on external powers as well as to redistribute resources within the group. These recent theoretical approaches seem more applicable to Latin America, in part because they focus more on the national level of analysis rather than on the regional ro group level. As Andrew Axline (1979) points out, regional integration efforts are viewed by the national governments as one of many development strategies available to them. As such, regional integration schemes reflect the development orientations of their constituent governments.

In the case of the Andean Pact, difficulties in reaching agreement on difficult economic issues may be attributed in part to the effects of regime change and changing development orientations of the group's members. In the late 1960s and early 1970s, most of the Andean Pact's member governments emphasized the need to reduce their dependency on external factors and clearly viewed the Andean Pact as one (of several) means of reducing that dependency. Petras and Morley (1978), for example, viewed the Andean Pact as a regional solution to dependency on external powers, but one requiring nationalistic member governments.

As the reformist governments in the Andean regime were replaced with more conservative ones in the early 1970s, there was less interest within the Andean Pact in overcoming dependency on foreign capital. Furthermore, economic difficulties in the member countries (Venezuela and Ecuador to a lesser extent) limited the regimes' abilities and willingness to bear the costs of integration. The distributional crisis experienced by the Pact was a function of diminished national capabilities to implement Pact programs.[3] Ernst Haas sees externalization as the logical outcome of the distributional crisis which occurs in the initial phases of integration efforts. As he states, "Externalization now appears in the guise of the *dependencia* doctrine: The members decide that they cannot obtain the right kind of economic growth unless they make common front vis-à-vis their major customers and suppliers of investment capital. . . . Having learned that they cannot grow without some members' incurring high integration costs, they attempt to intensify the integration process by shifting the cost to an external target—the 'center' of the world economic system, or the 'neocolonialist'" (1975: 10). Thus he argues, externalization can lead to increasing interactions within the region. Although the type of collectivization seems to have shifted away from an emphasis on common policies vis-a-vis multinational corporations toward the development of joint negotiating positions with respect to other governments, the Andean Pact's focus has indeed moved toward institutionalization of joint actions during the past ten years.

At the same time that changes in the Andean Pact were occurring as the result of diminished capabilities and changed developmental goals of the member governments, Brazil also began to shift its foreign policy toward one emphasizing Third World cooperation. Brazil's growing financial difficulties—particularly its rising foreign debt and increasing oil import bills—have inspired new Brazilian policies emphasizing Third World ties. Brazil's foreign debt may be as high as $57 billion and the 1980 cost of servicing its debt ($13 billion) and of importing its oil ($7 billion) exceeds its total exports (The Economist, 1980: 21). This shifting Brazilian foreign policy is manifest in Brazil's overture in proposing the Amazon Pact which seeks much more limited cooperation than the Andean Pact. It is argued here that both of these organizations must be understood in the context of the goals and capabilities of the members which comprise them rather than through analysis of integrative processes on the group level.

By examining the formation of the Amazon Pact and the changes occurring within the Andean Pact, insights will be gained into the relationship between regional cooperation schemes on the one hand and national capabilities and developmental orientations on the other. This study focuses on these two organizations from three perspectives: (1) the Brazilian initiative as a reflection of new directions in Brazilian foreign policy; (2) the effects of the Amazon treaty on the Andean Pact and the foreign policies of its members; and (3) the impact of the changing nature of Latin American regional organizations on foreign policy and integration in the region.[4]

The Andean Pact and the Amazon Treaty

Ever since its formation in 1968, scholars have been intrigued with the Andean Pact. Studies of the Pact abound (Avery, 1973: 549-556; Axline and Mytelka, 1976; Diaz-Alejandro, 1968; Fontaine, 1977; Fullmer, 1973: 1-17; Gálvez and Llosa, 1974, Kearns, 1972: 225-249; Kuczynski and Huelin, 1973; Milenky, 1971: 77-91; Morawetz, 1972; and Ferris, 1978). The agreement creating the Andean Pact was perhaps the most innovative and far-reaching attempt at regional integration in the Third World. The five members agreed on the creation of a free trade area by 1981, a common external tariff, harmonization of economic and social policies, common treatment of foreign investment, joint industrial programming, and a host of other programs. The accomplishments of the Andean Pact in implementing its economic programs have been mixed. There have been remarkable successes, at least relative to earlier attempts at Latin American integration, followed by long periods of stagnation. The primary purpose of the Andean Pact was to accelerate the economic development of its members. Against that standard, progress in the pact has been limited.

The Junta, or permanent technical board of the Andean Pact, issued a report in May 1979 in which the lack of national political support for the group was viewed as the major weakness of the Andean integration movement. The lack of national legislation to implement group decisions and the inability of member governments to compromise in order to reach joint agreements were viewed as the main obstacles to further progress in the group (Junta del Acuerdo de Cartagena, 1979; Latin America Economic Report, 1979a). A survey by *Business Latin America* (1979) clearly demonstrates that foreign investors doing business in the Andean Pact countries do not perceive that the pact has had much impact on their operations nor do they expect significant achievements by the group.

Progress in the Andean Pact has been hampered by serious political differences between the members. In the early 1970s, leaders of the Andean Pact nations represented progressive reformist governments; by the mid-1970s, most of these reformers had been replaced by right-wing military governments. Certainly officials in Andean countries in 1980 expected the pact to change as democratic regimes were planned, for the first time, in all five Andean Pact nations. However, the Bolivian military coup has changed these expectations. The Andean Pact received a boost in momentum on May 26, 1979, with the meeting of the presidents of the five member countries in Cartagena, Colombia. The presidents assessed the ten years of efforts toward subregional integration, reaffirmed their commitment to the Andean Pact, and resolved to establish an Andean Tribunal of Justice and other institutions.

Although foreign policy coordination was an early specified goal of Andean cooperation, it received little emphasis in the early years. The Acta Final of the first meeting of Andean Pact foreign ministers noted that one of the goals of the organization was to: "build up the negotiating capacity of our countries towards the great industrialized nations and in forums where trade and development problems are discussed" (as cited by Nun Peichihovici, 1971: 69-70). Junta officials negotiated trade (and other) policies with extraregional organizations on behalf of the Andean Pact, but differences between the member governments made meaningful coordination difficult. By May 1979, however, when the five Andean presidents met in Cartagena to reaffirm their commitment to integration, both international and domestic changes had occurred which gave a new impetus to the pact's foreign policy role.

A permanent council of foreign ministers was established to coordinate policies and the presidents committed themselves to formulating joint policies toward SELA (Latin American Economic System), LAFTA (Latin American Free Trade Association), and other international organizations and transnational enterprises seeking to create a new international economic order.

The Andean group took the lead in calling for the resignation of Anastasio Somoza of Nicaragua and pressing the Organization of American States to take a strong stand on the Nicaraguan Revolution. During the past year, the Andean Pact members have been outspoken in reaffirming democratic traditions and human rights in the region. During the political crisis in Bolivia during the fall of 1979, the other four Andean Pact nations were instrumental in calling on Colonel Natusch to step down and in supporting the restoration of democracy in the country. Although unable to prevent the military coup in 1980, they strongly condemned its occurrence. More recently, the foreign ministers of the five Andean Pact nations agreed to a joint code of conduct in their external relations. Among other things, this code of conduct "affirmed the principle that the defense of human rights in other countries was an obligation of governments under international law and was fully compatible with the equally valid principle of nonintervention in the affairs of other nations" (Latin America Weekly Report 1980a).

The Andean Pact is today undergoing its most serious crisis as a consequence of regime changes in Peru and Bolivia. The Belaúnde Administration, installed in July 1980, reaffirmed Peruvian commitment to Andean integration, while at the same time suggesting that changes be made in major pact programs. Officials formulating the regime's developmental programs are reportedly calling for modifications in the foreign investment code and renegotiation of the sectoral industrial programs already approved. Furthermore, the Belaúnde government's decision to lower tariffs on industrial products makes progress toward a common external tariff, already two years behind schedule, virtually impossible (Latin America Regional Reports, 1980b).

Belaúnde's opposition to the increasingly political orientation of the pact has caused some difficulty in formulating regional diplomatic positions on controversial issues. While the changes evolving in Peruvian policies toward the Andean Pact could well modify the group's direction, a much more serious challenge comes from the consequences of the 1980 Bolivian military coup.

Following the coup, the other four Andean Pact governments issued an immediate joint statement condemning the military takeover and discussed the use of joint economic sanctions against Bolivia. The government of General García Meza reacted to this condemnation by calling for closer ties with the governments of the Southern Cone and by threatening to withdraw from the pact.

Bolivian dissatisfaction with the distribution of benefits form Andean integration is well known. Coupled with resentment at perceived Andean intervention in Bolivian domestic affairs, Bolivian hostility and resentment toward the Andean Pact are increasing. The instability of the García Meza regime and the possibility that Argentina may withdraw its support from the Bolivia military regime create a great deal of uncertainty in analyzing the future of Bolivia's role in the pact. What is clear, however, is that the regime changes in both Peru and Bolivia will create changes in the political direction and economic programs of the pact.

The political role and the contemporary crisis over Bolivia, however, are recent developments. At the time of the Brazilian proposal, the Andean Pact was having problems reaching economic agreements and it is in this context that the Brazilian initiative takes on added significance. In the early months of 1976, ideas for the formation of an Amazon cooperation agreement began circulating in the Brazilian chancellory. In November 1976, Brazil formally proposed the creation of an organization to foster regional cooperation within the region and initiated a series of bilateral talks with each of the other potential member nations. During the year following the Brazilian initiative, doubts were raised by many Latin Americans who feared the possibility of Brazil's expansionist intentions—especially Peruvians and Venezuelans. In July 1977, Peru agreed to participate and in November 1977, while on a trip to Brazil, Venezuelan President Carlos Andrés Pérez agreed to participate. The representatives from the eight Amazon countries met in Rio de Janeiro in November 1977, again in Brasilia in March 1978, and in Caracas in May 1978, when the text of the treaty was approved. The treaty was signed by representatives of the eight member nations in a special ceremony in Brasilia on July 3, 1978.

The treaty itself is a very interesting document which must be understood in the context of Latin American geopolitics. Article XIX, for example, states that:

> Neither the signing of this Treaty nor its execution shall have any effect on any other international treaties in force between the Parties nor on any differences with regard to limits or territorial rights which may exist between the Parties nor shall the signing or implementation of this Treaty be interpreted or invoked to imply acceptance or renunciation, affirmation or modification, direct or indirect, express or tacit, of the position or interpretation that each Contracting Party may hold on these matters.

This article explicitly recognizes the prior existence of the Andean Pact and the obligations of the Andean member governments. It also carefully avoids taking sides in the Ecuador[ean]-Peru[vian] and Venezuela[n]-Guyana[n] border disputes.

In the Treaty of Amazon Cooperation, member governments agree to cooperate in furthering the economic and social development of the region, in preserving the environment, and in providing for the rational utilization of resources. Specifically, the agreement provides for cooperation between members with respect to: freedom of commercial navigation, promotion of research, including research by groups outside the region; a regular system for exchanging information, the coordination of health services in the Amazon region, the establishment and improvement of road, river, air and telecommunication links within the Amazon, and promotion of trade and tourism.

To carry out these joint efforts, the agreement provides for meetings of the foreign ministers of the member countries when "deemed opportune or advisable," in which basic guidelines for policies will be established. An Amazonian Cooperation Council comprised of top level diplomatic representatives will meet annually, beginning in 1981, to implement decisions made by the foreign ministers and to consider various plans for joint action. The treaty does not establish a permanent secretariat but rather provides that "the functions of the secretariat shall be performed *pro-tempore* by the Contracting Party in whose territory the next regular meeting of the Amazonian Cooperation Council is scheduled to be held." Finally, the member governments are charged with creating permanent national commissions to implement joint decisions and to further the goals of the Amazonian Pact.

As spelled out in the treaty, the goals of the Amazon agreement are relatively modest and restricted to joint cooperation in a clearly specified set of areas. In contrast to the clear specification of areas for cooperation, the mechanisms and organizations to provide that cooperation are quite vague. The lack of regular meetings for foreign ministers, the absence of a permanent secretariat, and the limited functions and provisions for selection of the Amazonian Cooperation Council clearly indicate that the scope and power of the group are intended to be modest.

As a relatively new agreement which will not become operative until ratified by all signatory governments, the participants are unsure of how the programs and mechanisms will evolve. Officials at Itamaraty, the Brazilian Foreign Ministry, were somewhat vague about how they expected the negotiations and meetings to proceed, stating that until the contracting parties formally meet, many of the provisions would continue to be ambiguous and unclear. The literature on the Amazon Treaty is sparse, hampering efforts to present definitive statements of how the treaty will evolve as an organization.[5] A logical first step in that direction is to consider the reasons behind the Brazilian initiative.

Proposing the Treaty: The View from Brasilia

The Brazilian initiative in proposing the Amazon Treaty of Cooperation reflects major changes in Brazil's perceptions of its role in the world. Following the military coup of April 1964, the Brazilian government's foreign policy came to be based on the doctrine of ideological frontiers and of Brazil's geopolitical position in the world. Brazil's foreign policy was designed to increase national power through the dual strategies of rapid economic development and increased relations with the advanced industrialized nations.[6] Brazil's ambitious plan to develop its vast Amazon territory involved a massive commitment of public funds and a corresponding dependence on foreign investment to develop the region. Brazil's neighbors became increasingly nervous as Brazil's development plan came to include the establishment of roads and military bases in the unexplored frontier areas.

Brazil carried out its ambitious economic development schemes with the support of extraregional actors—foreign investors from Europe, Japan, and the United States, foreign governments, and interantional financial institutions. Brazil's long-term foreign policy interests were clearly perceived as being linked with those of the developed nations, and support for regional organizations was minimal.

Brazilian foreign policy makers simply did not place much importance in fostering good relations with its neighbors. Within South America, Brazil's closest allies were other military governments. The Brazilian government made several initiatives, however, toward the smaller bordering states. Bolivia received large amounts of foreign investment from Brazilian companies, investments which were used to enable Bolivia to comply with its obligations in the Andean Pact. Brazilian support for the military coup which overthrew the liberal Torres government, replacing it with the more conservative Banzer regime, is widely believed to have been the decisive factor in the coup's success. Similarly, Brazilian support for the incipient separatist movement in Santa Cruz is perceived as being another means of asserting greater Brazilian control over Bolivia (Schilling, 1978). The 1980 Bolivian military coup was seen by most observers, however, as having close links with the Argentine military. Brazilians have been moving in great numbers to occupy Paraguayan lands bordering on Paraná, and certainly parts of Paraguay are inhabited by more Brazilians than Paraguayans and are more integrated into the Brazilian economy than that of Paraguay (Katzman, n.d.: ch. 4).

The direction of Brazilian foreign policy initiatives toward other Latin American nations during the decade of the 1960s was not one to inspire friendly overtures. In addition to fears of Brazilian expansionism, which were greatly intensified with the implementation of the Amazonian development scheme, and Brazil's obvious preference for dealing and perhaps identifying with the industrialized nations rather than Latin American ones, the past experiences of Latin American nations in dealing with Brazil in multilateral settings were not reassuring. In LAFTA, Latin American small and medium-sized nations found themselves at a significant disadvantage in dealing with the larger, more developed countries, particularly Argentina, Brazil, and Mexico. These three countries received most of the benefits of "integration," leaving a legacy of suspicion and the impetus to create a new subregional organization, the Andean Pact, which would exclude these major powers and thus be more attuned to the needs of the other nations.

Brazil's foreign policy has always been essentially pragmatic in nature, responding to changes in the international environment and to domestic political economic needs. By the mid-1970s, Brazil's foreign policies began to change direction. Increased friction with the United States over trade issues and over Brazil's nuclear agreement with West Germany led to more Brazilian foreign policy independence. Soaring oil prices threatened to slow Brazil's economic growth, and foreign policy measures were taken to reduce that danger. Brazil's pro-Israeli stance was quietly dropped, and relationships with OPEC members were given more attention. Oil exploration agreements with Egypt, Iraq, and Libya were signed as was a large oil trade agreement with Saudi Arabia. In the past few years, Brazil has moved to improve its relations with Black Africa. Whereas its African policy was once dominated by shared trade and security concerns with South Africa, today Brazil is busily extending foreign aid and encouraging investment in Angola, Nigeria, and other West African nations (Latin America Economic Report, 1977, 1979b).

In this context of a changed international environment and Brazil's pragmatic adoption of a "Third World" foreign policy stance, the Brazilian proposal for an Amazon Pact makes more sense. During the past several years, former President Geisel initiated presidential visits to many Latin American countries and encouraged greater cooperation and exchange. Increasingly, the Brazilian government perceives a clear economic advantage to closer ties with Latin America. Brazilian exports to other Latin American nations are rapidly increasing as Brazil seeks new markets for its exports in an effort to deal with its serious balance of payments difficulties. As *Latin America Regional Reports* (1980a) indicates, Brazilian exports to LAFTA have increased from 11.8% to 15% from 1976 to 1979 and to the Andean Pact nations from 4.2% to 6.2%. These economic reasons for closer regional cooperation were summarized by Brazilian Foreign Minister Ramiro Saraiva Guerreiro, who said: "This position of good neighborliness is more and more productive, to the extent that our world responsibility grows as do our options for business negotiations and cooperation" (O Estado de São Paulo, June 17, 1979).

In addition to Brazil's growing responsiveness to increasing its ties with Third World nations, and with Latin American nations in particular, as a response to economic difficulties, Brazil's relations with Argentina play an important role in determining Brazilian ties with other members in the region. Traditionally, Brazil and Argentina have viewed each other as rivals within Latin America, and for years Argentina has enjoyed better ties with the Andean Pact than has Brazil.

In the spring of 1980, however, Brazil and Argentina took significant steps to reduce chronic sources of friction between their governments. On May 14, 1980, Brazilian president João Baptista Figueredo visited Argentina and signed ten agreements, including provisions for joint cooperation in nuclear energy, hydroelectric construction efforts, satellites, armaments manufacture, and technological exchanges in alternative energy developments. This move toward increasing rapprochement between Brazil and Argentina seems to represent an attempt to increase Brazilian flexibility—to remove, as one observer writes, "a constant stumbling block of Brazil in other areas, especially in its relations with other Third World countries" (Latin America Weekly Report, 1980b).

The Brazilian proposal to create a new subregional group for the development of the Amazon seems inconsistent with its traditional emphasis on bilateral relations. Except for international organizations related to trade and primary products important to Brazil's economy, Brazilian participation in multilateral schemes has been less than enthusiastic. At least one Brazilian observer sees the Brazilian initiative in creating the Amazon Pact as an attempt to continue Brazilian emphasis on bilateral ties: "I don't think that the recently created Amazon Pact represents a significant innovation [in Brazilian foreign policy]. On the contrary, I think that the Amazon Pact is in line with the traditional style, trying to use a positive multilateral climate to facilitate bilateral understandings creating, above all, a climate of constructive cooperation in the Amazon Basin to balance the difficulties with Argentina sustained by the controversy of Itaipu" (Lafer, 1979: 56).

But while the Amazon Pact may serve the purpose of improving Brazil's bilateral ties with its neighbors, the Brazilian government appears to have had other objectives as well, including: (1) increasing development of the Amazon and preventing the possibility of unwanted outside intervention in the region; (2) reducing fears of Brazilian expansionism on the part of its neighbors; and thus (3) increasing its range of independent foreign policy action by acquiring closer allies, or at least less united opponents, on its borders.

Certainly the Brazilian initiative in proposing the Amazon Pact must be understood in the broader context of both its shifting overall foreign policy behavior in expanding relations with a wide variety of Third World nations and related to this, its worsening international economic position. Domestically, Brazil's ambitious national Amazon development plan was running into increased internal opposition with charges that foreign investors were exercising undue control over the area. Daniel Ludwig's operations in Jari were increasingly criticized and investigated as a Brazilian sellout (Latin America Economic

Report, 1979c). At the same time, Brazilians are aware that the Amazon region represents an increasingly valuable natural resource in a world where natural resources are becoming ever more scarce. Brazilians express fear at suggestions made in international forums that the Amazon be considered an international resource to be used for common goals such as providing homes for refugees from Indochina or other overpopulated areas; reference is frequently made to a proposal of the Hudson Institute which suggested that a huge lake be created in the Amazon basin (Mercado Jarrín 1978). Certainly one of the principal reasons for Brazil's national Amazon plan and for its suggestion of joint efforts to develop the region is its fear of external intervention. However, some representatives in Brazil's Congress were suspicious about the Amazon Pact, fearing that this was yet another effort to internationalize the region (O Globo, May 6, 1979).

Brazil's initial plans for the Amazon Treaty were more ambitious than the agreement which emerged. Specifically, the Brazilian Foreign Ministry had proposed the creation of duty-free zones in border areas and the eventual movement toward regional economic complementariness and physical integration. These provisions were eliminated because of the protests of the Andean Pact members who saw this as a clear challenge to the Andean organization.

The main reason for Brazil's proposal seems to be the fact that Brazil needs capital, international cooperation, and legal agreements to proceed with its plans for developing the Amazon. The need for international cooperation is especially acute in the areas of health, settlement, and contraband. Legal agreements are necessary if Brazil is to use the Amazon's water resources—both in navigation and generation of hydroelectric power. In addition to its need for international cooperation to develop the Amazon, the Brazilian government seems to have had broader intentions. *Latin America Economic Report* (1978) explicitly states: "Brazil has made no secret of its desire to step up its economic and commercial presence in Latin America and, more explicitly, of using the Amazon Pact as a 'back door' to the Andean markets."

From Brazil's perspective, however, the Amazon Treaty was not intended as a way of coopting or confronting the Andean Pact, but rather as a way of neutralizing possible negative consequences of remaining isolated from the Andean countries. The fact that the Andean Pact was going through a difficult time made such a Brazilian initiative more attractive to the pact's member governments.

Finally, as an effort to increase Brazil's foreign policy flexibility by emphasizing the nation's Third World ties, the Amazon Pact was explicitly presented in the context of Third World aspirations. In his speech at the signing of the Treaty of Amazon Cooperation, the Brazilian president underlined the international connotations by stressing the sovereignty of the Amazon nations over the region and by emphasizing this cooperation scheme in the context of the North-South division of the world.

> Against the attempts at internationalization, in the abrupt form of the past or the subtle interference of the present, the best antidote is the regionalization of the protection of the area. In Amazonia, I repeat, it is the countries which share it, and only they, who must have the exclusive responsibility for its development. . . .
>
> In order to overcome the dependence expressed in the vertical north-south axis, the effort to reform the structure of international commerce is not enough. Complementing reformist action, it is necessary to create, on a horizontal basis, among developing countries, the ties which will annul the distances artificially created by dependence. Towards the achievement of this objective, the Amazonic Treaty will be an efficient instrument for generating within the continent, areas of convergence and joint work [Geisel, 1978].

Thus, for Brazil, the proposal to create an Amazon Pact was more than a rhetorical gesture; it was, first of all, an attempt to increase national control over a valuable resource by acquiring regional allies; second, it represented a shift in foreign policy direction toward a Third World-oriented set of relationships. Brazil sought to reduce its isolation from the Andean countries by coopting them and to increase its flexibility in international relations. As Thomas Skidmore (1976) argues, Brazil will undoubtedly continue to play both sides—to be a supporter of Third World demands and to seek eventual OECD membership.

With its increasing economic difficulties, however, there is added incentive for Brazil to support Third World demands for a restructuring of the international financial system. And, indeed, during the United Nations Special Session on Development in September 1980, Brazil assumed a leadership role in pressing for Third World economic demands in negotiations with the industrialized countries.

The Amazon Pact thus represents one, among many, diplomatic initiatives taken by the Brazilian government to further its developmental goals in light of its diminished capabilities. Rather than reflecting a new-found ideological solidarity with Third World and Latin American developmental aspirations, the Brazilian proposal is a pragmatic move to increase the regime's foreign policy flexibility and to advance its developmental goals. Brazil's initiative depended on the acceptance of the other member countries, however, and as we shall see in the section that follows, this acceptance was not automatic, nor was it uniformly favorable.

Responding to Brazil: The View From the Andean Capitals

Initial reactions to Brazil's proposal ranged from enthusiasm on the part of some Andean Pact members to skepticism by others to outright opposition in the case of Venezuela. These reactions were clearly determined by *national* goals and capabilities rather than by concern for acting as members of an Andean *group*. Specifically, the Andean Pact member governments' responses to the proposed Amazon Treaty were determined by the priority of the development of the Amazon region in national developmental plans, possible strategic or geopolitical advantages to increasing cooperation with Brazil, the Third

World orientation of the governmental leaders, and finally, the costs of not participating. Since the Amazon Pact involves minimal commitments from the signatory nations and provides for an absolute veto by any member nation, the costs of remaining outside the treaty are perceived as being higher than the costs of joining. While the nations vary in the importance assigned to Amazon development, they share a fear of outside intervention and a common interest in developing the region.

Officials at the Andean Pact headquarters in Lima, as might be expected, expressed concern about the impact of the Amazon Pact on Andean cooperation. While some junta officials maintained that the Amazon Treaty embodied such a different form of regional cooperation that it would have no effect on the Andean Pact, other officials saw the Amazon Treaty as, at best, a challenge to the pact. One official expressed fear that Brazil would be more closely linked with each of the Andean countries than they were with one another. Another junta official saw the Amazon Treaty as an incentive for Andean cooperation and stressed the fact that the pact members had acted jointly in negotiating with Brazil and that members refused to allow the creation of an entity which would challenge the Andean organization. Certainly, the Andean Pact nations expressed concern about the impact of the Amazon Pact on Andean cooperation, but this response was determined more by national than by regional concerns. Venezuelan and Ecuadorean responses to the Amazon Pact present an interesting contrast in light of the fact that the governments of these two nations have probably benefited the most from Andean integration and are among the most enthusiastic supporters of Andean cooperation.

Robert Bond (1978a) notes that Venezuela's main objection to the Amazon Treaty came from its historic lack of close relations with Brazil, Brazil's traditional reluctance to enter multilateral agreements, Venezuela's concerns over the future of the Andean Pact, and the lack of the Amazon region as a high priority to the Venezuelan government. Furthermore, Venezuelan President Carlos Andrés Pérez actively sought a Third World leadership role for Venezuela and viewed Brazil as opposing, or at least not supporting, this role. Many Venezuelans also saw Brazil's initiative as an attempt to neutralize Venezuela's increased world power as a result of its oil wealth.

Interactions between Brazil and Venezuela have historically been at a low level, representing less than 2% of either's trade. Politically, Venezuela disagreed with Brazilian policy in a variety of areas. Pérez opposed Brazil's nuclear program, especially its failure to ratify the Nuclear Non-Proliferation Treaty, and, as a democratic nation, condemned the violation of human rights in Brazil. But by November 1977, when Pérez visited Brazil, many of these objections had been overcome. Pérez indicated Venezuelan acceptance of Brazil's nuclear program as peaceful and stated that human rights were matters of national concern. But, as Bond notes, only four of the eighteen agreements prepared by the Brazilian Foreign Ministry for the occasion were signed, indicating that the Venezuelan-Brazilian reconciliation was not total (Bond, 1978a: 635-636). In response to Venezuelan objections concerning the Amazon Treaty's effect on the Andean Pact, in which Venezuela currently plays a leadership role, some of the clauses of the original treaty's proposal were modified.

Relations between Brazil and Venezuela have improved since the signing of the treaty. In January 1979, then-president Carlos Andrés Pérez wrote, "the signing of the Amazonian Pact is important because it brings Brazil closer to our nations and compels us to regard Brazil without suspicion" (El Universal, January 28, 1979: 4). In November 1979, Brazilian President João Figueiredo made an official visit to Venezuela. This visit, his first abroad, resulted in the adoption of a joint communique recognizing Brazilian and Venezuelan commitments to principles such as human rights, nonintervention, and ideological pluralism. A framework for trade negotiations in diverse fields ranging from steel production, nuclear technology, oil and school lunch programs was established with the goal of increasing trade between the countries to some $2 billion.

Ecuador, in contrast to Venezuela, responded enthusiastically to the Brazilian proposal. Ecuador is also one of the prime beneficiaries of the Andean Pact in that membership (and especially the special treatment provided) has stimulated the creation of new industries designed to take advantage of the pact's provisions. Unlike some of the other Andean Pact members, the Ecuadorian government has been pursuing an active program of Amazon development, sparked in part by the discovery of oil in the region. Ecuador hopes to benefit from Brazil's technological experience in developing its Amazon region and to benefit from cooperative measures with respect to ecological issues and river navigation. Most of all, however, Ecuador's interests in the Amazon Pact are geopolitical. Ecuador hopes to use the Amazon Pact and closer relations with Brazil as a means of improving its position with respect to the territories claimed by Peru in 1941. As one Ecuadorian official noted, Ecuador is not bordered by Brazil and thus does not feel nearly as threatened by Brazil as the other countries do. Thus, Ecuadoreans reacted enthusiastically to Brazil's initiative in proposing the Amazon Pact, both for the economic advantages in cooperating to solve shared problems and because it perceived a clear geopolitical advantage.

Bolivia also saw geopolitical advantages to participation in the Amazon Pact in that it would give Bolivia increased access to the Atlantic without endangering its claim of access to the Pacific. Although since the coup, Bolivia has stressed its affinity with the Southern Cone, the Amazon Pact is not perceived as limiting Bolivian foreign policy flexibility.

Peru's initial response to the Brazilian initiative was quite hostile due to long-standing rivalries in the Amazon region; meetings between Brazilian President Geisel and Peruvian President Morales Bermúdez appear to have reduced some of these fears. Peruvian officials in foreign policy-making positions were particularly concerned about the possibility of Brazil's taking advantage of Bolivia's obsession with an outlet to the sea and possibly securing a Brazilian presence in the region. By 1976, Peru's unenviable financial situation and lack of resources to carry out its own plans for developing the Amazon made cooperation with Brazil appear a more attractive alternative.

The Amazon region of Colombia is very sparsely populated and the region—in spite of mineral wealth—is only minimally integrated into the country. There have been few reports of Colombia's reaction to the Brazilian initiative. Given its perceptible move away from being a leader of Andean integration toward less active participation in the group, it would appear that Colombia did not take an active role in either supporting or opposing the Amazon Pact. Surinam and Guyana have had special relationships with Brazil for some time; although these two nations have few resources, they may benefit from increased cooperation.

In looking at the foreign policies of the five Andean Pact members toward Brazil's proposal to create an organization for Amazon cooperation, it is important to remember that the Amazon region is largely uninhabited and unintegrated into the national economic and political systems. In virtually all of the countries, national plans to settle and develop the Amazon have fallen short of governmental goals. Brazil's efforts to build roads, to move colonists into the region, and to encourage large multinational corporations to operate in the region were viewed as somewhat threatening to the bordering nations. Participation in the Amazon Pact thus enables these governments not only to benefit from Brazil's superior expertise in developing the region, but also serves to keep them informed of Brazilian intentions and plans in the area. Thus, while Brazil may be seeking to coopt the Andean countries by including them in a Brazilian-dominated group, the Andean countries expect to realize clear political, as well as economic, benefits from this cooperative endeavor as well. Significantly, in January 1980, the foreign ministers of the five Andean Pact members met for the first time as the newly constituted Andean Council of Ministers. Immediately following this meeting, the ministers traveled to Lima, Peru, where they met with the Brazilian foreign minister to discuss possible areas for future cooperation.

The decision to create an organization to provide for cooperation in developing the Amazon region not only reflects some of the realities of Latin American international politics, but also suggests some implications for the future of regional organizations in the Latin American region.

Conclusions: Implications of Andean and Amazon Cooperation for Latin American Regional Politics

The peak of Latin American commitment to economic integration as a tool for achieving national economic development is commonly thought to have been reached in 1970-1971 with the inital heady successes of the Andean Pact. Today the Andean Pact is a very different organization than the one envisioned by its founders ten years ago; its momentum continues, though in a different direction than anticipated. Progress in sectoral programming and trade liberalization has been painfully slow while the group has taken rapid strides toward increased institutionalization of subregional cooperation. The creation of an Andean Tribunal of Justice and the forthcoming creation of an Andean Parliament indicate a willingness to continue the integrative process in spite of persistent difficulties in reaching agreements on collective economic policies requiring difficult national economic choices.

More importantly, the emergence of the Andean Pact as an outspoken advocate of reformist democratic solutions to Latin American problems represents a dramatic change for the region. The Andean foreign ministers are increasingly negotiating with external actors as a group and are emphasizing human rights and democracy in their bilateral ties and actions within multilateral organizations. The possibility of stagnation and crisis in the Andean Pact is, of course, ever-present. The effects of Bolivian dissatisfaction on the movement toward political unity are difficult to predict. Bolivian withdrawal from the group could weaken political cohesion or, conversely, increase the solidarity of the other members.

Further confounding the student of Latin American regional integration are attempts to revitalize LAFTA through creation of ALADI (Latin American Integration Association). It may be, as Ferguson (1980: 27) suggests, that a revitalized LAFTA (or SELA) will be one outcome of closer relations between Brazil and the Andean countries. Certainly changes in Brazil's relations with its Latin American neighbors have important implications for the international relations of the region as a whole. Its initiatives toward Argentina and Chile on the one hand and toward the Andean Pact on the other are evidence of increased Brazilian willingness to act as part of a Latin American group—a willingness which could give new vitality to regional cooperation schemes. These two trends—growing coordination of Andean foreign policies, particularly as advocates of reformist democratic principles, and Brazil's increased willingness to take an active regional role—are manifest in the two subregional organizations studied here. This study has suggested that analysis of the national foreign policies of the member nations is the most profitable avenue for understanding Latin American regional cooperation.

The linkages between domestic political and economic conditions and national foreign policy behavior offer exciting possibilities for further research. Domestic political changes, as in Brazil's *abertura* and lessening of political tension, affect other nations' willingness to pursue closer diplomatic relations. Changes in regimes, such as the Bolivian 1980 coup, similarly affect a nation's position in regional international politics both in terms of the regime's changing developmental orientations and its willingness to participate in group ventures. Changes in economic capabilities, particularly in the most common case of reduced governmental revenues to meet expanding needs, affect national participation in regional organizations in at least two ways. A decrease in capabilities makes it more difficult for a government to accept economic sacrifices required in reaching group decisions. Yet declining domestic capabilities may also increase the willingness of that government to seek political support from other like-minded governments in bargaining with external actors. Political support from such governments may also help generate domestic political support for regimes facing internal problems as in the case of Ecuadorean President Jaime Roldós' advocacy of increased human rights and Andean support for Bolivian territorial aspirations.

If, as tentatively suggested here, domestic economic adversity leads to increased regional cooperation, Latin American integrative efforts may well flourish in the coming years. And yet, development of integration schemes will clearly not be in the direction posited by integration theorists, but rather, like the Andean and Amazon Pacts, are likely to pursue either increased international power through common negotiating positions or limited cooperation or specific issues of mutual interest.

NOTES

1. The vast literature on integration is summarized and analyzed by Pentland (1973). Some of the major theoretical works include Axline (1971: 163-176), Barrera and Haas (1969: 150-161), Deutsch et al. (1957), DeVree (1972), Etzioni (1965), Haas (1971, 1975), Haas and Schmitter (1966) Lindberg (1970: 649-732), Nye (1968a: 855-880, 1968b, 1971), Puchala (1975: 496-520, Schmitter (1970b: 233-265), and Mitrany (1966).

2. Criticisms of integration theory as it relates to Latin America include Haas (1975), Haas and Schmitter (1966), Schmitter (1970a, 1970b, 1972), Milenky (1973), and Sloan (1971: 138-162). Several more recent efforts to discuss Latin American cooperative schemes include Milenky (1977: 73-96), Bond (1978b: 401-423), Grunwald (1976), and Hopkins (1977).

3. The crisis of distribution has been discussed by many authors including Nye (1971), Haas (1975), Sloan (1971), Schmitter (1970b, 1972), and Avery (1979).

4. This study is based on personal interviews carried out by the author in 1979 with officials in the Andean Pact's Junta, the Brazilian Foreign Ministry, Itamaraty, and officials in other Andean countries.

5. Some of the sources describing and analyzing the Amazon Treaty of Cooperation include Carrasco (1978: 19-25), Ricupero (1977), Mercado Jarrín (1978: 26-30), and Schilling (1978).

6. Brazil is one of the few Latin American nations whose foreign policy has been studied in some detail. Some of the principal works in this area include Storrs (1973), Bailey and Schneider (1974: 108-124), Rosenbaum (1968: 377-392, 1972: 58-84), Jaguaribe (1975), Selcher (1974, 1978), Gordon (1972: 621-631), Cline (1976: 63-68), Gall (1976: 155-201), Theberge and Fontaine (1977), Skidmore (1976: 9-40), Perry (1976), and Schneider (1977).

REFERENCES

AVERY, W. P. (1979) "The politics of cooperation and crisis in the Andean Common Market." Presented at the annual meeting of the International Studies Association.

——— (1973) "The extra-regional transfer of integrative behavior." International Organization 27 (Autumn): 549-556.

AXLINE, A. W. (1979) Carribbean Integration: The Politics of Regionalism. New York: Nichols.

——— (1971) "Common markets, free trade areas, and the comparative study of foreign policy." J. of Common Market Studies 10 (December): 163-176.

AXLINE, A. W. and L. K. MYTELKA (1976) "Dependence and regional integration: a comparison of the Andean Group and Caricom." Presented at the 17th Annual Meeting of the International Studies Association.

BAILEY, N. A. and R. M. SCHNEIDER (1974) "Brazil's foreign policy: a case study in upward mobility." Inter-American Economic Affairs 27 (Spring): 3-26.

BARRERA, M. and E. B. HAAS (1969) "The operationalization of some variables related to regional integration: a research note." International Organization 23 (Winter): 150-161.

BOND, R. D. (1978a) "Venezuela, Brazil, and the Amazon Basin." Orbis 2 (Fall): 645-646.

——— (1978b) "Regionalism in Latin America: prospects for the Latin American Economic System (SELA)." International Organization 32 (Spring): 401-423.

Business Latin America (1979) "Corporate survey points up Ancom's minimal impact on MNCs' operations." March 28.

CARRASCO, J. P. (1978) "El Tratado de Cooperación Amazónica." Nueva Sociedad 37 (julio/agosto): 19-25.

CLINE, W. R. (1976) "Brazil's emerging international economic role," pp. 63-68 in R. Roett (ed.) Brazil in the Seventies. Washington, DC: American Enterprise Institute.

DEUTSCH, K., S. A. BURRELL, R. A. KANN, M. LEE, M. LICHLERMAN, R. F. LINDGREN, F. L. LOWENHEIM, and R. W. VAN WAGENEN (1957) Political Community and the North Atlantic Area. New York: Greenwood Press.

DEVREE, J. K. (1972) Political Integration: The Formation of Theory and Its Problems. The Hague: Mouton & Company.

DIAZ-ALEJANDRO, C. F. (1968) "The Andean Group in the integration process of Latin America." Presented at the Conference on the Economic Integration of Latin America. Stanford, California.

The Economist [London] (1980) "And now, the Brazil crisis." May 17: 21.

O Estado de São Paulo (1979) June 17: 11.

ETZIONI, A. (1965) Political Unification: A Comparative Study of Leaders and Forces. New York: Holt, Rinehart & Winston.

FERGUSON, Y. H. (1980) "Latin American regional integration: an interim assessment." Presented at 1980 International Studies Association.

FERRIS, E. G. (1978) "The Andean Pact: a selected bibliography." Latin American Research Review 13 (Fall): 108-124.

FONTAINE, R. W. (1977) The Andean Pact: A Political Analysis. Center for Strategic and International Studies, Georgetown University, The Washington Papers 5, 45. Beverly Hills: Sage.

FULLMER, R. G. (1973) "The Andean Common Market: implications for U.S. business." Overseas Business Reports 73 (October): 1-17.

GALL, N. (1976) "Atoms for Brazil, dangers for all." Foreign Policy 26 (Summer): 155-201.

GALVEZ, J. L. and A. LLOSA (1974) Dinámica de la Integración Andina. Lima: Banco Popular del Peru.

GEISEL, E. (1978) "Speech at the signing of the Treaty of Amazonic Cooperation." (mimeo.)

O Globo (1979) May 6: 5.

GORDON, L. (1972) "Brazil's future world role." Orbis (Fall): 621-631.

GRUNWALD, T. [ed.] (1976) Latin America and the World Economy. Beverly Hills: Sage.

HAAS, E. B. (1975) The Obsolescence of Regional Integration Theory. Research Series No. 25. Berkeley: Institute of International Studies, University of California.

——— (1971) "The study of regional integration: reflections of the joy and anguish of pretheorizing," pp. 3-42 in L. Lindberg and S. Scheingold (eds.) Integration: Theory and Research. Cambridge: Harvard Univ. Press.

——— and P. SCHMITTER (1966) "Economics and differential patterns of political integration: projections about unity in Latin America," pp. 259-300 in International Political Communities. New York: Doubleday.

HOPKINS, T. W. (1977) Latin America in World Affairs. Woodbury, New York: Barron's Educational Series.

JAGUARIBE, H. (1975) "El Brazil y la América Latina." Estudios Internationales (January-March).

Junta del Acuerdo de Cartagena (1979) Evaluación del Progreso de Integración, 1969-1979. Lima: Junta.

KATZMAN, K. T. (n.d.) "Converting resources and economic power into political power." (mimeo.)

KEARNS, K. C. (1972) "The Andean common market: a new thrust at economic integration in Latin America." J. of Interamerican Studies 14 (February): 225-249.

KUCZYNSKI, M. and D. HUELIN (1973) The Andean Group: Trade, Industry, and Foreign Investment. London: Latin American Publications Fund.

LAFER, C. (1979) "Política exterior Brasileira: balanco e perspectivas." [Separata da Revista] Dados 22: 49-62.

Latin America Economic Report (1979a) "Ten years on, Andean Pact forces an uphill strategy." June 8: 174.

——— (1979b) "Brazil in Africa: radical politics boost business." June 22: 186.

——— (1979c) "Jari: poison or healthy medicine?" July 13: 211.

——— (1978) "The Amazon pact: a forest of problems." May 19: 147.

——— (1977) "Brazil strengthens the African connection." October 21: 178.

Latin America Regional Reports (1980a) January 14.

——— (1980b) October 3.

Latin America Weekly Report (1980a) March 21.

——— (1980b) May 9.

LINDBERG, L. (1970) "Political integration as a multidimensional phenomenon requiring multi-variable measurement." International Organization 24 (Autumn): 649-732.

MERCADO JARRIN E. (1978) "Pacto Amazónico: dominación o integración?" Nueva Sociedad 37 (julio/agosto): 26-30.

MILENKY, E. S. (1977) "Latin America's multilateral diplomacy: integration, disintegration, and interdependence." International Affairs (Royal Institute of International Affairs) 53 (January): 73-96.

——— (1973) The Politics of Regional Organization in Latin America: The Latin American Free Trade Association. New York: Praeger.

——— (1971) "From integration to developmental nationalism: the Andean Group 1965-1971." Inter-American Economic Affairs 25 (Winter): 77-91.

MITRANY, D. (1966) A Working Peace System. Chicago: Quadrangle.

MORAWETZ, D. (1972) Economic Integration Among Less Developed Countries With Special Reference to the Andean Group. Cambridge, Harvard University: Development Advisory Service.

MYTELKA, L. K. (1979) Regional Development and the Global Economy: The Multinational Corporation, Technology, and Andean Integration. New Haven, CT: Yale Univ. Press.

NUN PEICHIHOVICI, B. (1971) Integración Subregional Andina. Santiago: Editorial Andrés Bello: 69-70.

NYE, J. S. (1971) Peace in Parts: Integration and Conflict in Regional Organization. Boston: Little, Brown.

——— (1968a) "Patterns and catalysts in regional integration," pp. 333-349 in J.S. Nye (ed.) International Regionalism. Boston: Little, Brown.

——— (1968b) "Comparative regional integration: concept and measurement." International Organization 22 (Autumn): 855-880.

PENTLAND, C. (1973) International Theory and European Integration. New York: Macmillan.

PERRY, W. (1976) Contemporary Brazilian Foreign Policy: The International Strategy of an Emerging Power. Foreign Policy Papers 2, 6. Beverly Hills: Sage.

PETRAS, J. F. and M. H. MORLEY (1978) "The rise and fall of regional economic nationalism in the Andean countries, 1969-1977." Social and Economic Studies 27 (June): 153-170.

PUCHALA, D. J. (1975) "Domestic politics and regional harmonization in the European communities." World Politics 27 (July): 496-520.

RICUPERO, R. (1977) "A cooperacão regional na Amazonia." Itamaraty, November. (mimeo)

ROSENBAUM, J. H. (1972) "Brazil's foreign policy: developmentalism and beyond." Orbis 16 (Spring): 58-84.

——— (1968) "A critique of the Brazilian Foreign Service." J. of Developing Areas (April): 377-392.

SCHILLING, P. C. (1978) El Expansionismo Brasileño. Mexico: El Cid Editor.

SCHMITTER, P. (1972) "Autonomy or dependence as regional integration outcomes: Central America." Research Series 17. Berkeley: Institute of International Studies, University of California.

——— (1970a) "Central American integration: spill-over, spill-around, or encapsulation." J. of Common Market Studies 9 (September): 1-48.

——— (1970b) "A revised theory of regional integration." International Organization 24 (Autumn): 233-265.

SCHNEIDER, R. M. (1977) Foreign Policy of A Future World Power. Boulder, CO: Westview Press.

SELCHER, W. (1978). Brazil's Multilateral Relations: Between First and Third Worlds. Boulder, Colorado: Westview.

——— (1974) The Afro-Asian Dimension of Brazilian Foreign Policy, 1956-1972. Gainesville: Univ. of Florida Press.

SKIDMORE, E. T. (1976) "Brazil's changing role in the international system: implications for U.S. policy." pp. 9-40 in R. Roett (ed.) Brazil in the Seventies. Washington, DC: American Enterprise Institute.

SLOAN, J. J. (1971) "The strategy of developmental regionalism: benefits, distribution, obstacles, and capabilities." J. of Common Market Studies 10 (December): 138-162.

STORRS, K. (1973) Brazil's Independent Foreign Policy, 1964-1969. Ithaca: Cornell Univ. Press.

THEBERGE, J. D. and R. W. FONTAINE (1977) Latin America: Struggle for Progress. Lexington, MA: D. C. Heath.

Elizabeth G. Ferris, Assistant Professor of Political Science at Miami University, Oxford, Ohio, is the coeditor of Latin America's Foreign Policies: Global and Regional Dimensions *(Westview, 1981). Her articles on Latin American foreign policies have appeared in numerous journals.*

FRANCISCO E. THOUMI
Inter-American Development Bank
Washington, D.C.

HUMAN RIGHTS POLICY
Basic Human Needs and Economic Implications for LDCs

I. Introduction

Economic development—defined by growth of GNP per capita—among the poor countries of the world during the last 25 years has been higher than in almost any other period in mankind's history. Although this growth might have not been as high as that expected by some policy makers, the 1950-1975 period shows an overall improvement over the recent past. In spite of this apparent surge in growth, many policy makers and social scientists have shown disappointment and dismay at some characteristics of the recent increases in GNP (Morawetz, 1977).

First, absolute poverty is still widespread in most LDCs. It has been argued that growth in most countries has benefited only certain population groups whose income was substantially above poverty levels. Second, relative poverty has not declined in most LDCs, as the income distributions of most countries have not become more egalitarian. Furthermore, it has been argued that in some of the fastest growing LDCs income distribution has actually become more unequal. Third, the fast income growth of LDCs has taken place at a time when per capita income in the

AUTHOR'S NOTE: The opinions and ideas expressed in this article are those of the author only and do not represent the policies of the Inter-American Development Bank. The author acknowledges previous draft comments made by John Elac, Martin Lu, Miguel Urrutia, Jan Peter Wogart, and a journal referee.

Journal of Interamerican Studies and World Affairs, Vol. 23 No. 2, May 1981 177-201

MDCs was also growing. The actual dollar gap in per capita terms between LDCs and MDCs has actually increased. Fourth, the income growth process of LDCs has been accompanied by a fast change in social values.

"Modernization" has implied westernization. The change in social values has increased social tensions, intergeneration gaps, identity conflicts, and raised economic expectations. It can be argued that the introduction of new commodities to LDCs markets, the growth of the various media systems, the growth of advertising and other marketing techniques, the increased urbanization process, and other changes brought up by the development process have increased people's dissatisfaction, alienation and unhappiness in the presence of rising per capita income. In short, income growth per se has not solved some of the main development problems.

In view of the failure of income growth just described, governments, development institutions, and social scientists have in later years shifted emphasis from economic growth policies and recommendations toward policies, recommendations, and development measures that reflect other social goals and achievements. Thus, a more equal income distribution, the improved quality of life, the kind and magnitude of human rights enjoyed in a country and other social characteristics have become policy goals. The fact that goals other than income growth and of trade-offs between these goals and income growth are acknowledged, indicates that income growth is only one variable in the objective function of the governments.

While there is no consensus on the meaning and limitations of terms such as human rights, basic human needs, and social goals, governments and other policy-making institutions have proceeded pragmatically and have supported development programs that provide housing, health, nutrition, education, and other elements thought to be basic for the well-being of the poor. These policies are being followed on the belief that results will be achieved which are closer to the goals of a more equal and free society than the income growth policies followed until recently.

This article explores the concepts of human rights and basic human needs (BHN) and discusses some of the policy implications of accepting human rights and BHN as goals for an LDC.

II. Human Rights and Basic Human Needs Concepts

HUMAN RIGHTS

Human beings exercise their rights every time they choose some of their actions. Total absence of rights exists when somebody imposes on an individual a behavioral pattern which is completely determined. It is difficult to think of the complete absence of human rights except when the individual is killed; in any other circumstance, the individual has at least a minuscule amount of rights. For instance, a prisoner normally has the right of pacing inside his cell but might not have the right to walk out of it. While one might think of some of these rights as irrelevant, they are still rights. A citizen from an authoritarian nation may have the right to decide when and where to go within his city but might be required a permit to travel to a different city. In this case his intracity travel rights are greater than his intercity travel rights.

These examples are very useful in demonstrating that a basic relationship between human rights and individual choice exists. A right exists when individuals have alternatives—that is, when they can choose. *In a very general and abstract way, human rights can be defined simply as the alternatives and action included in the set of feasible choices of an individual. When an alternative is not in the individual's feasible set, that alternative is not a right.*[1]

The inclusion of an alternative in the individual's feasible set depends on various kinds of constraints which limit feasible choices. The power structure of the society restricts each individual's feasible set in various ways. The legal system indicates that some actions are not approved. The hierarchy of any society restricts and regulates the relations among human beings and thus limits their actions. The powerful can also impose behavioral constraints outside the legal system, as they sometimes can impose their own wills on the less powerful. There are also economic restrictions, such as the individual's wealth and income constraining the number of activities that he can undertake. It can be said, then, that every constraint defines a particular set of rights. The set of laws of a society determines whether the action is legal; the informal hierarchical and power patterns determine whether the action is approved; the economic constraints determine which actions can be financially undertaken. It can be said that there are legal, social, and economic rights. The definition of human rights as stated requires the conjunction of legal, social, and economic rights so that a right can be called a human right. In an abstract way, human rights are the intersection of the set of legal, social, and economic rights.

Besides the three external constraints on the individual's behavior described above, there is an internal restriction imposed by the individual's set of moral values. In terms of economic theory, this restriction may be introduced through the "utility function;" it separates the constraints imposed by factors external to the individual from the one imposed by the individual's own morals. The individual's morals may produce a situation in which actions and alternatives included in the human rights set are never undertaken as they are considered immoral, such as eating pork in the case of orthodox Moslems and Jews.

The constraints of the feasible set can be bent and broken by each individual. However, braking these constraints brings at least a threat of punishment, if not punishment itself. Breaking the rules set by the legal, hierarchical, and power systems of the society bring about a threat of reprisal on the individual. Breaking the economic constraints also brings the risk of punishment, as violations on somebody else's income and wealth are punished through the legal system.[2]

It could also be argued that the individual who breaks the behavior rules established by his own morals receives self-punishment as his conscience, which defines the morals, punishes the individual.[3]

All the constraints on personal behavior depend on the metaphysics of the individual and of the individuals in power. The moral restrictions self-imposed by individuals obviously depend on what the individuals' convictions about their behavior and role in society are. Restrictions imposed by the society's explicit and implicit behavior codes depend on the convictions of the individuals in power in that society. Finally, the economic constraints of an individual also depend on the metaphysics of the society, since the distribution of wealth and income are based on the fundamental convictions of the society—convictions on ownership and property rights, the combination of public and private goods to be produced, and in general, about the nature of the economic system adopted by the society. The society's economic constraint also depends on its capital stock and its production level plus or minus international transfers. Individuals have their own feasible set constrained by economic factors, as own wealth and income are limited.

The importance of metaphysics in determining human rights cannot be overstated. To illustrate this point, let us consider two polar sets of convictions about the nature of men and society. One can conceive the concept of a society in two fundamentally different ways: (1) as an association of free individuals who belong to the society because it is convenient for them to do so, or as (2) an entity in which each individual is assigned a position or function to maximize a concept of social well-being. The behavioral options open to members of societies regulated by laws and customs inspired by these two polar sets of convictions are quite different. In the society inspired by the former concept of society, each individual will have more freedom of movement, consumption ideology, and so on. In this kind of society, individuals are also less dependent on the society or central government. Their success or failure depends very much on themselves; he cannot easily blame the society for not succeeding. In the latter concept of society, each individual has less freedom of choice but can depend more on society. In extreme versions of this type of society, each individual's life is predetermined by birth, and present status does not depend on the individual's actions. As one always has to live in a society, one would like to make a choice between these two polar cases. However, this choice cannot be made on purely positive grounds. Any choice made depends unequivocally on the metaphysics of the individual choosing. In other words, a Martian without any convictions on what human life is all about cannot logically choose between the two models of society just described.

As seen above, the determination of human rights depends not only on the metaphysics, but also on the economic limitations of the society. The exercise of most human actions require the use and consumption of economic resources. In those cases, the informal and legal moral codes of a society determine what an individual may do, while the economic restrictions determine which choices among the morally and legally acceptable are actually exercised.

The economic constraint on human choices creates some interesting relationships among rights. For instance, a poor individual's legal right to eat cannot be exercised when he lacks income. In cases in which the exercise of rights directly consumes resources, trade-offs and complementarities among rights become clear. High-income individuals can exercise much more rights than low income individuals, however, they all have to choose which rights to exercise. This also indicates that citizens of rich countries on the average can exercise more rights than citizens of poor countries. As long as feasible choices and economic development are related, citizens of developed countries will enjoy a greater quantity and variety of human rights.

The economic limitations on human rights imply that the amount of human rights of each individual in a society depends also on the rights of other individuals, and that trade-offs among the rights of the various individuals exist. In other words, an individual's feasible set normally cannot be increased without diminishing somebody else's feasible set. However, this could be possible in cases where externalities are important, such as when the improved health of a society in general decreases the individuals' probability to catch an illness. Complementarities among rights are also possible: education and nutrition are complementary rights, since better nutrition increases the ability to learn.

There are also cases in which the trade-offs among various human rights are less obvious, but nonetheless real. Inasmuch as present feasible choice sets and consumption depend on what percentage of GNP is saved and invested and inasmuch as future feasible choice sets also depend on present investment, there is a trade-off between present and future consumption levels, and thus, between present and future rights exercised.

A more subtle trade-off may also exist between some rights, such as freedom of expression and of the press, and current and future consumption levels and future political freedoms. For example, it can be aruged that in a politically polarized country, political freedom can lead to strikes and violence that would cripple present output. More importantly, political freedom may lead to frequent government changes from extreme right to extreme left and vice versa, which can substantially lower total income, investment, and thus, future consumption and possibly future political freedoms. Unfortunately, while the existence of these trade-offs among rights can be acknowledged, their importance cannot be quantified. In other words, there is no knowledge about the magnitude of these trade-offs which could be used to formulate a policy not based on convictions.

The preceding discussion illustrates the need to differentiate two types of rights: legal and social rights and economic rights. Legislation and social values in many countries establish the right of an individual to do something. However, economic constraints on his feasible choice set actually prevent the individual from exercising those legal and socially approved alternatives. For example, the constitutions of some Latin American countries establish the right to obtain a minimum level of education. However, there are not enough schools, teachers, and so on, so that many individuals cannot exercise these legal rights. In these cases, one can argue that either legal rights are written into law to pay lip service to Western individualistic traditions or that they are actually policy goals of the society. The set of policies actually followed by the governments can be considered as their "revealed preference" so that the actual meaning of the legal rights can be established.

To summarize, and thinking about possible policy interpretations and recommendations, two main facts can be concluded from the above discussion. First, human rights cannot be determined or listed without making value judgments—that is, without appealing to metaphysical convictions. Second, human rights cannot be considered as free goods in the economic sense—that is, human rights are limited by economic restrictions. This second conclusion also implies that human rights with economic elements cannot be expanded indefinitely and that implicit or explicit trade-offs exist both among the kinds of human rights and among the people who have them. This last conclusion is very important from a policy viewpoint, as more of one economic right for a person or group of persons entails less rights for somebody else, except in some cases when externalities are present.

Legal rights, economic rights, and social rights can be defined as sets of alternatives and activities suitable to be realized by the individual. Human rights are then the intersection of the legal, social, and economic rights sets. A priori, there is no reason for either of these three sets of rights to be contained by their intersection, thus, it can be expected that some legal or social rights cannot be exercised because of economic constraints that do not permit them to be exercised, and vice versa, some economic rights cannot be exercised because of social and/or legal restrictions.

BASIC HUMAN NEEDS (BHN) AND POLICY GOALS

Basic human needs can be defined in various ways; most authors, however, shy away from commiting themselves to a rigorous definition[4] and define BHN simply as minimum requirements of certain elements which are required for people to survive, to reach an income level above poverty, to reach a decent standard of living, and so on. While BHN definitions in these terms are attractive from a policy point of view, they fail to explain what BHN is and how the concept is formed.

In orthodox economic theory there is no such a thing as BHN. Traditional welfare theory, based on the liberal ideas of the European philosophers of the eighteenth and nineteenth centuries, fundamentally accepts that humans are independent to choose and act by themselves. Consumer patterns and income distribution are not questioned. Ideally, within the theory, individual wealth and income depend on the way in which the individuals work and act as free entities in the society. The government should not attempt to change the distribution of income nor to affect consumer patterns, as these interventions would violate the right of individual freedom. Basically, orthodox welfare theory assumes that everyone is created equal and that the current incomes and wealth distribution depends on how the individual works in the society. Within this framework, there are no good and bad commodities, as no morals are attached to certain types of consumption. Luxury commodities are simply commodities with high-income elasticity, at high levels of income, while basic commodities are those in which a substantial proportion of the income is spent at low-income levels.

The acceptance of BHN implies a ranking among commodities and services. To obtain a definition of BHN one can proceed in the following way: first, take the addition of the sets of legal, social, and economic rights of a society; second, define a ranking among those rights—that is, establish a priority system among them. This ranking is not unique, and it would vary with the metaphysics of the individual or governemnt making it. Third, a line in the ranking is drawn. Rights with higher ranking or priority than the line drawn are then defined as basic needs. In this fashion, BHN is defined as a subset of the addition of legal, social, and economic rights. However, they are not necessarily a subset of any of the three added sets. In other words, BHN consists of rights that individuals have on moral grounds which might not be compatible with the legal, social and/or economic framework of the society.

THE EMPIRICAL ASPECTS OF BASIC NEEDS AND HUMAN RIGHTS

As shown above, the basic theoretical framework used to describe and analyze BHN and human rights is rather abstract but quite simple. In spite of the theoretical simplicity of these concepts, their empirical verification is very complex. To give empirical meaning to the BHN and human rights concepts, one needs to name the dimensions of the feasibility sets discussed above. As it will be shown, this is not easy. However, let us begin by looking carefully at some of the attempts to deal with this problem.

A recent United Nations publication (United Nations, 1977) classifies and ranks basic human needs. The classification is the following:

A. *Basic biological needs*

Adequate food;
Shelter and protection against climatic impacts;
Protection against disease and provision of a favorable health environment;
Protection against pollution of air, water and soil; and
Protection against noise.

B. *Economic needs*

Opportunity for work and job training;
Opportunity to improve living standards and satisfy basic biological needs;
Facilities to perform daily economic activities; and
Access to infrastructure facilities.

C. *Social needs*

(a) *Needs of the individual*

Responsive government and personal security;
Opportunity for social participation and interaction;
Opportunity for community cohesion and communication;
Provisions for social mobility and flexibility;
Opportunity for intellectual development and education;
Access to recreation for physical and mental health;
Opportunity to retain and develop specific cultural traditions;
Opportunity to fulfill spiritual needs; and
Opportunity to participate and enjoy visual and performing arts, art, and architecture.

(b) *Needs of families*

A home providing adequate space for privacy and social interaction;
Stability and affection;
Access to adequate child and family care facilities; and
Access to family planning information and assistance.

While acknowledging the hierarchical nature of basic needs, the U.N. publication does not commit itself to any specific ranking. It does seem that the priority of basic needs declines as one goes down on each of the categories A, B, C(a) and C(b) above. However, there is no hint as to how one can compare the ranking of say the third basic need of category "A" with the second of category "B."

It is also acknowledged that while one can list needs, their qualitative nature makes it impossible to establish positively "which goals and priorities are derived from actual needs" (United Nations, 1977: 10) and that "even less is known about the effectiveness of measures proposed in development plants to attain social goals" (1977: 10).

One striking characteristic of the attempts to spell out the basic needs is their lack of specificity. The classification written above includes repeatedly the words opportunity, protection, and adequate, without specifying the actual meaning of those words. Let us illustrate the complexities that arise when attempting to specify a basic need such as "adequate food." One can increase the degree of specificity by stating that adequate food is the amount and quality of food that allows people to survive. However, this definition is also very indefinite, as it does not delineate the length and quality of the survival. It is known that there is a minimum caloric intake required by the body to avoid death by starvation. Is this minimum amount useful to define basic needs? Medical science has determined other rather arbitrary criteria of minimum levels of food required to lead a "meaningful life." Can those criteria be used to define basic food needs? Further problems arise, as all food standards are established according to some nutritional characteristics of food, such as calories, vitamins, and so on, which are included in food and not in terms of specific goods. This type of definition raises the following issue: Should minimum nutritional requirements be supplied taking the current dietary patterns, or should they be supplied through other means? The answer to this question is extremely important from a policy point of view, as it would be a determining factor in establishing minimum income levels allowing individuals to satisfy their basic needs.

Similar problems arise when attempting to define basic needs in housing, health, clothing, and education. In general, there is no way in which those needs can be defined in a positive way—as adequate housing, health, and so on, are not concepts which can be defined absolutely.

Further difficulties arise when one considers that the satisfaction of one BHN might require the satisfaction of a previous one. For example, in today's world, opportunity for intellectual development and education (the fifth individual social need listed) requires the previous achievement of a minimum level of nutrition (the first basic biological need). Similarly, the actual exercise of many of the civil liberties so dear to Western-developed governments—such as freedom of the press and of ideas, free political participation, and freedom of mobility—can be exercised only by those individuals who are literate, well nourished, and healthy. In these situations, the emphasis by governments of some developed countries on the civil liberties in some LDCs, disregarding the satisfaction of other prerequired BHN, could lead to the ironic paradox of advocating the guarantee of some BHN which could be exercised only by a minority of citizens of LDC.

BASIC HUMAN NEEDS POLICY ISSUES

To set a BHN policy, it is necessary to tackle the following main issues at the beginning. First, as BHNs are rights, it is necessary to explain the empirical content of the word "rights." Different interpretations can be given: (1) A right can be something to which every individual is entitled; thus, every individual should have the capacity to obtain it; (2) A right is something which reflects a long-term social goal. In a way, it represents a characteristic of an ideal society, but not of today's society. Second, empirically workable definitions of BHN have to be established, for without them a policy cannot be stated.

To illustrate the importance of these issues and their policy implications, let us begin by empirically defining BHN as minimum standards of nutrition, shelter, education, health, transportation, clothing, and communications and estimating in a rough way their price tag as follows:[5]

(A) A study of poverty in 10 Latin American cities (Arellano, 1975) indicates that in 1969, given a basic diet of 27 items, it took approximately $110 a year to provide adequate nutrition to an individual in Colombia. At 1976 food prices, this figure is around $200.
(B) In the conference Habitat, an estimate of $4,000 was produced as the minimum capital needed to provide shelter to a family of 6. This estimate includes housing services excluding land. Assuming a 10% real rate of return, this is equivalent to a flow of $400 a year per family or $67 a year per capita.
(C) Rough education costs for Latin America indicate that the actual cost of elementary education for four years—the minimum necessary to teach a person to read and write so that illiteracy is eliminated—is $500 per student, or $50 per capita in flow terms.
(D) Costs of medicine are very difficult to determine. Our educated guess is that in order to guarantee pure water supply and minimum medical attention and treatment, $50 per year and per person are necessary.
(E) Transportation: minimum social costs can be estimated at 15¢ per urban bus ride. Assuming the equivalent of one ride per person/day, a figure of $45 per person/year is obtained.
(F) Clothing costs per person/year can be put at $20.
(G) Communication costs can be set at $10.

The previous figures are based on a few careful estimates and various ballpark estimates. However, they are useful to obtain a rough figure of $462 of 1976 dollars per capita as the requirement to provide a minimum set of BHN. These basic human needs include a diet of only 27 items, which is varied, but which includes less items than that found in the markets of Latin American countries. A more diversified diet providing the same nutrition is more expensive. The basic human needs estimated do not include any education beyond the fourth grade, except for that of the teachers and medical people; they do not include any transportation, except in public buses; and include only minimum expenditures in medical services, clothing, and communications. These minimum levels of basic needs do not include any infrastructure investments such as roads, telephone lines, and airports. They also exclude investments in some very capital-intensive industries such as petrochemicals, and in military, security, and internal order items. Still, the per capita cost of these basic needs is $462, which exceeds the per capita income of some countries.

As pointed out above, the policy implications of considering BHN as an entitlement vs. a goal are extremely important. To illustrate this point, let's look at what acceptance of the duty to satisfy basic needs would entail in the short-run in a medium-income country such as Colombia, with a $600 per capita income in 1976 dollars.

Let's assume that the income distribution of wage earners for 1964 has remained constant and that the wage earners and personal distributions are the same. Table 1, derived from Urrutia and Berry's work (1975), summarizes this distribution. In order to satsify basic needs, Colombia would have to spend approximately 77% of her total gross national product (462/600 = .77).

As Table 1 shows in column 5, the average income of the three poorest groups (61% of the population) is only 16%, 38%, and 59% of the national average and is clearly insufficient to satisfy the cost of the estimated BHN basket of 77% of the income per capita of the country. Thus, in order to guarantee these groups an income sufficient to cover their basic needs, a real transfer of income is necessary. This transfer is estimated in Table 2. The figure comes to 27.5% GNP. These transfers could be achieved by taxing away 83% of the after tax income of the richest 1.5% of the population which receives 20.2% of the GNP, and also by taxing away 30.8% of the income of the second richest group (9.3% of the population), which receives 29.2% of GNP. These taxes will still leave the top 10.8% of the population as the richest group, with an income of 2.11 times the national average.

Current total taxes in Colombia amount to 11% of GNP. This figure includes direct and indirect taxes. Direct taxes are about 7% of GNP. In order to transfer resources to the poorest 61% of the population so that they can satisfy their basic needs, a fourfold increase in direct taxes—all to be paid by the richest 10% of the population—is necessary.

TABLE 1
Colombia's Income Distribution

1 ACCUMULATED PERCENTAGE OF POPULATION	2 PERCENTAGE OF POPULATION IN GROUP	3 ACCUMULATED PERCENTAGE OF INCOME	4 PERCENTAGE OF INCOME P/GROUP	5 COLUMN 4 / COLUMN 2
0.0		0.0		
	25.0		4.0	.16
25.0		4.0		
	27.5		10.5	.38
52.5		14.5		
	8.5		5.0	.59
61.0		19.5		
	11.0		9.1	.83
72.0		28.6		
	8.0		8.3	1.04
80.0		36.9		
	9.2		13.7	1.49
89.2		50.6		
	9.3		29.2	3.14
98.5		79.8		
	1.5		20.2	13.47
100.0		100.0		

The magnitude of the income transfer effort required to satisfy basic needs in the short run is so great that many obvious questions are raised. Are these transfers politically feasible within the existing political system? If the government attempts to transfer that much income, would it destroy the entrepreneurial class? Would it cause the elimination of foreign investment flows? While the answers to these questions can only be empirically determined in that one does not positively know about them unless the transfers are actually attempted, I submit that there is consensus that changes of the magnitude required cannot take place in the short run within the political framework of most of the LDCs of America. What this fundamentally means is that the acceptance of the satisfaction of basic human needs of all the Colombian population in the short run cannot be achieved without a dramatic change in the Colombian political system and income distribution.

Note that the previous exercise includes only the satisfaction of a set of needs describing what can be considered as very primitive western life: minimal education, housing, food, clothing, transportation and communications. The scenario that arises if a

TABLE 2
Estimation of GNP Transfers Necessary to Guarantee Basic Needs Satisfaction

NATURE OF TRANSFERS	MAGNITUDE OF TRANSFERS
To poorest group per person:	462 - (600x.16) = 366
To second poorest group per person in group:	462 - (600x.38) = 234
To third poorest group per person in group:	462 - (600x.59) = 108
To poorest group as percentage of GNP:	$\frac{366}{600}$ x.25 = .153 or 15.3%
To second poorest group as percentage of GNP:	$\frac{234}{600}$ x .275 = .107 or 10.7%
To third poorest group as percentage of GNP	$\frac{108}{600}$ x .085 = .015 or 1.5%
Total as percentage of GNP	27.5%

SOURCE: Table 1.

country such as Colombia were to guarantee the satisfaction of BHN for all its citizens is one which differs dramatically from what many Colombians consider to be their minimum standards. The consumption pattern guaranteeing BHN satisfaction does not include: private cars, airplanes, household appliances, trips abroad, intermediate and superior education, liquor, entertainment, and so on. Actually what arises is the picture of a very austere and egalitarian society closer to a utopia, like the ones described by writers such as Skinner, More or Thoreau, than to a developed Western country.

The BHN whose cost was estimated does not include political rights. The explicit definition of political BHN and political rights encounters much greater difficulty than the definition of any economic rights. The preceding U.N. classification lists "responsive" government and "opportunity" for social participation and interaction as the premier social needs of the individual. These statements are vague enough so that governments of many ideologies could agree on the wording; thus, "opportunity for social participation and interaction" may be interpreted by a

Westerner to mean a right to oppose the government and to participate in electing it, and by a Communist as meaning that individuals have the right to participate in the political one-party system established in the country, following the rules created for that purpose.

Other difficulties arise even after the ideological obstacle is surpassed. Let us assume that the Western capitalist ideology is accepted. Should, then, elections be used as an indication for political BHN satisfaction? What about the power structure that determines the system through which candidates are nominated? What if out of three candidates in a presidential election, two are sons of past presidents and the third one a daughter? What is the meaning of elections in an environment in which 60% of the electorate is illiterate? In what measure does the media affect the way in which people vote? How can a simple majority vote be used to choose among three candidates when two have very similar characteristics, and the third one is very different? These questions do not have any answers, but do raise serious objections to the usefulness of elections as a system that provides political alternatives and that allows the expression of public opinion in many countries.

In spite of all these conceptual difficulties, it may be argued that many Western individual political rights "guaranteed" by the Colombian Constitution—such as freedom of speech and of participation in the elective system—require a larger economic resource commitment to BHN than the one estimated above, such as a higher level of education and higher communication costs. These higher costs could easily produce a situation in which a sum higher than the GNP has to be devoted to BHN satisfaction. In such an event, political rights might conflict with the satisfaction of basic economic needs in the short run, and governments, implicitly or explicitly, have to choose which of those needs to satisfy.

A similar conflicting situation arises when a group in the society determines that their BHN are at a higher level than the one discussed, and has the political power to achieve them. For example, a group in a society can consider that owning a private car, having the use of telephones, having a humanistic college education, traveling abroad at least once in a lifetime, eating beef once a day, and so on are "necessities" without which "they cannot live a decent life." If this group succeeds in guaranteeing their access to such commodities, implicitly they are denying other groups in the society the same items which they define as BHN!

One of the most difficult facts to come to grips with in economic development policy is the simple fact of poverty in a country as a whole. It is not only necessary to accept that there are poor people in a country and that policies should be designed to improve their lot, but it is also necessary to accept that the country in itself is poor—that the income per capita is only $200, $600, or $800, and that the feasible economic policies and goals are constrained by that income restriction. In other words, in a country with an income of only x dollars per capita, the government cannot achieve the goals of a set of policies that implicitly assume an income per capita of twice that amount.

It is also important to note that at higher income levels the conflict between political rights and economic ones may disappear, and actually, a complementary relationship between the two could develop. For instance, a situation of political freedom and representative democracy could be very fertile ground for the development of entrepreneurial activities and higher economic growth. However, at low levels of income, the discussed conflict does exist.

A basically different policy approach is obtained if it is assumed that an income sufficient to satisfy BHN is not a right to which every human is entitled today, but rather, a goal toward which the policy should be directed. In these terms, "BHN is a refocusing of development objectives to specifically reach the poor in LDC's" (Liepziger and Lewis, 1977: 5). "The concept (BHN) encompasses the following elements:

(1) The attainment of certain absolute minimum levels of private consumption for the world's population of food, shelter, and clothing;

(2) The access of the population to the minimum level of essential public services such as safe water, sanitation, health, education, and public transportation;
(3) The participation of the people in the decisions that affect their lives" [Liepziger and Lewis, 1977: 5].[6]

When BHN satisfaction is defined as a long-term goal without actually defining the time framework for the achievement of that goal, policy recommendations become varied, somewhat more general, and the policy trade-offs become blurred. In spite of this lack of specificity, a discussion of these policies is valuable, as it indicates the available alternatives to LDC governments.

First, a set of policies can be designed to lower the cost of BHN satisfaction. As BHN is defined in terms of the characteristics of various goods and not in terms of minimum consumption levels of specific goods, the actual cost of BHN satisfaction depends on the composition of the goods consumed.

It is very important as part of BHN policy to spread out and to increase the knowledge about BHN satisfaction. First, governments and citizens should become aware of facts such as: (1) dietary trade-offs which keep nutrition constant but change the composition of the diets; (2) transportation and housing costs depend on the layout of the cities (U.S. city layouts require higher amounts of energy, more transportation and larger sewage, electricity, water, and other infrastructure costs than traditional Latin American city layouts); (3) the relationship between education and malnutrition; and (4) the relationship between availability of pure drinking water and lower child death rates.

Many more examples of the knowledge required to actually estimate BHN "production functions" and "cost functions" come to mind. However, of fundamental importance is the acknowledgement that the government has to direct policy efforts in the direction of finding and spreading such knowledge.

Second, a set of policies designed to change consumption patterns must be implemented. Orthodox consumer theory shows how a consumer, faced with prices for every good and constrained by his income, maximizes his satisfaction when he is allowed to choose his consumption pattern freely. The theory demonstrates that consumers acting as sovereigns over their own consumption maximize their own well being. Thus, government should not question the consumer's choice. Why, then, should consumption patterns be altered? The orthodox consumption theory fails to justify the case for consumers' sovereignty in the following cases.

First, new commodities are being created constantly. The creation and invention of these goods constantly changes the utility function of every consumer. For example, a 1950 Latin American peasant's utility function did not include transistor radios, color or black and white television, jet airplane transportation, and so on which were included in his function in 1977. While there is no dynamic theory of consumption that explains how new commodities become variables in the utility function, there is a consensus that the increased knowledge of new commodities given a constant real income lowers utility. This is what is commonly known as the "demonstration effect." In the capitalist world, the introduction of new commodities into the utility functions of individuals has not been a subject of economic policy, as the private sector has not had any restrictions on the new commodities it has introduced or advertised. If the demonstration effect is strong enough, a situation in which an individual's real income increases and his utility decreases is possible. This leads to higher incomes and lower satisfaction. The issue of introducing new commodities should be a matter of policy in LDCs. Currently, most governments have a policy implemented by default: the introduction of new commodities is left to the decisions of the private sector. There is no theoretical reason to believe that this implicit policy leads to utility and welfare maximization through time.

Second, most consumers do not have complete knowledge about the effects of consuming many items. In other words, a commodity has characteristics $i=1, 2, ..., n$ in certain quantities, i.e., its impact on total consumption per unit is given by a vector of characteristics $(X_1, X_2, \ldots, X_n)$. However, the consumers do not necessarily perceive all those "n" characteristics and all the correct quantities. So, from the consumers' perception, one unit's consumption of the good could increase consumption by a vector (Y_1, Y_2, Y_3, . . ., Y_m), where $X_i \neq Y_i$ and $m \neq n$. In concrete terms, drinking polluted water satsifies thirst but also can have an effect on the health of the consumer. As the concept of bacteria ("a little animal in the water") is not understood by many ill-educated citizens, their water consumption pattern using their consumer's sovereignty could lead to lower utility than other consumer patterns imposed by a government.

Two kinds of nontraditional policies can be suggested to modify consumption patterns. First, advertising can be controlled and regulated. Private advertising is not designed to provide complete information about the characteristics of a commodity but only to maximize sales. Food advertising concentrates on "crunchiness," sparklingness, texture, taste, and so on, but normally does not give information about nutrition. Note that private advertising is explicitly created to change consumption patterns, thus, it should be required to provide full and accurate information so that consumers' choice can be based on real characteristics of the commodity consumed. Second, a more radical approach can be taken by imposing high consumption taxes and subsidies to alter consumption in a desired way. Depending on the political position of the government, bans can also be put into effect on certain types of consumption, such as limiting downtown transportation to using buses and bicycles.

Third, other traditional economic policies can be designed to increase the degree in which BHN can be satisfied. These traditional policy recommendations can be classified into various somewhat overlapping groups: (1) setting the prices "right;" (2) increasing taxes on the target group; (3) changing the composition of government expending to benefit the low-income target group; and (4) implementing urban and agrarian reforms entailing expropriations.[7]

All these policies coincide greatly with policies designed to improve income distribution. The actual discussion of these policies can be made quite lengthy; only a partial list, however, will be made here as an illustration.[8] These policies include subsidies on the production and consumption of wheat and other cereals; shifts in public expenditure to provide infrastructure for the poor in the urban and rural areas; expansion of public elementary education; development of health delivery systems in the urban poor and rural regions; decrease in military expenditure; elimination of capital subsidies which induce capital-intensive industries that generate few jobs; lowering of the high effective protection for capital intensive industries; income tax increases achieved through higher rates and/or improved collection; excise taxes on luxury items; agrarian reform; urban reform and planning, and so on.

This list can be expanded. However, what is relevant from a policy point of view is not so much to have an ever increasing list of theoretical alternatives, but to have criteria to choose among those alternatives. Economic policy is an art in which decisions are made with the help of economic models, but where general policy guidelines do not exist. The actual policy choice and implementation made will vary in each country depending on various elements, such as the governments' commitments to human rights and BHN satisfaction, the political power structure, and so on. It is important to point out that if a government is committed to BHN satisfaction and follows most of the policies included in the list above, the same government probably will have the political power to redistribute wealth and to achieve a more direct BHN satisfaction in the short run. The actual choice of policies, therefore, is determined on political grounds and not on economic efficiency grounds.

One important characteristic of all the policies listed above is their dependence on institutional and cultural factors. For example, when one recommends "developing health delivery systems," one is not giving a very specific recommendation but rather is suggesting a policy field in which the actual policy implementation will depend on community-specific characteristics, such as the way in which peasants of various countries and regions react to contact with outsiders, to scientific medical treatment, and so on. Today very little factual knowledge exists about the "how to" of BHN policies in most countries, thus, specific policy recommendations cannot be made.

III. Conclusions

This article has defined human rights as consisting of three elements: social, legal, and economic rights; it has then related BHN to human rights and explored a few of the policy issues that arise in attempting to satisfy BHN. The main points that are developed in this essay are:

1. There are trade-offs among the satisfaction of BHN which arise from the economic requirements of BHN. These trade-offs are of two kinds: among various BHN and among the BHN of the different individuals in a society.

2. There might be trade-offs between BHN and other human rights such as political freedom and free speech. However, no quantitative evidence can be given for these trade-offs. This is expected, as political freedom and free speech, and so on, are qualitative entities.

3. It can be strongly argued that BHN satisfaction is a prerequisite for the exercising of political rights. If this is so, a poor country can achieve political rights for a subgroup of citizens only at the expense of BHN satisfaction of other subgroups of citizens.

4. The policy requirements to satisfy BHN in the short run in LDCs are such that radical structural changes in the society are needed. Most existing governments are not likely to be able to implement those changes.

5. The choice of long term policies to satisfy BHN depend on political factors and cultural characteristics. Lack of knowledge about those, as well as the case-specific nature of many policies, prevents the finding of general policy prescriptions.

6. The choice between satisfying BHN in the short run vs. looking at BHN as a long-run policy goal cannot be made without

making metaphysical judgements: therefore, it cannot be looked at from a positive point of view alone. After all, when has mankind lived without metaphysics?

NOTES

1. This definition of human rights could differ from other definitions used by various philosphers, who sometimes differentiate between rights and freedoms, legal and de facto rights, and so on. I use this definition of human rights, in spite of possible complaints from some social scientists, because it complements economic theory and the theory of social choice. This definition does not preclude the possibility of developing different models using other definitions of human rights.

2. Income and wealth in this context do not have to be private, as violations against public wealth and property are also punishable.

3. Some economists could object to this statement, as they can claim that even when the individual's conscience "punishes" an individual, he is maximizing his utility when undertaking the action chosen. However, this does not mean that individual actions do not have internal moral approval or rejection.

4. See for example ILO (1977); Liepziger and Lewis (1977); Streeten and Burki (1978), where a BHN approach to economic development policy is discussed without actually defining BHN.

5. Estimates of the cost of BHN are frequently made in ways similar to the one used in this article. See for example the work of Altimir (1978).

6. A similar approach is followed by Streeten and Burki (1978).

7. Western European and U.S. economists frown on expropriations as policy suggestions. However, the moral foundations of private wealth today in the United States and Western Europe are very different from the foundations of private wealth in Latin America, where wealth is associated with privilege, and the ability to capture rents created by government intervention, and not with individual effort and achievement. Thus, a policy recommendation to redistribute wealth in Latin America is not morally equivalent to the same recommendation in the United States and Western Europe.

8. See Ahluwalia (1974) for a full discussion of these policies.

REFERENCES

AHLUWALIA, M. A. (1974) "The scope for policy intervention," pp. 73-90 in H. Chenery, M. S. Ahluwalia, C.L.G. Bell, J. H. Duloy, and R. Jolly (eds.) Redistribution with Growth. London: Oxford Univ. Press.

ALTIMIR, O. (1978) "La dimensión de la pobreza en América Latina." Santiago, Chile: ECLA [Economic Commission for Latin America]. (mimeo)

ARELLANO, A. (1975) "Hacia una canasta de consumo mínimo." Santiago, Chile: Universidad de Chile. (mimeo)

ILO [International Labor Organization] (1977) Employment Growth and Basic Needs: A One World Problem. New York: Praeger.

LIEPZIGER, D. M. and M. A. LEWIS (1977) "A basic needs approach to development." Washington, DC. (mimeo)

MORAWETZ, D. (1977) Twenty-five Years of Economic Development: 1950-1975. Washington, DC: The World Bank.

STREETEN, P. and S. J. BURKI (1978) "Basic needs: some issues." World Development 6, 3: 411-421.

United Nations (1977) The Social Impact of Housing: Goals, Standards, Social Indicators and Popular Participation. New York: Author.

URRUTIA, M. and R. A. BERRY (1975) La distribución del ingreso en Colombia. Medellín: La carreta.

Francisco E. Thoumi is Chief of the Social Studies Section of the Inter-American Development Bank in Washington, D.C. An economist with degrees from the Universidad de los Andes in Bogotá and the University of Minnesota, he has headed the Section of Industrial Studies in the Departamento Nacional de Planeación de Colombia, has been an economist with the World Bank, and an assistant professor of economics at George Washington University. His articles have appeared in several United States and Latin American economics journals.

REVIEW ESSAY

PORTRAITS OF VENEZUELA

Childers, Victor E. HUMAN RESOURCES DEVELOPMENT: VENEZUELA. Bloomington: International Development Research Center, 1974.

Margolies, Luise, ed. THE VENEZUELA PEASANT IN COUNTRY AND CITY. Caracas: EDIVA, 1979.

Martz, John D. and Enrique A. Baloyra. ELECTORAL MOBILIZATION AND PUBLIC OPINION: THE VENEZUELA CAMPAIGN OF 1973. Chapel Hill: University of North Carolina Press, 1976.

Martz, John D. and Enrique A. Baloyra. POLITICAL ATTITUDES IN VENEZUELA: SOCIETAL CLEAVAGES AND PUBLIC OPINION. Austin: University of Texas Press, 1979.

Steiner, Stan. IN SEARCH OF THE JAGUAR: GROWTH AND PARADOX IN VENEZUELA. New York: Times Books, 1979.

Zago, Angela. AQUI NO HA PASADO NADA. Caracas: Sintesis Dosmil, 1972.

I. General Perspectives

It is a well-worn truth that scholars and observers of Latin America are deeply marked with the imprint of the first country they have known in the region. Thus, people who came to intellectual maturity working in the bitter divisions of Argentina differ markedly in expectations, orientations, and general mood from those who came to know Latin America first through Venezuela. The observation is valid, but a moment's reflection reveals its limitations. Like all clichés, it oversimplifies, assuming that there is a single reality to any nation: one Venezuela, understood and experienced in identical ways by all who study her. But

Journal of Interamerican Studies and World Affairs, Vol. 23 No. 2, May 1981 203-223

like most nations, Venezuela has given cause for grief as well as joy, hope as well as disillusion. Only since World War II has a progressive and increasingly open set of institutions emerged and come to dominate national life. While steady, continuous change does mark recent Venezuela experience, such change has not come without hitches, reversals, contradictions, and deep disagreements over the meaning, form, and proper direction of national development.

Now as in the past there are many Venezuelas, and in a sense each observer finds the nation and people he seeks. Part of understanding Venezuela, or any nation, fully thus lies in bringing to consciousness the inevitable and necessary interaction of ourselves as observers with the changing society we study. In other words, we need to be conscious of the formation of our consciousness about Venezuela and, in this process of self-examination, consider the kind of difference the diverse mental sets brought to the study of Venezuela makes for understanding and analysis. Of course, such self-analysis must be matched with careful attention to the visible transformations of Venezuelan society and of the awareness Venezuelans display about the changes they and their nation have undergone in recent years. These changes are well known: the consolidation of democracy and of a remarkable degree of freedom in a country with strong authoritarian traditions; economic growth with continuing imbalances, inequalities, and dependence on petroleum; "modernization" (that loaded term) with all its associated changes in life-styles and perspectives—urbanization, patterns of mass culture, dress, music, literacy, and the like.

How to sort out the *real* Venezuela? A considerable literature now exists on Venezuela, and a look at this body of work reveals that different schools of thought have to a large extent seen what they came to see. The six books considered here reflect a fairly representative variety of perspectives, both on Venezuela and on social and political analysis as a whole.

An older tradition continues to see Venezuela as a romantic tropical paradise. This point of view is carried forward in Stan Steiner's ill-conceived work, which lays a thin veneer of contemporary economic and political concerns over a base of romantic self-deception. The two volumes by John Martz and Enrique Baloyra illustrate an opposite tendency. They do not idealize the supposed lost values of tropical innocence, but rather take to Venezuela the theories, concepts, tools of analysis, and images of self and society predominant in North American political science. To Martz and Baloyra, Venezuela is a crucial and fascinating laboratory of democracy—in some sense, a mini-United States. Victor Childers moves behind the social and political openness of Venezuela to pose a series of hard questions about benefits, distribution, and opportunities. He takes off from a tradition of analysis concerned to "fine tune" the planning of economic and physical development with human resource growth (e.g., factories to schools), but ends with considerations which point to the need for historical and institutional analysis to grasp more fully Venezuela's problems in human resources development.

The writers on Venezuela considered here address the nation's jarring combinations of vast wealth, social and political openness, and sustained inequalities in several ways. Each directs attention to the personal experience contained in (and often hidden by) such large collective processes as urbanization, migration, or the consolidation of democracy. The volume edited by Luise Margolies brings together Venezuelan and foreign scholars in a focus on the continuing transformations of rural life. Angela Zago's fine memoir of the guerrilla movement humanizes political experience in a similar way. We speak easily of the defeat of the guerrilla movement and the consolidation of democracy in Venezuela. But what did this experience mean to those involved? Who went to the guerrilla fronts? Why? What exactly happened there? Angela Zago's work provides a clearly etched portrait of the motivations, frustrations, and combined personal and political transformations of the generation which fought in the political and guerrilla struggles of the early 1960s.

In evaluating these six works, it is important to bear in mind that the impact of assumptions, concepts, and ideologies on research is normal and inevitable. Everyone—scholar, activist, and average citizen—operates with some conceptual and ideological baggage. The point is not to eliminate this in an illusory search for some single "objective" truth, but rather to work through the process with care and sensitivity to the relation between our consciousness about reality and reality itself. In so doing, we can evaluate different works both for factual accuracy and for the utility of the concepts and ideas they advance. What processes do they highlight? In what way do they make possible a systematic linkage of individual experience, community context, institutional organization, and national as well as international transformations? Are new areas for study and reflection opened? Are the authors themselves open to self-criticism and change? Do they reflect adequately the rich diversity of experience and the intensity of change and conflict characteristic of Venezuela since 1945? Let us see.

II. Studying Venezuelan Society

The six books reviewed here vary enormously in quality. I begin with the romantic image of Venezuela (never very accurate, to be sure) as represented by Stan Steiner's *In Search of the Jaguar.* This is quite simply a bad book—lacking any clear theoretical foundation or explanatory premises, riddled with inaccuracies, and presented in a confused and biased fashion. Steiner sees Venezuela as a sort of lost tropical paradise, a sultry Eden manqué. The descriptions of different towns and regions are full of images of sensuality denied. According to the dust jacket, this book "allows the many voices of Venezuela to speak for themselves," and in the process "portrays what happens when the legendary El Dorado takes on the far more exploitable facade of Arabia of the Americas." But of course the voices of Venezuela "speak" here in response to the questions the author poses. Steiner chooses and organizes material, and his obvious lack of information about Venezuela and understanding of how it came to its present state leads him to a half-baked romanticism which either glorifies the simple virtues of untainted poverty or contents itself with repeating local prejudices.

Several examples illustrate the problem. At one point, Steiner bemoans the fact that young women in the countryside no longer have the skill or inclination to fetch and carry water. He describes this task in lyrical terms, as a "stately procession that takes place every day in every village in the country; the pilgrimage of women to the springs and water holds to bring water to their families, and using that most beautiful tool of rural technology, their own bodies. It is lovely to see" (Steiner, 1970: 83). One wonders if Steiner has ever carried water, or performed this difficult and onerous task everyday. It is easy to romanticize other peoples' poverty.

The absence of theoretical criteria and historical knowledge about Venezuelan development leads Steiner into more serious errors. He repeats the clichés of upper-class conversation and takes their vision of lower classes as true without question. Thus, he quotes a personnel director in Ciudad Guayana who complains that no one tells migrants, especially their children, how to behave properly: They are corrupted by the city and live only for stealing and politics. Things were supposedly different in the countryside: "When something was wrong, they would go to their father and to their priest. In the city they have a political protest. Politics is the religion of the young people in the cities" (1979: 92). But this is pure upper-class prejudice, and Steiner's acceptance of these class-bound clichés betrays his scant understanding of the structure of both rural and urban society, and of the patterns of family life, religion, and politics characteristic of the Ciudad Guayana region and of the nation as a whole.[1]

Steiner does have a nice ear for language, and occasionally comes up with striking images as he describes Venezuela's different regions. He is particularly sensitive to the Americanization of culture in Caracas, and describes it well (Steiner, 1979: 110-114). But a somewhat contradictory theme pursued throughout the book is the persistence of the past. Thus, the antiquity of the Jewish cemetery in Coro is advanced as a possible explanation for the "quickness and restlessness" of Venezuelans (1979: 26). The African heritage of coastal populations receives particular attention and is offered as a basis for their characteristic dance, music, religion, and economic activity (1979: 60, 66). But all this assumes what must be accounted for. The persistence of the past is a historical process not a natural phenomenon, and must be explained, not simply taken for granted.

Finally, there are a number of annoying factual errors. Constant reference is made to the "Guájito" (Steiner, 1979: 45-54). But the area and its inhabitants are *Guajira* and *Guajiro* as a glance at any map would show. Steiner refers to the "dictator Jimenez" (1979: 159) whose proper name is Pérez Jiménez. He speaks of a planned trip to Cumaná to interview Bishop Parra León, to whom he had an introduction, and notes that the bishop is in his 80s (1979: 131), but unfortunately Bishop Parra León was born on August 13, 1911. Steiner despairs of certain knowledge about items like the size of Caracas (1979: 122), but seems to have invested little effort in research on this or other relatively straightforward points. Nagging little problems like these make one lose confidence in the author's judgment. All in all, this is not a useful guide to Venezuela. It purports to be a sensitive, humanizing account of that nation's soul—but in fact it simply advances a confused collection of prejudices, clichés, and half-truths. The subtitle of this book is, "Growth and Paradox in Venezuela," but surely the major paradox of this book is why it was published at all.

With Victor Childers we move into quite a different world. Statistical analysis replaces romantic images, and in some sense gives the lie to them. Childers looks at human resources development in Venezuela in two related senses: first, specific policies and programs in areas like health, education, labor, and nutrition; and second, the relation of such programs to physical development projects. In his view, human resources development is both a result of economic growth and a stimulus to such growth, as a healthy, well-educated population can both produce and consume at higher levels. Childers notes at the outset that these questions take on special and difficult dimensions in Venezuela, where the distortions of the petroleum economy make for an incongruous combination of high aggregate and per capita levels on many standard indices of development along with a series of features more typical of a "dual economy" (Childers, 1974: vii).

A number of key issues and areas in human resources development are explored: labor and the labor market (chapter 1), education (chapter 2), health and nutrition (chapter 3), and family life (chapter 4). Childers' analyses are occasionally noteworthy. With respect to labor, for example, he shows how the capital-intensive focus of development in Venezuela leads both the widespread unemployment and a notable skills shortage. This is partly a matter of inadequate training and partly a result of social attitudes which fail to dignify and reward skilled labor (Childers, 1974: 17, 33). Problems in the labor market are closely tied to educational policies and programs, which Childers sees, somewhat drily, as "a primary processor of human resources and as the supplier of skilled personnel to the productive sector" (1974: 55). He documents the significant quantitative expansion of education in Venezuela, but notes the persistent problem of dropouts.

In terms of health and nutrition, Childers wisely stresses the importance of "positive health," going beyond simple treatment of illness. While the death rate has declined and a number of diseases have been brought under control, the general health of the Venezuelan population is still widely undermined by anemia and parasitic infection. Such problems are closely tied to income and mortality: poor people are more malnourished, more susceptible to disease, and more likely to die young (1974: 98, especially 102, 103). The extent and effect of malnutrition are graphically described: "Between 40% and 50% of Venezuela's pre-school population is estimated to be vulnerable to malnutrition. Severe malnutrition [during infancy] may restrict development of the brain, resulting in permanent mental retardation and below normal intersensory integrative ability. Malnutrition and infection interact in a synergistic manner to undermine the health and development of much of the child population in the world's developing areas. Venezuela's population is not exceptional" (1974: 133).

Childers argues that future development planning must go beyond a concern with expanding the nation's stock of physical capital to a more broadly-based program of human resource development. This involves attention both to quantitative measures (numbers of schools, teachers, innoculations, vitamins, and the like) and to matters of quality: how are teachers trained? What is taught in schools? What values are imparted in the classroom? In the family?

The link of education to the labor market is a particularly good illustration of the problems of human resource planning. It is very difficult to "fine tune" the relation of school graduates to labor market needs. Accurate projections are hard to make, and it is costly in political terms to reorient staff and services to a broader vision of human resources. It is far simpler to build a dam, a mill, or a schoolhouse. Physical projects are visible and the payoffs tangible and immediate, while investments in human resources take longer to mature and are often difficult to see and evaluate.

In closing, Childers (1974: 180) argues that existing development plans, and the structure of the labor market in particular, overemphasize physical projects and thus exacerbate the mismatch of jobs to skills. The scale and type of project need to be reconsidered, as does the quality of education and the need to invest heavily in areas related to success in school, such as health and nutrition.

Institutional factors clearly make a difference here. Thus, a full understanding of human resources development in Venezuela must be grounded in analysis of the evolution and operation of key economic, social, cultural, and political institutions. The attitudes and values crystallized in institutions such as family, church, school, business, and bureaucracy shape the way plans are turned into collective efforts and outcomes. Childers provides a useful baseline, but further analysis must go "behind the quantitative facade" (McGinn and Davis, 1969: 34) to look more closely at the formation and implementation of development plans and at the kind of personal experiences only suggested by the numbers Childers piles up in such impressive fashion. Ideally, his work should be read in conjunction with a body of analysis like the Ciudad Guayana studies, which confront plans, planners, institutions, and processes of economic, social, cultural, and political change in a systematic and fruitful way (see Peattie, 1972; McGinn and Davis, 1969; or Rodwin, 1969).

III. Studying Venezuela Politics

One way to move behind the quantitative facade is to look closely at politics: at ideologies, organizations, participation, careers, and conflicts. Politics is a crucial area for the organization of human experience, providing orientations, meanings, and a sense of identity, and grounding these in structures of collective action which knit individuals and groups together in common effort. The transformation of politics in all these senses has been central to recent change in Venezuela. The formation, consolidation, and persistence of democracy is of great value to Venezuelans, and is, as Robert Alexander has recently argued (1980: 241) "one of the most important things to have happened in Latin America since World War Two." How can we best understand politics in Venezuela?

The two volumes by Martz and Baloyra address politics in Venezuela through examination of organizations, ideologies, and public opinion during a process central to democratic political life—an election campaign. The two books should be read together. The first, *Electoral Mobilization and Public Opinion,* examines the 1973 presidential campaign from the perspective of candidates, party organizations, ideologies, strategies and tactics, and the like. The second, *Political Attitudes in Venezuela,* looks more closely at the attitudes and values of mass publics through a survey conducted during the same election year. The authors bring to both works a commitment to seeing, understanding, and explaining Venezuelan politics using the concepts and tools of analysis of North American political science. How successful are they?

The results are mixed. While the second volume is considerably stronger, both suffer to some extent from a lack of historical depth and a tendency to limit analysis either to the elaboration of definitions, typologies, categories, and taxonomies (especially true in *Electoral Mobilization*), or borrowing selectively from a very limited body of theory, presenting this as *the* theory against which analysis must be set. This latter problem is particularly apparent in *Political Attitudes,* whose findings are often set against a clearly overvalued stock of theory, including attempts to ascribe a "monistic" political tradition to Latin America (Martz and Baloyra, 1979: 46-48), a modernization theory (1979: 95-98 and passim) or such shopworn hypotheses as Lipsett's notions on working-class authoritarianism (1979: 46, 47, 62).

Electoral Mobilization has four parts: The Political Setting (chapters 1-2), The Mobilization of Forces (chapters 3-6), Campaign Implementation (chapters 7-9), and Conclusions on "The Significance of Political Campaigns." Massive amounts of information are presented throughout the book, including useful data on the electoral system, the operation of key electoral institutions, regional differences, candidate selection, and the details of party platforms. The book is basically a narrative account of these various aspects of the campaign, and the chapters have a fairly standard format. Some guiding hypothesis or set of definitions is stated, and then the experience of major and minor groups, parties, and candidates will be reviewed in these terms. The analysis of ideologies and programs in chapter 6 is a case in point: The speeches and platforms of the different parties and candidates are reviewed *seriatim,* in terms of some distinctions laid out at the head of the chapter.

This is perhaps useful as documentation, but does not really contribute much to analysis or understanding. Close examination reveals that most of the "hypotheses" and "propositions" advanced throughout the book are simply definitions.[2] More disturbing, despite the authors' obvious concern with classification and definition, some of the definitions advanced are surprisingly unsatisfying. Thus, "democratic campaigning," which is surely central to this book's very purpose, is left essentially without substance: "Democratic political campaigning is a transitory political system that intermittently appears in competitive party systems" (Martz and Baloyra; 1976: xl).

Clearly, political campaigning is a valid subject, and it is particularly appropriate for Venezuela, one of the few nations in Latin America where campaigns do make a difference. But the book is disappointing. The authors rarely go beyond the elaboration of taxonomies and the "fitting" of data into the boxes their categories provide. But while classification is useful, it should be subordinate to explanation: if typoligies have no link to theory, classification becomes an end in itself, and our understanding of social and political processes is not advanced. We have more categories, but no clearer vision of how and why the different elements fit together. Work of this sort promises more than it can deliver—for while claiming to explain, it simply provides a list of elements to look at. Moreover, the lack of a clear theoretical focus makes for scatter. There is insufficient selectivity here, and much of the book's enormous detail runs to trivia, gossip, and anecdotes of dubious and undemonstrated relevance.

Political Attitudes is quite a different matter. The analysis is clearer, more focused, and much more rigorous. In seven chapters the authors, discuss topics such as the social context of political opinion and organizations (Martz and Baloyra, 1979: ch. 2, 3), cultural diversity and political cleavages as reflected in community formation (1979: ch. 4) and ideology (1979: ch. 5), and the nature and sources of partisanship which receives a rich and suggestive analysis in chapter 6. Seven appendices provide extensive data on the survey, including a full Spanish text of the instrument itself. As with the earlier volume, there is no bibliography, but once again the notes are extensive.

To this reader, the most noteworthy discussions in this book concern (1) the relationship between social class and partisanship and party affiliation; (2) the impact of subcultural diversity and community formation (especially the changing structure of regionalism) on party formation; and (3) the suggestive analysis of age differences in partisanship. Martz and Baloyra demonstrate convincingly that party ties cut across class divisions in Venezuela. Thus, although class consciousness exists, it is not translated into a major political force (1979: 36). There is no significant difference in support of democracy or evaluation of particular groups or policies by social class (1979: 57, 60). There is a close relationship between class and party membership, for partisan political participation is a more important means for the expression of interest among lower-class groups than among their better-off compatriots. Thus, as the authors suggest, making voting obligatory stimulates lower-class political activity:

> It could be argued that critics and discontents of the upper strata participate less because they can afford to, since their higher levels of capacity reflect successful experiences in other areas. By contrast, the lower strata, in spite of their less successful experiences, seem to maximize their participatory rates, especially in the partisan mode, as if to create conditions of obligation that may allow them greater access to influencing public policy. That is, their involvement suggests an attempt to create a network of influence, not available otherwise due to their low social condition [Martz and Baloyra, 1979: 70-71].

Concerning regional differences, Martz and Baloyra address the impact on political life of the well-known changes in regional patterns in Venezuela, which stem from the generalized modernization and massive internal migrations of recent years. They view region as a basis for action, self-image, and community formation and conclude, overall, that its impact in Venezuelan political life is declining. The differences they do find between regions suggest "the permanence of a 'remnant' which expresses a uniqueness of the regional communities," but these differences "do not indicate a marked impact of the regional factor" (1979: 92).

How to account for and understand the impact of region on political life? Martz and Baloyra consider the question in terms of "modernization theory," and find a "theoretical blemish" (1979: 95): "high levels of support for elections and greater frequency of party membership are more characteristic of the more peripheral and rural regions, no matter how one examines them" (1979: 95). Here, the perspectives of "modernization theory" and "social mobilization theory" provide little help, and the authors are forced to conclude that *"modernization is not a critical threshold for participation"* (1979: 98, italics in original). They apparently find this hard to accept (1979: 98, 187), but there is no inherent problem here. Many communities, in Venezuela and elsewhere, have engaged in strenuous, sustained participation of all kinds while remaining low on standard indices of "modernization."

Issues of organization, ideology, and the historical circumstances of change could be considered here, but the authors' devotion to setting their findings against a particular brand of theory makes them sidestep such considerations. This is too bad, for both men are extremely knowledgeable about Venezuelan history and about the evolution, operation, strengths, and weaknesses of the nation's political structures. Their own data on age differences in political participation point in the direction of institutional and historical analysis. Thus, they note that younger voters are more influenced by socioeconomic distinctions than by community context (1979: 163). Older individuals are more oriented to political parties, and indeed, *"have a general orientation to parties which sets them off from the rest of the electorate"* (1979: 163, italics in original). Perhaps older Venezuelans remain tied to the original, vigorous thrust of party organization, ties, and loyalties. They came to political maturity earlier and continue to see politics more through the lens of community structures and party organization than do the new generations which grew up in a more fluid social and political situation.

The final chapter of *Political Attitudes* is less a set of conclusions than a recapitulation of the materials presented throughout the book. Martz and Baloyra note that political attitudes and partisanship present contradictions:

> Lower strata are more critical and cynical, less likely to support coups, more anti-communistic, more supportive of AD, more militantly partisan, less supportive of *desarrollismo*, and less efficacious and capable. Thus, *the social aspect of the contradiction is that those who are yet to benefit from the present state of affairs are least likely to support extremist solutions* (read coups and communism) outside the framework of the democratic regime. In addition, they seem to participate more as if to compensate for their low level of political capacity [Martz and Baloyra, 1979: 186-187, italics in original].

Disregarding the cryptic nature of the last sentence, it is clear that Martz and Baloyra have isolated an important political outcome: The consolidation of democracy has been compatible with relatively unspectacular social and economic redistributions. This suggests that partisanship and democracy are themselves important values and that "the system" clearly manages to retain loyalties (both active commitments and passive grants of legitimacy) without massive social reorganization.

The data and conclusions of *Political Attitudes* suggest the need for further consideration of two sets of questions: (1) the historical formation of regions and communities, and the way this process affects social and political organizations; and (2) the meaning of "the consolidation of democracy" in Venezuela. These matters are addressed in the last two works reviewed here, Luise Margolies' collection of essays on *The Venezuela Peasant in Country and City* and Angela Zago's *Aqui No Ha Pasado Nada.*

IV. Venezuela Experiences: Peasants and Revolutionaries

The Venezuela Peasant in Country and City is a valuable contribution to our understanding of the continuing transformation of the nation's rural population through the spectacular and highly visible migration to the cities. Also through the little noted but important process of intrarural migration and change within the agricultural economies of particular regions, and as part of the general citification of the countryside brought about by the availability of better transportation, media, material goods of all sorts, and the increased presence of a host of national institutions in once isolated towns and villages. As Margolies notes in her introduction, "These processes have wrought qualitative as well as quantitative changes in the nature of the Venezuelan peasantry and have also been responsible for the partial effacement of regional diversities which had been so vigorous in the past" (Margolies, 1979: 7). The volume is handsomely produced, with a number of helpful maps and striking photographs. There is no bibliography or index, but each paper has extensive notes and references.

Three contributions in particular stand out for the light they shed on the inner structure and personal meaning of large-scale processes such as urbanization, migration, and economic transformation: Angelina Pollak-Eltz' paper on "Migration from Barlovento to Caracas" (Margolies, 1979: 29-40); Luise Margolies' "Urbanization and the Family Farm: Structural Antagonism in the Venezuelan Andes" (1979: 55-91); and William Roseberry's illuminating study of the rise and decline of the Andean coffee economy in "On the Economic Formation of Bocono" (1979: 92-114).

Pollak-Eltz sets the process of migration from Barlovento to the capital in a context of the gradual decline of traditional plantation agriculture in the Barlovento region. Migration out of this area is nothing new—since the abolition of slavery, black peasants seeking a better life have abandoned the farms of Barlovento either for work in the surrounding towns or for life in the capital itself. The author traces patterns of migration carefully, noting that the region's proximity to Caracas makes it possible for migrants to begin as individual commuters and thus settle into urban life gradually. Contact with village of origin is maintained through regular visits, participation in local religious life, and a steady flow of remittances. The gradual transition to city life is further evidenced in the housing preference of Barlovento natives in Caracas, who choose *barrios* and *rancho* dwellings reminiscent of former housing whenever possible.

Despite these elements of continuity, Pollak-Eltz acknowledges the great attractiveness of city life for migrants and notes the long-term, perhaps irreversible process of transformation, which is now under way. Migrants "overwhelmingly feel that their economic situation has improved since moving to the metropolitan area" (1979: 38) and praise everything from the street life, nightlights and television of the city, to its schools, health care, and transportation facilities. Initially, migrants maintain many traditional beliefs, and are politically conservative, respecting authority and order (1979: 38), but many of these traits disappear with the second generation, as ties to Balovento decline, religious values and practices lose importance, and political views become more radical (1979: 39). Pollak-Eltz provides a particularly useful insight into the very long-term nature of the migration process and the way in which ties with rural life are shed only slowly, and in a selective manner.

Margolies and Roseberry examine the historical formation and continuing transformations of rural life in the Andean region. Before the advent of petroleum, the Andes were Venezuela's most prosperous region: a refuge from the civil wars which devastated other areas and a source of opportunity and wealth in the growing coffee trade. Coffee was the nation's leading export until well into the 1920s, continuing for some time thereafter to provide income to many. As Margolies (1979: 65) notes, "Between 1873, the year of the first national census, and 1926, the Andean population increased by 120%, and its mean annual growth rate was almost double the national rate." Moreover, under conditions of relatively abundant, fertile, and previously unexploited land, crop yields were high and agricultural livelihoods secure. The large fluctuations in yield caused by soil exhaustion and the irregular rainfall associated with deforestation were still in the future (1979: 75).

With the petroleum boom and the collapse of coffee prices after 1929, the Andean region began a long decline, becoming an "expulsion zone" (Margolies, 1979: 67) with migrants leaving the farms both for other regions and for the growing Andean cities. In this context of decline, Margolies considers the fate of the family farm. Family farms were the basis of the agricultural boom, linked by credit, finance, and marketing relationships to regional and national centers of trade. The world depression destroyed this economy. Even though yields remained high, it became extremely difficult to make a living on the family farm, and a slow process of migration began, gradually increasing and changing in character:

> The migratory process was irreversible and seemingly imperceptible. In town, a certain number of families left yearly to be supplanted by migrants from the rural hamlets. By the 1960s, nearly all the original townspeople had departed, their places taken by ex-peasants. By the late 1950s, a period marked by rapid urbanization on a national scale, the peasants had begun to bypass the town, migrating directly to the large urban areas. Whereas movement to the town had been accomplished by the entire family, the direct movement to the cities fell predominantly to the younger members of the peasant household. Just as the town "suddenly" appeared to be populated by large numbers of ex-peasants, only in the sixties did the peasants pessimistically verbalize the irrevocable reality of the changing family farm, now sustained by a sharply reduced household [1979: 73].

What happens to the farms and families left behind? The departure of children and young adults leads to a manpower shortage, increasing the uncertainties of family farming. Moreover, "migration breeds migration" (Margolies, 1979: 77) as the push of poor living conditions is amplified by the pull of city lights and a culture which denigrates the peasant and rural life in general. The family farm is in decline, and the local cultures based on it are fading out. As Margolies suggests, the future of agriculture lies in the spread of larger, more technologically sophisticated commercial farms. These do not grow out of the transformation of family farms, but rather replace them, for the seed, tools, credits, and technical assistance essential to large-scale farming are not available to the small producer.

Roseberry's work on the Boconó District of Trujillo State complements Margolies by stressing the need to look at continuing agrarian transformations over time. He shows that the coffee economy has never been completely replaced by petroleum and needs to be seen in a dynamic, historical way. Thus, he rejects an exclusive focus either on peasants or on the decline of coffee relative to petroleum. The peasant sector cannot be studied in isolation, but must be seen in the context of its many links with the nonpeasant economy of trade, transport, and credit. Moreover, a prepetroleum/postpetroleum view of Venezuelan agriculture is unsatisfactory, for it leads to "an inevitable tendency to see the prepetroleum-coffee economy as static, as a 'given' which received an external stimulus from the petroleum economy. This would ignore the fact that the coffee economy itself was a historical product, the result of a social process of formation with an explainable trajectory and potential (Margolies, 1979: 94).

Roseberry's discussion of the historical formation of the coffee economy is excellent. He links the evolution of landed property (Margolies, 1979: 95-96, 100) and of coffee production in the nineteenth century both to external demand and to migration into the Andes, as Venezuelans from other regions fled from civil wars while Italian and Spanish immigrants came to the mountain valleys to engage in commerce and farming (1979: 97). He documents the intricate links between exporters, regional buyers, local traders, and producers (1979: 98-99), with particular stress placed on the provision of long-term credit, the development of transportation, and the growth of a local market for goods imported from the outside. This kind of detailed historical analysis allows us to see the rural economy not as a static point from which change begins, but rather as part of a dynamic process of continuing change. Patterns of migration and remaining social relationships become clearer in this light, as do the continued inequalities in the countryside which lead, in the long term, to greater and greater concentrations of land, resources, and access to the benefits of public programs (1979: 106-107), laying the basis for commercial agriculture, which Margolies sees as the "inevitable" successor to the family farm.

The consolidation of democracy in Venezuela has attracted considerable scholarly and popular attention. But in celebrating the undoubted virtues of Venezuelan democracy, it is important not to overlook the costs of this process. In the current tranquility, it is all too convenient to scrub from memory the violence, turmoil, and revolutionary euphoria of the early 1960s. With the defeat of the left, much of this experience was quickly and deliberately forgotten—in politics and in cultural life in general. In the words of Alfredo Chacón (1970: 49):

> The defeat of the Left, which became apparent with Acción Democrática's second electoral victory [1963] and the divisions among revolutionary groups, had an immediate and visible impact on the revolution's cultural contingent. Despite efforts at survival which lasted until 1965 or 1966, in 1964 the intellectual advance guard lost the drive which had characterized its best moments. Its members were overcome by a demoralization comparable in scope and depth only to their own earlier revolutionary euphoria, and the group fell apart.[3]

Angela Zago's beautifully written and insightful memoir of the guerrilla movement, *Aquí No Ha Pasado Nada,* brings this period vividly to life. While the life of a *guerrillera* is of course not typical of the population as a whole, Zago's memoir is important as a reflection of the experience of a group of Venezuelans who set out with high hopes to make a revolution, met with defeat, frustration, unexpected personal conflicts, and failed.[4] Celebrating her twenty-first birthday while under intense attack by government troops, she recalls:

> Eulogio looks at me without speaking. He does not understand my joy, or the stupid things I am saying. Grown up. A full citizen of the Republic. Come girl, can you tell me what you will be when you are grown up? When I was little, I thought that at 21 I would be working for the revolutionary system. When I was little I believed in God [Zago, 1972: 174].

Angela Zago went to the mountains at the age of 20 and stayed for 18 months until sickness led her to return to the city. When she left the city, she had already been a militant of the Communist party for many years ("All I know since the age of 13 is the Party" [Zago, 1972: 85]). She went to the hills because the party decided she was needed there. But in more human terms, her willingness to go to the guerrilla front was also an expression of hatred of inequality and injustic, hopes for change, and a great deal of youthful enthusiasm. At one point she notes that thirty years of *life* is far preferable to sixty years of vegetating (1972: 80). A desire for creative action and a deep commitment to humanizing society are visible throughout. Toward the end of the book, she sums up her motivations this way:

> To the informer who is about to talk. To the comrade who forgot about the meeting and forgot about us. To the old woman who hopes and prays for a good match for

> her daughter. To the women and men of the world: Liiiiiisten. Listen. Excuse me for stopping you. I just wanted to tell you that in many parts of the world we are a group—big, small—of human beings who only want a more human society. Look: that's all it is. You know? Hungry children depress us. Not being able to cry out terrifies us. Protocol suffocates us. Indifference crushes us. Liiiiisten. Excuse me. But you know, here in your country there are young men who torture young men and women. Here in your country there is a plot against the human race, and they want to turn us into animals. Listen. Please don't turn away: it's your race [1972: 198].

Her personal ideals were clearly wrapped up in and subordinate to the party and the revolution. The isolation of life in the guerrilla front amplified the difficulties of integrating such an all-consuming devotion to the party with the normal stresses of personal life. Moreover, as a woman she found herself sexually suspect at all points and expected to conform to a rigid code of morality resembling nothing so much as the views of the "petty bourgeois" society she was struggling to overthrow (Zago, 1972: 53). Revolution came first, and notes of personal affection depress and confuse her: "It is hard to explain. I am afraid of hurting my comrades. I know their problem is basically the same as mine. We are all young. We have all led a life which limits the most simple emotions, and we need someone to give our love to, someone to talk with about our doubts" (1972: 90).

An understandable need. But in fact it was difficult even to acknowledge the existence of personal concerns, let alone their close relation to political commitment. These dilemmas were only expressed and considered freely in Zago's friendship with Argimirio Gabaldón, the guerrilla commander whose letters to her—stressing the need to combine personal warmth and sensitivity with revolutionary commitment—are central to the book (see pp. 94-96). The author was about to join Gabaldón's brigade when the commander was accidentally killed, and from this point on, everything seems to go downhill for Zago. Some time later, after the capture and presumed death of her close friend and comrade Marcelo, Zago reflects at length on the difficulties of combining personal and political commitments:

> It has been so difficult to speak openly. I now remember that we never really managed it. I was always afraid to step over the line, to break our morale. But I also wonder. Can you be a revolutionary while always constraining your feelings? Who is right? Was the Commandante [Argimirio Gabaldón] not a good revolutionary? But these things undermine morale. A revolutionary has no right to think of his own things. Big contradiction. Are my things not the things of the revolution? How have I managed to separate the two? The revolution here, my life there, for later. For when the revolution no longer needs me. And when will the revolution no longer need me? [1972: 188].

What is life like in the guerrilla movement? On her way to the hills, Zago mulls over a romantic image: "Clearly, I might as well be on the moon, I don't have the slightest idea of what a guerrilla front is like. I imagine a file of men in olive green welcoming me. It's bound to be like that. We love theater so much . . . how we enjoy a ceremony. I bet there will be songs and all that" (Zago, 1972: 10-11). In the front itself, Zago was responsible for building the social bases of party organization, and her accounts of developing contacts and groups, dealing with schools, dispensaries, and with such local problems as alcoholism or marital infidelity provide revealing insights into the unspectacular day-to-day work of trying to make a revolution. Occasionally the idyllic image returns, and life in the guerrilla front resembles nothing so much as an armed summer camp (1972: 130-131). But as time passes, Zago's reflections become more somber: There is constant tension and fear, ties to the city are few, and isolation and a sense of stagnation take a growing toll.

Toward the end of the book, Zago describes in detail the experience of struggle against a government encirclement. Troops arrive, occupy the area, and search the villages, fields, and hills. She and her companions narrowly escape death. At one point they are hiding in a field of reeds, which is systematically burned and sprayed with machine gun fire. They are saved only because some local residents were flushed out of hiding in the same operation and were confused with *guerrillos*. Zago conveys a powerful sense of the fear and disorientation felt under the weight of overwhelmingly attack. While evading the troops, she is separated from her companions. Isolated and fearful, she falls prey to nightmares and hallucinations and finally manages to send a note, which expresses her sense of isolation and fear:

> Dear Comrade Marcelo: SOS
>
> Greetings. SOS. I have been alone and without a guide for many days. SOS. I would love to have news of you. SOS. If you have decided to go to the city, or if the enemy has trapped you, please let me know. SOS. I am alone. SOS. I am alone. SOS. I am alone. SOS. I am alone. SOS. SOS.
>
> Greetings. SOS [Zago, 1972: 175].

These passages should be required reading for anyone seriously interested in understanding the guerrilla movement in Venezuela—the hopes on which it rested, the day-to-day activities of its members, and the personal as well as political costs of this difficult and dangerous life. Zago's problems in reconciling her personal and political commitments led to disillusion, but it is important to realize that the disillusion she recounts was not with the idea of revolution, to which she remained strongly committed, but with the party and with the efficacy of the particular strategies and programs of revolutionary action it carried out.

The experience of military encirclement, isolation, and narrow escape from death, along with the death of many friends and comrades, left Angela Zago depressed and seriously ill. "The Party" decides to bring her to the capital for medical treatment. The trip to Caracas, like the book as a whole, is presented in writing of great power. As she suggests, the trip itself was sufficiently surreal to have been described by Breton (Zagos, 1972: 203). Finally, she transfers to a taxi, arrives in Caracas, and confronts the city once again in a scene of enormous depth and emotion with which the book closes.

> I began to walk toward the Plaza Venezuela and I stopped at the corner of the Gran Avenida. Lots of cars passed by. There was a lot of noise. People passed without noticing me. Movement. Movement. Gasoline and dust. And me with my worn yellow dress, of cheap material and down to the middle of my leg. With my rubber-soled shoes. My raggedly cut hair. My eyebrows grown together. My broad shoulders and muscular legs. Me with a torn paper bag and a box of sanitary napkins for sale in any pharmacy or grocery store but which seemed vital to me. Me with two enormous panties in the paper bag, and a great feeling of timidity. I walked near some girls in my own age, with short skirts, powdered faces, lipstick, plucked eyebrows, lashes with mascara and fancy hairdos, carrying books I envied and talking about discoteques while I wondered: "how can I make contact with the Party"? I saw my same city. My city without war. And I thought, before returning to form part of it: *Nothing has happened here* [1972: 204-205, italics in original].

V. Conclusion

Angela Zago's memoir uncovers the personal side of political struggle and suggests that our conventional understandings of "the defeat of the guerrilla movement" and the "consolidation of democracy" may not do justice to the experiences of the period. Perhaps we need other names, other words to capture more truly the quality of experience as lived and understood. What is Venezuela *really* like, after all? What concepts and categories can organize and explain recent Venezuelan life and faithfully reflect the consciousness of Venezuelans themselves as they have undertaken and lived through the striking transformations of the past 35 years? The answer is difficult and elusive, for as I have suggested here, scholars and observers of many kinds have come to Venezuela with very different goals, concepts, and tools of analysis. All in all, the results are mixed, and with Pablo Neruda (1976: 69) we might well say:

> I loved Venezuela but she was not there.
> I sought her among all the names that lived:
> I called and called and no one responded,
> The submerged nation did not respond.

—Daniel H. Levine

NOTES

1. Not surprisingly, Steiner is particularly vulnerable to the myth of Latin "spirituality" being corrupted by *yanqui* technology. Thus, he quotes the production chief of a major oil refinery: "The man who has no philosophy of life is not Venezuelan. In our country, many of the technical people are a little ashamed of being technicians . . . in our hearts we do not want to be a technological power. Secretly we first want to be philosophers and poets. In the refinery you may see technicians wearing safety helmets, but in their back pockets they may have books of poems,' he says a little shyly, as if he is describing himself" (Steiner, 1979: 29).

2. At various points the authors acknowledge the taxonomic nature of their work (1976: 264), and describe it as a "research inventory" (1976: xl), a list of items for study. They also note the tautological quality of many of their arguments (1976: xlii). But more often they see themselves as engaged in "theorizing," "theory building," and work of a "theoretical" nature.

3. Editor's note: The translations of Chacon and Zago are by the author of this article, Daniel H. Levine.

4. A Venezuelan novel which deals with this experience well is Adriano González León's *País Portátil* (1968: 253-254).

REFERENCES

ALEXANDER, R. (1980) "Democracy in Venezuela." Latin American Research Rev. 15 (Summer): 241-247.

CHACON, A. (1970) La Izquierda Cultural Venezolana 1958-1968. Ensayo y Antología. Caracas: Editorial Domingo Fuentes.

GONZALEZ LEON, A. (1968) País Portátil. Barcelona: Editorial Seix Barral, S.A.

McGINN, N. F. and DAVIS, R. G. (1969) Build a Mill, Build a City, Build a School. Industrialization, Urbanization, and Education in Ciudad Cuayana. Cambridge: MIT Press.

NERUDA, P. (1976) "For Venezuela," pp. 69-70 in P. Neruda, Song of Protest. New York: William Morrow.

PEATTIE, L. (1972) The View From the Barrio. Ann Arbor: Univ. of Michigan Press.
RODWIN, L. [ed.] (1969) Planning Urban Growth and Regional Development: The Experience of the Guayana Program of Venezuela. Cambridge: MIT Press.

Daniel H. Levine is Associate Professor of Political Science at the University of Michigan. His research interest in the religious, political, and social life in Latin America, particularly in Venezuela and Colombia, is reflected in two of his recent books, Churches and Politics in Latin America *(Sage, 1980) and* Religion and Politics in Latin America: The Catholic Church in Venezuela and Colombia *(Princeton, forthcoming 1981), as well as numerous articles.*

REVIEW ESSAY

EDUCATION, ETHNICITY, AND HUMANISM
Recent Trends in Mexican Intellectual History

Weinstein, Michael A. THE POLARITY OF MEXICAN THOUGHT: INSTRUMENTALISM AND FINALISM. University Park and London: Pennsylvania State University Press, 1976.

Llinás Alvarez, Edgar. REVOLUCION, EDUCACION Y MEXICANIDAD: LA BUSQUEDA DE LA IDENTIDAD NACIONAL EN EL PENSAMIENTO EDUCATIVO MEXICANO. México: Universidad Nacional Autónoma de Mexico, 1979.

Lipp, Solomon. LEOPOLDO ZEA: FROM MEXICANIDAD TO A PHILOSOPHY OF HISTORY. Waterloo, Ontario: Wilfrid Laurier University Press, 1980.

Krauze, Enrique. DANIEL COSIO VILLEGAS: UNA BIOGRAFIA INTELECTUAL. México: Joaquín Mortiz, 1980.

Béjar Navarro, Raúl. EL MEXICANO: ASPECTOS CULTURALES Y PSICOSOCIALES. México: Universidad Nacional Autónoma de México, 1979.

Mexico has one of the richest and most exciting intellectual histories in the Western hemisphere, its roots stretching back to the 1520s when the first scholar-friars arrived as representatives of the Erasmian age in Spain. Its tight, undeviating history is characterized by service to authority centralized in Mexico City—initially the church, later the secular state—and a rugged, critical alternative to established power. The study of this history has not fared so well as its subject, the professional investment in the field yielding irregular returns ranging from marginal to mainstream. Moreover, the historiography reveals a set of pervasive imbalances—an emphasis on luminaries at the expense of

Journal of Interamerican Studies and World Affairs, Vol. 23 No. 2, May 1981 225-232

lesser figures and on intellectual history from a topical rather than a holistic perspective, an ignorance of intellectual life in the other major cities, a disregard for mentor and institutional relationships, and a seeming reluctance to identify and to use archival source materials.

There are signs, however, that this state of the craft may be changing. Since intellectuals became highly visible during the Echeverría sexennium (1970-1976), there has been renewed interest in Mexican intellectual history. Recently it has been the theme of symposia from Perpignan, France, to Pella, Iowa, as it will be for the VI Conference of United States and Mexican Historians. The books under review, while exhibiting the deficiencies of the discipline, may be read for their successful isolation and explanation of some of the abstract, though no less vital, themes of civilization.

Mexico has long attracted outside attention from non-Mexicanists. Travelers, savants, novelists, and humanists have provided us with insights into Mexico as valuable as those of formal scholarship. The list includes Humboldt, Artaud, Lawrence, Northrop, and Fromm. To this company may be added Michael A. Weinstein. A philosopher by profession but not a trained Mexicanist, Weinstein understandably was first drawn to Mexican culture by reading F.S.C. Northrop's *Meeting of East and West.* Teaching himself to read Spanish with "an introductory grammar, a dictionary, and the collected works of Vasconcelos" (Weinstein, 1976: ix), he went to Mexico in the 1970s to test the hypothesis that Mexican philosophy might be useful in formulating a critique of United States political and behavior theories. From the start his approach was unique, for he drank at the font of information not primarily in Mexico City but in Monterrey with Agustín Basave Fernández del Valle, the highly respected scholar at the University of Nuevo León. The book that resulted from his efforts, *The Polarity of Mexican Thought*, offers cogent testimony to the intellectual values he found in Mexico.

The author's thesis is that twentieth-century Mexican philosophy is a reaction to the materialism of the Porfiriato, associated with positivism, utilitarianism, and evolutionism, and its modern-day continuation in liberalism and Marxism. Weinstein terms the material view of life "instrumentalism," which denotes the human experience derived from egoism, the substitution of means for ends, the calculation of advantage, and the will to power. In both personal and public relations, instrumentalism leads to contingency and exploitation.

Standing in a polar relationship to instrumentalism is "finalism," which describes human action occurring as intrinsic value, disinterest, and spontaneous good. This thesis is elaborated from Antonio Caso's *Existence as Economy and as Charity*, published in 1919. Weinstein treats Caso (1883-1946) both as a finalist and an existentialist, citing José Gaos that Caso's thought anticipated that of Gabriel Marcel. Caso sought to build an ethic founded on the principle of "maximum effort and no advantage." However, he recognized the fact that disinterest could also be interest, though "in the object for itself" and not for ulterior motives. Thus, for Caso the highest human good is reached through charity, "an active renunciation of interest in favor of a fully committed creative action" (Weinstein, 1976: 37).

Both Antonio Caso and José Vasconcelos as leaders of the anti-positivist movement in Mexico were influenced by Henri Bergson's revolt against nineteenth-century absolutisms through his notion of "creative freedom." Vasconcelos, however, departed from Caso's concern with the ethical realm of finalism and articulated a "constructive," or "aesthetic," version of finalism contained in his idea of "organic logic," which precedes instrumental or formal logic. In this philosophy emotion and reason are subordinated to imagination, while "objects of experience" are preserved in their "integrity" and coordinated into a meaningful whole. Weinstein demonstrates how Vasconcelos's universalism is still alive today in Basave's "cosmovision," and he sees finalism at work in the heretofore unstudied thought of sociologist Lucio Mendieta y Núñez.

Weinstein constantly argues the relevance of his theme of the polarization of Mexican thought to understanding the contemporary world. The Mexican thinkers have transferred the nineteenth-century instrumentalism to the imperialism of the twentieth-century, he contends, and he extends the theme to the universal conflict between absolutism and freedom. Although his critique of Mexican thought lies somewhere between a New Left and a greening-of-Mexico approach, Weinstein locates a spiritual center in post-Revolutionary ideas that in fact informs the deepest levels of Mexican experience from art to foreign policy.

José Vasconcelos (1889-1959) is the prototypical intellectual of twentieth-century Mexico. A member of the Ateneo de la Juventud group that since 1906 had been attacking positivism, precipitating the intellectual revolution before the political one, Vasconcelos from the start was involved with politics and the new Revolutionary state. He became one of the few intellectuals who managed to implement an arching vision. As rector of the National University and minister of education in the 1920s, he established the basic relationship of education and the state that exists today. Recently there has been a spate of articles and books (1) embracing the myth of Vasconcelos when they are uncritical studies, and (2) explaining the mystique of the culture hero when they are dispassionate analyses. *Revolución, educación y mexicanidad* by Edgar Llinás Alvarez falls in the middle.

Llinás argues that until 1910, Mexican education was dichotomized by Hispanic and Euro-American traditions. Hispanic education was derived from the culture of the conquest and was centered in the church. Euro-American, or non-Hispanic, models of education were first implanted in Mexico as a result of the Enlightenment and were oriented toward the state. The nineteenth century reinforced the secular, anti-Hispanist ideology, notably through institutional channels like the Literary Institute of Toluca, the National Preparatory School, the Academy of Sciences and Literature, and the National Conferences of Public Instruction held in 1889 and 1890. During the years between the Reform and the Revolution, however, there was still a Hispanist school represented by Trinidad Sánchez Santos, Mariano Cuevas, and Carlos Pereyra that clung to the Catholic basis of social cohesion and decried the French and United States influence in Mexico.

The 1910 Revolution brought the conflict of traditions to a head. The Mexicans, as Llinás explains, knew categorically that they did not want to be Spanish and that they were decidedly not Euro-Americans. Discovering themselves as Mexicans, they were now faced with the question of "what is a Mexican?" Calling the idea of *lo mexicano* the "dominant one in national life" (Llinás, 1979: 19), Llinás traces education's link to national identity, especially in the period 1910-1930. Using concepts of ethnicity, Mexicans groped their way toward an understanding of their cultural *mestizaje* and the roles of the Indian, the mestizo, and the European in their society. But the violent phase of the Revolution left the institutional base of education in a state of flux, and theory could hardly be wedded to practice. Furthermore, in 1917 President Carranza defederalized education and placed it in the hands of municipal authorities. Still there was no revolution in education. The first Michoacán Pedagogical Congress in 1919 reached two conclusions as to the future course of Mexican education: it should be nationalist and predicated on the knowledge of Mexico, and it should selectively utilize worthwhile elements in foreign culture. It remained for Vasconcelos to generate action from this educational synthesis.

If Octavio Paz's idea of the Mexican Revolution as a fiesta has validity, then it is also a useful metaphor for Vasconcelos's embodiment of the Revolution and education in the 1920s. Llinás captures the excitement and dynamism of Vasconcelos's ambitious program for the educational redemption of the masses. He underscores the fact that in his transforming fervor Vaconcelos was adept at using politics and publicity to stimulate social change in matters as diverse as eating habits and musical taste. Vasconcelos, Linás assures us, solved the dilemma of identity by incorporating the Hispanic tradition into Euro-American values; and the Mexicans ceased being the "Yankees of the South" and became "themselves." The author uses his sources skillfully, but it is disappointing that he did not employ SEP archival documentation or at least tell us if it is available.

Among the distinguished intellectual successors of Caso and Vasconcelos in Daniel Cosío Villegas (1898-1976). There is no area of the post-Revolutionary cultural experience in which Cosío did not participate. Widely known for his scholarship, political criticism, and the institutions he developed, he left a myriad of achievements that must be carefully sorted out in order to penetrate the logic of his intellectual commitment to Mexico. This task is ably discharged by Enrique Krauze in his biography of Cosío.

Cosío matured in the creativity of the Mexican 1920s. Even more influential than Caso or Vasconcelos as intellectual mentors were Pedro Henríquez Ureña and, indirectly, Alfonso Reyes. These influences had a profound effect on Cosío with regard to the functions of the writer and the moralist in society. Cosío soon learned the art of cultural survival and could turn his pen to literature as well as to banking reports. He also spent considerable time abroad studying economics. By age 34, he had found a utopian freedom in Spain, where low on funds but high on confidence, he considered advertising his services as an expert researcher, willing to work in Europe on any assignment.

Two years alter Cosío had abandoned his *Wanderjahre* and had returned to Mexico to cope with the educational problems of the post-Revolutionary state. In the space of five years he founded the Fondo de Cultural Económica, the hemispherically important publishing house, and helped organize the Casa de España, an advanced school of liberal arts partially staffed by Spanish Republican exiles, which in 1940 became El Colegio de México. Cosío was a Mexican Walter Lippmann, combining service to the government with moral rigor. He brought order, goals, schedules, thoroughness, and productivity to his institutional work, and not forgetting the lessons of his mentors, he regarded noninvolvement as a supreme value in intellectual activity. In 1947 his essay, "The Mexican Crisis," became a classic point of departure for the critical analysis of post-Revolutionary Mexico, and a year later he conceived his team-written *Historia moderna de México*. His final intellectual contribution came in the last eight years of his life, when he was the leading political commentator during the moral crisis following Tlatelolco.

In this his second study of Mexican intellectuals, Krauze again displays his talent for collecting information from private archives and through interviews to construct unusually intimate portraits of Mexico's "cultural entrepreneurs." Perhaps because of this very ability, his sensitive and earthy account of Cosío's career is marred by its misconception as an "intellectual biography." Some of the anecdotes, while appropriate for a complete biography, intrude upon a story that emphasizes Cosío's intellectuality. More serious is the book's sparse internal analysis of Cosío's thought, especially the scant attention given to his seminal essays in the 1920s. Krauze tells us what but not who Cosío was, since he provides no framework of comparative Mexican intellectual traditions that might reveal Cosío's full meaning. In terms of the organizing principles in Cosío's life, however, the moral one underlying the broad spectrum of Cosío's activities is sharply delineated by Krauze. For the reader sufficiently grounded in the Mexican intellectual experience, this book is a delight.

The diversity of post-Revolutionary intellectual traditions is well illustrated by the case of Leopoldo Zea. His work reflects the legacy of Caso and Vasconcelos, but nevertheless is unique among contemporaries in stressing a hemispheric over a national perspective and in combining the roles of both scholar and originator of ideas. The modern study of Mexican intellectual history began in 1943 with Zea's elucidation of positivism. His next book, on nineteenth-century Latin American thought, lacked the scholarly precision of the first, and with the exception of several smaller works on Mexican ideas, he turned increasingly to the role of pensador, sacrificing in the process most of his research potential. It is primarily Zea's function as philosopher rather than historian of philosophy that is the subject of the book by Solomon Lipp.

In the late 1940s, Zea momentarily left his quest for a Latin American philosophy to spur the academic movement of *lo mexicano*, which, as Llinás argues, was needed to posit a national identity in orienting the institutional policies of the post-Revolution. Much of the preoccupation with defining the Mexican attempted to clarify the implications of ethnicity and to articulate a national social psychology. Thus Zea, taking his cues from the perspectivism of José Ortega y Gasset and Samuel Ramos, wrote articles, organized symposia, and edited books on putative national characteristics and the historical significance of *mestizaje*. But as Zea was to write: Mexicanism was only a "point of departure toward a broader and more responsible task" (Krauze, 1980: 48), and by the late 1950s, when *lo mexicano* was no longer of major concern to intellectuals, Zea returned to his philosophical study of Latin American history.

Ultimately Zea conceives of Mexican and Latin American history in a western context, laying aside, for instance, the question of a possible indigenous or even a mestizo basis to development. For Zea, the dilemma of Latin America resides in the schism produced by the Reformation when northern Europe evolved its modernity contingent upon concepts of the individual's freedom from social and religious restraints. Latin America, however, inherited the older Iberian, Catholic tradition, with its non-Protestant indifference to progress, and by the nineteenth century was unfit to enter the world order as an equal partner. In the ensuing pattern of power relationships, western Europe and especially the United States became the exploiters. Zea made his interpretation in the wake of post-World War II decolonization, which sharpened the world disparity in opportunity already present. By the 1960s he had become the principal Mexican Third World philosopher, noting that Latin America had long ago faced the problems of modernizing according to alien criteria.

Lipp easily sees through Zea's often simplistic, cosmic assessment of western civilization, and indeed his warmth and urbanity frequently rescue Zea from overstatement and rigidity. In explicating Zea's thought, Lipp performs excellently, although he does not consistently place it in historical sequence. The relationship is not clear between the *lo mexicano* intellectuals in the first part of the book and Zea, who only enters the book in the second part. Do the thinkers who precede Zea constitute a roots linkage to him, and are the thinkers posterior to Zea influenced by him? Lipp does not tell us. He also fails to establish Zea's discipleship to Caso, Ramos, and especially Gaos. This stems from Lipp's subordination of the internal history of ideas to a synchronic exegesis of the writings of the dominant thinkers. The book's strength lies in presenting the Latin American perspective of Zea's thought, the author finding, like Weinstein, that Zea argues for a position beyond the limiting elements of socialism and capitalism, envisioning a Latin American freedom wherein community replaces alienation and marginalization.

It is incumbent upon the student of Mexican intellectual history to monitor the dialogue between the national and the international that has always underpinned the growth of culture in Mexico. *El Mexicano* by Raúl Béjar Navarro suggests that if the concrete Mexican was redeemed by the post-Revolutionary intellectuals, his meaning is not yet a closed issue. Béjar's essays, though insubstantial, indicate some of the present concerns of Mexican intellectuals, such as their inclusion of the chicano within their Mexicanist orbit and their challenge to the state, or "official," version of culture.

In one respect, however, Béjar's focus allows for continuity with the past. The book's principal essay treats the theme of the Mexican character and the question of whether a "Mexican" exists. In a familiar story the author of the introduction, Héctor Manuel Capello, bemoans the lack of study of the "distinctive Mexican being" (Béjar, 1979: 16), echoing a plea made by Ezequiel Chávez in 1901.

These books bear witness to the ecumenical as well as to the parochial in Mexican thought. All have certain common themes: A philosophy of man couched in both his particular and generic circumstances, an evaluation of the state in its relationship to human resources, the acknowledgement of the moral as well as the material basis of society, and the assumption that education must be directed toward qualitative ends. All attest to the Mexican's conviction in resolving his problems through the efficacious and humanistic enhancement of the nation as a comprehensive but just polity.

—*Henry C. Schmidt*

Henry C. Schmidt is an Associate Professor teaching Latin American History at Texas A & M University. The author of The Roots of Lo Mexicano: Self and Society in Mexican Thought *(Texas A & M University Press, 1978), he has also published in various journals. His specialization is Mexican culture and thought.*

BOOKS RECEIVED

GENERAL AND REGIONAL LATIN AMERICA

Brown, Lyle C., ed. RELIGION IN LATIN AMERICAN LIFE AND LITERATURE. Waco, TX: Markham Press Fund, 1980. Index. x, 426 pp.

CEDAL [Centro de Estudios Democráticos de América Latina] SINDALISMO, SOCIALISMO Y DEMOCRATICO. San José, Costa Rica: CEDAL, 1979. Colección Seminarios y Documentos. 116 pp. Paper.

——— SOCIALISMO DEMOCRATICO. Postulados Básicos. San José, Costa Rica: CEDAL, 1979. Colección Seminarios y Documentos. 89 pp. Paper.

Crow, John A. THE EPIC OF LATIN AMERICA. Third edition, expanded and updated. Berkeley, CA: University of California Press, 1980. References, bibliographical essay, index, two maps. xxvi, 929 pp. $29.95 cloth, $14.95 paper.

Das, Man Singh and Clinton J. Jesser, eds. THE FAMILY IN LATIN AMERICA. New Delhi, India: Vikas Publishing House Pvt. Ltd., 1980. U.S. distributor, Advent Books, New York. xvii, 430 pp. $40.00.

ECLA [Economic Commission for Latin America] ECONOMIC SURVEY OF LATIN AMERICA, 1978. Santiago, Chile: United Nations, 1980. 589 pp. Paper.

Ferno, Renate and Wolfgang Grenz, bearb. HANDBUCH DER DEUTSCHEN LATEINAMERIKA-FORSCHUNG: INSTITUTIONEN, WISSENSCHAFTER UND EXPERTEN IN DER BUNDESREPUBLIK DEUTSCHLAND UND BERLIN (WEST). NEUERE VEROFFENTLICHUNGEN. Hamburg: Institut fur Iberoamerika-Kunde. Dokumentations-Leitstelle Lateinamerika (ADOK) und Bonn: Deutscher Akademischer Austauschdienst (DAAD), 1980. Appendices, indices. xvii, 483 pp.

Fitzgibbon, Russell H. and Julio A. Fernández. LATIN AMERICA: POLITICAL CULTURE AND DEVELOPMENT. Second edition. Englewood Cliffs, NJ: Prentice-Hall, 1981. Bibliography, index. vi, 374 pp. $12.95 paper.

Ford, Thomas R., Joseph S. Vandiver, and Man Singh Das, eds. A LEGACY OF KNOWLEDGE: SOCIOLOGICAL CONTRIBUTIONS OF T. LYNN SMITH. New Delhi, India: Vikas Publishing House Pvt. Ltd., 1980. U.S. distributor: Advent Books, Inc., New York. Appendix, notes on contributors, index. xxxi, 301 pp. $25.00.

González, Nelly S. DOCTORAL DISSERTATIONS ON LATIN AMERICA AND THE CARIBBEAN: AN ANALYSIS AND BIBLIOGRAPHY OF DISSERTATIONS ACCEPTED AT AMERICAN AND CANADIAN UNIVERSITIES, 1966-1970. Urbana, IL: CLASP [Consortium of Latin American Studies Programs, Publication No. 10], 1980. List of figures and tables, indices, appendices, xxviii, 198 pp. Paper.

ILDIS [Instituto Latinoamericano de Investigaciones Sociales] EL CONTROL POLITICO EN EL CONO SUR. México, D.F.: Siglo Veintiuno Editores, 1978. 302 pp. Paper.

——— LA VIVIENDA POPULAR EN AMERICA LATINA. México, D.F.: FUNDACOMUN [Fundación para el Desarrollo de la Comunidad y Fomento Municipal]—ILDIS, 1979. 400 pp. Paper.

Interamerican Development Bank. ECONOMIC AND SOCIAL PROGRESS IN LATIN AMERICA. 1979 Report. Washington, DC: Interamerican Development Bank, 1979. Statistical appendix with index of tables. 458 pp. Paper.

Levine, Robert M. RACE AND ETHNIC RELATIONS IN LATIN AMERICA AND THE CARIBBEAN: AN HISTORICAL DICTIONARY AND BIBLIOGRAPHY. Bibliography, subject index. viii, 252 pp. $13.50.

Martin, Dolores Moyano, ed. HANDBOOK OF LATIN AMERICAN STUDIES: SOCIAL SCIENCES. No. 41. Austin: University of Texas Press, 1980. Indexes, including abbreviations and acronyms, title list of journals indexed, subject and author index. xvii, 796 pp. $55.00.

OAS [Organization of American States] HANDBOOK OF EXISTING RULES PERTAINING TO HUMAN RIGHTS. Washington, DC: OAS, 1980. 147 pp. Paper.

Obregon Valverde, Enrique. POR UNA SOCIAL DEMOCRACIA LATINOAMERICANA. San José, Costa Rica: CEDAL, 1979. Colección Seminarios y Documentos. 120 pp. Paper.

Orlove, Benjamin S. and Glynn Custred, eds. LAND AND POWER IN LATIN AMERICA: AGRARIAN ECONOMIES AND SOCIAL PROCESSES IN THE ANDES. New York: Holmes & Meier, 1980. Glossary, bibliography, list of contributors, index. 258 pp. $35.50.

Palerm, Angel. ANTROPOLOGIA Y MARXISMO. México, D.F.: CIS-INAH [Centro de Investigaciones Superiores del Instituto Nacional de Antropología e Historia] and Editorial Nueva Imagen, S.A., 1980. 224 pp. Paper.

Rietti Matheu, Mario. MONEDA Y BANCA: SU EVOLUCION EN AMERICA LATINA. Bogotá, Colombia: Biblioteca Felaban [Federación Latinoamericana de Bancos], 1979. Anexo estadístico, estructura del sistema financiero, bibliografía. xvi, 280 pp. Paper.

Rossi, Ernest E. and Jack C. Plano. THE LATIN AMERICAN POLITICAL DICTIONARY. Santa Barbara, CA: ABC-Clio, 1980. Index. xi, 261 pp. $25.25.

Weaver, Frederick Stirton. CLASS, STATE, AND INDUSTRIAL STRUCTURE: THE HISTORICAL PROCESS OF SOUTH AMERICAN INDUSTRIAL GROWTH. Contributions in Economics and Economic History, No. 32. Westport, CT: Greenwood Press, 1980. Tables, illustrations, appendix, bibliography, index. xiv, 247 pp. $28.50.

Woods, Richard D. REFERENCE MATERIALS ON LATIN AMERICA IN ENGLISH: THE HUMANITIES. Metuchen, JN: Scarecrow Press, 1980. Addendum, author, title and subject indexes. xii, 639 pp. $32.50.

ARGENTINA

Andrews, George Reid. THE AFRO-ARGENTINES OF BUENOS AIRES, 1800-1900. Madison: University of Wisconsin Press, 1980. Illustrations, tables and figures, glossy, appendices, notes, bibliography, index. xiv, 286 pp. $21.50.

Cavarozzi, Marcelo. CONSOLIDACION DEL SINDICALISMO PERONISTA Y EMERGENCIA DE LA FORMULA POLITICA ARGENTINA DURANTE EL GOBIERNO FRONDIZISTA. Buenos Aires: CEDES [El Centro de Estudios de Estado y Sociedad], 1979. Vol. 2, No. 7/8. Referencias. 83 pp. Paper.

Frenkel, Roberto. EL DESARROLLO RECIENTE DEL MERCADO DE CAPITALES EN ARGENTINA. Buenos Aires: CEDES [El Centro de Estudios de Estado y Sociedad], Vol. 2, No. 10, 1979. Referencias. 55 pp. Paper.

OAS. REPORT ON THE SITUATION OF HUMAN RIGHTS IN ARGENTINA. Washington, DC: General Secretariat, OAS, 1980. iii, 266 pp.

Potash, Robert A. THE ARMY AND POLITICS IN ARGENTINA, 1945-1962: PERON TO FRONDIZI. Stanford, CA: Stanford University Press, 1980. Bibliography, index, photographs. ix, 418 pp. $25.00

Romero, José Luis. LA EXPERIENCIA ARGENTINA Y OTROS ENSAYOS. Buenos Aires: Editorial de Belgrano, 1980. xvi, 522 pp. Paper.

BRAZIL

Burns, E. Bradford. A HISTORY OF BRAZIL. Second edition. New York: Columbia University Press, 1980. Appendices, glossary of Portuguese words, reading suggestions, index. x, 579 pp. $32.50 cloth, $10.00 paper.

Colonelli, Cristina Argenton. BIBLIOGRAFIA DO FOLCLORE BRASILEIRO. São Paulo: Conselho Estadual de Artes e Ciencias Humanas, 1979. Abreviaturas, indice. 294 pp. Paper.

Holloway, Thomas H. IMMIGRANTS ON THE LAND: COFFEE AND SOCIETY IN SAO PAULO, 1886-1934. Chapel Hill, NC: University of North Carolina Press, 1980. Notes, bibliography, index, lists of illustrations, tables, figures. xviii, 218 pp. $21.00.

Love, Joseph L. SAO PAULO IN THE BRAZILIAN FEDERATION, 1889-1937. Stanford, CA: Stanford University Press, 1980. Appendices, notes, bibliography, index, list of figures and tables. xx, 398 pp.

Tyler, William G. ADVANCED DEVELOPING COUNTRIES AS EXPORT COMPETITORS IN THIRD WORLD MARKETS: THE BRAZILIAN EXPERIENCE. Significant Issues Series, U.S. Export Competitiveness Project, Vol. II, No. 8. Washington, DC: Center for Strategic and International Studies, Georgetown University, 1980. vi, 87 pp. Paper.

Uricoechea, Fernando. THE PATRIMONIAL FOUNDATIONS OF THE BRAZILIAN BUREAUCRATIC STATE. Berkeley: University of California Press, 1980. List of tables and abbreviations used in references, sources, index. xvii, 233 pp. $16.50.

CARIBBEAN REGION

Brana-Shute, Rosemary and Gary Brana-Shute, eds. CRIME AND PUNISHMENT IN THE CARIBBEAN. Gainesville, FL: Center for Latin American Studies, 1980. Index, list of tables and figures. x, 146 pp. $6.00 paper.

Hippolyte-Manigat, Mirlande. HAITI AND THE CARIBBEAN COMMUNITY: PROFILE OF AN APPLICANT AND THE PROBLEMATIQUE OF WIDENING THE INTEGRATION MOVEMENT. Kingston, Jamaica: Institute of Social and Economic Research, University of the West Indies, 1980. Bibliography, index. xiii, 256 pp. Paper.

Levy, Claude. EMANCIPATION, SUGAR, AND FEDERALISM: BARBADOS AND THE WEST INDIES, 1833-1876. Gainesville, FL: University Press of Florida, 1980. Latin American Monographs, Second Series, No. 25. Center for Latin American Studies, University of Florida. Notes, appendixes, bibliography, index. vii, 206 pp. $13.50.

Nicholls, David. FROM DESSALINES TO DUVALIER: RACE, COLOUR AND NATIONAL INDEPENDENCE IN HAITI. Cambridge Latin American Studies 34. New York and Cambridge: Cambridge University Press, 1979. Notes on terminology, notes, bibliography, index. xi, 357 pp. Cloth.

OAS. SIXTH REPORT ON THE SITUATION OF POLITICAL PRISONERS IN CUBA. Washington, DC: General Secretariat, OAS, 1980. 39 pp. Paper.

OAS. REPORT ON THE SITUATION OF HUMAN RIGHTS IN HAITI. Washington, DC: OAS, 1979, ii, 81 pp. Paper.

CHILE

Nuñez P., Ivan. TRADICION REFORMAS Y ALTERNATIVAS EDUCACIONALES EN CHILE, 1925-1973. Estudios VECTOR I. Santiago, Chile: VECTOR, 1980. Referencias bibliográficas. 48 pp. Paper.

Vigorito, Raúl, Diego Portales, Juan E. Herrera, y Juan Morales. TRANSNACIONALIZACION DE LO ECONOMIA CHILENA. Estudios VECTOR 2. Santiago, Chile: VECTOR [Centro de Estudios Económicos y Sociales] y ILET [Instituto Latinoamericano de Estudios Transnacionales], 1980. 207 pp. Paper.

COLOMBIA

Meldau, Elke C. BENEFIT INCIDENCE: PUBLIC HEALTH EXPENDITURES AND INCOME DISTRIBUTION: A CASE STUDY OF COLOMBIA. North Quincy, MA: Christopher Publishing House, 1980. Appendixes, selected bibliography, index. 224 pp. $9.75.

Ospina Vásquez, Luis. INDUSTRIA Y PROTECCION EN COLOMBIA, 1810-1930. Third ed. First edition, 1955. Medellín: Fondo Rotatorio de Publicaciones FAES, Editorial Lealón, 1979. 576 pp. Paper.

Restrepo, Vicente. ESTUDIO SOBRE LAS MINAS DE ORO Y PLATA EN COLOMBIA. Fifth ed. First edition, 1883. Medellín: Fondo Rotatorio de Publicaciones FAES, Editorial Lealón, 1979. Appendices. 259 pp. Paper.

MEXICO

González, Luis. HISTORIA DE LA REVOLUCION MEXICANA, PERIODO 1934-1940: LOS ARTIFICES DEL CARDENISMO. No. 14. México, D.F: El Colegio de México, 1979. Publicaciones citadas, índice analítico. vii, 271 pp. Paper.

Hernández Chavez, Alicia. HISTORIA DE LA REVOLUCION MEXICANA, PERIODO 1934-1940: LA MECANICA CARDENISTA. No. 16. México, D.F.: El Colegio de México, 1979. Anexos, bibliografía, índice analítico. ix, 236 pp. Paper.

Krauze, Enrique. DANIEL COSIO VILLEGAS: UNA BIOGRAFIA INTELECTUAL. México, D.F.: Joaquin Mortiz, 1980. Notas, índice de nombres, índice de láminas. 318 pp. Paper.

Lerner, Victoria. HISTORIA DE LA REVOLUCION MEXICANA, PERIODO 1934-1940: LA EDUCACION SOCIALISTA. No. 17. Bibliografía, índice de nombres. vi, 199 pp. Paper.

Medina, Luis. HISTORIA DE LA REVOLUCION MEXICANA, PERIODO 1940-1952: No. 20. CIVILISMO Y MODERNIZACION DEL AUTORITARISMO. No. 20. México, D.F.: El Colegio de México, 1979. Epilogo, índice analítico. ii, 205 pp. Paper.

——— HISTORIA DE LA REVOLUCION MEXICANA, PERIODO 1940-1952. DEL CARDENISMO AL AVILACAMACHISMO. No. 18. México, D.F.: El Colegio de México, 1978. Indice de nombres. ix, 410 pp. Paper.

Sinkin, Richard N. THE MEXICAN REFORM, 1855-1876: A STUDY IN LIBERAL NATION-BUILDING. Austin: Institute of Latin American Studies, University of Texas, 1979. Appendices, notes, bibliography, index. x, 263 pp. $18.95 cloth, $7.50 paper.

Torres Ramírez, Blanca. HISTORIA DE LA REVOLUCION MEXICANA, PERIODO 1940-1952: MEXICO EN LA SEGUNDA GUERRA MUNDIAL. No. 19. México, D.F.: El Colegio de México, 1979. Indice analítico. vii, 380 pp. Paper.

Ulloa, Berta. HISTORIA DE LA REVOLUCION MEXICANA, PERIODO 1914-1917: LA ENCRUCIJADA DE 1915. No. 5. México, D.F.: El Colegio de México, 1979. Anexos, bibliografía, índice de nombres. viii, 267 pp. Paper.

——— HISTORIA DE LA REVOLUCION MEXICANA, PERIODO 1914-1917: LA REVOLUCION ESCINDIDA. No. 4. México, D.F.: El Colegio de México, 1979. Bibliografía, índice analítico. 178 pp. Paper.

PERU

Bernales, Enrique. CRISIS POLITICA: SOLUCION ELECTORAL? ANALISIS DE LOS RESULTADOS DE LAS ELECCIONES PARA LA ASAMBLEA CONTITUYENTE DE 1978. Lima: DESCO, 1980. Bibliografía, índice de cuadros. 132 pp. Paper.

Cavanagh, Jonathan. REFLECTIONS ON CLASS THEORY SUGGESTED BY ANALYSES OF THE PERUVIAN MILITARY REGIME: 1968-1979. Gottingen, Germany: Birte Fries, 1980. Appendices, bibliography. 558 pp. Paper.

García Sayan, Diego and Fernando Eguren. ARGO: CLASES, CAMPESINADO Y REVOLUCION. Lima: DESCO, 1980. Bibliografía y referencias bibliograficas. 160 pp. Paper.

Gasparini, Graziano and Luise Margolies. INCA ARCHITECTURE. Bloomington, IN: Indiana University Press, 1980. Notes, references, glossary, credits for photographs and plans, index. xv, 350 pp. $32.50.

González Vigil, Fernando, Carlos Parodi Zevallos and Fabian Tume Torres. ALIMENTOS Y TRANSNACIONALES. Lima: DESCO, 1980. Bibliografía. 286 pp. Paper.

Junta del Acuerdo de Cartagena. DECISION 146: PROGRAMA SECTORIAL DE DESARROLLO DE LA INDUSTRIA METALMECANICA. Lima, Peru: Junta del Acuerdo de Cartagena, 1980. 178 pp. Paper.

——— DOCUMENTOS: REUNION DE LOS PRESIDENTES DE LOS PAISES ANDINOS: CARTAGENA, 26 AL 28 DE MAYO DE 1979. Lima, Peru: Junta del Acuerdo de Cartagena, 1979. 93 pp. Paper.

——— EVALUACION DEL PROCESO DE INTEGRACION, 1969-1979. Lima, Peru: Junta de Acuerdo de Cartagena, 1979. Anexo estadístico. 172 pp. Paper.

——— MEMORIAS DEL PRIMER SEMINARIO ANDINO DE FUNDICION FERROSA. Lima: Junta del Acuerdo de Cartagena, 1979. 290 pp. Paper.

Riofrio, Gustavo and Alfredo Rodríguez. DE INVASORES A INVADIDOS (2): 10 ANOS DE AUTODESARROLLO EN UNA BARRIADA. Lima: DESCO, 1980. Anexos. 125 pp. Paper.

Stein, Steve. POPULISM IN PERU: THE EMERGENCE OF THE MASSES AND THE POLITICS OF SOCIAL CONTROL. Madison, WI: University of Wisconsin Press, 1980. Notes, selected bibliography, lists of tables, figures, and charts. xvi, 296 pp.

VENEZUELA

Herman, Donald L. CHRISTIAN DEMOCRACY IN VENEZUELA. Chapel Hill, NC: University of North Carolina Press, 1980. Appendix, notes, bibliography, index, list of tables, maps, and charts. xiv, 289 pp. $24.00.

MONTALBAN. Caracas: Universidad Catolica Andrés Bello (UCAB No. 9), 1979. 1,004 pp. Paper.

MISCELLANEOUS

ANUARIO DE ESTUDIOS AMERICANOS XXXIV. Sevilla, Spain: Escuela de Estudios Hispano-Americanos, 1977 [1980 publication date]. Serie 1. Annuario. xiv, 902 pp. Paper.

Balán, Jorge and Elizabeth Jelin. LA ESTRUCTURA SOCIAL EN LA BIOGRAFIA PERSONAL. Buenos Aires: CEDES [El Centro de Estudios de Estado y Sociedad], Vol. 2, No. 9, 1979. Bibliografía. 25 pp. Paper.

Bruce-Novoa, Juan D. CHICANO AUTHORS: INQUIRY BY INTERVIEW. Austin: University of Texas Press, 1980. Selected bibliography. xii, 292 pp.

Child, John. UNEQUAL ALLIANCE: THE INTER-AMERICAN MILITARY SYSTEM, 1938-1978. Boulder, CO: Westview Press, 1980. Bibliography. x, 253 pp. $22.00.

Daleski, Richard J. DEFENSE MANAGEMENT IN THE 1980s: THE ROLE OF THE SERVICE SECRETARIES. Monograph Series No. 80-8. Washington, DC: National Defense University, 1980. Appendix, endnotes, figures, table. vi, 57 pp. Paper.

Elliott, Charles F. and Carl A. Linden, eds. MARXISM IN THE CONTEMPORARY WEST. A Westview Special Study. Boulder, CO: Westview Press, 1980. Index. xii, 177 pp. $19.00.

Franko, Lawrence G. and Sherry Stephenson. FRENCH EXPORT BEHAVIOR IN THIRD WORLD MARKETS. Significant Issues Series, Vol. II, No. 6, U.S. Export Competitiveness Project. Washington, DC: Center for Strategic and International Studies, Georgetown University, 1980. Appendix, selected bibliography. ii, 96 pp. Paper.

García, Indes and Alberto Adrianzen. NO ALINEADOS: NUEVA FUERZA INTERNACIONAL. Lima: DESCO, 1980. Praxis No. 15. Anexos. 172 pp. Paper.

Keliher, John G. THE NEGOTIATIONS ON MUTUAL AND BALANCED FORCE REDUCTIONS: THE SEARCH FOR ARMS CONTROL IN CENTRAL EUROPE. New York: Pergamon, 1980. Published in cooperation with the National Defense University. Notes, bibliography, index. x, 203 pp.

Lagos Matus, Gustavo, ed. LAS RELACIONES ENTRE AMERICA LATINA, ESTADOS UNIDOS Y EUROPA OCCIDENTAL. Santiago, Chile: Instituto de Estudios Internacionales de la Universidad de Child, Editorial Universitaria, 1979. 173 pp. Paper.

Margiotta, Franklin D., ed. EVOLVING STRATEGIC REALITIES: IMPLICATIONS FOR U.S. POLICYMAKERS. Washington, DC: National Defense University Press (The National Security Affairs Institute, 1979-1980 seminar series), 1980. Endnotes, bibliography, seminar participants. xi, 222 pp.

Orrego Vicuña, Francisco, ed., con la asistencia de Gloria Echeverria Duco. LA COMUNIDAD DEL PACIFICO EN PERSPECTIVA. 2 volumenes. Santiago, Chile: Instituto de Estudios Internacionales de la Universidad de Chile, Editorial Universitaria, 1980. Vol. 1: 357 pp.; Vol. 2: 229 pp. Paper.

Sauer, Carol O. SEVENTEENTH CENTURY NORTH AMERICA. Berkeley: Turtle Island Foundation, 1980. List of figures, bibliography, index. 296 pp. $19.95 cloth, $9.95 paper.

U.S. Arms Control and Disarmament Agency. ARMS CONTROL AND DISARMAMENT AGREEMENTS: TEXTS AND HISTORIES OF NEGOTIATIONS. Washington, DC: U.S. Arms Control and Disarmament Agency, 1980. vii, 239 pp.

Vol. 23 No. 3
August 1981

JOURNAL OF INTERAMERICAN STUDIES

and WORLD AFFAIRS

A Publication of the Center for Advanced International Studies,
The University of Miami

SAGE PUBLICATIONS

Journal of INTERAMERICAN STUDIES and WORLD AFFAIRS

The editors and publisher wish to acknowledge with gratitude the assistance and encouragement of the Center for Advanced International Studies, University of Miami, in providing ancillary services and support for this journal.

Journal of
INTERAMERICAN
STUDIES
and WORLD AFFAIRS

Vol. 23
No. 3
August
1981

CONTENTS

Colombian Narcotics and United States-Colombian Relations
RICHARD B. CRAIG 243

The Costeños and the Revolution in Nicaragua
PHILIP A. DENNIS 271

Intellectuals: Agents of Change in Mexico?
RODERIC A. CAMP 297

Brazilian Elites and the Descendants of the German, Italian, and Japanese Immigrants
GLENN A. NICHOLS and PHILIP S. SNYDER 321

REVIEW ESSAYS

Centralism as Pragmatic Tradition: A Critique
MARIO VARGAS LLOSA
Translated by LYSANDER KEMP 345

Reinterpreting Colombian Economic History
WILLIAM PAUL McGREEVEY 352

A. Curtis Wilgus: 1897-1981
JOHN P. HARRISON 364

BOOKS RECEIVED 365

SAGE PUBLICATIONS / *Beverly Hills London New Delhi*

Policy: The **JOURNAL OF INTERAMERICAN STUDIES AND WORLD AFFAIRS** reflects the interests of the scholarly community and interested public concerned with the social, economic, political, and cultural aspects of life in Latin America (including the Caribbean), particularly in those instances where the subject is of concern to more than one of the traditional disciplines. As these concerns change, so will the content of the journal.

Articles which have special relevance for interrelationships between American nations and of those nations with the rest of the world will be given special consideration. An effort will be made to include occasional articles that state an unusual or even discordant position on a subject of broad interest to be supplemented by critical comments of authorities representing differing positions on the topic. The editors continue to welcome articles by scholars from all parts of the world.

Manuscripts should be submitted in duplicate to: Editor, **JOURNAL OF INTERAMERICAN STUDIES AND WORLD AFFAIRS,** Box 24-8134, University of Miami, Coral Gables, Florida 33124. Manuscripts should be typewritten, double-spaced, with footnotes, references, tables, and charts on separate pages, and should follow the current journal style. A brief biographical paragraph describing each author's current affiliation, research interests, and recent publications should accompany the manuscript.

Correspondence regarding book reviews should be sent directly to: Book Review Editor, **JOURNAL OF INTERAMERICAN STUDIES AND WORLD AFFAIRS,** Box 24-8134, University of Miami, Coral Gables, Florida 33124.

JOURNAL OF INTERAMERICAN STUDIES AND WORLD AFFAIRS is published four times annually—in February, May, August, and November.

Subscriptions: Regular institutional rate $42.00 per year. Individuals may subscribe at a one-year rate of $20.00. Add $2.00 for subscriptions outside the United States. Orders from the U.K., Europe, the Middle East, and Africa should be sent to the London address (below). Orders from India should be sent to the New Delhi address (below). Noninstitutional orders **must** be paid by personal check.

Second class postage paid at Beverly Hills, California. ISSN 0022-1937

This journal is abstracted or indexed in **Historical Abstracts, Human Resources Abstracts, Sage Urban Studies Abstracts, International Political Science Abstracts, Public Affairs Information Service, Current Contents, Social Sciences Citation Index, Social Sciences Index, ABC POL SCI,** and **United States Political Science Documents**.

Back Issues: Information about availability and prices of back issues may be obtained from the publisher's order department (address below). Write to London office for sterling prices.

Inquiries: Address all correspondence and permissions requests to SAGE PUBLICATIONS, Inc., 275 South Beverly Drive, Beverly Hills, California 90212. Inquiries and subscriptions from the U.K., Europe, the Middle East, and Africa should be sent to SAGE PUBLICATIONS Ltd, 28 Banner Street, London EC1Y 8QE, England. From India, write to SAGE INDIA, P.O. Box 3605, New Delhi 110 024 India. Other orders should be sent to the Beverly Hills office.

Advertising: Current rates and specifications may be obtained by writing to the Advertising Manager at the Beverly Hills office (address above).

Claims: Claims for undelivered copies must be made no later than three months following month of publication. The publisher will supply missing copies when losses have been sustained in transit and when the reserve stock will permit.

Change of Address: Six weeks' advance notice must be given when notifying of change of address. Please send old address label along with the new address to insure proper identification. Please specify name of journal. POSTMASTER: Send change of address to: Journal name, c/o 275 South Beverly Drive, Beverly Hills, CA 90212.

RICHARD B. CRAIG
Department of Political Science
Kent State University
Kent, Ohio

COLOMBIAN NARCOTICS AND UNITED STATES-COLOMBIAN RELATIONS

In recent years Latin America has become the principal source of narcotic drugs on the illicit United States market. Five of the nine countries granted top-priority status in State Department narcopolitics are located in Latin America. Mexico, having earlier supplied 80% of the heroin used by American addicts, is currently the source of approximately 40% of the drug. Coca grown primarily in Bolivia and Peru, shipped through Ecuador, and processed into cocaine in Colombia monopolizes the world market. In the wake of Mexico's highly successful herbicide campaign, Colombian marijuana has come to dominate the American pot scene. And again in response to U.S. demand, Colombia has become the world's foremost manufacturer of illicit methaqualone. Is it any wonder, then, that control of drug cultivation, processing, and shipment constitutes the paramount issue of contemporary U.S.-Colombian relations?

Analysis of Colombian-United States narcopolitics reveals a complex, delicate set of problems at international, national, and subnational levels. Solutions, if indeed they are to be found, will require greater ingenuity, patience, funding, and cooperation than in the past. Fundamental changes may be required in both

---

AUTHOR'S NOTE: This is a revised version of a paper presented before the Latin American Studies Association in Bloomington, Indiana, on October 17, 1980.

Journal of Interamerican Studies and World Affairs, Vol. 23 No. 3, August 1981 243-270

countries. If they are not forthcoming, damage to the social fabric of American and Colombian societies may prove irreparable.

The Colombian Drug Scene

Colombia's rise to prominence as the world's drug-smuggling capital has been nothing short of meteoric. The country which 10 years ago shipped relatively small amounts of marijuana and cocaine currently exports some 25 to 32 metric *tons* of cocaine and somewhere between 20,000 and 75,000 *tons* of marijuana to the United States alone. Addition of the tons of marijuana and cocaine smuggled to Canada and Western Europe yields a truly staggering total. How and why, it must be asked, did Colombian drug cultivation, processing, and trafficking become almost overnight the most lucrative "cottage industry" in history, an activity so enormous as to threaten indirectly the very existence of one of Latin America's rare democratic systems?

Any analysis of cocaine must begin in Bolivia and Peru, countries best known for their glorious Inca heritage, grinding poverty, political instability, and coca. The use of coca is deeply ingrained in the culture of both countries and predates even the Inca period by several hundred years. "Coca chewing in Bolivia is generally accepted," notes South (1977: 22), "and is as commonplace among some segments of the population as the coffee break or tea time of other cultures."

The hearty coca tree thrives where other crops often cannot survive, growing to maturity in 18 months and remaining productive for 30 to 40 years. With three to four annual harvests, the Andean campesino can produce over 3,000 pounds of leaf per acre. Once the leaves are dried, a three-step process leads to the production of cocaine. First, the leaves are mixed with water, kerosene, and other chemicals to produce coca paste. The paste is then reduced to cocaine base at a 3:1 ratio. Third, the base is converted to cocaine hydrochloride, usually at a 1:1 ratio. Unlike the first two stages, conversion from base to cocaine requires the skill of a chemist; until recent years it was not the specialty of Andean traffickers.

It is noteworthy that Peru and Bolivia are the world's only licit producers of coca. The principal problem in both countries is overproduction and diversion. According to U.S. Drug Enforcement Administration (DEA) estimates (mimeographed), Peru produced a total of some 25 million kilos of coca leaf in 1977, while Bolivia produced 30 million kilos. However, of the Peruvian total, only 7,951,000 kilos of leaf were accounted for, leaving some 17 million "potentially unaccountable." By the same process of elimination, some 15.5 million kilos of Bolivian leaf were unaccounted for. Both countries are obviously producing *far* more coca leaf than is necessary for domestic industrial or medical use, export, and chewing. Much of the overproduction is either illicitly converted to cocaine hydrochloride or smuggled for processing in base form into Colombia via Ecuador.

Clandestine laboratories capable of processing base or paste into cocaine are located throughout Colombia but most are found in Cali, Medellín, and Pasto. The majority of these facilities are operated by 10 major refining groups which specialize in producing the finished product. "They don't do anything else in the leaf-to-street cycle," according to a well-informed DEA agent (Interview, 1980a). Apparently no one, American or Colombian, has any real idea how many of these "kitchen labs" are in operation and for a good reason.

> I honestly couldn't even give you a good guesstimate of how many there are even in Cali because look, these are really "pots and pans" operations in the literal sense. Not only are they extremely portable, but the very same utensils used in making coke from base are often used a few hours later to cook supper in.

Primitive or modern, these "chemists" produce more than enough cocaine to meet world demand. Colombian drug traffickers are world renowned for skill and daring, and their sophisticated smuggling networks see to it that some 95% of the cocaine leaving the country reaches its foreign destination. Much the same can be said for marijuana.

Under incessant pressure from Washington and fearing their potential domestic effects, Mexico launched a massive eradication campaign against marijuana and opium poppies in the fall of 1975, an unprecedented effort which continues to this day (Craig, 1978, 1980). As thousands of plots were destroyed or contaminated by the airborne offensive, the supply and popularity of Mexican marijuana dwindled rapidly. Demand, on the other hand, increased, and well-organized Colombian criminal syndicates in league with their American counterparts wasted no time in taking advantage of an enormously lucrative opportunity. Almost overnight the ton replaced the kilogram as the standard measure of Colombia's marijuana production.

Colombian drug entrepreneurs did not, however, rest content with a monopoly over two drugs; they quickly captured a third: methaqualone. The primary source of illicit Quāālude, Rohrer's methaqualone, has until very recently been diversion from the legitimate market. It is now Colombia.

Quāālude base is a controlled substance in Colombia, yet the operators of clandestine laboratories apparently have little difficulty in obtaining it from abroad. Most of the illegal base originates in, of all places, Hungary. From there it is clandestinely shipped through the free port of Hamburg in 100-pound barrels. These in turn are smuggled through northern Colombian ports under false invoice, then shipped inland for processing. Some 15 presses annually turn out millions of tablets for the U.S. black market labelled "Lemmon-714" and "Rohrer 714," exactly like the original legal versions. These presses may in fact be the same ones used by Lemmon and Rohrer when they legally manufactured methaqualone a few years ago (Interview, 1980a). The entire Quāālude cycle is another clear example of why Colombian drug traffickers are so grudgingly admired by narcotics agents. They are, indeed, master smugglers. Yet even the greatest of talents requires a proper arena in which to perform. In this regard, Colombia constitutes a virtual amphitheater.

From the viewpoint of geography and climate, it offers an excellent locale for raising, processing, and smuggling narcotic drugs. Marijuana can be, and probably is, grown in every region in the country. The northern provinces of Bolívar, Atlántico, Magdelena, César, and Guajira are well-suited climatically and topographically for cultivating marijuana, so much so that a *canabicultura* has all but replaced such traditional pursuits as farming, pasturing, mining, and fishing. Colombia's northern coastline is ideal for smuggling by sea, while literally hundreds of rough clandestine landing strips accommodate daring airborne smugglers. Much of the area is remote, inhospitable, and inaccessible, making it very difficult to police. It is truly a smuggler's paradise with a legendary history of clandestine activity.

Contraband is, however, not the exclusive province of the north. Colombia itself is characterized by the contraband *ambiente.* Notwithstanding official posturing to the contrary, the sale of smuggled goods is so widespread as to be accepted as normal in the eyes of most citizens. Millions of tax dollars are lost annually from illegal sales of coffee, sugar, cattle, cement, cigarettes, electronic appliances, emeralds, and even decals of Walt Disney characters. Such is the extent of contraband activity that Colombians have been hard-pressed to coin a truly appropriate phrase to describe its collective impact. But they have not been idle, as witness the following: parallel economy, black market, unofficial economy, second economy, informal economy, unregistered economic activity, and, perhaps most appropriately, *la otra economía.*

Inseparable from "the other economy" is the ubiquitous nature of corruption, a phenomenon so commonplace as to be accepted as a way of life and nothing out of the ordinary. The jokes, stories, charges, and countercharges involving corruption of Colombian officials at all levels and in all branches of government, military, private, and even religious life are legendary. Even such a personage as Attorney General Serrano Rueda frankly admitted in May 1977 that the problem could hardly get any worse, especially at the administrative level. It was necessary to "make a diagnosis of Colombia," he contended, because corruption had reached its "maximum level." The country had "passed from the hands of the Sacred Heart to those of the hands of the mafias" (Excelsior, 1977b).

Thus, it is no accident that in recent years many Colombianos have come to refer to their own politicians and police as "gangsters" and "mafiosos." It is equally obvious that the nation could not have achieved such international notoriety in narcotics if many officials were not on the drug "take." And the "take" is enormous, with bribes in the thousands of dollars being commonplace. In this regard, money is truly no object to Colombian *traficantes,* and neither is violence.

Violence and organized drug traffic are all but inseparable, and Colombia has intermittently enjoyed an infamous reputation for violence which peaked during the period of *La Violencia* (1946-1957), subsided during the National Front (1958-1974), only to return in new forms during the mid-1970s. A climate of fear has recently spread from the countryside to the city. Guerrilla groups and common criminals have attacked the system and its citizenry with increasing frequency. Such was the extent of kidnapping in the mid-1970s that Colombians sarcastically referred to it as *el nuevo deporte nacional.* Murder, assault, robbery, and kidnapping in major cities reached the stage where personal security was an important issue in the 1978 national elections.

Drug traffickers not only complement this generally violent ambience but also personify and exaggerate it. In a profession known for its violence, Colombian *marimberos* (traffickers) stand out. Recalcitrant farmers are murdered, rival traffickers savagely eliminated, uncooperative judges killed and/or their property destroyed. "I've worked in narcotics for many years in several countries," remarked a DEA official in Mexico City (Interview, 1980d), "but never have I seen anything like the Colombian trafficker. He is really one mean bastard." In league with highly lucrative bribes, the murder of Colombian judges, narcotics agents, and lawyers constitutes a crucial factor in explaining why so few major drug figures are convicted and sent to prison.

Regionalism and rural poverty combine to constitute another key factor in Colombia's emergence as a massive drug center. It is no mere coincidence that pivotal areas of marijuana cultivation are also scenes of grinding poverty. The Guajira Indians, for example, have long been known for their fierce pride, tribal loyalties, independent ways, and smuggling expertise as well as their poverty (Aschmann, 1960). Like the vast majority of rural inhabitants, they too have been bypassed by the nation's steady development.

National progress has, in fact, been decidedly one-sided in favor of urban areas and marked by half-hearted agrarian reforms and a highly skewed distribution of income in which the bottom 20% of the population receives only 3% of the income.

According to Berry (1978), 10% of the nation's farmers owned slightly more than 80% of the land in 1970, while the bottom 20% owned only .327%. Given such figures, which reinforce Colombia's rigid class lines in rural areas, it is logical that the campesino —like his brothers in Mexico, Bolivia, and Peru—is all too often abjectly poor and without hope. When offered the opportunity by a trafficker to earn $1000 or more annually for raising marijuana, he does so because it often means a chance to earn a decent living for the first time in his life. Engaging in an illegal activity is of little or no consequence to someone who has absolutely nothing to lose. The fact that some 100,000 Colombian families are directly or indirectly supported by narcotics incomes attests to this truism (U.S. Senate, 1979a: 212).

Narcopolitics and Colombia's Antidrug Campaign

As a result of such factors, Colombia has become a polydrug nation whose citizens annually manufacture at least 25 tons of cocaine from Bolivian and Peruvian base, act exclusively as smuggling conduits for increasing amounts of the finished product from these two Andean nations, and are themselves turning more and more toward cultivating the coca bush and thereby controlling the entire coca-cocaine cycle. Colombian campesinos are farming an estimated 200,000 acres of high-quality marijuana whose potency, or THC content, is three and four times greater than the Mexican variety, this while "chemists" in Bogotá and Cali stamp out millions of Quāālude tablets annually. All these illicit activities are of particular interest to U.S. officials for one overriding reason—some 70% of this cocaine, marijuana, and methaqualone is ingested by American drug users.

With the possible exception of heroin use, which appears to be somewhat in decline due to Mexico's herbicide campaign, Americans are abusing narcotic drugs at unprecedented levels and ever-younger ages. Estimates—or perhaps more appropriately "calculated guesstimates"—vary. But in 1977, if one uses midrange figures, there were at least 1.5 million regular cocaine users and 15 million marijuana smokers, while 10 million admitted that they had at one time snorted cocaine and 43 million had smoked marijuana (Strategy Council on Drug Abuse, 1979). All indications are that these abuse figures have subsequently been exceeded. The national drug problem is no longer described as "very serious"; it is now "pandemic." However, as the problem worsens, the most popular solution remains essentially unchanged: Shut it off at the source. With rare exceptions, the source is foreign. With no exceptions, the agency ultimately charged with the difficult, delicate, and extraordinary task of "screwing tight the foreign tap" is the Department of State.

Since 1969, State has given high priority to the flow into the United States of narcotics from foreign sources. That priority has risen with each passing year in proportion to escalating domestic drug abuse. The position of Senior Advisor for International Narcotics Matters was created in 1971 and accorded assistant secretarial rank in an effort to "bring narcotics control considerations to bear systematically on the development of foreign policy." The senior advisor, representing the Secretary of State, directs the Bureau of International Narcotics Matters with its annual budget of $40 million for bilateral and multilateral control programs (Office of Drug Abuse Policy, 1978).

Policies are implemented through State's regional bureaus and at the embassy level. As regards Latin America, the Bureau of Inter-American Affairs and respective embassies play a crucial coordination-support role. A Deputy Assistant Secretary of State supervises drug-related activities in the Bureau of Inter-American Affairs, while functional responsibility is vested in a narcotics coordinator. A senior diplomatic officer acts as narcotics coordinator within most embassies, chairing a working committee generally composed of representatives from DEA, Customs, Agency for International Development, Agriculture, Defense, CIA, Legal Affairs, and United States International Communications Agency. In Mexico and Colombia, with their large drug production, Foreign Service officers work full-time on narcotics matters, acting as special assistants to the ambassador. Their primary objective is to "create an awareness and gain the commitment of the host government to take action against illegal drug cultivation and trafficking." Once this is accomplished, State Department narcotics control funds "act as a catalyst to illicit drug producing and transit nations to begin supply reduction and enforcement operations" (U.S. Senate, 1978: 26). Colombian officials have been made aware, and they have taken action. It remains to be seen, first, whether they have taken the correct actions and, second, if American funds will ever be used most effectively.

Convincing Colombian presidents, cabinet officials, and military officers that a concerted antidrug effort on their part is first and foremost in their nation's own best interest has not been an easy task for U.S. diplomats. Terrence Todman, Assistant Secretary of State for Inter-American Affairs, epitomized their approach during the 1970s when he remarked (U.S. House, 1977: 310-311): "One fact that we tried to get across . . . is that it is a threat to the very existence of any nation because if they permit trafficking in narcotics it builds a sort of shadow government that can bring down any government because the traffic is large, the money that's involved is large, and the temptations are great." This line of reasoning was coupled with strong reminders that one of the several results from a tremendous narcotics dollar flow is "inflation and a wrecking of government's economic plans." Both warnings are undeniably true, and they are still being reiterated. Yet it required an inordinate amount of time for Colombian officials to heed them.

President Alfonso López-Michelsen (1974-1978) was fond of reminding America's public, its diplomats, presidents, and presidential wives that the root problem was theirs, not Colombia's. Drug traffic "never would have acquired its actual dimensions," he stated in February 1978, "if a permanent number of customers did not exist in the United States who supply large international chains with financing that have their origin only in the very same United States" (Excelsior, 1978d).

American narcotics officials had heard the López lament many times before. It was, in fact, a very familiar refrain for anyone who had earlier served in Turkey or Mexico. And depending on which came first, the chicken of U.S. demand or the egg of Colombian production, they knew he was correct. Yet by the spring of 1978 such remarks amounted to political window dressing, because López had already decided the time for action had come. Decisions during his last year in power laid the groundwork for a frontal assault by his successor.

Calendar 1977 saw 7,342 persons arrested on drug charges by Colombian authorities, who also claimed to have confiscated 529,491 pounds of marijuana and 15,604 pounds of cocaine (Washington Post, 1978). An antinarcotics unit specializing in cocaine cases was created within the attorney general's office in December 1977. Its power and that of other units was augmented when López issued a decree virtually absolving all security forces of liability for injury or death in actions against drug traffickers and kidnappers (New York Times, 1978). On April 26, 1978, somewhere between 574 and 680 tons of marijuana were seized in a single cooperative raid. Colombian authorities, acting on DEA leads, then seized more than a million pounds of pot in the same Guajira region, neatly packaged in bales and ready for shipment during the next three days.[1] Colombians, meanwhile, were listening to presidential campaign rhetoric, and López-Michelsen was negotiating an antidrug aid package with the United States. He had obviously become convinced the problem posed a serious domestic threat. However, he was not convinced the situation was as bad as the U.S. General Accounting Office (GAO) and CBS television made it out to be.

A March 29 GAO study on drug control in South America singled out corruption in the Colombian government as a major cause of the massive trafficking problem (GAO, 1978). Four days later, in the thick of presidential campaigning, commentator Morley Safer of CBS's "60 Minutes" unloaded a second political bombshell by revealing that a confidential memorandum to President Carter from Dr. Peter Bourne, his soon-to-be-disgraced special assistant on drug abuse, charged three prominent Colombian politicians with involvement in narcotics: General Abraham Varón Valencia, Minister of Defense; Oscar M. Montoya, Minister of Labor; and Julio César Turbay Ayala, ex-ambassador to the United States and the frontrunning Liberal Party candidate who would be elected president of the republic within a month (CBS, 1978). Their denials of the allegations were categoric and swift.

General Varón (Miami Herald, 1978a) rejected the charges and told U.S. Ambassador Diego Asencio that they were based on "false information which has caused notorious damage to the prestige of the country, its government, and its armed forces."

Spokesmen for several Latin American embassies joined the Colombian press in staunchly supporting López-Michelsen's denial of the accusations and his retort that it was the American government that was "corrupting the peoples of Latin America" (Times of the Americas, 1978). Turbay Ayala, in a sharply worded letter to Ambassador Asencio, stated: "Both President López and Mr. Bourne categorically denied the false allegations, which are the result of the dirty campaign against my reputation." Turbay also made public Asencio's reply, which read in part: "It is the position of my government that there is no proof that you may have had any part in the drug traffic. I find incomprehensible and absurd the use of any allegation of your participation in the drug traffic" (Miami Herald, 1978b).

The timing of these two exposés could not have been worse for overall U.S.-Colombian relations and narcotics diplomacy in particular. "I think," lamented one American diplomat (Miami Herald, 1978a), "relations between the two countries are now at their lowest level in recent years." He was essentially correct, but once Turbay overcame these and other challenges to become president in August 1978, relations improved and Colombia's *campaña antidroga* took on a dramatically different character.

Turbay sounded an ominous note for revolutionary groups, common criminals, and drug entrepreneurs in his inaugural address of August 7. He pledged, first, to wage an "implacable crusade" against narcotics traffickers and noted, second, that "my Government proposes to study the feasibility of a legal statute pertaining to the security of the State that would permit (democratic) institutions to function and defend themselves against the dangers that threaten them" (El Tiempo, 1978b). The study was not a prolonged one. On September 6, the government promulgated what it termed a "statute of security." Officials initially denied that the law was aimed at drug smugglers. According to the new defense minister, General Luis Carlos Camacho-Leyva (Excelsior, 1978b) it "certainly does not include concrete measures against narcotics traffic." Official pronouncements aside, the Turbay administration wasted no time in launching a truly unprecedented campaign against growers, processors, and traffickers. It would become, claimed Procurator General Guillermo González Charry (Excelsior, 1978a), "a battle without quarter against the two principal problems of immorality that plague Colombia: administrative corruption and narcotics traffic."

An initial important step involved the government's use of the media in a soul-searching effort to reveal the true extent of the drug problem. Responsible officials informed the public of the dangers posed by massive cultivation, manufacture, and traffic of marijuana and cocaine. They admitted that such activities were far larger than heretofore had been imagined. The dangers they posed to Colombians, their government, economy, international image, and societal fabric were openly discussed. A lion's share of the blame was still laid at Washington's feet, but Bogotá accepted its share for the first time.

Second, and perhaps most important, Turbay ordered the military and particularly the Army to assume a major role in the *campaña.* Army units had played only a minor, indirect part in previous feeble programs. With the Army as the phalanx of a combined military effort in the Guajira the government pledged to avoid the *"fracasos"* that characterized "innumerable campaigns of the previous government" (Excelsior 1978c). In what came to be known in October 1978 as "Operation Fulminante," some 4,000 military personnel—including three infantry batallions, one cavalry group, one artillery unit, two military vessels, and nine aircraft—launched a frontal assault against marijuana cultivation, drug smuggling, and guerrilla activities in the northern provinces.

Airborne smugglers were forewarned late in October when the Air Force announced that flights over the "security corridor" of northern Colombia would be permitted only between the hours of 7:00 AM and 5:00 PM. Pilots attempting to traverse the area at other times or at altitudes below 2,000 meters would "without hesitation" be challenged and their planes "intercepted or shot down." Clandestine landing strips and maritime ports would be bombed and marijuana fields destroyed (El Tiempo, 1978a).

Third, the antinarcotics unit of the Judicial Police within the attorney general's office was increased in size, given greater responsibility and training, and granted substantial salary increases. Drug-related activities of the national police, the Department of Administrative Security, and the Bureau of Customs were accelerated and agent salaries increased (U.S. Senate, 1979b; Interview, 1980c). Such pay hikes were absolutely necessary if the corruptive impact of trafficker bribes were to be reduced.

Fourth, the Turbay administration signed a new narcotics pact with the United States. A continuation of existing agreements, it called for further cooperation and coordination, especially in the two-peninsula campaign launched in November 1978 which successfully coordinated "Operation Fulminante" in the Guajira peninsula with a similar operation by U.S. enforcement agencies in the Florida peninsula. The pact also included additional U.S. training and equipment for Colombian agents. In fiscal 1979, Washington contributed $3.8 million to Colombia's effort, with $2.4 million going specifically to the north coast campaign (U.S. Senate, 1979b).

Bogotá's contribution in terms of money, equipment, and personnel was considerably greater. And the results were very impressive, at least on paper. From October 15, 1978, to August 31, 1979, Colombian armed forces seized 2,765 tons of marijuana and reportedly burned twice that amount in the field; confiscated 85 airplanes, 294 vehicles, and 76 boats; arrested 1,481 persons on drug-related charges: 1,278 nationals and 203 foreigners, the majority of whom were Americans. Retail value of the seized marijuana alone was put by Ambassador Asencio (U.S. Senate, 1979b) at almost $4 billion. These were impressive figures. When coupled with Asencio's persuasive arguments and those of Senator Laughton Chiles, whose native Florida was being inundated with Colombian narcotics, they resulted in a record $16 million aid package for fiscal 1980.

Analyzing the Campaign: Two-Way Street or Cul d'Sac?

Antidrug campaign statistics, no matter the country or agency of origin, are invariably most impressive to those who want to be impressed. Buoyed by the initial results of the military's Guajira program, the government issued a special *informe* on February 4, 1979, proclaiming a victory in the battle against narcotics traffic. The same bulletin (Excelsior, 1979b) gave even more attention to successful antiguerrilla activities during Turbay's first six months in office, claiming that subversion had been all but eliminated. Subsequent events have shown this initial reaction to be somewhat overly optimistic on both counts. The *informe* is important, however, in seeking to explain why the new regime moved so swiftly and decisively against drug smuggling.

Most American officials believe, as they did in the case of Mexico's decision in the mid-1970s, that U.S. pressure was the key to explaining Colombia's massive frontal assault against drug traffickers, especially on the north coast. "They will surely deny it," said a veteran DEA officer (Interview, 1980d), "but without our incessant pushing, our constant reminders of how huge the problem had become, and yes our financial support, the Colombians might never have taken the whole thing seriously." Undoubtedly, there is some measure of truth in such reasoning. But the impact of U.S. pressure, while important, was only indirectly responsible for Turbay's 1978 *campaña.*[2] And it played virtually no part in the government's subsequent decision to alter dramatically the program's nature.

The same could be said about the role of Colombia's domestic drug problem. While not comparable to America's overall situation, drug abuse is a rapidly growing problem in Colombia, especially among students and urban poor. Trends indicate increased use of marijuana, barbiturates, and cocaine.[3] Politicians, meanwhile, have paid lip-service to the problem but failed to take it seriously. According to one Colombian drug rehabilitation organization, which claims 70% of all the citizenry has tried marijuana, the government has done virtually nothing about drug abuse: "A good image before the United States in its fight against the drug market has been more important for Colombia and the government than our own addicted youth" (Excelsior, 1979a).

Negative international imagery can also go only so far in explaining Colombia's revitalized campaign. Laymen and politicians alike are keenly aware of their country's increasingly negative reputation due to drug trafficking and other contraband. "How do you think it feels," asked an exchange student whose father is a prominent local politician in Cali, "to instantly recognize that knowing smile when I tell another student here that I'm a Colombian? They almost always want to know if I brought any good grass." When asked whether concern over the nation's reputation played an important role in the antidrug program, he smiled knowingly and replied: "Not really; Turbay and the Liberals and the Army acted because they were afraid just like the rest of us" (Interview, 1979).

It must be recalled that one of the few issues which kept Colombians awake during the otherwise ho-hum elections of 1978 was public order and fear: fear of revolutionaries, kidnappers, common criminals, and in some areas narcotics traffickers.[4] Turbay pledged to attack vigorously such problems and, armed with a "statute of security," proceeded to do just that. He is an astute politician and, above all, he knew that lawlessness in its many forms had reached the point of threatening Colombia's democratic institutions and perhaps even its tradition of civilian government. Had the new president not registered impressive early gains against kidnappers, urban guerillas, and drug smugglers, had he not brought about a renewed sense of citizen security, his administration would have been placed under enormous strain. No one needed to tell Turbay this, especially outsiders. And when it came to narcotics dealers, no one needed to clarify the obvious: Their economic power and all that it implied had become a serious threat to the status quo system which has governed Colombia so effectively in recent years.

In economic terms, the impact of Colombian drug dollars has been profound. Just how profound depends on one's source. No one really knows, for example, how much money Colombians actually earn from marijuana, cocaine, and Quāalude sales. The range is wide: from $1 billion to $8 billion annually. Ambassador Asencio (U.S. Senate, 1979a) best analyzed this calculated guessing game in his December 1979 Senate testimony: "My numbers are at best educated guesses," he said. "So, I must emphasize, are everybody else's." The total, by any standard, is "a whole lot," which to him meant over $3 billion in 1979. The popular diplomat succinctly linked economic effects of this enormous sum to its sociopolitical ramifications and then posed a fundamental question for his own countrymen:

> Colombia has been facing a severe economic challenge from narcotics traffickers. The integrity of its financial institutions has been placed in jeopardy. A growing inflation rate has been accelerated by illegal monies. Legitimate business enterprises have had to defend themselves from absorption by criminals. Land values, both agricultural and residential, are soaring, leaving farmers and middle-class home buyers in a quandary. The specter of corruption remains ever present. The very bases of the political power structure have been challenged by criminals. Obviously, none of this is healthy for a democracy. Colombia has become painfully aware that it is in its own best interest to confront the situation with the limited resources at its disposal. Can we do less?

Asencio's closing query is crucial, for despite its $16 million aid package in fiscal 1980, there are many objective observers in both countries who feel strongly that the United States could do far more for its part. And they turn the tables on critics of Colombia's campaign by asking several logical and often embarrassing questions concerning the true extent of America's commitment against narcotic drugs.

WILL THE REAL U.S. DRUG ABUSE PROGRAM PLEASE STAND UP?

Students of the American drug scene are often puzzled over the true nature of Washington's antinarcotics program and its approach to marijuana and cocaine in particular. All indicators point to serious health problems resulting from regular use of these drugs, yet equally reliable statistics document quantum increases in the number of pot smokers and coke snorters. Meanwhile, one administration after another has failed to present and then vigorously pursue a coherent policy on either. In the undeniably clear words of Congressman Lester Wolff, Chairman of the House Select Committee on Narcotics Abuse and Control: "We have made a definite statement on tobacco today and we have not made one on marijuana" (U.S. House, 1979: 442).

Colombians are puzzled by a lack of consistency and a series of apparent contradictions in Washington's stance on marijuana: They are confused by pronouncements about the proven ill effects of the drug and the leniency shown traffickers in U.S. courts; they are surprised that 11 state governments have decriminalized—which to them means "legalized"—without a challenge from Washington;[5] they are amused at the publicity by the American press of random calls for marijuana legalization in Colombia when there is *apparently* no chance of such proposals ever being enacted;[6] and they are ever alert in reminding Americans that Colombia's current marijuana production will decline, independent of their own law enforcement efforts, in direct proportion to reduced usage by U.S. smokers. Such a reduction will not occur, however, so long as prevention is second-rated to law enforcement and so long as the latter is itself plagued by serious problems.

IS THE UNITED STATES REALLY SERIOUS?

Even if one stretches the point and accepts Washington's claim that a balanced, fully coordinated national drug abuse program does exist, he still must question its sincerity and depth. It is one thing for the U.S. government to attack the problem at its foreign source instead of in its own back yard; it is quite another if the effort is underfinanced, poorly coordinated, and hamstrung by numerous legal restrictions.

Prior to its special, one-time-only commitment of $16 million in fiscal 1980, Washington had been rather parsimonious in aiding Colombia's *campaña*, contributing less than $4 million in each of the two preceding fiscal years. Is this the mark of a country seriously committed to helping the primary source nation attack a monumental problem whose wellsprings are distinctly North American? Even the $16 million figure is "chicken feed" vis-à-vis the enormous economic and social costs to both the United States and Colombia of marijuana and cocaine smuggling. "The leading power in the Western world," remarked President Turbay in a New York *Times* interview (1980a), "with its millions has confiscated less in its territory than Colombia with its limited resources has in its. If the United States would only make a substantial investment in Colombia to match the contribution by the Colombian government, drug traffic would be reduced in a very large way."

Bear in mind that $16 million does not approach the U.S. street value of any one of several cocaine seizures by Colombian agents in recent years.[7] Consider, second, that this "truly extraordinary sum in terms of our past funding experience" is, according to Ambassador Asencio (U.S. Senate, 1979b), about the same as the budget of the Birmingham, Alabama Police Department. Note, third, that the worldwide budget of the Bureau of International Narcotics Matters of the State Department is actually "less than half the budget of the Baltimore Police Department." If this were not reminder enough, recall finally, the perennial lament of U.S. enforcement agents, who interdict at best only 10% of all drug shipments, that they are outfinanced, outgunned, and outsophisticated by their trafficking adversaries. Clearly, it will cost the American taxpayer far more if the drug problem is to be combatted successfully at the foreign source or along the nation's borders. It will also require greater coordination and cooperation among U.S. antidrug forces.

Knowledgeable Americans have correctly noted the major flaws in Colombia's *campaña:* corruption, interagency squabbles, jurisdictional disputes, and a lack of necessary equipment. Many of these same sources also decry the lack of cooperation and at times open friction between the DEA and the Bureau of Customs and between DEA and the Internal Revenue Service. They find it hard to believe (U.S. House, 1979: 238) that cooperation between DEA and Customs has improved markedly in recent months, as agency spokesmen claim, when only 3% of the latter's drug seizures are intelligence related.[8] They hear IRS agents swear (U.S. Senate, 1979a) that their organization actually discourages cooperation with the DEA on tax fraud cases. And they are well aware of the jurisdictional disputes, lack of cooperation, hoarding of information, and open hostility which too often characterize relations between federal agents and their state and local counterparts.

Equally puzzling to the outside observer are numerous legal provisions which seriously hamper America's drug enforcement programs, in particular the *possee comitatus* dictum, curbs on DEA activities in foreign countries, restrictions on IRS tax disclosures, and amendments to the Foreign Assistance Act. Colombians are amazed at the inability of the United States, with all its sophisticated equipment and technology, to stem the narcotics tide from abroad. Explanations by U.S. diplomats (U.S. Senate, 1979b) that the *possee comitatus* doctrine effectively prohibits military participation in civilian law enforcement fail to impress Colombians. Turbay took a calculated risk, they reason, by deeply involving the army in a traditionally nonmilitary and unpopular role in the Guajira campaign. Why cannot U.S. officials make a reciprocal effort by modifying *possee comitatus* to allow at least the use of military intelligence for interdicting drug shipments?[9]

In the wake of accusations that they were involved in coerced confessions from American citizens in Mexico, the activities of DEA agents in foreign countries were sharply curtailed by an amendment to the International Security Assistance and Arms Control Act of 1976 (P.L. 94-329). The so-called Mansfield amendment provides that "no officer or employee of the United States may engage or participate in any direct police arrest in a foreign country with respect to narcotics control efforts." Virtually impossible to enforce in certain cases, the amendment nevertheless puts a crimp in DEA activities abroad. If allowed by the host governments, why should the United States bar its agents from participating in arrest actions in a foreign country?

Congress sought in the 1976 Tax Reform Act to ensure taxpayers more privacy over information provided the IRS by restricting access rights of other government agencies to tax information. At the same time, and perhaps unknowingly, it seriously affected the government's ability to prosecute major drug traffickers on tax fraud charges. It had, according to a former area manager for the Criminal Investigation Division of the IRS, "a devastating and debilitating effect." If, for example, incriminating information is obtained from "a taxpayer, the taxpayer's records, or the taxpayer's representative, IRS cannot alert the Attorney General or other federal agency heads of the crime, regardless of its seriousness" (U.S. Senate, 1979a: 291 and 308). Is it unreasonable to assume that the act's secrecy article and its restrictive summons provisions could be amended to allow federal attorneys to attack the very lifeblood of major drug dealers—money—while still protecting the legitimate taxpayer's privacy? Even more to the point, is it logical or even fair to demand that Colombia substantially curtail marijuana production and simultaneously deny her the best means of doing so?

In its unprecedented aid package of fiscal 1980, Congress stipulated that the funds could be used only in the interdiction of drug traffic and in that regard only for fixed radar equipment, helicopters, patrol vessels, transport vehicles, fuel, and agent training. "That's it," emphasized a knowledgeable State Department narcotics officer (Interview, 1980c), "nothing else, period." No weapons, no airplanes, no high-level multispectral photography equipment, no airborne radar, no communications equipment, no spraying rigs, and, most important, nothing to spray. According to one diplomat (New York Times, 1980b), "It's like asking someone to build a house but telling him he cannot use any hammers, saws or nails. These guys in Congress are like janitors playing brain surgeons."

Their major incision was made in a 1978 amendment to the International Security Assistance Act of 1961. The so-called Percy amendment (U.S. House, 1980) bans the use of foreign funds in any program utilizing the herbicide paraquat. The prohibition became complete when the Department of Health, Education and Welfare (HEW) subsequently concluded that persistent smoking of paraquat-contaminated marijuana was likely to cause fibrosis of the lung. Although HEW's findings are still being appealed by the State Department, the United States cannot currently allow its aid funds to be spent on paraquat unless some type of dye or marker is used to identify the contaminated pot. The substance has not been developed, and Colombia has in effect been denied the best means of helping American diplomats achieve their primary goal—destruction or contamination of drugs at the source to preclude their importation and use.

Whither La Campaña Colombiana?

President Turbay Ayala has waged truly unprecedented campaigns against drug traffickers, common criminals, and subversives. While surely not eliminated, the threat posed to citizen and government by bank robbers, kidnappers, and revolutionaries has been eased. Turbay's antidrug efforts were perhaps even more impressive, particularly when compared to those of his predecessors. Unfortunately, recent developments have raised serious doubts about the *campaña*, leaving it and U.S.-Colombian narcopolitics in a state of limbo.

In the spring of 1980, having decided it really was not well-suited to chop down, burn, or interdict marijuana in transit, the army pulled out if its lead role in the much-publicized north coast campaign. The pillar of Operation Fulminante was undeniably the Colombian army. No one is sure what the pillar is today, but some informed sources think they know what it might be tomorrow.

Of the numerous explanations offered for the army's crucial decision, three seem most logical. First, the army was ordered out by Turbay, who felt the soldiers could better be used in other tasks, especially counterinsurgency operations. It should be recalled that the withdrawal decision came in the midst of a two-month seige of the Dominican embassy by Colombia's most publicized revolutionaries, the M-19. Second, army commanders saw their role in the campaign as a no-win proposition; they had made only minimal headway against growers and traffickers while their public image in rural areas—which heretofore had been positive—had declined markedly. After all, no one relishes depriving a lowly campesino of the first real income and human dignity he and his family have ever known. Third, and probably most important, the army, which had intermittently been plagued with corruption before the drug era, simply could not escape the enormous corruptive influence of narcotics dollars.

Turbay and the man directly in charge of Colombia's antidrug campaign, Minister of Defense General Luis Carlos Camacho-Leyva, apparently agreed that it was time to reorganize the entire program. The first stage of that revision called for replacement of the army by three 600-man units of the National Police. These select groups would be specially trained in narcotics interdiction; headquartered in Cali, Medellín, and the Guajira; and commanded by Camacho-Leyva, who also heads the recently created National Narcotics Coordinating Committee. Assisting the National Police force would be their own intelligence service, members of the Federal Judicial Police, and an unspecified number of army units acting "in a low-profile, support capacity" (Interview, 1980a).

American diplomats and narcotics officers initially assumed a wait-and-see attitude on Colombia's reorganized effort. Their response to the army's withdrawal was none too enthusiastic, and they were most disgruntled in the fall of 1980 when Bogotá refused to activate the first 600-man unit because Washington refused to foot the bill. In the interim, cooperative efforts between the two countries were rendered even more difficult by the absence of a U.S. ambassador in Bogotá from February 27, 1980, when Diego Asencio was taken hostage, to October, 2 when his successor Thomas Boyatt was approved by the Senate. The fact that seven months passed without a successor being named reinforces the belief that Washington is not really serious about its nation's drug problem. "I must admit that Colombia's preoccupation with things other than drugs has been marked since the embassy seizure," said one career diplomat in July 1980, "and the fact that they've done very little against narcotics shipments this year can within reason be blamed on the lack of an ambassador; nobody's been pushing them" (Interview: 1980b).

Campaign reorganization and ambassadorial absence have not meant an idleness on the part of Colombian and American officials or their trafficking adversaries, however. Of potentially major importance were the recent signings of extradition and mutual assistance agreements between the two nations. Both will undoubtedly be approved in the wake of Ronald Reagan's landslide, and they could greatly enhance efforts to immobilize major traffickers who currently remain untouchable. In the interim, while cocaine continues to gain in popularity and Colombian pot supplies 70% of the American market, reduced numbers of soldiers attempt the thankless and hopeless task of slashing and burning thousands of acres of marijuana.[10]

As regards the ever popular cannabis, which is increasingly thought to be quite harmful to heavy smokers, one would perforce be smitten with acute naiveté to believe law enforcement alone capable of solving the problem. If America's marijuana consumption is indeed to be reduced substantially, either one or both of the following must occur: A combined and concerted demand reduction-law enforcement program in the United States and/or a massive herbicide campaign in Colombia. While the odds on option one remain long, the compulsive gambler might reasonably risk a few dollars on option two.

Colombian officials were on the verge of launching a Mexico-like paraquat program in the fall of 1979. Yet after visits to Mexico by both the National Council on Dangerous Drugs and President Turbay Ayala, during which the Mexican eradication program was examined at length, it was officially decided not to use the herbicide for three reasons: (1) its threat to legitimate food crops often grown in conjunction with marijuana; (2) its potentially damaging effects on smokers; and (3) its possibly harmful ecological impact. Unofficially, however, it appears that Bogotá chose not to spray because Washington would not pay for the paraquat or for anything else if Colombia chose to go it alone (Interview: 1980a, 1980c).

American officials have remained remarkably diplomatic in the midst of this classical Catch-22 scenario. Most obviously realize, as they did in constantly pressuring the Mexicans to spray in the mid-1970s, that without a herbicide program, there is *no* currently feasible way to reduce substantially the enormous flow of Colombian marijuana and its serious negative impacts on both countries. Still, they seem to parrot almost religiously the official government line that we will "cut off our nose to spite our face" if Colombia decides to go it alone on paraquat as did Mexico. Sounding almost like a tape recording of Ambassador Asencio's testimony before the Senate in December 1979, a State Department narcotics expert contended (Interview: 1980c):

> Herbicides are not really necessary when you get right down to it. Most of the problem could be solved by interdiction if we and the Colombians really wanted to pay the price. Just look at the

thousands of pounds the Coast Guard has seized recently, and just think what they alone could do with a real budget.

It is no mean task to reconcile such reasoning with the traditional contention that "you either stop it in the field or you don't stop it at all." It will be far more difficult for U.S. diplomats, however, if Colombia should decide to launch a herbicide program, reasoning that the economic and social impact of marijuana trafficking poses a greater national threat than the termination of any amount of U.S. aid. That diplomatically sensitive possibility could of course be avoided by one of three developments. First, some ingenious chemist could come forth with an identifiable agent to mix with the paraquat, thereby meeting the standards of the Percy amendment. The best efforts of several chemical firms have thus far produced only what an American official called "an agent so obnoxious that I've tabbed it odor of skunk." Second, an appellate court could reverse the lower court's upholding of HEW's decision on paraquat's toxic effects. Third, the new Republican-controlled Senate could again amend the 1961 International Security Assistant Act by eliminating Senator Percy's amendment.

The question of whether Colombia will or will not spray may eventually prove moot. Ultimately, with or without Washington's assistance, it must confront head-on the problems of drug cultivation, processing, and shipment. This must be done not to please the United States, but to insure the survival of the nation's institutions.

It can be argued that narcotics traffickers, their political and social satraps, and their millions of dollars constitute the greatest single threat to Colombian democracy since *La Violencia* of the 1940s. Economically, drug dollars are the prime contributor to mounting inflation, *la otra economía*, spiraling land and real estate values, reduced legitimate exports, and cutbacks in government spending for sorely needed development projects. Placed in stark relief by Slater (1980), who uses midrange estimates that many would consider conservative, the combined 1977 export value of marijuana and cocaine alone would constitute 16% of

Colombia's gross national product, 126% of all legal exports, and 583% of Colombia's legal exports to the United States.

Politically, drug trafficking organizations have assumed de facto control of several cities on the north coast. Their money is said to have financed some surprising victories in the 1978 congressional elections. It has, in league with real and threatened violence, made a mockery of the judicial process whenever *traficantes* stand accused and rendered most precarious the lives of honest judges, lawyers, and their families. Socially, illicit drug earnings are creating a nouveau riche that is buying and bullying its way into the nation's class-conscious society. And perhaps most important, trafficker mores and money are corrupting the very fabric of Colombian society at all levels in ways totally unacceptable to the average citizen who generally shrugs off corruption as perfectly normal.

The cumulative effect of these developments is nothing short of profound. It would appear to demand that the government act resolutely and reduce substantially the volume of narcotics traffic. On the other hand, an all-out frontal assault against marijuana cultivation would itself pose some problems for Colombian officials. Assuming that it largely succeeded, what would the thousands of campesinos do who currently farm *la yerba*? Employment opportunities are scarce in the Guajira and along the Atlantic coast. Would their inhabitants willingly return to a bare subsistence lifestyle, give up the only *dignidad* they have ever known? Would their response not in fact be violent and politically destabilizing at a time when national and regional politicians sorely need stability?

In the long run Colombia's drug phenomenon will require future administration to address its domestic *raison d'être*. For just as the United States must ultimately admit that drug abuse constitutes a fundamental national problem and attack it with the primary goal of demand reduction, so, too, must Colombian politicians address the issues of poverty, rural neglect, and maldistribution of income. To do otherwise could mean that future United States diplomats would deal with Colombian generals in their quest to solve America's drug problem at its foreign source.

NOTES

1. Confusion reigns over the actual amount. DEA reported 574 tons; UPI listed 647 tons; Procurator General Jaime Serrano said his scales showed 680 tons. Such conflicting reports are very typical of narcotic statistics; all too often it boils down to a game of "pick 'em."

2. According to a strategically placed Colombian official who wrote to me and requested that his name be withheld: "It was not U.S. insistence that made the operation possible but the fact that the country began to be aware of the problem."

3. A 1975 U.S. government report (Blutstein et al., 1977) found that an astounding 43.3% of all Colombian secondary students regularly used drugs; a rate which, *if* accurate, is higher than those in the United States and Western Europe.

4. For an excellent analysis of the 1978 elections, see Ruhl (1978).

5. Colombians should no longer claim puzzlement over U.S. decriminalization laws following a recent Supreme Court ruling. Colombia's highest court upheld a general trend in Latin American countries by declaring (Miami Herald, 1980) legal the possession of small amounts of marijuana (28 grams) and hashish (10 grams).

6. Although improbable, legalization is still a possibility. It has been openly recommended on several occasions by Ernesto Samper Pizano, president of the prestigious Asociación Nacional de Instituciones Financieras (ANIF) and is scheduled for congressional debate in 1981. For the prolegalization position, note in particular ANIF (1979).

7. For example, a coordinated raid in Bogotá on September 11, 1979, netted some 700 kilograms of cocaine worth an estimated $500 million (El Tiempo, 1979).

8. Top Customs officials are particularly resentful of DEA's power, so much so that 15 of them recently journeyed to Washington to attend a secret meeting on the problem. According to columnist Maxine Cheshire (Washington Post, 1980), they came from all over the nation at their own expense to "declare war on the Drug Enforcement Administration."

9. It appears that *possee comitatus* is being circumvented, at least in part, by a cooperative Department of Defense-Customs program that allows Customs agents to monitor AWACS radar information on suspected smuggling flights. The arrangement will in all likelihood soon be challenged in court.

10. The futility of such primitive methods was exemplified by a May 1977 dispatch (Excelsior, 1977a) from the Guajira, where authorities had discovered a marijuana plantation of some 1,500 hectares. They estimated that the destruction of this one farm alone would require "the collaboration of no less than 500 persons during several weeks."

REFERENCES

ANIF [Asociación Nacional de Instituciones Financieras] (1979) Marihuana: legalización o represión. Bogotá: Biblioteca ANIF.

ASCHMANN, H. (1960) "Indian pastoralists of the Guajira peninsula." Annals of the Association of American Geographers 50: 408-418.

BERRY, A. (1978) "Rural poverty in twentieth century Colombia." J. of Interamerican Studies and World Affairs 20: 355-376.

BLUTSTEIN, H., J. D. EDWARDS, K. T. JOHNSTON, D. S. McMORRIS, and J. D. RUDOLPH (1977) Area Handbook for Colombia. Washington, DC: Government Printing Office.

CBS Television Network (1978) "60 minutes: The cocaine memorandum." April 2.

CRAIG, R. B. (1980) "Operation condor: Mexico's antidrug campaign enters a new era." J. of Interamerican Studies and World Affairs 22: 345-363.

——— (1978) "La campaña permanente: Mexico's antidrug campaign." J. of Interamerican Studies and World Affairs 20: 107-131.

Excelsior [Mexico City] (1979a) March 13.

——— (1979b) February 5.

——— (1978a) September 22.

——— (1978b) September 8.

——— (1978c) August 22.

——— (1978d) February 14.

——— (1977a) May 25.

——— (1977b) May 21.

GAO [U.S. General Accounting Office] (1978) Drug Control in South America Having Limited Success—Some Progress but Problems are Formidable. Washington, DC: Government Printing Office.

Interview (1980a) July 25. Washington, DC: Drug Enforcement Administration.

——— (1980b) July 25. Washington, DC: Department of State.

——— (1980c) July 24. Washington, DC: Department of State.

——— (1980d) March 28. Mexico, D.F.: U.S. Embassy.

——— (1979) May 9. Kent, OH: Kent State University.

Miami Herald (1980) May 13.

——— (1978a) April 8.

——— (1978b) April 5.

New York Times (1980a) November 3.

——— (1980b) April 3.

——— (1978) March 19.

Office of Drug Abuse Policy (1978) International Narcotics Control Policy. Washington, DC: Government Printing Office.

RUHL, J. M. (1978) "Party system in crisis? An analysis of Colombia's 1978 elections." Inter-American Economic Affairs 32 (Winter): 29-45.

SLATER, L. (1980) "Colombia: The cinderella of cannabis and coke." Unpublished manuscript, University of Texas at El Paso.

SOUTH, S. B. (1977) "Coca in Bolivia." Geographical Rev. 67 (January): 22-33.

Strategy Council on Drug Abuse (1979) Federal Strategy for Drug Abuse and Drug Traffic Prevention 1979. Washington DC: Government Printing Office.

El Tiempo [Bogotá] (1979) September 12.

——— (1978a) October 5.

——— (1978b) August 8.

Times of the Americas (1978) April 26.

U.S. House (1980) The Use of Paraquat to Eradicate Illicit Marihuana Crops and the Health Implications of Paraquat-Contaminated Marihuana on the U.S. Market. A Report. Select Committee on Narcotics Abuse and Control. Washington, DC: Government Printing Office.

——— (1979) Oversight Hearings on Federal Drug Strategy (May and June).

——— (1977) T. A. Todman testimony before the House Select Committee on Narcotics

Abuse and Control. Oversight Hearings. Washington, DC: Government Printing Office.

U.S. Senate (1979a) D. C. Asencio testimony before the Permanent Subcommittee on Investigations of the Senate Committee on Governmental Affairs, Illegal Narcotics Profits. December 12: 204-219. Washington, DC: Government Printing Office.

——— (1979b) D. C. Asencio testimony before the Subcommittee on Criminal Justice of the Senate Judiciary Committee. September 19. Washington, DC: U.S. Government Printing Office.

——— (1978) Stopping "Mother Ships"—A Loophole in Drug Enforcement. J. H. Linnemann testimony before the Subcommittee to Investigate Juvenile Delinquency of the Senate Committee on the Judiciary. August 22: 25-26. Washington, DC: Government Printing Office.

Washington Post (1980) November 12.

——— (1978) March 11.

Richard B. Craig is Associate Professor of Political Science at Kent State University. Author of The Bracero Program: Interest Groups and Foreign Policy *(University of Texas Press), he is currently involved in researching the impact of narcotics traffic on U.S.-Latin American relations and has published several articles on the problem.*

PHILIP A. DENNIS
Department of Anthropology
Texas Tech University

THE COSTEÑOS AND THE REVOLUTION IN NICARAGUA

In Nicaragua in July 1979, the Sandinista popular revolutionary movement finally succeeded in overthrowing the dictatorship of the Somoza family, which had been placed in power and then supported for many years by the U.S. government. Analysis of the revolution, even in conservative U.S. government sources (LeoGrande, 1979; Montgomery, 1980), has noted the greed and corruption of the Somoza dynasty and the poverty, illiteracy, and poor health of Nicaragua's masses. More liberal sources (Koeppel and Harvey, 1980; Burbach and Draimin, 1980) comment favorably on the democratic and social justice orientation of the new revolutionary government. Coverage of the revolution, however, has barely mentioned the east coast, an isolated, ethnically complex, and fascinating part of the country. The problems of communication, ethnic diversity, and political integration posed by

AUTHOR'S NOTE: My fieldwork in Nicaragua in 1978-1979 was supported by an NIMH Postdoctoral Fellowship through the Department of Anthropology, Michigan State University. Funds from the Department of Anthropology and the Dean of the Graduate School, Texas Tech, made possible my brief trip to Nicaragua in June 1980.

In Nicaragua, I would especially like to thank Myrna Cunningham, Galio Gurdián, Olga Marta Montiel, and Douglas Stevens for their ideas and their hospitality.

This article was originally presented at the Midwest Association for Latin American Studies at Michigan State on October 11-13, 1979. Tani Adams, Anna Rubbo, Arthur Rubel, Michael Tussig, and Richard Vengroff are among those who provided helpful comments.

Journal of Interamerican Studies and World Affairs, Vol. 23 No. 3, August 1981 271-296

the east coast are common to other Latin American countries and will have to be faced by the new government in Managua.

In this article I hope to provide a different perspective on the revolution by sketching the history and general background of Nicaragua's east coast. My interest stems from 10 months' ethnographic fieldwork among the Miskito people of this area in 1978-1979. I lived in the village of Awastara, about 20 miles north of Puerto Cabezas (see Figure 1), learning the Miskito language and collecting information on various aspects of Miskito culture. A brief trip to the coast in June 1980 provided some additional information and impressions of what has happened since the revolution.

The Coast: Geography and Population

Geographically, the lagoon-fringed coast is an area of rain forest-clad hills and of pine savannas and gallery forests along the large rivers which flow eastward from the interior. Travel has traditionally taken place along the rivers, the numerous swamps and streams making overland communication almost impossible in the rainy season. "The coast" is virtually synonomous with the department of Zelaya, which—with an area of 59,094 square kilometers—includes about 45% of Nicaragua's territory (Incer, 1975: 234). Although enormous in area, Zelaya is sparsely populated. In 1971 the population was 149,016, or about 7.5% of the national total (Incer, 1975: 178).

In many ways the east coast is completely different from the Spanish-speaking nation to the west. LANICA's one daily flight in an old C-87 from Managua to Bluefields, Corn Island, Puerto Cabezas, Waspam, Bonanza-La Rosita, Siuna, and back is the only reasonably efficient means of communication. Otherwise, passengers and freight must go down the highway to Rama and from there be ferried down the sluggish Rio Escondido to Bluefields and El Bluff. From there they may go north by boat to Puerto Cabezas and other points along the coast. The isolation of the area can be seen in the fact that it is a good deal cheaper to fly

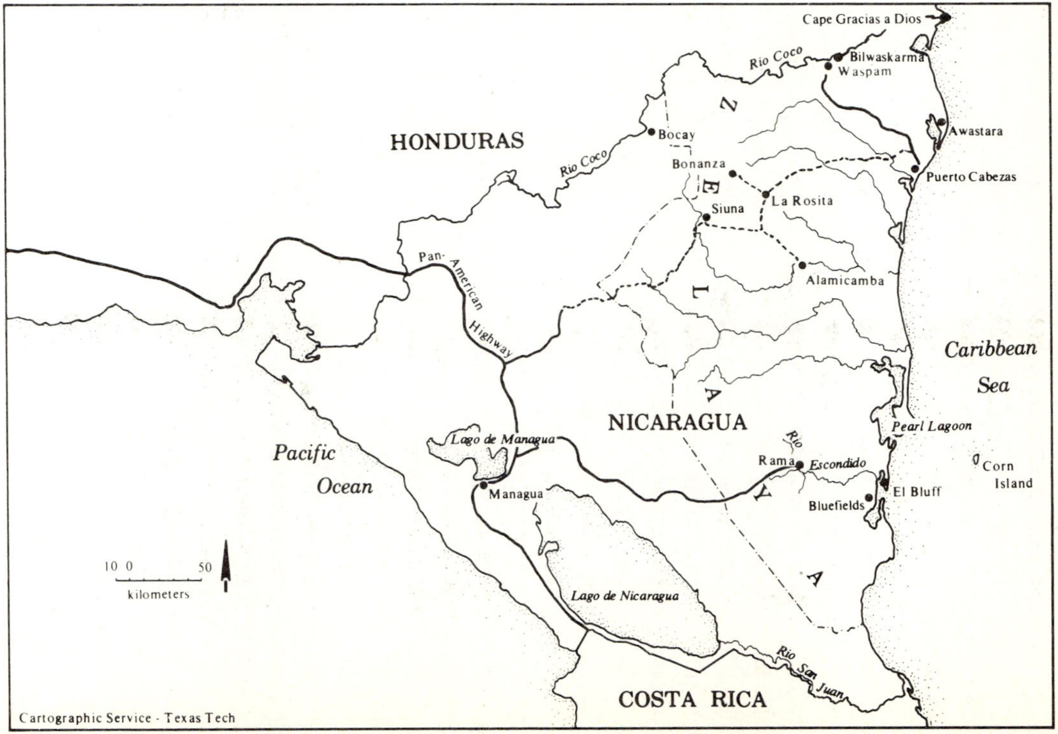
Cape Gracias a Dios
Rio Coco
Bilwaskarma
Waspam
Awastara
Puerto Cabezas
HONDURAS
Bocay
Rio Coco
Bonanza
La Rosita
Siuna
Alamicamba
Z
E
L
A
Y
A
Pan-American Highway
Caribbean Sea
NICARAGUA
Pearl Lagoon
Rio Escondido
Rama
Corn Island
El Bluff
Bluefields
Lago de Managua
Managua
Pacific Ocean
Lago de Nicaragua
Rio San Juan
COSTA RICA
10 0 50
kilometers
Cartographic Service - Texas Tech

Figure 1.

from Managua to San José, Costa Rica—about 75 córdobas—than from Managua to the coast, about 175 córdobas. A new road, opened in recent years, connects Managua to the coast via the mines in the Siuna area, but it is open only during the dry season. This road promises to bring major changes to the coast in the near future, as it is further improved and becomes more heavily traveled.

The coast is not only geographically isolated but has a different history, culture, and language from Hispanic Nicaragua to the west. Traditionally under the realm and influence of the British Caribbean, the coastal population is largely Protestant and English is its lingua franca.

Ethnically, the population is very diverse. Miskito-speaking villagers probably form the numerical majority. They occupy two major areas: the coast itself, from Bluefields north to Cape Gracias a Dios, and the Río Coco, where Miskito villages line the river from near its mouth to Bocay. A third Miskito-speaking area is outside Nicaragua, across the Río Coco in southeastern Honduras. In the interior of Zelaya are a number of Sumu Indian villages. These people have not been studied by anthropologists and little is known about them.

Black, English-speaking people originally from the West Indies are the majority population on the south coast and in the Bluefields area. They are known in the Miskito area as creoles, and this is the sense in which this word is used in this essay. Chinese families in lesser numbers are spread throughout the area. The Spanish-speaking population is relatively small and recently arrived from the west. It is growing rapidly, however, as poor peasant farmers from the Pacific zone arrive to colonize available lands, especially in the Siuna-La Bonanza mining districts.

The creole population came originally from Jamaica and other parts of the Caribbean to work on banana and coconut plantations around Bluefields, Pearl Lagoon, and Corn Island. More recently, an ethnic frontier seems to be moving northward from the Bluefields area, as creole men have gone there for work and as prosperous creole families have moved north to fill positions in the Moravian church and in the service professions. There is a prestigious creole middle class associated with the Moravian church in the coastal towns. In the villages, many creole men have married Miskito women, and the creole population has been a continuing source of Miskito contact with Caribbean English culture.

The Chinese population is small but economically powerful. In 1979 most of the stores and restaurants in Puerto Cabezas were Chinese-owned. Chinese shopkeepers were completely fluent in Spanish, English, and Miskito as well as their native Chinese. Some were wealthy enough to send their children to the United States and elsewhere to school. The Chinese were occasionally accused of price-fixing and were resented by the local population, but as is so often the case with overseas Chinese, they were relatively uninvolved politically. Their primary preoccupation seemed to be making money, not supporting or opposing the Somoza government. In communities with sufficient business to support a store, there was often a Chinese shopkeeper in residence, usually with a Miskito wife and children who would bear his Chinese surname. In Awastara, there had been a Chinese shopkeeper during the 1940s when the oil company operated there, but he had moved to the more prosperous area around the mines when the drillers left, taking his Miskito wife and children with him.

History of the Miskito

At the time of the first European contact, the native inhabitants of the coast were small groups of people who lived by hunting and fishing and slash and burn agriculture, and who spoke languages of the Macro-Chibchan family, related to those along the northern coast of South America (Helms, 1971: 14-15). English buccaneers established friendly relations with these people and enlisted them in their conflicts with the Spanish. Together, the English and their Miskito allies attacked Spanish shipping and traveled up the rivers to attack Spanish settlements far in the interior (Floyd, 1967). A mutual-advantage relationship developed between the buccaneers and the Miskito. The Miskito got arms, tools, rum, and clothing, while the buccaneers got lumber, skins, food (including turtles, which the Miskito were adept at catching), and sexual access to Miskito women.

One possible etymology for the name *Miskito* is from the English word musket, as it was through acquiring muskets that the Miskito subjugated other groups and spread up and down the coast and up the Río Coco (Helms, 1971: 16). Miskito hegemony extended as far south as Costa Rica. The remnants of other groups, collectively known as Sumu, live today up some of the coastal rivers, where they were pushed by Miskito expansion. Miskito dominance on the coast for several hundred years can be traced to their successful contacts with Europeans and to their position as middlemen in the trade between the English and the Sumu tribes in the interior (Helms, 1969).

The Miskito "kings," who ruled from 1661 to 1894, were essentially English puppets (see Helms, 1969). With a Miskito king "ruling," the English could oppose Spanish claims to the coast by arguing they were defending the interests of their loyal Miskito allies. The kings also served as a symbolic focus of Miskito ethnic identity and solidarity in their conflicts with neighboring Sumu peoples and with the Spanish. The memory of their kings still remains, and in some of the coastal communities a modern "king" returns with a message for his people during a festival at New Years.

Relations between the Miskito and the English buccaneers and traders were good. Words, concepts, and items of material culture passed from the English to be permanently integrated into Miskito culture. Such Miskito words as *rokbus* (gun, from early English arquebus) and *grapling* (anchor) can easily be traced to English, but are "traditional" Miskito words today. The Miskito language, like Miskito culture in general, is sometimes mentioned in disparaging terms. It is true that the sources of many linguistic and cultural items are clearly from the outside, but there is no reason this fact should imply inferiority. Instead, from the positive point of view, one can emphasize the flexibility and adaptability of Miskito culture, as demonstrated by its ability to incorporate so many foreign items and make them authentically Miskito. Miskito culture today is vigorous, although rapidly changing, and the number of Miskito speakers increases every year.

Other reasons besides its adaptability help account for the persistence of Miskito culture. As Helms points out, until recently the Miskito have been left alone in their coastal and riverine environment, in control of their own land and able to interact on reasonably favorable terms with outsiders. In addition, their matrilocal pattern of social organization has kept a core of related Miskito women together, raising their children as Miskito and speaking the Miskito language (Helms, 1968: 459-464). Miskito men were free to travel and work elsewhere, bringing home or sending home their earnings. Another common pattern has been for English, creole, Chinese, and other men to live with Miskito women, leaving behind children who would be raised as Miskito and who would join the "mainstream of Miskito culture." As a result, the diversity of physical types among the modern Miskito is remarkable, from tall, light-skinned individuals to individuals with African appearing features to oriental. Surnames among the Miskito include Hoppington, Webster, Kingsman, Wong, Chow, and Muellar, as well as such Spanish names as Renales and López.

Other events have also been important in forging the patterns in contemporary Miskito culture. In 1849, Moravian missionaries made their appearance on the coast. They learned the Miskito language and translated the Bible, and in 1881 successfully converted large numbers of people up and down the coast in a mass experience known as the Great Awakening. The missionaries introduced items important to Miskito life today, such as houses made of sawed lumber, breadfruit trees, and new varieties of rice. They worked diligently for improvement in Miskito technology and health, and they vigorously opposed aspects of Miskito culture they found immoral, such as shamanism, polygyny, and drunkenness on ritual occasions. By the turn of the century there were missionaries living in many of the coastal communities, and today the Moravian church is the strongest religious group on the coast.

The Miskito themselves are the missionaries today. Almost every village has its Moravian lay pastor trained at the Instituto Bíblico in Bilwaskarma. The position of lay pastor carries a great deal of prestige and, prior to the 1979 revolution, attending the Instituto Bíblico was one of the main upward mobility channels for bright Miskito youths. Besides learning the Bible and Christian religious dogma, lay pastors were exposed to middle-class American practices—such as wearing white shirts and ties to church and exchanging Sunday dinner invitations—and to conservative political views, which included anticommunist and antirevolutionary rhetoric. The lay pastors were rotated from village to village every 2 to 3 years and theoretically were not allowed to serve in their home village, to prevent their being drawn into factional village disputes. Interestingly, although the lay pastors are mostly Miskito, in 1979 all but two of the Moravian bishops were creole. This de facto creole control of the church hierarchy was resented by the Miskito, especially by the more ambitious lay pastors.

Along the Río Coco, the Catholic missionaries have been a major influence. In general, they seem to have placed more emphasis on development activities than the Moravians, at least in recent years. A cooperative to buy and sell rice and beans, major products of the Río Coco area, was started by a Catholic missionary and was successful for a number of years. It was the immediate precursor of Alianza Para el Desarrollo Miskito y Sumu (ALPROMISU), the Miskito self-determination organization. The health program along the Río Coco, a joint effort by the Catholics and local Nicaraguan officials, has been quite successful and has been recognized by such groups as the International Red Cross. Health and development efforts in the area around Puerto Cabezas have been led by various church organizations and by the University of Wisconsin CENDER program.

Given the rise to power of the Sandinista government, it is interesting to note that the only development group with any leftist sympathies has been the Catholics. The Catholic position is not surprising given the strong anti-Somoza stand taken by the church in western Nicaragua and the social justice orientation of the Church in other parts of rural Latin America. For the immediate future, the Sandinistas will be forced to continue working with the church-led development agencies on the coast, but it seems likely that the group most likely to be supported will be the Catholics.

In the late 19th century the Miskito involvement with the world economy began shifting from that of middlemen to that of wage laborers. Economic enterprises on the coast, controlled by Americans and Europeans, included mining, lumbering, and banana raising. Helms (1971: 29) diagrams the waxing and waning of each of these booms as they affected the Miskito. Their general effect was to draw the Miskito farther away from subsistence agriculture and gathering and to make them dependent on the wages they earned as laborers. The Miskito had easy access to manufactured tools, clothes, and medicines at company commissaries, and purchased foodstuffs such as flour, sugar, and coffee became prominent in the Miskito diet. The Miskito seem to have found a sense of well-being from earning good wages and having well-stocked stores in which to spend them. Helms (1971: 156) says that the Miskito of Asang *feel* poor when there are no company jobs, and I found the same feeling in Awastara. Surrounded by lagoons and rivers full of fish and forests and savannas full of exploitable animals and plants on which they once survived, the Miskito feel poor if they are not making good wages working for a company. However romantically appealing it may be, they are uninterested in going back to subsistence farming, hunting and fishing as a way of life. They are deeply involved in selling the product of their labor on the outside and anxious to have more of the consumer goods their wages will buy. This seems to be a fact of life for the Miskito, as it has become for many other horticultural and hunting and gathering peoples.

The last great boom, in the late 1960s and 1970s, involved selling turtles and lobsters from the coastal waters. The Miskito had traditionally fished turtles, but when two foreign companies began buying them in large numbers, the Miskito intensified their efforts and began seriously depleting the turtle population. The turtles who feed off the east coast of Nicaragua represent the last large green turtle population in the Caribbean, and, finally, through the efforts of conservationists, the Nicaraguan government banned the foreign companies' operations in 1977. Nietschmann (1973) shows how the boom-and-bust cycle centered around turtle fishing, unlike previous cycles, led to the depletion of an important subsistence resource and had serious repercussions within Miskito coastal villages. A more recent article (Nietschmann, 1979) discusses inflation, out-migration from Miskito villages, and other aspects of the Miskito dependence on wage income.

Ironically, the Miskito themselves resent the recent government ban on foreign turtle companies, since it took away a major source of cash income for them. The concede the long-term damage caused by overfishing, but argue that there still *seem* to be plenty of turtles off the coast and point out how seriously the ban has affected the local turtle fishermen. Miskito history reflects a willingness to exploit their environment for all it is worth, greatly altering the people/environment equilibrium patterns at several times in the past.

In 1978-1979, jobs as lobster divers and sailors on shrimp fishing boats provided a major source of employment for young Miskito men. These boats, many owned by Somoza, were working the coastal waters intensively, threatening destruction of the shrimp and lobster fishery in the area. Like other earlier enterprises on the coast, the fishing companies were interested in a quick profit and not in sustained yield of the resource for the future. Shrimp and lobster were shipped off to U.S. markets where they commanded a high price, while the Miskito divers (mostly boys in their late teens and early twenties) quickly spent their wages on rum at the Chinese stores. Planning for the future was nowhere in evidence. It remains for the new Sandinista government to create development plans that will emphasize not only the protection of natural resources but also their rational development for the benefit of the local population.

The Miskito and the Somoza Government

Politically, the Miskito area has been a part of Nicaragua only since 1894. In 1860 Great Britain gave up her territorial aspirations to the coast through the Treaty of Managua. The treaty created a Miskito Reserve along the east coast, within which the Miskito were to be free to govern themselves. But in 1894 General Rigoberto Cabezas occupied Bluefields, bringing to an end the reign of the last Miskito king, Robert Henry Clarence, and "reincorporating" the Mosquitia into Nicaragua as the Department of Zelaya. The incorporation document did grant certain privileges to the Miskito inhabitants: They were to be free from military service and from taxes, and all revenues from the area were to remain there for the benefit of the coastal population. A later agreement, in 1905, allowed Miskito and creole people to gain legal title to lands occupied before 1894 (copies of these legal documents are appended to Bourgeois and Gruenberg, 1980: 97-108). However, the general attitude about the incorporation among Miskito people has been that they were tricked into giving up their "independence" (as represented by the king) and forced to swear allegiance to a country they disliked. Some old Miskito men argue that Nicaragua was to have power for only 50 years, until the Miskito could control their own affairs, and "their country" would then be given back for them to rule. Such an event never happened, of course, and in the meantime the growth of the creole and Spanish-speaking population has complicated the question of land ownership along the coast.

In Miskito history the "Spaniards," as Spanish-speaking Nicaraguans continue to be called, have been the traditional enemies. At the same time, there has been a long tradition of friendly relations with English-speaking foreigners, beginning with the buccaneers and extending through the missionaries and company foremen of recent times. Given these patterns, it is interesting to note how the recently deposed dictator fit into them. Educated in U.S. military schools, Anastasio Somoza, Jr., spoke fluent English and had an (estranged) American wife. He occasionally visited the coast, where he gave speeches in English, urged people not to forget their English, and emphasized his friendship with the creole and Miskito people. He liked to boast that "everyone on the coast is a Liberal" (his own party). In a situation of ethnic antagonism, Somoza could legitimately claim to be not entirely

Spanish, thus using his bilingualism and his ties to the United States for his own political advantage.

Most Miskito probably sympathized with Somoza for other reasons as well. They had never been effectively incorporated into a Spanish or English jurisdiction and had no tradition of expecting services from a central government. Thus, the little that the Somoza government did provide in the way of schools and health services was duly appreciated but not measured against any other standard of expected government services. And there was relatively little interference in local affairs in this isolated area.

The Miskito had had no opportunity to learn about Sandinista type socialism as a political philosophy, and they probably had substantial prejudice against it through the influence of conservative Christian missionaries. The Moravians and other Protestant churches on the coast all worked with the Somoza government and generally regarded him, however objectionable some of his policies may have been, as a bulwark against a "Communist takeover" in Central America. He portrayed himself in this role and seemed to be taken at face value by the churches. I heard sermons in villages (delivered by lay pastors, but obviously repeating the opinions of higher level missionaries) warning that if Somoza left, the Communists would gain control and religion would be outlawed. One dramatic warning was that the communists would "take away a man's sailing dory or his animals, which he had worked so hard to acquire, and give them to his lazy neighbor across the village, who never worked at all." Ironically, this is exactly what was accomplished by the traditional Miskito kinship system, which insisted on reciprocal sharing of fish, turtles, and other products between kinsmen.

Many Miskito also seemed to admire Somoza as a strongman. The Miskito pattern of leadership is for an ambitious strongman to gather around him a circle of relatives and supporters and to rely on eloquence, persuasion, and skillful manipulation to accomplish his ends. Miskito political organization is not democratic, but is based on competition between such charismatic figures. The Miskito are also proud, independent, and outspoken.

These aspects of the "Miskito character" have been noted from early times:

> They are a fine set of men, lively, intelligent, and high spirited; but they have learnt no good from the intercourse of English and American sailors. . . . They are a violent, quarrelsome set of Indians, and most terrible drinkers. From the king being of their tribe, and the remembrance of the deeds of former days, they have still a great propensity to plunder and illuse the surrounding tribes, in spite of all the king can do to prevent them. They are lazy, insolent, and have a most overweening idea of their own consequence and capabilities; yet these questionable propensities show an impulsive nature with some character [Bell, 1862: 250].

Although the Miskito admire successful strongmen, they are usually cynical about the political pretensions of those who are not their own relatives. The Awastara headman during my fieldwork tried to conduct local affairs by haranguing, threatening, and flying into a rage at his fellow villagers. He often wore National Guard fatigues and a commando ranger type hat and presented a striking figure as he strode up and down in front of those assembled for Sunday afternoon meetings. A common response, however, was to disregard him or even ridicule him for his pretensions. His attempts to play the role of a Somoza-style strongman was obviously unsuccessful. An older and politically more astute former headman was almost as flamboyant a speaker, but seemed to be more effective. He also had close ties with higher officials in the Somoza government, as did various Miskito political leaders along the coast. As far as I know, there were no Miskito leaders with close ties to the Sandinistas. Thus, even the Miskito who were cynical about the Somoza government saw the dictator himself as an extremely successful strongman who could provide valuable favors to those who worked with him.

Another factor which contributed to Miskito political attitudes was that for them, the original experience with the Sandinistas along the Río Coco had been negative. They personally knew American plantation managers and other foreigners, whom they generally admired, who were killed by the guerrillas. Sandinista attacks devastated the Standard Fruit Company installations in April 1931, which directly hurt the Miskito smallholders who sold bananas to the company. Far from feeling exploited by Standard Fruit, the Miskito were delighted to have a market for their products and a chance to buy consumer goods in the company commissary at Puerto Cabo Gracias a Dios. Drawn into the wage economy during the last 100 years, the Miskito strongly identified with the companies and with their foreign managers. Miskito men in Awastara spoke admiringly of their former bosses. They also compared what they regarded as the good wages and the fair treatment as equals they had received from them, with the poor wages and treatment as social inferiors they say they receive from current Spanish-speaking Nicaraguan employers. In general, the Miskito did not feel exploited or oppressed by the foreign companies and did not share the Sandinista interpretation of them as class enemies of the people. In fact, one of their main concerns today is to bring the companies back so they can have jobs and good wages again.

One widely known incident took place in March 1931, when a German Moravian missionary was executed and then beheaded by the Sandinista guerrillas (Macaulay, 1967: 190). As the Miskito tell the story, he asked as a final favor to be allowed to sing a hymn from the Moravian hymnbook. Such courage made him a minor martyr in Miskito eyes.

The situation on the coast, then, was very different from that in the western part of the country, where the first Sandinistas were most often viewed as patriotic, nationalist revolutionaries. The Miskito instead shared with the Standard and United Fruit Companies and the Moravian church their view of the Sandinistas as bandits and murderers. During the Sandino period, guerrillas along the upper Río Coco did confiscate some cattle (see, for instance, Helms, 1971: 147) and other village property for their own use. Such confiscation was viewed as outright robbery by the Miskito and was greatly resented.

Portraying himself as a loyal friend of the Miskito people, Somoza himself helped fund ALPROMISU. A large appropriation from the Somoza government had been set aside to sponsor the regional meeting of the Congress of Indigenous Peoples in May 1979 and to help with other ALPROMISU projects. ALPROMISU's aims were to earn scholarships for Miskito students, secure some kind of formal Miskito representation in the government, defend Miskito land claims, and to promote the general welfare of the Miskito people. One major issue which had developed in 1979 was timber-cutting regulations promulgated by INFONAC, the government forestry development organization. The Miskito believed that INFONAC was appropriating Miskito lands and selling the timber resources which rightfully belonged to the Miskito. A young Miskito lawyer active in ALPROMISU vigorously defended his people's claims.

To some extent ALPROMISU was a controversial organization because of the way it promoted Miskito rights, as opposed to those of creole and Spanish-speaking people in the area. These latter people considered themselves as much costeños as the Miskito, and many regarded ALPROMISU as a divisive force and thought some overall costeño organization, not based on ethnicity, would be better for promoting development. Some of the Río Coco Miskito also felt unrepresented in ALPROMISU, which tended to be dominated by a few prominent Miskito individuals from Puerto Cabezas.

Some older Miskito men in the villages mistakenly thought ALPROMISU was trying once more to establish an independent Miskito nation to drive out the "Spaniards" and return to the legendary days of Miskito dominance. The idea of a new Miskito kingdom on the coast, or of a new English-speaking country with close ties to Britain and the United States, also occurs occasionally in the Nicaraguan popular press. There is no practical possibility of such an occurrence, but reactions to the idea reflect the history of the area: Some creoles and Miskito people speak wistfully of the possibility, while Spanish Nicaraguans mention it with scorn and resentment. General Somoza's generous support of ALPROMISU was obviously intended to control ethnic political developments on the coast by supporting a seemingly harmless Miskito organization.

After the revolution, ALPROMISU changed its name to MISURASATA, or Miskito, Sumu, Rama, Sandinista Aslatakanka ("united together"). At a dramatic meeting in Puerto Cabezas, Sandinista Comandante Daniel Ortega addressed the organization's annual meeting in November 1979 and spoke in favor of a change in name and organizational structure to include the some 200 Rama Indians (but still excluding creoles, Chinese, and "Spaniards"). He emphasized that being poor and being Nicaraguan were more important than being Indian, but nevertheless encouraged the Miskito to respect their own cultural heritage (Adams, 1979). Given this mandate, MISURASATA has since been recognized as a legitimate people's organization, among the Asociación de Trabajadores del Campo (ATC), Comités de Defensa Sandinista (CDS), and other types of organizations created by the revolution.

MISURASATA has also been granted a seat on the ruling council of the revolutionary government, thus gaining a remarkable degree of formal recognition. MISURASATA seems to be gaining strength in the Miskito villages and has become increasingly vocal in defending Miskito rights and acting as spokesman for the Miskito as a whole, within the framework of loyalty to the revolution. A major victory was won when MISURASATA was allowed to direct the mass literacy campaign in the Miskito area and to alphabetize in Miskito. Literacy materials in Miskito had just arrived on the coast in June 1980.

Its vocal, almost strident pro-Miskito stance seemed likely to bring MISURASATA into conflict with the Sandinista government in the near future over issues such as land ownership and colonization by poor Nicaraguans in the Miskito area. Behind the official government tolerance for MISURASATA, one sensed the attitude that "those irritating Miskito" were again causing trouble and that their clamor for ethnic identity might soon go too far.

MISURASATA's ability to survive and prosper under the new government, in spite of its close ties with the previous regime, has interesting implications. On the one hand, it demonstrates the Sandinista government's official tolerance of ethnic self-determination, as well as the political realization that any repression of the organization might fan anti-Spanish and anti-Sandinista sentiments on the coast into an open explosion. On the other hand, from the Miskito point of view it shows an interesting Miskito cultural ability to adapt and survive in a completely changed political situation. MISURASATA is now an official Sandinista organization which supports the revolution and can campaign for its share of government resources. To some extent this new political sophistication may reflect centuries of successful accommodation to outsiders and adjustment to the changes they have introduced. The Sandinista government and its programs in this sense may be seen as simply the latest wave of foreign influence to arrive on the coast imposing new living patterns for the Miskito.

Migration from the west and colonization are rapidly taking place in the interior of Zelaya. An Instituto Nicaraguense de Reforma Agraria (INRA; 1980) report describes this recent colonization in some detail. The migration began in the 1930s and 1940s, with mining activity and rubber-gathering attracting poor Nicaraguans from the Pacific. The major influx began in the 1950s, however, as small agriculturalists began pushing along the dirt tracks that were being built into the area. The typical pattern has been for a man to arrive first and clear a patch of land and then send for his family. In time, other relatives and friends arrive to settle nearby. The original pioneer may sell the improvements on his land, thus obtaining a modest lump sum of working capital, and move on to a more distant piece of undisturbed forest. In this way, the whole interior zone near the Siuna-La Rosita mines is being settled. About 1970, the Catholic Church began a program organizing these settlers into congregations, with "delegates of the word" as lay evangelizers in each one. The program was apparently quite successful and laid the foundation for settler cooperation with the Sandinista guerrillas, who began operating in the area a few years later.

Interior Zelaya is thus quite different than the coast proper, in that it is becoming populated with Spanish-speaking peasant farmers, many of whom have been politicized to some degree through the efforts of leftist Catholic missionaries. Many of these settlers also cooperated with the revolutionaries and can thus logically expect benefits from the new government. The success of this spontaneous colonization process is also interesting, compared with the failure of many planned colonization projects in other parts of lowland Latin America.

The continuing colonization promises to bring poor Spanish-speaking peasants into increasing conflict with the Miskito along the coast and along the Río Coco. The indigenous Sumu communities have apparently been severely disrupted and, despite armed conflict, appear to present no serious obstacle to Spanish colonization in the interior, but this will not be the case along the coast itself. In June 1980 conflicts between Miskito villagers and encroaching Spanish colonists were occurring in Alamicamba, and MISURASATA vigorously defended the Miskito land claims. The legal status of the Miskito claims was in some doubt, since not all communities formalized their title deeds in the 1905 period. Land ownership granted under British protection in the last century could also be dismissed as an imperialist anachronism. Traditional use rights have so far been respected, and the new government has made great efforts to be fair and just toward the Miskito. Nevertheless, one can foresee pressure from Spanish-speaking colonists with ties to the revolutionary government for access to Miskito lands.

In 1978-1979, there was a genuine desire among costeños in general for a bigger share of the country's resources and for more political leverage. In January 1979 a conference was held in Puerto Cabezas, in an ex-convent recently acquired as a branch campus of the Universidad Nacional Autónoma de Nicaragua (UNAN) to plan for development on the coast. Representatives of the various development agencies spoke there, as well as university professors and people in the service professions. One of the themes that emerged was a common sense of identity as costeños, whether of Miskito, creole, or Spanish-speaking background. Another theme was resentment of the coast's abandonment by the central government and its exploitation by foreign companies. Costeños in general felt that the Somoza government had not complied with the 1905 agreement to use coastal revenues for the economic development of the region and for the benefit of the local population.

After the conference, a plan emerged to found a new, separate university of the coast, which would specialize in subjects directly related to local problems, for example, fisheries and forestry management and interethnic relations. Hopes were high among intellectuals on the coast when support was found in the Somoza government for the plan. It was easy for Somoza to divert funds to the coast from the central UNAN in Managua, since it was a major center of leftist student activity and where the population generally supported the Somoza government. Since the revolution, plans for the new university are said to have been dropped, although the UNAN branch campus was scheduled to reopen in September 1980.

In June 1980 there seemed, predictably enough, to be a great deal of dissatisfaction with the revolution on the coast. A number of the large Chinese shopkeepers had left, but those who remained continued their economic hold on the region. One Miskito small shopkeeper reported, however, that the new government price controls allowed him to compete successfully with the Chinese for the first time. Daily laborers working for the government were also being paid higher wages than ever before, and this new money in circulation seemed to result in more activity in the Puerto Cabezas marketplace. The Moravian church and the church-related development groups seemed somewhat marginalized and disgruntled with the general pattern of developments. A plethora of new government agencies had arrived on the coast, as elsewhere in the country, to bring the benefits of the revolution to the people. Social science research aimed at helping the new agencies accomplish their tasks was being encouraged, and some reports had already been prepared (Bourgeois and Gruenberg, 1980; INRA, 1980). Many of the young people working for the new bureaucracies seemed sincere and idealistic and genuinely concerned with gaining the support of local people. The formal apparatus of government in general seemed to be monopolized by young people, replacing the older power structure of village headmen, local political bosses, and Moravian lay pastors. A meeting of town authorities which I attended in La Rosita seemed to be all idealistic youths under 30. Many individuals connected with the Somoza government had lost their positions, and in some cases, at least, their practical experience seemed to be badly needed. Syndicates of workers—turtle fishermen, for example—had been formed in the Miskito villages, and some Miskito (I talked to) were cautiously optimistic about the possible benefits the new government might bring.

There was concern among Sandinista leaders that the east coast might provide a staging ground for counterrevolutionary groups seeking to undermine the new government. These fears were not unfounded, since ex-National Guard officers and other former Somocistas have threatened to retake the country from their bases in Honduras. In October 1980 a three-day strike in Bluefields resulted in several arrests of counterrevolutionary leaders. The strike itself apparently indicated the unhappiness of creole residents over the presence of Cuban teachers and doctors and over the government's failure to better conditions on the coast (Latin America Weekly Report, 1980).

During the revolutionary struggle, the general Sandinista position about the Miskito self-determination movement had been that the hope of the future lay not in such movements, but in joining the national struggle for liberation. As have many leftist groups around the world, the Sandinistas argued that ethnic differences were tools used by the ruling class to divide and maintain control over a disadvantaged population. This point of view emphasizes the common structural position of poor, oppressed peoples and views the cultural differences between them as secondary. Ethnic differences become barriers perpetuated by the ruling class, which prevent oppressed peoples from recognizing their common, powerless position and from uniting in a common effort to overthrow those in power. On the coast, official Sandinista pronouncements have been that the revolution was made for poor, exploited peoples like the Miskito. The Sandinistas hope that once the Miskito are shown the reality of their class position, they can be persuaded to join wholeheartedly in the struggle for change.

Appealing as such arguments for class solidarity may be, they underestimate the importance of cultural differences. To local people like the Miskito, their language, their beliefs, their kinship system, and their history as they understand it are social realities as important as their disadvantaged class position. Furthermore, it is difficult to unite with their oppressed brothers (in this case "Spaniards" to the west), who have long been the object of animosity and conflict. Finally, Miskito political ambitions, so far as they exist at all, center on self-determination for themselves, not on creating a "new Nicaragua."

Given the potential for conflict, it is interesting to note that the official Sandinista position has been to encourage the Miskito self-determination movement. Cultural Survival, a U.S.-based organization which has funded recent MISURASATA activities, notes important Miskito gains since the revolution:

> An expensive bilingual component was added to the impoverished nation's literacy campaign. A national Indian organization has a seat on the Council of State. The government has accepted the Indians' right to their traditional land and is presently negotiating the limits of that territory. These are rights which most indigenous people in Latin America do not enjoy [Cultural Survival, 1980: 9].

At least at an ideological level, the new government seems tolerant of the Miskito ethnic presence. An interesting view is expressed by two scholars strongly sympathetic to the Sandinista government, who see ethnic consciousness evolving naturally into class consciousness over time:

> The conservation, and even the accentuation of Miskito identity, not only does not contradict the formation of class consciousness, but acts as a catalyst for it. The process of reaffirmation of ethnic identity by a colonized people leads to a new class consciousness which supercedes the defensive ethnocentrism which occurs at first [Bourgeois and Gruenberg, 1980: 78; my translation].

This, like the Sandinista revolution in general, seems hopeful and idealistic.

The Costeños, The Guardia, and The Revolution

The Guardia Nacional de Nicaragua was organized by the U.S. Marines in 1927. After the assassination of Sandino at the instigation of Somoza in 1934, the Guardia served effectively as a personal army for the Somoza dynasty (Millett, 1977). In the late

1970s, the violence and cruelty practiced by the Guardia included mass executions of peasants in villages suspected of cooperating with the Sandinistas and of young men in poor barrios of the cities. By the time of the Sandinista victory, the Guardia was hated and feared by most of the population in the western part of the country.

An interesting question, not dealt with by Millett or by military analysts (Dyer, 1979), is where the rank and file of Guardia troops were recruited. Certainly there was a strong effort to recruit creole and Miskito men from the coast, and many did serve, although I have not been able to find hard data on the numbers of costeños in the Guardia. My own impressions, from casual observation and from knowing many Miskito families with Guard members, were that the Miskito were strongly represented. The salary and benefits were attractive to young Miskito men, and they found the possibility of combat exciting. With a proud military tradition since the days of the buccaneers, the Miskito were not averse to fighting their traditional enemies, the "Spaniards." The problem of killing other Nicaraguans was not acute for the Miskito, since traditionally they had not regarded "Spaniards" as countrymen. For Somoza, the Miskito and the creole populations provided soldiers with a useful ethnic background.

Selective recruitment for the military among sympathetic ethnic groups is of course a common political strategy. The Ghurka units from India in the British army and the Cossack cavalry in the Russian Czar's army are well-known examples. Many of the new governments in Africa have also relied on selective military recruitment. For example, General Amin's army in Uganda seems to have consisted mostly of Nubian soldiers from the north, who were antagonistic toward the majority population in southern Uganda.

> Yet the Nubi have been an essentially marginal group in Uganda for nearly 90 years, feeling superior to others, yet regarded by them as alien. Extolled for their loyalty, stamina, and military virtues, "admirable and cheap material," overworked and underpaid in the early years, they remained an odd minority. . . . If ever there was fertile ground for pent-up frustration and aggression it was here [Southall, 1975: 89].

The usefulness of marginal ethnic groups in civil conflict is obvious: Traditional antipathies can be enlisted against an existing enemy, the rival ethnic group. The problem for those recruited is that their future may depend on the outcome of the conflict. In modern Africa, particularly, genocide seems to have become increasingly common as a way of punishing ethnic groups for their political sins.

In U.S. history, the unhappy experience of the Iroquois provides another comparison. For over 200 years, the Iroquois dominated the area which is now western New York State, northern Pennsylvania, and adjacent areas. The league which united their six nations served in some measure as a model for the U.S. constitution and allowed them to maintain a united front against the invading colonial powers, the English and the French. They successfully survived the colonial period, skillfully playing off the British against the French, proud of their mastery of diplomacy and warfare. The Revolutionary War divided them, however, and served as a turning point in Iroquois history. The western four nations fought as allies of the British during the war and controlled the western territory when the war ended in 1784. However, the wartime hostilities between American settlers and the Indians, along with resentment of the Iroquois's pro-British position, played a major role in their subsequent downfall. Divided by the war, overwhelmed by hostile settlers flooding in from the east, cheated out of their land in a series of treaties and deals based on the premise that they were a defeated enemy, the Iroquois never recovered (Wallace, 1972: 111-183). The reservation system in which they were confined created what Wallace calls "slums in the wilderness, where no traditional Indian culture could long survive and where only the least useful aspects of white culture could easily penetrate" (1972: 184).

The Iroquois example is perhaps extreme, but there are some parallels with the Miskito situation. The Miskito fought with Somoza's army against the Sandinistas, they harbor a long tradition of antagonism toward "Spaniards," and they enjoy the land and resources needed by a developing nation.

A predictable result of involvement of individual Miskitos with Somoza's Guardia was to deepen the ethnic antagonisms that already existed. People in the west were not surprised that "sambos" from the coast were involved in killing civilians, reducing the cities to rubble, and the general destruction perpetrated by the Guard. After all, Spanish Nicaraguans "knew" that Miskito and black costeños were savage and bloodthirsty. On the other side, there were no Miskito Sandinistas and little understanding of the Miskito point of view by the revolutionaries. Currently, there is some legitimate worry that costeños might be recruited for a counterrevolutionary force to topple the Sandinista government.

The Future

One may venture a few predictions about the Miskito and the east coast under the new Sandinista government. First, in spite of the revolutionary rhetoric emphasizing the solidarity of those who had been disenfranchised, it seems unlikely that old antagonisms will disappear. To the Miskito, the Sandinistas are "Spaniards" from the west, their traditional enemies, and furthermore they are Spaniards previously labelled as communist, antireligious bandits. To the Sandinistas themselves, the bitter memory remains of fighting against Guardia troops, many of whom were Miskito and creoles from the coast. Practically, it also seems probable that areas which actively supported the revolution will have first priority in receiving its benefits. This may include interior Zelaya with its peasant Spanish-speaking population, but probably not the Miskito and creole areas along the coast and the Río Coco.

On the other hand, the resources of the east coast will have to play a major role in future development plans by any Nicaraguan government. Lumbering, gold mining, fishing, and cattle raising are all important activities on the coast and will continue to be mainstays of the economy. The pine savannas and the tropical rain forest in the interior, in particular, will be exploited more intensively in the near future. In 1979, INFONAC lumbering regulations and activities in the pine savannas were already creating serious conflict with the Miskito. As more Spanish-speaking settlers come to the coast along the newly opened road, additional conflict will develop. For the Miskito, as long as they themselves do not control the exploitation of their natural resources, their position will continue to be that of marginalized wage laborers. Education of Miskito youth, a major preoccupation of Miskito families already, seems to be the only possibility of gaining this kind of control over their own affairs. A hopeful sign is that the Sandinista government, among its many positive and forward-looking steps so far, has announced that education will be a major public goal. The current literacy campaign has been announced as only the first step in providing educational opportunities for the people. For the first time in eastern Nicaragua, a national government seems to be making a serious commitment to provide social services for the population. This kind of effort will not go unappreciated, even by a cynical Miskito and creole population.

In general, the most hopeful projection is that the Sandinista government will show itself to be sophisticated in its understanding of the east coast's history and generous in its attempts to integrate the country and create a new Nicaragua. Let us hope that should this happen, the Miskito will not suffer the fate of the Iroquois and, long-time successful opportunists in foreign affairs that they are, will have a chance to adapt to their new situation.

REFERENCES

ADAMS, R. N. (1979) "Notes on Nicaragua: The Atlantic coast." (mimeo)

BELL, C. N. (1862) "Remarks on the Mosquito territory, its climate, people, productions, etc., etc., with a map." J. of the Royal Geographical Society 32: 242-268.

BOURGEOIS, P. and J. GRUENBERG (1980) "La Mosquitia y la revolución: Informe de una investigación rural en la Costa Atlántica Norte." Siuna, Nicaragua: Instituto Nicaraguense de Reforma Agraria. (mimeo)

BURBACH, R. and T. DRAIMIN (1980) "Nicaragua's revolution." New York: North American Congress on Latin America Report on the Americas 14 (May-June): 2-35.

Cultural Survival, Inc. (1980) "Nicaragua." Cambridge, MA: Cultural Survival Newsletter 4 (Fall): 8-9.

DYER, G. (1979) "Nicaragua," pp. 507-512 in J. Keegan (ed.), World Armies. New York: Facts on File.

FLOYD, T. S. (1967) The Anglo-Spanish Struggle for Mosquitia. Alburquerque: Univ. of New Mexico Press.

KOEPPEL, B. and D. HARVEY (1980) "Nicaragua rebuilds: A new model is emerging from the ruins left by Somoza and civil war." Progressive 44(May): 42-46.

HELMS, M. W. (1971) Asang: Adaptations to Culture Contact in a Miskito Community. Gainesville: Univ. of Florida Press.

——— (1969) "The cultural ecology of a colonial tribe." Ethnology 8: 76-84.

——— (1968) "Matrilocality and the maintenance of ethnic identity: The Miskito of eastern Nicaragua and Honduras." Stuttgart-Munchen, Germany: Verhandlungen des XXXVIII Internationalen Amerikanistenkongresses: 459-464.

INCER, J. (1975) Geografía Ilustrada de Nicaragua. Bogotá: Colombia: Italgraf, S.A.

Instituto Nicaraguense de Reforma Agraria (1980) "La frontera agrícola: notas sobre el campesinado español." Siuna, Nicaragua. (mimeo)

Latin American Weekly Report (1980) "Atlantic Coast disturbances ring alarm bells in Managua." Oct. 17: 7.

LEOGRANDE, W. M. (1979) "The revolution in Nicaragua: Another Cuba?" Foreign Affairs 58 (Fall): 28-50.

MACAULAY, N. (1967) The Sandino Affair. Chicago: Quadrangle.

MILLETT, R. (1977) Guardians of the Dynasty: A history of the U.S. Created Guardia Nacional de Nicaragua and the Somoza Family. Maryknoll, NY: Orbis Books.

MONTGOMERY, R. N. (1980) "The fall of Somoza; anatomy of a revolution." Parameters: J. of the U.S. Army War College 10(March): 47-57.

NIETSCHMANN, B. (1979) "Ecological change, inflation, and migration in the far western Caribbean." Geographical Rev. 69(January): 1-24.

——— (1973) Between Land and Water: The Subsistence Ecology of the Miskito Indians, Eastern Nicaragua. New York: Seminar Press.

SOUTHALL, A. (1975) "General Amin and the coup: Great man or historical inevitability?" J. of Modern African Studies 13(1): 85-105.

WALLACE, A.F.C. (1972) [orig. ed. 1969] The Death and Rebirth of the Seneca. New York: Vintage Books.

Philip A. Dennis is Associate Professor of Anthropology at Texas Tech University. The results of earlier fieldwork on intervillage feuding in Oaxaca, Mexico, have appeared in article form in English and as a monograph, Conflictos por Tierras en el Valle de Oaxaca *(INI [Instituto Nacional Indigenista], Colección SEP-INI, 1976). His most recent fieldwork was among the Miskito of east Nicaragua on a dramatic culture-bound syndrome which has created major public health problems.*

RODERIC A. CAMP
Department of Political Science
Central College
Pella, Iowa

INTELLECTUALS
Agents of Change in Mexico?

Intellectuals have always played a role in the political development of their societies. Their role, however, has fluctuated with changes in time and place, and in the 20th century the intellectual's function in society seems ambiguous both to the intellectual himself and to those who have studied him. In spite of this ambiguity, there is a consensus in recent literature that the ability of intellectuals to influence elite groups and the government itself is on the increase (Ladd and Lipset, 1976: 309). The reasons for this increased influence are several, and although there is recognition of the expanding importance of men of knowledge, there are few serious examinations of this group and its role (Marsal and Arent, 1970: 466; Marsal, 1966: 36; Friedmann, 1960: 540-541). This essay will examine explanations for the increased importance of intellectuals, suggest why they could be essential to Mexico's future, and, given their contemporary image, their own structural characteristics, and their relationship to the political system, argue that it is unlikely that the Mexican intellectual will be an agent of change.

Explanations for the increased important of intellectuals since World War II generally fall into five categories: the demand for

---

AUTHOR'S NOTE: I would like to acknowledge the assistance of a National Endowment for the Humanities Foundation Grant and a Fulbright-Hays Post-Doctoral Research Fellowship for making this research possible and the suggestions and criticisms of William B. Julian, James W. Wilkie, Alexander Wilde, and Edward J. Williams.

Journal of Interamerican Studies and World Affairs, Vol. 23 No. 3, August 1981 297-320

intellectuals as communicators between (1) politicians and technicians and (2) the rest of society, a need for holders of knowledge in an increasingly specialized world, the use of intellectuals as propagandists for their governments, the expanded role of thinkers as pragmatic leaders of opposition movements, and the traditional function of men of knowledge as creators and disseminators of values. Let us examine each of these explanations in order to better understand the importance of the intellectual in today's society.

As the social and economic complexities of societies have increased, roles have become more specialized; in the educated class, an intelligentsia of specialists, technicians if you will, has emerged. At the same time, political and social pragmatists have continued their leadership roles in the realm of practical politics. Although a few talented individuals have played both general and specialized roles, a gradual separation has formed between people focusing on the use of knowledge to find the most efficient solutions to problems and those more concerned with the social and political realities of administering solutions to a society.

The intellectual, a creative thinker who takes a critical posture in searching for more humane and rational solutions to contemporary problems from a perspective of transcendental values and transmits these ideas to a broad audience, has the necessary skills to serve as a bridge between these two groups. The conflict between normative and behavioral thinking has brought about a gap between the language of the technicians and the pragmatists, in terms of both forms of expression and commonly understood meanings. The most careful student of this phenomenon, Alvin Gouldner (1976: 191), argues that modern politics will become increasingly ineffective unless we can find ways to bridge the discourse between those two groups. But not only might the intellectual bridge this critical gap among two elite groups in most societies he is also the most logical person to communicate many of the views of the experts and the politicians to a mass audience (Hayek, 1960: 373).

The knowledge which gives intellectuals an opportunity to serve as special communicators in their societies also increases the likelihood that they will be called upon in larger numbers to serve in government positions, the second of our general explanations for their importance. We are moving into what Zbigniew Brzezinski (1968: 18) described as a technetronic age, in which "knowledge becomes a tool of power and the effective mobilization of talent an important way for acquiring power" (Birnbaum, 1971: 622; Eulau, 1977: 70; Gouldnee, 1975-1976: 6). This trend is complemented by an extraordinary growth in all activities related to knowledge production in the United States and elsewhere (Machlup, 1962: 374; Lipset and Dobson, 1972: 175). Intellectuals will be drawn to establishment activities within the public sector not solely because of their preparation for increasingly specialized tasks but also as suggested by our third explanation because governments need more "experts in the art of speech" (Aron, 1957: 205). As Raymond Aron (1957) argues, the theorist and the propagandist have become combined, and the man of ideas is no longer separate from the man of action. Governments need articulate propagandists for very practical reasons: The less they use intellectual means, the more they must resort to force (Kolakowski, 1972).

Many countries have suffered political turmoil since their independence, and it has often been turmoil caused by a national inability to legitimize political and economic norms and resolve pressing problems, which has led to a fourth reason why intellectuals are important. One of the obvious outcomes of this has been widespread political violence and the presence of groups and organizations who use violent means to achieve their political and social goals. Revolutionary activities are particularly attractive to and suited to intellectuals because they are "apt to be sensitive to discrepancies between distant ideals and contemporary realities" (Putnam, 1976: 194). Recognizing this, governments have encouraged many forms of antiintellectualism to inhibit their abilities to organize or lead antigovernment activities (Gordon, 1955: 522). From a revolutionary's point of view, the intellectual contributes to a movement which cannot be acquired from practical experience as a guerrilla (Lenin, 1969: 74). Regardless of whether the intellectual's role in revolutionary activities is as a direct leader or as a theoretical advisor, he exists as a possible viable threat to existing governments.

Last, intellectuals continue to play an important traditional role as creators and disseminators of values. They are crucial to the formation of cultural symbols which determine man's identity and that of his society (Lipset and Dobson, 1972: 175, 178). This is increasingly critical to cultures and governments which are attempting to mold or restructure their societies following non-traditional principles. Intellectuals do this not only through their creation of cultural resources; in most societies, they play the role of gate-keepers and socializers in the certification of other elites because of their control over the formal institutions of higher education.

All of the above are explanations important to increasing our understanding of intellectuals in general. The purpose of this essay, however, is to understand the implication of these patterns in Mexico. Mexico provides an important setting for examining the recent role of the intellectual because it is a nation in the midst of serious social, political, and economic problems which will test the durability of its unique political system. The reality of Mexico's situation has been noted both by critical observers and by Mexicans who are currently in positions to make or influence decisions which will determine its future (Guzman, 1978: 6; Gordon, 1978; Lyons, 1977: 55; Urquidi, 1977: 7; Solís, 1977: 4-6; Johnson, 1978: 244; Koslow, 1977: 1; Williams, 1977: 1; Williams, 1978: 210-211).[1] In the opinion of both groups, Mexico must resolve its problems in the next decade or it will once again be confronted with a major social revolution. This important juncture in Mexico's development has serious implications for the United States because it is becoming clear that Mexico is no longer solely dependent economically on the United States; the United State and Mexico have become dependent, if unequally, on each other (*Uno más uno*, 1978). Further, the Mexican-American population,in absolute numbers, is the fastest growing minority in the United States; thus, the future development of Mexico and possibly the stability of United States border regions, and perhaps of the United States as a whole, depend upon Mexico's determination and capacity to overcome these problems.

When the violence of the 1910 Revolution in Mexico subsided in 1920, intellectuals began to make major contributions to the transformation of postrevolutionary Mexico, in the creation of major institutions, in the formation of policies, and in the generation of ideas (Krauze, 1976; Krauze, 1977). Today, because of their training and breadth of perception, intellectuals remain among the people best equipped to provide solutions to Mexico's problems and to offer the leadership and critical evaluations which might prevent Mexico from making fatal policy errors. The following pages will examine the presence of conditions in Mexico which affect the ability of intellectuals to play some of the roles described above, and we may be able to speculate on the likelihood of intellectuals' providing real alternatives, both in terms of leadership and ideas, for resolving Mexico's problems. Specifically, the historical and contemporary image of the intellectual, the structure of intellectual life, and the relationship of the intellectual to the political system in Mexico will be examined, all of which are essential to any discussion of Mexican intellectuals (Kadushin, 1974: 335).

Historically, intellectuals have been accorded a considerable amount of prestige in Latin America. Unlike in North American politics, intellectuals have been highly successful in electoral endeavors and political parties. Some authors think that the intellectual has been so highly esteemed in Latin America that politicians who want to increase their popularity attempt to invent formal intellectual qualifications if they are without them (Harrison, 1964: 27). Furthermore, Latin Americans have traditionally had a high regard for humanistic education, the source of most intellectual education, and this interest has extended to the literary activities in which most intellectuals are involved (Ellison, 1964: 88). Mexico is no exception to this general historical pattern, since beginning with the 1810 Revolution, Mexico has had numerous distinguished intellectuals who were both political theorists and activists (Careaga, 1971: 47; Schlesinger,

1972: 77). But in the 20th century, Mexican politics has not been characterized by a predominance of intellectual leaders (Ross, 1977: 430).[2] Even the attitude of the government seems to have considerable impact on the image of the intellectual in his society as does the self-image intellectuals themselves have. Arthur Schlesinger (1959: 488) argues, for example, that when intellectuals are more fully involved in the political elite during a government administration, the intellectual has a much higher status. Although Schlesinger's statement was directed toward the United States, it applies to other situations, including that of Mexico. For example, most intellectuals described the Gustavo Díaz Ordaz administration (1964-1970) as one which depreciated their prestige and that of his successor, Luis Echeverría (1970-1976), as an administration which improved their image.[3]

In spite of certain traditional cultural factors which contributed positively to the image of intellectuals, there is a strongly held belief among some intellectuals and many political elites that the word *intellectual* has a negative connotation in the Mexican scene. As one prominent Mexican writer commented: "In Mexico, intellectuals are spoken of in a pejorative way, in a joking tone. It is almost an insult to be called an intellectual."[4] Not all intellectuals share this view, but such negative views have eroded the intellectual's self-confidence. Some Mexican political leaders are also quick to promote this bias, although not publicly. When I asked several individuals for an interview to discuss Mexican intellectuals, they would reply, in a not entirely humorous vein, "What intellectuals?"

Although the intellectuals' lack of self-confidence may be cyclical and typical of many cultures, it is indicative of a more serious problem, usually identified by those intellectuals having close ties with public life. A Mexican poet best expressed this concern in his comment that "today, the word is used in an ambience in which there is some distrust concerning the intellectual, whether it is from the point of view of the masses or the political leaders. I think a dangerous situation has emerged in which the intellectual is becoming part of an elite."[5] The significance of this is that intellectuals run the risk of isolating themselves, both from the political decision makers who will guide

Mexico's future and from the masses for whom intellectuals might provide some leadership.

The intellectual's role in his society is not only affected by his image and self-image; equally important, and rarely discussed, is the dichotomy present in the definition of an intellectual in Mexico and elsewhere. Intellectuals and political elites have different perceptions of the role of the intellectual in public life. Intellectuals themselves share this dual view, some believing that an intellectual must promote his ideas in the government sector, or at least become politically active, while others believe he should remain outside of public life (Cosio Villegas, 1976; Hale, 1978: 133). In part, this became an issue in the resignation of five prominent intellectuals from the magazine *Politica* in the early 1960s. Those who resigned claimed they wanted independence from the prevailing political views carried by the magazine. Those who remained criticized these intellectuals for abandoning their political positions (Rico Galan, 1964: 25; Abreu Gómez, 1964: 26; Coccioli, 1965: 113). This uncertainty in the definition of an intellectual is not just semantic; indeed, it causes a significant structural weakness within intellectual life. This major rift among intellectuals promotes disunity. Because intellectuals themselves cannot agree on the role they should play in Mexican society, they weaken their collective voice on other ideological issues, and in fact each intellectual may choose to support the position of a colleague on the basis of that individual's position on political activism. Such divisions lessen the intellectual's ability to function in a pressure group, a condition which can be skillfully manipulated by political leaders.

Because political leaders see intellectuals in a different light, due to their emphasis on action, they consider a *different* group of intellectuals to be important. Many intellectuals feel that they are not being heard, which is correct. While politicians are not allergic to intellectuals as a group, many resent intellectuals who remain outside of public life. Therefore, politicians may be listening to one group of intellectuals, while the intellectuals look to another group, those outside public life, as their own leaders. Thus, suspicion will grow between the two groups, and the gap between public policy and intellectual life may widen if politicians' and intellectuals' perceptions of each other cannot be reconciled and their relationship clarified.

Intellectual self-image and definition, as well as the image and definition of intellectuals held by society as a whole, particularly political leaders, directly affect the intellectual's role and his ability to play a specific role. Equally important in determining the role intellectuals play is the growth of literacy and the expansion of libraries and cultural materials. Historically, in other countries, the requirement of mandatory primary education was accompanied by increased literacy (Brzezinski, 1968: 19-20). Paralleling this development was the expansion of circulating libraries, which in turn aided the growth of literature (Coser, 1965: 6, 44). Not only are these developments essential for increasing the demand for the goods produced by intellectuals but more important they are essential to the expansion of the independent intellectual, that is, the individual who is not dependent upon the government for his welfare. Furthermore, in the absence of these trends, there would be an increased probability that intellectuals, as they have traditionally in Latin America, would come from the upper social classes, those who have had access to education and have the economic independence to support their intellectual proclivities (Hodara, 1972: 33). Of the more than 50 prominent intellectuals in Mexico from 1920 to 1980, as selected by intellectuals, scholars, and politicians, only 4 were known to have lower class background (Camp, 1979).

In Mexico, the literacy rate has increased since the end of World War II, and it is obvious to any consistent visitor that the number of bookstores in Mexico City, and to a lesser extent in other important cities, has expanded rapidly. However, the level of functional illiteracy leaves a large portion of the Mexican masses outside the reach of intellectual writing, indicated by the low sales figures for nonfiction best sellers. While it is rare for a serious work published by a commercial press to sell more than 5,000 copies,[6] certain issues of comic books, which stress escapist themes, are read by between 1.5 and 3 million persons, many of whom are from the middle class (Hinds, 1977: 31-32). As of 1978, the mosts commercially successful book ever sold in

Mexico was *A Calzon Quitado*, an autobiographical exposé by the former mistress of President Díaz Ordaz, actress and singer Irma Serrano (Morett, 1978: 87).

The increased availability of education and books in Mexico contributes to a parallel pattern in the development and strength of other media: newspapers, magazines, radio, and television. These media are concentrated heavily in large urban centers, particularly Mexico City. Newspapers and magazines—whose columns provide an extra source of income for the intellectuals who write and are the major forum for the expression of ideas, given the realistic alternatives in the Mexican book-publishing world—have certain characteristics which determine the form of collaboration and access of intellectuals. Most important, 64% of the magazines and newspapers are published in the Federal District, which, in spite of being the most highly urbanized region in Mexico, accounts for only 14% of the population (Jiménez de Ottalengo, 1974: 778). In turn, newspapers in the provinces are dominated by several chains (Jiménez de Ottalengo, 1974: 771, 777-779; Cole, 1972: 105). Although the government actually owned only 2 of the 201 major newspapers in Mexico in 1970, the government can and does exert indirect influence over privately owned newspapers.

Government influence on newspapers and magazines stems from its control over the sales and distribution of newsprint and its role as an advertiser. The government agency known as PIPSA is the only agency authorized to import paper into Mexico (Cole, 1972: 69). It has been argued that PIPSA has never actually suspended newsprint to a publisher critical of the government, but it can either sell the publisher a poorer quality paper or, in the recent case of *Por Qué?*, force it to buy newsprint on the open market at a substantially more expensive, unsubsidized price (Underwood, 1965: 118; Erlandson, 1964: 235; Johnson, 1978: 158). Furthermore, the government is a major advertiser, accounting for an estimated 20% to 30% of all advertising copy (Russell, 1977: 141; Cole, 1972: 79). Elimination of government advertising would mean economic disaster for most newspapers and magazines.[7]

Radio could provide intellectuals with a mass audience, since 89% of Mexican homes in cities of more than 50,000 people have radios, but the quality of news and informational programs has been low, making intellectual participation unlikely (Maza, 1969: 98-99; Cole, 1972: 131). Television, which has recently begun to have talk shows and interviews, has for the most part programs of similar quality as radio. As one writer suggests, the freedom of expression on the subject of political affairs in Mexico seems to be in direct relationship to the level of education required to comprehend it and the number of people who might be reached by the particular medium. This accounts for the fact that books are the freest from control, while radio, television, and movies receive the most censorship (Garibay and Leñero, 1972: 35).[8]

The government, in addition to providing support for and indirect control over activities which employ intellectuals and disseminate their ideas, has been the supporter of the single-most important publisher in Mexico, the semiofficial Fondo de Cultura Económica. Many of the intellectuals in Mexico were first published by this press. But in 1965, after publishing Oscar Lewis's *The Children of Sánchez*, a highly realistic but critical view of Mexican poverty, the Fondo was faced with a suit against the publisher. Although the suit was later thrown out of court, the director general and his closest collaborators were dismissed, partly as a punishment for publishing Lewis, Georg Lukacs, and other "subversive" writers (Durán, 1967: 60). Mexican intellectuals responded with criticism of the dismissals in the press and by the withdrawal of their manuscripts from the Fondo, charging supression of freedom of thought (Russell, 1971: 35; Careaga, 1971: 107). Since that date, the Fondo has stayed away from publishing controversial contemporary analyses and criticisms of Mexican politics (Fondo, 1980).

The characteristics of the Mexican media, both in terms of their structure and their lack of freedom to print any author, has obvious implications for intellectuals. Although Mexican intellectual activities are no more neglected by their major newspapers than is true elsewhere in the world (Maza, 1969: 92), newspapers and magazines vary considerably in terms of what they will publish and, more important, whom they will publish. In particular, major publishers, newspapers, and intellectual journals wield considerable economic influence over the career development of young and well-established intellectuals. Charles Kadushin has argued that journals exercise power "through the clique and star system, the ability to publish some people and not others, and the ability to select some ideas and not others" (Kadushin, 1974: 51). This is not just a North American phenomenon, as was pointed out by one prominent Mexican poet: "These intellectual journals are very much closed. If you belong to one group you cannot exchange ideas in another group's journal. I could give you the names of 50 people who would never appear in *Vuelta* or in *Excélsior*. An excellent recent example was the reporting on Carlos Chávez's (one of Mexico's foremost composers) funeral. Octavio Paz gave the main oration and his name was not even mentioned in the *Excélsior* articles.... We have a name for this in Mexico, *ninguneo*, a word which refers to the policy of never mentioning someone's name in the history of literature or art."[9]

The policy of not publishing a person's work, or even mentioning his or her name, not only affects one's ability to make a living but also dramatically affects whether he or she will ever receive recognition from other intellectuals and readers of intellectual reviews, a critical factor in developing the reputation necessary for editorial acceptance of manuscripts. It also has another serious implication for Mexican intellectual life, since it directly relates to the ability of intellectual journals to survive, because the readership is splintered among journals which are controlled by particular personalities who express restricted points of views. This pattern not only divides the intellectuals themselves but also politicians often succumb to reading certain reviews and ignoring others, since they too are members of political cliques, led by single personalities, many of whom have ties with intellectual cliques. They find it difficult to follow numerous journals, instead of one or two expressing a narrow range of intellectual views. Last, these parochial orientations, in combination with the control of distribution by a few individuals, have severely restricted intellectual journals from reaching a mass audience, even in Mexico City.[10]

The concentration of the media and publishing houses in Mexico City has in turn contributed to its continued attraction of cultural activities and intellectuals. Mexico City is the undisputed political, economic, and social capital of the country, and the geographic centralization of intellectual activity, as is true in Paris and in London, is a factor contributing to increased cultural homogeneity among intellectuals, even of different ideological or philosophical views (Coser, 1967: 5-6). Coser (1967: 6) goes so far as to argue that not only do intellectuals communicate with each other more rapidly in such close proximity, but, more important, they come into constant social contact with politicians, an interaction which he believes helps both groups "develop a set of common assumptions transcending institutional affiliations and functional divisions." Although this assumption would be more applicable to a society in which the political system had reached a stage of maturity in which its legitimacy was well-established, Mexico is not immune from this influence. It was quite apparent from the interview process, both in the arranging of interviews and in talks with intellectuals and politicians, that many of them were acquainted with one another, even to the extent of having intimate friendships.[11] Furthermore, the concentration of intellectual activity in one small region of the country and its resulting homogeneous cultural overtones implies that most other regions of the country are neglected in terms of intellectual attention; and equally important, talented minds who fail to emigrate from the provinces are unknown to or ignored by the intellectuals of the capital and the publishers who popularize them. None of the 50 intellectuals selected as most prominent in Mexico (from 1920 to 1980) by intellectuals and politicians worked and lived outside of Mexico City.

The structural patterns engendered by this centralization of intellectual activities leads us to one last element in intellectual life, their recruitment, that is, how they make it into prominent intellectual circles. Intellectuals, as alluded to in the above passages about journals, are joined in coteries. Of the intellectuals interviewed, only one claimed to be independent of group connections, and only one other was seen as independent by other intellectuals. They are recruited in one of two ways: (1) either on the sole basis of their work, through the vehicles of several provincial literary reviews, or, more important, by winning national prizes or (2) on the basis of a mentor-student relationship, most frequently developed at the university. But whether a person is first recognized and recruited (1) in the classroom or from personal contact or (2) through the notoriety of his work, someone had to make the decision to recruit him into an intellectual circle. Both Coser (1967: 8) and Kadushin (1974: 25), in their studies of Europe and North America, found that young intellectuals were sponsored by older, well-established intellectuals.[12] In this regard, Mexican intellectuals have more in common with English intellectuals. Most English writers and literary critics started their careers as Oxbridge undergraduates (Coser, 1967: 7), and for Mexican intellectuals, the National University serves a similar function, both as a highly centralized, selective educational sieve, and for socializing and certifying future intellectuals. An analysis of the 50 most prominent Mexican intellectuals from 1920 to 1980 demonstrates quite clearly that: Most of the younger ones were disciples or students of older intellectuals; nearly all of the intellectuals were college educated and not self-educated; most of the intellectuals had taught or were teaching at the National University or, in more recent years, the Colegio de México; and the majority had also been students at the University.[13]

These educational patterns are significant because they demonstrate the importance of a single cultural institution, the National University, in certifying and selecting intellectuals. Because the National University is a public institution, and because it has and does employ a substantial number of intellectuals, it is important to understand its relationship to the state and the influence of the state on employing intellectuals as teachers (Birnbaum, 1971: 620-621; Gouldner, 1976: 185; Hansen, 1969: 328; Uricoechea, 1969: 17-18). While the university in theory has an autonomous relationship with the state, in reality it is only semiautonomous. This semiautonomous relationship stems from the fact that the funds for the university come from the state and are subject to control by the state. Through that means, extensive manipulation is possible. In practice, however, the state has frozen funds to the university for political reasons only once in recent years (Levy, 1977: 13, Barros Sierra, 1976: 99; Burke, 1977: 262). On a different level, the leadership of the university, that is the president, or rector, and the governing board, has been subject to varying governmental influence. This influence depends on the make-up of the board, which since the 1940s has been dominated by prominent professor-public men, and by the personal inclinations of Mexican presidents (Barros Sierra, 1976: 47, 116; Silva Herzog, 1974; Silva Herzog, 1972: 139). Despite these indirect controls over the university, most of which are seldom applied, intellectuals prefer to be employed there, both because their alternatives elsewhere are limited and because in Mexico the university is seen as a "clean institutional haven for intellectuals who do not want to be contaminated by the corruption present in government agencies."[14]

One cannot understand the importance of the university system to intellectual life unless its peculiar environment is also understood. As Gouldner suggests, the public education system "becomes a major *cosmopolitanizing* influence on its students, with their corresponding distancing from *localistic* interests and values," and it may well have a distinct socializing influence on the groups who attend (Gouldner, 1975-1976: 14). This view is confirmed by Mexican interpretations which see the National University as the builder of ideological, moral, and political foundations of the Mexican national ethos and which see it as providing a cultural and ideological experience distinct from private universities or from the small, prestigious university, the Colegio de México (Lomnitz, 1977: 316).

Conclusions

The image of the intellectual, the extensiveness and characteristics of the media, the peculiarities of intellectual recruitment, and the importance of a single, national university in intellectual life are the results of and contributors to the relationship between intellectuals and politicians in Mexico. These factors allow intellectuals and politicians to provide alternative leadership and ideas to each other. The most important mediating factor to these conditions in Mexico, and therefore to the relationship between politicians and intellectuals, is the nature of the political system. Mexico is characterized by a political structure which has been increasingly described as authoritarian (Purcell, 1973; Stevens, 1977). Although some scholars have attempted to fit Mexico into precise categories for theoretical purposes, it can best be described without the benefit of hypothetical frameworks as a unique system controlled by an informal, hierarchical arrangement of overlapping and competing political cliques who are dominated by the most important of clique leaders, the president of Mexico (Johnson, 1978: 57; Fagen and Tuohy, 1972; Grindle, 1977; Camp, 1976). The very nature of this system, tied to the vagaries of personalistic, reciprocal relationships, is both difficult to predict and to analyze.

In spite of analytical problems, several characteristics of the Mexican system have clearly emerged, and they have a profound impact on the relationship between intellectuals and politicians. In the first place, historically speaking, intellectuals have never shied away from holding public office in Latin America or Mexico, contrary to the more typical pattern of separate roles in the United States. Furthermore, the Mexican Revolution provided numerous opportunities for Mexicans with every conceivable skill to enter public service and occupy leadership roles, since a void was created by the fact that most well-educated ideologists had been supporters of the Porfiriato (Eggleston, 1972: 41). Many young intellectuals answered the call as supporters of the revolution and visionaries of a new Mexico. It has not been until recently that intellectuals have split decisively about the acceptability and desirability of holding public office.[15]

In addition to recognizing historical patterns, one must acknowledge that there have not been realistic incentives for intellectuals' staying in the private sector. Few intellectuals have come from or had the opportunity to enter business careers, both because of their humanistic training and orientation and because until recently business was a family-dominated enterprise, closed to outsiders in the management-level positions. More important, it has been the government, and not the private sector, which has been the leader in the creation and growth of cultural institutions, such as schools, art museums, research institutes, and publishing houses, all of which have been the primary employers of Mexican intellectuals. These cultural institutions have been subject to varying degrees of political influence, both in terms of budget and personnel (Scott, 1964: 335; Beltran, 1977).

The effective control of a small circulating group of elites in Mexico, at least since 1929, has produced a dampening effect on the growth and success of opposition parties as viable alternatives for the political ideas of various intellectuals. This fact, combined with the readiness of the established political leadership to repeatedly attempt co-opting the most effective and capable opposition leaders, has made it difficult for all but the most independent of intellectuals to remain outside the public sector. This can be concretely demonstrated by a careful examination of the careers of the leaders of every major opposition movement in Mexico since 1923, most of whom have joined the government (Camp, 1977). Similarly, the careers of individual intellectuals have often followed the same pattern of first criticizing and then working for the government, despite protestations to the contrary.

The self-image, historical pattern, and political monopoly by a small group of elites have a twofold effect on the relationship between intellectuals and politicians. The first effect is unifying and results from both traditional reasons and the government's active recruitment of intellectuals to public service. The second effect is divisive, resulting from the recent disagreement among Mexican intellectuals, following a general 20th-century pattern, over whether they should play a solely antiestablishment role. Compounding the situation, politicians select only those intellectuals who are establishment participants, omitting others whom intellectuals consider not important. As to the effect both patterns have had, or will continue to have, experience suggests that the integrative pattern has not resulted in intellectuals' making significant contributions to changes in government policy.[16] The divisive pattern, which will continue for some time and grow as the system stumbles over an increasing number of social problems, only reconfirms the past ineffectual role of intellectuals: Many public men and establishment intellectuals may be ignoring those to whom it may be most important to listen.

The peculiarities of the media and the formation of intellectual groups also affect the relationship between Mexican politicians and intellectuals and the role intellectuals can have as agents of change. To begin with, there are numerous similarities between (1) the formation of intellectual groups and their control over journals and (2) the formation of bureaucratic groups and their control over public resources. The government censorship of media (both through control of newsprint and advertising and more direct control over certain media stations and licensing procedures), although powerful, does not appear to be heavily used, rather it hangs like a threatening sword of Damocles. But this in itself is important because the government, through censorship and through its inability to increase functional literacy at a faster pace, has in effect channeled intellectual appeals toward the middle and upper classes, those who most frequently buy and read the media in which intellectuals write. This means, therefore, that for the moment, political leaders do not have to worry about or feel threatened by intellectuals' taking control of mass mobilization, an area they and their party vehicle, the Institutional Revolutionary Party, dominate.

The failure of intellectuals to appeal to the masses is significant, primarily because there is a parallel development within the Mexican political system. As I have argued elsewhere, the Mexican political system has de-emphasized the political activist, who is rapidly being displaced by the bureaucratic technician—an individual with few ideological interests and no skills for dealing with large groups (Camp, 1980: 9; Chávez, 1978: 20).

The technocrat has obtained his position because of his ability in interpersonal, small group relationships, not mobilization of the masses. This weak point in the present political system is one which most intellectuals, either through inability or role perception, are not willing to exploit. If intellectuals could provide skillful leadership to bridge the gap between the lower and middle classes, they could have the ability to change both the structure and the output of the political system in Mexico (Paz, 1972).

Few people recognize the large part intellectuals have had in weakening their own interrelationships and thus their effect on public life. In one sense, intellectuals appear to be far worse culprits than the government in effectively censoring their own kind through group domination of various journals and newspapers. This has less effect on ideas not getting a hearing than on *where* they are published and *who* hears them. Furthermore, the continuation of this informal censorship among intellectual groups emphasizes and exacerbates differences among the intellectuals, thus weakening their collective voice for change and making them more susceptible to government exploitation. Although on rare occasions, when intellectual outrage toward a governmental policy is universal, such as the *Children of Sánchez* case or, more notably, the 1968 repression of students, intellectuals will temporarily maintain a united front, but these instances have never been of long duration.

A further congribution to the intellectual's relationship to the politician stems from the noted importance of the National University. The university, which is extremely important to the formation and recruitment of intellectuals, is equally dominant in the formation and recruitment of national political leaders (Camp, 1974, 1975, 1976, 1978). The university has been historically important for both groups and, not surprisingly, it has been the source of many opposition leaders, too (Alonso, 1976: 125). The centralization of recruitment, both in one city and in one institution, demonstrates rather clearly that the majority of intellectuals and national political leaders have been educated, socialized, and recruited in the same environment, and in many cases, those important to them as mentors, both in the development of their ideas and in the success of their careers, have been the same individuals (Camp, 1980).

If Lewis Coser and Charles Kadushin can argue that this homogeneous cultural milieu is important to intellectuals as a group, it can also be argued that it is important in establishing some overlapping values among both groups (Camp, 1978a). This does not mean that politicians and intellectuals in Mexico think alike, but that there are more similarities in the basis for their value frameworks than meets the eye. Because both intellectuals and politicians absorb personal and institutional modes of behavior in their respective careers, and in most cases are changed by them, their attitudes may well reflect the dominant beliefs among their professional peers, rather than the significant differences they had before entering those careers.

It seems that both public men and intellectuals seek public power; and prestige in Mexico and Latin America is measured in part by one's success in having access to or influence over public power (Dealy, 1977: 8-12). Because both the politician and the intellectual must maintain professionalism in order to succeed, both have accepted certain rules which condition their behavior and make possible their personal and professional familial security. Neither the politician nor the intellectual can easily confront the system head on, and those who do must be economically and socially independent, something extremely difficult to be because of the many factors which come to play in the structure of intellectual and political life. The intellectual, like the politician, has in his own way become economically and socially part of the middle and upper classes in Mexico. It is not likely that he will be inclined to in terms of personal sacrifice and values, nor have the ability to convince the political leadership of the need for, or himself bring about through his own leadership, substantial changes in government policy. This will be possible only if fissures appear in the structure of intellectual and political life, changing the conditions which have governed, and will continue to govern, the relationship between politicians and intellectuals in Mexico.

NOTES

1. This is also based on more than 60 interviews with current cabinet members and prominent intellectuals, May 15, 1978 to September 2, 1978.

2. Standard works on Mexico do not even mention intellectuals, let alone discuss them. See, for example, Leon Padgett (1976).

3. Both intellectuals and politicians, regardless of their views of the two administrations, generally agreed on this point in interviews.

4. From an interview with a prominent Mexican author, Mexico City, June 30, 1978. For a similar view expressed among some Latin American intellectuals, see Ellison (1964: 89); and for the implications of this self-image on role performance, see Seeman (1958: 35).

5. Interview, Mexico City, July 4, 1978.

6. From interviews with two managing editors of leading Mexican reviews, Mexico City, August 9, 1978, and August 28, 1978.

7. The government is not the only source of censorship through advertising. Russell (1977: 141) reports a case in 1972 of a group of advertisers organizing a boycott against *Excélsior,* driving it from first to fourth in the nation in ad copy in just three months.

8. For a clear example of how the government can control films by denying an actor or producer permission to make a movie, see Irma Serrano (1978: 192ff).

9. Interview, Mexico City, August 4, 1978. Also see José Luis Cuevas's (a controversial Mexican writer) interview with James Fortson (1978: 8), where he notes that on returning to Mexico from Paris in 1977, his answers to political questions at a press conference were not published by the media, with the exception of two magazines with well-known political views. Censorship through partial omission is another form used in Mexico and elsewhere. For censorship of even the powerful in Mexico, see the *Los Angeles Times* (1978: 7-10).

10. Interviews with editors or past editors of five leading intellectual reviews, Mexico City, summer 1978.

11. Politicians were equally helpful in arranging interviews with antiestablishment intellectuals, as were intellectuals themselves. I was surprised on more than one occasion to find a high public official phoning even the most critical of intellectuals in my presence.

12. I was able to establish mentor identities for nearly 40 of the 50 prominent intellectuals noted above, of whom the majority were also part of this same select group, but of the older generation.

13. This is on the basis of biographical data obtained from correspondence and interviews with these intellectuals, their students, or relatives and on the basis of Camp (1980).

14. Interview with a Mexican anthropologist, Mexican City, July 12, 1978, and other Mexican intellectuals. Also see Trilling (1959: 20), who suggests the intellectual is generally most attracted to the university.

15. Both intellectuals and politicians agreed that while this trend had already begun, the events of 1968 were critical in suddenly widening the gap between the two. This is just one of the many implications of 1968 which needs to be examined.

16. The majority of intellectuals and politicians interviewed agreed on this fact. One of the most frequently mentioned exceptions was José Vasconcelos and his contribution to educational policy in Mexico.

REFERENCES

ABREAU GOMEZ, E. (1964) "'Política' y la política de los intelectuales." Política 5, 104 (August 15): 26.

ALONSO, J. (1976) La dialéctica clases-élites en México. Méexico, D.F.: Centro de Investigaciones Superiores del INAH.

ARON, R. (1957) The Opium of the Intellectuals. New York: Doubleday.

BARROS SIERRA, J. and G. GARCIA CANTU (1976) 1968. México, D.F.: Siglo XXI.

BELTRAN, E. (1977) Medio siglo de recuerdos de un biólogo mexicano. México, D.F.: Sociedad Mexicana de Historia Natural.

BIRNBAUM, N. (1971) "Problem of a knowledge elite." Massachusetts Rev. 12: 620-636.

BRZEZINSKI, Z. (1968) "America in the technetronic age." Encounter 30 (January): 16-26.

BURKE, M. E. (1977) "The University of Mexico and the revolution, 1910-1940." Americas 34: 252-273.

CAMP, R. (1980) Mexico's Leaders, Their Education and Recruitment. Tucson: Univ. of Arizona Press.

——— (1979) "Los intelectuales y la política en el México postrevolucionario, el caso de los profesores," pp. 523-552 in Instituto Mexicano de Cultura. Sociología de la Paz y de la Guerra. México, D.F.

——— (1978a) "The education of Mexico's political elite." Center Discussion Paper Series. Milwaukee: Univ. of Wisconsin.

——— (1978b) "The elitelore of Mexico's revolutionary family." J. of Latin Amer. Lore 4: 149-182.

——— (1977) "La campaña presidencial de 1929 y el liderazgo político en México." Historia Mexicana 27: 231-259.

——— (1976a) "El sistema mexicano y las decisiones sobre el personal político." Foro Internacional 65 (July-Sept.): 51-82.

——— (1976b) "Education and political recruitment in Mexico: The Alemán generation." J. of Interamerican Studies and World Affairs 18: 295-321.

——— (1975) "The national school of economics and public life in Mexico." Latin Amer. Research Rev. 10 (Fall): 137-151.

——— (1974) "Mexican governors since Cárdenas, education and career contacts." J. of Interamerican Studies and World Affairs 16: 454-481.

CAREAGA, G. (1971) Los intelectuales y la política en México. México, D.F.: Edit. Extemporaneos.

CHAVEZ, E. (1978) "Burocracia y tecnocracia en el poder." Proceso 92 (August 7): 18-21.

COCCIOLI, C. (1965) "Mexico's wobbling left." Atlas (The Magazine of the World Press) 9(February): 113-114. Tr. from Carriere de la Sera, Milan.

COLE, R. (1972) "The mass media of Mexico: Ownership and control." Ph.D. dissertation, University of Minnesota, Minneapolis.

COSER, L. (1967) "The differing roles of intellectuals in contemporary France, England and America." Symposium on Sociology of the Intellectuals, Buenos Aires.

——— (1965) Men of Ideas: A Sociologist's View. New York: Free Press.

COSIO VILLEGAS, D. (1976) Memorias. México, D.F.: Joaquín Mortiz.

DEALY, G. (1977) The Public Man, an Interpretation of Latin and Other Catholic Countries. Amherst: Univ. of Massachusetts Press.

DURAN, M. (1960) "The beleaguered Latin American intellectual: A success story." Ventures 7(Fall): 55-60.

EGGLESTON, R. (1972) "Legitimacy and ideology in a corporatist state: A case study of post-1910 Mexico." Ph.D. dissertation, Syracuse University.

ELLISON, F. (1964) "The writer," pp. 79-100 in J. J. Johnson (ed.) Continuity and Change in Latin America. Stanford, CA: Stanford Univ. Press.

ERLANDSON, E. H. (1964) "The press in Mexico: Past, present and future." Journalism Q. 41: 232-236.

ERLAU, H. (1977) Technology and Civility, the Skill Revolution in Politics. Stanford, CA: Hoover Institution.

FAGEN, R. and W. TUOHY (1972) Politics and Privilege in a Mexican City. Stanford, CA: Stanford Univ. Press.

Fondo de Cultura Económica (1980) Libro conmemorativo del 45 aniversario del Fondo de Cultura Económica. México, D.F.: Author.

FORTSON, J. (1978) "Tintes fascistoides en México: Cuevas." Ecelsior (June 23): 1, 8.

FREIDMANN, J. (1960) "Intellectuals in developing societies." Kyklos 13: 531-544.

GARIBAY, R. and V. LENERO (1972) "México 1972: Los escritores y la política." Plural (November): 34-35.

GORDON, D. (1978) "Mexico, a survey." Economist, special supplement (April 22): 1-34.

GORDON, M. (1954) "Social class and American intellectuals." A.A.U.P. Bull. 40: 517-528.

GOULDNER, A. (1976) The Dialectic of Ideology and Technology. New York: Seabury Press.

——— (1975-1976) "Prologue to a theory of revolutionary intellectuals." Telos (Winter): 3-36.

GRINDLE, M. (1977) "Patrons and clients in the bureaucracy: Career networks in Mexico." Latin Amer. Research Rev. 12: 37-66.

GUZMAN, R. (1978) "La organización política independiente, única vía de cambio sin violencia: Villoro." Proceso 93 (August 14): 6-8.

HALE, C. A. (1978) "Review of Daniel Cosio Villegas, *Memorias.*" Hispanic Amer. Historical Rev. 58: 132-133.

HANSEN, G. (1969) "Intellect and power: Some notes on the intellectual as a political type." J. of Politics 31: 311-328.

HARRISON, J. P. (1964) "The role of the intellectual in fomenting change: The university," pp. 27-42 in J. J. TePaske and S. Nettleton Fisher (eds.) Explosive Forces in Latin America: Columbus: Ohio State Univ. Press.

HAYEK, F. (1960) "The intellectuals and socialism," pp. 371-384 in G. B. De Huzar (ed.) The Intellectuals, A Controversial Portrait. New York: Free Press.

HINDS, H. (1977) "Literatura popular: Kalimán." Hispamérica 6(18): 31-43.

HODARA, J. (1972) "El fin de los intelectuales?" Aportes 25 (July): 31-43.

JIMENEZ DE OTTALENGO, R. (1974) "El periódico mexicano, su situación social y sus fuentes de información." Revista Mexicana de Sociología 36: 767-806.

JOHNSON, K. (1978) Mexican Democracy: A Critical View. New York: Praeger.

KADUSHIN, C. (1974) American Intellectual Elite. Boston: Little, Brown.

KOLAKOWSKI, L. (1972) "Intellectuals against intellect." Daedalus 101(Summer): 1-15.

KOSLOW, L. (1977) The Future of Mexico. Tempe: Arizona State Univ. Press.

KRAUZE, E. (1977) "La rectoría de Gómez Morín." Vuelta 3: 26-32.

——— (1976) Caudillos culturales en la revolución mexicana. México, D.F.: Siglo XXI.

LADD, E. and S. M. LIPSET (1976) The Divided Academy, Professors and Politics. New York: Norton.

LENIN, V. I. (1969) What Is To Be Done? New York: International Publishers.

LEVY, D. (1977) "Limits on government's financial control of the university: Mexico." New Haven, CT: Yale Higher Education Research Group.

LIPSET, S. M. and R. B. DOBSON (1972) "The intellectual as critic and rebel: with special reference to the United States and the Soviet Union." Daedalus 101(Summer): 137-198.

LOMNITZ, L. (1977) "Conflict and mediation in a Latin American university." J. of Interamerican Studies and World Affairs 19: 315-338.

Los Angeles Times (1978) May 19: 7-10.

LYONS, G. (1977) "Inside the volcano." Harper's 254, 1525 (June): 41-46, 51-55.

MACHLUP, F. (1962) Production and Distribution of Knowledge in the United States. Princeton, NJ: Princeton Univ. Press.

MARSAL, J. F. (1966) "Los intelectuales latinoamericanos y el cambio social." Desarrollo Económico (July-December): 295-317.

——— and M. J. ARENT (1970) "Right-wing intelligentsia in Argentina: An analysis of its ideology and political activity." Social Research 37: 447-481

MAZA, E. (1969) Los medios de información colectiva en México. Mexico, D.F.: n.p.

MORETT, J. (1978) "Con tinta negra." Teleguia (July 27): 87.

PADGETT, L. (1976) The Mexican Political System. Boston: Houghton Mifflin.

PAZ, O. (1972) The Other Mexico: Critique of the Pyramid. New York: Grove Press.

PURCELL, S. K. (1973) "Decision-making in an authoritarian regime: Theoretical implications from a Mexican case study." World Politics 26: 28-54.

PUTNAM, R. D. (1976) The Comparative Study of Political Elites. Englewood Cliffs, NJ: Prentice-Hall.

REYNOLDS, C. (1977) "Growth, distribution and structural change in Mexico: Recent trends and future prospects," pp. 19-33 in L. Koslow (ed.) The Future of Mexico. Tempe: Arizona State Univ. Press.

RICO GALAN, V. (1964) "Pero . . . Qué entienden los intelectuales por periodismo?" Política 5, 104 (August 15): 25.

ROSS, S. R. (1977) "La protesta de los intelectuales ante México y su revolución." Historia Mexicana 26: 396-437.

RUSSELL, P. (1977) Mexico in Transition. Austin, TX: Colorado River Press.

RUSSELL, S. E. (1971) "The fondo de cultura económica: A Mexican publishing house." Ph.D. dissertation, University of Texas at Austin.

SCHLESINGER, A. M. Jr. (1972) "El intelectual y la sociedad norteamericana," pp. 75-114 in G. Careaga (ed.) Los Intelectuales y el Poder. Meéxico, D.F.: Sepsetentas.

——— (1959) "Comments on 'American intellectuals: Their politics and status.'" Daedalus 88: 487-488.

SCOTT, R. E. (1964) Mexican Government in Transition. Urbana: Univ. of Illinois Press.

SEEMAN, M. (1958) "The intellectual and the language of minorities." Amer. J. of Sociology 64(July): 25-35.

SERRANO, I. (1978) A Calzon Amarrado. México, D.F.: n.p.

SILVA HERZOG, J. (1974) Una historia de la Universidad de México y sus problemas. México, F.F.: Siglo XXI.

——— (1972) Una vida en la vida de México. México, D.F.: Siglo XXI.

SOLIS, L. (1977) "Fracaso de los economistas mexicanos." Vuelta 11: 4-6.

STEVENS, E. P. (1977) "Mexico's PRI: The institutionalization of corporatism?" pp. 227-258 in J. Malloy (ed.) Authoritarianism and Corporatism in Latin America. Pittsburgh, PA: Univ. of Pittsburgh Press.

TRILLING, L. (1959) "Mind and market in academic life." New Leader 42(February): 19-23.

UNDERWOOD, R. B. (1965) "A survey of contemporary newspapers of Mexico." Ph.D. dissertation, Univ. of Missouri—St. Louis.

Uno Más uno (1978) August 4:1.

URICOECHEA, F. (1969) Intelectuales y desarrollo en América Latina. Buenos Aires: Centro Editor de America Latina.

URQUIDI, V. (1977) "Mexico en la encrucizade." Vuelta 1: 5-7.

WILLIAMS, E. J. (1978a) "Oil in Mexican-U.S. relations: Analysis and bargaining scenario." Orbis 22: 201-216.

——— (1978b) "Petroleum policy and Mexican domestic politics: Left opposition, regional dissidence, and official apostasy." Presented at the meeting of the Southern Economic Association, Washington, D.C.

Roderic A. Camp is Chairman of Political Science and Director of Latin American Studies at Central College, Pella, Iowa. He is the author of numerous articles and several books on Mexico, including Mexico's Leaders: Their Education and Recruitment *(University of Arizona Press, 1980).*

GLENN A. NICHOLS
Department of Political Science
Texas Southern University

PHILIP S. SNYDER
Houston, Texas

BRAZILIAN ELITES AND THE DESCENDANTS OF THE GERMAN, ITALIAN, AND JAPANESE IMMIGRANTS

A growing realization on the part of scholars and the general public has been the increasing interdependence of the world. Technology and communications have narrowed distance and time between diverse cultures, resulting in increased contact, if not increased cultural harmony.

The immigration of millions of persons to new homes has heightened this interdependence. In the Western Hemisphere not only the United States but also Mexico, Brazil, Argentina, and Chile received substantial numbers of immigrants.

Brazil, alone, was the recipient of more than 5 million immigrants. The majority of the immigrants, apart from those of the Iberian Peninsula, came from Germany, Italy, and Japan. Chronologically, the Germans arrived first, the Italians second, and the Japanese third. Numerically, Italy has contributed 1.5 million, Germany 300,000, and Japan 170,000 to date.

The study of interethnic contact in Brazil constitutes an important contribution to the general literature on immigration and its consequences. Much of the general literature and the theories evolved have concentrated on the experience of the United States. A general theory concerning interethnic contact must be built not only on the experience of the United States but

Journal of Interamerican Studies and World Affairs, Vol. 23 No. 3, August 1981 321-344

on other cultures as well. Brazil is especially important in this regard because it differs from the United States in terms of culture, level of economic development, and the degree of social pluralism exhibited in the host society. Not only may the outcome of immigration be different from that in the United States but also the Brazilian case may help sharpen our understanding of the variables that influence intercultural harmony.

It is difficult, however, to assess interethnic relations in Brazil because, since 1950, ethnic groups have not been surveyed in the Brazilian Census and, even in 1950, census data were less than complete. As a consequence of this data shortage, postwar ethnic studies have tended to focus on family histories or, at best, study groups within select localities. The few nationwide studies that exist tend to be general, often impressionistic, and nonquantitative in nature.[1] An additional problem is the relative lack of comparative studies by which the patterns of any one group could be gauged in relation to other groups. This scarcity of comparative data has hindered the development of fruitful hypotheses regarding the outcome of cultural contact in Brazil. Because of these problems, this article will focus on the degree to which the German, Italian, and Japanese populations have penetrated the elite levels of Brazilian society. The question of general behavior will have to await extensive research in Brazil itself.

Consideration of the consequences of intercultural contact leads to the question of what is meant by the concepts of "assimilation," "accommodation," and "acculturation." A survey of the literature indicates a lack of general agreement on a precise definition of these terms. Some students (Berry, 1965; Park and Burgess, 1924; Gordon, 1964; Vander Zanden, 1963) treat these concepts as if they were virtually synonymous. Others distinguish between them but often define them differently. For example, Goodman and Marx (1978) define accommodation as a process whereby the cultures of groups are synthesized. Assimilation is treated as a process whereby one group imposes its culture on another. In contrast, King and Koller (1975) treat assimilation as a synthesis of two cultures. Despite these problems of terminology, there does, nevertheless, seem to be a consensus on the outcomes of cultural contact:

(1) the migrant group could adopt the culture of the host country while shedding its own
(2) the host country could adopt the culture of the immigrant group
(3) there could be a syntheses or blending of cultures so that a new culture is formed
(4) the groups could maintain their cultural identity while cooperating within the larger society, that is, cultural pluralism
(5) two or more cultures could initially meet and then live separately.

There is greater agreement regarding the variables influencing intercultural harmony. Apart from factors rooted in psychological behavior (Dollard et al., 1939; Adorno et al., 1950), the literature emphasizes external and internal variables concerning the immigrant group. External factors include relations between the host state and the immigrants' ancestral state (Gordon, 1978: 87). If relations are good, better relations between the cultures are more likely to result. Another external factor concerns the degree of democracy and pluralism in the host state (Schermerhorn, 1970: 186-187). A democratic society is said to be more conducive to intercultural harmony. An internal variable is the extent to which the immigrant population tends to concentrate or cluster (Gordon, 1978: 85). Clustering impedes better relations. The size of the immigrant group relative to the host population is also a factor (Gordon, 1978: 85). The larger the immigrant group, the more likely relations will be poor. Blalock (1967) has attempted to develop a formula for immigrant group size relative to that of the host population. An additional factor is racial and cultural distance between the immigrant group and the host society. The greater the distance, the worse relations are likely to be (Gordon, 1978: 85; Dworkin and Dworkin, 1976: 34-35; Warner and Srole, 1945).

The focus of this article is not whether the immigrant populations have become like Luso-Brazilians (Brazilians of Portuguese descent), whether a synthesis has been produced, or whether a level of cultural pluralism has been reached, but the degree to which the Brazilian elite has been penetrated by the descendants of German, Italian, and Japanese immigrants. It is a more limited study than that of the general population, but one that is interesting in its own right. Our concern is the extent to which the immigrant populations participate in the social, economic, and political institutions of power in Brazil. The task undertaken here is twofold. First, we seek to identify the social, economic, and political elite. Second, we attempt to ascertain whether these ethnic groups are represented in the elite in proportion to their share of the total population.[2] Although elite analysis is not a substitute for a study of the general population, knowledge learned about the elite can be useful for understanding the population as a whole. First, any definitive study of the German, Italian, and Japanese populations of Brazil would require an assessment of whether they are included in the elite. Second, Brazil is an especially elitist and authoritarian society (Jaguaribe, 1966: 55-69; Motta, 1971; Roett, 1972), and in such a society elites may play an extraordinary role in providing opportunities and access to their respective populations. Third, while the focus of this study is on elites, we do possess some limited data on the general population which generally parallels and reinforces our findings on the elite.

In the remainder of this article we will examine, first, the social elite; second, the economic elite; and, third, the political elite.

Findings

THE SOCIAL ELITE

All societies, except possibly primitive ones, possess a social elite. By social elite we do not mean only the members of an exclusive group such as the Yacht Club or Jockey Club, but a wider population whose members are not only likely to possess prestige but also are likely to possess a disproportionate share of the economic and political power. It is probable that future economic and political leaders will be drawn from this group.

How should the Brazilian social elite be identified? What is employed here is membership in three volumes of *Who's Who* over a 20-year period. A common criticism of the use of such sources is that they omit members of the "real" elite while, on the other hand, they include people whose elite status is questionable. However, there is no other generally agreed on method to identify elites. Three approaches have been used to identify elites and each possesses inherent limitations. One method, the decisional, studies who it is that makes social, economic, and political decisions and then argues that such decision makers are the elite. The approach has been criticized for ignoring nondecisions (who decides what is not to be decided) and for the problems of identifying "key" decisions. Only participants in "key" decisions would constitute the elite.

How should a "key" decision be isolated? Consultation of newspapers suffers from the problem that the newspapers may be misinformed. Consultation of elites, apart from being a tautology, suffers from the possibility that elites are not telling the truth or are biased (Bachrach and Baratz, 1970). A second approach, the positional, has been even more criticized. In essence, this approach studies formal offices and argues that these officeholders are the elite. In fact, this is not always the case: Formal power is not always actual power (Garson, 1977: 62-65). A final approach, the reputational, of which this study is an example, contends that elites can be identified by nonelites. This is done by either consulting lower strata or by using some kind of listing such as *Who's Who*. The criticism is that lower strata may not identify correctly (Garson, 1977: 67-71).

In sum, then, there is no way to identify elites that does not contain problems. It is possible to argue that none of these approaches correctly identifies the "real" elite. As a consequence, for the researcher, there are only two choices. In the absence of a perfect approach, he or she could reject the study of elites or admit the limitations of the approach being used and couch his or her conclusions cautiously and tentatively. The second course is pursued here.

There is a second defense of the use of *Who's Who* sources. One author of this article has spent some time in Brazil and has seen

TABLE 1

German, Italian, and Japanese Representation in the Brazilian Who's Who of 1953, 1963, and 1973[a]

	1953		1963		1973		Percent of
	No.[b]	Percent	No.	Percent	No.	Percent	Total Pop.[c]
Germans	86	5.09	292	8.76	430	8.78	2
Italians	145	8.84	446	13.39	528	10.78	5-7
Japanese	0	0	35	1.05	67	1.37	0.48
Luso-Brazilians[d]	1160	75.06	1971	59.15	2863	58.45	
Others[e]	297	11.01	588	17.65	1077	21.99	
Total[f]	1688	100	3332	100	4898	100	

SOURCE: Sociedade Brasiliera de Expansão Comercial Ltda. (1951, 1963); Who's Who in Brazil Editorial Ltda. (1973-1974). Population base figures are from Cenni (1975: 405); Fouquet (1974: 183); and Comissão de Recenseamento do Colona Japonesa (1964: 6).

a. Care should be taken with regard to this and other tables because of the use of surnames. In addition to the other problems inherent in surname identification, is the fact that Brazilians often take the name of collatoral ancestors and use mixed names. Moreover, surname identification favors males. We do not believe that these factors bias our data in favor of a particular ethnic group, but the data should be taken tentatively.

b. Number.

c. Percent of total population.

d. The Luso-Brazilian category is not pure because of other nationalities who have taken Luso-Brazilian surnames.

e. Included within "other" are other immigrant populations such as Spaniards, Poles, Jews, Syrians, Lebanese, French, English, and so on. We could not count these groups individually because of the absence of population base figures.

f. Numbers may not add to 100 because of rounding.

several Brazilians use such a listing as a measure of one's status. In other words, in the absence of an alternative national listing that is published at several points in time, membership in *Who's Who* takes on a reality of its own. As one student of elites puts it, "Reputation for power may be self-fulfilling. True, the reputational approach may reflect the effect of national myths, propaganda, and popular desires about how politics *should* be. But people commonly act on the basis of their *perceptions* of reality, even when these perceptions are based on 'myths'" (Garson, 1977: 70).

Our concern here is whether the descendants of German, Italian, and Japanese immigrants are represented in the social elite in proportion to their share of the national population. Table 1 contains information with respect to the inclusion of Germans,

Italians, and Japanese in several volumes of *Who's Who.* Surnames were counted for 1953, 1963, and 1973. The table indicates that persons of German descent were overrepresented in all three editions, and in 1963 and 1973 they were overrepresented almost five-fold. The Italians and Japanese (except for 1953) are also represented in excess of their proportion of the total population but not to the same extent. In the aggregate, the three immigrant groups are about 10% of the population, but have 21% of the listings in 1973. To the extent that inclusion in *Who's Who* represents status, we can say that all three immigrant groups have been socially successful.

A crucial measure of social penetration is intermarriage. A very interesting, yet limited, finding is presented in Table 2, which was compiled by listing by national origin marriages among Germans, Italians, and Japanese in the *Who's Who of 1973-1974.* This was done by examining the surnames of spouses, in most cases the maiden names of women. The total figures do not match the 1973-1974 entries in Table 1 because of persons who remained single and the difficulty of categorizing some surnames. For these reasons the findings must be regarded as tentative.

What Table 2 suggests is that Germans and Italians are about equally likely to marry outside their ethnic group. In both cases, over 40% of the marriages are with Luso-Brazilians. Neither group marries the other to any extent. This is at least in part due to the fact that Germans and Italians tend to live in different localities.

The Japanese, on the other hand, present a different pattern. Three-quarters of the Japanese married a Japanese spouse, while only one-fifth wed Luso-Brazilians. This supports what has been learned about the Japanese in other studies. In a São Paulo university society, it was reported that Japanese students marry other Japanese almost exclusively (Shimidu, 1973: 480). And, census material compiled about the Japanese in 1964 by the University of Tokyo reveals that only 18% of Japanese-Brazilian males marry Luso-Brazilians while 8% of Japanese-Brazilian females marry Luso-Brazilians (Comissão de Recenseamento, 1964: 356). This additional research suggests that our marriage statistics may be essentially correct.

TABLE 2

Intermarriage Among Nationalities[a]

	Germans		Italians		Japanese		Luso-Brazilians		Total	
	No.[b]	Percent	No.	Percent	No.	Percent	No.	Percent	No.	Percent
Germans	103	52.02	7	3.54	0	0	88	44.44	198	100[c]
Italians	14	5.62	131	52.61	0	0	104	41.77	249	100
Japanese	2	3.57	0	0	43	76.00	11	19.64	56	100

SOURCE: Who's Who in Brazil Editorial Ltda. (1973-1974).

a. See Table 1 for additional comments.

b. Number.

c. Numbers may not add to 100 because of rounding.

TABLE 3
German, Italian, and Japanese Listings in the Economic *Who's Who* of 1967[a]

	Number	Percent	Percent Total Population
Germans	130	15.00	2.00
Italians	134	15.00	5-7.00
Japanese	9	1.00	0.48
Luso-Brazilians	427	48.00	
Others	192	21.00	
Total	892	100.00[b]	

SOURCE: Sociedade Brasileira de Publicacoẽs Culturais e Economicas (1967).
a. See Table 1 for additional comments.
b. Numbers may not add to 100 because of rounding.

In sum, we can say that all three groups have had some success in entering the Brazilian social elite, but the Japanese appear to have been less successful than the Germans and Italians. As indicated later, this may in part be due to racial and cultural distance from Luso-Brazilians.

THE ECONOMIC ELITE

In earlier studies, both Warren Dean (1969) and Joseph Love (1971) found that, at the turn of the century, immigrant groups in Brazil possessed a disproportionate share of the ownership of industry and, therefore, could be said to have penetrated part of the economic elite. At the present time, the dynamic economic activities in Brazil are centered in industry and commerce. Have the immigrant populations continued to enjoy their initial advantage?

In 1967, a *Who's Who* was published which listed the leaders in the industrial and commercial sectors of Brazil. Table 3 was constructed from those entries. What Table 3 indicates is that all three groups are mentioned in excess of their share of the total population. The Germans are overrepresented sevenfold, the Italians between two- and threefold, and the Japanese twofold. These findings suggest that the German, Italian, and Japanese populations have all been successful in penetrating the economic elite, but that the Germans have been the most successful.

Until now, we have been dealing exclusively with elites. We do possess, however, some tentative data concerning occupational distribution for the general population. This material is presented in Tables 4 to 7.

Tables 4 to 7 were compiled by counting identifiable surnames within selected occupations in the Sao Paulo and Porto Alegre telephone yellow pages. Those businesses with identifiable surnames do not constitute the total number of businesses, because many are listed by other names. While we recognize that telephone distribution is not widespread in Brazil, even in the urban areas measured, there is no reason we know of to assume that, within the same occupational category, one ethnic group is more likely to employ surnames or to possess a telephone than another. In other words, we believe that German mechanics, lawyers, and doctors are as likely to possess a telephone and to identify their business by surnames as their Luso-Brazilian counterparts. The telephone items selected were used because personal names predominate.

In a tentative sense, a pattern of occupational distribution may be discerned. If we compare differences (difference from the Luso-Brazilian percentage) in the total between Germans, Italians, and Japanese, respectively, and Luso-Brazilians, a measure of occupational congruity can be derived. In other words, we are seeking to ascertain which groups most closely fit the occupational distribution of the Luso-Brazilians. When the total difference from the Luso-Brazilians is considered, we can compare the three immigrant groups. In the São Paulo listings, Germans were less like the Luso-Brazilian distribution in 1966 than were the Italians, but by 1974 the two groups deviated an equal 32 points. In Porto Alegre, Germans more closely followed the Luso-Brazilian distribution in both years. The Japanese could not be measured in Porto Alegre, but the São Paulo data suggest that they are the least economically similar to the Luso-Brazilians.[3]

In sum, we find an economic pattern not unlike the social one. All three immigrant groups are proportionately overrepresented in the Economic *Who's Who*. The Germans are especially overrepresented. As regards urban occupational distribution, the Germans and Italians are approximately equidistant to that of the Luso-Brazilians, while the Japanese are much more distant.

(text continued on page 335)

TABLE 4

Occupational Listings in Terms of the *Paginas Amarelas* (yellow pages) of the São Paulo Telephone Directory, 1966

Occupation	Germans No.[a]	Germans Percent	DLB[b]	Italians No.	Italians Percent	DLB	Japanese No.	Japanese Percent	DLB	Luzo-Brazilians No.	Luzo-Brazilians Percent
Butchers	4	1	0	44	3	+ 2	3	3	+ 2	52	1
Lawyers	67	24	-18	272	24	-18	14	13	-28	1800	42
Clothing Store	9	3	+ 1	27	2	0	2	2	0	70	2
Architects	10	4	+ 3	19	2	+ 1	3	3	+ 2	55	1
Auto Dealers	6	2	- 1	45	4	+ 1	5	5	+ 2	133	3
Bars and Cafes	7	3	- 6	52	5	- 4	5	5	- 4	361	9
Shoe Stores	2	1	0	40	4	+ 3	1	1	0	47	1
Carpenters	1	1	0	3	1	0	0	0	- 1	9	- 1
Accountants	6	2	- 1	32	3	0	7	7	+ 4	106	3
Dentists	45	16	+ 4	114	10	- 2	18	18	+ 6	528	12
Despachantes[c]	6	2	- 1	35	3	0	4	4	+ 1	139	3
Electricians	7	3	+ 2	28	2	+ 1	5	5	+ 4	47	1
Economists	4	1	0	14	1	0	2	2	+ 1	36	1
Engineers	49	18	+10	120	11	+ 3	14	13	+ 5	326	8
Mechanics	24	9	+ 5	109	10	+ 6	10	10	+ 6	135	4
Doctors	30	11	+ 2	169	15	+ 6	8	8	- 1	394	9
Total[d]	277	100	54	1123	100	47	101	100	67	4238	100

SOURCE: Telephone Directory of São Paulo, 1966.

a. Number.

b. DLB = Percentage Difference from the Luso-Brazilian Percentage.

c. A go-between operating between the bureaucracy and the individual.

d. Numbers may not add to 100 because of rounding.

TABLE 5

Occupational Listings in Terms of the *Paginas Amarelas* (yellow pages) of the São Paulo Telephone Directory, 1974

Occupation	Germans No.[a]	Germans Percent	Germans DLB[b]	Italians No.	Italians Percent	Italians DLB	Japanese No.	Japanese Percent	Japanese DLB	Luzo-Brazilians No.	Luzo-Brazilians Percent
Butchers	6	2	0	45	3	+ 1	1	- 1	- 1	105	2
Lawyers	101	29	-10	377	28	-11	33	14	-25	2161	39
Clothing Store	7	2	- 1	19	1	- 2	3	1	- 2	182	3
Architects	12	3	+ 1	36	3	+ 1	9	4	+ 2	135	2
Automobile Dealers	13	4	- 1	91	7	+ 2	10	4	- 1	256	5
Bars and Cafes	5	1	- 3	34	3	- 1	4	2	- 2	242	4
Shoe Stores	6	2	0	36	3	+ 1	1	- 1	- 1	115	2
Carpenters	4	1	+ 1	18	1	+ 1	4	2	+ 2	38	- 1
Accountants	4	1	0	31	2	+ 1	18	8	+ 7	77	1
Dentists	61	17	0	227	17	0	90	37	+20	937	17
Despachantes[c]	10	3	+ 1	45	3	+ 1	3	1	- 1	109	2
Electricians	4	1	+ 1	29	2	+ 2	5	2	+ 2	51	- 1
Economists	6	2	+ 1	16	1	0	3	1	0	56	1
Engineers	46	13	+ 6	88	6	- 1	18	8	+ 1	392	7
Mechanics	28	8	+ 4	151	11	+ 7	17	7	+ 3	225	4
Doctors	36	10	+ 2	112	8	0	18	8	0	432	8
Total[d]	349	100	32	1355	100	32	237	100	70	5513	100

SOURCE: Telephone Directory of São Paulo, 1974.

a. Number.

b. DLB = Percentage Difference from the Luso-Brazilian Percentage.

c. A go-between operating between the bureaucracy and the individual.

d. Numbers may not add to 100 because of rounding.

TABLE 6

Occupational Listings in Terms of the *Paginas Amarelas* (yellow pages) of the Porto Alegre Telephone Directory, 1962

	Germans			Italians			Luzo-Brazilians	
Occupation	No.[a]	Percent	DLB	No.	Percent	DLB	No.	Percent
Butchers	3	1	- 1	20	13	+11	17	2
Lawyers	56	20	-10	31	20	-10	309	30
Clothing Stores	13	5	+ 2	2	1	- 2	33	3
Architects	6	2	+ 1	5	3	+ 2	14	1
Automobile Dealers	6	2	0	3	2	0	17	2
Bars and Cafes	4	1	- 4	8	5	0	55	5
Shoe Stores	9	3	0	4	2	- 1	30	3
Carpenters	7	2	+ 1	2	1	0	9	1
Accountants	17	6	+ 4	7	5	+ 3	18	2
Dentists	37	13	+ 4	9	6	- 3	88	9
Despachantes[c]	5	2	- 1	3	2	- 1	29	3
Electricians	8	3	+ 2	2	1	0	3	1
Economists	8	3	+ 2	4	2	+ 1	11	1
Engineers	12	4	- 1	8	5	0	52	5
Mechanics	7	2	+ 1	1	1	0	4	1
Doctors	84	30	- 3	43	28	- 5	333	33
Total[d]	282	100	37	152	100	39	1022	100

SOURCE: Telephone Directory of Porto Alegre, 1962.

a. Number.

b. DLB = Percentage Difference from the Luzo-Brazilian Percentage.

c. A go-between operating between the bureaucracy and the individual.

d. Numbers may not add to 100 because of rounding.

TABLE 7

Occupational Listings in Terms of the *Paginas Amarelas* (yellow pages) of the Porto Alegre Telephone Directory, 1972

Occupation	Germans No.[a]	Germans Percent	Germans DLB[b]	Italians No.	Italians Percent	Italians DLB	Luzo-Brazilians No.	Luzo-Brazilians Percent
Butchers	3	1	- 1	11	5	+ 3	18	2
Lawyers	94	33	-14	64	32	-15	428	47
Clothing Stores	8	3	+ 1	6	3	+ 1	16	2
Architects	14	5	+ 1	13	6	+ 2	34	4
Automobile Dealers	7	2	- 1	10	5	+ 2	27	3
Bars and Cafes	7	2	0	8	3	+ 1	16	2
Shoe Stores	7	2	0	7	3	+ 1	20	2
Carpenters	2	1	0	1	1	0	3	1
Accountants	7	2	0	7	3	+ 1	17	2
Dentists	61	22	+ 5	36	18	+ 1	158	17
Despachantes[c]	5	2	- 2	3	1	- 3	35	4
Electricians	2	1	0	3	1	0	3	1
Economists	8	3	+ 2	3	1	0	13	1
Engineers	17	6	+ 2	6	3	- 1	40	4
Mechanics	13	4	+ 1	6	3	0	24	3
Doctors	27	9	+ 2	18	9	+ 2	62	7
Total[d]	282	100	32	203	100	33	914	100

SOURCE: Telephone Directory of Porto Alegre, 1972.

a. Number.

b. DLB = Percentage Difference from the Luzo-Brazilian Percentage.

c. A go-between operating between the bureaucracy and the individual.

d. Numbers may not add to 100 because of rounding.

THE POLITICAL ELITE

Have the German, Italian, and Japanese populations been as equally successful in penetrating the political power structure? Three measures are employed here to gauge this. First, we will look at German, Italian, and Japanese representation in the Chamber of Deputies. Second, we will examine the immigrant groups in terms of the Brazilian Cabinet. And, third, we will look at immigrant representation in the Army Officer Corps.

Table 8 contains information with respect to Germans, Italians, and Japanese in the Camber of Deputies. Considering the Chamber of Deputies since 1930 (1930 is usually taken as the beginning of modern Brazil), the Germans are represented approximately in proportion to their population size. The Japanese and Italians, however, are underrepresented until the 1970s. We may say that all three groups have penetrated the margins of political power in the 1970s. It is important, however, to bear in mind that the Chamber of Deputies tends to be a symbolic office rather than a powerful one. This has especially been the case since the military assumed power in 1964.

Table 9 contains information with respect to German, Italian, and Japanese representation in the Brazilian Cabinet since 1930. The Cabinet is a far more powerful and sensitive political post than the Chamber of Deputies. With respect to the Cabinet, the Germans are overrepresented during the period 1930-1938 (the early Vargas years) but have no further representation until 1945-1954. There were not any Italians in the Cabinet until 1945-1954. The Japanese were not represented until 1965-1975—the period of military rule. If we focus on the period of military rule since 1964, the Germans have been overrepresented, the Japanese about equally represented, and the Italians slightly underrepresented. As with the Chamber of Deputies, a trend can be discerned in recent years toward greater representation of all three immigrant groups.

Those familiar with the politics of Brazil know that the real locus of power is not the legislature or the Cabinet, but the military officer corps. Apart from Super-Ministers, since 1964 real power has been concentrated in the military. A crucial institution in the military centers around the *Escola Superior de*

TABLE 8

German, Italian, and Japanese Membership in the Chamber of Deputies, 1930-1976[a]

	1930-1940		1940-1950		1950-1960		1960-1970		1970-1976		Percent of Total Pop.[c]
	No.[b]	Percent	No.	Percent	No.	Percent	No.	Percent	No.	Percent	
Germans	9	1.93	8	2.55	23	2.73	25	3.10	14	2.74	2
Italians	7	1.50	2	.64	16	1.90	28	3.47	30	5.87	5-7
Japanese	0	0	0	0	1	.12	1	.12	3	.59	0.48
Luso-Brazilians	410	87.79	275	87.58	720	85.51	671	83.25	407	79.65	
Others	41	8.78	29	9.24	82	9.74	81	10.05	57	11.15	
Total[d]	467	100	314	100	842	100	806	100	511	100	

SOURCE: Câmara dos Deputados (1976).

a. See Table 1 for additional comments.

b. Number.

c. Percent of total population.

d. Numbers may not add to 100 because of rounding.

TABLE 9

German, Italian, and Japanese Representation in the Brazilian Cabinet, 1930-1975[a]

	1930-1938		1940-1945		1946-1954		1955-1964		1965-1975		Percent Total Population
	No.[b]	Percent	No.	Percent	No.	Percent	No.	Percent	No.	Percent	
Germans	2	4.88	0	0	2	2.08	8	6.40	14	7.41	2.00
Italians	0	0	0	0	1	1.04	8	6.40	12	6.35	5-7.00
Japanese	0	0	0	0	0	0	0	0	1	.53	.48
Luso-Brazilians	39	95.12	54	100	86	89.58	101	80.20	150	79.37	
Others	0	0	0	0	7	7.29	8	6.40	12	6.35	
Total[c]	41	100	54	100	96	100	125	100	189	100	

SOURCE: Council on Foreign Relations (1930-1975).

a. See Table 1 for additional comments.

b. Number.

c. Numbers may not add to 100 because of rounding.

Guerra (Superior War College). We do not possess a listing for that entity but data are available for the army officer corps. These data are presented in Table 10.

Table 10 demonstrates the extent to which Germans, Italians, and the Japanese have penetrated the army officer corps. The Germans have been the most successful of the three groups and are the only group overrepresented in the ranks of colonels and generals. The Italians, except among generals, are represented according to their share of the population. The Japanese have apparently just begun to penetrate the officer corps and are overrepresented in the lower ranks. The German success may be due to their longer residence in Brazil.

Our overall political findings can be briefly summarized. Descendants of German, Italian, and Japanese immigrants are relatively well-represented in the Chamber of Deputies and the Cabinet. Germans, alone, seem to be overrepresented in the higher military ranks. It should also be noted that two recent presidents have been of Italian (President Médici) and German (President Geisel) extraction.

Conclusions

The focus of this article has been on the degree to which German, Italian, and Japanese populations have penetrated the Brazilian elite. In general all three groups are represented in the elite disproportionate to their population size. They are overrepresented in a social, economic, and political sense. Although general success is discernible, the Germans and Italians seem to have been more successful at becoming members of the elite than the Japanese. And, the Germans are either equal to or slightly ahead of the Italians. This is especially to be noticed in the army officer corps, which may be regarded as at least a primary center of power in contemporary Brazil.

Our data on the Germans are surprising because many earlier studies suggest that the Germans were marginal to Brazilian society. Prior to World War II, the Germans were often presented as marginals. Emilo Willems's (1940) work was almost an

TABLE 10

German, Italian, and Japanese Representation in the Army Officer Corps[a]

Rank	Germans No.[b]	Germans Percent	Italians No.	Italians Percent	Japanese No.	Japanese Percent	Luso-Brazilians No.	Luso-Brazilians Percent	Other No.	Other Percent	Total
Lieutenant	58	5.09	68	5.98	14	1.23	898	79.17	98	8.63	1136
Captain	44	3.31	74	5.57	14	1.05	1082	81.49	114	8.58	1328
Major	60	3.86	74	4.77	6	.39	1320	84.99	93	5.99	1553
Lieutenant Colonel	61	4.27	71	4.97	0	0	1189	83.21	108	7.55	1429
Colonel	32	5.69	35	6.40	0	0	446	79.19	49	8.72	562
General	10	6.76	4	2.70	0	0	125	84.46	9	6.08	148
Total	265		326		34		5060		471		
Percent of Total Population		2		5-7		.48					

SOURCE: Ministério do Exercito (1978).

a. See Table 1 for additional comments. Army figures are for the combat arms.

b. Number.

apology for the Germans' failure to enter the mainstream. Barm-Haltzer (1970) also stressed their isolation. Cortes (1974) underlined their political isolation and manipulation. And, Roche (1959) contended that the rural German communities were marginal as late as the 1950s.

In view of these earlier studies, one must ask why the Germans have succeeded so well. The nature of our data, as indicated previously, prevents the drawing of firm conclusions. Yet, in the light of the general literature concerning assimilation and acculturation, we might suggest some tentative explanations.

Some explanations advanced in the general literature are of little help here. Explanations grounded in psychological frustration as a cause of prejudice (Dollard et al., 1939; Adorno et al., 1950) are simply outside the bounds of this study. Likewise, explanations emphasizing host country pluralism (Schermerhorn, 1970) and host-ancestral state relations (Gordon, 1978: 87) cannot explain the variance between the German, Italian, and Japanese descendants in Brazil. Of more utility are the socioeconomic explanations, but even here nont alone constitutes a complete explanation. For example, Gordon (1978: 85) has argued that the size of the immigrant population relative to the native population may retard absorption into the larger society. After a certain threshold, the larger a group becomes, the less likely it will be assimilated. This explanation may partially account for the greater German success than that of the Italians but it does not account for the relatively less successful Japanese. Explanations which argue that urban settlement facilitates absorption into the larger society are also limited. In our study the Germans seem to have been more successful in penetrating elite institutions, although the Italians settled in more urban areas (Baily, 1978: 321-340). Another explanation contends that the greater a group's cultural and racial difference from that of the host society, the more obstacles the group will encounter (Gordon, 1978: 85; Kinloch, 1979: 59-60; Dworkin and Dworkin, 1976: 34-35). This explanation may account for the Japanese, but why do the culturally more removed Germans seem more successful than the Italians?

A more promising explanation rests on the fact that economic and political power and success are not the equivalent of absorption into the larger society. A group, such as Jews, may be successful in penetrating elite structures, but significantly less successful in entering society at large. Although many students point to immigrant group clustering as a factor that impedes assimilation (Inglis, 1975: 338; Baily, 1978: 321-340), some argue that clustering and togetherness may enable a group to achieve economic and political power (Petersen, 1971: 232; Dworkin and Dworkin, 1976: 37). Scholars point to clustering among Germans prior to World War II. Perhaps, this clustering which may have impeded general assimilation is responsible for German success with respect to elite institutions. Extensive field work, however, will be needed to determine whether this is the case.

NOTES

1. The literature on immigration and assimilation in Brazil is extensive and cannot be fully cited here. The list provided contains the more representative and important works (Cenni, 1975; Comissão de Recenseamento do Colona Japonesa, 1964; Delhaes, 1964: 473-494; Roche, 1959; Delhaes, 1973; Fouquet, 1974; Ilg, 1972; Oberacker, 1955; Cortes, 1974; Sims, 1973; Smith et al., 1967; Fuju, 1959; Haskins, 1969: 32-53; Saito, 1961; Becker, 1967: 45-79; Pinsdorf, 1976; Laytano, 1968: 3-32; Tigner, 1961: 515-532; Schaden, 1956: 41-46; Willems, 1940; Maeyama, 1972: 151-182; Oberacker, 1977: 383-432; Willems, 1946).

2. There is, of course, the possibility of a "hidden elite." There is no way to prove or disprove this argument, but we believe that the groups examined here, particularly the political elite, are what most scholars of Brazil would call the elite.

3. If upper status occupations are considered separately (lawyers, architects, accountants, dentists, economists, engineers, and medical doctors), the Italian pattern is marginally closer to that of the Luso-Brazilians than the Germans. On the other hand, if occupations of a lower status (butchers, cafe owners, carpenters, electricians, and mechanics) are considered separately, the Germans are more congruent with the Luso-Brazilian pattern than are the Italians.

REFERENCES

ADORNO, T. W., E. FRANKEL-BRUNSWICK, D. LEVINSON, and N. SANFORD (1950) The Authoritarian Personality. New York: Harper & Row.

BACHRACH, P. and M. BARATZ (1970) Power and Poverty: Theory and Practice. New York: Oxford Univ. Press.

BAILY, S. (1978) "The role of two newspapers in the assimilation of Italians in Buenos Aires and São Paulo, 1893-1913." Intl. Migration Rev. (Fall): 321-340.

BARM-HALTZER, K. (1970) Die Nationalisierung der deutschen Einwanderer und ihrer Nachkommen in Brasilien als Problem der deutsch-brasilianischen Beziehungen 1930-1938. Berlin: Colloquium Verlag. Vol. XIV of Bibliotheca Ibero-Americana, Veröeffentlichungen des Ibero-Amerikanischen Instituts.

BECKER, V. (1967) 'Um Povado Teuto Brasileiro." Estudos Leopoldense: 45-79.

BERRY, B. (1965) Race and Ethnic Relations. Boston: Houghton-Mifflin.

BLALOCK, H. M. (1967) Toward a Theory of Minority Group Relations. New York: Wiley.

Câmara Dos Deputados (1976) Deputados Brasileiros, 1826-1976. Brasilia: Author.

CENNI, F. (1975) Italianos no Brasil. São Paulo: Editora da Universidade de São Paulo.

Comissao de Recenseamento do Colona Japonesa (1964) The Japanese Immigrant in Brazil. Tokyo: Univ. of Tokyo Press.

CORTES, C. (1974) Gaucho Politics in Brazil: The Politics of Rio Grande do Sul, 1930-1964. Albuquerque: Univ. of New Mexico Press.

Council on Foreign Relations (1930-1975) Political Handbook and Atlas of the World. New York: Council on Foreign Relations.

DEAN, W. (1969) The Industrialization of São Paulo, 1880-1945. Austin: Univ. of Texas Press.

DELHAES, G. D. v. (1973) Industrialisierung in Sudbrasilien. Die deutsche Einwanderung und die Anfaenge der Industrialisierung in Rio Grande do Sul. Cologne: Boehlau Verlag.

——— (1964) "Ein Jahrhundert italienische Answanderung nach Brasilien: Betrachtungen ueber die Gesamtauswanderung und deren Anfaenge." Jahrbuch fuer Geschichte von Staat, Wirtschaft und Gesellschaft Lateinamerikas: 473-494.

DOLLARD, J., N. MILLER, L. DOOB, D. H. MOWRER, and R. SEARS (1939) Frustration and Aggression. New Haven, CT: Yale Univ. Press.

DWORKIN, A. and R. DWORKIN (1976) The Minority Report. New York: Praeger.

FOUQUET, K. (1974) Der deutsche Einwanderer und seine Nachkommen in Brasilien, 1808-1824-1974. São Paulo: n.p.

FUJU, Y. (1959) The Acculturation of the Japanese Immigrants in Brazil. Gainesville: Univ. of Florida Press.

GARSON, G. D. (1977) Power and Politics in the United States. Lexington, MA: D. C. Heath.

GOODMAN, N. and G. MARX (1978) Sociology Today. New York: Random House.

GORDON, M. M. (1978) Human Nature, Class, and Ethnicity. New York: Oxford Univ. Press.

——— (1964) Assimilation in American Life. New York: Oxford Univ. Press.

HASKINS, D. (1969) "Japanese emigration and assimilation in Brazil." Intl. Migration Rev. (Spring): 32-53.

ILG, K. (1972) Pioniere in Brasilein. Innsbruck, Vienna, and Munich: Tyrolia-Verlag.

INGLIS, C. (1975) "Some recent Australian writing on immigration and assimilation." Intl. Migration Rev. (Fall): 335-344.

JAGUARIBE, H. (1966) "Brazilian nationalism and the dynamics of its political development." Studies in Comparative Intl. Development: 55-69.

KING, D. and M. KOLLER (1975) Foundations of Sociology. New York: Holt, Rinehart and Winston.

KINLOCH, G. C., (1979) The Sociology of Minority Group Relations. Englewood Cliffs, NJ: Prentice-Hall.

LAYTANO, D. (1968) "O japonês no Rio Grande do Sul." Revista de Instituto Historico e Geografico Brasileira: 3-32.

LOVE, J. (1971) Rio Grande do Sul and Brazilian Regionalism, 1882-1930. Stanford, CA: Stanford Univ. Press.

MAEYAMA, T. (1972) "Ancestor, emperor, and immigrant: Religion and group identification of the Japanese in rural Brazil, 1908-1950." J. of Interamerican studies and World Affairs 14: 151-182.

Ministerior do exercito (1978) Almanaque de Oficiais paro o Ano de 1978. Brasilia: Author.

MOTTA, R. (1971) Movimentos Partidarios no Brasil. Rio de Janeiro: Fundacão Getulio Vargas.

OBERACKER, C. H., Jr. (1977) "Transformacão da lingua alema no Brasil," pp. 383-432 in E. Schaden, Homem, Cultura e Sociedade no Brasil. Petropolis: Editora Vozes.

——— (1955) Der deutsche Beitrag zum Aufbau der brasilianichen Nation. São Paulo: Herder.

PARK, R. E. and E. W. BURGESS (1924) Introduction to the Science of Society. Chicago: Univ. of Chicago Press.

PETERSEN, W. (1971) Japanese Americans. New York: Random House.

PINSDORF, M. (1976) "German speaking immigrants: Builders of business in Brazil south." Ph.D. dissertation, New York University.

ROCHE, J. (1959) La colonisation Allemande et le Rio Grande do Sul. Paris: Institut des Hautes Etudes de l'Amérique Latine.

ROETT, R. (1972) Brazil: Politics in a Patrimonial Society. Boston: Allyn and Bacon.

SAITO, H. (1961) O Japonês no Brasil. São Paulo: Fundacão Escola de Sociología e Politica de São Paulo.

SCHADEN, E. (1956) "Acculturacão de Alemães e Japonêses no Brasil." Revista de Antropologia (June): 41-46.

SCHERMERHORN, R. A. (1970) Comparative Ethnic Relations. New York: Random House.

SHIMIDU, A. H. (1973) "Assimilacão dos estudantes universitarios nisseis em São Paulo," in T. Maeyana and H. Saito, Assimilacão e Integracão dos Japonêses no Brasil. São Paulo: Editora Paulo.

SIMS, H. D. (1973) Japanese Postwar Migration to Brazil: An Analysis of Data Presently Available. Pittsburgh: n.p.

SMITH, R. J., J. B. CORNELL, H. SAITO, and T. MAEYAMA (1967) The Japanese and Their Descendants in Brazil: An Annotated Bibliography. São Paulo: Centro de Estudos Nipo-Brasileiros.

Sociedade Brasileira de Expansão Comercial itda. (1951, 1963) Quem e Quem no Brasil. Sao Paulo: Author.

Sociedade Brasileira de Publicacões Culturais e Economicas (1967) Who's Who in Brazilian Economic Life. São Paulo: Author.

Telephone Directory (1966, 1974) São Paulo: n.p.

——— (1962, 1972) Porto Alegre: n.p.

TIGNER, J. L. (1961) "Shindō Remmei: Japanese Nationalism in Brazil." Hispanic Amer. Historical Rev.: 515-532.

VANDER ZANDEN, J. (1963) American Minority Relations. New York: Ronald Press.

WARNER, L. and L. SROLE (1945) The Social Systems of American Elite Groups. New Haven, CT: Yale Univ. Press.

Who's Who in Brazil Editorial Ltda. (1973-1974) Who's Who in Brazil. São Paulo: Author.

WILLEMS, E. (1946) A Aculturacão dos Alemaes no Brasil. São Paulo: Companhia Editoria Nacional.

——— (1940) Assimilacão e Populacões Marginais no Brasil. São Paulo: Companhia Editora Nacional.

Glenn A. Nichols is Assistant Professor of Political Science at Texas Southern University. His articles have been published in various journals, including Luso-Brazilian Review, Georgia Political Science Association Journal, *and this one.*

Philip S. Snyder received his Ph.D. in Central European history from Rice University in 1974 and, after several years in private business, is now employed by the city of Houston.

REVIEW ESSAY

CENTRALISM AS PRAGMATIC TRADITION
A Critique

Véliz, Claudio. THE CENTRALIST TRADITION OF LATIN AMERICA. Princeton, NJ: Princeton University Press, 1980.

Like many Latin American intellectuals, the Chilean historian Claudio Véliz practices his profession in various countries. When I first met him, some 20 years ago, he was working at Chatham House, in London, in an office next to Arnold Toynbee's; later he returned to Santiago to establish the Institute of International Studies at the University of Chile; still later I ran across him in the outskirts of Melbourne, where he headed the Department of Sociology at La Trobe University; and last year he was at Harvard. Now, I believe, he is back in England, a country he openly admires and feels indebted to.* These many years of living in other worlds have not cooled his passionate interest in the affairs of Latin America. But, perhaps, they have contributed to his more hemispheric, less local and fragmentary view of the region and to his efforts to study it as a unity—which is what he has done in the ambitious and polemical book he has recently published, *The Centralist Tradition of Latin America.*

His book is ambitious because of its thesis and the wide variety of fields in which he wants to prove it: economics, social institutions, politics, religion, art and architecture, history, and even psychology. And it is polemical because the thesis is so daring that its implications contradict many of the ideas about life and society in Latin America that are considered almost axiomatic by a good many scholars.

According to Professor Véliz, there is a deep-rooted "centralist" tradition in our countries that has been the main factor in their historical evolution and has given a common stamp to their societies, despite the

---

*Editor's Note: After his stay in England, Professor Véliz is again resident in his academic home of La Trobe University.

Journal of Interamerican Studies and World Affairs, Vol. 23 No. 3, August 1981 345-351

many differences. This "centralism" is their common denominator and has given them certain characteristics that differentiate them from the rest of the world. It may be civilian or military but it is always bureaucratic and legalistic; it is generated by an avid and ubiquitous state that can reach its tentacles into every area of social life but can also be so pliant as to seem invisible. It has been, Véliz argues, the principal determinant of our historical and community existence, the force that has shaped our institutions, our laws, our economies, our cultural creations, and our political conditions.

Foreseeing objections to this thesis, Professor Véliz begins by declining to provide a clear-cut, unequivocal definition of what he means by "centralism": The phenomenon, he says, is neither just this nor just that. He prefers to let the book as a whole reveal the full complexity of the sense in which he uses this concept, which for him is something specifically Latin American, what is prototypical of our countries. He even states that the centralism he describes is not an ideology but rather a "pragmatic tradition," a mode of organization more detectable in practice than in theory, that resulted from certain historical and social circumstances exterior to Latin America, not from deliberate choice. As proof that centralism is devoid of ideology, he offers the fact that, regardless of the aims of their leaders, the great upheavals in Latin America in the 20th century, without exception, have ended up by strengthening the vertical structure of political power, that is, the center. This is certainly true of the revolutions in Mexico (1910), Bolivia (1952), Cuba (1958), and Nicaragua (1979), and of course the same may be said of all the authoritarian regimes, past and present, that have been imposed by coups d'etat. This downgrading of ideology as a decisive factor in the historical and social reality of Latin America is an important part of the originality of Véliz's book, and gives it a rather refreshing air in a realm like that of the social sciences, which have been so contaminated by ideological disputes in the last decade.

However, perhaps the most daring aspect of the thesis is not its downgrading of ideology but its reassessment of the influence of Spain and Portugal on the make-up of our character as countries. Although his perspective differs from that of the so-called Hispanists, Professor Véliz maintains, as they did, that the Iberian inheritance is an essential part of our lives and customs and that Brazil and Spanish America have derived their personality from Iberia. The longest and most thoroughly documented argument in the book (and also the most impassioned, because a very South American dialectical fervor throbs under Véliz's calm English prose) is his effort to demonstrate that the foundations of our centralist system were laid during the conquest and the colonial period and that the coming of independence did nothing whatever to alter it—that, on the contrary, the new republics, from the very outset, accentuated and strengthened the centralist tradition initiated under Spanish and Portuguese rule, perfecting it to the point of making it, in an almost ontological sense, their very nature.

The most attractive and imaginative passages in the book are those in which the author shows us how the intellectuals and ruling classes of 19th-century Latin America were fascinated by France, England, and the United States; how, in the 20th century, the intellectuals and the revolutionary ideologues and leaders have been bewitched by ideological models derived from those same countries (along with Soviet Russia and the People's Republic of China); how, again and again, they have tried to transplant those countries' institutions, political parties, doctrines, and tactics in the Americas in order to achieve by such means—that is, by means of the federal system of the United States, or British economic liberalism, or French positivist radicalism, or German or Italian Christian democracy, or Soviet or Chinese socialism—the goals of modernization, economic development, and social justice; and how all of their attempts have failed. According to Véliz, the reason why they failed is that the intellectual elites were blind to the nature of their own historical ground. What they transplanted either died or grew malformed because the soil was not right for it. And while these minorities strove to fit their countries to the model of Paris, London, New York, Moscow, or Peking, Latin American society went right on developing within certain patterns established centuries earlier by the conquistadors, who never suspected how long those patterns would prevail. (Perhaps they should be called administrators, not conquistadors.) Véliz epitomizes the beginning of the process of institutional centralization in the victory of La Gasca—a functionary obedient to the imperial political center—over Pizarro, whose rebellion was the first in a long series of frustrated anticentralist efforts throughout the course of our history.

The centralist process that Véliz describes has something of the impersonal nature that ideological conceptions of history attribute to historical processes, and no doubt this is somewhat contradictory in an author opposed to ideological explanations. But Véliz makes no pretense of giving his thesis a rigid, prognosticatory form, of presenting centralism as an inevitable historical phenomenon. Things happened this way because of an amalgamation of historical circumstances, many of them accidental (which means that things could have happened differently). Also, he makes no attempt to derive general conclusions applicable to other worlds. He limits his argument to a defense of this conviction; that the basic cause of the failure of every experiment aimed at modernizing and developing Latin America has been the mistake of considering these countries as a tabula rasa on which history can be started from scratch. Not so: They are societies that have developed their own system, one that is old, powerful, and very difficult to replace.

Among the factors that have shaped the social and political system of Latin America—its vertical, centralized, authoritarian structure—Professor Véliz emphasizes four, all of them negative; the absence of feudalism, the lack of religious nonconformity, and the fact that the region never experienced anything comparable to either the Industrial Revolution in England or the radical transformations brought about by the French revolution. He also underlines two phenomena that he considers typically Latin American: (1) the development of an urban culture that, unlike those of Europe, was not created by industrial growth but instead was antecedent to it and (2) the establishment of a system of "bureaucratization and rationalization" of the state before—again—the growth of industry. It is the interaction of all these elements that, according to his thesis, has given our countries their primordial characteristic: centralism.

Although Professor Véliz's scrupulous analysis of each of these elements can be judged properly only by specialists, even a layman like the present writer will notice the debatable aspects of some of his hypotheses and theories (all of which, it should be said, he presents skillfully, elegantly, and with plentiful documentation).

There is no difficulty, for example, in accepting his statements about the lack of religous nonconformity and the sociopolitical consequences he derives from that fact. The wars and quarrels between liberals and conservatives during the 19th century often appeared to be religious but actually were not, and in any case they never succeeded in undermining Catholicism's absolute hegemony over society. However, his conviction that the Spanish and Portuguese colonies never experienced anything that can correctly be called feudalism is more questionable. True, there was no feudalism if we accept the limited definition that Professor Véliz sets forth (and that suits his thesis): a feudal political power, operating from the periphery, that forced the monarch—as in England—to surrender some of his prerogatives, grant concessions to the nobles, and thus decentralize society. In this sense, feudalism unquestionably did not exist in Spain, in Portugal, or in their American possessions. But are we really to believe that the triming of royal power by the landowning nobles was the only or even the most important characteristic of the feudal system?

In Latin America the agrarian periphery never confronted the power of the center with demands for concessions, either in the colonial period or after, because, quite simply, it had no need to do so: That power was never hostile to the "feudal" landowners. The latter never had reason to feel that either their economic interests or their social autonomy was threatened by the central government; on the contrary, they were its natural representatives on the local level. Within its domains, Latin American feudalism ruled absolutely and could make decisions about lives and properties with guaranteed impunity. This in no way impaired the power of the center; instead, it reinforced it. The feudal system did not consist only in a certain kind of relationship between the barons and the king but also in a specific kind of link between the lord and the land and the lord and the vassal. The Latin American version of the system not only took root throughout the region but even survives today in a good number of our countries and has only recently been left behind in others. The existence of a system of feudal relationships in the agrarian periphery is not at all inconsistent with the centralist character of Latin American societies; feudalism and centralism have been complementary. The former, whose oppressive force paralyzes all initiative, was the most effective agent of the latter, which, for a number of reasons, was unable to extend the fiscal and legal arms of the state into all corners of society. In England, the feudal lords, to protect their rights, forced concessions from the crown that later would benefit the whole society in that they helped to democratize it. In Spanish and Portuguese America, the feudal lords protected their rights by strengthening the power of the center while at the same time serving as its principal base of support in the periphery.

This was due, not to chance or caprice but to one of the most significant factors in Latin American reality—a factor that Professor Véliz almost ignores: the native cultures, the Indian masses. The many aboriginal cultures actually made up the overwhelming majority of the population in the major colonial possessions; just as important, some of them—as in Mexico and Perü—had attained a very high level of development and cohesion. Although natives were officially excluded from economic, political, and social life when the colonial system was instituted, their "invisible" presence had a profound effect on the shape that the system assumed. The colonial governments not only deprived indigenous society of all standing and participation but also set about exploiting it in a methodical fashion, and to do so they had to create a means of overseeing it and keeping it in a state of total submission and servitude. This was the function of agrarian feudalism. It was regressive, isolationist, and hostile to any hint of modernization, not only because this suited the interests of the feudal lord but also because it was the only way of maintaining the continued helplessness of the enormous peasant masses (whom the republican as well as the colonial governments deliberately avoided integrating into the rest of society), because, in other words, it also served the interests of the center. The almost total lack of reference to the social, political, and cultural problems created by the presence of an "indigenous world" in many parts of our countries is all the more noteworthy in Professor Véliz's study for the very reason that he has dealt so justly with so many other aspects of Latin American reality.

There is also some reason to question what might be called the author's excessive pessimism. According to him, every effort to apply a form of organization derived from Europe or the United States to the countries of Latin America has failed because these forms have been incompatible with our centralist nature, whereas the proliferation of authoritarian regimes has been fostered by this same mode of political conduct, this "secular tradition." It would appear that if we accept these premises, we must then conclude that democratic and representative forms of government will continue indefinitely to be a chimera for Latin America and that authoritarian regimes will return over and over again, since the weight of a historical tradition will always frustrate any decentralizing efforts to disperse power and promote freedom, goodwill, and tolerance. But there is evidence of a more optimistic nature to set against this lugubrious outlook. Whenever the people of Latin America have been given a genuine opportunity to vote, they have almost invariably favored democratic civilian formulas that roundly contradict the authoritarian centralist tradition. And, again almost invariably, our repressive regimes have been imposed by military coups with the support of only a small—sometimes even minuscule—segment of the population. What Latin American dictatorship has had the popular support enjoyed by Italian fascism or German nazism? On the other hand, European countries as little inclined historically toward the democratic system as Spain, Portugal, Germany, and Italy are now societies that have embraced that system. These encouraging examples tell us that, no matter how powerful and fateful the force of a tradition may seem—including the centralist tradition Professor Véliz describes so effectively in this book—it can never be an unsuperable obstacle to a country's desire to learn how to live in freedom.

—*Mario Vargas Llosa*
(translated by Lysander Kemp)

Mario Vargas Llosa has experienced and observed a variety of centralized governments, both civil and military. Two of his four major novels have been concerned with the military in Peruvian society. The locale of his forthcoming novel is the Serao of the Brazilian northeast during the long struggle in the 1890s of Antonio Conselheiro and his messianic followers with the forces of the state. Vargas Llosa received a doctorate from the University of Madrid in 1958. Recently he has been a resident fellow at The Wilson Center of the Smithsonian Institution.

REVIEW ESSAY

REINTERPRETING COLOMBIAN ECONOMIC HISTORY

Arango, M. CAFE E INDUSTRIA, 1850-1930. Bogotá: Carlos Valencia Editores, 1977.

Bergquist, C. W. COFFEE AND CONFLICT IN COLOMBIA, 1886-1910. Durham, NC: Duke Univ. Press, 1978.

Brew, R. EL DESARROLLO ECONÓMICO DE ANTIOQUIA DESDE LA INDEPENDENCIA HASTA 1920. Bogotá: Banco de la República, Archivo de la Economía Nacional, 1977.

Palacios, M. COFFEE IN COLOMBIA, 1850-1970. Cambridge, England: Cambridge Univ. Press, 1980.

Palacios, M. EL CAFE EN COLOMBIA, 1850-1970: UNA HISTORIA ECONÓMICA, SOCIAL Y POLÍTICA. Bogotá: Editorial Presencia Ltda., 1979.

Luis Ospina Vásquez changed the study of Colombian economic history with the publication of *Industria y protección, 1810-1930* (1955). The size and density of his 531-page book slowed its absorption by even the professional historians and economists most interested in its contents. Nonetheless, the personal presence of the author, frequently found in the basement of the Luis Angel Arango library until his much-lamented death on April 12, 1977, promoted the slow but certain diffusion of his work.

Despite its title, the book has a wider concern than the growth of manufactures. Compare it, for example, to *A luta pela industrialização do Brasil, 1808 a 1930* by Luz (1961), a good book in itself but with a scope fitting to its title. Ospina Vásquez treated tariff and manufactures

AUTHOR'S NOTE: The views expressed in this review are those of the author and should not be attributed to the World Bank.

Journal of Interamerican Studies and World Affairs, Vol. 23 No. 3, August 1981 352-363

to be sure, but he also dealt with land policy, cycles of export products, and trade in general. Perhaps most important, in his long closing chapter, he examines the sparse data available on long-term trends in levels of living for rural Colombian workers, citing data from the early 18th through the end of the 19th century. His work set a standard of scholarship which has influenced most writing on Colombian economic history over the past quarter century.

What made his work special—and a watershed in Colombian historiography—was that he applied the principles of scholarly research on economic issues in a rigorous way. Since that time it has been easier to distinguish clearly between scholarship and polemic. There could not now be written an *Economía y cultura en la historia de Colombia* of the sort that Luis Eduardo Nieto Arteta (1942) first published, a work interesting in design but with a cavalier attitude toward sources and statistical data.

Despite its value, the work of Ospina Vásquez had one pernicious influence on historical work, an influence implicit in his table of contents, a simple chronological listing of time periods for Chapters II through VIII. The sequential design of his work enable him to avoid analytical arrangements that might otherwise have yielded a more satisfactory set of conclusions from his vast research effort. The historians of Colombia's economic history have too often avoided the important job of building and examining hypotheses about causal relations between events. With ever more detailed searchings for facts and many more facts having been found, there has been too little design which could hold together a coherent picture of how the economy evolved and what facts and factors may have caused that evolution to occur as it did and not in some alternative way. The books under review here are among the best at avoiding pure historicism, yet several of them depart from the guidance of design and hypothesis to present unorganized detail. This was not the manner of Luis Ospina Vásquez, but some of his successors may have read his attention to detail as guidance for an absence of theory. The organizing theme is subtle in the master's work; in some later writers it may be absent altogether.

These latest books rework ground covered before, particularly the nature of the major export industry of coffee and its interactive relationship to domestic politics and international influence. Perhaps the most significant advance in unearthing new historical detail and providing a coherent framework for it is Bergquist's (1978) study of the War of the Thousand Days, 1899-1902.

Professor Bergquist's book is a most welcome addition to the literature on Colombian history. It might fairly be called political history in the new style rather than economic history per se, given its careful attention to the decisions and events surrounding the war. Nonetheless, in a fashion reminiscent of other historians seeking to link political to economic events, Bergquist draws out for the reader the association between the war and misfortunes in the international market for Colombian coffee. Unlike some other authors on Colombian history who seem to get stuck in the period before important events happen.[1] Bergquist concentrates on the critical period and the manner in which political and economic interactions set the stage for a long period of change thereafter.

No other author had dug through the archival details of *fin-de-siècle* Colombia to give us so clear a picture of the events which transpired. How many historians and social critics have cited the estimate of 100,000 deaths in the war, and how few have even the slightest idea where the estimate originated. In the Rippy translation of the Henao and Arrubla *Historia de Colombia* (1936) is the first place I saw the number appear. Everett E. Hagen (1962: 379) took it from p.519 of the Rippy translation and observed that the numbers killed relative to total population were far higher than the death rate experienced in the U.S. Civil War. Colombians have compared deaths during the Thousand Days War with the supposed 300,000 who died during the *violencia* of 1948 to 1963 (Guzman et al., 1962: Vol. 1, 292). Bergquist (1978: 208) quotes from an ultimatum of resignation submitted by Aristides Fernández and José Joaquín Casa, that "blood still [May 10, 1903] flowed and the bones of more than one hundred thousand Colombians bleached unburied." This source, if queried as was one recent U.S. president, "What did they know, and when did they know it?" would have to admit to guesswork and supposition at best. There were no Vietnam-like body counts, most military deaths are by disease rather than battle wounds, and all sides must surely have had excellent reasons to exaggerate or minimize their armies, their gains, and their losses. Bergquist has traced an important number back to a key ministerial statement. It remains for him, or another generation of scholars, to do the job Philip Curtin (1969) did on rechecking sources for estimating

African migrations under slavery. Bergquist's solidly based and intellectually sound work provides an excellent basis for that next round of investigation.

A book less successful in its execution, flawed by unnecessary conflict with previous publications, yet offering an important contribution by reason of enormous inputs of energy in the examination of unpublished archival material is that of Marco Palacios. His work appears in a 429-page Spanish-language edition (1979) with 65 tables and charts and a 338-page (plus 15) English edition (1980) with 48 tables and charts. Professor Palacios, now a faculty member of El Colegio de México in Mexico City, spent six years on the work, much of that time being in archives outside the usual settings in Bogotá. The result is a fuller picture of the details of change in the coffee zones, particularly the areas of Sasaima and Viotá in Cundinamarca and Fredonia [Hacienda Jónas] in Antioquia. It is unfortunate that the historicist approach, the conscious unwillingness to impose conceptual frameworks on the mass of information, led Professor Palacios to limit his potentially valuable inquiry to a rather undigested flock of facts.

That this failure is fundamental to his work, Palacios himself makes clear for the discerning reader in a preface where he writes,

> I have consciously avoided a systematic quantitative treatment, not so much becasue of my own ignorance of quantitative methods—an ignorance easily corrected in this age of computers—but because of the incongruence and the slight reliability offered by all Colombian statistical publications at all times [Palacios, 1980: xi].

This is a strange statement from an author who offers scores of tables and whose critiques of other authors—principally Bustamante, Urrutia, and McGreevey—hinge on numbers and their interpretation. How one reaches the facile conclusion that uncorrected ignorance is advantageous, and the more so the worse the data, must make any reader wonder at the clarity of vision remaining after six years of poring over old account books.

Nonetheless, one may readily admit that despite all the numbers he presents, Professor Palacios did not offer a systematic story. There are few statistics per se, in the sense, for example, of numerical descriptions born of theory, as averages, means, dispersions, time series, and the other simple descriptive data that constitute what Durkheim called social facts and which, by their nature as intellectual creations, are different from raw facts. Palacios does delve into the issue of profit rates for Hacienda Santa Barbara and hence does get into statistics and social facts there. But his entry is far from complete. He does engage in careful scrutiny of the data where other analysts have offered suggestive hypotheses, which Palacios seems determined to expose rather than to replace. The most significant of these is concerned with whether the issuance of paper money in the Regeneration, 1880-1895, encouraged economic growth. I was unable to see, finally, how Palacios actually advanced that debate other than to maintain, in a manner perhaps consistent with and a consequence of his agnostic approach to research, that the policies were "marked by incoherence" (Palacios, 1980: 129). All public policy making has a good deal of incoherence in it, given its origin in the give and take of the political arena. Analysis—and in this Marxists and neoclassical economists do not differ—consists of finding the pattern where, to the untrained and uninformed eye, no pattern seems to exist. Historicism can refute theory with inconvenient facts, but it is in essence destructive as it offers no alternative theory.

The search of archives does have its rewards. An important find by Professor Palacios was a recording in the Hacienda Jónas records of the day laborer's normal daily ration, which Palacios calculates to be equivalent to 3,578 kcal, an amount well above the average of 2,364 consumed in Colombia in 1977 (World Bank, 1980: Table 22, 152),[2] a recent year for which data are at hand. How is it that Professor Palacios fails to comment on this high level of rations, an amount sufficient for an adult and perhaps one child? Further, his data show substantially lower rations for two other haciendas in the 1930s. Do these data imply a trend? Is there any logic to the placement of data in the table? The text offers no answer. Curiously, Professor Palacios did not make reference to another source of nutritional intake data for the 1890s, namely, the study by Manual Cotes (1893). Cotes describes daily food intake for a day laborer as 600 grams of *mazamorra;* 360 of bread; 3,575 of *chicha;* and 40 of chocolate. Meat was available to them only on occasion (Cotes, 1893: 31). If the 600 grams of *mazamorra* contain the same number of kcals per 100 grams as does the maize which appears in the Palacios table, and if *chicha* has the same caloric content as *guarapo,* one finds calorie avaliability on the sabana in the neighborhood of 2,800 kcals,a level lower than that of the Hacienda Jónas but still strikingly high. There may be an error in my calculation—and hence also in that of Professor Palacios—if maize and *mazamorra* rations were a watered gruel rather than corn itself. The issue is an important one because Cotes—and, for that matter, Miguel Samper, (1867)—thought the poor were starving to death at a time in which the above figures imply quite adequate food intake. It will not do for an author simply to put numbers before the public without some guidance on their interpretation, especially on a matter of such central concern.

A comment this reviewer could not let pass is Professor Palacios's (1980: 148) suggestion that the impact of the railways on coffee expansion had been "exaggerated" in an earlier work. He went so far as to cite a page of such exaggeration which proves on examination to be a graphic representation of the relationship between the number of kilometers of railway in use in Colombia and the quantum of coffee exports each year for which data were available between 1885 and 1934 (McGreevey, 1971: 254). How can the presentation of social facts flowing from a theory linking coffee and transportation, a theory explicit in one of the best and earliest works on the topic (Beyer, 1947),[3] in any sense represent an exaggeration? To arrange facts in a matter consistent with theory is at the heart of the work of analytical history. Compare fact arrangement with the cavalier statement by Professor Palacios (1980: 149) that "Table 23 shows that, compared to the price of coffee, transport costs did not fall to any great extent." A glance at the table mentioned above shows, among other things, that from 1905 to 1932 a bag of Cundinamarca coffee fell in price by 30% while the cost of transport was falling by 74%. Transport's share in delivered cost fell from 22% to 8% in that period. Of course, a bag of coffee cost more than moving it around. It is at the margin of cost change, however, that one finds the notable impact on economic choice. Rather than worrying about the exaggeration of other writers, Professor Palacios might consider the elasticity of response of coffee growers implicit in their expansion of production due to the decline in transport costs. Elasticity, however, may be interpreted as a "statistical" matter and hence outside his concern.

It is not in the arena of numerical manipulation that Professor Palacios makes his most telling contribution: It is in his consideration of the conditions which led to a decline of the large haciendas of the coffee speculators in Cundinamarca and the subsequent—though unconnected in his work—risk of the Federación Nacional de Cafeteros. Given Professor Palacio's historicist bent, he does not proffer theories connecting the decline of the one and the rise of the other. Palacios and his mentor, Malcolm Deas—in related writings (Deas, 1977, 1979)—tell the doleful tale of the decline of Hacienda Santa Barbara in Sasaima and the eventual ejection of major landholders generally from the management and ownership of coffee estates. The evidence provided by these authors seems to indicate that this change resulted from the unsuitability of coffee as grown in Colombia for management in units larger than those formed by the individual *arrendatarios*, who received a plot of land in exchange for labor in coffee cultivation. Those workers executed work agreements for weeding, cultivation, care, and harvesting of the coffee plants, which all parties recognized as belonging to the so-called coffee speculators. These agreements produced substantial profits in the 1890s—or until the rise in wages began to eat into the profitability of coffee growing—and the expansion of smallholder production acros the Magdalena in Tolima and southern Caldas offered competition in product and factors markets, that is, by limiting coffee prices due to expanded supply and in raising wages of seasonal and *arrendatario* workers by offering a feasible work alternative in open lands.

By the 1920s many *arrendatarios* had learned all they needed to know to cultivate coffee for their own account. These kulaks, as Palacios is tempted to call them, pressed for the breaking up of the estates in Viotá and other coffee-growing areas of Cundinamarca. The break-up, moreover, was not effectively resisted because the speculators of the 1890s or, more likely, their heirs by one or two generations recognized by the mid-1930s that the estate-labor system was not feasible under conditions of labor scarcity. The estate system was not able to sustain the support of the federal government, and it could not rely on the scarcity of opportunity to maintain low wages. The Quindío was populated by Antioqueños in the later 19th century, but there was still room for expansion through the early stage of the *violencia*, that is, the late 1940s. Thus, that area provided a place for labor to go to earn a return equal to the total product which could be offered by coffee production through the estate system of the *tierra templada* of Cundinamarca.

The distribution of the product between capital and labor is among the oldest themes of economic analysis. The particulars of the Colombian coffee economy of the period 1890-1950 offer one large example of what happens when innovation occurs and offers returns not to a factor of production but rather to the act of innovation itself. The innovators get their return only until others learn to copy the innovation. There was, perhaps, never a return to the ownership of land; there was, rather, a return to the innovative act of planting, cultivating, processing, and marketing coffee.

Leaders and innovators—whatever one may wish to call the Ospinas, Uribes, Angel Arangos, and Lopez—began to see that the distribution of the product from coffee did not involve a substantial return to land per se, because it was not a truly scarce factor of production. They sought other mechanisms by which to expand their share of the income produced by the coffee industry. That mechanism was the Federación Nacional de Cafeteros, the trade organization, first, of the larger coffee growers in the 1920s, then, subsequently, the marketing organization that controlled the purchase, resale, and rationalization of coffee cultivation in the country as a whole. It was in the years of crisis for the coffee industry, that is, from 1928 to 1936, that a crisis of labor shortage and protest drove the coffee speculators from Viotá and other coffee-growing areas of Cundinamarca. A crisis of lower coffee prices emerged when Brazil abandoned the coffee price-maintenance scheme that prevailed from 1907 to 1928. The Federación Nacional de Cafeteros arose as an instrument of the coffee elite to organize the industry. It was the mechanism, in other words, which replaced ownership and control of land as the technique by which a few could realize substantial gains from the coffee industry as a whole. It is an adage in economics that control of price requires control of supply. How better to control supply than to do it on a national scale, such as organizing the industry as a whole, rather than retaining an atomistic system of what were essentially still rather small estates. Let production units fall back to their natural size, roughly that which could be managed and cultivated by a single *arrendatario* and his family along with a crew of seasonal workers. Restrict the access of those producers to the market by filtering their product and sales through a national organization controlled by the nation's senior economic leadership. Operate the sytem not for individual gain but for a class of senior executives identified by the industry as a whole. Such a cartel arrangement, so strange to North Americans, would seem perfectly natural to any European or Japanese businessman.

This story is left implicit in the work of Palacios. The advantage of leaving theory and hypothesis in the shadow is presumably that uncomfortable facts are never allowed to be swept under the rug. The disadvantage is that significant patterns are left unexplored.

The works of Arango and Brew, unlike the previous works considered, fit more nearly the term *monograph* than *book*. They are detailed presentations of specific themes already explored in earlier works by Parsons (1968) and Ospina Vásquez (1955).

Arango's work divides into three chapters dealing with (1) the early history of coffee cultivation in the three regions of Santander, Cundinamarca, and areas of Antioqueño colonization; (2) labor and management systems for coffee cultivation; and (3) the linkages between coffee export and, first, cottage and, later, factory-based manufacturing activities. Though an interesting reorganization of information, particularly with respect to data on employment and capital equipment in the manufacturing establishments of Medellín, Arango's study is flawed by the incompleteness of his material. He did not have access to the 1918 census or to the study done by P.L. Bell (U.S. Department of Commerce, 1921).[4] Perhaps more important he does not refer to the text by Albert Hirschman that gave rise to the notion of forward and backward linkages in industry, inspired in large measure by Hirschman's (1958: 98-119) experience as a consulting economist in Colombia. Since Arango is centrally interested in that theme, it is sad to see that he has missed out on Professor Hirschman's perceptive analysis, available now for nearly as long as we have had the book of Luis Ospina Vásquez.

Arango (1977) offers in his Table II.8—which presents coffee production by department for the selected years of 1874 to 1943—data for 1892 from a census of exportable products and for 1925 from the book of Diego Monsalve, *Colombia Cafetera* (1927). Neither set of figures is complete. Their presentation in this table has the advantage of making their understatements of the totals clear. That is a singular advantage of such time series information. By being able to compare such data with earlier and later figures, an analyst can generate some hypotheses to explain the limitations of the data. Arango, in a footnote to the table, explains that certain provinces were left out of the count for the 1892 data; perhaps he could have made the additional step of making estimates for those provinces and hence have improved on the figures of the original source. Unfortunately, he uses the 1892 data as if they were complete in other parts of his work.

Roger Brew's (1977) monograph, based on his D.Phil. thesis at Oxford directed by Malcolm Deas, is more than twice as long as Parsons's study of the Antioqueños and about half as interesting. It lacks that element of reality the French would have historians infuse into their work, a reality which Parsons achieved by months of walking and seeing, hearing and smelling Antioquia. Mr. Brew, now unfortunately deceased, breathed too much archival dust and not enough trail dust.

Interesting data show up in his Table 6 on what is called the distribution of income in Medellín in 1853. The source is a cadastral survey of the city carried out, presumably, for purposes of levying a property tax. Such a survey would normally yield information on the value of real estate within the locality but offer no information on income from that property, from property outside the bounds of the locality, or from wages and profits from other sources. Thus, unless the author had some means of adjusting data from the cadastre, one could hardly suppose that his table describes income in the normal sense of the word. Nonetheless, the data are useful in identifying the owners of substantial properties, and personal residence is perhaps as good an indicator of elite status as one can find. Having identified the elite, it would have been extraordinarily useful if Brew had drawn some family trees based on the 1853 data to link those families to the elite of the 20th century.

Brew's work is to be admired for the impressive array of additional facts, both numerical and contextual, which he has brought to general attention with this monograph. It can usefully be consulted along with Ann Twinam's (1976) work on an earlier period. It remains for some analyst to put all the pieces of information into some coherent framework.

Just as it appears that Mariano Arango in Medellín did not have easy access to some U.S. publications, so it happens that a North American reviewer is late in receiving books from Colombia. Word has arrived of books published by the Instituto de Estudios Colombianos (1979),[5] the Centro de Investigaciones Económicas at the Universidad de Antioquia, Medellín,[6] and Fedesarrollo (Urrutia, 1979, 1980). An important addition to the literature is an article by José Antonio Ocampo (1980), which returns to original sources in an effort to rebuild sound estimates of Colombian foreign trade in the 19th and 20th centuries.

There are thus entries in the historiography of Colombian economic history which will correct some of the flaws identified in the books under review. There is evidence of a serious return to original sources aimed at rebuilding the data base. Such a return is likely to be unproductive unless it is informed by conceptual frames of reference that permit aggressive adjustment and correction of those sources on the basis of the superior information which we now have. That process now seems to have been effectively adopted by a generation of economists with a serious interest in economic history. Good historians like Arango, Bergquist, and Palacios will in the future have their counterparts in economists like R. Albert Berry, Ocampo, and Urrutia. The result should be a continuation of interesting debates.

—*William Paul McGreevey*

NOTES

1. A prominent case is Frank Safford (1976), whose topic could more practically have been addressed by examination of 20th century materials rather than the thin and sparse sources for the 19th, which he has so exhaustively treated. Safford was apparently unable to come forward in time from the lair of his antebellum expertise. (Editor's Note: Safford and Bergquist put forward their differing approaches to the interrelationships of social structure, politics, and the economy of Colombia during the 19th century in LARR, 1978.)

2. Average requirements suggested by the World Health Organization are 2,300 kcal daily.

3. This work is among the few doctoral dissertations which should have been published and was not.

4. This study summarizes and extends information from a 1915 manufacturing survey.

5. This work includes papers presented at the 1975 conference on economic history of Colombia.

6. Professor James J. Parsons has sent notices of monographs by Jorge Villegas and Mariano Arango from the center, which also has published a series of monographs on 20th century economic trends.

REFERENCES

BEYER, R. C. (1947) "the Colombian coffee industry: Origins and major trends, 1774-1940." Ph.D. dissertation, University of Minnesota, Minneapolis.

COTES, M. (1893) Régimen Alimenticio de los Jornaleros de la Sabana de Bogotá. Bogotá: Imprenta La Luz.

CURTIN, P. (1969) The Atlantic Slave Trade, A Census. Madison: Univ. of Wisconsin Press.

DEAS, M. (1979) "Poverty, civil war and politics: Ricardo Gaitán Obeso and his Magdalena River campaign, 1885." Nova Americana 2: 263-303.

——— (1977— "A Colombian coffee estate: Santa Barbara, Cundinamarca, 1870-1912," pp. 269-298 in K. Duncan and I. Rutledge (eds.) Land and Labour in Latin America. Cambridge, England: Cambridge Univ. Press.

GUZMAN CAMPOS, G., O. FALS BORDA, and E. Umana (1962) La Violencia en Colombia. Bogotá: Ediciones Tercer Mundo.

HAGEN, E. E. (1962) On the Theory of Social Change. Homewood. IL: Dorsey Press.

HENAO, J. M. and G. ARRULA (1963) Historia de Colombia [Bogotá], tr. by J.F. Rippy. Chapel Hill: Univ. of North Carolina Press.

HIRSCHMAN, A. (1958) The Strategy of Economic Development. New Haven, CT: Yale Univ. Press.

Instituto de Estudios Colombianos (1979) Historia Económica de Colombia: Un Debate en Marcha. Bogotá: Biblioteca Banco Popular.

LARR [Latin American Research Review] (1978) Response by Frank Safford to review essay by Charles W. Bergquist, "On Paradigms and the Pursuit of the Practical," in Safford's book, The Ideal of the Practical: Colombia's Struggle to Form a Technical Elite. LARR 13: 247-260.

LUZ, N V. (1961) A la luta pela industrialização do Brasil, 1808 a 1930. São Paulo: Difusao Européia do Livro.

McGREEVEY, W. P. (1971) An Economic History of Colombia, 1845-1930. Cambridge, England: Cambridge Univ. Press.

MONSALVE, D. (1927) Colombia Cafetera. Barcelona: Artes Gráficas.

NIETO ARTETA, L. E. (1942) Economía y cultura en la historia de Colombia. Bogotá. n.p.

OCAMPO, J.A. (1980) "La exportaciones colombianas en el siglo XIX." Desarrollo Sociedad 4(Julio): 165-226.

OSPINA VASQUEZ, L. (1955) Industria y protección, 1810-1930. Medellín, Colombia: E.S.F. [Editorial Santa Fe].

PARSONS, J. J. (1968) [orig. ed. 1949] Antioqueno Colonization in Western Colombia. Berkeley: Univ. of California Press.

SAFFORD, F. (1976) The Ideal of the Practical: Colombia's Struggle To Form a Technical Elite. Austin: Univ. of Texas Press.

SAMPER, M. (1867) La miseria en Bogotá. Bogotá: n.p.

TWINAM, A. (1976) "Miners, merchants and farmers: The roots of entrepreneurship in Antioquia, 1763-1810." Ph.D. dissertation, Yale University.

URRUTIA, M. [ed.] (1980) Ensayos sobre historia económica colombiana. Bogotá: FEDESARROLLO [Fundación para la Educación Superior y Desarrollo].

——— (1979) 50 anos de desarrollo económico colombiano. Bogotá: La Carreta.

U.S. Department of Commerce (1912) Colombia: A Commercial and Industrial Handbook. Washington, DC: Government Printing Office.

World Bank (1980) World Development Report, 1980. Washington, DC: Author.

William Paul McGreevey is a senior economist at the World Bank's Development Research Center. He is the editor of Third World Poverty: New Strategies for Measuring Developing Progress *(Lexington Books 1980) and is currently preparing an article on the transition to economic growth in Colombia for inclusion in a book to be edited by Roberto Cortes Conde and Shane Hunt on Latin American economic history. A previous article and lengthy bibiliography on Colombia appear in Roberto Cortes Conde and Stanley J. Stein, eds.,* Latin America: A Guide to Economic History, 1830-1930 *(University of California Press, 1977).*

A. CURTIS WILGUS: 1897-1981

This Journal does not publish obituaries, in part because of limitations of space, but also because the careers of major scholars of Latin America who have recently died are fully recounted elsewhere. It seems appropriate, however, to bring to the attention of our readership that Dr. A. Curtis Wilgus—the founder of the *Journal of Interamerican Studies* together with its first editor, Dr. Robert McNicoll—died in his Miami home of a heart attack at the age of 83 on January 23, 1981. The relationship of Dr. Wilgus with the Journal from its inception in January 1959 until 1969 is briefly but, I think, adequately recounted in the introduction to the *Cumulative Index: Journal of Interamerican Studies and World Affairs, 1959-1978* (Sage Publications, 1979). The changes in the editorial policy of the Journal since 1972—when a new publisher, Sage, and a new editorial board at the University of Miami assumed responsibility—are also apparent from the *Index*.

Dr. Wilgus was one of those fortunate individuals who remained fully and effectively active as scholar, bibliographer, and academic entrepreneur until his sudden and unexpected death. The volume of his contributions, particularly in the field of bibliography, as supervising editor of a substantial series of historical dictionaries of the nations of Latin America, and in the reissuing of fundamental books long out of print, actually accelerated after his retirement from the University of Florida. In this work he was fortunate not only in the enjoyment of exceptional health but also in the active professional collaboration of his wife Karna, who will complete the editorial work on his final book, *Latin America: A Guide to Illustrations*, and see it through publication.

—John P. Harrison
Editor

BOOKS RECEIVED

GENERAL AND REGIONAL LATIN AMERICA

Crow, John A. THE EPIC OF LATIN AMERICA, third ed., expanded and updated. Berkeley: Univ. of California Press, 1980. References, bibliographical essay, index. xxvi, 929 pp. $14.95 paper.

DESCO. AMERICA LATINA 80: DEMOCRACIA Y MOVIMIENTO POPULAR. Lima, Perú: DESCO [Centro de Estudios y Promoción del Desarrollo], 1981. 508 pp. Paper.

Herd, Jan, ed. THE AUTOMOTIVE INDUSTRY IN LATIN AMERICA. Latin American Monograph Series No. 12. Erie: Northwestern Pennsylvania Institute for Latin American Studies, Mercyhurst College, 1980. 180 pp. Paper.

OAS. ANNUAL REPORT OF THE INTERAMERICAN COMMISSION ON HUMAN RIGHTS, 1979-1980. Washington, DC: Author,1980. 153 pp. Paper.

OAS. STATISTICAL BULLETIN OF THE OAS. (The external debt and Latin American economic development; regional statistics; country tables.) Washington, DC: Author, 1980. Vol. 2, No. 1-2, January-June. 220 pp. Paper.

Pagano, Carlos. EXTERNAL FINANCING PROSPECTS OF LATIN AMERICA'S DEVELOPMENT BANKING SYSTEM. Washington, DC: Inter-American Development Bank, 1980. Annexes, bibliography, list of tables. 96 pp. Paper.

Puig, Juan Carlos. DOCTRINAS INTERNACIONALES Y AUTONOMIA LATINOAMERICANA. Caracas: Universidad Simón Bolívar, Instituto de Altos Estudios de América Latina, 1980. Apéndice, índice onomástico y temático. 316 pp. Paper.

TePaske, John J., coordinating ed. RESEARCH GUIDE TO ANDEAN HISTORY: BOLIVIA, CHILE, ECUADOR, AND PERU. Durham, NC: Duke University Press, 1981. Index. xiii, 346 pp. $18.75.

ARGENTINA

Frenkel, Roberto. EL DESARROLLO RECIENTE DEL MERCADO DE CAPITALES EN ARGENTINA. Buenos Aires: CEDES [Centro de Estudios de Estado y Sociedad], Vol. 2, No. 10, 1979. Referencias. 55 pp. Paper.

BRAZIL

Levine, Robert M. BRAZIL SINCE 1930: AN ANNOTATED BIBLIOGRAPHY FOR SOCIAL HISTORIANS. New York and London: Garland, 1980. Indexes. xvii, 336 pp. $35.00.

CARIBBEAN REGION

Lent, John A. CARIBBEAN MASS COMMUNICATIONS: A COMPREHENSIVE BIBLIOGRAPHY. Waltham, MA: ASA-Crossroads Press, 1981. Addendum, author index. 152 pp. $20.00 paper.

Philipson, Lorrin and Rafael Llerena. FREEDOM FLIGHTS: CUBAN REFUGEES TALK ABOUT LIFE UNDER CASTRO AND HOW THEY FLED HIS REGIME. New York: Random House, 1981. Appendix. xxix, 201 pp. $12.95.

Tata, Robert J. STRUCTURAL CHANGES IN PUERTO RICO'S ECONOMY, 1947-1976. Papers in International Studies, Latin America Series No. 9. Athens: Latin America Program, Ohio University Center for International Studies, 1980. List of figures and tables, references. xiii, 104 pp. Paper.

CENTRAL AMERICA

El Colegio de México. CENTROAMERICA EN CRISIS. México, D.F.: Centro de Estudios Internacionales, El Colegio de México, 1980. 226 pp. Paper.

Somoza, Anastasio, as told to Jack Cox. NICARAGUA BETRAYED. Boston and Los Angeles: Western Islands Publishers, 1980. Appendices, index. xii, 431 pp.

COLOMBIA

Delpar, Helen. RED AGAINST BLUE: THE LIBERAL PARTY IN COLOMBIAN POLITICS, 1863-1899. University: University of Alabama Press, 1981. List of tables, notes, bibliography, index. xiii, 262 pp. $23.50.

Palacios, Marco. COFFEE IN COLOMBIA, 1850-1970: AN ECONOMIC, SOCIAL, AND POLITICAL HISTORY. Cambridge Latin American Studies 36. New York: Cambridge University Press, 1980. Appendices, weights and measures, glossary, notes, bibliography, index, lists of tables, figures, maps. xv, 338 pp. $34.50.

ECUADOR

Hurtado, Osvaldo. POLITICAL POWER IN ECUADOR, tr. by Nick D. Mills. Albuquerque: University of New Mexico Press, 1981. Illustrations, notes, bibliography, supplementary bibliography, index. xxv, 398 pp. $29.95.

MEXICO

Berry, Charles R. THE REFORM IN OAXACA, 1856-76: A MICROHISTORY OF THE LIBERAL REVOLUTION. Lincoln: University of Nebraska Press, 1981. Lists of maps and tables, appendices, list of abbreviations, notes, bibliography, index. xviii, 282 pp. $20.00.

García, Juan Ramón. OPERATION WETBACK: THE MASS DEPORTATION OF MEXICAN UNDOCUMENTED WORKERS IN 1954. Contributions in Ethnic Studies, No. 2. Westport, CT: Greenwood Press, 1980. Tables and figures, illustrations, appendices, bibliography, index. xviii, 268 pp. $25.00

Goldman, Shifra M. CONTEMPORARY MEXICAN PAINTING IN A TIME OF CHANGE. The Texas Pan American Series. Austin: University of Texas Press, 1981. Appendix, notes, bibliography, index, list of illustrations. xxvi, 229 pp. $30.00.

Henderson, Peter V. N. FELIX DIAZ, THE PORFIRIANS, AND THE MEXICAN REVOLUTION. Lincoln: University of Nebraska Press, 1981. Appendices, list of abbreviations, notes, selected bibliography, index. xi, 239 pp. $18.50

Hopgood, James F. SETTLERS OF BAJAVISTA: SOCIAL AND ECONOMIC ADAPTATION IN A MEXICAN SQUATTER SETTLEMENT. Papers in International Studies, Latin American Series No. 7. Athens: Ohio University Press, 1979. Ohio University Center for International Studies, Latin America Program. Lists of figures and tables, references. xi, 145 pp. $11.00 paper.

Lehr, Volker G. DER MEXIKANISCHE AUTORITARISMUS: PARTEIEN, WAHLEN, HERRSCHAFTSSICHERUNG UND KRISENPOTENTIAL. Lateinamerika Studien 8. Muenchen: Wilhelm Fink Verlag, 1981. Anhang, literaturverzeichnis, verzeichnis der tabellen und schaubilder im text. 375 pp. Paper.

PERU

Burkholder, Mark A. POLITICS OF A COLONIAL CAREER: JOSE BAQUIJANO AND THE AUDIENCIA OF LIMA. Albuquerque: University of New Mexico Press, 1981. Appendices, notes, glossary of Spanish terms used, bibliography, index. xi, 184 pp. $20.00.

Devlin, Robert. LOS BANCOS TRANSNACIONALES Y EL FINANCIAMIENTO EXTERNO DE AMERICA LATINA: LA EXPERIENCIA DEL PERU, 1965-1976. Santiago de Chile: CEPAL [Comisión Económica para América Latina] Naciones Unidas, 1980. Anexos, bibliografía. x, 265 pp. Paper.

Flores Galindo, Alberto. LA AGONIA DE MARIATEGUI: LA POLEMICA CON LA KOMINTERN. Lima, Perú: DESCO [Centro de Estudios y Promoción del Desarrollo] 1980. Anexos. 134 pp. Paper.

Pease García, Henry y Alfredo Filomeno. PERU 1979: CRONOLOGIA POLITICA. Tomo VII. Lima: DESCO, 1980. Indices temáticos.

Roncagliolo, Rafael. QUIEN GANO? ELECCIONES 1931-1980. Lima: DESCO, 1980. Indices de cuadros, gráficos, mapas. 135 pp. Paper.

Rubio, C. Marcial and Enrique B. Bernales, PERU: CONSTITUCION Y SOCIEDAD POLITICA. Lima: DESCO, 1981. Bibliografía, índice de tratamiento del articulado constitucional según las páginas del libro. 686 pp. Paper.

VENEZUELA

Ellner, Steve. LOS PARTIDOS POLITICOS Y SU DISPUTA POR EL CONTROL DEL MOVIMIENTO SINDICAL EN VENEZUELA, 1936-1948. Caracas-San Cristóbal: Universidad Católica Andrés Bello, 1980. Cronología, siglas, bibliografía. 181 pp. Paper.

Penniman, Howard R., ed. VENEZUELA AT THE POLLS: THE NATIONAL ELECTIONS OF 1978. Washington, DC: American Enterprise Institute for Public Policy Research, 1980. Abbreviations, appendices, index. xvi, 287 pp. Paper.

MISCELLANEOUS

Bathrick, David D. AGRICULTURAL CREDIT FOR SMALL FARM DEVELOPMENT: POLICIES AND PRACTICES. Boulder, CO: Westview Press, 1981. Includes an integrated agricultural development case study of Nicaragua. Appendices, references, glossary, list of tables and figures. xviii, 170 pp. $17.50.

Donaldson, Robert H., ed. THE SOVIET UNION IN THE THIRD WORLD: SUCCESSES AND FAILURES. Part I—Soviet Union and Latin America, 3 chapters. Boulder, CO: Westview Press, 1981. List of tables. xiv, 458 pp. $25 cloth, $12 paper.

McGreevey, William Paul. THIRD-WORLD POVERTY: NEW STRATEGIES FOR MEASURING DEVELOPMENT PROGRESS. Lexington, MA: Lexington Books, 1980. Lists of figures and tables, bibliography, index. xx, 215 pp.

OECD. GEOGRAPHICAL DISTRIBUTION OF FINANCIAL FLOWS TO DEVELOPING COUNTRIES: 1976-1979. Disbursements, commitments, external debt, economic indicators. Paris: OECD [Organization for Economic Cooperation and Development], 1980. Summary tables. xxvi, 209 pp. Paper.

OECD. DEVELOPMENT COOPERATION: EFFORTS AND POLICIES OF THE MEMBERS OF THE DEVELOPMENT ASSISTANCE COMMITTEE (report by John P. Lewis), 1980 Review. Paris: OECD, 1980. Statistical annex, text tables and charts. 241 pp. Paper.

Rodack, Madeline Turrell, ed. and translator. ADOLPH F. BANDELIER'S THE DISCOVERY OF NEW MEXICO by the Franciscan Monk, Friar Marços de Niza in 1539. Tucson: University of Arizona Press, 1981. Maps, selected bibliography, index. 135 pp. $10.95.

Roth, Russell. MUDDY GLORY: AMERICA'S "INDIAN WARS" IN THE PHILIPPINES, 1899-1935. West Hanover, MA: Christopher Publishing House, 1981. Illustrations, notes, bibliography, index. 281 pp. $12.95.

U.S. Arms Control and Disarmament Agency. WORLD MILITARY EXPENDITURES AND ARMS TRANSFERS, 1969-1978. Washington, DC: Arms Control and Disarmament Agency, 1980. Statistical notes and sources, tables. iii, 166 pp. Paper.

Vol. 23 No. 4
November 1981

JOURNAL OF INTERAMERICAN STUDIES

and WORLD AFFAIRS

A Publication of the Center for Advanced International Studies,

The University of Miami

SAGE PUBLICATIONS

Journal of INTERAMERICAN STUDIES and WORLD AFFAIRS

The editors and publisher wish to acknowledge with gratitude the assistance and encouragement of the Center for Advanced International Studies, University of Miami, in providing ancillary services and support for this journal.

Journal of
INTERAMERICAN
STUDIES
and WORLD AFFAIRS

Vol. 23
No. 4
November
1981

CONTENTS

Labor-Industrial Conflict and the Collapse of Uruguayan Democracy
HOWARD HANDELMAN 371

Military Radicalism in Latin America
MILES D. WOLPIN 395

Political Assassination in Guatemala: A Case of Institutionalized Terror
DANIEL L. PREMO 429

Japanese Immigration into Latin America: A Survey
JAMES L. TIGNER 457

REVIEW ESSAY

Diverse Influences on the Venezuelan Left: Five Books by Venezuelan Leftists
STEVE ELLNER 483

Index to Volume 23 495

SAGE PUBLICATIONS / *Beverly Hills* *London* *New Delhi*

Policy: The **JOURNAL OF INTERAMERICAN STUDIES AND WORLD AFFAIRS** reflects the interests of the scholarly community and interested public concerned with the social, economic, political, and cultural aspects of life in Latin America (including the Caribbean), particularly in those instances where the subject is of concern to more than one of the traditional disciplines. As these concerns change, so will the content of the journal.

Articles which have special relevance for interrelationships between American nations and of those nations with the rest of the world will be given special consideration. An effort will be made to include occasional articles that state an unusual or even discordant position on a subject of broad interest to be supplemented by critical comments of authorities representing differing positions on the topic. The editors continue to welcome articles by scholars from all parts of the world.

Manuscripts should be submitted in duplicate to: Editor, **JOURNAL OF INTERAMERICAN STUDIES AND WORLD AFFAIRS**, Box 24-8134, University of Miami, Coral Gables, Florida 33124. Manuscripts should be typewritten, double-spaced, with footnotes, references, tables, and charts on separate pages, and should follow the current journal style. A brief biographical paragraph describing each author's current affiliation, research interests, and recent publications should accompany the manuscript.

Correspondence regarding book reviews should be sent directly to: Book Review Editor, **JOURNAL OF INTERAMERICAN STUDIES AND WORLD AFFAIRS**, Box 24-8134, University of Miami, Coral Gables, Florida 33124.

JOURNAL OF INTERAMERICAN STUDIES AND WORLD AFFAIRS is published four times annually—in February, May, August, and November.

Subscriptions: Regular institutional rate $42.00 per year. Individuals may subscribe at a one-year rate of $20.00. Add $4.00 for subscriptions outside the United States. Orders from the U.K., Europe, the Middle East, and Africa should be sent to London address (below). Orders from India should be sent to the New Delhi address (below). Noninstitutional orders **must** be paid by personal check.

Second class postage paid at Beverly Hills, California. ISSN 0022-1937

This journal is abstracted or indexed in **Historical Abstracts, Human Resources Abstracts, Sage Urban Studies Abstracts, International Political Science Abstracts, Public Affairs Information Service, Current Contents, Social Sciences Citation Index, Social Sciences Index, ABC POL SCI,** and **United States Political Science Documents.**

Back Issues: Information about availability and prices of back issues may be obtained from the publisher's order department (address below). Write to London office for sterling prices.

Inquiries: Address all correspondence and permissions requests to SAGE PUBLICATIONS, Inc., 275 South Beverly Drive, Beverly Hills, California 90212. Inquiries and subscriptions from the U.K., Europe, the Middle East, and Africa should be sent to SAGE PUBLICATIONS Ltd, 28 Banner Street, London EC1Y 8QE, England. From India, write to SAGE PUBLICATIONS INDIA Pvt. Ltd, P.O. Box 3605, New Delhi 110 024 India. Other orders should be sent to the Beverly Hills office.

Advertising: Current rates and specifications may be obtained by writing to the Advertising Manager at the Beverly Hills office (address above).

Claims: Claims for undelivered copies must be made no later than three months following month of publication. The publisher will supply missing copies when losses have been sustained in transit and when the reserve stock will permit.

Change of Address: Six weeks' advance notice must be given when notifying of change of address. Please send old address label along with the new address to insure proper identification. Please specify name of journal. POSTMASTER: Send change of address to: Journal name, c/o 275 South Beverly Drive, Beverly Hills, CA 90212.

HOWARD HANDELMAN
Department of Political Science
University of Wisconsin
Milwaukee, Wisconsin

LABOR-INDUSTRIAL CONFLICT AND THE COLLAPSE OF URUGUAYAN DEMOCRACY

During the 1960s and early 1970s, the collapse of civilian democracies in several of Latin America's most socioeconomically developed nations and the rise of highly institutionalized, repressive regimes raised serious questions about the nature of political development and political decay in that region. Neither advanced social indicators (Argentina, Chile, Uruguay), nor an extensive, modern-industrial economic sector (Argentina, Brazil), nor a sustained period of representative government (Chile, Uruguay) seemed to be guarantees of continued civilian-democratic rule. Indeed, scholars such as Guillermo O'Donnell have suggested that the nature of economic growth and industrialization in Latin America—most notably in the "Southern Cone"—had resulted in increased class conflict, intense political strains, and the rise of bureaucratic-authoritarian (B-A) regimes.

The spread of dictatorships (only recently challenged by pressures for "redemocratization") focused scholarly attention on "the new authoritarianism" (Collier, 1979) and the "B-A phenomenon" (O'Donnell, 1973, 1978). Primarily this literature has

---

AUTHOR'S NOTE: This article is partially based on field research conducted in Uruguay from June to December 1976, with funds provided by the Midwest Universities Consortium for International Activities (MUCIA) and the Graduate Research Committee of the University of Wisconsin, Milwaukee.

Journal of Interamerican Studies and World Affairs, Vol. 23 No. 4, November 1981 371-394

focused on Argentina, Brazil, and Chile, while some political scientists have extended the paradigm to include Peru, Mexico, and Colombia (Malloy, 1977; Collier, 1979). Yet very little has been written on the rise of authoritarian rule in Uruguay. Although McDonald (1975) and Weinstein (1975) have discussed the demise of Uruguayan democracy, neither placed it into the broader B-A literature. Conversely, most of the major theoretical works on authoritarianism (save Kaufman, 1979) largely ignore Uruguay, with scarcely a parenthetical footnote.

Given Uruguay's small size and the limited number of political scientists who have been able to work in that nation since its 1973 military takeover, this omission is understandable. However, examination of the collapse of Uruguayan democracy is important for two reasons. First, given the small number of nations that have been analyzed within the B-A model, any additional case studies can enrich our understanding of the phenomenon. Second, becuase Uruguay once enjoyed one of the highest standards of living in Latin America, one of the region's most advanced levels of social development (literacy, education, development of an urban middle class), and one of its most democratic political systems, the rise of its highly repressive, civil-military dictatorship merits further examination.

Nearly two decades ago, Philip Taylor (1962) observed that Uruguay was embroiled in a growing economic and political crisis, but that it still enjoyed one of the highest levels of civil liberties in Latin America. A series of polls conducted by Russell Fitzgibbon (later joined by Kenneth Johnson) from 1945 through the mid-1960s indicated that Latin American experts in the United States consistently ranked Uruguay as the most democratic nation in the region (Fitzgibbon, 1967).

On June 27, 1973, the last vestiges of Uruguayan democracy came to an end as President Juan María Bordaberry dissolved the nation's Congress and formally established a military-dominated dictatorship. Since that time, perhaps 55,000 persons have been detained for varying lengths of time for political reasons. Constituting approximately 1 out of every 30 adults, Uruguay's portion of political detainees is probably the highest in the world.[1]

How is it that a country whose degree of civil liberties and democratic political participation only recently compared well with any nation in the world has become one of Latin America's more repressive regimes? The purpose of this article is to examine the rise of authoritarian rule in Uruguay and its relation to the suppression of the nation's labor movement. I will suggest that the decay of Uruguayan democracy, beginning in the late 1960s and formally completed in June 1973, was integrally related to the decline of working class living standards and the resulting trade union militancy and class conflict.

The Rise of the Uruguayan Labor Movement

The origins of Uruguay's trade union movement can be traced to the last quarter of the nineteenth century with a huge influx of Spanish and Italian immigrants to Montevideo. As in much of Latin America, early organization of the incipient working class (mostly artisans) was led by anarchist militants. During the last two decades of the century, these men created the International Association of Workers and its successor, the Local Federation of Uruguayan Workers (D'Elia, 1969: 3). The trade union movement was nurtured by the intense wave of immigration, which not only increased the size of the working class, but brought many European workers with socialist or anarchist backgrounds.[2] Unlike many other Latin American labor movements developing in this period, Uruguay's trade unions did not subsequently form links with either populist political leaders or dominant political parties. By 1929 the socialists, communists, and anarchists each had their own labor federations.

Yet despite the Marxist (or anarchist) rhetoric of its leadership, the working class offered no radical challenge to the national political system. While workers might choose leftist trade union leaders, they voted in national elections primarily for the middle class-dominated Colorado Party, propelling that party to over 50 years of electoral dominance, from 1904 to 1958. In fact, Colorado policies reflected an enduring alliance between the working class and the nation's industrial bourgeoisie, with the latter group benefitting from trade protectionism and the former from a well-developed welfare state.

The moderate behavior of Uruguayan labor and its electoral alliance with the Montevideo middle class might be attributed to three factors: first, the organized working class constituted a relatively small portion of the nation's urban population relative to the extensive middle class of small businessmen, white collar employees, and government bureaucrats (Rama, 1960; Solari, 1966); second, Uruguayan industrial units have generally been extremely limited in scale, with over 90% of industrial firms employing fewer than 20 workers (Berenson, 1975). The direct, paternalistic relationship between many employers and their workers in very small firms was not conducive to a high degree of militancy;[3] finally, the Colorado welfare state satisfied worker aspirations sufficiently to keep them content with middle-class political control.

The Post-Korean Economic Crisis and the Rise of Worker Militancy

The political alliance which President José Batlle y Ordóñez forged at the start of the twentieth century between the state, the Uruguayan working class, the dependent middle class (largely government bureaucrats), and the industrial bourgeoisie was to last nearly 50 years. But it was a somewhat fragile coalition, based on the capacity of the nation's meat and wool exporters to finance a large (and inefficient) bureaucracy, a welfare state, and a protected (and inefficient) industrial sector. So long as Uruguay remained prosperous and retained the highest standard of living in Latin America, class conflict could readily be contained.

However, with the close of the Korean war, Uruguay entered a prolonged period of economic decline. The industrial sector—based on import substitution and fostered by extreme protectionist measures—proved increasingly inefficient and noncompetitive. More important, the nation's ranching elite failed to make the necessary capital investments in grazing land (Uruguay has an extremely low level of fertilized pasture) and animal stock to match the productivity of its competitors in the world wool and meat markets (see Kirby, 1975). Lacking guaranteed foreign markets, and unable to match the productivity levels of Australia and New Zealand, Uruguay's capacity to export wool and meat decreased steadily. The stagnation of the traditional export sector triggered a general decline in the national economy and undermined the base of the urban welfare state. From 1956 through 1972, the country's Gross National Product fell 12% (McDonald, 1972: 34). Falling output was accompanied by one of the highest inflation rates in Latin America, reaching levels of 135% in 1967 and 67% in 1963.

The country's economic decline reduced significantly the real income of the working class. From 1957 through 1967, real salaries dropped nearly 24%. Public employees were particularly hard hit during this period, experiencing a decline in real income of some 40% (Weinstein, 1975: 119). Given these circumstances, it is not surprising that labor militancy increased sharply. The discontent of blue- and white-collar workers was expressed in two forms: first, the spread of trade unionism among formerly unorganized or inactive sectors of the work force. The most dramatic advances in this area came among the dependent middle class—bank employees, government bureaucrats, and other white-collar workers.[4] Because public employees (mostly white-collar) had absorbed by far the greatest decline in real income, they became the most militant element of the labor union movement. During the 1960s, union leadership became increasingly consolidated in the hands of the Communist Party. By 1966, most of the nation's unions had joined together in a national labor confederation, the National Workers Convention (CNT), primarily under Communist leadership.

Increased working-class discontent also expressed itself in a growing number of strikes. The total man-days lost through strikes rose from 1,200,000 per year in the mid-1950s to 2,500,000 in 1963 (Weinstein, 1975: 119). By the mid-1960s, labor-management conflict had reached crisis proportions. Militant unions representing textile, construction, chemical, and bank workers struck for weeks, or months, on end. Even those industries with relatively good labor relations were closed periodically due to frequent transportation strikes and recurring general or sympathy strikes. Finally, in industries such as leather tanning or chemical products, work stoppages of several hours repeatedly brought production to a halt.

The Response of the Industrial Elite

What was the effect of increased labor tensions on the political perceptions of the nation's economic elite? While objective statistical data on the number of work stoppages, strikes, and general strikes during the decade preceding the 1973 coup are revealing,[5] they do not fully reflect the extent to which labor-management conflict produced a growing polarization of Uruguayan society. To more fully appreciate the forces contributing to the current level of political repression in Uruguay, one must understand the effect which class conflict had on the political attitudes of the nation's industrial elite, and the extent to which that sector came to condone repressive measures in controlling the country's labor force.

During the last six months of 1976, I interviewed over 100 of Uruguay's most important industrial, commercial, and agricultural leaders. This elite sample included the current and preceding officers of the nation's most influential economic interest groups (the National Chamber of Commerce, the Uruguayan Chamber of Industry, the Association of Bankers, the Rural Federation, and the Rural Association), as well as the officers of Uruguay's largest industrial and commercial firms.[6] A significant proportion of these men, particularly at the firm level, had held their posts in the years preceding the coup.[7] From these interviews I was able to gather important insights into the attitudes of my respondents in these areas. It should be noted that shortly before that time, many of these men had participated in a series of conferences sponsored by the Uruguayan military high command

(ESMACO) regarding the future of labor-management relations in that country.

Given the limited size of my sample, and more importantly, the strained political atmosphere in which the interviews were conducted, these observations must be viewed with caution. Yet the results coincided with the impressions of Uruguayan sociologists and economists with whom I worked, as well as with the observations of those members of the economic elite with whom I was able to discuss these issues candidly. It was clear from my interviews that the degree of support or enthusiasm for the military takeover varied considerably between sectors of the economic elite. Representatives of the landed aristocracy—the nation's leading ranching families—tended to be fairly critical of government economic policy since 1973, and did not view the military's political *or* economic policy since 1973 as being beneficial to their sector. Spokesmen for the banking and commercial sector were generally supportive of the "Chicago School" economic policies introduced by civilian Finance Minister Alejandro Vegh Villegas (discussed below), but not particularly positive about the military's repressive political policies. Industrial leaders were clearly the most supportive of the current government's policies, and were most positive about the role of the military in the regime.

While the reasons for these attitudinal divisions are complex, the interviews revealed that the majority of the industrial elite felt that the dissolution of Congress and the elimination of democratic processes in 1973 was necessary for the nation's political and economic survival. It is impossible to quantify the traumatic effect which labor unrest had produced among these industrialists. Questions regarding unions and labor relations prior to 1973 often elicited highly emotional, at times almost hysterical responses. The president of one major corporation removed from his wall safe a scrapbook which he had kept of "slanderous attacks" made by his workers' union against him.

Other industrial leaders claimed that they feared for their personal safety during the years preceding the coup. Often these respondents saw a link between labor union activity and the kidnappings conducted by the Tupamaros. In fact, responses often suggested a conspiratorial view of the left which failed to distinguish between differing (and often hostile) leftist factions or divisions within the labor movement. Finally, there was a tendency among industrial leaders to significantly overstate the number of strikes that took place and the number of work-days lost in the years preceding the coup. While this might have been partially a conscious attempt to justify their position, I think that it also reflected the paranoia which labor conflict instilled in the industrial elite during this period.

In a larger survey of 300 industrialists, respondents were asked to indicate the most important accomplishments of the present regime.[8] Fifty-two percent included "control of labor unrest," making that the most frequently selected accomplishment. Within my subsample of *major* industrial leaders, those respondents who felt that the country was on the verge of collapse in 1973—and that, consequently, military intervention was necessary—were most likely to cite the CNT, and not the Tupamaros, as the major subversive threat in Uruguay. And, as indicated previously, of those who did mention the Tupamaros, nearly one-half saw the guerrilla movement and labor strife as part of a single, coordinated conspiracy of the left.

In short, if these responses are reflective of attitudes prevalent in the year preceding the collapse of Uruguayan democracy—and I believe that they are—then the interviews suggest that there is a close relationship between the degree to which sectors of the economic elite were threatened by labor unrest and the extent of their support for both the military takeover and the repressive measures which both preceded and followed the coup.

The concern of Uruguay's industrialists over increased class conflict during the late 1960s manifested itself in two areas. First, a more direct involvement in the nation's political process. Up until this point, the nation's economic elite had generally not been heavily involved directly in the political system (in terms of actual participation in the Parliament, the Cabinet, and so forth), especially when compared to other Latin American nations. Following the inauguration of President Jorge Pacheco Areco in

1967, that pattern began to change (Macadar et al., 1971). In 1968, Pacheco appointed "a cabinet integrally composed of entrepreneurs, bankers, large ranchers, and lawyers representing foreign industrial banking interests" (Instituto de Economía, 1969: 366). The formation of that cabinet was quickly followed by the introduction of a series of repressive government actions directed against the labor unions (see below).

The second important development during this period was the forging of links between the industrial elite and the military. While a significant portion of the Uruguayan officer corps is of rural origin, their middle-class background is more compatible with the nation's industrial leadership than with the more "aristocratic" commercial and agricultural elites. During the late 1960s, a significant number of inactive military officers were hired by private industry as security consultants. Leaders of various industrial interest groups (including the Uruguayan Chamber of Industry and the Association of Automotive Vehicle Manufacturers) indicated to me that they felt an especially close link between the industrial sector and the nation's military.

In short, as the industrial elite became increasingly concerned with labor confrontations, and as these industrialists extended their direct political involvement, they were forging ever closer ties with the armed forces. The evidence seems to suggest that from the mid-1960s on, Uruguay was moving toward what José Nun (1967) has called a "middle-class military coup," or more precisely, a coup partially instituted in response to the needs of the nation's industrial elite.[9]

1968-1973: The Decay of Democratic Institutions[10]

Unlike Chile, where political repression was introduced suddenly and explosively in September of 1973, the decay of democratic practices in Uruguay was a gradual process extending over a period of five years or more.

The debilitating effects of growing social tension and unrest on civil liberties are clearly illustrated in the treatment of "criminal suspects" and prisoners. Given Uruguay's extended history of relative political tranquility and its extremely low crime rate, the country's penological practices were fairly enlightened prior to 1960. It is worth noting, for example, that administration of the nation's major prisons was placed in the hands of the Ministry of Education. By the early 1960s, however, conditions had begun to deteriorate. Philip Agee (1975), a leading CIA operative in Montevideo during this period, notes that police were already engaging in the torture of "common criminals" and, less frequently, of political dissidents.

More significantly, the accelerating level of labor unrest, coupled with student demonstrations and periodic "terrorist" activities (bank robberies, bombings), induced more stringent political controls. In October 1965, following a series of extended strikes by government employees and general strikes, the National Government Council (Uruguay's collegial executive body) enacted a state of siege, referred to in Uruguayan law as "Prompt Security Measures." Under the terms of the decree, all strikes and all meetings for the promotion of strikes were prohibited. Extensive arrests of union leaders soon followed, and by the end of the month most CNT officials, as well as the leaders of individual labor unions, were in hiding. The purpose of the security measures seemed to be twofold: first, to enable the government to better control already existing labor unrest; and second, to provide stand-by powers before the government announced economic stabilization measures which were designed to secure IMF loans. In addition to their antistrike provisions, the "Prompt Security Measures" also enabled the government to shut down CNT or Communist-controlled newspapers and radio stations that were charged with contributing to labor unrest. The measures were renewed several months later and extended through the end of 1965. In fact, the government's action established a precedent which was to be repeated almost continually from 1968 onward: states of siege—instituted for 60 to 90 days and renewed for extended periods of time—soon became a standard government response to labor unrest.

In 1966, more fundamental changes were introduced into the Uruguayan political system. Under the terms of a new constitution, supported by both traditional parties, the collegial executive was abolished and Uruguay returned to a presidential executive system. Jorge Batlle, a leader of the Colorado Party and a leading proponent of the new constitution, clearly indicated the purpose of the constitutional change. He suggested that only a strong, centralized executive could control labor demands sufficiently so that the government could stabilize the nation's currency, halt protracted inflation, and restore economic growth. Only then, Batlle, argued, could the real income of the working class once again begin to rise.

Thus, even before the 1966 presidential elections, there was clear evidence of a growing level of class conflict and political polarization which undermined the traditional labor-industrialist base of the Colorado Party. It was not until 1968, however, that the future course of Uruguayan politics was firmly set. Following the death of Colorado President Oscar Gestido in 1967, the relatively unknown vice-president, Jorge Pacheco Areco, a former editor of the liberal Batllista newspaper *El Día*, assumed the presidency. During his first week in office, Pacheco issued a decree banning the Socialist party and several other small leftist factions. The Socialist party newsweekly, *El Sol*, and the leftist newspaper, *Epica*, were closed down as well.

On June 13, 1968, President Pacheco invoked Article 168 of the new Constitution to decree a limited state of siege under the terms of the "Prompt Security Measures." Once again, the event precipitating the state of siege (as in 1965) was labor unrest—specifically, a prolonged strike of bank tellers. Under the terms of the decree, Pacheco Areco froze prices and wages, banned further strikes, and drafted the striking bank workers into the armed forces. While the "Prompt Security Measures" had been invoked before, the 1968 decree was far more serious for two reasons: first, it was used for more extensive arrests of trade unionists and repression of union activity; second, from that point onward, emergency ("state of siege") powers were used by Pacheco and by his successor, Juan María Bordaberry, almost continuously until the 1973 "coup."

In the words of Uruguayan sociologist Enrique Cárpena (1970: 61), "1968 seemed to mark the end of Batllista ideology, the end of the democratic illusion. . . . The state began the systematic use of violence; . . . the 'Prompt Security Measures' became the norm and liberal democracy became the exception."

The labor movement's objections to the "Security Measures" were not limited to the decree's most manifestly repressive aspects. Even the seemingly innocuous wage and price freeze was seen as a move against the working class. Indeed, since wage increases secured during the period of intense inflation preceding the decree had not nearly matched spiraling prices, the CNT viewed Pacheco's action as a means of maintaining the workers' loss of real income. The *Instituto de Economía* of the National University argued (1969: 363): "the decree of June 28, 1968, freezing wages and prices instituted a new stage in the national political and economic process, generating a real qualitative change . . . in conflict between social groups and classes."

Thus, whatever Pacheco's intention, the "Prompt Security Measures" failed to put an end to labor conflict. Tension was particularly high in government-owned industries where, as we have seen, employees had suffered the sharpest decreases in real income. In early 1969, the government dissolved the administrative council of the state-owned *Frigorífico Nacional* (National Packing House). The council had provided for worker participation in the administration of the packing house, and its dissolution represented an escalation of government-union conflict. In April, 14,000 meat workers went on strike. Violent confrontations between strikers and police resulted in the shooting of several workers. On June 11, as the meat workers' strike entered its third month, the CNT called a general strike resulting in the arrest of 5,000 workers.

At this point, the Pacheco administration reinstituted the state of siege which had lapsed for three months (April-June, 1969), one of the only times under Pacheco that those controls had been relaxed. On June 28, employees of the UTE (the state-owned telephone company) struck. Once again, striking workers were drafted. In fact, at this point all state employees, as well as bank workers (perennially on strike) were militarized. Thousands of workers who failed to return to work were imprisoned, particularly in the banking sector.

By mid-1969, police mistreatment of labor leaders and strikers had become routine. Hundreds of striking UTE workers were forced to stand for up to 18 hours in the waterfront area near the central UTE offices. Imprisoned union leaders such as Hugo Cares, president of the Bank Employees Union and vice-president of the CNT, were subjected to extended beatings and other forms of torture. On October 2, Carlos Cárpena, jailed UTE worker, died while under detention. From July onwards, CNT leaders operated from clandestine headquarters.

President Pacheco's repeated use of extraordinary powers against the labor movement reflected a basic shift in political power within the Uruguayan state during the period of 1968-1973. With the police totally incapable of controlling the Tupamaros or other radical political groups, the size and budget of the nation's armed forces increased dramatically. In a five-year period, the military component of the government budget increased from 13.9% to 26.2% (Weinstein, 1975: 129).[11] Disgusted with the apparent ineptitude of civilian leadership, the colonels and generals became increasingly politicized. In a few short years, the Uruguayan armed forces—heretofore the least interventionist in Latin America—became the dominant force in the nation's political system.

The growth of military influence occurred in the context of increasing tension between Uruguay's executive and legislative branches. To the extent that the civil liberties of political dissidents and imprisoned trade unionists received any government protection at all, it came from the nation's Congress. Periodically, the liberal faction of the Blanco Party, a few dissident Colorados, the Christian Democrats, and of course, the parties of the left, spoke out against violations of human rights and other government excesses. As Pacheco Areco and the Congress clashed over the use of exceptional presidential powers, the military's growing influence was used to intimidate the legislative branch. Under these circumstances, the President could ignore congressional attempts to limit his powers.

In August 1969, when Congress rescinded Pacheco's military draft of bank employees, the President simply reissued his decree.

Similarly, two years later, in 1971, Congress voted to terminate three years of a nearly continuous state of siege. Once again, Pacheco ignored congressional intent and immediately reimposed the "Prompt Security Measures"—this time in clear defiance of the Constitution. On each occasion, faced with the spectre of military intervention, Congress accepted its secondary role.

As the nation approached the 1971 presidential and congressional elections, the political polarization was intensified by the creation of a left-of-center electoral coalition, the *Frente Amplio* (Broad Front). The Frente brought together several dissident Colorado and Blanco political leaders, Christian Democrats, Socialists, and Communists. Enjoying significant support among Montevideo's professional, white-collar, and working-class voters (and ultimately winning 30% of the vote in the nation's capital), Frente presidential candidate, Liber Seregni, appeared at earlier points in the campaign to offer a viable challenge to the long-standing electoral dominance of the Blancos and Colorados. Though Seregni's support outside of Montevideo faded as the election approached (he received only 18% of the national vote), the spectre of an electoral challenge from the left added to the fears of the military and economic elites.

The inauguration in early 1972 of President Juan María Bordaberry, Pacheco Areco's Colorado ally, led to a brief period of improved executive-legislative relationships. Shortly after Bordaberry assumed office, Congress lifted emergency antiunion measures which had been in effect almost continuously since June 1968. Restrictions on labor's right of assembly and on strikes were removed with the President's acquiescence. However, less than one month later, in April 1972, a renewed Tupamaro offensive and a CNT general strike induced the Congress to accede once again to extraordinary presidential powers. Bordaberry decreed a "state of internal war" which eliminated virtually all protection of civil liberties. While the decree was originally issued for a period of only 30 days, strong military pressure on the Congress resulted in continuous extensions of the "state of war" into 1973.

From May through November of 1972, the Uruguayan armed forces used the powers of this decree to launch an all-out war on the Tupamaros. Through massive arrests and the torture of captured guerrilla suspects, the military broke the back of the movement. By June 30, 700 alleged Tupamaros had been captured, 23 were known dead, the guerrillas' "people's prison" and hospital had been captured, and the organization's infrastructure broken. Thus, by the middle of 1972, the Tupamaros were clearly on the defensive, and by the end of the year they had obviously been beaten.

Yet the success of the antiguerrilla campaign failed to bring a corresponding reduction in government repression. Quite to the contrary, in July 1972, strong military pressure induced the Congress to pass a "Public Order Law" whose provisions were far more draconian than the "Prompt Security Measures" which had been employed in previous years. In November, the "state of internal war" was extended for a period of 90 additional days.

In fact, by early 1973 the movement toward a highly authoritarian state had achieved a momentum of its own, divorced from the campaign against the Tupamaros. In February of that year, the armed forces established the *Consejo de Seguridad Nacional*, a military-civilian council (with obvious military dominance), to review all major government policy decisions. "Bitter February," as it has since become known, established unquestioned military dominance over both the legislative and the executive branches. And on June 27, the last vestiges of liberal democracy came to an end with the dissolution of the Uruguayan national Congress. The suppression of Congress was followed in short order by the total repression of an opposition press, the suspension of political party activity, and the dissolution of the CNT.

Why the Coup?: Causes of Political Repression

It is often assumed that the collapse of Uruguayan democracy, culminating in the 1973 military takeover, was primarily precipitated by Tupamaro activity. To be sure, the Pacheco and Bordaberry regimes justified repressive measures instituted before and after the coup in terms of the alleged guerrilla threat. In

June 1972, Uruguayan government spokesmen stated that the "Prompt Security Measures" were necessary to control the urban guerrillas, and that once the Tupamaros were crushed the measures could be lifted.

Undoubtedly, the activities of the "Tupas" and associated student unrest did contribute to a conservative backlash. However, a careful examination of the chronology of events leading up to the dissolution of Congress suggests that growing political repression was directed at least equally toward breaking the labor union movement. The first "Prompt Security Measures" were invoked in 1965, nearly two years *before* the Tupamaros began widespread revolutionary activity. The imposition of a new state of siege in June 1968, and the ensuing wage-price freeze, were not directed at the guerrillas, but at prolonged strikes of government and bank employees. The same was true of the reinstitution of the "Prompt Security Measures" in June 1969. In fact, except for the declaration of an "internal state of war" in April 1972 (following a major guerrilla offensive), almost every escalation of government repression prior to the coup was more closely connected with labor unrest than with an upsurge of Tupamaro activity. Finally, it is significant that the ultimate steps toward military domination of the Uruguayan political system from February through June 1973 were taken *after* all of the top Tupamaro leadership had been captured and the guerrilla movement broken.

Obviously, one cannot definitively infer the motivation for the government's politically repressive measures solely from a chronological analysis such as this. However, these conclusions coincide with impressions drawn from interviews with leading industrialists as well as spokesmen for the former legitimate political opposition. Several former leaders of the left Frente Amplio and of the liberal Ferreira wing of the Blancos interviewed in Montevideo and Buenos Aires suggested to me that "if there had been no Tupamaro movement, Pacheco, Bordaberry, and the military would have had to invent one."[12] A former leader of the Socialist Party insisted that there was evidence that two spectacular prison escapes of nearly 100 Tupamaro leaders in August and September 1971 were permitted by the government, presumably in order to keep the "guerrilla threat" alive. "Without the Tupamaros," he told me, "it would have been far harder to justify the continued state of siege." Bizarre as this theory may appear, it is worth noting that months before the escapes, the police found (and apparently ignored) excavation equipment and frogmen's wet suits in the sewers, which were later used by the escaping prisoners. In any event, the guerrillas served as a convenient justification for the implementation of legislation which was designed as much to repress labor unrest and the "legitimate" left as to control the Tupamaros.

The Coup and its Aftermath

Within hours of the dissolution of Congress on June 27, 1973, the CNT declared a general strike. Throughout Montevideo, plants and construction sites were seized by their workers, most dramatically at ANCAP, the state-owned petroleum-refining operation. The general strike lasted for 15 days, but was weakened from the start by the indecisiveness of high-ranking CNT and Communist Party officials. In the months preceding the coup, an apparently populist faction of the armed forces had issued a series of military communiqués calling for socioeconomic reforms. Based on these pronouncements, some of the CNT leadership were apparently captivated by the hope that the coup might bring to power a progressive ("Peruvianist") military government. Thus, despite considerable rank-and-file commitment to resisting the coup, the general strike was easily broken for lack of leadership.

Whatever confusion existed in the minds of CNT officials, President Bordaberry and the military quickly made their position toward the unions clear. In the days following the dissolution of Congress, hundreds of CNT leaders were arrested. On July 2, 1973, the CNT was officially dissolved, though many affiliated unions were temporarily allowed to continue limited operations. President Bordaberry announced that the government had liberated the unions "from the dictatorship of the

Communists." He warned that the "old unionism" would not be tolerated. Two days later, a government decree gave all employers, public and private, the right to summarily dismiss any workers who failed to return to work.

In early August, the government issued a decree calling for union elections designed to allow the rank and file to choose new, non-Communist leadership. During elections that were held in September and October of 1973, members of militant unions such as the textile workers defied military rule and tried to reelect their recently deposed officials. Consequently, in October the government suspended further elections.

At the individual plant level, the breaking of almost all unions and the decree permitting firing of strikers led to widespread dismissals. Over 40% of the major industrial firms whose officers I interviewed in 1976 indicated that they had taken advantage of the situation following the coup to dismiss militant trade unionists and other "agitators." Some company officials conceded that they had used the opportunity to get rid of "excess labor force." In plants such as FUNSA (Uruguay's largest industrial firm, producing tires and auto accessories) and General Electric, hundreds of workers were dismissed.

The Position of Labor Since 1973

The government's failure to force a change of leadership in Uruguay's most militant unions led to the suspension of activity among all of the CNT's largest member unions—the textile workers, chemical workers, construction workers, and so on. While a limited number of smaller, less militant unions have continued to exist on paper, their activities have been of no consequence since collective bargaining and strikes were totally prohibited. The limited opportunities which did exist for union input into government economic policy prior to 1973 have since been eliminated as well. For example, the government's wage and price board (COPRIN), which previously included representatives of labor and industry, was stripped of all associational interest group representation.

In the early months of 1976, massive arrests of former Communist Party activists and trade union officials terminated any remaining activity among former CNT affiliates. In my interviews with industrial officials, I was able to discover only one union still functioning at the industrywide level in 1976: the Tobacco Workers Union, a very moderate union, never affiliated with the CNT, that had continued to meet periodically with management to discuss working conditions.

At the level of the individual factory or firm, a number of union locals continue to operate in sub rosa fashion. Several industrialists whom I interviewed indicated that a de facto (though illegal) union exists in their firm and meets periodically with management. These, however, constituted a very small fraction of the labor force. And even in these few cases (as with the more open activity of the Tobacco Workers Union), "union activity" was limited to the function of a communications link between labor and management. In no case was the union serving as an agent of collective bargaining.

Thus, government repression of Uruguay's labor movement currently expresses itself in two distinct forms: first, the imprisonment and brutalization of former union officials and activists. While precise data is obviously unavailable, these people constitute a large proportion, possibly a majority, of Uruguay's political prisoners since the coup. According to knowledgeable persons whom I spoke to, next to the Tupamaros, labor activists are the political prisoners most likely to be subjected to torture or other forms of mistreatment. Of the 22 persons whom Amnesty International identified as having died of torture prior to July 1975, at least 8 were trade unionists.[13]

On a more general level, the repression of trade unions, the elimination of collective bargaining, and the prohibition of strikes have meant that most workers now receive no more than the minimum salary required by law. In fact, prior to July 1976, employers were prohibited from granting their workers wage increases which exceeded the cost of living percentage periodically decreed by the government. A government directive issued in 1976 "freeing wages" from state controls has had little meaning, since most employers have no incentive or need to offer their workers higher wages. Only in a few industries enjoying an export boom (most notably leather tanning and manufacturing) has competition for skilled labor induced employers to pay more than the minimum salary decreed for their sector. And in a significant number of firms, particularly smaller ones, even the legal minimum wage is still not paid.

Thus, in the years since the dissolution of Congress and the CNT, the standard of living of the working class has been entrusted completely to the government. The negative consequences for labor are apparent. In 1974, direction of Uruguay's economy was assumed by Finance Minister Alejandro Vegh Villegas, an American-trained economist with "Chicago School" orientations. In order to control the country's chronic inflation and attract foreign investment, Vegh instituted an austerity program placing the brunt of economic sacrifice squarely on the shoulders of the working class. From 1973-1979, real income of the nation's workers fell nearly 30%. Nor is there any question that this decline is the result of conscious government policy. In an August 1975 newspaper interview, Vegh Villegas stated that although real wages had decreased sharply, it was necessary that they drop even further so that inflation could be brought under control.[14]

Conclusions

Events of the last two decades have had a sobering effect on Latin America and on students of that region's political process. The path toward economic and political development now appears to be far more difficult and torturous than had previously been imagined. Ironically, it has been the nations with the more advanced indicators of socioeconomic development—Argentina, Chile, Uruguay, and Brazil—where the most repressive bureaucratic-authoritarian regimes have been instituted. As greater mass political participation produced pressures for redistributory economic policies, and as the economies of some of the Southern Cone nations have stagnated, class conflict has intensified. This has been particularly true when austerity programs have been introduced designed to bring runaway inflation under control.

To be sure, the particular characteristics of authoritarian governments in each of the Southern Cone nations have varied somewhat. Yet there do seem to be certain important similarities in the origins of bureaucratic-authoritarianism in the area, which suggest the utility of including Uruguay within Guillermo O'Donnell's B-A thesis. O'Donnell (1973, 1978) associates the rise of such regimes with attempts by the economic and military elite to resolve political crises which, in turn, can be traced to bottlenecks in the economy. The combination of sharp inflation, recession, and elite perception of a radicalized (hence "dangerous") labor movement inspires both an attempt to restructure the economy and a repressive political reaction from above. All of these elements were clearly present in the Uruguayan case.[15]

In a study of Argentine and Chilean antiinflationary policies, Epstein (1978) has demonstrated that it is the working class that has been asked to make the major sacrifices. The situation has been no different in Uruguay. Under such circumstances, democratic political processes are untenable. As one leading Uruguayan industrialist admitted to me, it is impossible to impose "Chicago School" deflationary wage policies on the working class while permitting the free organization of trade unions and the right to strike. With the recent referendum defeat of the military regime's proposed constitution calling for a highly cosmetic transition to civilian government, Uruguay still finds itself far removed from an end to military-authoritarian rule. Ultimately, when that transition does come, it must somehow come to grips with the problems of labor-industrial relations and the working class's share of the economic pie.

NOTES

1. Data on the number of political prisoners are based on figures from Amnesty International. The estimate of 55,000 political detainees includes all persons held for whatever length of time since the 1973 dissolution of Congress. It also includes persons

interrogated for brief periods of time and released. The long-term political prisoner figure ranged from 5,000-10,000 for most of the 1970s. It may now be 2,000-3,000.

2. From 1860-1904, Uruguay's population rose by 500% (see Weinstein, 1975: 20).

3. See Hamilton (1967) for a discussion of the relationship between factory size and the level of worker radicalism.

4. Dependent middle class is used here to mean salaried employees, as opposed to independent professionals and businessmen.

5. Officially, the Uruguayan government does not recognize that a coup took place in June 1973. Technically, a constitutionally elected president, Juan María Bordaberry, simply dissolved Congress. However, as one colonel whom I interviewed stated, "there is really nothing else you can call what happened, but a *golpe*."

6. Of the persons interviewed, 67 were from the industrial sector, 21 from the commercial sector, and 15 from the rural elite.

7. With the exception of foreign-owned corporations and one or two Uruguayan firms—notably FUNSA—almost all Uruguayan industrial and commercial firms are family-owned. Consequently, there is a very low rate of turnover among top officers.

8. In addition to the in-depth interviews conducted with over 100 members of the economic elite, a survey was conducted of some 300 industrial and commercial firms. However, the scope of the more extensive survey was far more limited, and few questions could be asked in the area of industrial-labor relations because of the political sensitivity of that issue.

9. When speaking of a "middle class coup," we must distinguish between the independent middle class (i.e., industrialists and commercial businessmen who own the means of production), who are more aptly included in what John Johnson called the "middle sector" than in the middle class per se, and the dependent middle class (white-collar workers, government bureaucrats, teachers, and so on). I am not suggesting (nor does Nun) that all of the middle class supports what Nun calls a "middle class military coup." In Uruguay, the dependent middle class were among the strongest electoral supporters of the leftist Frente Amplio and undoubtedly among the greatest foes of the coup. However, I am suggesting close links between the military and the industrial bourgeoisie.

10. This section is based heavily on the Uruguayan journal *Marcha* and on the newsletter, *Latin America* (London).

11. The size of the current military budget is not known even to the U.S. embassy. However, it is estimated to be between 40% and 50% of the total. McDonald (1975) notes that in 1965, Uruguay had ranked 91st of 121 countries in the world in terms of percentage of GNP spent on the military.

12. Among Uruguay's two traditional parties, the liberal wing of the Blanco Party, led by Senator Wilson Ferreira Aldunate, was most outspoken against many aspects of political repression. In 1975-1976, I interviewed Wilson Ferreira, former Frente leader Zelmar Michelini (since murdered), and other exile leaders in Buenos Aires, as well as various former Frente and Blanco spokesmen still in Montevideo.

13. The number of trade unionists may be higher, since the Amnesty International data did not include occupational information on all of the persons who have died under torture.

14. By 1976, the decrease in real income had become sharp enough to seriously disturb Uruguayan industrialists and merchants whose firms serve the domestic market. Most of

the economic elite to whom I spoke from that sector—as opposed to those who produce primarily for export—indicated to me that the time had come to begin to raise real wages. The government had begun to indicate that it also felt that further declines might be counterproductive. These same sentiments were conveyed to me by Vegh Villegas himself in an October 1976 interview. Yet real incomes have continued to decline through 1980.

15. For an analysis of post-1973 attempts to restructure the economy, particularly to stimulate nontraditional, industrial exports, see Handelman (1981).

REFERENCES

AGEE, P. (1975) Inside the Factory: CIA Diary. New York: Penguin.

BERENSON, W. (1975) Group Politics in Uruguay: The Development, Political Activity and Effectiveness of Uruguayan Trade Associations. Ph.D. dissertation, Vanderbilt University, Nashville.

CÁRPENA, E. (1970) "Clase social, ideología y opinión pública," pp. 55-74 in Cuadernos de Ciencias Sociales. Montevideo: Instituto de Estudios Sociales.

COLLIER, D. [ed.] (1979) The New Authoritarianism in Latin America. Princeton, NJ: Princeton Univ. Press.

D'ELIA, G. (1969) El Movimiento Sindical. Montevideo: Nuestra Tierra.

EPSTEIN, E. (1978) "Anti-inflationary policies in Argentina and Chile: or who pays the cost?" Comparative Pol. Studies 11 (July): 211-230.

FITZGIBBON, R. (1967) "Measuring democratic change in Latin America." J. of Politics 29 (February): 129-166.

HAMILTON, R. (1967) Affluence and the French Worker in the Fourth Republic. Princeton, NJ: Princeton Univ. Press.

HANDELMAN, H. (1981) "Economic policy and elite pressures in Uruguay," in H. Handelman and T. Sanders (eds.) Military Governments and the Movement Toward Democracy in South America. Bloomington: Indiana Univ. Press.

Instituto de Economía (1969) El Proceso Económico del Uruguay. Montevideo: Universidad de la República.

KAUFMAN, R. (1979) "Industrial change and authoritarian rule in Latin America," pp. 165-254 in D. Collier (ed.) The New Authoritarianism in Latin America. Princeton, NJ: Princeton Univ. Press.

KIRBY, J. (1975) "On the viability of small countries: Uruguay and New Zealand compared." J. of Interamerican Studies and World Affairs 17 (August): 259-280.

MACADAR, L., N. REIG, and J. E. SANTIAS (1971) "Una economía Latinoamericana," pp. 35-142 in Uruguay Hoy. Buenos Aires: Siglo XXI.

MALLOY, J. [ed.] (1977) Authoritarianism and Corporatism in Latin America. Pittsburgh: Univ. of Pittsburgh Press.

McDONALD, R. (1975) "The rise of military politics in Uruguay." Inter-American Economic Affairs 29 (Spring): 25-43.

——— (1972) "Electoral politics and Uruguayan political decay." Inter-American Economic Affairs 26 (Summer): 25-45.

NUN, J. (1967) "The middle class military coup," pp. 66-118 in C. Veliz (ed.) The Politics of Conformity in Latin America. New York: Oxford Univ. Press.

O'DONNELL, G. (1978) "Reflections on the patterns of change in the bureaucratic-authoritarian state." Latin America Research Rev. 12 (Winter): 3-38.

——— (1973) Modernization and Bureaucratic-Authoritarianism: Studies in South American Politics. Berkeley: University of California, Institute of International Studies.

RAMA, C. (1960) Las Clases Sociales en el Uruguay. Montevideo: Neutro Tiempo.

SOLARI, A. (1966) Uruguay en Cifras. Montevideo: Universidad de la República.

TAYLOR, P. (1962) Government and Politics of Uruguay. New Orleans LA: Tulane Univ. Press.

WEINSTEIN, M. (1975) Uruguay: The Politics of Failure. Westport, CT: Greenwood Press.

Howard Handelman is Professor of Political Science at the University of Wisconsin, Milwaukee and a member of its Center for Latin America. He is coeditor (with Thomas Sanders) of Military Government and the Movement Toward Democracy in South America *(Indiana University Press, 1981) and editor of* The Politics of Agrarian Change in Asia and Latin America *(Indiana University Press, forthcoming). He is currently Director of the American University Field Staff's (AUFS) "Politics of Food" Project and is engaged in research in that area.*

MILES D. WOLPIN
Department of Political Science
SUNY—Potsdam
Potsdam, New York

MILITARY RADICALISM IN LATIN AMERICA

Analyses of military roles in Latin America during the two decades following World War II often assumed the military were both isolated or apart from politics, and hence amenable to civilian control. The resurgence of militarism since the early Sixties has been reflected in scholarly works reassessing these assumptions. Whereas the pioneers in this field, such as Lieuwen (1964) and Needler (1969), are clearly civilianist—reflecting a democratic and distinctly liberal bias in their values—students of Latin American militarism in the late Sixties and Seventies have increasingly, if tacitly, assumed the unviability of civilian hegemony and tended to downplay the democratic normative issue. Terms such as militarism, democracy, and civilian supremacy have been virtually eclipsed from analyses of military intervention (Johnson, 1964; Einaudi, 1969; Ropp, 1970; Stepan, 1971; Rankin, 1974; Needler, 1975; Fitch, 1979).

Regardless of how one assesses the legitimacy of domestic militarism, the new scholarship has undoubtedly increased the precision and extended the range of our understanding. The armed forces are conceptualized as an integral component of Latin American political systems rather than as an isolated,

---

AUTHOR'S NOTE: The author wishes to express his appreciation to John Saxe Fernández and Octavio Rodríguez Aranjo of UNAM for facilitating this research, and to Liisa North for her criticism.

Journal of Interamerican Studies and World Affairs, Vol. 23 No. 4, November 1981 395-428

nonpolitical institution. At the same time, there has been a healthy decline in reification as the focus of analysis is refined to include intramilitary factional, and even individual, actors. As Stepan (1971) demonstrated in his superb study of the Brazilian Armed Forces, even within one service, career experiences and socialization may vary so markedly that, given appropriate leadership, one faction is prepared to use arms in defense of increasingly radical leftist policies.

The present study's objective is to ascertain what cluster of career and background characteristics is most likely to be associated with military radicalism of the left and right. In doing this, there is an assumption that ideologically, armed forces, regardless of the degree of professionalization, are neither invariably unified nor isolated from other political sectors. While it may well be true (Vagts, 1959; Nun, 1969; Lang, 1972; Abrahamsson, 1972) that insofar as they become politicized, military officers are more likely to opt for the right, this is not necessarily engendered by conservativism inherent in the professional "military mind" or ethos. Although Huntington (1959) associates political conservativism with such military professionalism, I shall argue that this is the result of a particular combination of recruitment, socialization, and historical factors rather than of the professional function itself. It will be shown that radically leftist, as well as radically rightist, orientations are consonant with the military ethos or calling.

After specifying those professional values which may be furthered by leftist or rightist goals, I shall briefly identify background, institutional, and career variables which analysts in recent years have regarded as predisposing officers in one direction or another. I shall then turn to studies of particular Latin American military interventions that clearly differentiate the characteristics of left-wing and right-wing military factional elites. Finally, I shall contrast the attributes of 20 prominent Latin American rightist military leaders with about the same number of leftists who have emerged since the Bolshevik revolution signaled the presence of socialism as a major world force. The focus of this study, then, is the small minority of outstanding officers who play a catalytic role in transforming government policies. There is no implication that other sociopolitical forces are of lesser importance when changes are made. If "great men" do not remake societies by themselves, neither do "social forces" lacking effective leaders.

Professionalism and Radicalism

One such social force of paramount and growing importance is militarism, and more generally, the role of the armed forces in society. The minority of military radicals must appeal to or at least secure the acquiescence of their professional colleagues.[1] While it is true that during periods of crisis, the number of politicized officers grows, the preponderance remain preoccupied with bureaucratic or institutional concerns. Hence, to ensure corporate backing, radical elites must, through new "national security" doctrines, appear to harmonize their goals of a "national interest" or "class" character with what Needler (1975) has identified as the military's core institutional interests: armed forces unity, command authority, monopoly over armed force, special military privileges or status, current spending levels as a minimum, autonomy over promotions and seniority, prestige and dignity of the armed forces, good relations with the population, border defense and preparedness, and internal order. Although pursuit of some of these may involve conflict with others, it is customarily rationalized within a framework of professional values given in Huntington's classic statement on the characteristics of military professionalism (1959): (1) promotion of expertise; (2) a sense of responsibility to society rather than a desire for financial gain as the basis for using one's expertise ("his responsibility is the military security of his client, society. . . . The motivations of the officers are a technical love for his craft and the sense of social obligation to utilize this craft for the benefit of society"); and (3) corporate consciousness and loyalty ("a sense of organic unity and consciousness of themselves as a group apart from laymen").

Officers, of course, vary immensely in their degree of professionalism, as do members of other professions. Thus, Huntington stresses that "an officer corps is professional only to the extent to which its loyalty is to the military ideal. This perspective premised upon the degree to which such values are internalized and exhibited in actual behavior is both historically derived and useful for those who would 'pierce the corporate veil'." Hence, without appropriate skills, attitudes, and policy preferences, the fact that one military possesses more schools, journals, equipment, or effectives does not necessarily indicate greater professionalism. Nor, for that matter, does the facile imitation of foreign logistical or training modes (Fitch, 1979). Unfortunately, it is quite difficult to differentiate between professional form and content short of actual combat. And as Lieuwen (1963: 114) has noted, Latin American armed forces have an aversion for external combat missions, while exhibiting an unprofessional propensity for internecine warfare. Military forces in the region have employed their weapons routinely to suppress civilian populists, especially the socialist left, whether or not the latter was engaged in overt guerrilla or revolutionary struggle.

If being an extreme rightist implies principled opposition to egalitarian structural change, it is obvious that such officers will interpret their function within the existing oligarchic system—one where the distribution of wealth and ownership of the means of production are concentrated in a small, upper-class sector. Given such orientation, the left will be viewed not only as a threat to national unity, but as Needler (1963) noted in the case of Ecuador, a number of officers involved in deposing that country's mildly reformist government claimed they had feared the army itself would be abolished because of alleged Fidelista influence. Thus the preservation of existing expertise and armed strength, along with the defense of corporate autonomy, imply internal preservation of the existing order against those seeking some form of socialist structural change. Populists and social reformers are often perceived as unwitting accomplices of the socialist left. Even when fear of communism does not obliterate such distinctions, "ill-conceived" social reforms are often viewed as likely to diminish both the incentives of capitalists to invest as well as available resources for such purposes, thus reducing the economic growth and overall strength of the nation. Worse still, the *ambiente* of reformist political conflict involves demonstrations, strikes, and so on, considered a source of societal disunity, and therefore weakness. Reformist programs are often perceived as potentially threatening to military budgetary aspirations, and leftists are regarded as undermining the dignity or prestige of the military when they criticize the armed forces for external ties to the Pentagon. Occasional leftist attempts to proselytize officers and especially enlisted ranks excite professional animosity because they undermine the command structure and thus are a threat to military unity. Stepan (1971) has identified this as a significant catalytic factor in the overthrow of Goulart. The same can be said of attempts to arm workers in Perón's Argentina, Arbenz's Guatemala, and more problematically, in Allende's Chile. Although militias threaten some of the institutional interests identified by Needler, they do not directly contravene Huntington's professional ethos. Only insofar as they are associated with the furtherance of *other* leftist policies can such opposition be alleged to flow from a professional concern.

While the internalization of professional values and a commitment to the military's institutional interests may be consonant with such rightist perspectives among officers, can it be argued that the converse is also true? Is it possible that officers equally or even more strongly identified with the "military ethos" will believe that egalitarian changes in socioeconomic structures are imperative for Latin American societies, regardless of their level of relative development? Well over a decade ago in discussing Brazil, a North American journalist (Gunther, 1968: 71) recounted

> roughly 100,000 conscripts out of 2,500,000 available are inducted every year at the age of eighteen; half are illiterate, and roughly 40 percent of those called up have to be rejected on grounds of ill-health, caused principally by malnutrition.

Under a succession of repressive rightist regimes, the social problem in that important nation has, if anything, worsened over the dozen or so years which have elapsed. The existence of such a state of affairs under regimes of dependent capitalism is not, of course, limited to the relatively industrialized Latin American nations. If anything, it is more pronounced in countries characterized by less advantageous resource endowments, lower levels of industrialization, and (it may be added) lower levels of external debt burdens. Given the relatively heavy and rapidly rising external indebtedness for most Latin American states, however, under existing structures the future is likely to entail more rather than less mass austerity and deprivation.

This situation, and the widening socioeconomic gap with the industrialized "North," contravenes professional military goals in three specific ways. First, it restricts the quality and quantity of available manpower (Finer, 1975: 27). Second, failure to develop and employ human resources deprives the military of potentially greater wealth to draw upon, therefore constricting the economic basis of long-run military potential.[2] Third, political alienation inhibits national unity or civic integration by predisposing lower classes to participate in domestic disorders and less anomic forms of violent conflict. This, of course, applies equally to a good number of self-styled reformist politicians who cooperate with transnational corporations, their local associates, and indigenous oligarchic sectors. Hence, the social existence of "two nations" within a framework of dependent capitalism strikes at the very heart of the military professional's nationalism. Whereas the "open door" economic policy bias of rightist officers actually contradicts their nationalist aspirations, this is not the case for leftist officers, distinguished by support for both nationalization of transnational subsidiaries and a dominant role for the state in defending natural resources (Stepan, 1971: 246; Janowitz, 1964: 64).[3]

From the Bolshevik revolution until the 1960s, it was more difficult to argue persuasively that professional military values were better promoted by radically leftist rather than extreme rightist policies. For approximately a half century, beliefs were widespread that public ownership of the means of production was inherently inferior to an "open door" for transnational capital which would transfer technology, invest capital, and develop resources optimally in accord with the theory of comparative advantage. The role of the state then was to promote accumulation through taxation and through borrowing for infrastructure, in order to attract investors. Similarly, a propitious climate for foreign and domestic capitalists would be engendered by the suppression of wages, labor militancy, and leftist agitators. Since the early Sixties and particularly as the crisis—symbolized by skyrocketing external indebtedness, inflation, and economic stagnation—of dependent and world capitalism emerged in the Seventies, it has become ever more widely recognized in the "South" that the "open door" is a strategy for the mastery of technology, balanced development, control of very extensive corruption, and for coping with the problems of mass poverty. At the same time, state socialist systems appear to have experienced greater *relative* success (Wolpin, 1981) in raising mass living standards and sociocultural levels, while simultaneously creating strong and highly trained armed forces.[4] The geographic constriction of the dependent capitalist world has been marked by rising capitalist national rivalry, unprecedented balance of payments deficits, intensified North/South antagonism, and a renewed process of U.S.-sponsored militarization. This will contribute to long-run American economic decline (Melman, 1974, 1979) and military weakness by diverting vitally needed capital and scientific resources from socioeconomic and cultural areas, thus intensifying political alienation and domestic cleavages. Hence, if there could be serious doubt about the past, in the 1980s socialist developmental mobilization is more consonant with professional values such as maximizing long-run strength and social responsibility, than is reaction and transnational capitalist subordination.

Analytic Perspectives

In relative terms, socialist mobilization also offers greater congruence with what Janowitz (1964: 64) sees as "anti-corruption" and "antidecadence" orientations of younger officers. Although his focus was upon the "new nations," recruitment changes and "modern" organizational characteristics which he identifies have become increasingly relevant to military roles in Latin America since World War I, especially during the last two decades. Thus, on recruitment he notes:

> the military establishment is recruited from the middle and lower-middle classes, drawn from rural areas or hinterlands. In comparison with Western European professional armies, there is a marked absence of a history of feudal domination. As a result the military profession does not have strong allegiance to an integrated upper class which it accepts as its political leader nor does it have a pervasive conservative outlook. . . . Either by selection or by training, emerging military officers are generally without strong religious concerns. This is markedly different from the devout overtones of the military establishment in Western countries, where religion, particularly high social-status religion, supplied an element of professional identity and a bridge to aristocratic and, subsequently, to other ruling elites [Janowitz, 1964: 64].

Whereas in the 19th and early 20th centuries, neofeudal social relations persisted, as did upper- and upper middle-class recruitment in many regions of Latin America, it can be surmised that armed forces expansion and capitalist labor market relations to hinterland rural sectors have enhanced both social mobility and the proportion of officers not socially interlocked with the large property-owning upper classes. Hence, we would predict, as far as these and the religious factors are concerned, a greater openness to socially egalitarian ideas among such officers.

A related recruitment factor stressed by Janowitz (1964: 55) is the father's occupation. While some "are small landholders," he acknowledges "an occupational inheritance factor—a confrontation of sons whose fathers have served in the government either in the military, in minor civil service posts, or as teachers. Their sons have had the model of success in bureaucratic rather than in free professions." Hence, if "the absence of an aristocratic social tradition implies that the military has less of a stake in the existing social structure . . . its middle-class social origins . . . do contribute to a bureaucratic and managerial outlook which is congenial to gradual modernization and social change."

Stephen Ropp (1970) maintains that rising urban recruitment is a key factor in moving the Latin American military toward a more pronounced reformist orientation in the future. Studying the 1967-1968 graduating army cadet classes for Chile, Uruguay, Guatemala, Nicaragua, and Honduras, he found disproportionate urban representation extending to unusually high recruitment from the capital itself. Ropp (1970: 30) argues:

> there seems to be a general consensus that the urban environment exerts a "liberalizing" influence. Irving Horowitz maintains that the Latin American urban complex is a center of reform because it contains the bulk of the reform-minded social sectors. The opposite side of the urban-progressive coin is the association of rural areas with conservatism. The military officer orientated toward rural society is viewed as hostile to "self-indulgent urban values." This general orientation in turn seems congruent with the institutional values of the military. Both tend to stress certain "fundamentalist" beliefs in the correct ordering of the social system.

This would seem to be consistent with Janowitz's previously mentioned stress upon the absence of a strong identification with traditional high status religion—a tendency which is less pronounced in urban settings. Yet Ropp's demographic criterion for urbanism was 5,000, a level which more appropriately might be designated as semirural, given the cultural ambience of such towns when they are not suburban appendages of large cities. Furthermore, the work of Imaz (1964) casts doubt upon an equation of urban origins with military reformism, as does that by North and Korovkin (1981).

From a comparative standpoint, it may be worth noting that the analyses by Janowitz and Ropp refer to a number of characteristics which Rejai (1973: 138) found to be associated with largely civilian leaders of the French, Bolivian, and Vietnamese revolutions. In addition to customarily having indigenous origins, "revolutionary leaders are overwhelmingly middle class, with a sprinkling of upper and lower classes." Rejai stresses:

> in contrast to the predominantly urban background of the Bolivian and French revolutionaries, the Vietminh leaders came almost exclusively from rural areas. It would seem, moreover, that regardless of geographic origin, early involvement in national politics in urban areas is a uniform pattern in the development of revolutionary elites.

Additional characteristics discovered by Rejai were "moderate exposure to foreign cultures," high educational attainment, and a disproportionate representation of intellectuals and professionals "in the forefront of revolutionary movements." Relative youth, another attribute, is also stressed by Janowitz who notes:

> Younger officers with less seniority have fewer vested interests in the military system. They are less involved in the social and political status quo and more involved in contemporary political currents, with the result that they are inclined toward a more radical outlook.

This, he adds, may be reinforced by slow or disorderly promotion in a milieu where few more attractive options exist outside the armed forces for the lower middle-class recruit.

If social origins and premilitary exposure are an initial source of values, attitudes and affinities, most contemporary analysts view them as less significant than socialization resulting from lengthy intramilitary career experiences which may begin as early as the age of fourteen. One consequence of this socialization process according to Janowitz (1964: 43) is "a strong sense of public service . . . reinforced by its concept of heroic leadership." Analogous to Huntington's ethos of "social responsibility," this dedication is likely according to Janowitz to operate in conjunction with youth and bureaucratic lower middle-class social origins to dispose officers toward "gradual social change and modernization."

The institutional socialization process functions at a general level to affect all officers, although unusual or "adaptive" career experiences may be necessary for the small minority who become radical political leaders concerned with broader societal issues. Both of the previous mentioned scholars, along with others such as Lucien Pye (1962: 78-79), have argued that exposure to more advanced technology in a comparative context is likely to make officers in Third World nations acutely sensitive to the need for modernization. While this may occur within various countries through "education," discrepancies between actuality and potential are highlighted by foreign tours and training. Discussing U.S. foreign assistance, Janowitz (1964: 96-97) reports:

> There is ample evidence, however, that new nations' officers sent to the service academies and staff and command schools are deeply touched by the close personal contacts they develop and by the sense of public service they see among cadets and officers. U.S. military assistance officers, operating in the new nations, are personally well received, mainly because they have been carefully selected and are prepared to make themselves useful in day-to-day operational problems. Occasionally an enterprising American officer will seek to develop, in his new-nation counterparts, a sense of the modernizing functions that armies might play.

In tandem with exposure to corruption, mass poverty, socialist ideas, and the situation described in note 5, such career experiences may account for the leftist radicalization of a small proportion of ex-trainees. Yet radical rightist reinforcement is certainly a more ubiquitous consequence of this external socialization (Wolpin, 1973; Etchison, 1975) which posits "open door" capitalism as the only viable route to development while denigrating nonalignment, and targeting both "socialism" and "Communism" as the enemies of the Free World. Referring to the Fifties, and particularly the Kennedy era, Janowitz recalls:

> Gradually, over the years United States political and military authorities have become aware that such programs have domestic political implications for new nations. They have become concerned that these programs help develop pro-American loyalties among the officers of new nations. To this end, for example, more than one thousand U.S. military assistance officers were given special training before they were sent abroad.

His conclusion, however, like that of Fitch (1979) a decade and a half later, is that such indoctrination has but a marginal impact. Fitch (1979), Einaudi (1969), Miguens (1970-1971), Stepan (1971), and Astiz (1973) maintain, as does Rankin (1974) in his review of their conclusions, that *indigenous* war colleges and other educational processes have been the primary source of new internal political (i.e., "developmental") missions. Fitch contends that nations with the highest proportion of U.S.-trained officers are the *least professionalized,* because their limited budgetary resources preclude the most sophisticated weapons and logistical systems, along with a full array of journals, higher educational institutions, and so on. Yet he is honest enough to concede the possibility that U.S. indoctrination may affect Latin American officers indirectly through war college instructional programs as in Ecuador, where the United States played a major role in organizing the institution.

Because officer corps are seldom cohesive when it comes to enforcing radical policies upon a civilian population, explanation requires analysis of divergent as well as common experimental patterns. One of the very few scholars who, along with Stepan (1971), has placed a great stress upon personal characteristics and subinstitutional factionalism in Latin America—as a consequence of differential career experiences and socialization—is Robert Potash (1969), who in Rankin's (1974: 95) view "decries the abstract depersonalization of the military." Potash stresses what Astiz touches upon: the military is composed of numerous factions and subfactions. For Potash,

> Argentine history during the period from 1928 to 1945 is a composite of various factions momentarily coalescing into a single unit, usually to intervene in the political process, and then renewing their divisions.

According to Janowitz (1964: 29), such divisions occur because of "differences in training, indoctrination, operational experience, and intergenerational cleavages." The significance of such subcorporate factional concerns is underlined, and has been substantiated recently in a study which found that between 1946 and

1970, corporate motives were absent in 65% of the coups against civilian governments, and in 81% of those against military regimes. By employing Janowitz's (1964: 45-49) career typology for leftists and rightists—routine, prescribed, and adaptive—an analysis can be made of the sharp divergences in socialization patterns of radical officers.

The overwhelming majority of officers follow "routine" or "prescribed" career patterns. Whereas the former channels one into a technical specialty and often early retirement, the latter involves appropriate "ticket punching" and cooptative sponsorship, which yields a "proper balance of command and staff assignment, attendance at the higher staff schools and careful avoidance of excessive specialization."

Socialization of "adaptive" officers is markedly different and experienced by "the very small minority . . . who supply the politically oriented leadership." After observing that some may have entered the armed forces with political ambitions and been subsequently sought out by civilian political leaders, Janowitz stresses that "career experiences are just as crucial in fashioning and developing these adaptive and politically involved officers." At the core of such career experiences is contact with civilians and/or other exposure to political ideas reinforced by "friendship patterns." Thus, Janowitz (1964: 46-48) emphasizes that:

> experience at staff college and exposure to intellectual and political discussions which make up so much of the curriculum of these institutions . . . are, together, important sensitizing experiences. . . . Service abroad as an officer in training, or a special political-military assignment, also contributes to this type of career. As in industrialized nations, politically oriented officers are associated with new weapons. . . . Often they were officers who, early in their careers, had unique educational or political-military assignments. Although such assignments were thought to be barriers to a successful career, in the end they helped these officers to enter the military elite because they taught negotiative and innovative skills. . . . These officers were concerned not only with technical management of the military but with relating the military to the broader society and to the role of violence in the conduct of foreign affairs.

If such career patterns differentiate the politically active elite with an intense concern for broader issues from their more narrowly politicized colleagues, to what extent can it be said that prior studies of Latin American ideological factions are consonant with Janowitz's "adaptive career" thesis? Do the "adaptive" careers of "progressive" officers differ markedly from those of "reactionaries?"

Analyses of Ideological Factions

The two major studies to date of military ideological factionalization are by Stepan (1971) and North and Korovkin (1981). Their conclusions—along with more limited findings by several others—are consistent with some of the relationships already set forth. Stepan stresses the crucial nature of *different* socialization patterns for distinct factional groups. In addition to social origins and the environment, he places great emphasis upon the totality or "cluster" of career experiences rather than on any single activity, such as U.S. training tours (1971: 238-239).

> When the core group of ten generals supporting the Castelo Branco government of 1964 was compared with the 92 other generals completing the universe of 102 and with the pro-Goulart subgroup of twenty generals who were purged after the 1964 revolution, several striking differences emerged. The variables associated most highly with membership in the core group were: participation on the permanent staff of the Superior War College, attendance at foreign schools, graduation as number one in the class at one of the three major army schools, and membership in the most technically advanced branch of the services of the army.
>
> The concept of cluster is important, because the experiences were interrelated and mutually reinforcing. Five of the ten generals (50 percent of the core group) had all participated in World War II in FEB, been on the permanent staff of the Superior War College, attended foreign schools, and graduated first in one of the three major army schools. Of the remainder of the universe, only one of the 92 had done all four. The statistical probability of such a difference in proportions occurring by chance are one in a thousand.

TABLE 1
Career Experiences of Brazilian Generals, 1974

	Castello Branco "Core Group" N = 10	Goulart Constitutionalists N = 20
FEB Participant	60%	25%
ESG Student	90	50
ESG Staff	70	18*
Grad. 1st in Class	100	20
Att. Mil. School Abroad	100	20
Att. Mil. School in USA	100	20

SOURCE: Stepan, 1971: 241.
*Data missing for 3.

As Table 1 indicates, the dichotomy is especially striking when the ten generals in the Castelo Branco "core" group are compared with the 20 Constitutionalist pro-Goulart generals who were purged. It is important to note the "American connection" of this "core" group. While Stepan fails to acknowledge that Washington was actively endeavoring to "destabilize" the Goulart administration (Black, 1978; Parker, 1979) for many months prior to the coup, and dispatched the CIA's Colonel Vernon Walters—a friend of Castelo Branco's since the latter was Walters' student at Fort Leavenworth during the early World War II years—he does concede that:

> One other feature made the core group distinctive. One hundred percent of the group had attended foreign schools, 80 percent actually going to schools in the United States, whereas only 24 percent of the generals who were not in the core group had attended foreign military schools. Certainly the data do not support the contention that U.S. military training of Latin American officers inculcates apolitical professional values among the officers. *Prima facie,* it could be argued that dislike of emotional nationalism, as well as the active anti-Communist and openly pro-American stance of the 1964-1967 Castelo Branco government was a result of, or was related to, their American training. Certainly it is a major goal of much—some would say all—American sponsored training to contribute to such attitudes.

While Stepan suggests that such training operated in the context of "political contacts and life style," it is worth emphasizing that the FEB (Fôrça Expedicionária Brasileira) operated under direct American command both in combat and retraining. According to Gunther (1968: 55), Castelo Branco "has been inflexibly pro-American ever since" his days at the U.S. Command and Staff College. In Italy he shared quarters with Walters, his former instructor at Ft. Leavenworth. While other officers played a more prominent initial role from late 1962 in organizing the conspiracy, Janowitz's (1964) emphasis upon "friendship patterns" of "adaptive and politically involved officers" is underscored.

A similar American role is in the 1956 creation of Ecuador's war college. Fitch's (1979) findings—that officers who attended that institution were just as supportive of the 1963 "anti-Communist" coup against that country's constitutional government as were those who had U.S. training—do not mitigate the significance of external socialization. Indirect mechanisms may even be more effective because of their "national" symbolism for certain purposes. This was the policy perspective of CIA Deputy Director Richard Bissell (1968) when he addressed a meeting of the influential Council on Foreign Relations. Nor is it without some irony that Augusto Pinochet was reassigned from his diplomatic post in Washington to the new U.S.-organized Ecuadorean war college for its first two years (1956-1958).

While multifaceted external socialization is obviously more effective than limited exposure, this can be misconstrued by those like Luigi Einaudi (1969), who point to a substantial percentage of Peru's 1968 junta receiving U.S. training and conclude that it was nugatory. What this obscures is that as North and Korovkin (1981) demonstrate, the Velasquista coalition was itself sharply divided along ideological lines, and became more so until Velasco and the socially radical nationalist faction with whom he increasingly sympathized was forcibly deposed in 1975. These factional background differences were more pronounced, yet paralleled those between the Velasquista coalition as a whole and the remainder of the army, with respect to such factors as U.S. and other foreign training, higher military education in Peru, service branch, and even social background. Thus, shortly after

Belaunde Terry was overthrown, Petras and Rimensnyder (1970: 19) reported:

> All of the fourteen cabinet ministers graduated from one of the three Peruvian military academies during the late 1930s or early 1940s. Several members of the government were contemporaries at Chorillos as administrators or instructors during their subsequent military careers. Only two members of the government came from upper-class families, and few married outside their social background, which was exclusively middle-class. All of this suggests that we are dealing with a homogeneous, close-knit group.

Trimberger (1978) also underscores the importance of a hiatus with the social upper class, while North and Korovkin's (1981) data supported their conclusion that there was no "solid connection between Velasquistas and the Peruvian upper class society or business worlds." Among them, none were recruited from the upper class while 40% of other senior officers were! At the same time, 40% of the former were from "popular" backgrounds, as compared to 5% of the latter. A much smaller percentage (10%) of the Velasquistas were from Lima, while 40% of counterpart officers were. Similarly, Velasquistas were evenly divided between rural and urban origins, while other officers were twice as likely to be urban. Of Velasquistas, 80% served in the infantry, whereas this was true of only 20% of other officers. As for education, the Velasquistas were much less likely to have attended the CAEM (Centro de Altos Estudios Militares), 33% vs 70%, and slightly less likely to have experienced foreign training, 75% vs 85%.

These findings by North and Korovkin are consistent with Monteforte Toledo's (1970: 41-43) contention that the CAEM did not have a "decisive influence," but that it played an indirect role as one of the factors contributing to a new military outlook. He argues that the Army Intelligence School had a "much greater influence" in conjunction with the impact of direct exposure to atrocities and peasant misery during the 1962-1965 counterinsurgency campaign. North and Korovkin also conclude that army officers "necessarily felt the impact of the peasant movements and the guerrilla fronts of the 1960s more directly than their fellow officers in the navy and air force. . . . The army's specific military (counterinsurgency) role heightened the awareness of its officers concerning the contradictions between the maintenance of the traditional system of oligarchic domination and the needs of internal security which, in the final analysis, rested on a modicum of popular support." The new socially radical mission was, of course, justified in terms of professional values through the elaboration of a new national security doctrine by the CAEM's Mercado Jarrín and others.[5]

The dynamics of the revolutionary process involved not only confrontation with the United States and allied indigenous corporate upper-class sectors, but also greater interaction with radical civilian leftists. This culminated during the last year or so of the Velasco regime in a sharp split between a socially radical subfaction of seven officers who were open to "socialist" ideas, and others with a "moderate" procapitalist bias. The latter eventually joined more conservative officers in deposing Velasco and purging first some and then, in 1976, the remaining leftists. With respect to the latter and Velasco himself, Monteforte Toledo (1970: 43) stresses the radicalization *consequential* to struggle for social reform: "Since the seizure of power in 1968, the governing team has advanced ideologically more quickly than the remainder of the armed forces—even to the degree that some ministers believe the CAEM has joined the reactionaries." North and Korovkin found that the seven leftist "core" officers were exclusively from the infantry (excepting Admiral Dellepiane), none had been born in Lima, only one had been trained in the United States, two had no foreign training, two who did had been to France, and five had no CAEM background. On all of these indicators, they differed from about the same number of those in the centrist and rightist factions of the Velasquista coalition. While the numbers are small, the pattern is consistent with Stepan's data, and with mine (to be presented shortly). Further, the CAEM curricula was socially reformist, open to at least some forms of collectivism, and while anti-Communist, this last was neither stressed to the extent it was in the Brazilian ESG (Escola Superior de Guerra), nor was it equated with private sector oligarchic interests. Predictably, after Velasco's ouster, the Morales regime was far more moderate than the reactionary entourage over which Castello Branco presided.

What can be said of such factors as age and rank? The Velasquistas and Brazilian constitutionalists were purged as colonels and generals respectively; Janowitz and others have reasonably hypothesized that youthfulness and junior rank are more likely to be associated with radical leftism. The *tenentes,* the November 19th Movement in Guatemala, and the Uruguayan officers who sought to follow the Peruvian model between February 1973 and their ouster in October, were for the most part quite young and low in rank. Many Velasquistas had risen in rank to colonel only in the immediately preceding period of combat against the revolutionary guerrillas—an experience which also radicalized young Portuguese officers in Angola. As for the Brazilians, approximately 70% of those purged after Goulart's overthrow were not general officers, and at least some of the latter had been promoted recently by the Brazilian president in an abortive attempt to ensure military loyalty. It is probable that a combination of sociopolitical discrimination in the cooptative promotion process, reinforced by rightist ideological indoctrination and material perquisites, accounts for the relative paucity of officers who are open to radical leftist perspectives at higher ranks.

RADICAL PRAETORIAN LEADERS

In an attempt to extend the findings of the Stepan and North and Korovkin studies, along with more limited research by Monteforte Toledo (1970), Fitch (1979), Astiz (1969), Einaudi (1969), and Potash (1969), I have assembled sociobiographical career experience data for 20 Latin American rightists and an equal number of leftists. As officers, they played a major role in national political crises during the contemporary revolutionary era. They were selected *because of their prominence* and the consequential availability of data from biographical sources and country studies. Although several countries are underrepresented, and some data are missing for a number of officers, the results are suggestive, and when interpreted in light of the patterns already described, they may provide some basis for appraising earlier propositions elaborated above, as well as those for future research.[6]

Both the left-wing and the right-wing military leaders shared a number of important characteristics. As Table 2 indicates, most of them entered the military through national service academies. A very small number went to foreign academies, and a similar proportion enlisted as soldiers, though here we find slightly more among the leftists. About 90% of both groups were army men, though of the remainder, three rightists were air force, while two leftists belonged to the navy. With respect to those in the army, about three-fourths of both groups were infantry. Beyond that, the leftists had artillery backgrounds, while their rightist counterparts had served in the more prestigious cavalry/armor. About a quarter of both groups had some combat experience, though this was of an international character only for some of the Brazilians and two Bolivian leftists. Most of those for whom information could be obtained had attended higher military education, with equal proportions serving as instructors, assistant directors, or directors at military academies, staff, or war colleges. Of the small minority who had no higher military education, substantially more were rightists. Foreign exposure through visits, participation in conferences and tours as trainees, attachés, or instructors characterized almost all for whom information was available. About half of the latter had been exposed to more than one foreign culture. Finally, within their own country—as Table 3 makes clear—there is a common pattern of interaction with civilians, most frequently with leaders or activists in political parties.

One of the most interesting discoveries was that these officers differed to a moderate or great degree on at least ten prerecruitment and experiential indicators. Urban geographical origins tended to be associated with rightists, while a substantially higher

TABLE 2
Similar Career Experiences of Leftist and Rightist Latin American Officers

	Leftists (%) N = 20	Rightists (%) N = 20
Mode of Entry****		
Enlisted*	15	10
National Military Academy	70	75
Foreign Military Academy**	5	10
Direct Commission	5	5
No information	20	5
Service and Branch		
Air Force	-	15
Navy	10	-
Army	90	85
Infantry	60	65
Armor/Cavalry	-	15
Artillery***	20	5
Intelligence, Alpine, Engineers	15	-
Combat Experience		
Foreign	15	25
Domestic	10	5
None	40	50
No Information	35	20
Higher Military Education****		
Command & Staff or War College	30	55
Prof., Asst. Dir. or Director of Military School	65	55
None	5	15
No Information	30	30
Foreign Exposure: Number of Nations		
None	10	5
One	25	45
Two	20	5
Three or More	20	35
No Information	25	10

SOURCES: See Table 3.
*All Accept Batista subsequently attended a Military Academy.
**Haina in the Dominican Republic is "foreign" during U.S. occupation.
***Marmaduke Grove's branch is artillery, though he headed the air force for several months in 1925 and 1932. For about 30 years prior to the 1925 golpe, he served in the army.
****Nonexclusive categories.

percentage of leftists were characterized by rural and semirural backgrounds. The latter also differed by being much less indigenous in terms of recent ancestry and/or marriage patterns. Their marginality—to use Janowitz's concept—was also reflected by lifestyle differentiation. Leftist officers were more prone to be

TABLE 3
Differential Recruitment and Career Experiences of Leftist and Rightist Latin American Officers

	Leftists (%) N = 20	Rightists (%) N = 20
Geographic Origins		
Urban	15	25
Semi-Rural (Hinterland Town)	40	30
Rural (Village)	30	15
No Information	15	30
Ethnic Origins		
Dominant Indigenous	5	30
Marginal*	40	15
No Information	55	55
Class Origins		
Life Style		
Upper Middle or Upper	10	35
Middle (Unprosperous)	45	5
Lower (Popular)	30	25
No Information	15	35
Occupational		
Self-Employed Prosperous Business	5	20
Military Bureaucratic	5	10
Civil Bureaucratic	10	-
Free Professions	15	-
Marginal shopkeeper, peasant, etc.	30	25
No Information	35	45
Security/Mobility		
Secure Middle or Upper	30	45
Popular or Downwardly Mobile Middle	55	25
No Information	15	30
Civilian Interaction****		
Upper Class Sectors	-	20
Popular Sectors	20	5
Political Activist Relatives	35	15
Leftist Intellectuals & Pol. Leaders	55	-
Student or Trade Union Leaders	20	-
Guerrilla Leaders	10	-
Rightist Political Leaders	-	55
U.S. Corporate, Diplomatic or C.I.A.	-	25
No Information	15	30
Foreign Exposure		
U.S. Only**	5	35
U.S. and Latin American	15	25
U.S., Europe and Latin American	-	10
U.S. and Europe	5	-
Canal Zone and Latin American	5	-
Canal Zone, Latin American and Africa	5	-
Europe Only	15	-
Latin America Only***	10	15
None	10	-
No Information	30	15

(continued)

TABLE 3 (Continued)

	Leftists (%) N = 20	Rightists (%) N = 20
Personal Attributes****		
Trauma with Socio-economic Aspects	50	15
Neurotic Symptoms	15	-
Non-Authoritarian Personality	30	-
Very High Intelligence	45	15
Intellectual Interests	35	5
Socially Adept & Extroverted	50	25
Probity	30	5
Corruption	5	25
Social Pretentiousness and Upward Mobility Aspirations	5	30
Brutality	-	50
Disoluteness (Orgies, Drinking, etc.)	5	15

NOTE: This table is a composite derived from sources which include the major authorities on militarism in Latin America. Specifics are available from the author on request.

*Recent familial immigration, foreign wife; exploited racial group.

**Includes Pinochet's instructional assignment in U.S.-organized War College in Quito, 1956-1958. Pinochet left his assignment in Washington to assume this position.

***Includes German Busch's exposure to Paraguayan forces in Chaco War.

****Nonexclusive categories.

recruits from "popular" poverty-stricken families or from unprosperous middle-class backgrounds. They were less commonly from upper middle-class or bourgeois homes than rightist officers. In addition, only among leftists was there evidence of downward social mobility for parents, and a markedly higher proportion of leftist officers appear to have experienced major personal traumas *which could be attributed by them to an unjust socioeconomic order.*

Differences in other areas were equally striking. Leftists were on the average about four years younger—43 at the time of political emergence—and their rank was often lower and more commonly of field grade. There is greater evidence of very high intelligence and even intellectual interests among progressive officers, who also tended to be distinguished by personal attractiveness, sociopolitical skills, probity, informal or democratic personal style, to a lesser degree by unpretentiousness, and in three cases by neurotic symptoms. Their right-wing counterparts were more prone to engage in embezzling, brutality, single or multiple marriages to upper-class women, to acquire business investments, and in a few cases to be socially dissolute.

While as noted earlier, both groups were highly interactive with civilians, the rightists were far more likely to associate with conservative politicians, Pentagon or CIA agents, and the upper classes of their societies. Leftist officers were more directly exposed to lower class misery, and tended to come into contact with leaders of trade unions, student organizations, populist or socialist political movements, and nationalist intellectuals. Interaction with politically active civilians who were wives, fathers, brothers, or offspring appears to have been especially pronounced among progressive officers.

A final distinction emerging from their career patterns is the significance of tours, training, and assignments in the United States. A far higher percentage of rightists visited *only* the United States, and a greater proportion were exposed to countries in addition to the United States. A small number of leftists, on the other hand, were exposed to only Europe, while this was not the case for any right-wing officers.

Experiential Patterns and Analytic Perspectives

The premilitary backgrounds which North and Korovkin found among the Velasquistas, along with those of leftist officers in my sample, suggest such leaders are likely to have been directly opposed to, if not personally immersed in poverty and social oppression. Contrasts between great wealth and destitution are especially vivid in rural areas, where there is also greater propensity for physical proximity, social contact, and at times even personal relationships. Thus, both Horowitz (1969) and Ropp (1970) may be unduly optimistic with respect to the hypothesized association between urban *origins* and reformist inclinations. Rejai's contention that regardless of geographical background, subsequent exposure to urban political activists is essential, does seem to be well taken. Naturally, such contact is most likely when off-base or during foreign assignments. Yet as we have seen in the Peruvian case, direct interaction with guerrillas may be influential, as it also was for Major Rubén Sánchez of Bolivia, an enlistee from a lower-class background.

While North and Korovkin found a larger proportion of leftists originating in lower-class families, what is especially striking is that neither in their Velasquista faction nor in my sample were many progressives recruited from *acomodada* backgrounds. This contrasted in both instances with rightists, whose upper middle-class fathers tended to be prosperous, self-employed business owners or successful military officers. Those leftist fathers who were middle class tended to be either civil bureaucrats (e.g., school teachers or postal clerks) or nonprosperous members of the free professions. Combined with the traumas often experienced by children (e.g., the fathers of Cardenas and Arbenz committed suicide after business failures) and frequent nonindigenous family origins or marital characteristics, it would seem that many radicals were clearly marginated from the entrenched upper classes, and at least *predisposed* to empathize with those whose hardship was more stressful. These parameters, and a general lack of importance attached to traditional religious ritual, suggest that Janowitz's emphasis upon lower middle-class rural or hinterland origins and reformist potential is well placed.[7]

The foregoing characteristics do no more than enhance the probability that military men from such backgrounds will respond favorably to subsequent leftist appeals. The same may be said with regard to some, if not all, of the personal characteristics distinguishing progressive officers. Thus, Rejai found that revolutionaries tended to be intellectuals or professionals, while Keniston (1968) and others who have studied leaders of the U.S. anti-Vietnam movement discerned a pattern of high intelligence and a primary base for the protest movement at elite national universities. It seems obvious that a critical interpretation of established societal structures and routines is far more intellectually demanding than one that accepts existing values, and that attributes mass discontent to Communist subversives manipulated by the Soviet Union or revolutionary Cuba. It also seems that younger officers, characterized by probity, informality, dynamic oratorical skills, and so on, are more open to mass-oriented reformist movements than officers distinguished by contrary traits. Relative youthfulness, also observed in a number of twentieth-century junior officer rebellions, may be related not only to a greater openness to leftist ideas, but also to a paucity of the lifestyle perquisites generally associated with senior rank. Material privileges and status were emphasized by Needler (1963) in his analysis of the rightist Ecuadorean coup, and by Stepan more tangentially with respect to the Castelo Branco conspiracy. Finer (1975) stresses such attributes, as did Adams, in his analysis of the Guatemalan officer corps. The propensity of rightist officers for upper-class mobility suggests a personal style inhibiting them from responding affectively to leftist ideas.

Exposure to socially radical nationalist (or even socialist) perspectives may be the result of intramilitary socialization, though this commonly tends to be antileftist. Hence, factional differences associated with distinct military education patterns found by Stepan and North and Korovkin, are especially significant. The variation they identified in foreign training experiences, particularly the relationship between U.S. exposure and rightism, was duplicated in my sample. This underscores the impact of U.S.-orientation tours and other indoctrination, whether or not, as Stepan argues, it is merely reinforcement. Further, reinforcement *can* intensify hostility to the left, and it may operate through the ESG, the Ecuadorean War College, and other similar institutions that have been influenced in one way or another by U.S. contacts. Hence, it may not be coincidental that North and Korovkin, Urriza, and Petras and Rimensnyder found the Velasquistas centered around the Chorillos Military Academy and the Army Intelligence School rather than CAEM which, while not structured by the United States, was, as Monteforte Toledo (1970: 42) stresses, saturated with U.S. anti-Communist counterinsurgency propaganda. The only qualification in a "Cold War" era is that the content of foreign exposure may vary enormously.

Certainly, civilian-military relationships help undermine the myth that "the military" are in some fundamental respect isolated from civilian society. As Woddis (1977) and Carranza (1978) convincingly argue, they have never been isolated or, for that matter, politically uninvolved. Obviously this is a variable, and both the degree and the scope of such interaction grow during periods of crisis. Thus, North and Korovkin found that civilian contacts and alliance formation increased as the political crisis and factional conflicts within the Velasquista coalition intensified.

THE "ADAPTIVE CAREERS" OF RADICAL ELITES

Although data is no more than tentative, the studies by Stepan, North and Korovkin, and myself are consistent with Janowitz's hypothesis that officer politicians would in some sense be "adaptive" rather than followers of prescribed routine careers. Their foreign experiences and the incidence of politically relevant civilian interactions set them apart, as did the fact that many had served in diplomatic roles or as instructors, assistant directors, or directors at military education institutions. A good number were also assigned to work with government ministers or chiefs of staff.

One may hypothesize that, given the relative paucity of wars in Latin America or participation in extracontinental conflicts, a disproportionate percentage of these officers boasted combat experience. While in a few cases, the wars were conventional, in others the fighting brought officers into personal and even sympathetic contact with peasants, workers, students, and insurgent revolutionary leaders. Reinforcing perceptions acquired through campaigns or contacts with civilians and foreign or war-college experiences, were *experiential friendship cliques*. The latter occurred as a result of the Chaco War for Busch, World War II, Fort Leavenworth, and the ESG for Castelo Branco; the Mendoza Mountain Division for Perón; Chorillos and the School of Intelligence for the Velasquistas; Tachira and the

Márquez Military Academy for Pérez Jiménez. Both Potash and Janowitz have stressed the role of such personal ties for generational cohorts.

It is difficult to ascertain on the basis of available data in what other ways the careers of these activists deviated from those of more typical officers. Their professionalism is implied by common military academy backgrounds, an average of 23 years between award of commission and political emergence, and extensive higher military education, reinforced by exposure to often more advanced military establishments in other countries. This suggests that relatively high professionalism was consistent with both leftist and rightist political radicalism. Such symmetry is more problematic in the decades ahead.

Historical and Structural Parameters

While prediction is hazardous when syncretic change is involved, it seems reasonable to anticipate that during the Eighties, those officers most likely to link professional values and institutional interests to a rejection of dependent capitalism will be men in junior ranks who, as youths, were directly exposed to the massive resource underdevelopment and social alienation so pervasive in Latin America. This should affect even the rising proportion recruited from urban surroundings, as the rural poor have migrated in unprecedented numbers to the cities, where their presence has become increasingly visible. Such pre- and even intramilitary (when on leave) exposure, along with the proportional decline in recruitment from prosperous and secure upper middle classes, may predispose increasing numbers of junior officers to be receptive to "socialist" ideas.

At the same time, failure of antileftist, quasipermanent, "developmental" military regimes to acquire legitimacy, provide capable political leadership, or to catalyze balanced and self-sustaining growth—let alone cope with rising mass impoverishment—has intensified factional antagonisms leading to what may be slow and unsteady extrication in Peru, Panama, Argentina,

Honduras, and Uruguay. Populist and socialist elements in those countries have (or are about to resume) more active roles as disseminators of ideas reinforced by the regional and global expansion of both state socialism and state capitalism. Of equal importance, America's dramatic decline as a socially integrated and prosperous world power will contribute to an increasingly receptive environment for military assimilation of economically nationalist and leftist ideas. Ironically, the socioeconomic crisis afflicting the United States and, in lesser measure, the world capitalist system will be accentuated during the Eighties by the diversion of vitally needed resources to underwrite the renewed militarization that Washington embarked upon even before Reagan's election. Deemphasis of human rights, coupled with active support for "open door"-oriented rightist sectors, is unlikely to neutralize intensified nationalist sentiment in Latin America—a development that Horowitz and Trimberger (1976) presciently anticipated in the mid-seventies. Such renewed nationalism will be manifested in military educational curricula, a process of aid diversification which is already well underway, and in a diminished role for U.S. training programs.

Hence, the traditional tendency of the armed forces to function in sociopolitical crises as a Bonapartist trustee for a nonhegemonic bourgeoisie (Nun, 1969) may diminish appreciably. In the Eighties, integration of heretofore "national" indigenous entrepreneurial sectors into dependency relationships with transnational corporate conglomerates will finally deprive this sector of its pretentions to being national and progressive. Nationalist leadership in the region will be based increasingly on radicalized leftist elites in the civil and military state sectors, with support from intellectuals, party activists, students, and organized trade unions.

Well over a decade ago, Huntington (1968) predicted that the military would play a progressive or leftist role in societies with a weak and small bourgeoisie, principally in Africa and some Middle Eastern countries. Where "middle classes" were relatively sizable and well organized, one could expect social interaction and reference group identification by the officer corps. Yet he did not foresee the situation in which the integration of such enlarged classes into a transnational capitalist system effectively denationalizes the former, whose policies result in a disastrous flow of vitally needed wealth abroad, increasingly unsustainable external indebtedness, widening and frequently intensified impoverishment, deepening technological dependence, a growing welfare gap with the OECD nations—in short, an unviable developmental strategy. Nationalist officers will more readily acknowledge the necessity for structural change if their long-run professional and associated institutional interests are to be promoted.

NOTES

1. The term "radical" distinguishes these officers from those whose outlook is centrist, "moderate," and incremental—often those who lead caretaker or transitional governments. When leftist, radicals are "extremists" (from the perspective of business and landowning classes) committed to implementing within a relatively short time policies of an "antioligarchic" and "antiimperialist" character.

2. Human resource underdevelopment is also manifested by an inability to produce, maintain, and effectively operate sophisticated modern weapons systems in the absence of foreign dependence. Thus, Wulf (1979: 248-249) warns that "increased imports and greater production of modern military equipment in the periphery were necessarily based on a multiplication of the number of technicians, engineers, and scientists from industrial countries working there. Without their services, it is impossible to keep the equipment operational according to the pattern of industrialized countries. The independent decision-making in the military sector which is hoped for and expected through indigenous arms production, cannot be attained since local production is crucially reliant on the delivery of technology and personnel from abroad. Besides the fact that modern equipment often lies rusting in ports or stores, since it cannot be maintained in actual fighting between peripheral countries, sophisticated carrier systems like fighter-bombers and main battle tanks have often proved a handicap. Because of poor logistics (like shortage of munition supplies), lack of special military infrastructures (like airfields and fortified bridges), and inferior training of soldiers, the modern equipment can be used only marginally or even not at all."

3. For an incisive analysis of the historical relationships of arms to dependency and underdevelopment, see Albrecht et al. (1974), Petras (1978), and Roxborough (1979).

4. The only Third World armies strong enough to confront those of advanced capitalist nations have been created by state socialist regimes: China versus the United States (1950-1953); Vietnam versus the United States (1968-1974); and Cuba versus South Africa (1975-1976). In 1943, the Soviet Union—then a relatively backward developing country—astonished the world by halting the Nazi advance at Stalingrad, turning the German offensive into a retreat that ended about two years later in Berlin.

5. When he addressed the Tenth Conference of American Armies at Caracas in September 1973, General Edgardo Mercado Jarrín (Prime Minister, Minister of War, and Commander-in-Chief of the Peruvian army) suggested that the components of national security for nonaligned Latin American nations were antithetical to some important U.S. foreign policy goals: "For the United States, security means the maintenance of powerful military forces that underpin its policy of world hegemony and the preservation of its way of life. For Latin American countries that form part of the 'Third World' bloc, this same concept of security signifies—in addition to its traditional meaning—the sovereign right to control one's natural resources, one's primary commodities, and the acquisition of sufficient financial and technological capacity to bring about the integral (multifaceted) development of its population by adopting a policy independent of the major world powers. From this standpoint we cannot unquestioningly accept the limited conception of the traditional functions of the state, which imply that security represents no more than territorial defense without at the same time considering the sources of socio-economic disequilibrium, the complex phenomenon of external dependence and all those factors of a domestic or external origin which vitally affect the welfare of a nation. A national security policy must be geared to security goals which are national in character and that enable us to transcend—within a just framework—the deeply rooted social and economic problems of internal and external origin that jeopardize national goals and the development of policies to solve both the underlying problems as well as the concomitant hostilities and pressures which they engender."

6. Classification as "leftist" or "rightist" was premised upon active support—involving risk and often loss of one's position—for the policies delineated in note 1. The leftists were: Adm. Candido Aragao da Costa (Brazil); Col. Jacobo Arbenz (Guatemala); Col. German Busch (Bolivia); Gen. Lazaro Cardenas (Mexico); Adm. Jorge Dellepiane (Peru); Gen. Jorge Fernández Maldonado (Peru); Gen. Miguel Angel De La Flor Valle (Peru); Col. Samuel Gallardo (Bolivia); Gen. Enrique Gallegos Venero (Peru); Lt. Col. Marmaduke Grove Vallejo (Chile); Col. Juan Domingo Perón (Argentina); Gen. Carlos Prats González (Chile); Lt. Luis Carlos Prestes (Brazil); Gen. Leonidas Rodriguez Figueroa (Peru); Maj. Ruben Sánchez Valdivia (Bolivia); Gen. Juan José Torres Gonzáles (Bolivia); Gen. Omar Torrijos Herrera (Panama); Maj. Gen. Juan Velasco Alvarado (Peru); Gen. Gualberto Villaroel (Bolivia); and Gen. Liber Seregni (Uruguay).

The rightists were: Gen. Carlos Manuel Arana Osorio (Guatemala); Col. Juan Ayora (Bolivia); Gen. Hugo Banzer Suárez (Bolivia); Gen. Rene Barrientos Ortuno (Bolivia); Col. Fulgencio Batista Zaldivar (Cuba); Gen. Humberto de Alencar Castelo Branco (Brazil); Gen. Oswaldo Cordeiro de Farias (Brazil); Gen. Arthur Da Costa y Silva (Brazil); Gen. Odylio Denys (Brazil); Gen. Gustavo Leigh Guzman (Chile); Lt. Gen. Juan Carlos Ongania (Argentina); Gen. Enrique Peralta Azurdia (Guatemala); Lt. Col. Marcos Pérez Jiménez (Venezuela); Gen. Augusto Pinochet Ugarte (Chile); Gen. Pedro Rodríguez Echevarría (Dominican Republic); Gen. Anastasio Somoza Sr. (Nicaragua); Gen. Anastasio Somoza Jr. (Nicaragua); Gen. Alfredo Stroessner (Paraguay); Gen. Rafael Trujillo Molina (Dominican Republic); and Lt. Gen. Jorge Rafael Videla (Argentina).

7. While little evidence for religious leanings was found among the military, under certain circumstances, exposure to the "social gospel" can be a catalyst for officers otherwise predisposed to the left. Thus, Urriza (1978: 91) points out that participation in the short courses on Christianity was frequent among the more radicalized officers, one noteworthy consequence being General Jorge Fernández Maldonado's publication, "The Armed Forces, Christianity and Revolution."

REFERENCES

ABRAHAMSSON, B. (1972) Military Professionalization and Political Power. Beverly Hills, CA: Sage.

ALBRECHT, U., D. ERNST, P. LOCK, and H. WULF (1974) "Armaments and underdevelopment." Bull. of Peace Proposals 5: 173-185.

ASTIZ, C. (1973) "The military establishment as a political elite: the Peruvian case," pp. 203-229 in D. H. Pollack and A.R.M. Ritter (eds.) Latin American Prospects for the 1970s: What Kinds of Revolutions? New York: Praeger.

——— (1969) "The Argentine armed forces: their role and political involvement." Western Pol. Q. 22: 862-878.

BISSELL, R. (1968) Intelligence and Foreign Policy. Cambridge, MA: Africa Research Group.

BLACK, J. N. (1978) United States Penetration of Brazil. Philadelphia: Univ. of Pennsylvania Press.

CARRANZA, M. E. (1978) Fuerzas armadas y estado de excepción en América Latina. Mexico: Siglo XXI Editores.

EINAUDI, L. R. (1969) The Peruvian Military: A Summary Political Analysis. Santa Monica, CA: The Rand Corporation.

ETCHISON, D. L. (1975) The United States and Militarism in Central America. New York: Praeger.

FINER, S. E. (1975) The Man on Horseback: The Role of the Military in Politics. Harmondsworth, Eng.: Penguin Books, 2nd Ed.

FITCH, J. S. (1979) "The political impact of U.S. military aid to Latin America: institutional and individual effects." Armed Forces and Society 5 (Spring): 360-386.

GUNTHER, J. (1968) Inside South America. New York: Simon & Schuster.

——— (1941) Inside Latin America. New York: Harper & Row.

HOROWITZ, I. L. (1969) "The socioeconomic pivot," pp. 3-231 in I. L. Horowitz et al. (eds.) Latin American Radicalism. New York: Random House.

——— and E. K. TRIMBERGER (1976) "State power and military nationalism in Latin America." Comparative Politics 8 (January): 223-243.

HUNTINGTON, S. P. (1968) Political Order in Changing Societies. New Haven, CT: Yale Univ. Press.

——— (1959) The Soldier and the State. Cambridge, MA: Harvard Univ. Press.

IMAZ, J. L. (1964) Los que mandan. Buenos Aires: Editorial Buenos Aires.

JANOWITZ, M. (1964) The Military in the Political Development of New Nations. Chicago: Univ. of Chicago Press.

JOHNSON, J. J. (1964) The Military and Society in Latin America. Stanford, CA: Stanford Univ. Press.

KENISTON, K. (1968) The Young Radicals. Cambridge, MA: Harvard Univ. Press.

LANG, K. (1972) Military Institutions and the Sociology of War: A Review of the Literature with Annotated Bibliography. Beverly Hills, CA: Sage.

LIEUWEN, E. (1964) Generals vs. Presidents: Neomilitarism in Latin America. New York: Praeger.

——— (1963) "New-militarism in Latin America: the Kennedy administration's inadequate response." Inter-American Econ. Affairs 16 (Spring): 11-20.

MELMAN, S. (1979) "Inflation and unemployment as products of war economy." Bull. of Peace Proposals 9: 359-374.

——— (1974) The Permanent War Economy: American Capitalism in Decline. New York: Simon & Schuster.

MIGUENS, J. E. (1970-1971) "The new Latin American military coup." Studies in Comparative International Development 6: 4-5.

MONTEFORTE TOLEDO, M. (1970) La solución militar a la peruana: 1968-1970. Mexico: UNAM.

NEEDLER, M. C. (1975) "Military motivations in the seizure of power." Latin American Research Review 10 (Fall): 63-79.

——— (1969) "The Latin American military: predatory reactionaries or modernizing patriots?" J. of Interamerican Studies 11 (April): 237-244.

——— (1963) Anatomy of a Coup D'Etat: Ecuador. Washington, DC: Institute for the Comparative Study of Political Systems.

NORTH, L. and T. KOROVKIN (1981) The Peruvian Revolution: Reform Policies and Ideological Orientations of the Officers in Power, 1968-1976. Montreal: McGill University Centre for Developing Area Studies. Monograph Series No. 15.

NUN, J. (1969) Latin America: The Hegemonic Crisis and the Military Coup. Berkeley, CA: University of California, Institutional Studies, Politics of Modernization Series, No. 7.

PARKER, P. R. (1979) Brazil and the Quiet Intervention, 1964. Austin: Univ. of Texas Press.

PETRAS, J. (1978) Critical Perspectives on Imperialism and Social Class in the Third World. New York: Monthly Review Press.

——— and N. RIMENSNYDER (1970) "What is happening in Peru?" Monthly Review 21 (February): 15-28.

POTASH, R. A. (1969) The Army Politics in Argentina, 1928-1945. Stanford, CA: Stanford Univ. Press.

PYE, L. W. (1962) "Armies in the process of political modernization," pp. 69-89 in J. J. Johnson (ed.) The Role of the Military in Underdeveloped Countries. Princeton, NJ: Princeton Univ. Press.

RANKIN, R. C. (1974) "The expanding institutional concerns of the Latin American military establishments: a review article." Latin American Research Rev. 9 (Spring): 81-108.

REJAI, M. (1973) The Strategy of Political Revolution. Garden City, NY: Doubleday Anchor.

ROPP, S. C. (1970) "The military and urbanization in Latin America: some implications of trends in recruitment." Inter-American Econ. Affairs 24 (Autumn): 27-35.

ROXBOROUGH, A. (1979) Theories of Underdevelopment. Atlantic Highlands, NJ: Humanities Press.

STEPAN, A. (1971) The Military in Politics: Changing Patterns in Brazil. Princeton, NJ: Princeton Univ. Press.

TRIMBERGER, E. K. (1978) Revolution From Above: Military Bureaucrats in Japan, Turkey, Egypt, and Peru. New Brunswick, NJ: Transaction Books.

URRIZA, M. (1978) Peru: Cuando los militares se van. Caracas: Editorial Cidal.

VAGTS, A. (1959) A History of Militarism. New York: Free Press.

WODDIS, J. (1977) Armies and Politics. London: Lawrence & Wishart.

WOLPIN, M. D. (1981) Militarization and Social Revolution in the Third World. Montclair, NJ: Allanheld, Osmun & Co.

——— (1973) Military Aid and Counterrevolution in the Third World. Lexington, MA: D. C. Heath.

WULF, H. (1979) "Dependent militarism in the periphery and possible alternative concepts," in S. G. Newman and R. E. Harkavy (eds.) Arms Transfers in the Modern World. New York: Praeger.

Miles D. Wolpin, Associate Professor of Political Science at the State University of New York, Potsdam, is Militarization Project Director for the International Peace Research Institute (PRIO) in Oslo, Norway, while on leave from his university post. His research has focused on comparative military roles in the East, West, and Third World, and on dependency and revolutionary strategies. He is the author of Militarism and Social Revolution in the Third World *(Allanheld and Osmun Press, 1981) as well as numerous articles and books.*

DANIEL L. PREMO
Department of Political Science
and International Studies
Washington College
Chestertown, Maryland

POLITICAL ASSASSINATION IN GUATEMALA
A Case of Institutionalized Terror

> There was but one side to politics in Guatemala. Both parties have a beautiful way of producing unanimity of opinion, by driving out of the country all who do not agree with them.
>
> —John Lloyd Stephens (1839)

The concepts of "political assassination" and "terrorism" are fraught with definitional problems. For purposes of this study, the former will be defined simply as "murder for political motives." It is one of a series of acts that collectively are intended to produce a psychological state of fear and uncertainty within the general population, i.e., "terrorism," in an effort to direct political activity through intimidation.

Assassination is usually thought of as a terroristic act associated with opposition political groups. This article examines its use as a mechanism of control by government and private groups who perceive a threat to their privileged position in society.

The systematic elimination of leaders representing trade unions, as well as peasant, student, professional, and other "popular sectors" has reached an unprecedented level in Guatemala's turbulent history. The use of assassination as an instrument of repression is a recognition of failure to achieve a more benign politics of conciliation or cooptation. In the case of Guatemala, terror by assassination has become a deliberate policy alternative in recent decades for suppressing popular demands to broaden political participation, and to avoid the

Journal of Interamerican Studies and World Affairs, Vol. 23 No. 4, November 1981 429-456

implementation of structural reforms needed to alleviate long-standing social and economic antagonisms.

The Study of Assassination

The literature on assassination tends to emphasize the political murder of high-level officials, e.g., the head of state or chief executive. There is a paucity of studies on middle- and low-level assassination. What studies do exist tend to link assassination with guerrilla warfare, or to portray it as an adjunct of terrorism (Havens et al., 1977). In Latin America, this has led to a focus in recent years on rural guerrilla movements and urban terrorist groups.

In contrast, little attention has been given to the use of assassination by governmental authorities as a mechanism of control and repression. To be sure, the history of the region is filled with examples of regimes whose survival has relied on the extensive use of force and violence, including selective assassination. Rosas in Argentina, Díaz in Mexico, Trujillo in the Dominican Republic, Batista in Cuba, Duvalier in Haiti, or any of a number of reactionary military regimes presently in power immediately come to mind. However, in these instances, the "government" made (or makes) little effort to conceal its direct control in determining the nature of the violence to be employed or the intended victims. Indeed, it has long been considered an essential ingredient of the caudillo's personalist rule to exercise and accept responsibility for whatever degree of violence may have been necessary to seize control of government and to maintain his authority.

With the advent of guerrilla warfare, one of the problems confronting governments in Western liberal democracies is that "there is no coherent and generally accepted philosophy in the name of which force can be organized against the violence offered by the terrorist" (Burton, 1975: 212). In combatting terrorism, governments—especially those lacking broad-based popular support—may be forced to adopt repressive measures, including the use of counterterrorist squads. Karl Schmitt (1969: 539) has noted that a weak government is tempted to remove its opponents by murder rather than by due process of law. He suggests that the incidence of low-level assassination is determined more by the presence or absence of respected government authority than the existence of rivalries based on economic, political, or ideological issues.

In resorting to the use of paramilitary forces, or in condoning their existence, the government may contribute to the erosion of its own authority by overreacting to the real or imagined threat of "subversive activity." Descending to the same level as the terrorist makes the government appear more repressive, and it carries the additional risk of allowing the terrorist or common criminal elements to commit violent acts and blame them on the paramilitary groups. As we shall see, over a period of time, counterterrorist groups become difficult to control, and tend to pursue vendettas without regard to the overall political situation (Burton, 1975: 26).

Using Guatemala as a case study, this article examines the hypothesis that a government's systematic use of assassination directed against nonmilitary combatants will succeed in suppressing popular opposition and support for guerrilla movements in the short run. However, it is posited that the continuation of such a policy will eventually prove to be counterproductive. In the absence of meaningful socioeconomic reforms, social and political antagonisms will be exacerbated, political groups will become increasingly polarized, and the government will be required to intensify the use of repressive measures, thereby weakening its claim to legitimacy and undermining the entire political fabric.

The key phrase in the preceding paragraph is "nonmilitary combatants." There is no question of government's right to use force when confronted with a legitimate threat to its survival. Military operations carried out against guerrilla bands, or police actions taken against terrorist groups have become a disturbingly common feature of political life in contemporary society (Laquer, 1977). However, when the presence of guerrilla activity is used by the government and members of the private sector to maintain the political and economic status quo by the systematic elimination of its civilian political opponents, assassination becomes a mechanism of control and repression incompatible with any notion of due process of law, and contradictory to the most rudimentary principles of a democratic society.

In order to understand the nature of assassination in Guatemala today, we must first examine salient features of the country's social and economic class structure, together with a survey of its recent political history.

Social and Economic Class Structure

With a land area of 42,042 square miles (roughly the size of Tennessee), Guatemala is the most populous nation in Central America, with an estimated 7.2 million people in 1981. The country's dominant geographic region is the highlands, extending southeast from Mexico, where over 80% of the total population resides in about one-fifth of the national territory. Guatemala City, the capital, displays all of the characteristics typical of the "primate city" phenomenon among Central American countries (Micklin, 1969).

Ethnicity is an important structural and cultural feature of national life. The 1964 census separates Guatemalans into two social categories; criollo and Hispanicized indigenous groups, commonly known as *ladinos,* and the various subordinate Indian groups descended from the Maya. The Maya comprise an estimated 40-45% of the population. The average life expectancy is 57.8 for the population as a whole. However, when broken down by ethnic group, the average life expectancy for ladinos in 1970 was approximately 60.5, while that for Indians was only 44.5 (Barrios Klee, 1979). The overall illiteracy level of 70% is second only to that of Haiti in all of Latin America. In brief, Guatemala is a country that, viewed from virtually any statistic, demonstrates low socioeconomic and cultural indices, especially in the rural area, where 70% of the population still resides. The problems of integrating the traditional Indian communities of the highlands into national life have been one of the underlying structural factors contributing to the country's turbulent political history.

Guatemala's basic social and economic class structure is primarily a consequence of the structural relationships established during the colonial period. The early appearance of the *latifundia* system concentrated land ownership in the hands of a few colonists who formed the nucleus of a wealthy upper class. The privileged position of this landed elite was reinforced by a class structure that relegated nonwhite groups to sharply inferior social and economic positions (Martínez Peláez, 1976). The nature and effects of these social and economic relationships are still visible today. Political and economic power in Guatemala is concentrated in the hands of a small group of large landowners, industrialists, and other interrelated groups of common self-interest. Historically, these groups have been allied with the military and backed by both representatives of foreign corporations and the hierarchy of the Catholic Church. According to the 1964 census, 2% of the total number of landowners hold title to 63% of the cultivated area in Guatemala. In contrast, 87% of the total number of farms occupy only 19% of the country's arable land area, and average less than 2.5 acres each in size (Jonas and Tobis, 1974: 14).

The problem of *minifundia* has been exacerbated in recent decades by population pressures and the inability or unwillingness of the existing power elite to provide for a more equitable distribution of land. In the highlands, 50% of the landholdings are smaller than three acres, and are often fragmented into various noncontiguous plots. The majority of *minifundistas* are illiterate Indians, divorced from national life, who subsist on the production of corn. AID reported in 1979 that an estimated 60% of the rural population had a per capita income of less than $80 a year. As a result, some 200,000 landless peasants and an estimated 400,000 Indian minifundistas are forced by poverty and tenancy agreements to migrate to the southern coastal areas every year at harvest time to supplement their incomes by picking cotton or cutting cane on the rich latifundia.

In the mid-1970s, President Laugerud García discreetly supported a movement originally founded by Catholic priests to establish cooperatives among poor Indian farmers in the highlands. Large landowners strongly opposed the policy, as did the two right-wing parties that provided the main civilian backing for the regime, the Institutional Democratic Party (PID) and the National Liberation Movement (MLN). The latter's outspoken leader (and the country's vice-president at the time), Mario Sandoval Alarcón, likened cooperativism to communism. What might have developed into an authentic rural movement was aborted by the disastrous earthquake of February 4, 1976, which claimed an estimated 25,000 lives. The greatest damage and loss of life occurred precisely in the highland areas where cooperatives were being developed.

The present government of General Fernando Romeo Lucas García has turned its attention away from cooperatives to a modest colonization program in the jungle areas of El Petén. However, conflict over land ownership long common in the highland region has erupted in the development area known as the Northern Transversal Strip. Stimulated by the discovery of oil, road and pipeline construction, and the exploitation of nickel deposits, land speculators quickly established title to much of the land before the resettlement program was even under way. The result is that would-be colonizers have ended up working as peons on the large farms now appearing in the area (Riding, 1979).[1]

In 1970, Richard Adams wrote that economic change was occurring in Guatemala. However, he added that such change was, if anything, "reinforcing the existing power structure, not substantially modifying it" (Adams, 1970: 125). Nothing has happened in the past decade to challenge the validity of Adam's assessment. If we understand by economic development an improvement in the standard of living for the majority of inhabitants of a country, the conclusion is inescapable that such development is not at present a reality in Guatemala. A succession of governmental failures since 1954 to meet the demands of a growing population has resulted in the aggravation of social and economic tensions. These, in turn, have manifested themselves in the rapid polarization of political forces that since the mid-1960s have not hesitated to make calculated use of assassination and terror in pursuit of their objectives.

The Political Environment

In order to be properly understood, contemporary political developments, particularly as they relate to the study of assassination, must be placed in historical perspective.

Guatemala's political history has been dominated by long periods of personalist dictatorships alternating with much shorter periods of political instability. In the 105 years preceding the overthrow of Jorge Ubico in 1944, 4 men had occupied the presidency for a total of 73 years. Of the country's last 7 president's, 6 have been career military officers, supported by an array of reactionary, moderate, and centrist political parties, none of which existed prior to 1955. Beginning with Carlos Arana Osorio in 1970, Guatemala's military presidents have all been supported by precarious electoral minorities whose common ideological thread has been their support for the status quo and their staunch anticommunism.[2]

The issue of communism in Guatemala is a highly volatile one, dating back to the reformist governments of Juan José Arévalo (1945-1950) and Jacobo Arbenz Guzmán (1950-1954). Although Arévalo was widely denounced in the United States as a communist, his actions in office underscore the nationalist character of his government. The case of Arbenz is admittedly more complex, beginning with the fact that his government granted legal recognition to the Guatemalan Communist Party (PGT) in 1951 (Schneider, 1958).[3] Viewed from the perspective of the international cold war, and the militant anticommunism that existed in the United States in the early 1950s, the Eisenhower administration concluded that the Arbenz regime represented a "communist threat," and conspired for its overthrow (Taylor, 1956; Gordon, 1971). Many observers date the beginning of Guatemala's current violence and polarization to the exile invasion, supported by the CIA, that ousted the Arbenz government in June 1954. The counterrevolution carried out by the self-proclaimed groups of "Liberationists" swiftly negated the reforms introduced by Arévalo and Arbenz. Castillo Armas and his supporters also established the principle that political opposition to governmental policy was tantamount to "communist subversion."

Although street demonstrations led by students and trade unionists occurred sporadically under the governments of Castillo Armas and Ydígoras Fuentes, no sustained violent opposition arose until the appearance of several left-wing guerrilla groups during the rule of Colonel Peralta Azurdia (Gott, 1970). The military's inability to suppress guerrillas operating in Zacapa and Izabal departments in 1966 led to the adoption of a policy of systematic repression of groups thought to be supporting them. One such group, of course, was the PGT, which had been forced to operate underground since 1954. On March 6, 1966, 28 PGT leaders and trade unionists "disappeared" following their arrest while attending a clandestine meeting.

Colonel Arana Osorio was appointed military commander of Zacapa following Méndez Montenegro's election in 1966. Shortly thereafter, anticommunist civilians drawn from among participants in the 1954 coup were integrated into the military's security apparatus. The first in a series of right-wing paramilitary groups commenced operations. In the beginning, such groups as the National Organized Anti-Communist Movement (MANO), the New Anti-Communist Organization (NOA), and the "Eye for an Eye" (OJO) chose their victims from individuals who could be associated with the Arévalo-Arbenz years, or with the more recent guerrilla insurgency. However, under cover of antiguerrilla activity, noncommunist leftists were sought out by right-wing terrorist groups and eliminated. Leaflets appeared, threatening not only prominent members within the PGT and rebel groups, but also students, intellectuals, trade unionists, and professional people who sought to organize or protest against what they considered social injustice (Johnson, 1973; Booth, 1980). Between October 1966 and March 1968, an estimated 3,000-8,000 Guatemalans were reportedly killed in the Zacapa-Izabal campaign. The use of counterterror methods by civilian paramilitary groups is credited for much of the success against guerrillas and their suspected supporters (Amnesty International, 1976).

With the destruction of rural guerrilla movements in the late 1960s, left-wing opposition moved into urban areas and began to resort increasingly to acts of individual terror. Arana Osorio was elected President in 1970 on a campaign of "law and order," in which he promised to eradicate the urban guerrillas. During the first three years of his presidency, the incidence of murders and disappearances reached unprecedented levels. Depending on the source, the estimates of victims, many of whose mutilated corpses made identification impossible, range from 3,500 to 15,000 (Menton et al., 1973).

Although there was a general lessening of political violence in the period preceding the 1974 elections, the inauguration of General Kjell Laugerud García was followed by a rash of killings by paramilitary groups. Acts of violence by leftist organizations and clandestine movements of the right occurred with alarming frequency in 1975 in both urban and rural areas. MANO, NOA, and OJO gave way to the appearance of self-styled death squads, whose avowed purpose was to eliminate "antisocial elements" and anyone who cooperated with "subversive organizations." Between 1972 and 1976, Amnesty International documented a total of 1105 individual cases of executions and disappearances (7 Días, 1979). The largest identifiable group of victims were peasants. Others included members and leaders of opposition parties, among them all 7 members of the PGT's Executive Committee who "disappeared" in September 1972; trade unionists and journalists; university professors and students; and assorted professionals. For the same period, Guatemalan newspapers reported a high incidence of left-wing political violence, including 149 murders of members of security forces, other government personnel, businessmen, and large landowners and their employees.

For the better part of a decade, politically motivated killings involving leftist groups and right-wing paramilitary organizations had been a common feature of Guatemalan daily life. Although the military had succeeded in destroying the guerrilla movement in Zacapa and Izabal, right-wing paramilitary forces continued to freelance in the name of "counterinsurgency" with no visible attempt by the government to control them. Moderate leaders of the political opposition and spokesmen for trade union, university, and other popular sectors were openly assassinated or "disappeared," never to be seen again.

With the emergence of the Guerrilla Army of the Poor (EGP) in late 1975, the country began a new cycle of guerrilla warfare, terror, and counterterror whose effects have deeply split Guatemalan society and have yet to run their course.

Guerrilla Warfare and Generalized Violence, 1976-1978

The reappearance of rural guerrillas provided the backdrop for a resurgence of official repression, including assassination. Government talk of a renewal of guerrilla activity in the highland regions of El Quiché, Huehuetenango, Alta Verapaz, and Chiquimula occurred as early as July 1975. However, Defense Minister General Lucas García announced that the guerrillas were "too few in number" to pose a threat to the nation, and their attempt to indoctrinate peasants in El Quiché had been "quickly discovered and dispersed" (El Imparcial, 1975).

The most active and largest of the guerrilla organizations operating in Guatemala is the Guerrilla Army of the Poor. Its membership has increased in number from about 300 in 1975 to an estimated 1200 by the end of 1980. The EGP has been most active in propaganda and organizing in El Quiché; near Escuintla, along the tropical Pacific Coast; and to a lesser extent in Zacapa. Prior to 1980, the EGP generally followed a policy of avoiding large-scale armed confrontation, and concentrated its efforts on indoctrination, especially among the Indian population. Reports in recent years suggest that Indians, including women, have become increasingly active in guerrilla units operating in the northwest (Prensa Libre, 1979; New York Times, 1980; Washington Report, 1980).

A second guerrilla group, the self-styled Armed People's Organization (ORPA), has been engaged in military action since

September 1979. ORPA's political affiliation, strength, and leadership hierarchy are undetermined. However, guerrilla units of up to 150 members have occupied villages and carried out propaganda activities in various departments.

The pro-Soviet PGT has vacillated in its support of guerrilla warfare. Factionalism has undermined the PGT's internal cohesion between those who seek to regain legal status and those who advocate the primacy of armed struggle. According to statements attributed to the party's general secretary, there is no indication that the PGT is eager to endorse an immediate appeal to arms, despite its belief that a further escalation of repression and terror is "inevitable" (Gonzales, 1979).[4]

Apart from the renewal of guerrilla activity in 1975, the existence of nonideological groups of common criminals, and the continued operations of right-wing extremist organizations contributed to the climate of political violence. Rampant looting that followed the 1976 earthquake necessitated the immediate declaration of a National State of Emergency. Although spokesmen for the National Police continued to deny its existence, the death squad resumed its vigilante actions against known and suspected criminal elements.

The resurgence of violence created concern among political leaders of all tendencies. Death threats were reported by leaders within both opposition and progovernment parties. Assassination victims during this period were by no means limited to high ranking politicians and members of the military. Persons with little influence in the nation's political or economic life, but with some standing in their local communities, were also singled out for torture and murder by unidentified assailants.

During a news conference in San José, Costa Rica, President Laugerud accused international communism of "dragging the country into a bloodbath." When asked about his responsibility for the violence in Guatemala in recent years, he replied that it was brought into the country by "communists who are being directed, financed, and incited by the Cuban Government" (El Imparcial, 1976a). In a remarkably candid assessment, Government Minister General Vassaux Martínez declared at a press interview several days later that the nation's most recent surge of violence was the consequence of long-standing social and economic problems "that cannot be eradicated simply by means of coercive measures." He added that the principal cause of violence resides in "the failure for many years to extend an effective system of social justice to all the people" (El Imparcial, 1976b).

Although President Laugerud attempted to dissociate his administration from right-wing violence, the government's inability to account for the disappearance and assassination of individuals with leftist sympathies led to continued criticism of the state of human rights. The principal instrument of right-wing assassination was the Secret Anti-Communist Army (ESA). In its first communique issued on June 22, 1977, the ESA announced its intention of "protecting social classes attacked by communist gangs." The new organization stated that it would wage a "bitter struggle" against extreme leftist groups such as the PGT and the EGP, warning that it had already begun to judge "the most prominent communists who promote terror in the country" (El Imparcial, 1977). The emergence of the ESA reintroduced an element of counterterror reminiscent of the extremist operations of the MANO, NOA, and the OJO in the early 1970s.

The ESA took credit for several key assassinations in 1977 that contributed to, if not initiated, a new "cycle of polarization" between extremist groups.[5] On June 8, Mario López Larrave, a prominent labor lawyer, founding member in 1976 of the National Committee of Labor Unity (CNUS) and a candidate for the post of rector of San Carlos University, was assassinated. University officials and CNUS, which encompasses the largest labor confederations and peasant leagues, accused the government of an "obvious inability to guarantee human rights" (Prensa Libre, 1977). High School and university student agitation escalated in August following the kidnapping, torture, and murder of Aníbal Caballero Ramírez, vice-president of the Students Association at the Rafael Aqueche Institute, and the similar disappearance and murder of university leader Robín García.

In what appears to have been direct retaliation for the students' deaths, no fewer than seven MLN leaders were assassinated in various parts of the country in August. In October, the ESA issued "death sentences" against union leaders and members for their alleged communist affiliation, and directed similar threats against newsmen. By the end of President Laugerud's term of office, the conditions appeared to be present for a return to the politics of terror that characterized the Arana Osorio era. The EGP had effectively increased the scope of its operations in the northwestern highlands. Guerrilla forces had also embarrassed the Laugerud administration by kidnapping Roberto Herrera Ibarguen, a personal friend and adviser to the President.[6] In addition, the Rebel Armed Forces (FAR), which had been quiescent for several years, announced the resumption of guerrilla activities in February. The ESA and the death squad responded in kind. Amnesty International issued a list of 113 persons either killed or presumed to be kidnapped for political reasons by paramilitary groups during the last three months of 1977 (New York Times, 1978).

Violence and Assassination Under the Lucas García Presidency

Following President Lucas García's inauguration on July 1, 1978, Guatemala's police chief announced "a harsh campaign" against guerrilla groups. By the end of the President's first month in office, the government admitted that "a new wave of violence" was sweeping the country. In October, workers and students demonstrated in opposition to a proposed increase in urban bus fares. In a ten-day period between October 2-12, at least 30 persons were killed, 350 injured, and 600 arrested. A general labor strike led by CNUS quickly spread throughout the country. Governmental authorities charged that "well-organized agitators" were following instructions from political groups identified with the extreme left and were "taking advantage of disorders in the capital in an attempt to overthrow the government" (El Imparcial, 1978).

On October 19, the ESA published a "death list" containing the names of 37 labor, university, and opposition political leaders, and reiterated its determination "to fight international communism to the death." The following day, the secretary general of the Association of University Students (AEU), Oliverio Castañeda de León, was machinegunned within two blocks of the Central Park where he had just spoken at a rally commemorating the anniversary of the October 1944 "Revolution." The impact of Castañeda's assassination exceeded that of Robín García's murder or any other student leader previously killed. Castañeda occupied the highest position of student leadership at the University of San Carlos. His assassination in full view of the public was clearly intended to intimidate the entire university community in particular, and all "agitators" and government critics in general. The university's response was to intensify its condemnation of the government's inability to control right-wing paramilitary violence.[7]

Political life has become increasingly violent under the Lucas García administration, especially since the January 1979 fall of Somoza in Nicaragua. During the first six months of his government, more than 500 victims of violence were reported, over 200 of whom displayed signs of torture. Amnesty International (1979) reported in September 1979 that political murder and repression had taken 2,000 lives in the previous 16 months, many of them government opponents murdered by "semiclandestine death squads" (New York Times, 1979). While the information provided through the local press is not always complete nor necessarily accurate, 546 murders clearly identified as politically motivated were reported during a period of less than two months at the beginning of 1979 (Torres Rivas, 1979). By the end of 1980, an average of 10 bodies were being found daily in or within a short distance of Guatemala City. In addition, clandestine gravesites had been discovered in rural areas with as many as 30 bodies. In its most recent report, Amnesty International states that between January and November 1980, some 3,000 people described by government officials as "subversives" and "criminals" were either assassinated or seized and murdered later; another 364 "disappeared" in this period and have yet to be accounted for (Amnesty International, 1981). Estimates of political murders committed during the Lucas García regime run as high as 5,000-6,000 (Hoge, 1981; Washington Report, 1981; Update Latin America, 1981).

Victims and Assassins

The raw data, while a crude index of the generally violent nature of Guatemalan political life today, do not tell us much about either the victims or the assassins. With respect to the former, it is possible to classify assassination victims in accordance with their position on the political spectrum. We can determine with reasonable accuracy those individuals who have been singled out as the target for assassination by right-wing extremists, as opposed to those who have been claimed as victims by left-wing groups. By including occupation as a second variable, we can formulate some tentative assumptions concerning the qualitative use of assassination as an instrument of control, repression, terror, and counter-terror (see Table 1).

It is evident that since 1978, top leaders of the moderate political left have been assassinated in an effort to prevent the organization and legal representation of opposition parties. The most prominent victims to date have been Alberto Fuentes Mohr, former foreign minister under Méndez Montenegro and leader of the small Social Democratic Party (PSD), who was murdered on January 25, 1979; and Manuel Colóm Argueta, head of the United Revolutionary Front (FUR), who was assassinated on March 22, 1979.[8] On July 13, 1979, Feliciano Acevedo and Arnoldo Oliva, both of whom had participated in the organization of the PSD, were assassinated in an apparent resumption of the execution of leftist opposition leaders by the ESA. On October 5, 1979, Gerard Méndez, a member of the FUR's political council, was kidnapped and warned to leave the country. By April 1980, 11 of FUR's national and regional leaders had been assassinated. In addition to the PGT, the FUR, and the PSD, the ranks of the Christian Democratic Party (PDC) have been decimated by kidnappings and murders in recent years. The

TABLE 1

Targets of Right-Wing Assassination Groups

1. Opposition Political Leaders

   A. Guatemalan Labor Party (PGT)
   B. Christian Democratic Party (PDC)
   C. Guatemalan Socialist Party (PSD)
   D. United Revolutionary Front (FUR)

2. Labor Leaders and Trade Unionists
3. University Professors and Officials
4. University and High School Student Leaders
5. Journalists and Newsmen
6. Peasant Leaders
7. Intellectuals and Professionals
8. Priests who sympathize with the Indians' status

Targets of Left-Wing Assassination Groups

1. Political Leaders, e.g., MLN
2. Foreign Diplomats, e.g., Nicaraguan Ambassador
3. Military and National Police Officials

   A. Associated with regimes prior to 1978
   B. On active duty

4. Civilian Government Officials

   A. Associated with regimes prior to 1978
   B. Current officials and advisers

5. Peasant Informers
6. Businessmen, Industrialists, and other professionals associated with the government or its closest allies within the private sector

party's secretary general, Vinicio Cerezo, himself the target of several assassination attempts, informed U.S. officials in May 1981 that 76 Christian Democratic leaders had been killed in the previous 10 months (Dickey, 1981). The political center is rapidly disappearing in Guatemala. Indications are that both the Christian and Social Democratic parties have been terrorized into not participating in elections scheduled for 1982.

The growth of trade unionism in Guatemala has also been a factor in the resurgence of right-wing paramilitary activity. The Lucas government inherited a legacy of labor activism that contributed to the confrontation with authorities during the

October 1978 strikes. In addition to seeking higher wages, trade union leaders have been especially active in attempting to secure collective bargaining concessions from employers.[9]

At least 6 trade unionists were assassinated and 2 kidnapped between June 1977 and June 1978. In the ensuing 15 months, 12 more unionists were murdered and 9 disappeared (Amnesty International, 1979). The assassination of labor leaders, especially those serving in the capacity of secretary general or president of their respective unions, was even more intense in 1980. Between March 12 and June 29, at least 11 labor leaders were slain, including several active in the communist-dominated Autonomous Labor Federation. A recent source (Update Latin America, 1981) places the total number of union victims for the year at 110. Moreover, on June 21, 1980, 27 members of the National Confederation of Workers (CNT) were kidnapped by "unidentified persons" who raided the union's headquarters in Guatemala City. An additional 17 CNT members "disappeared" from the union's conference center in Palín, Escuintla, on August 24. As yet, none of the 44 missing have been accounted for.

Agricultural union leaders have suffered an even greater toll. According to figures provided by the Democratic Front Against Repression, 311 peasant leaders were killed in 1980 by government security forces and their civilian auxiliaries (Update, 1981). Government repression has been directed especially against suspected collaborators of the Peasant Unity Committee (CUC), an Indian-dominated union founded in 1978 that has been forced to operate underground since late 1979.

Evidence of the persecution of peasants active in the organization of peasant leagues and rural cooperatives continues to mount, especially in areas where guerrilla groups are active. Dramatic improvements in *minifundia* yields have been achieved in recent years through the use of fertilizer (Olson, 1981). Unfortunately, while the distribution of fertilizer through rural cooperatives holds some promise of self-sufficiency for Indians, it works to the disadvantage of plantation owners, who depend on the availability of cheap labor. Indians who display leadership potential eventually find their names appearing on "death lists." According to one observer (Luhan, 1981), half the adult and adolescent male population of San Juan Comalapa, a community of 8,000 Indians located 40 miles northwest of Guatemala City, has been intimidated into fleeing the village for the anonymity of the capital or permanent migration to the southern coast.

University students, professors, and officials have also been the victims of political violence. The University of San Carlos and its regional affiliates have long been considered centers of "leftist subversion." Law school professors especially have played a leading role in advising trade unions and peasant organizations concerning legal registration and questions of land rights. The Lucas García government has also looked with disfavor on the contribution of student leaders and professors in the organization of the Democratic Front Against Repression.

The academic sector's continued involvement with groups that oppose the current regime has made it a prime target for kidnappings and murder. On March 10, 1980, the AEU reported that more than 30 youths had been kidnapped and killed since the first of the year, and accused the government of "continuing a wave of repression directed against the university" (7 Días, 1980a). During March and April, 24 students and professors were murdered, prompting the University's Superior Council to conclude that either the government is incapable of guaranteeing the safety and rights of its citizens, or it has failed to take the necessary action to halt the current violence (7 Días, 1980b).

Following the abduction and murder of two students in May 1980, the AEU issued a bulletin demanding that the University adopt "measures of defense" and "denounce the government for pursuing a policy which seeks to impose terror among the students and the rest of the popular forces" (7 Días, 1980c). On May 31, the ESA revealed a list of some 100 students, professors, and labor leaders it had "sentenced to death" for being communists. During June and July the ESA took credit for the murder of at least 4 university students whom it accused of belonging to the Robín García Student Front. Two professors and 5 students were killed on July 14, in retaliation for the murder of police chief Colonel Miguel Angel Girón Natareño. By the end of 1980, over 50 professors and officials associated with San Carlos and more than 100 students had been assassinated. Numerous others, including the university's rector, had fled into exile. In reviewing the number of assassinations, disappearances, and threats directed against the university, it is difficult not to agree with the Superior Council's conclusion that, from its perspective, Guatemala is presently experiencing the highest levels of violence in its history.[10]

Newspapermen, journalists, and radio newsmen comprise another category of persons capable of generating a source of resistance to the government by their ability to criticize officials and policies. Their freedom to do so without censorship or fear of reprisal has been brought under serious question by the number in their profession who received threats, were assassinated, or disappeared in 1980, as well as earlier years. In discussing a report that at least 40 newsmen had been threatened, the President's public relations secretary stated on April 17, 1980, that if there have been threats against journalists, "it should be the newspapers in the country that should investigate the situation, to find the way to protect their journalists and to file charges against the persons who issue the threats" (Prensa Libre, 1980a).

While the focus of this study has been on the escalation of right-wing assassinations against leaders within the popular sectors, it should be pointed out that left-wing extremist groups, especially the EGP's urban unit, have also intensified their acts of violence against the government. During the 1970s, a large number of the targets of left-wing assassinations appear to have been singled out for their alleged collaboration with previous administrations. Most victims, whether civilian or military operations and other repressive actions against guerrilla movements and those individuals accused of supporting them in the late 1960s and early 1970s. For example, the EGP's first operation in Guatemala City was the murder of Jorge Hernández Castellón. Hernández, an MLN congressman from Chiquimula, had been one of Arana Osorio's principal security advisers, and thought to have been responsible for the disappearance of many leftists. The EGP took credit in 1976 for the murder of Colonel Edmundo Ramírez Cervantes, who served as chief of the regional police during the Arana presidency, and Miguel Sánchez Herrador, an ex-army officer who was responsible for supervision of military operations on the southern coast. The element of revenge also stands out in the assassinations of Rafael Arreaga Bosque, former defense minister under Méndez Montenegro, and Colonel Samuel Ramírez Lima, presidential chief of staff under Arana.

Much as the assassination of Oliverio Castañeda de León in October 1978 acted as a catalyst in producing a strong reaction among left-wing groups and centrist parties, it could be argued that the murder of Major General David Cancinos on June 11, 1979 generated a similar sense of indignation and resolve within government circles. As Army Chief of Staff, Cancinos was considered next in line for Minister of Defense and a possible presidential candidate for the 1982 elections. The EGP claimed credit for Cancinos's death, charging him with being one of the principal organizers of the death squad. Cancinos's murder marked a significant escalation in the targets of left-wing assassinations. Victims have come increasingly from the ranks of military officers on active duty and civilians presently in government service. Equally important is the higher rank of both the officers and public officials. During the recent violence in Guatemala, there has occurred rather quickly a transition from middle- to high-level assassination. The country's third-ranking army chief and the police chief of the IV Corps of the National Police were assassinated in February and July 1980, respectively. Government Minister Donaldo Alvarez Ruíz survived an assassination attempt in February 1980, as did his Deputy Minister in August. Other government advisers, industrialists, and professionals in the service of private business have been less fortunate. In a communiqué distributed to the Guatemalan media in March 1981, the EGP, ORPA, and PGT claimed credit for 23 execution operations of "repressive officials," including the former deputy chief of judicial police (Prensa Libre, 1981). The assassinations not only continue, but it would appear that no one short of the President himself is now considered "untouchable."

The official position of the Guatemalan government has been to deny any complicity in the organization or activities of any of the paramilitary groups or death squads such as the Secret Anti-Communist Army. Exactly who is behind such groups is still a matter of conjecture. A tendency has been to blame the MLN and its passionately anticommunist leader, Sandoval Alarcón, as the most likely protagonists. However, opposition leaders are more inclined to accuse those officials closer to the center of power, namely the National Police Chief, the Minister of Government, and the Defense Minister. Moreover, they argue that only the private sector could compile such comprehensive information on those involved in union activities. CACIF is frequently cited by Guatemalan intellectuals as the type of "reactionary" group with sufficient resources, contacts and motive to preserve the status quo. University sources have pointed out that various murders and abductions have occurred in the presence of police and by persons driving vehicles with official license plates. From this, they have concluded that it is the government, acting at times on information provided by the business sector, that is primarily responsible for the systematic elimination of opposition.

To date, the most serious attempt to research the Guatemalan government's involvement in right-wing terrorism has been carried out by Amnesty International. In February 1981, Amnesty stated categorically that "routine assassinations, secret detentions and summary executions are part of a clearly defined program of government in Guatemala . . . carried out by a specialized agency under the direct supervision of President Lucas García" (Amnesty International, 1981: 7).[11]

While we cannot declare with absolute certainty that any single group is more responsible for Guatemala's political violence than another, it is more than coincidence that the overwhelming majority of assassination victims have been student, peasant, and trade union leaders, professors and intellectuals, and politicians who have attempted to organize parties of the moderate left. All of these victims and those individuals whose names appear on the most recent "death lists" are considered "communists" by government officials and members of the business, banking, and agro-export elites. Under such an elastic definition, Guatemalans in increasing numbers are subject to classification as "communists." Among them there are doubtlessly some who have come to believe that their only recourse is to support a form of armed struggle similar to that which occurred in Nicaragua, and which is now taking place in El Salvador.

Summary and Conclusions

The increase in generalized violence in Guatemala is at least to some degree a function of the political uncertainty existing in Central America. Political divisions within the country have been accentuated by the Sandinist victory in Nicaragua and the current leftist insurgency in El Salvador. Guatemalan officials, including military spokesmen, believe that Guatemala is the target of an international communist plan which seeks to destroy the country's image and unleash a guerrilla struggle aimed at seizing power. Guatemalan officials claim to have detected Cuban mercenaries operating with the guerrillas in El Quiché. Guerrillas are also thought to be receiving training in Cuba and the Soviet Union, which, according to Guatemala's Government Minister, accounts for the increase in subversive activity at the beginning of 1980 (Prensa Libre, 1980b). For the most part, the Guatemalan military's response to increasing domestic criticism has been to close ranks with the private sector in an effort to insulate the country against "the communist plague." However, in July 1980 the Education Ministry announced that it was preparing a nation-wide literacy campaign intended to reach "at least one million persons." The government declared in April 1981 that state-owned farms would be turned over to some 25,000 peasant families as part of the administration's policy of "encouraging free enterprise and private property" (El Imparcial, 1981b). While such programs may well prove to be another case of "too little, too late," they are an indication at least that the government is not impervious to the reformist activity occurring in Nicaragua and El Salvador.

The study of assassination in Guatemala is complicated by the fact that the Guatemalan government is presently engaged in combatting rural and urban guerrilla units through the use of conventional counterinsurgency tactics. Accounts of the mass murder of Indians and newly discovered gravesites continue to circulate (Hoge, 1981). The military appears determined to use any means necessary to discourage the rural population from heeding guerrilla appeals for support. While guerrilla activity in rural areas has increased, the hardline approach adopted by the Lucas García government may ultimately prove to be strategically counterproductive. There is no evidence that the military's repressive action directed against indigenous noncombatants has diminished the ranks of the guerrillas. On the contrary, it has probably aided their recruiting efforts and contributed to the gradual radicalization of the Indians.

Although irrefutable evidence is lacking, it is widely believed that off-duty members of the national police and the army, supported by funds and personnel from the private business sector, engage in clandestine paramilitary operations intended to eliminate civilian opposition to the government. In rural areas, special army forces known as *Kaibiles* are those most frequently accused of arbitrary detentions, "disappearances," and killings. Through both the selective and, at times, apparently indiscriminate choice of victims targeted for assassination, the government has attempted to paralyze all mass activity. To some degree, it has succeeded in creating a climate of terror among key sectors of the population, namely, trade unions, opposition politicians, university professors and student leaders, journalists, professionals, peasant leaders, and even priests who have expressed sympathy with the underprivileged sectors of society.

While some of the assassination victims may well have been committed to the violent overthrow of the existing regime and thus engaged in "subversive activity," it is not always possible to separate such individuals from the greater number of victims whose political opposition was expressed through legal channels. The study of assassination is further complicated by the existence of self-proclaimed death squads that dispense vigilante justice against criminals and other "anti-social" elements. It is this writer's contention that right-wing extremist groups in Guatemala have adopted the tactics of the death squads in recent years to increase the fear of torture and mutilation among potential victims, thereby contributing toward the institutionalization of terror. However, political assassinations patterned after the modus operandi of the death squads usually display one important distinction; the bodies of the victims who "disappear" and are later found along the roadside are not generally mutilated beyond recognition. The victim must be identifiable to serve effectively as a warning. There are also those who "disappear" and are never heard from again.

Some assassinations are carried out in congested areas in broad daylight for the express purpose of demonstrating the victim's complete vulnerability and the impotence (or unwillingness) of governmental authorities to guarantee personal safety. In short, they are designed to achieve a demonstration effect whose message is strikingly simple: no one can ensure adequate safeguards for himself or his family. When such groups as the Secret Anti-Communist Army are permitted to operate with seeming impunity, the mere publication of a "death list" of individuals slated for execution may be sufficient to deter political activity. Political acquiescence is achieved through a combination of attrition by assassination and intimidation that frequently results in voluntary exile. The operation of the death squads contributes an additional element believed to be necessary to create a climate of terror—the apparent indiscriminate assassination, the victims of which have little or no association with militant groups. This serves to create the generalized impression or fear that any person could become the target of a terrorist group (Aguilera Peralta, 1979: 101).

One cannot help but feel a sense of deep concern at the number of assassinations, "disappearances," and threats directed against both progovernment and various popular sectors during the past two years. Guatemala is currently experiencing the highest levels of political violence and abuse of personal rights in its history. A review of that history suggests that the root of the country's political crisis remains the capacity of an archaic economic and social structure in preventing the Indian campesino or urban laborer from readjusting upward their abysmal share of the nation's wealth. Apart from the literacy campaign and modest land redistribution program, there is little indication that either the military or the private sector is willing to consider broadening the political process and undertaking the social and economic reforms that might conceivably alleviate existing tensions.

In very few countries of the world is it as dangerous to struggle for individual self-betterment or in support of the simplest democratic rights as it is today in Guatemala. The question is no longer whether or not there will be change, but the degree to which this change takes place peacefully or violently. The disintegration of the established order is not likely to occur as rapidly in Guatemala as appears to have been the case in Nicaragua and now seems imminent in El Salvador. For one thing, there is no symbol against which diverse opposition groups can unite. For another, apart from the capital, the population is still overwhelmingly Indian, illiterate, and politically unsophisticated. The extreme left has yet to demonstrate conclusively that Guatemala's Indians are not just as susceptible to mobilization in support of the status quo as they are to oppose it. Finally, the Guatemalan military has developed a corporate tradition of independent conservatism, supported by an equally conservative private sector that is disposed to assist in the repression of popular movements in order to retain its monopoly over the benefits of economic growth.[12] The result is a continuing accentuation of social antagonisms and polarization of political forces.

The old "rules of the game" in Guatemalan politics have changed drastically in the past two decades. The country is presently engaged in a politics of attrition, intimidation, and terror in which middle- and high-level assassinations play a major role. It is a form of politics in which there can be no real winners in the short term, only victims.

NOTES

1. The dispossession of Indians from their ancestral lands and other forms of injustice which they are caused to suffer are at the root of several recent tragic confrontations with authorities: namely, the Panzós "massacre" in Alta Verapaz on May 29, 1978, in which over 100 Indians were killed by troops; and the government's precipitous assault on the Spanish embassy on January 31, 1980, after its occupation by a delegation of Indians from El Quiché. At least three instances of mass violence involving Indians and special army units have been reported in 1981.

2. The military does not have its own political party. However, since 1970 it has put forth its own presidential candidates. To ensure their election, it has been sufficient to secure a temporary alliance with one or a coalition of rightist parties. In 1970, Colonel Carlos Arana Osorio drew his support from the MLN, the most reactionary of the three major right-wing parties. In 1974, an MLN-PID coalition threw its support behind General Laugerud García in elections that are generally considered to rank among the most fraudulent in Guatemala's modern history. In 1978 the PID and the Revolutionary Party (PR) formed an electoral alliance to support General Lucas García. In 1970 the PR appeared in the "opposition," after having provided the country with its first civilian president since Arévalo, Julio César Méndez Montenegro (1966-1970). Since 1978, the

opposition role has been carried out by the MLN. From the military's point of view, any one or combination of the three parties serves its purpose equally well.

3. In 1952, the party adopted the name Guatemalan Party of Labor (Partido Guatemalteco del Trabajo; PGT), which it has continued to use.

4. In May 1980, a militant faction of the party denounced the Central Committee for disavowing any responsibility for the March 22 assassination of Colonel Máximo Zepeda Martínez, who fought against leftist guerrillas in the 1960s, or the murder of Alberto Habie Mishaan, business leader and president of the influential Association of Agricultural, Trade, Industrial, and Financial Chambers (CACIF).

5. The concept of "polarization" as used by Leo Kuper is especially appropriate to the situation in Guatemala (Kuper, 1977). In its most extreme form, the state of polarization is one in which there is no longer the possibility of understanding, dialogue, or the adjustment of interests between mutually exclusive hostile camps. Violence becomes endemic, going beyond the interrogations, tortures, terrorism, and counterterrorism of which assassination is a part. Through premeditated and involuntary action and reaction, violence moves to higher levels of destruction through escalating cycles of polarization.

6. As a condition for Herrera's release, the EGP demanded the publication of his activities as Government Minister with details concerning kidnappings, assassinations, and torture of "revolutionary" elements.

7. See, for example, the special issue of the University of San Carlos Review dedicated to Castañeda, *Oliverio Castañeda de León: Homenaje* (University of San Carlos Review, 1978).

8. Colóm Argueta survived an earlier assassination attempt in March 1976. A former popular mayor of Guatemala City (1970-1974), he was considered by many to be the best hope of the combined opposition to lead a future centrist government. An outspoken critic of what he termed the government's "selective repression," Colóm reportedly stated in an interview shortly before his murder that "I've been told that my head is the price for FUR's registration" (Latin America Political Report, 1979).

9. The Guatemalan Bottling Plant Union is a prime example of union repression. After gaining recognition in February 1978, the union became a leader in the trade union movement. Since then, at least four union officials, including two secretary generals, and eleven workers have been assassinated, while others have chosen exile after receiving repeated death threats. The company's personnel chief and security head were assassinated by leftist groups in 1980.

10. The university continues to publish a weekly newspaper, *7 Días en la USAC.* However, since late 1980 it has been devoid of political content, apparently a victim of voluntary censorship through intimidation.

11. AI's report also asserts that no evidence has been found to support the government claims that "death squads" exist independently of the regular security services. According to a former press representative of the Ministry of the Interior, Guatemala's death lists are prepared from the records of Military Intelligence and the National Police, and approved at meetings held at the National Palace. Amnesty's evidence indicates a pattern of selective repression. Targets for extreme governmental violence tend to be selected from "grassroots organizations outside official control" (Amnesty International, 1981). For its part, the Guatemalan government has described AI's report as "biased, ridiculous and childish." A presidential spokesman said that AI has been trying to discredit the Guatemalan government for years with "false news and biased statements," and in doing so has become "a spokesman of international communism" (El Imparcial, 1981a).

12. For a discussion of additional factors that have contributed to the predominance of the right in Guatemala, see Millett (1980).

REFERENCES

ADAMS, R. N. (1970) Crucifixion by Power. Austin: Univ. of Texas Press.
AGUILERA PERALTA, G. (1979) Violencia y Contraviolencia. Guatemala: Editorial Universitaria.
Amnesty International (1981) Guatemala: A Government Program of Political Murder. London: Amnesty International.
——— (1979) "Memorandum to the government of Guatemala, 10 to 15 August." London: Mimeograph.
——— (1976) Guatemala. London: Amnesty International.
de BARRIOS KLEE, E. R. (1979) "En Guatemala." 7 Días en la USAC (February 26): 8.
BOOTH, J. A. (1980) "A Guatemalan nightmare: levels of political violence, 1966-1972." J. of Interamerican Studies and World Affairs 22 (May): 195-223.
BURTON, A. (1975) Urban Terrorism: Theory, Practice and Response. New York: Free Press.
DICKEY, C. (1981) "Haig's emissary, in Guatemala, discounts charges of rights abuse." Washington Post (May 14): 16.
GONZALES, C. (1979) "Revolution: the ways to it." World Marxist Rev. (October): 57-60.
GORDON, M. (1971) "A case history of U.S. subversion: Guatemala, 1954." Science and Society 35 (Summer): 129-155.
GOTT, R. (1970) Guerrilla Movements in Latin America. New York: Doubleday.
HAVENS, M. C., C. LEIDEN and K. M. SCHMITT (1977) Assassinations and Terrorism: Their Modern Dimensions. Manchaca: Sterling Swift.
HOGE, W. (1981) "Repression increases in Guatemala as U.S. tries to improve relations." New York Times (May 3): 20.
El Imparcial [Guatemala City] (1981a) February 20: 1.
——— (1981b) April 4: 1.
——— (1980) March 28: 7.
——— (1978) October 5: 1.
——— (1977) June 23: 4.
——— (1976a) May 18: 1.
——— (1976b) May 22: 6.
——— (1975) August 6: 1.
JOHNSON, K. F. (1973) "On the Guatemalan political violence." Politics and Society (Fall): 55-82.
JONAS, S. and D. TOBIS [eds.] (1974) Guatemala. Berkeley, CA: North American Congress on Latin America.
KUPER, L. (1977) The Pity of It All: Polarisation of Racial and Ethnic Relations. Minneapolis: Univ. of Minnesota Press.
LAQUER, W. (1977) Terrorism: A Study of National and International Political Violence. Boston: Little, Brown.
Latin America Political Report [London] (1979) March 30: 6.
LUHAN, J. M. (1981) "The next El Salvador." The New Republic 184 (April 11): 23-25.
MARTINEZ PELAEZ, S. (1976) La Patria del Criollo. San José: Editorial Universitaria Centroamericana.
MENTON, S., J. N. GOODSELL and S. JONAS (1973) Ad Hoc Committee on Guatemala. Gainesville, FL: Latin American Studies Association.
MICKLIN, M. (1969) "Urbanization, technology, and traditional values in Guatemala: some consequences of a changing social structure." Social Forces 47 (June): 438-446.

MILLETT, R. (1980) "Central American paralysis." Foreign Policy 39 (Summer): 99-117.

New York Times (1980) January 28: 4.

——— (1979) December 6: 9.

——— (1978) February 23: 14.

OLSON, S. (1981) "In Guatemala, under foot." New York Times (April 8): 27.

Prensa Libre [Guatemala City] (1981) March 31: 4.

——— (1980a) April 18: 1.

——— (1980b) March 7: 2.

——— (1979) May 5: 1.

——— (1977) June 9: 3.

RIDING, A. (1979) "Guatemala opening new lands, but best goes to the rich." New York Times (April 5): 5.

SCHMITT, K. M. (1969) "Assassination in Latin America," in J. F. Kirkham et al. (eds.) Assassination and Political Violence: A Report to the National Commission on the Causes and Prevention of Violence. Washington, DC: U.S. Government Printing Office.

SCHNEIDER, R. M. (1958) Communism in Guatemala, 1944-1954. New York: Praeger.

7 Días en la USAC [Guatemala City] (1980a) March 17: 1.

——— (1980b) April 21: 3.

——— (1980c) May 26: 2.

——— (1979) May 7: 8.

TAYLOR, P. B., Jr. (1956) "Guatemalan affair: a critique of U.S. foreign policy." Amer. Pol. Sci. Rev. 50 (Summer): 787-806.

TORRES RIVAS, E. (1979) "Vida y muerte en Guatemala: reflexiones sobre la violencia." 7 Días en la USAC (October 20): 6.

University of San Carlos Review (1979) Oliverio Castañeda de León: Homenaje. Guatemala: University of San Carlos.

Update Latin America [Washington] (1981) March/April: 5.

Washington Report on the Hemisphere (1981) April 7: 1.

——— (1980) November 11: 8.

Daniel L. Premo is Associate Professor of Political Science and History at Washington College. He has been a regular contributor to the Yearbook on International Communist Affairs *since 1973 and is currently writing a monograph on contemporary Colombian politics.*

JAMES L. TIGNER
Department of History
University of Nevada
Reno, Nevada

JAPANESE IMMIGRATION INTO LATIN AMERICA
A Survey

The early relations of Latin America and Japan, representing a distinct chapter in the discovery of East Asia by the West, are attributable to the initial thrust of West European expansion beginning in the late fifteenth century, led by Portugal and Spain. Magellan claimed the Philippines for Spain in 1521, and following the conquest of Mexico, and later Peru, Spain sought to establish a trans-Pacific route for communication and commerce. The conquest of the Philippines, carried on from 1565 to 1571 under the leadership of Miguel López de Legaspi, foreshadowed the beginning of the Manila-Acapulco trade, which was subsequently carried on until 1815. In 1606 there were 3,000 Japanese colonists in Manila, and 15,000 in Dilao, which included Manila. Some Japanese, as well as Chinese, served as crew members on the Spanish galleons, and it is probable that these Japanese were the first in recorded history to reach the Americas (Ishii, 1937: 88; Bradley, 1942: 11; Meskill et al., 1971: 74-86; Schurz, 1939: 99-128).

Portuguese and Spanish vessels reached Japan in the period 1542-1580, but it was not until 1592 that the first formal contact occurred between the Spanish and Japanese at Manila. The Shogun of Japan, Tokugawa Iyeyasu, desired Western technology and trade, but Japan was not important to Spain at that time, which was then seeking the islands of Rica de Oro and Rico de Plata. Japanese missions were dispatched to New Spain to

Journal of Interamerican Studies and World Affairs, Vol. 23 No. 4, November 1981 457-482

promote trade with the Spanish colony, but little was achieved, partly because the economic and commercial life in the Philippines suffered from the restrictions imposed by the severe mercantilist policy of the mother country (Stephens and Bolton, 1917: 467-480; Haring, 1947: 79; Dixon, 1911: 211-247).

The Tokugawa Shogunate, soon perceiving the menace of Western imperialism and the potential impact of Christianity on the stability of the state, gradually applied a policy of antiforeignism and seclusion, beginning in 1612. From 1638 to 1868, Japanese leaving the country did so on the pain of death, and the same penalty applied to any Japanese who, having left, returned. The Dutch alone among the Western powers enjoyed trading privileges with the Japanese between 1638 and 1854. Thus, for more than two centuries, Japanese contacts with the New World remained infrequent and largely accidental (Sansom, 1950: 171-180, 1963: 44; Schurz, 1939: 110; Davis, 1872: 353-360).

The expedition of Commodore Matthew C. Perry was instrumental in reestablishing Japan's relations with the West. And following the restoration in 1868 of the Meiji Emperor, Mitsuhito, Japanese were encouraged to seek knowledge throughout the world. Emigration from Japan was legalized in 1885 as the government became concerned about the implications of population increase on available resources (Wilcox, 1931: 618; Beckman, 1962: 244-275; Yoshida, 1909: 157-167).

The first phase of emigration—the Meiji era, from 1868 to 1912—started in 1885, when 945 persons left Japan for Hawaii. These were contract immigrants, hired to work on sugar plantations and in sugar mills for a period of three years. Transportation expenses were paid by the employers. While emigration to the United States began about the same time, these immigrants were classified as "free immigrants" who paid their own passage. Laws in the United States prevented the entry of contract immigrants. Canada ranked third in the number of emigrants received in the period prior to 1900, followed by Australia, Mexico, Peru, New Caledonia, and the Fiji Islands (Japan, Ministry of Foreign Affairs, 1951: 2).[1]

The second phase of Japanese emigration—the Taisho era, from 1912 to 1926—began near the close of the first decade of the present century, following passage of restrictive legislation on Asian immigration to the United States, Mexico, Hawaii, Canada, Australia, and South Africa. In this period, new emigration outlets were sought. The most notable developments in this phase were the shift in destinations of the majority of Japanese emigrants from North America to Latin America, and the spectacular rise of Brazil and Peru as the leading immigration countries for Japanese in the Western Hemisphere (Normano, 1938: 7; Vieira, 1973: 40-41).

The third phase of Japanese emigration—the Showa era (1926-?)—witnessed the peak in Japanese emigration to Latin America in the late 1920s and early 1930s, followed by a decline in the mid-1930s. Although Japanese immigrants had been generally well received in Latin America, and quickly gained a reputation for honesty, diligence, and respect for the law, their position was prejudiced by the emergence of Japan as an imperialist nation. Moreover, by the 1930s the failure of the Japanese to assimilate was evident, and while highly regarded as individuals, their group-exclusiveness aroused suspicion. To these fears and suspicions were added economic rivalry, Japan's trade policies, and the growth of nationalism in Latin America. The combination of these factors led to a drastic curtailment of Japanese migration to the main immigration countries of Brazil and Peru in 1934 and 1936, respectively. Thus, the direction of Japanese emigration changed to East Asia, particularly to Manchuria and China Proper.

In summary, the total number of Japanese residents abroad in 1940 stood at 1,718,258. Of this number, 1,229,016 or 71% were located in Asia. Among the balance of 489,242, a total of 234, 574 resided in Latin American countries (Japan, Ministry of Foreign Affairs, 1951: 5; Normano and Gerbi, 1943: 11; Japan, Colonial Ministry, 1937: Table 14, 18-20; Taeuber, 1958: 199; Tigner, 1955: 1-656).

From the time of their independence early in the nineteenth century until the 1930s, it was the common policy of Latin American countries to foster immigration, which included Orientals. The abolition of the African slave trade gave rise to the Chinese coolie traffic, which began with the introduction of 800

Chinese to Cuba in 1847; by 1874, when the traffic was suppressed, 114,081 had been admitted to the island. Between 1849 and 1874 some 87,000 entered Peru to work on coastal sugar plantations, in the guano deposits, and railroad construction projects. Chinese entered Mexico to labor on the henequen and sugar cane plantations, and the number there attained a total of almost 19,000 persons. By the 1890s, Chinese emigration to Latin America had begun to decline steeply in most areas because of rising immigration restrictions. The addiction of some Chinese to opium, and their tendency to mingle with the native populations, producing large numbers of unattended offspring, created disturbing social problems. Moreover, the competition they offered in small business and the trades engendered progressive hostility and resulting anti-Chinese movements. After witnessing the extraordinary progress of Japan's modernization and westernization by the end of the century, the Latin Americans concluded that East Asia was composed of different peoples, and the Japanese were encouraged to emigrate on the assumption that they might prove superior to the Chinese. Consequently, after the turn of the century Chinese immigration was largely superseded by that cf the Japanese (Bradley, 1942: 46-50, 113; Paz Soldán y Unanue, 1891: 73-77; García, 1909: 23; Cosía Villegas, 1957: 167; MacNair, 1935: 96-100; Lubbock, 1935: 24-35; Stewart, 1951).

When the Japanese first became interested in Latin America as a field for emigration, their attention was centered on the Pacific coast, mainly Mexico and Peru, where immigration began in 1898 and 1899, respectively. But the great impetus to Japanese emigration came with World War I, for emigration from Europe declined sharply and agricultural workers were in great demand, especially in Brazil. Because of these circumstances, the mechanics of emigration were centralized in Japan for more efficient operation. Prior to the war, emigration had been carried on by several emigration and colonization companies. To achieve more effective operation, the Japanese government in 1917 sponsored the merger of these firms into the Overseas Development Company, Ltd. (Kaigai Kogyo Kabushiki Kaisha), although some of the firms retained their original names. The Nippon Yusen Kaisha and the Osaka Shosen Kaisha, both government-subsidized steamship companies, carried out the overseas transportation of emigrants to the Western Hemisphere (Japan, Ministry of Foreign Affairs, 1951: 3).[2]

Efforts were made coincidentally to organize emigration more efficiently on the local and prefectural levels. In 1915, Overseas Societies (Kaigai Kyokai) were established in the prefectures of Hiroshima and Kumamoto; they were followed by similar societies in other prefectures in 1918. The Japanese government, beset by economic crises and a growing unemployable population after World War I, vigorously pushed overseas migration. The Overseas Emigration Societies Act of 1927 provided for the establishment of Emigration Cooperative Societies (Kaigai Iju Kumiai) along the lines of traditional Japanese guilds. The purpose of these organizations was to form groups with spiritual as well as economic bonds for joint emigration. In 1927, the Kobe Emigration Center was opened and the newly designated, so-called farm settlers were sent abroad. Unlike the worker-settlers who had previously been sent abroad, these farm settlers were supposed to buy land and develop their own farms. The Federation of Emigration Cooperatives, a central organization for emigration administration, was established to facilitate emigration (Normano and Gerbi, 1943: 24, 30; Ohara, 1967: 12-13).[3]

Beginning in 1921, the Overseas Development Company received direct financial assistance from the Japanese government. This was an annual subsidy of from 100,000 to 250,000 *yen,* plus a contribution amounting to the cost of passage for emigrants. In the period from 1923 to 1933, the peak of the Brazilian traffic, government subsidies totaled 16,364,000 yen. Commencing in 1923, the transportation of individual emigrants was subsidized up to 60%, and after 1930-1931 it was subsidized in full. Additionally, the emigrant was given a travel allowance of 50 yen. Normally this applied to "free immigrants" who went to Peru after contract immigration was abolished there in 1923, as well as to "free immigrants" and "contract immigrants," who migrated to Brazil and other Latin American countries through 1940. By 1934, the government subsidy averaged 1300-1400 yen per family. Few women migrated to Latin America, except to Brazil, until this aid was given (Bradley, 1942: 54-55; Japan, Ministry of Foreign Affairs, 1951: 4).

TABLE 1
Remittances Sent to Japan in 1937 by Japanese Immigrants in Latin American Countries

COUNTRY	YEN
Brazil	1,730,372
Peru	911,134
Mexico	302,139
Argentina	199,557
Chile	18,023
Panama	11,815
Colombia	11,300
Cuba	8,769
Bolivia	1,939
Uruguay	1,380
Venezuela	750
TOTAL	3,197,178

NOTE: One yen, valued at about $1.00 in the early Meiji period, dropped to $.50 in the first decade of the present century, and to $.25 by 1941.

Immigrants sent private remittances to the homeland for a variety of purposes, including assistance to family members or relatives, donations, contributions, loans, repayments of debt, and investments. The following data record the amount of remittances sent to Japan in 1937, a representative year, by Japanese immigrants in Latin American countries (Japan, Ministry of Foreign Affairs, 1937: Table 1).[4]

Organized Japanese emigration to Latin America began in 1898 and continued until interrupted by World War II. The majority of some 235,000 Japanese who emigrated there during this period were poor farmers under contract to work in agriculture in Mexico, Peru, and Brazil. Brazil alone received almost 190,000 of these immigrants. Contracts ranged from six months to three years in duration.

In the aftermath of the short-lived Japanese colony of Esquintla, Chiapas in 1898, a program of contract immigration acceptable to Mexico and Japan was adopted in 1902, and the first group of workers recruited for the project reached Mexico the following year. Immigrants entering Mexico from 1903 to 1907 were assigned to coal mines in the state of Coahuila, sugar plantations in Oaxaca, and several railroad construction projects (Cortés, 1974: 110-111, 124-127; González Navarro, 1960: 77; Unno, 1941: 179-183).

These experiments proved to be dismal failures, comparable to the first decade of the program in Peru. More than one-third of the plantation workers died from disease in the first year, and the remainder dispersed. Less than half of the coal miners fulfilled their contracts, as a result of disease and the frequency of mining accidents. In summary, about 15,000 Japanese migrated to Mexico prior to 1941; today less than 4,000 including descendants, remain there. Most of the Japanese are located in the Federal District and the states of Sonora, Coahuila, Chihuahua, Sinaloa, Veracruz, and Jalisco. Only 24 Japanese immigrants entered Mexico in the period from 1951 to 1970 (Japan, Colonial Ministry, 1937: 18-20; Okinawa, G.R.I., 1952: 1, 3-5; Okinawa, Prefectural Office, 1939b: 61, Table 43; Japan, Emigration Service, 1971: 31-32).

Economic progress among the Japanese in Mexico has never been sustained or vigorous, owing to the revolution and its aftermath, anti-Asiatic disorders and discriminatory legislation, the world economic depression, and the forced evacuation of Japanese from sites of established residence during World War II. Most Japanese are engaged in small business enterprises, and the few in agriculture are principally truck gardeners or farm laborers. The largest Japanese agricultural community, including Okinawans, developed near Mexicali in the 1920s, when cotton cultivation was especially profitable (Barnhart, 1962a: 297-332; Izawa, 1971: 206-210).[5]

The assimilation of the Japanese in Mexico, both racially and culturally, is farther advanced than elsewhere in Latin America, except in Bolivia. This is explained by the small size of the colony and the high proportion (60%) of Japanese who have taken Mexican wives. The increasing pace of intermarriage among *Nisei* (born in Mexico) of both sexes seems to insure that the *Sansei* (third generation) will eventually lose the characteristics of Japanese nationality and spirit.

The countries of Central America and the Caribbean were among the first to impose restrictions on Asiatic immigration, initially concerning the Chinese, and later the Japanese: Costa

Rica in 1896, Guatemala in 1909. Others followed, and by the early 1930s all of the countries in the region had on their statute books either general or racially discriminatory limitations, or absolute prohibitions, on Japanese immigration. In 1936, there were 368 Japanese in Panama, 2 in Honduras, 7 in El Salvador, and 597 in Cuba (Bradley, 1942: 65, 112; Japan, Colonial Ministry, 1937: Table 14; Japan, Ministry of Foreign Affairs, 1951: 2-3).

During World War II, all five Central American countries and Panama sent Japanese nationals to the United States for internment, suspended constitutional guarantees of Axis nationals, froze funds, and "blacklisted" individuals and firms. In the postwar years, Japanese emigration to the region virtually ceased. In general, it may be concluded that Japan's relations with the Central American nations have been predominantly economic in character. Less than 2000 Japanese are located in Central America and the Caribbean region today, chiefly in Panama, Cuba, and the Dominican Republic (Gardiner, 1972: 15-47; Barnhart, 1962a: 297-332; Ohara, 1967: 15).[6]

The countries of northern South America—Venezuela, Colombia and Ecuador—raised similar barriers to Asiatic immigration, and few Chinese or Japanese have migrated there. However, efforts were made by Tokyo to introduce immigrants and to establish a colonization project. In 1915, the government of Japan, then headed by Okuma Shigenobu, sought to arrange through agreement with the government of Ecuador for the right of residence and property ownership there for Japanese citizens. The agreement was concluded, but only eight Japanese had established residence there by 1939, thanks to progressively stringent barriers to Asian immigration; as late as 1963, Ecuador still had only nine Japanese residents.

An agreement was made by the governments of Japan and Colombia in 1929 authorizing the Overseas Development Company, Ltd. (KKKK) of Japan to acquire 204 hectares of land near Cali. Small groups of families were introduced to grow vegetables for local markets, and in 1936 the Japanese population stood at 215. Japanese and their descendants numbered 600 in 1951, and by the late 1960s the total had risen to an estimated 1,000. Venezuela had 10 Japanese residents in 1936, 30 in 1951, and in the period from 1952 to 1965, 32 immigrants were introduced there. By the late 1960s, the Japanese and their descendants totaled some 300 persons (Bradley, 1942: 63-64; Japan, Ministry of Foreign Affairs, 1951: 9; Japan, Office of the Prime Minister, 1964: 3; Japan, Colonial Ministry, 1937: Table 14; Ohara, 1967: 15-17; Barnhart, 1962a: 297-332).[7]

Peru, in 1877, was first among the Latin American republics to establish diplomatic relations with the Japanese Empire. In 1898, the Peruvian government issued a decree authorizing the immigration of contract laborers, and a group arrived the next year. Manual labor at sugar plantations and mills was the principal work. The net income of the immigrants proved to be much less than expected, and many were mistreated by plantation owners and managers. Within a year after arriving in Peru, the majority had migrated to the cities, notably Lima and Callao.

Japanese immigration was brought almost to a standstill by the Peruvian Supreme Decree of 1936. At the close of 1941, when immigration was halted completely by World War II, the total number of Japanese immigrants was approximately 29,000, with one-third originating from the island of Okinawa (Markham, 1892: 376; Irie, 1951: 656-659; Sacurai, 1935: 40, 1940: 116-117; Japan, Colonial Ministry, 1937: Table 14; Gardiner, 1975; Tigner, 1978: 20-44).[8]

The latent antagonism toward the Japanese erupted in mob attacks on them and their property in Lima and Callao in 1940. During the course of the war, some 1800 Japanese (one-half of whom were Ryukyuans) were sent to the United States and held in controlled camps; only 800 have been readmitted to Peru since 1945 (Emmerson, 1977: 40-47, 56; Barnhart, 1962b: 169-178).[9]

Approximately 95% of the Japanese are located in the Lima Department, the remainder being mainly in the departments of Libertad, Ancash, Junín, Ica, and Arequipa. Like most Peruvians, still fewer Japanese have been attracted to the frontier life in the *montaña*, although several attempts have been made to establish colonies there. The present Japanese *(naichi-jin)* population in Peru is estimated to total 48,000, 40% of which is from the Ryukyus. Most are owners or operators of small shops such as bars, cafés, grocery stores, bakeries, and bazaars. Since the war, about 500 households have moved into the fertile valleys near

Lima to grow cotton (Okinawa, G.R.I., 1961: 126; Japan, Emigration Service, 1966: 1-34, 1971: 31-32, 1972: 35-36).[10]

Although the Japanese have gained notable economic success in Peru and have made a significant contribution to the Peruvian economy, the prospects for immigration in the foreseeable future appear negligible. Anti-Japanese feeling can be attributed to the relatively small area of cultivable land and the economic rivalry produced by keen competition in the two major urban centers, the fear of Japanese imperialism and the unfavorable balance of trade with Japan prior to World War II, the stigma of Chinese immigration, World War II, and the resistance of the Japanese to racial and cultural assimilation.

The introduction of Japanese into Bolivia coincided with Peruvian immigration, as a large proportion of the first groups fled from the plantations and moved into the forests of Eastern Bolivia to work as rubber gatherers. A few migrated there under contract during the "Rubber Boom" (1911-1912), but most were remigrants from Peru or were "summoned" by friends or relatives. About 500 migrated to Bolivia between 1900 and 1941, and this has been augmented by an estimated 4000 since 1945. The current Japanese population, including descendants, totals approximately 6000, with 3600 (60%) Ryukyuans, and is distributed mainly in La Paz, Riberalta, Santa Cruz, and Trinidad. The outstanding characteristics of their occupational pattern are the dominance of urban pursuits among the inhabitants of the Altiplano, and the high proportion of farmers among those living in the Oriente (Tigner, 1963: 206-229; Japan, Colonial Ministry, 1937: Table 14; Ohara, 1967: 15-17; Barnhart, 1962a: 297-332).

The status of Naichi-jin and Ryukyuans was affected only slightly by World War II. Corresponding to events in Peru and Central America, some Japanese were deported to the United States for internment during the war. Sent to controlled camps in Crystal City, Texas, 28 Japanese were allowed to return to Bolivia at the end of the war.[11]

The assimilation of Japanese has progressed farther in Bolivia than in any other of the Latin American states. This is demonstrated impressively by the extent of intermarriage. Excluding postwar immigrants, about 85% of the *Issei* (born in Japan) married Bolivian women, with an even higher percentage among the second generation. Cultural assimilation is similarly advanced, and the general acceptance of the Japanese is perhaps unequalled on the continent. The conclusion of a Migration Agreement in 1956, as well as the distribution of free land and governmental assistance to Japanese and Ryukyuans in the Santa Cruz region since 1953, testify to this attitude.

Japanese immigration in Chile has been insignificant, although a diplomatic mission was established in 1911 and the Japanese government thereafter encouraged emigration. About 500 Japanese entered Chile during the period 1903-1925, but in the latter year Japanese were excluded from the quotas (Wilcox, 1931: 938; Japan, Colonial Ministry, 1937: Table 14).

Chile severed relations with the Axis powers in January 1943, and the Japanese were almost immediately affected. Fifty Japanese were evacuated from the coastal zone, all branches of Japanese firms were closed, and although private concerns owned by resident Japanese were permitted to function, they were put on the "black list." The Japanese who had been evacuated from the coast were allowed to return to their homes soon after the cessation of hostilities in 1945. Thirty Nisei were in Japan at the outbreak of the war, and after its close, eight were recalled by their families, since Chilean law allowed those born in the country to reenter.

The major factor limiting Japanese settlement in Chile prior to 1925 was the lack of opportunity in agriculture: the absence of labor contracts and the great cost and scarcity of productive farm land. Currently, less than 200 Japanese of the first generation remain in Chile, and the total population falls between 900 and 1000. Intermarriage is rare. Most of the Japanese have small shops in Santiago and its suburbs, and the few in agriculture have nurseries or truck gardens. Eleven Japanese migrated to Chile in 1952-1965 (Ohara, 1967: 16; Rippy, 1949: 63; Barnhart, 1962a: 297-332).

The majority of some 2000 Japanese who had settled in Argentina prior to 1920 were immigrants who had reemigrated from either Brazil or Peru. Contract immigration was never operative in Argentina, and after 1918 most of the immigrants were "summoned" by friends or relatives in residence there. The early migrants worked in a variety of occupations as unskilled laborers, but beginning in 1918 they became interested in the laundry business, to which was subsequently added a dry cleaning section. The operation of *tintorerias* is the single largest occupation of the Japanese in Argentina, with truck gardening in second place. An estimated 4,400 had entered the country by 1941. The current Japanese population in Argentina is about 18,000, of which 12,000 (65%) are Ryukyuans. These figures include 5,084 immigrants since 1945. Of the total number, about 90% is located in the city of Buenos Aires and its suburbs. Lesser groups are found in Rosario, Córdoba, Tucumán, Resistencia, Santa Fe, and Corrientes (Tigner, 1967: 203-224; Gashu, 1951: 1; Japan, Colonial Ministry, 1937: Table 14; Okinawa, Prefectural Office, 1939a: 6; Yamamoto, 1932: 179; Japan, Ministry of Foreign Affairs, 1949: 42; Ohara, 1967: 15-17; Japan, Emigration Service, 1971: 31-32; Barnhart, 1962a: 297-332).

The processes of assimilation and acculturation among the Japanese are remarkably advanced in Argentina. This can be attributed to several factors: (1) government-subsidized contract immigration was not carried on there; wives or "picture brides" were "called" at the "caller's" expense, and the number was consequently limited; (2) widespread conditions have favored urbanization as opposed to resettlement in rural areas, which predisposes Japanese immigrants to form cluster settlements.

Japanese residents of Argentina suffered little more than inconvenience during World War II because of the pro-Axis sympathies of the Argentine government. Argentina's declaration of war against Japan and Germany occurred in March 1945, and soon thereafter the government decreed that Japanese and Germans were to be known officially as "foreigners under vigilance." The publication of three Japanese-language newspapers was suspended, and Japanese-operated schools and organizations were closed. All restrictions were raised in 1947. No Japanese or Ryukyuans were arrested or relocated or suffered any loss of property.

Paraguay's immigration law of 1903 specifically banned persons of the "yellow race." This restriction was lifted in 1924, but there was no organized immigration of Orientals there until 1935, when the Japanese colony of La Colmena was established. This was the first of a series of colonies developed cooperatively by the Japanese and Paraguayan governments and a private Japanese colonization assertion. La Colmena, located 81 miles southeast of Asunción, was planned as an agrarian community in which immigrant families were to acquire, develop, and occupy relatively large parcels of land.

Between 1936 and 1941, 138 families comprising 844 persons formed the original colony. The colonists were recruited mainly from the northern and central part of Japan, and in addition, 12 Japanese families were brought from the frontier regions in southern Brazil and distributed throughout the colony. Cotton has been the dominant crop in acreage and value; however, a multicrop system was adopted in an effort to minimize the risks of monoculture. Japan's interest in Paraguay was related in part to changes of immigration policy in Brazil. In 1934 Brazil, the principal recipient of Japanese emigration in Latin America, set strict quotas on Oriental immigration, and Japan was compelled to seek other outlets for her surplus population (Ohara, 1967: 15-17; Japan, Office of the Prime Minister, 1964: 43; Fretz, 1962: 54-56; Stewart, 1967: 79-176; Barnhart, 1962a: 297-332).[12]

World War II struck in the Pacific before a second colony could be established, and it was not until 1955 that the second colony, Frederico Cháves, was founded. The third and fourth colonies, Fram and Pedro Juan Caballero, respectively, were organized in 1956. A migration agreement was concluded with Paraguay in 1959, which provided for a quota of 85,000 Japanese immigrants over a 30-year period. In 1952-1965, 6,358 Japanese emigrants were introduced to Paraguay; however, 94 families totaling 552 persons, have returned to Japan. In general, it appears that although the colonies have not attained the level of prosperity of Japanese colonies in Brazil, notably in São Paulo and Paraná, they do reflect a continuous, if modest, growth. The Japanese and their descendants in Paraguay are now estimated to total some 8,000 persons.

The Japanese presence in Brazil began in 1908, when the first group of 779 pioneer immigrants arrived in Santos aboard the *Kasato Maru*. Excluding the period from 1941 to 1950 (World War II and its immediate aftermath), the flow has been uninterrupted, but diminishing markedly since the early 1960s. Except for a few initial failures in São Paulo and the colonization projects in the Amazon region, it has been eminently successful. The need for workers on coffee *fazendas* in the state of São Paulo was largely responsible for the introduction of Japanese through 1941, whereas in the postwar era immigrants with technical or more specialized education backgrounds are found together with agriculturists (Rocha Nogueira, 1973: 37-69, 107-149; Koyama, 1949: 428; Saito, 1976: 183-197; Neiva, 1945: 22-25; Carneiro, 1950: 61; Sims, 1972: 246-265; Tanaka, 1947: 2-21; de Mello Carvalho, 1940: 725).

Prior to World War I, the majority of Japanese immigrants were contract laborers; the decade from 1915 to 1925 saw efforts to establish agricultural colonies; and following 1925, Japanese immigration and resettlement involved governmental organization and direction and capital migration. The government of São Paulo state subsidized the entry of Japanese immigrants until 1921; from 1925 onward, the Japanese government largely financed the emigration to Brazil.

The years from 1908 to 1925 were regarded as the experimental period, when some 40,000 Japanese were introduced to Brazil, most of whom were assigned to coffee plantations. Japanese emigration to Brazil received its first major impetus when the Overseas Development Company was established in 1917 with a capital of 9 million yen. The suspension of migration from Europe, resulting from the World War, provided further stimulus. Thanks to these developments, the number of Japanese immigrants increased from 165 in 1916 to 899 in 1917; to 5,522 in 1918; to 3,022 in 1919 (Koyama, 1949: 428; Yamamoto, 1927: 52-62; Japan, Ministry of Foreign Affairs, 1941: 179-180.[13]

The second phase, from 1925 to 1941, saw the crest of the flow, with 1933 being the peak year when 23,299 Japanese entered the country. Approximately 150,000 Japanese came during this period. While most were placed on the São Paulo coffee fazendas, lesser numbers formed agricultural settlements in Sãõ Paulo, Paraná, Mato Grosso, and Amazonas. After World War II the third phase, from 1951 to the present, began a period which has seen some 60,000 Japanese immigrants settle in Brazil (Saito, 1976: 184-185; Defontaines, 1938: 388; Okinawa, G.R.I., 1957: 4-7, 10; Japan, Ministry of Foreign Affairs, 1951: 3-4; Becu, 1943:

58-65; New York Times, 1942, 1945a; Barnhart, 1962a: 297-332).[14]

The total of 250,000 Japanese immigrants who entered the country between 1908 and 1975 has increased to an estimated 750,000, 10% of whom originated in the Ryukyu Islands. In 1958, a census carried out by the Japanese residents of Brazil to commemorate the 50th anniversary of immigration disclosed that at that time, of a total of 430,151 Japanese and their descendants (223,794 men; 206,357 women), 291,398 were Nisei, and 138,636 Issei, a ratio of 210 Nisei to 100 Issei. Within the current total of 750,000, it is estimated that about 75% are to be found in São Paulo state, 18% in Paraná, and lesser numbers in Mato Grosso, Minas Gerais, Goiás, Pará, Amazonas, Santa Catarina, Rio Grande do Sul, and Rio de Janeiro. Both Issei and Nisei in Brazil are still predominantly farmers: however, the Nisei and Sansei are being drawn in steadily increasing numbers to urban occupations (Hastings, 1969: 33-53; Saito, 1976: 185; Shiroma, 1959).

Although Brazil has received more Japanese immigrants than any other country in Latin America, their presence has not been accepted without incident. There were two major outbreaks of anti-Japanese sentiment in Brazil prior to World War II: the first in 1923-1924 and the second in 1933-1934, at which time the government of Brazil adopted the pattern on immigration quotas designed in fact (if not in theory) chiefly to restrict Japanese immigration.

Japanese immigration into Brazil was resumed in 1951; as noted, it gained momentum in the 1950s, but declined abruptly in the 1960s, owing mainly to the improvement of Japan's domestic economy. About one-fifth of the 60,000 Japanese immigrants who were introduced through 1975 came from the Ryukyu Islands. The postwar arrivals included technicians, "free immigrants," and colonists, who settled in an area designated by the Brazilian government under a fixed ratio. (A treaty of Migration and Settlement signed in 1960 became effective in 1963.)

Outwardly, except for language, the Japanese and their descendants have been well blended into the Brazilian scene. Growing trends in social mobility, industrialization, and urbanization contribute constantly to the process. However, the Issei generally and the Nisei and Sansei in rural areas, remain Japanese in spirit and loyalty, and consciously resist any racial and cultural losses. Mixed marriages among the Issei in Brazil are almost unknown, and less than 5% have become naturalized citizens. The failure of the Japanese to assimilate was brought clearly into focus by the *Shindo Remmei* (Way of the Subjects of the Emperor League) phenomenon which emerged during World War II. This movement was a manifestation of extreme nationalism directed toward the mass return-migration of all Japanese to the homeland at the conclusion of the war. After the War, it was used by racketeers within the colony as a means of economic exploitation of their countrymen who refused to accept the fact of Japan's defeat. Terrorist organizations were formed to assassinate the Issei who made a public admission that Japan had lost the war. The antagonism engendered by the Shindo Remmei movement was largely dissipated by the early 1960s; this doubtless influenced the ratification of the immigration agreement, mentioned previously, by the Brazilian Congress (Willems and Saito, 1947: 133-152; Tigner, 1961: 515-532; Hastings, 1969: 33-53: Vieira, 1973: 75-114; Sims, 1972: 246-265).[15]

After Japan regained sovereign status in 1952, the government gave high priority to the organization and implementation of an overseas emigration program. In 1953, an Emigration Section was established in the Ministry of Foreign Affairs; one year later the Federation of Japan Emigration Associations was organized and charged by the Ministry of Foreign Affairs with migrant recruitment, training, shipping, education, settlement assistance, travel loans, and subsidies. A Five Year Plan was adopted in 1958, which envisioned placing 100,000 emigrants in Latin America. In 1963 the Overseas Emigration Service was established to carry on research, disseminate information and advice, and to provide emigrants with lectures and other training activities. Funds were supplied by the government, private sources, and banks in the United States. Despite these efforts, emigration to Latin America declined after 1960. Although a population of more than 100 million was still seen as too large for the small territory of Japan, the economic growth of the country by the 1960s led to an acute shortage of labor, and it became counterproductive to send overseas on a large scale labor badly needed by the domestic economy. Concurrently, economic growth raised the Japanese standard of living to a level that made emigration, with all of its uncertainties, no longer attractive. Under these circumstances, the idea of emigration has changed. Before World War II, emigration tended to be a partial solution for Japan's surplus population; it is now regarded as an ambitious project for independent, adventurous people who are challenged by new environments. The Japanese government still maintains an active role in the administration of emigration activities, but offers little more than travel loans, information about possible host countries, and educational and health assistance (Ohara, 1967: 17-20; New York Times, 1977).

It should be mentioned that while the decrease in the number of emigrants is largely explained by Japan's expanding economy and unprecedented prosperity, conditions in Latin America have also discouraged immigration. Economic instability caused by rampant inflation, political upheavals, the rapid population increase, the low standard of living in rural districts and low wages of farm workers, together with more selective immigration policies, have also been a deterrent.

Emigration from the Ryukyu Islands to Latin America was a major problem of the Ryukyuan government and the United States Civil Administration of the Ryukyu Islands during the U.S. occupation of the Ryukyus from 1945 to 1972. Being an economically deficit area and suffering from extreme population pressure, a large proportion of the population applied for emigration to Latin America in the aftermath of World War II. In response to these circumstances, a survey was made of Ryukyuan communities in Latin America by the author, and possibilities for further settlement were explored. Bolivia was selected for the first experiment; in 1953, the Bolivian government approved a 10-year program for the settlement of Ryukyuan immigrant farmers in the Santa Cruz region. This included the granting of 125,000 acres of free land, and assistance by the Bolivian Development Corporation. The program was coordinated with the U.S. Department of State, and funds were supplied by the Foreign Operations Administration and the Department of the Army. Since then, the Japanese government has become involved and the project has steadily expanded.

The chief objectives and motives of the emigration policy of Japan after the Meiji Restoration (1868) and prior to World War II fall into three groups: (1) relief of population pressure; (2) economic expansion; (3) political strategy. Group one had general and consistent application, whereas groups two and three varied in accordance with time and place. In Latin America, the policy was largely based upon the three groups in combination, with perhaps less emphasis on the third. A few remarks should be made about group one, omitting groups two and three, which are beyond the scope of this article.

After World War I, Japan became seriously concerned about the specter of overpopulation, for the birthrate stood at 36.2 per thousand in 1920 and remained above 34 per thousand for the next few years. In view of the progressive increase in both population and the volume of food imports in a period when the national economy was no longer expanding, anxiety over the future of the population was natural. The solution to overpopulation faced barriers of considerable magnitude. First, Japan rejected biological methods of dealing with the problem, for they conflicted with religious and social ideas (the family system) and with the mercantilist policies of the state. A large population was considered essential for a strong state. Second, the Japanese are a "stay-at-home" people; although they went abroad, there was a general tendency for them to return eventually. Third, the world was already divided, and no country—not even one as vast and underpopulated as Brazil—would accept millions of Japanese immigrants. A corollary to the problem was the general imposition of immigration restrictions. Japanese immigration was less restricted in Asia, but that area was already overpopulated. Because of the limited number of immigration outlets available to the Japanese, the government turned to industrialization as a means of coping with population increase. This afforded a means of relieving congestion in rural areas, and provided a way to increase the food supply through industrial exports. In light of these circumstances, emigration and colonization became a secondary means of dealing with the problem of overpopulation. It is also clear that the Japanese never left their country in sufficient numbers to produce any but the most minimal response to the problems of a growing population.

What Japan gained most from emigration to Latin America came under the heading of morale. In periods of economic depression and national disasters—e.g., the collapse of the sugar market in the 1920s and its impact on the industry in the Ryukyus, destruction from typhoons, the earthquake of 1923, the agricultural depression of the 1930s, the aftermath of the devastation of World War II—the emigration process aided the rehabilitation of those who suffered most desperately. A family reduced to poverty could look forward to improving its economic status by emigrating as a group or by sending abroad its sons who, because of loyalty to the family, could be relied upon to remit most of their earnings. In this way, also, emigration has functioned as a mechanism whereby the frustrated younger generation could satisfy personal ambition.

An appraisal of Japanese immigration in the main host countries of Latin America must stress the negative character of their assimilation, both racially and culturally. Although the bases for their resistance to assimilation are diverse and complex, the following topics are useful in seeking an explanation: (1) nationalistic education; (2) the concepts of temporary immigration and dual nationality; (3) the Japanese "association"; (4) Japanese-language newspapers and periodicals; (5) the patriarchal structure of the Japanese family; (6) geographical isolation.

Apart from nonassimilation, it is evident that the Japanese have made an important contribution to the solution of the labor problem and the advancement of the national economies in the principal countries of immigration, Brazil and Peru. The Japanese immigrant entering Brazil as a contract laborer quickly became an independent proprietor of land, which he bought, rented, or sharecropped. In so doing, the Japanese became a familiar figure on the "boca de Sertão," the entrance to uninhabited areas such as the pioneer fringes of São Paulo, Paraná, and Mato Grosso. There he established a reputation as a skillful farmer, a generally trustworthy individual, and one who was inclined to experiment and innovate. The Japanese have consistently been on the perimeter of the expanding coffee frontier in Brazil since the first decade of this century. Indeed, Japanese (Okinawans, to be specific) made the first large-scale coffee plantings in southern Mato Grosso. By demonstrating in Brazil that small-farming was profitable, the Japanese have helped to create the relatively new middle-class farmer.

In recognition of their contributions, a Brazilian official speaking in Japan said "many of them have accomplished acts of true heroism, clearing virgin forests, planting with the sweat of their bodies and the vigor of their arms coffee plantations, and introducing into Brazil new cultures. . . . Japanese people have experimented with new techniques and methods in Japan, and taken them to Brazil for the benefit of the Brazilian people . . . emigrants from some countries have tried to exploit Brazilian resources for the benefit of their own country, but Japanese immigrants have done just the opposite" (Japan Times, 1958).

A survey completed in 1958 disclosed that Japanese farmers in São Paulo were responsible for the production of 94% of the state's tomatoes, 43% of the peanuts, 68% of the potatoes, 37% of the eggs, 27% of the cotton, 7% of the coffee, 22% of the bananas, 92% of the tea, and 8% of the rice. Perhaps the Japanese may be credited with helping to enrich the Brazilian diet (Commissão de Recenseamento do Colônia Japonesa, 1964: 162; New York Times, 1958).

In Peru, the Japanese produced some 25% of the cotton crop in the late 1930s, but there they have contributed most positively in the urban sector of the economy. Modern merchandising methods and advertising techniques, efficient operation, fair prices, higher ethical standards, and improved cleanliness and sanitation in food processing and distribution are attributes of the Japanese businessman, which Peruvians have been forced to copy in order to survive.

Throughout Latin America, with the qualified exception of Mexico, the income and standard of living of the Japanese is substantially above average. Other than in Mexico, where a small number continue to work as field hands, the Japanese are employers of native labor. They are better off financially in Brazil and Peru than elsewhere, but it is in the former that their success has been most spectacular, where several are millionaires.

In conclusion, immigration generally, and of Japanese in particular will probably continue in Latin America on a restrictionist and selective basis as a supplement for developmental programs, and as a means for implementing social and economic change. There is little likelihood of a return to the laissez-faire policies that prevailed until the 1930s. It seems most probable that the remaining frontiers will be settled by the rapidly growing native population and by internal, rather than international, migration.

NOTES

1. *Meiji* designated an era that would extend until the Emperor's death in 1912. The announcement of the era of enlightened rule was joined with the statement that henceforth there would be only one era name per sovereign. History was to unfold in emperor-sized units thereafter. *Showa* (Enlightened Peace) is the era name for the present Emperor's reign. Hirohito will be known posthumously as Emperor Showa.

2. The major emigration and colonization companies affected by the consolidation were the Oriental Emigration Company *(Toyo Imin Goshi Kaisha)*; the Continental Emigration Company *(Tairiku Imin Kaisha)*; the Morioka Emigration Company *(Morioka Imin Gomei Kaisha)*; the Kokoku Colonization Company *(Kokoku Shokumin Kaisha)*; the Takemura Colonization and Bonding Company *(Takemura Shokumin Shokan)*; the Nambei Colonization Company *(Nambei Shokumin Kabushiki Kaisha).*

Under the aegis of the Overseas Development Company, emphasis shifted from contract immigrants to colonist-settlers, and colonization was attempted on a broader scale.

3. Among the 47 prefectures of Japan reporting their residents abroad in the period 1908-1938, the major contributors of Japanese immigrants in Latin America, in order of importance, were as follows: Kumamoto, Fukuoka; Okinawa; Hiroshima; Hokkaido; Fukushima.

4. From the data cited, it may be concluded that the volume of remittances from Japanese immigrants in Latin America had very little influence on the international balance of payments of Japan. However, Japanese immigrants have nevertheless been involved in Japanese investments in the region. When Japanese firms establish subsidiary companies in Latin America, local Japanese immigrants, or their descendants, often participate in the companies as partners. Local Japanese are also employed by such firms, and facilitate labor management by aiding in communication between local employees and Japanese business representatives from Japan.

5. Japanese and Naichi-jin are terms used interchangeably in contradistinction to Ryukyuan or Okinawan. Naichi-jin identifies Japanese from the four main islands (Hokkaido, Honshu, Shikoku, and Kyushu), in contrast to the Ryukyuan (or Okinawan) —*Honseki-jin*—who occupy the Ryukyu Archipelago. The latter, however, regard themselves as Japanese. Latin Americans are generally unaware of this distinction among Japanese. *Latentiki Nihon-jin* refers to Latin-Japanese, an individual who is ethnically Japanese, but in nationality belongs to one of the nations of Latin America.

Mexico severed diplomatic relations with Japan on December 8, 1941, and with Germany and Italy on December 11. The Mexican Congress voted that a state of war existed with the Axis Powers as of May 22, 1942; President Avila Camacho formally declared the fact on June 1, 1942. All Axis aliens were evacuated to Guadalajara and Mexico City, except for a small number held in the controlled camp at Perote, state of Vera Cruz; none were sent to the United States for internment. All restrictions were lifted in 1946.

During World War II, 16 Latin American republics interned at least 8500 persons, many of whom lost their citizenship by wartime measures. Twelve of these states—Bolivia, Colombia, Costa Rica, the Dominican Republic, Ecuador, El Salvador, Guatemala, Haiti, Honduras, Nicaragua, Panama, and Peru—sent all or part of the Axis internees to the United States for internment as enemy aliens.

6. A total of 1325 Japanese emigrated to the Dominican Republic after World War II, but many returned to Japan in 1961-1962.

It was not until 1934 that Japan accredited its Minister to Mexico to each of the five Central American states. Japan's first diplomatic appointment directly to a Central American nation occurred in 1958, when Tokyo named a Minister to El Salvador. In 1963, the first Japanese embassy was established in Central America, also in El Salvador (Gardiner, 1972: 15-47).

7. Colombia broke diplomatic relations with the Axis powers in July 1942, followed by a declaration of war in November 1943. Ecuador broke diplomatic relations with the Axis powers in January 1942.

8. The Ryukyu Islands, forming an archipelago comprising 140 islands of 1803 square miles, lie in the extreme Western Pacific between Formosa and Kyushu Island, Japan. Okinawa is the largest island in the archipelago. The Japanese period of occupation, 1938-1945, was followed by that of the United States, 1945-1972, after which Japanese sovereignty was again restored.

9. Peru severed diplomatic relations with Germany, Italy, and Japan on January 24, 1942, and soon thereafter froze the accounts and holdings of citizens of Axis countries. Peru declared war on Germany and Japan on February 12, 1945, and Peruvian Japanese who had been forcibly interned in the United States faced serious problems at the end of the war. On September 12, 1945, the United States, by presidential proclamation, authorized the Secretary of State "to remove to destinations outside the limits . . . all alien enemies brought to the United States from other American republics who are within the territory of the United States without admission under the immigration laws." Meanwhile, the Peruvian government decreed that it would permit the return of no Japanese who had been deported from its territory; therefore, the Japanese could neither return to Peru nor remain in the United States. In time, some were allowed to return to Peru, many remained in the United States, and others returned to Japan (Gardiner, 1975; Emmerson, 1977: 40-47, 56).

10. For critical analysis of the Naichi-jin-Ryukyuan relationship, see U.S. Government, Office of Strategic Services (1944) and Tohama and Ikeda (1944: 51-56).

11. Bolivia severed relations with the Axis Powers in January 1942 and issued a declaration of war in April 1943.

12. At the outset of World War II, Paraguay prohibited the naturalization of Axis aliens by presidential decree, and provided for strict control over enemy aliens. Paraguay broke with the Axis in 1942, declared war, and joined the United Nations in 1945.

13. In the period 1917-1940, 164,718 Japanese entered Brazil under the auspices of the Overseas Development Company (KKKK).

14. An immigration law was enacted in Brazil in 1934, which specified that the number of foreigners of any one nationality who might enter the nation during any one year should

not exceed 2% of the immigration from that country during the period 1884-1933. The maximum number of Japanese immigrants per year was thereby limited to 2,849 (Becu, 1943: 58-65).

Brazil declared war on Germany and Italy in August 1942, but this action against Japan was delayed until June 1945; during the interim, the same restrictions imposed on Germans and Italians applied to Japanese. Although some Japanese were evacuated from coastal areas and antisubversive measures carried out, relatively few Japanese in Brazil suffered any real hardship as a result of the war. The Brazilian declaration of war on Japan in June 1945 had no apparent effect on their treatment or status.

15. Coping with the growing complexity of the Japanese ethnic group is a problem of great magnitude. Not only must distinctions be made between Naichi-Jin and Ryukyuans, but also between three generations of each—Issei, Nisei, and Sansei—together with the "New Japanese," those who came after World War II. A dichotomy among Nisei must be considered: those with traditional values, and those who identify with the values of Brazilian society; finally, there is differentiation of all Japanese classified as urban and rural.

REFERENCES

BARNHART, E. N. (1962a) "Citizenship and political tests in Latin American republics in World War II." Hispanic Amer. Hist. Rev. (hereinafter cited as HAHR) 42 (August): 297-332.

——— (1962b) "Japanese internees from Peru." Pacific Hist. Rev. 30 (May): 169-178.

BECKMAN, G. M. (1962) The Modernization of China and Japan. New York: Harper & Row.

BECU, H. Z. (1943) El problema del extranjero en el reciente legislación Latin Americano. Buenos Aires: Guillermo Kraft.

BRADLEY, A. (1942) Trans-Pacific Relations of Latin America. New York: Institute of Pacific Relations.

CARNEIRO, F. (1950) Imigração e colonização no Brasil. Rio de Janiero: Avulsa.

Commissão de Recenseamento de Colônia Japonesa [São Paulo, Brasil] (1964) The Japanese Immigrant in Brazil: Statistical Tables. Tokyo: Tokyo Univ. Press.

CORTES, E. G. (1974) "Mexican-Japanese relations during the Díaz years." Ph.D. dissertation, University of Southern California.

COSÍO VILLEGAS, D. [ed.] (1957) Historia moderna de Mexico, 4 El porfiriato, la vida social. Mexico: Hermes.

DAVIS, H. (1872) "Japanese wrecks in American water." Overland Monthly (October): 353-360.

DEFONTAINES, P. (1938) "The origin and growth of the Brazilian network of towns." Geographical Rev. 27 (July): 379-399.

DIXON, J. M. (1911) "Early Mexican and California relations with Japan." Annual Publications of the Historical Society of Southern California 7: 211-227.

EMMERSON, J. K. (1977) "Japanese and Americans in Peru, 1942-1943." Foreign Service J. (May): 40-47, 56.

FRETZ, J. W. (1962) Immigrant Group Settlements in Paraguay. North Newton, KS: Bethel College Press.

GARCIA, E. L. (1909) Las razas en Lima. Lima: Imp. Sanmarti y Cia.

GARDINER, C. H. (1975) The Japanese and Peru, 1873-1973. Albuquerque: Univ. of New Mexico Press.

——— (1972) "The Japanese and Central America." J. of Inter-American Studies and World Affairs 14 (February): 15-47.

GASHU, K. (1951) Los japoneses en la Argentina. Buenos Aires: Japanese Association.

GONZÁLEZ NAVARRO, M. (1960) La colonización en México, 1877-1910. Mexico: Talleres de Impression de Estampillas y Valores.

HARING, C. H. (1947) The Spanish Empire in America. New York: Oxford Univ. Press.

HASTINGS, D. (1969) "Japanese emigration and assimilation in Brazil." Int. Migration Rev. 3 (Spring): 32-52.

IRIE, T. (1951) "History of Japanese migration to Peru." HAHR 31 (November): 648-664.

ISHII, R. (1937) Population Pressure and Economic Life in Japan. Chicago: Univ. of Chicago Press.

IZAWA, M. [ed.] (1971) Nihonjin Mexico Ijushi [The History of Japanese Immigrants in Mexico]. Tokyo: Hensan Inkai.

Japan, Colonial Ministry (1937) Kaigai Iju Tokei, Showa 11 nen 10th month, Takumusho Takumuka [Overseas Emigration Statistics at the end of October 1936]. Tokyo: Colonial Ministry, Dept. of Colonization.

Japan, Emigration Service (1972) Kaigai Iju Tokei, Showa 27-45 [Overseas Emigration Statistics, 1952-1970]. Tokyo: Emigration Service.

——— (1971) Kaigai Iju Tokei, Showa 27-44 [Overseas Emigration Statistics, 1952-1969]. Tokyo: Emigration Service.

——— (1966) Kaigai Zairyu Hojin Si To Sengo Iju No Keiko [Overseas Japanese in the Americas and Postwar Emigration Trends]. Tokyo: Emigration Service.

Japan, Ministry of Foreign Affairs (1951) Japanese Emigration: Past and Present. Tokyo: Ministry of Foreign Affairs.

——— (1949) Nihonjin No Kaigai Katsudo Jurai No Keika [The Development of Japanese Activities Abroad]. Tokyo: Ministry of Foreign Affairs.

——— (1941) Brazil Ni Okeru Nipponjin Hatten-shi. Latin America Chuokai Kanko Inkai. Tokyo Gaimusho America Kyoku, Showa 16 [History of Japanese Development in Brazil] Edited by Editorial Committee of Central Society on Latin America. Tokyo: Ministry of Foreign Affairs.

——— (1937) Kaigai Zairyu Hompojin Sokingaku Chosa Showa 12 nen [Inquiry of Remittance from Japanese Abroad]. Tokyo: Ministry of Foreign Affairs.

Japan, Office of the Prime Minister (1964) Japan Statistical Yearbook, 1963. Tokyo: Office of the Prime Minister.

Japan Times (1958) September 7.

KOYAMA, R. (1949) Imin Yonjunenshi [History of Forty Years of Japanese Immigration]. São Paulo: Japanese Association of São Paulo.

LUBBOCK, A. B. (1935) Coolie Ships and Oil Sailers. Boston: Charles E. Lauriat.

MacNAIR, H . F. (1935) The Chinese Abroad: Their Position and Protection. Shanghai: Commercial Press.

MARKHAM, C. R. (1892) A History of Peru. Chicago: Sergel & Co.

de MELLO CARVALHO, P. (1940) "A legislação imigratória do Brasil, e sua evolução." Revista de imigracão e colonizacão 4 (October).

MESKILL, J. M., J. MESKILL, and A. T. EMBREE (1971) The Non-European World, 1500-1800. Glenview, IL: Scott-Foresman.

NEIVA, A. H. (1945) "O problema imigratorio Brasileiro." Revista de imigração e colonização 5 (October).

New York Times (1977) November 7.
——— (1958) June 15.
——— (1945a) July 13.
——— (1945b) June 7.
——— (1942) August 23.
NORMANO, J. F. (1938) "Japanese emigration to Latin America." Genus 3.
——— and A. GERBI (1943) The Japanese in South America. New York: John Day.
OHARA, Y. (1967) Japan and Latin America. Santa Monica, CA: Rand Corporation
Okinawa, G.R.I. [Government of the Ryukyu Islands] (1961) Nambei Ijuchi Gijo [Status of the Immigration Areas in Latin America]. Naha: GRI.
——— (1957) Nambei Iminchi Chosa Hokokusho [Inspection Report on the Immigration Areas in Latin America]. Naha: GRI.
——— (1952) Bureau of Social Affairs. Record of Okinawan Emigration. Naha: GRI.
Okinawa, Prefectural Office (1939a) Gaikoku Toko Kyoka Jinin [Number of Persons Permitted to Go Abroad]. Naha: Okinawa, Prefectural Office, Dept. of General Affairs, Division of Statistics.
——— (1939b) Okinawa Ken Tokei Sho [Statistics of Okinawa Prefecture]. Naha: Okinawa, Prefectural Office.
PAZ SOLDAN y UNANUE, P. (1891) La inmigración en el Perú. Lima: Imp. del Universo de Carlos Prince.
RIPPY, J. F. (1949) "Japanese in Latin America." Interamerican Econ. Affairs 3: 50-65.
ROCHA NOGUEIRA, A. (1973) A imigração japonesa para lavoura cafeeira paulista, 1908-1922. São Paulo: Univ. of São Paulo Press.
SACURAI, S. (1940) Ishokumin No Rakudo [Paradise of Immigrants]. Tokyo: Kyodo Insatsu Press.
——— (1935) Zaihi Doho Nenkan [Almanac of Resident Japanese in Peru]. Tokyo: Kyodo Insatsu Press.
SAITO, H. (1976) "The integration and participation of the Japanese and their descendants in Brazilian society." Int. Migration 14: 183-197.
SANSOM, SIR G. B. (1963) A History of Japan, 1615-1687. Stanford, CA: Stanford Univ. Press.
——— (1950) The Western World and Japan: A Study in the Interaction of European and Asiatic Cultures. New York: Knopf.
SCHURZ, W. L. (1939) The Manila Galleon. New York: E. P. Dutton.
SHIROMA, Z. (1959) Zaihaku Okinawa Kenjin Sonen No Ayuma [History of Fifty Years of Okinawan Immigrants in Brazil]. São Paulo: Okinawa Cultural and Relief Association.
SIMS, H. D. (1972) "Japanese postwar migration to Brazil: an analysis of data presently available." Int. Migration Rev. 6 (Fall): 246-265.
STEPHENS, H. M. and H. E. BOLTON [eds.] (1917) The Pacific Ocean in History. Presented at the Panama-Pacific Historical Congress. New York: Macmillan.
STEWART, N. R. (1967) Japanese Colonization in Eastern Paraguay. Washington, DC: National Academy of Sciences.
STEWART, W. (1951) Chinese Bondage in Peru. Durham, NC: Duke Univ. Press.
TAEUBER, I. (1958) The Population of Japan. Princeton, NJ: Princeton Univ. Press.
TANAKA, K. (1947) "Japanese immigrants in Amazonia and their future." Kobe Univ. Econ. Rev. 3: 2-21.
TIGNER, J. L. (1978) "The Ryukyuans in Peru, 1906-1952." The Americas 25 (July): 20-44.

——— (1967) "The Ryukyuans in Argentina." HAHR 47 (May): 203-224.

——— (1963) "The Ryukyuans in Bolivia." HAHR 43 (May): 206-229.

——— (1961) "Shindo Remmei: Japanese nationalism in Brazil." HAHR 41 (November): 515-532.

——— (1955) The Okinawans in Latin America. Washington, DC: National Academy of Sciences.

TOHAMA, H. and K. IKEDA (1944) "The Okinawa-Naichi relationship." Social Process in Hawaii: 51-56.

UNNO, M. (1941) Mexico Chubei Taikan [General View of Mexico and Central America]. Mexico: Algarin Mexico Press.

U.S. Government, Office of Strategic Services (1944) The Okinawans of the Loo Choo Islands: A Japanese Minority Group. Honolulu: Office of Strategic Services, Research and Analysis Branch.

VIEIRA, F.I.S. (1973) O japonês na frente de expansão paulista: O processo de absorção de japones em Marília. Sao Paulo: Centro de Estudos Nipo-Brasileiros.

WILCOX, W. F. [ed.] (1931) International Migrations. New York: National Bureau of Economic Research.

WILLEMS, E. and H. SAITO (1947) "Shindo Remmei, um problema de aculturacão." Revista Sociologia 9: 133-152.

YAMAMOTO, M. (1927) "The question of population in Japan." Kyoto Imperial University Econ. Rev. (July): 52-62.

YAMAMOTO, S. [ed.] (1932) Nihon Chiri Fuzoku Taikei [An Outline of Japanese Geography and Customs]. Tokyo: Editorial Committee of Central Society on Latin America.

YOSHIDA, Y. (1909) "Sources and causes of Japanese emigration." American Academy of Political and Social Science Annals 34 (September): 157-167.

James L. Tigner is Professor of History at the University of Nevada, Reno and a specialist on Latin America and East Asia, with his recent research focusing on the Japanese in Mexico. Along with numerous articles on the Ryukyuans in various Latin American countries, he has contributed extensively to Encyclopedia Britannica *on Latin American topics (1960-1978), co-authored* Latin America and the United States *with Graham H. Stuart (Englewood Cliffs, 1975) and wrote* The Okinawans in Latin America *(National Academy of Sciences, Washington, 1955).*

REVIEW ESSAY

DIVERSE INFLUENCES ON THE VENEZUELAN LEFT

Five Books by Venezuelan Leftists

Blanco Muñoz, A. (interviewer) LA LUCHA ARMADA: HABLAN 5 JEFES. Caracas: Facultad de Ciencias Económicas y Sociales, Universidad Central de Venezuela, 1980.

Iarrazábal, R. ESTRATEGIA DE PODER. Caracas: Editorial Ateneo de Caracas, 1979.

Proceso Político. CAP: 5 AÑOS: UN JUICIO CRITICO. Caracas: Editorial Ateneo de Caracas, 1978.

Rangel, J. V. SEGURIDAD DEFENSA Y DEMOCRACIA: UN TEMA PARA CIVILES Y MILITARES. Caracas: Ediciones Centauro 80, 1980.

Silva Michelana, J. A. and H. R. Sonntag, EL PROCESO ELECTORAL DE 1978: SU PERSPECTIVA HISTÓRICA ESTRUCTURAL. Caracas: Editorial Ateneo de Caracas, 1979.

Diverse theoretical currents have thoroughly transformed the dogmatic Marxism embraced by the Venezuelan left during the guerrilla warfare years of the 1960s. Although leftist leaders generally deny that their parties are replicas of foreign models, the Eurocommunist movement, and particularly the works of the Italian Communist Antonio Gramsci, have left an indelible mark (Cortés, 1979: 88-89). Venezuelan leftists have also been receptive to the issues raised by

AUTHOR'S NOTE: The author is grateful for critical comments from Richard Parker, Susan Thompson-Berglund, and Kathy Waldron.

Journal of Interamerican Studies and World Affairs, Vol. 23 No. 4, November 1981 483-493

dependentista economists regarding new forms of integration into the world capitalist system. Indeed, the left's intellectual productivity is impressive relative to its modest following, as reflected in the 8% of the vote it received in the 1978 presidential elections. Part of the reason for this poor showing was that each of the four main leftist parties (the pro-Moscow Partido Comunista de Venezuela—PCV; the Eurocommunist Movimiento al Socialismo—MAS; the Movimiento de la Izquierda Revolucionaria—MIR; and the Movimiento Electoral del Pueblo—MEP) ran separate candidates. In contrast, the social democratic Acción Democrática (AD) and the social Christian Copei, which together drew 90%, have failed to match the left's efforts on the ideological front, in spite of the fact that both parties have raised the banner of "renovation."

José Agustín Silva Michelena, who belongs to MAS, and the unaffiliated Heinz Rudolf Sonntag accept Gramsci's tenet that in certain well-established democracies, legitimacy and not force constitutes the state's most important underpinning. The authors maintain that in developed societies, the viability of the economic system and the strong influence of certain cultural symbols play a critical role in justifying the state's right to exist. In developing democratic nations, on the other hand, legitimacy derives first and foremost from electoral politics. This observation is perhaps most applicable to Venezuela, where presidential campaigns attain high levels of participation (Baloyra and Martz, 1979: 218-219) and absorb an inordinate amount of national attention over an extended period of time (Salinger, 1978: 97-98). As Silva Michelena and Sonntag note, electorally oriented political parties in Venezuela have preempted almost all forms of interest articulation. The authors hypothesize that although elections shore up the system, they also serve as a mechanism to vent social frustration, providing members of the ruling class with an acceptable arena to fight out their internal differences. As soon as elections are over, however, a new accommodation is reached as manifested in the consensus between AD and Copei over questions of primary importance. These parties, recognizing the critical legitimizing role played by democratic politics, have tacitly agreed to soft-pedal denunciations of administrative corruption in an effort to avoid erosion of public confidence.

The authors devote a chapter to the Supreme Electoral Commission (CSE) to show how the system guarantees electoral impartiality, without which elections would not be able to fulfill their legitimizing function. This point is valid with regard to vote-counting but it is overdrawn, perhaps to allow the authors to demonstrate the validity of another allegedly *gramscian* proposition,[1] namely the relative autonomy of state institutions vis-à-vis the dominant elites. The CSE, controlled by the two major parties, is hardly impervious to partisan influence. Its most glaring failure is its inability or unwillingness to enforce the eight-month presidential campaign limit, as well as to regulate campaign spending (Wells, 1980: 45).

The authors' functional explanation of electoral politics is intended to answer a number of important questions and to help chart a course for the Venezuelan left. The authors criticize the four major leftist parties for abiding by rules which are designed to fortify the prevailing system. These parties have failed to expose corruption in the government thoroughly, it is argued, because they implicitly accept the need to preserve the legitimacy of the democratic system. Furthermore, they followed the tone set by AD, Copei, and their respective North American publicity consultants in the 1978 campaign, in which issues were submerged. This observation echoes a more thoroughgoing criticism leveled by the radical fringe[2] against the mainstream left for subordinating daily struggles to the task of winning elections, both at national and institutional levels (Bravo, 1978: 120-121; Rodríguez, 1979: 208-210).

The authors also address themselves to the perplexing situation of two parties of similar ideological and programmatic orientations locked in an acute and bitter rivalry. Some political independents have suggested that this infighting between AD and Copei has recently reached uncontrollable limits and that, contrary to the aims of party leaders, it threatens the stability of the democratic system. Certain leftists, on the other hand, see the discord as a subterfuge designed to create the appearance of healthy competition between the two parties. The authors of *El proceso electoral* reject both of these viewpoints. Silva Michelena and Sonntag deny that the AD-Copei rivalry is programmed, since it derives from the system's built-in mechanism for expressing intra- and interclass tensions. At the same time, AD-Copei disharmony, far from surpassing tolerable limits, helps buttress the system by drawing attention away from the smaller parties to their left, a policy which the authors claim was consciously pursued in the 1978 elections.

Most Venezuelan leftists view their nation's bourgeoisie as divided between a traditional sector and an emerging one. The latter group was encouraged by the AD government of Carlos Andrés Pérez (1974-1979), which channeled increased oil revenue into state and private enterprises, and nationalized key extractive industries. One independent leftist writer (Duno, 1975) has popularized the term "twelve apostles" to refer to the most prominent representatives of the emerging bourgeoisie, including several allegedly corrupt officials of the Pérez administration.[3] The books by Silva Michelena-Sonntag, Proceso Político (which is the name of a fledgling political organization), and PCV leader Radamés Larrazábal, reflect general leftist thinking regarding the inextricable ties between all sectors of the Venezuelan bourgeoisie and foreign capital. This near uniformity on the left was first reached during the late 1960s, when the PCV struck the term "antiimperialist national bourgeoisie" from its nomenclature, partly in response to the negligible role played by that group in the Cuban revolution.

Despite this underlying agreement, the three above-mentioned books exhibit differences regarding the role of the emerging bourgeoisie and Venezuela's place within the worldwide configuration of dependent capitalism. Proceso Político views this sector as the "principal enemy" (Proceso Político, 1978: 88) in Venezuela. According to the authors, the emerging bourgeoisie is distinguished by its support for authoritarian measures at home and an aggressive foreign policy. Thus the Tinoco Plan, devised by one of the "twelve apostles" in 1975, would have turned over the state sector of the economy to experienced businessmen, under the pretext that too much oil-derived revenue was at stake to entrust to inefficient government bureaucrats.[4] The proposed technocracy, removed from public pressure, would have further nurtured the emerging elite. In addition, Carlos Andrés Pérez's nationalistic foreign policy expressed the ambitions of this sector of the bourgeoisie to convert the Andean Pact nations and the neighboring Caribbean into Venezuela's sphere of influence (Lanza, 1980: 100-166).

El proceso electoral and *Estrategia de poder* present a different analysis of the policies pursued under Pérez. Unlike Proceso Político, these leftists view Pérez's third world position as a challenge to U.S. economic and political interests. Although the entire Venezuelan left sharply criticized Pérez's nationalization of the oil and iron industries for failing to break ties with the multinational companies, Larrazábal admits that it represented "the first step in a larger struggle for the control of our natural resources." (Larrazábal, 1979: 94). The PCV reasoned that the takeovers would make it easier for a truly popular government to completely sever dependency ties at a future date (Carrera, 1979: 51). In order to prop up the state sector, Larrazábal admonishes against excessive labor conflict in government-run enterprises, a position reminiscent of his party's no-strike policy during World War II.

These different opinions of the emerging bourgeoisie and of the policies initiated under Pérez have important implications for leftist strategy. In theory, all parties on the left condemn AD and Copei for being faithful representatives of the dominant classes. Nevertheless, several of them—including the group "Vanguardia Comunista"—tacitly supported Copei's presidential candidate in the 1978 elections (García Ponce, 1977: 222-232), and subsequently favored committing the left's swing vote in Congress to the *copeyano* program. Larrazábal attributes this strategy to the notion that the left can eliminate Copei-AD polarization by lining up with the former to strike a blow at the latter, which is allegedly the more reactionary of the two parties. In spite of Larrazábal's plea for equal treatment of the two foes, the PCV came to ex-President Pérez's defense when corruption charges against him threatened to reach Watergate proportions. The PCV's attitude was admittedly influenced by Pérez's support for the Sandinistas and the personal praise extended to him by Fidel Castro.

José Vicente Rangel's reevaluation of the role of the armed forces in the nation's life rests on unorthodox arguments for a leftist. The traditional Marxist position, put forward by the Communist party in the 1960s, viewed the military as "subordinate to the policies of North American imperialists, the oligarchy and the commercial bourgeoisie" (Plaza, 1978: 171), although in practice the Venezuelan left did not abide by such a rigid dogma. Rangel praises military personnel for technical and administrative skills, which have been underutilized by the nation, and for a willingness to take appropriate measures in cases of corruption. He calls for the participation of the armed forces in national debate, and its incorporation into the decisionmaking process. This positive view of the military, like Silva Michelena-Sonntag's analysis of the CSE, reflects a more general position embraced by MAS, which twice postulated Rangel as its presidential candidate. According to MAS, the maturity of the political system and the insulation of state institutions from the direct control of the dominant classes place Venezuelan democracy in a category with the advanced European nations, which had served as the basis of Gramsci's analysis (Petkoff, 1976: 93-94, 121-127).

One of the most controversial aspects of Rangel's thesis on the renovation of the armed forces is the proposal to extend the right to vote to military personnel. AD and Copei have staunchly opposed the idea, since it violates the concept of an "apolitical" military as stipulated in the nation's constitution (Peña, 1980: 31). Rangel, in the final passage of his book, denigrates this "antiquated [*notion*] of apoliticism . . . which only serves the defiled ends of established groups." The role of the armed forces is a particularly delicate topic, and those who participate in the debate undoubtedly leave much unsaid. Political leaders of all tendencies privately confess a distrust of the military—an attitude which is not surprising given the nation's history—but this apprehension has not surfaced in public debate. Furthermore, all politicians pay lip service to the need to place qualified military personnel in administrative posts, but without mentioning the incompatibility between the authoritarian formation of officers and the brokerage role of democratic institutions. Finally, the motives of Rangel and fellow leftist leaders are open to conjecture. Given the apparent politicization of the armed forces, does the left seek to carve out its own following among junior officers who would be most receptive to the positions assumed by Rangel? Is leftist strategy designed to win over the military to socialism, or—as Allende attempted to do—to neutralize the institution through support of a "legalist" faction which could be counted on to defend a future socialist government?[5]

Some of Rangel's statements are astonishingly similar to positions forwarded by those on the other end of the political spectrum. Indeed, shortly after the publication of *Seguridad, defensa y democracia,* Rangel made common cause with ultraconservatives who were opposed to ceding a part of the disputed Gulf of Venezuela to Colombia. In this work, Rangel sharply criticizes the government for failing to implement an effective border policy or to prevent out-migration from strategic areas. He points to the vulnerability of the Orinoco oil belt region due to its lack of a transportation infrastructure. Brazil, on the other hand, has promoted development and settlement in its Amazonic borderlands. Venezuelan security is also menaced by the growing military influence in Colombia, and by the general acceptance in that nation of massive emmigration as an acceptable escape valve for mounting social tensions. Although these remarks are unconventional enough for a leftist, Rangel occasionally qualifies them in order to avoid confusion regarding his political identity. Thus, he warns against assuming an anti-Colombian attitude, which is currently all too prevalent in Venezuela. He views a strong government capable of providing for national security as the only viable alternative to the inefficacity of the present one, but adds that such strength does not necessarily imply the absence of democratic liberties. He also asserts a leftist position in stating that Venezuela needs to beef up its defenses to protect its oil reserves from possible U.S. intervention.

Just as discussion regarding the role of the military had been practically taboo prior to the publication of Rangel's book, the left up until recently avoided mention of the guerrilla fiasco of the 1960s. *La lucha armada: Hablan 5 jefes,* along with several other works (Peña, 1978a, 1978b), departs from this tradition. These five interviews with PCV leaders of the 1960s demonstrate that the emergence of MAS and Vanguardia Comunista in 1971 and 1974 stemmed from different perceptions of that shattering experience. Teodoro Petkoff and Pompeyo Márquez, president and secretary general of MAS, indicate that their party's call for a "Venezuelan road to socialism" was a reaction to the tendency to accept uncritically imported theories. Thus, in 1962 and 1963, the PCV followed an "incoherent" (Blanco, 1980: 133) policy of promoting urban terrorism, rural guerrilla warfare, military coups, and parliamentary activity in an attempt to carry out Lenin's dictum on the need to combine different forms of struggle. The following year, a greatly debilitated Communist party embraced Mao's strategy of the "prolonged war" beginning in rural areas, without taking into consideration the relatively small size of the Venezuelan peasant population, as well as its pro-AD leanings. Petkoff and Márquez were particularly bitter about Fidel Castro's public attack against the PCV in 1967 for abandoning the armed struggle. Shortly thereafter, the USSR, which had previously quietly disapproved of the PCV's guerrilla strategy, encouraged party leaders to take measures against Petkoff for openly criticizing the Soviet invasion of Czechoslovakia (Petkoff, 1969).

Differences within the PCV over the best way to disengage from the armed struggle and problems related to internal democratic norms also presaged the MAS split. According to Petkoff and Márquez, the PCV "bureaucrats"—which included Gustavo Machado and García Ponce (Blanco, 1980: 242)—issued a simple communiqué ordering rank-and-file members to cease guerrilla activity. The two interviewees rejected this approach as too mechanistic, in that it failed to allow for debate within the party. Their own call for a more protracted "orderly withdrawal" (Blanco, 1980: 222), however, was seen by some as a cover for their real intentions of resuming the armed struggle at a future date. Petkoff notes that the PCV's refusal to air general discussion regarding sanctions taken against himself for his position on Czechoslovakia was what convinced veteran Communist leaders like Márquez to leave the

PCV (Petkoff and other younger members, on the other hand, had privately decided at an earlier date to split the party, which they considered beyond renovation). MAS has attempted to avoid the rigidity in the decisionmaking process which characterized these incidents. The party's commitment to open debate is marked by its acceptance of the existence of internal factions, a policy which the more disciplined PCV spurns (Myers, 1980: 17).

The interview with Guillermo García Ponce clarifies the origins of Vanguardia Comunista, the party which he heads. García Ponce's discussion of his role as "military chief" of the PCV is telling of the close relationship between military strategy and political objectives. At the time, he favored working closely within the armed forces and concentrating efforts in urban areas, in order to create a disruptive climate conducive to a coup. This "putchist tendency" viewed the replacement of the AD government as the primary task of the moment instead of the more "extremist" (Blanco, 1980: 333) objective of "national liberation." García Ponce maintains in retrospect that had the left adhered to the slogan "New Government Now" rather than promoting a program of far-reaching reforms, it could have toppled the AD government. Vanguardia Comunista has inherited this anti-AD disposition, and does not discard the possibility of supporting a Copeyano "national candidate" (Blanco, 1980: 391) in order to deal an overwhelming blow to AD.

The PCV, MAS, and Vanguardia Comunista, which are represented in this selection of interviews, are currently dedicated to electoral politics, and MAS in particular has gone to great pains to emphasize its democratic orientation (Ellner, 1980: 70). Nevertheless, none of the five interviewees criticize the left's decision to launch guerrilla warfare on grounds that it attempted to overthrow a democratically elected government. Indeed, there is a consensus that after the fall of the Pérez Jiménez dictatorship in 1958, the PCV was overly anxious to hold elections, as demonstrated by its slogan "Elections Now" (Nuñez, 1979: 77-78). Instead, leftists should have insisted on representation in the Military Junta headed by Wolfgang Larrazábal, in recognition of their key role in the clandestine struggle against Pérez Jiménez. Had elections not been rushed, Larrazábal could have implemented far-reaching reforms, and thus enhanced his prospects and those of the PCV, which backed him in the upcoming elections. Even Pedro Ortega Díaz, the only PCV national leader who openly opposed the guerrilla struggle, acknowledges his support for a military conspiracy involving Larrazábal's brother Carlos on grounds that this scheme alone offered a fair possibility of success. These comments would appear to be at odds with the democratic commitment of these political actors over the last decade.

The shock of guerrilla defeat galvanized a process of reflection whereby hitherto vague differences on the left became clearly defined. The dynamics of interleft competition in the 1970s compelled individual parties to further refine their positions. The negative side to this rivalry is the disunity which has cost the left dearly in elections both at national and institutional levels. Nevertheless, a recently reached consensus recognizes the need to agree upon a common program and candidate for the 1983 presidential elections. The left's decision to combine forces for the June 1979 municipal elections, when it duplicated its vote over the previous presidential race, demonstrated that the unity strategy is feasible in spite of the outstanding differences which have been discussed in this essay. Even the pro-Moscow PCV has accepted the pluralistic Eurocommunist position that the construction of a socialist society requires the collaboration of different parties (Hernández, 1981: C-1). Should the left be able to build upon this mutual understanding and respect, Venezuela may soon by presented with the historically unusual situation of a host of relatively small leftist parties emerging as serious contenders to power.

—*Steve Ellner*

NOTES

1. Carl Boggs (1980: 22) claims that the "semiautonomy" concept of state institutions is based on a misinterpretation of Gramsci, and that the concept is really attributable to his successor, Palmiro Togliatti. For a general discussion of this theory, see Holloway and Picciotto (1978: 5-8).

2. The Partido de la Revolución Venezolana (PRV), led by ex-PCV guerrilla leader Douglas Bravo, and the Liga Socialista (LS) have put forward this critique of the four major leftist parties. The PRV and LS (which split off from MIR) were founded by leftists who favored continuation of guerrilla warfare in the mid- and late 1960s, although more recently both groups have abandoned the armed struggle.

3. Among the "twelve apostles" who held important government posts are: Pedro Tinoco (Finance Minister under President Rafael Caldera), Gumersindo Rodríguez (Minister of the Central Office of Coordination and Planning, Cordiplan, under President Pérez), Diego Arria (Governor of the Federal District and Minister of Information and Tourism under Pérez), and Carmelo Lauría (president of the Central Bank under Pérez).

4. Pedro Tinoco's proposal for the technocratic organization of government was first formulated in the 1960s, and was staunchly opposed by a faction within AD, which in 1967 split off and formed the left-leaning MEP (Blank, 1971: 92).

5. One student of the military in Latin America, Manfred Kossok, has argued that the attempt to promote a socialist faction within the armed forces offers little possibility of success: "The necessity to take offensive action in isolated instances (rebellions of Carapano [sic] and Puerto Cabello in Venezuela in 1962) or to seek links with the guerrilla movement (Guatemala) underlines the objective impossibility of revolutionizing the important parts of the armed forces from the inside . . . Thus, the field of action for progressive activity on the part of the armed forces, as a potential motive force of politicosocial change in Latin America is largely restricted to national reformist tendencies" (Kossok, 1972: 396).

REFERENCES

BALOYRA, E. A. and J. D. MARTZ (1979) Political Attitudes in Venezuela: Societal Cleavages and Political Opinion. Austin: Univ. of Texas Press.

BLANK, D. E. (1971) "Political conflict and industrial planning in Venezuela," pp. 84-106 in Phillip B. Taylor (ed.) Venezuela: 1969. Analysis of Progress. Washington, DC: School of Advanced International Studies, Johns Hopkins University.

BOGGS, C. (1980) "Gramsci and eurocommunism." Radical America (May-June): 7-23.

BRAVO, A. (1978) Crisis elecciones y violencia. Caracas: Editorial Ruptura.

CARRERA, J. (1979) "Una nacionalización que no ha resuelto los problemas claves," pp. 43-57 in Jesús Faría and Carrera (eds.) Venezuela en el mundo de hoy. Prague: Editorial Internacional "Paz y Socialismo."

CORTES, R. J. (1979) El MAS: Desbandada hacia la derecha. Caracas: Ediciones Centauro 79.

DUNO, P. (1975) Los doce apóstoles: Proceso a la degradación política. Valencia: Vadell Hermanos.

ELLNER, S. (1980) "Venezucommunism: learning the lesson of Chile?" Commonweal (February 15): 69-70.

GARCÍA PONCE, G. (1977) El país, la izqueirda y las elecciones de 1978. Caracas: Miguel Angel García e Hijo.

HERNÁNDEZ, R. [interviewer] (1981) "Eduardo Gallegos Mancera en los 50 años del PCV: la revolución venezolana no será obra de un solo partido." El Nacional, March 8: C-1.

HOLLOWAY, J. and C. PICCIOTTO (1978) "Introduction" in Holloway and Picciotto (eds.) State and Capital: A Marxist Debate. Austin: Univ. of Texas Press.

KOSSOK, M. (1972) "The armed forces in Latin America: potential for changes in political and social functions." J. of Interamerican Studies and World Affairs (Nov.): 375-398.

LANZA, E. (1980) El sub-imperialismo venezolano, Caracas: Editorial "Carlos Aponte."

MYERS, D. J. (1980) "Venezuela's MAS." Problems of Communism (Sept. -Oct.): 16-27.

NUÑEZ TENORIO, J. R. (1979) La Izqueirda y la lucha por el poder en Venezuela. Caracas: Editorial Ateneo de Caracas.

PEÑA, A. [interviewer] (1980) Corrupción y golpe de estado. Caracas: Editorial Ateneo de Caracas.
——— [interviewer] (1978a) Conversaciones con Américo Martin. Caracas: Editorial Ateneo de Caracas.
——— [interviewer] (1978b) Conversaciones con Douglas Bravo. Caracas: Editorial Ateneo de Caracas.
PETKOFF, T. (1976) Proceso a la izqueirda. Barcelona, Spain: Editorial Planeta.
——— (1969) Checoeslovaquia: El socialismo como problema. Caracas: Editorial Fuentes.
PLAZA, H. (1978) El 23 de enero de 1958 y el proceso de consolidación de la democracia representativa en Venezuela. Caracas: G&T Editores.
RODRIGUEZ, J. (1979) El pensamiento de Jorge Rodríguez. Caracas: Editorial Ateneo de Caracas.
SALINGER, P. (1978) Cuadernos venezolanos: Viajes y conversaciones con Carlos Andrés Pérez. Barcelona: Editorial Seix Barral.
WELLS, H. (1980) "The conduct of Venezuelan elections: rules and practice," pp. 30-55 in Howard R. Penniman (ed.) Venezuela at the Polls: The National Elections of 1978. Washington, DC: American Enterprise Institute for Public Policy Research.

Steve Ellner, Assistant Professor in the Department of Economics at the Universidad de Oriente at Puerto La Cruz, Venezuela, is the author of Los Partidos Políticos y Su Disputa por el Control de Movimiento Sindical en Venezuela, 1936-1948 *(Universidad Católica Andrés Bello, 1980). He received his Ph.D. in 1979 from the University of New Mexico.*

INDEX

to

JOURNAL OF INTERAMERICAN STUDIES

AND WORLD AFFAIRS

VOLUME 23

Number 1 (February 1981) pp. 1-120
Number 2 (May 1981) pp. 121-240
Number 3 (August 1981) pp. 241-368
Number 4 (November 1981) pp. 369-496

Authors:

ABBOTT, GEORGE, C., "The Associated States and Independence," 69.

CAMP, RODERIC A., "Intellectuals: Agents of Change in Mexico?" 297.

CRAIG, RICHARD B., "Colombian Narcotics and United States-Colombian Relations," 243.

DENNIS, PHILIP A., "The Costenos and the Revolution in Nicaragua," 271.

ELLNER, STEVE, "Diverse Influences on the Venezuelan Left: Five Books by Venezuelan Leftists" [Review Essay], 483.

FERRIS, ELIZABETH G., "The Andean Pact and the Amazon Treaty: Reflections of Changing Latin American Relations," 147.

HANDELMAN, HOWARD, "Labor-Industrial Conflict and the Collapse of Uruguyan Democracy," 371.

KUCZYNSKI, PEDRO-PABLO, "The Peruvian External Debt: Problem and Prospect," 3.

LEVINE, DANIEL H., "Portraits of Venezuela" [Review Essay], 203.

LLOSA, MARIO VARGAS, "Centralism as Pragmatic Tradition: A Critique" (Lysander Kemp, trans.) [Review Essay], 345.

MAYO, JOHN, "Britain and Chile, 1851-1886: Anatomy of a Relationship," 95.

McGREEVEY, WILLIAM PAUL, "Reinterpreting Colombian Economic History" [Review Essay], 352.

MONETA, CARLOS J., "Antarctica, Latin America, and the International System in the 1980s: Toward a New Antarctic Order?" (Marjory Mattingly Urquidi, trans.) 29.

NICHOLS, GLENN A. and PHILIP S. SNYDER, "Brazilian Elites and the Descendants of the German, Italian, and Japanese Immigrants," 321.

PREMO, DANIEL L., "Political Assassination in Guatemala: A Case of Institutionalized Terror," 429.

RUHL, J. MARK, "Civil-Military Relations in Colombia: A Societal Explanation," 123.

SCHMIDT, HENRY C., "Education, Ethnicity, and Humanism: Recent Trends in Mexican Intellectual History" [Review Essay], 225.

SNYDER, PHILIP S., see Nichols, Glenn A.
THOUMI, FRANCISCO E., "Human Rights Policy: Basic Human Needs and Economic Implications for LDCs," 177.
TIGNER, JAMES L., "Japanese Immigration into Latin America: A Survey," 457.
WOLPIN, MILES D., "Military Radicalism in Latin America," 395.

Articles:

"The Andean Pact and the Amazon Treaty: Reflections of Changing Latin American Relations," Ferris, 147.
"Antarctica, Latin America, and the International System in the 1980s: Toward a New Antarctic Order?" Moneta, 29.
"The Associated States and Independence," Abbott, 69.
"Brazilian Elites and the Descendants of the German, Italian, and Japanese Immigrants," Nichols and Snyder, 321.
"Britain and Chile, 1851-1886: Anatomy of a Relationship," Mayo, 95.
"Civil-Military Relations in Colombia: A Societal Explanation," Ruhl, 123.
"Colombian Narcotics and United States-Colombian Relations," Craig, 243.
"The Costeños and the Revolution in Nicaragua," Dennis, 271.
"Human Rights Policy: Basic Human Needs and Economic Implications for LDCs," Thoumi, 177.
"Intellectuals: Agents of Change in Mexico?" Camp, 297.
"Japanese Immigration into Latin America: A Survey," Tigner, 457.
"Labor-Industrial Conflict and the Collapse of Uruguyan Democracy," Handelman, 371.
"Military Radicalism in Latin America," Wolpin, 395.
"The Peruvian External Debt: Problem and Prospect," Kuczynski, 3.
"Political Assassination in Guatemala: A Case of Institutionalized Terror," Premo, 429.

Review Essays:

"Centralism as Pragmatic Tradition: A Critique," Llosa, 345.
"Diverse Influences on the Venezuelan Left: Five Books by Venezuelan Leftists," Ellner, 483.
"Education, Ethnicity, and Humanism: Recent Trends in Mexican Intellectual History," Schmidt, 225.
"Portraits of Venezuela," Levine, 203.
"Reinterpreting Colombian Economic History," McGreevey, 352.

Books Received:

233,365